Zhang Time Discretization (ZTD) Formulas and Applications

The book aims to solve the discrete implementation problems of continuous-time neural network models while improving the performance of neural networks by using various Zhang time discretization (ZTD) formulas.

The authors summarize and present the systematic derivations and complete research works of ZTD formulas from special 3S-ZTD formulas to general NS-ZTD formulas. These finally lead to their proposed discrete-time Zhang neural network (DTZNN) algorithms, which are more efficient, accurate, and elegant. The book will open the door to scientific and engineering applications of ZTD formulas and neural networks and will be a major inspiration for studies in neural network modeling, numerical algorithm design, prediction, and robot manipulator control.

The book will benefit engineers, senior undergraduates, graduate students, and researchers in the fields of neural networks, computer mathematics, computer science, artificial intelligence, numerical algorithms, optimization, robotics, and simulation modeling.

Yunong Zhang earned his B.S. degree from Huazhong University of Science and Technology, Wuhan, China, in 1996; his M.S. degree from South China University of Technology, Guangzhou, China, in 1999; and his Ph.D. from the Chinese University of Hong Kong, Shatin, Hong Kong, China, in 2003. He is currently a professor at the School of Computer Science and Engineering, Sun Yat-sen University, Guangzhou, China. Dr. Zhang was supported by the Program for New Century Excellent Talents in Universities in 2007. He received the Best Paper Award from International Symposium on Systems and Control in Aeronautics and Astronautics (ISSCAA) in 2008 and the Best Paper Award from the International Conference on Automation and Logistics (ICAL) in 2011. He was among the Highly Cited Scholars of China selected and published by Elsevier from 2014 to 2022.

Jinjin Guo earned her B.E. degree in measurement technology and instrument from Nanchang University, Nanchang, China, in 2016; her M.E. degree in control engineering from Sun Yat-sen University, Guangzhou, China, in 2018; and her Ph.D. in computer science and technology from Sun Yat-sen University, Guangzhou, China, in 2022. She is currently a lecturer at the School of Computer Science, Guangdong Polytechnic Normal University, Guangzhou, China. Her main research interests include neural networks, numerical computation, and tracking control.

Zhang Time Discretization (ZTD) Formulas and Applications

Yunong Zhang
Jinjin Guo

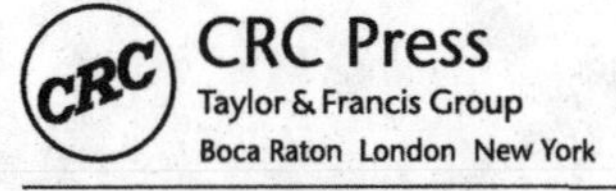

CRC Press is an imprint of the
Taylor & Francis Group, an **informa** business

Designed cover image: © Min C. Chiu

First edition published 2025
by CRC Press
2385 NW Executive Center Drive, Suite 320, Boca Raton FL 33431

and by CRC Press
4 Park Square, Milton Park, Abingdon, Oxon, OX14 4RN

CRC Press is an imprint of Taylor & Francis Group, LLC

ISBN: 978-1-032-80624-2 (hbk)
ISBN: 978-1-032-80735-5 (pbk)
ISBN: 978-1-003-49778-3 (ebk)

DOI: 10.1201/9781003497783

Typeset in CMR10
by KnowledgeWorks Global Ltd.

To our parents and
ancestors, as always

Contents

Figures

Tables

Preface

In recent decades, with the characteristics of distributed-storage and high-speed parallel processing, superior performance in large-scale online applications, and convenience of hardware implementations, neural networks have widely arisen in scientific computation and optimization, drawing extensive interest and investigation of researchers. Due to the in-depth research in neural networks, the approaches based on recurrent neural networks (RNNs) are now regarded as powerful alternatives, which can online solve various mathematical and engineering problems. Generally, these RNNs can be divided into two classes: the continuous-time RNNs and the discrete-time RNNs.

As a special class of RNNs, originating and extending from the research of Hopfield neural network, zeroing neural network (also termed as Zhang neural network, ZNN) was proposed by Zhang *et al.* ZNN has been developed and investigated as a systematic and efficient method to solve various time-dependent problems in real time, and it differs from conventional gradient-based RNNs in terms of the problem to be solved, error function, design formula, dynamic equation, and the utilization of derivative information. ZNN can perfectly track the time-dependent solution by fully exploiting the derivative information of time-dependent parameters.

The hardware implementations of continuous-time models are often based on analogue very large scale integration (VLSI), which have some typical weaknesses, such as accuracy, design time, and cost. To overcome those weaknesses, it is necessary to investigate the discretization of continuous-time models. In addition, discrete-time algorithms are easier to implement industrially in current hardware (e.g., digital VLSI or digital computer) than continuous-time models. Thus, it is very important for the discretization of continuous-time ZNN (CTZNN) models to obtain discrete-time ZNN (DTZNN) algorithms.

To approximate the first-order derivative and then discretize the CTZNN models, there exist numerous numerical-differentiation formulas that we can consider. However, notice that the following three facts. (1) Backward numerical-differentiation formulas (also termed as backward difference formulas) may not adapt to the fast variational rate of the first-order derivative of the target function. (2) Central numerical-differentiation formulas (also termed as central difference formulas) cannot approximate the first-order derivative of the target function without enough number of data points in either side. (3) A numerical-differentiation formula does not necessarily generate a stable and convergent DTZNN algorithm (not to mention a high-accuracy one). Thus, effective numerical-differentiation formulas are urgently needed, which are different from those existing in the numerical ordinary differential equation (ODE) literature. Note that effective numerical-differentiation formulas must be one-step-ahead, i.e., approximating $\zeta(t_k)$ by $\zeta(t_{k+1})$, $\zeta(t_k)$, $\zeta(t_{k-1})$, $\zeta(t_{k-2})$, $\cdots$, where k denotes the updating index. In addition, effective numerical-differentiation formulas must lead to zero-stable algorithms. That is, effective numerical-differentiation formulas must satisfy strict conditions.

It is known that the classical Euler forward formula is usually considered as the first and also the simplest one-step-ahead numerical-differentiation formula, proposed in 1755 and widely applied in recent decades. Besides, there exists another one-step-ahead numerical-differentiation formula usable and effective for time discretization with higher precision than the Euler forward formula, termed as Zhang–Taylor discretization formula in this book, as proposed in 2014 (i.e., 259 years later since 1755). They can predict the future solutions of problems on the basis of present or previous data information in an effective and accurate manner. In recent years, a class of numerical-differentiation formulas usable and effective for time discretization has been proposed, established finally, and termed as Zhang time discretization (ZTD) formula, which can be used for the first-order derivative approximation and, more importantly, the CTZNN model discretization. For convenience and also for consistency, if a ZTD formula has N steps, we might as well term it as an N-step ZTD (NS-ZTD) formula in this book. It is noted that the Euler forward formula is actually a one-step ZTD (1S-ZTD) formula and that the Zhang–Taylor discretization formula is actually a three-step ZTD (3S-ZTD) formula. Thereafter, a number of ZTD formulas have been developed within such a framework. However, these ZTD formulas (e.g., the Zhang–Taylor discretization formula) are actually isolated and scattered, which have been developed via many relatively blind attempts. It is difficult to know how many ZTD formulas exist, not to mention the optimal formulas with respect to the stability. With continuing advance, general ZTD formulas (e.g., general 3S-ZTD formula) have been developed and investigated, which can construct numerous-specific ZTD formulas. Note that the different choices of parameters in the general ZTD formulas lead to different general or specific ZTD formulas and corresponding DTZNN algorithms. These DTZNN algorithms can be used for solving discrete time-dependent (also termed as future) problems.

In this book, the resultant various DTZNN algorithms are designed, proposed, developed, analyzed, simulated, and compared for real-time and high-precision solutions of future problems, such as future matrix pseudoinversion (including matrix left pseudoinversion and right pseudoinversion), future equality-constrained quadratic programming, future matrix inversion, future constrained nonlinear optimization, future unconstrained nonlinear optimization, future different-layer inequation-equation system, future matrix square root finding, future different-layer equation system, and future matrix equations. The main contributions lie in the following facts.

- This is the first book on the ZTD formulas and applications, which systematically introduces the first-order derivative approximation by ZTD formulas as well as various future problems solving by DTZNN algorithms.
- This book summarizes and presents the systematic derivations and complete research works of ZTD formulas from special 3S-ZTD formulas to general NS-ZTD formulas, as well as the corresponding DTZNN algorithms, starting from those with low computational precision to those with high computational precision.
- This book presents the complete mathematical foundations, such as the Taylor expansion, bilinear transformation, and Routh stability criterion, as well as the detailed theoretical analyses on zero-stability, consistency, and convergence of DTZNN algorithms.
- This book provides abundant and comparative numerical experimental results, as well as real-world applications (e.g., physical experiments based on a Kinova Jaco^2 manipulator), which further substantiate the effectiveness, high precision, superiority, and practicability of DTZNN algorithms.

The idea for this book on discretization and applications of neural networks was conceived during the classroom teaching as well as the research discussion in the laboratory and at international scientific meetings. Most of the materials of this book are derived from the authors' papers published in journals and proceedings of the international conferences. In fact, since the early 1980s, the field of neural networks has undergone the phases of exponential growth, generating many new theoretical concepts and algorithms (including the authors' ones). At the same time, these theoretical results and algorithms have been applied successfully to many practical applications. Our first priority is thus to cover each central topic in enough details to make the material clear and coherent; in other words, each part (and even each chapter) is written in a relatively self-contained manner.

This book contains 16 chapters, which are classified into the following seven parts.

Part I: Zhang–Taylor Discretization Formula and Applications (Chapters 1 and 2);

Part II: ZTD 6321 Formula and Applications (Chapters 3 and 4);

Part III: General Formulas and Applications of ZTD (Chapters 5–8);

Part IV: $\mathscr{O}(g^3)$ ZTD Formulas and Applications (Chapters 9 and 10);

Part V: $\mathscr{O}(g^4)$ ZTD Formulas and Applications (Chapters 11 and 12);

Part VI: $\mathscr{O}(g^5)$ ZTD Formulas and Applications (Chapters 13 and 14);

Part VII: Miscellaneous (Chapters 15 and 16).

Chapter 1—In this chapter, via the Zhang–Taylor discretization formula, two Zhang–Taylor DTZNN (ZT-DTZNN) algorithms are presented, developed, and investigated for future matrix right pseudoinversion (FMRP). For comparison as well as for illustration, Euler-type DTZNN (ET-DTZNN) algorithms and Newton iteration (NI) algorithm are presented. In addition, according to the criterion of whether the time-derivative information of the time-dependent matrix is explicitly known or not, these DTZNN algorithms are classified into two categories: (1) algorithms with time-derivative information known and (2) algorithms with time-derivative information unknown. Moreover, theoretical analyses show that maximal steady-state residual errors (MSSREs) synthesized by the ZT-DTZNN algorithms have $\mathscr{O}(g^3)$ patterns, the MSSREs synthesized by the ET-DTZNN algorithms have $\mathscr{O}(g^2)$ patterns, whereas the MSSRE synthesized by the NI algorithm has an $\mathscr{O}(g)$ pattern, with g denoting the sampling gap. Finally, two illustrative numerical experiments and an application example to manipulator motion generation are executed to substantiate the efficacy of the presented ZT-DTZNN algorithms for the FMRP.

Chapter 2—In this chapter, a problem called future equality-constrained quadratic programming (FECQP) is developed and discussed. For the FECQP solving, the corresponding continuous time-dependent equality-constrained quadratic programming (CTDECQP) is presented and its CTZNN model is obtained. Then, the Zhang–Taylor discretization formula is presented to discretize the CTZNN model and obtain higher computational accuracy. On the basis of the Zhang–Taylor discretization formula, two ZT-DTZNN algorithms are presented and discussed to perform the FECQP. For comparison, ET-DTZNN algorithms and NI algorithm, with interesting links being found, are also presented. It is proven that the MSSREs synthesized by the presented ZT-DTZNN algorithms, ET-DTZNN algorithms, and NI algorithm have patterns of $\mathscr{O}(g^3)$, $\mathscr{O}(g^2)$, and $\mathscr{O}(g)$, respectively. Numerical experiments (including the application examples) are carried out, of which the results further substantiate the theoretical findings and the efficacy of the ZT-DTZNN algorithms. Finally, the comparisons with Zhang–Taylor discrete-time derivative dynamics (ZT-DTDD) algorithm and Lagrange-type DTZNN (LT-DTZNN) algorithms for the FECQP solving substantiate the superiority of the presented ZT-DTZNN algorithms once again.

Chapter 3—In this chapter, a discrete-time enhanced ZNN (DTEZNN) algorithm is presented, analyzed, and investigated for future matrix inversion (FMI). For comparison, a discrete-time conventional ZNN (DTCZNN) algorithm is presented. Note that the DTEZNN algorithm is superior to the DTCZNN algorithm in suppressing various kinds of bias noises. Moreover, theoretical analyses show the convergence of the presented DTEZNN algorithm under various kinds of bias noises. In addition, numerical experiments, including an application to manipulator motion planning, are executed to substantiate the efficacy and superiority of the presented DTEZNN algorithm for the FMI.

Chapter 4—In this chapter, a 3S-ZTD formula, termed as the ZTD 6321 formula, is presented, which obtains higher computational precision in approximating the first-order derivative. Then, the ZTD 6321 formula is used for the discretization of the CTZNN model and it can greatly overcome the limitation of the conventional formulas in CTZNN discretization. On the basis of the ZTD 6321 formula, a DTZNN 6321 algorithm is presented and investigated for future matrix pseudoinversion (FMP), which is further divided into future matrix left pseudoinversion (FMLP) and FMRP. Numerical experimental results further validate the feasibility, effectiveness, and superiority of the presented DTZNN 6321 algorithm for the FMLP. Moreover, the presented DTZNN 6321 algorithm is applied to the manipulator control, which involves an FMRP problem. The physical experimental results based on a four-link redundant manipulator substantiate the realizability and effectiveness of the presented DTZNN 6321 algorithm.

Chapter 5—In this chapter, general ZTD formulas are developed via the idea of the second-order derivative elimination (SODE). All existing ZTD formulas in the previous works are included in the framework of the general ZTD formulas. The connections and differences of various general formulas are also discussed. Furthermore, the general ZTD formulas are used to solve future constrained nonlinear optimization (FCNO), and corresponding general DTZNN algorithms are developed. The general DTZNN algorithms have at least one parameter to adjust, thereby determining their zero-stability. Thus, the parameter domains are obtained by restricting the zero-stability. Finally, numerous comparative numerical experiments, including the motion control of PUMA560 manipulator, are executed to substantiate theoretical results and their superiority to the conventional Euler forward formula.

Chapter 6—In this chapter, a continuous-time derivative dynamics (CTDD) model is developed for solving continuous time-dependent unconstrained nonlinear optimization (CTDUNO) problem. Furthermore, aiming to remedy the weaknesses of the CTDD model, a CTZNN model is presented and investigated. For potential digital hardware realization, by using bilinear transformation, a general four-step ZTD (4S-ZTD) formula is presented and applied to the discretization of both the CTDD and CTZNN models. For solving future unconstrained nonlinear optimization (FUNO) problem, a general four-step discrete-time derivative dynamics (4S-DTDD) algorithm and a general four-step DTZNN (4S-DTZNN) algorithm are presented on the basis of the general 4S-ZTD formula. Further theoretical analyses indicate that the general 4S-DTZNN algorithm is zero-stable, consistent, and convergent with the truncation error of $\mathbf{O}(g^4)$, which denotes a vector with elements being $\mathscr{O}(g^4)$. Theoretical analyses also indicate that the MSSRE synthesized by the general 4S-DTZNN algorithm has an $\mathscr{O}(g^4)$ pattern confirmedly. The efficacy and accuracy of the general 4S-DTDD algorithm and the general 4S-DTZNN algorithm are further verified by numerical experimental results.

Chapter 7—In this chapter, a challenging problem called future different-layer inequation–equation system (FDLIES) is developed and investigated. To solve the FDLIES, the corresponding continuous time-dependent different-layer inequation-equation system (CTDDLIES) is first analyzed, and then a CTZNN model for solving the CTDDLIES is developed. To obtain a DTZNN algorithm for solving the FDLIES, a high-precision general six-step ZTD (6S-ZTD) formula for the first-order derivative approximation is developed. Furthermore, by applying the general 6S-ZTD formula to discretize the CTZNN model, a general six-step DTZNN (6S-DTZNN) algorithm is thus developed for solving the FDLIES. For comparison, by using three other ZTD formulas, three other DTZNN algorithms are also developed. Meanwhile, theoretical analyses guarantee the efficacy and superiority of the general 6S-DTZNN algorithm compared with the three other DTZNN algorithms for solving the FDLIES. Finally, several comparative numerical experiments, including the motion control of a five-link redundant manipulator, are provided to substantiate the efficacy and superiority of the general 6S-ZTD formula and the corresponding 6S-DTZNN algorithm.

Chapter 8—In this chapter, on the basis of previous works, by using the ZNN method, a CTZNN model is developed for continuous time-dependent matrix square root finding (CTDMSRF). Besides, a general nine-step ZTD (9S-ZTD) formula is derived, constructed, and investigated, and the corresponding theoretical analysis is provided. Next, by applying the general 9S-ZTD formula to discretize the CTZNN model, a general nine-step DTZNN (9S-DTZNN) algorithm is further obtained. For comparison, four other DTZNN algorithms are also acquired and presented, respectively, by using other ZTD formulas. Finally, the effectiveness and correctness of the presented four other DTZNN algorithms for future matrix square root finding (FMSRF) are further substantiated by numerical experimental results.

Chapter 9—In this chapter, a look-ahead scheme of ZNN is established to achieve the real-time tracking control of both serial and parallel manipulators. With the exploitation of current and previous data, the control inputs generated by DTZNN algorithms never lead to lagging errors caused by the inevitable computing time. To reduce prediction errors synthesized by DTZNN algorithms, a high-precision discretization formula, as an essential part of DTZNN algorithms, is presented to confine the prediction error in an ignorable range compared with lagging errors.

Chapter 10—In this chapter, a five-step ZTD (5S-ZTD) formula with high precision is presented to approximate the first-order derivative. Then, such a formula is studied to discretize two continuous-time neural network models, i.e., a CTZNN model and a continuous-time gradient neural network (CTGNN) model. Subsequently, two discrete-time neural network algorithms, i.e., a five-step DTZNN (5S-DTZNN) algorithm and a five-step discrete-time gradient neural network (5S-DTGNN) algorithm, are developed and investigated for the FMI. In addition to analyze a usual situation that the coefficient matrix is always nonsingular, this chapter investigates another situation that the coefficient matrix is sometimes singular for the FMI. Finally, two illustrative numerical examples, including an application to the inverse-kinematic control of PUMA560 manipulator, are provided to show the respective characteristics and advantages of the 5S-DTZNN algorithm and the 5S-DTGNN algorithm for the FMI in different situations, where the coefficient matrix to be inverted is always nonsingular or sometimes singular during time evolution.

Chapter 11—In this chapter, the repetitive motion control of redundant manipulators is investigated. First, a repetitive motion control problem is presented, and a CTZNN model is obtained for solving the problem. Meanwhile, the development of a DTZNN algorithm is desired for convenient computational processing. On the basis of this, the chapter presents a 6S-ZTD formula, which has high precision. By using the 6S-ZTD formula and the four-step backward numerical-differentiation formula, a 6S-DTZNN algorithm is further developed to solve the repetitive motion control problem. Theoretical analyses verify the efficacy of the 6S-DTZNN algorithm. Additionally, some discrete-time forms of conventional models are developed for comparison. Numerical experiments based on the four-link redundant manipulator are carried out, verifying the theoretical results and showing the efficacy of the 6S-DTZNN algorithm. Finally, physical experimental results based on the Kinova Jaco^2 manipulator substantiate the practicability of the 6S-DTZNN algorithm.

Chapter 12—In this chapter, future different-layer equation system (FDLES) is investigated. First, on the basis of the ZNN method, a zeroing equivalency (ZE) theorem is presented. Then, a CTZNN model is developed for continuous time-dependent different-layer equation system (CTD-DLES) solving. Next, a seven-step ZTD (7S-ZTD) formula is presented to discretize the CTZNN model, and thus a seven-step DTZNN (7S-DTZNN) algorithm is developed for the FDLES solving. 4S-DTZNN and three-step DTZNN (3S-DTZNN) algorithms are also developed for the same problem solving. Besides, numerical experiments are executed to substantiate the validity and superiority of the developed 7S-DTZNN algorithm. Finally, the path-tracking control problem of a four-link redundant manipulator is formulated as a specific FDLES problem and can thus be solved by the three DTZNN algorithms. Comparative numerical experimental results further indicate the developed 7S-DTZNN algorithm is much superior to the two other DTZNN algorithms.

Chapter 13—In this chapter, time-dependent matrix equation problems, including the Lyapunov equation, matrix inversion, and generalized matrix inversion, are investigated in a future (or say, discrete time-dependent) perspective. Then, in order to develop a unified solution algorithm for the above three future problems, a future matrix equation (FME) is investigated. The discrete-time unified solution algorithm, which is based on the ZNN method and an eight-step ZTD (8S-ZTD) formula, is thus developed and termed as eight-step DTZNN (8S-DTZNN) algorithm. Meanwhile, theoretical analyses on the stability and precision of the 8S-DTZNN algorithm are provided. In addition, other DTZNN algorithms obtained from the Euler forward formula, the Zhang–Taylor discretization formula, and a 6S-ZTD formula are also presented for comparison. Furthermore, numerical experiments, including the manipulator motion generation, are conducted and analyzed to substantiate the efficacy and superiority of the 8S-DTZNN algorithm.

Chapter 14—In this chapter, the problem of velocity-layer minimum joint motion control (VLMJMC) of redundant manipulators is solved in a discrete-time form. First, by applying the approach of Lagrange multipliers and the ZNN method, a CTZNN model is presented. Additionally, a 9S-ZTD formula is derived, constructed, and investigated. Second, by adopting the 9S-ZTD formula and other ZTD formulas with less steps, five DTZNN algorithms are further acquired and presented, with the corresponding theoretical analyses. Finally, numerical and physical experimental results both verify the feasibility, effectiveness, and correctness of the five DTZNN algorithms.

Chapter 15—In this chapter, a general two-step ZTD (2S-ZTD) formula with truncation error proportional to the sampling gap is presented and investigated. To begin with, the stability and accuracy of the general 2S-ZTD formula are ensured by strict proof. Then, the general 2S-ZTD formula is used for the first-order derivative approximation, and numerical experimental results verify its stability and accuracy. Besides, the general 2S-ZTD formula is applied to discretizing CTZNN model, and thus the general two-step DTZNN (2S-DTZNN) algorithm with square precision is developed for solving future minimization problem. Numerical experimental results verify the stability and accuracy of the general 2S-DTZNN algorithm again.

Chapter 16—In this chapter, in order to achieve higher computational precision in approximating the first-order derivative of the target point, Lagrange numerical-differentiation formulas (also known as one-step-ahead numerical-differentiation formulas) are presented. These formulas greatly remedy some intrinsic weaknesses of backward numerical-differentiation formulas and overcome limitation of central numerical-differentiation formulas. In addition, a group of formulas are proposed to obtain the optimal sampling gaps. Moreover, the error analyses of Lagrange numerical-differentiation formulas and backward numerical-differentiation formulas are further investigated. Numerical experimental results show that the proposed optimal sampling-gap formulas are effective, and the approximation performance of Lagrange numerical-differentiation formulas is much better than that of backward numerical-differentiation formulas.

This book is written for graduate students as well as academic and industrial researchers studying in the developing fields of neural networks, computer mathematics, computer science, artificial intelligence, numerical algorithms, optimization, robot technology, and simulation modeling. It provides a comprehensive view of the combined research of these fields, in addition to its accomplishments, potentials, and perspectives. We do hope that this book will generate curiosity and also happiness to its readers for learning more in the fields and the research and that it will provide new challenges to seek new theoretical tools and practical applications. It may promise to become a major inspiration for both studies and research works in neural network modeling, numerical algorithm design, prediction, and robot manipulator control. Without doubt, this book can be extended. Any comments or suggestions are welcome. The authors can be contacted via Dr. Zhang's web page at `http://cse.sysu.edu.cn/content/2477`.

Acknowledgments

This book basically comprises the results of many original research articles of the authors' research group, in which many authors of these original articles have done a great deal of detailed and creative research work. Therefore, we are much obliged to our contributing authors for their high-quality work. During the work on this book, we have had the pleasure of discussing its various aspects and results with many cooperators and students. We highly appreciate their contributions, which particularly allowed us to improve the presentation and quality of this book considerably. Especially valuable help was provided by Liangjie Ming, Wuyi Yang, Zanyu Tang, Zhuosong Fu, Litian Li, Dongqing Wu, Min Yang, Wenqi Wu, Kangze Zheng, Jielong Chen, Xiao Liu, and Zhenyu Li. We are grateful to them for their help and suggestions.

The continuous support of our research by the National Natural Science Foundation of China (61976230), by the Project Supported by Guangdong Province Universities and Colleges Pearl River Scholar Funded Scheme (2018), by the Key-Area Research and Development Program of Guangzhou (202007030004), by the start-up funding from Guangdong Polytechnic Normal University (2023SDKYA006), and also by the Scientific Research Platforms and Projects of Guangdong Provincial Education Department (2022ZDZX1012) is gratefully acknowledged under "Funding" section.

To all these wonderful people we owe a deep sense of gratitude especially now when the research projects and the book have been completed.

Part I

Zhang–Taylor Discretization Formula and Applications

Chapter 1

Future Matrix Right Pseudoinversion

Abstract

In addition to the high-speed parallel-distributed processing property, neural networks can be readily implemented by hardware and thus have been applied widely in various fields. In this chapter, via Zhang–Taylor discretization formula, two Zhang–Taylor discrete-time zeroing neural network (ZT-DTZNN) algorithms are presented, developed, and investigated for future matrix right pseudoinversion (FMRP). For comparison as well as for illustration, Euler-type DTZNN (ET-DTZNN) algorithms and Newton iteration (NI) algorithm are presented. In addition, according to the criterion of whether the time-derivative information of the time-dependent matrix is explicitly known or not, these DTZNN algorithms are classified into two categories: (1) algorithms with time-derivative information known and (2) algorithms with time-derivative information unknown. Moreover, theoretical analyses show that maximal steady-state residual errors (MSSREs) synthesized by the ZT-DTZNN algorithms have $\mathscr{O}(g^3)$ patterns, the MSSREs synthesized by the ET-DTZNN algorithms have $\mathscr{O}(g^2)$ patterns, whereas the MSSRE synthesized by the NI algorithm has an $\mathscr{O}(g)$ pattern, with g denoting the sampling gap. Finally, two illustrative numerical experiments and an application example to manipulator motion generation are provided and analyzed to substantiate the efficacy of the presented ZT-DTZNN algorithms for the FMRP.

1.1 Introduction

Matrix pseudoinversion (also known as Moore–Penrose inversion) is considered to be one of the basic problems widely encountered in a variety of scientific and engineering fields, e.g., robotics [1], machine learning [2], associative memories [3], and optimization [4]. Owing to its fundamental roles, much effort has been devoted to the fast solution and high accuracy of the matrix pseudoinversion, and many algorithms have been put forward by researchers [5–8]. Huang and Zhang [5] showed that the Newton iteration (NI) method can be used to compute the weighted Moore–Penrose inverse of an arbitrary matrix. Courrieu [7] proposed an algorithm based on a full-rank Cholesky factorization for fast computation of Moore–Penrose generalized inverse matrices. When solving the time-dependent matrix pseudoinverse, many conventional algorithms generally suppose the short-time invariance of the matrix and compute at each single time instant, where the change trend of the

DOI: 10.1201/9781003497783-1

time-dependent matrix is not exploited [1, 9]. The computed results are then directly used for the next time instant, and lagging errors may thus be generated between the obtained solution and the theoretical solution. Additionally, most numerical algorithms may not be efficient enough in large-scale online applications due to their serial-processing nature. Especially, when applied to the online solution of the time-dependent matrix pseudoinverse, these related numerical algorithms should be fulfilled within every sampling gap, and the algorithms fail when the sampling rate is too high to allow the algorithms to complete the computation in a single sampling gap, not to mention more challenging situations.

In recent decades, with the characteristics of distributed-storage and high-speed parallel processing, superior performance in large-scale online applications, and convenience of hardware implementations, neural networks have widely arisen in scientific computation and optimization, drawing extensive interest and investigation of researchers [10–14]. Due to the in-depth research in neural networks, the neural-dynamic approaches based on recurrent neural networks (RNNs) are now regarded as powerful alternatives [11–15], which can solve many mathematical and engineering problems with time-dependent coefficients.

Zeroing neural network (ZNN) is a special class of RNNs, which originates from the research of Hopfield neural network; it is proposed as a systematic approach to solve online time-dependent problems; it differs from conventional gradient-based RNNs in terms of the problem to be solved, error function, design formula, dynamic equation, and the utilization of time derivatives [16–19]. Liao and Zhang proposed several continuous-time ZNN (CTZNN) models for time-dependent matrix pseudoinversion, which can be accelerated to finite-time convergence via Li activation functions [19]. However, in view of the variation of the time step, the continuous-time models are difficult for digital computers to be implemented directly, which often demand constant time step (i.e., the sampling gap, g, is a constant in a certain calculating process). Thus, it is necessary to develop the corresponding discrete-time algorithms for discrete time-dependent (also termed as future) matrix pseudoinversion.

For obtaining the first-order derivative approximation and then discretizing the CTZNN model, there exist many numerical-differentiation formulas that we can consider. However, notice the following three facts [20]. (1) Backward numerical-differentiation formulas (also termed as backward difference formulas) may not adapt to the fast variational rate of the first-order derivative of the target function. (2) Central numerical-differentiation formulas (also termed as central difference formulas) cannot approximate the first-order derivative of the target function without enough number of data points in either side. (3) A numerical-differentiation formula does not necessarily generate a stable and convergent discrete-time ZNN (DTZNN) algorithm (not to mention a high-accuracy one). Thus, an effective numerical-differentiation formula is needed. In light of this analysis, a one-step-ahead numerical-differentiation formula, termed as Zhang–Taylor discretization formula, is thus constructed for the first-order derivative approximation. Furthermore, adopting the Zhang–Taylor discretization formula, we present two Zhang–Taylor DTZNN (ZT-DTZNN) algorithms for the future matrix right pseudoinversion (FMRP). These ZT-DTZNN algorithms are derived from the CTZNN model with time-derivative information known and with time-derivative information unknown but approximated by using backward numerical-differentiation formulas. It is theoretically proved that the two ZT-DTZNN algorithms converge toward the time-dependent theoretical solution of the FMRP problem with $\mathcal{O}(g^3)$ residual error patterns. Besides, for purposes of comparison, two Euler-type DTZNN (ET-DTZNN) algorithms and the conventional NI algorithm, together with their convergence performance analyses, are also presented. Through the numerical experiments, the theoretical results and the efficacy of the presented algorithms for the FMRP are well substantiated.

1.2 Problem Formulation and CTZNN Model

In order to lay a basis for further investigation, the preliminaries, the problem formulation of FMRP, and the CTZNN model are presented in this section.

Definition 1 *[15,19,21–24] For a given time-dependent matrix $A(t) \in \mathbb{R}^{m\times n}$, if $X(t) \in \mathbb{R}^{n\times m}$ satisfies at least one of the following four Penrose equations:*

$$A(t)X(t)A(t) = A(t), \quad X(t)A(t)X(t) = X(t),$$
$$(A(t)X(t))^{\mathrm{T}} = A(t)X(t), \quad (X(t)A(t))^{\mathrm{T}} = X(t)A(t),$$

where the superscript ^{T} denotes the transpose operator of a matrix, $X(t)$ is called the generalized inverse of $A(t)$. If matrix $X(t)$ satisfies all of the Penrose equations, then matrix $X(t)$ is called the pseudoinverse of matrix $A(t)$, which is often denoted by $A^{\dagger}(t)$.

Note that the time-dependent pseudoinverse $A^{\dagger}(t)$ always exists and is unique [19]. Specially, if matrix $A(t) \in \mathbb{R}^{m\times n}$ is of full rank at any time instant t, i.e., $\mathrm{rank}(A(t)) = \min\{m,n\}, \forall t \in [0,\infty)$, we have the following lemma to obtain the time-dependent pseudoinverse of $A(t)$.

Lemma 1 *[19, 21, 22] For any time-dependent matrix $A(t) \in \mathbb{R}^{m\times n}$, if $\mathrm{rank}(A(t)) = \min\{m,n\}, \forall t \in [0,\infty)$, then the unique time-dependent pseudoinverse $A^{\dagger}(t)$ can be given as*

$$A^{\dagger}(t) = \begin{cases} A^{\mathrm{T}}(t)\left(A(t)A^{\mathrm{T}}(t)\right)^{-1}, & \text{if } m < n, \\ \left(A^{\mathrm{T}}(t)A(t)\right)^{-1}A^{\mathrm{T}}(t), & \text{if } m \geq n. \end{cases} \tag{1.1}$$

When $m < n$, $A^{\dagger}(t)$ corresponds to the right pseudoinverse of $A(t)$. In the case of $m = n$, we have $A^{\dagger}(t) = A^{-1}(t) = A^{\mathrm{T}}(t)\left(A(t)A^{\mathrm{T}}(t)\right)^{-1} = \left(A^{\mathrm{T}}(t)A(t)\right)^{-1}A^{\mathrm{T}}(t)$. Note that for $m \geq n$, the procedure of obtaining the time-dependent pseudoinverse of $A(t)$ is similar to that of $m < n$ and thus omitted. This chapter [22] mainly considers the situation that $m < n$, i.e., the FMRP problem.

1.2.1 Problem formulation

Let us consider the following FMRP problem with X_{k+1} to be computed at each computational time interval $[t_k, t_{k+1}) = [kg, (k+1)g) \subset [t_{\mathrm{ini}}, t_{\mathrm{fin}}] \subset [0, +\infty)$:

$$A_{k+1} - X_{k+1}^{\dagger} = O_{m\times n} \in \mathbb{R}^{m\times n}, \tag{1.2}$$

where t_{ini} and t_{fin} represent the initial and final time instants, respectively; $O_{m\times n}$ denotes an $m \times n$ zero matrix. Besides, $A_{k+1} \in \mathbb{R}^{m\times n}$ being of full row rank is generated or measured from the smoothly time-dependent matrix $A(t) \in \mathbb{R}^{m\times n}$ by sampling at time instant $t_{k+1} = (k+1)g$, and $X_{k+1} \in \mathbb{R}^{n\times m}$ is the unknown matrix obtained during $[t_k, t_{k+1})$. Note that $k = 0, 1, 2, \cdots$ denotes the updating index. In the online solution process of the FMRP problem (1.2), computation has to be performed based on the present or previous data. For example, at time instant t_k, we can only use known information such as A_k and its derivative, instead of unknown information such as A_{k+1} and its derivative, for computing the unknown matrix X_{k+1} during the computational time interval $[kg, (k+1)g)$. Thus, the objective of this chapter [22] is, through the present or previous data, to find the unknown matrix X_{k+1} during $[t_k, t_{k+1})$, such that (1.2) holds true at each time instant.

1.2.2 CTZNN model

To develop DTZNN algorithms effectively for solving (1.2) (which is an actually unknown matrix pseudoinversion problem), the CTZNN model can firstly be generated by exploiting the ZNN method. Now, let us consider the following continuous time-dependent matrix right pseudoinversion problem as the continuation of (1.2): $A(t) - X^{\dagger}(t) = O_{m\times n}$. Then, a matrix-valued zeroing function (ZF) can be defined as $Z(t) = A(t) - X^{\dagger}(t)$. By adopting the ZNN design formula $\dot{Z}(t) = -\eta Z(t)$, we obtain $\dot{A}(t) - \dot{X}^{\dagger}(t) = -\eta\left(A(t) - X^{\dagger}(t)\right)$, where $\eta > 0$ is used to scale the convergence rate of the neural network and should be set as large as the hardware would permit [18]. By employing Lemma 3 in [19], the above equation can be further modified as $X^{\dagger}(t)\dot{X}(t)X^{\dagger}(t) = -\dot{A}(t) - \eta\left(A(t) - X^{\dagger}(t)\right)$. Reformulating the above equation, we have

$$\dot{X}(t) = -X(t)\dot{A}(t)X(t) - \eta(X(t)A(t)X(t) - X(t)), \tag{1.3}$$

of which the exponential convergence was proved in [19]. Note that (1.3) is the fifth CTZNN model with linear activation function in [19], which is exactly the Getz–Marsden dynamic system for the online solution of the time-dependent matrix pseudoinverse. It is also worth pointing out that there are five CTZNN models in [19], of which the first four are depicted in implicit dynamics that are difficult to be discretized directly (e.g., $A^{\mathrm{T}}(t)A(t)\dot{X}(t) = \cdots$). On the contrary, the fifth CTZNN model (i.e., (1.3)) is depicted in explicit dynamics, i.e., $\dot{X}(t) = \cdots$, which can be discretized directly and the corresponding discrete-time algorithms can be readily implemented by digital hardware.

Remark 1 *Before constructing specific discrete-time neural networks from (1.3) for solving (1.2), the main characteristics, difficulties, and even challenges of the FMRP, which are evidently different from time-independent case, are discussed here. (1) In view of the time variation of matrix $A(t)$, how to develop the discrete-time algorithm(s) without using future data is a key point for the FMRP. In other words, at the present time instant t_k, we have no mathematical function to express deterministically the future such as A_{k+1}, but we have to find in advance an optimal solution to it. (2) Computation consumes time inevitably; time is precious especially for the FMRP. Thus, how to design a simple discrete-time algorithm with higher accuracy is important. In other words, the discrete-time algorithm should satisfy the requirement of real-time computation.*

1.3 Zhang–Taylor ZNN Discretization

The Zhang–Taylor discretization formula is presented in this section, which is used to discretize the CTZNN model (1.3). Two ZT-DTZNN algorithms are thus presented for solving the FMRP problem (1.2), of which the stability and convergence are proved theoretically as well.

1.3.1 Effective $\mathcal{O}(g^2)$ formula

A Taylor series is an infinite sum of terms that are computed from the values of derivatives of a function at a single point. In scientific and engineering fields, the partial sums can be accumulated until an approximation to the function is obtained that achieves the specified accuracy. Consequently, the Zhang–Taylor discretization (also termed as Taylor–Zhang discretization, previously) formula is constructed in this subsection for the first-order derivative approximation by eliminating the second-order derivative, which can achieve higher computational accuracy in the application of ZNN discretization.

Theorem 1 *With the sufficiently small sampling gap $g \in (0,1)$, let $\mathcal{O}(g^2)$ denote the error (especially, the truncation error) positively or negatively proportional to g^2, i.e., of the order of g^2.*

Suppose that $\zeta(t)$ is sufficiently smooth. With $\zeta_{k+1} = \zeta(t_{k+1}) = \zeta((k+1)g)$, the Zhang–Taylor discretization formula is formulated as

$$\dot{\zeta}_k = \frac{2\zeta_{k+1} - 3\zeta_k + 2\zeta_{k-1} - \zeta_{k-2}}{2g} + \mathcal{O}(g^2). \tag{1.4}$$

Proof. The proof is presented in Appendix A. □

On the basis of Theorem 1, an effective $\mathcal{O}(g^2)$ formula is obtained for the first-order derivative approximation, which is expected to be applied for ZNN discretization for a higher accuracy in comparison with the ET-DTZNN with $\dot{A}_k$ known (ET-DTZNN-K) algorithm, the ET-DTZNN with $\dot{A}_k$ unknown (ET-DTZNN-U) algorithm, and the NI algorithm. In the next subsection, the ZT-DTZNN with $\dot{A}_k$ known (ZT-DTZNN-K) algorithm and the ZT-DTZNN with $\dot{A}_k$ unknown (ZT-DTZNN-U) algorithm are presented.

1.3.2 ZT-DTZNN-K and ZT-DTZNN-U algorithms

On the basis of the presented Zhang–Taylor discretization formula (1.4), two DTZNN algorithms are developed and investigated in this subsection. Specifically, it follows from (1.3) that

$$X_{k+1} \doteq -gX_k\dot{A}_kX_k - \hbar(X_kA_kX_k - X_k) + \frac{3}{2}X_k - X_{k-1} + \frac{1}{2}X_{k-2}, \tag{1.5}$$

with $\doteq$ denoting the computational assignment operator and $\hbar = g\eta$ representing the step length. For presentation convenience, (1.5) is called the ZT-DTZNN-K algorithm.

As we know, it may be difficult to know or obtain the value of $\dot{A}(t)$ directly in certain real-world applications. Thus, it is worth investigating the ZT-DTZNN-U algorithm. In this situation, $\dot{A}(t)$ can be estimated from $A(t)$ by employing the backward numerical-differentiation formula of the first derivative with a third-order accuracy [20]:

$$\dot{\zeta}_k = \frac{11\zeta_k - 18\zeta_{k-1} + 9\zeta_{k-2} - 2\zeta_{k-3}}{6g} + \mathcal{O}(g^3), \tag{1.6}$$

where $\mathcal{O}(g^3)$ denotes the truncation error. Thus, the ZT-DTZNN-U algorithm can be formulated as

$$\begin{aligned} X_{k+1} \doteq &-X_k\left(\frac{11}{6}A_k - 3A_{k-1} + \frac{3}{2}A_{k-2} - \frac{1}{3}A_{k-3}\right)X_k \\ &- \hbar(X_kA_kX_k - X_k) + \frac{3}{2}X_k - X_{k-1} + \frac{1}{2}X_{k-2}. \end{aligned} \tag{1.7}$$

1.3.3 Theoretical analyses

Before investigating the performance of the ZT-DTZNN-K algorithm (1.5) and the ZT-DTZNN-U algorithm (1.7), the following definitions are provided as a basis for further discussion [25].

Definition 2 *An N-step method/formula $\sum_{j=0}^{N}\alpha_j\chi_{k+j} = g\sum_{j=0}^{N}\beta_j\xi_{k+j}$ can be checked for zero-stability by determining the roots of the characteristic polynomial $\Gamma_N(\iota) = \sum_{j=0}^{N}\alpha_j\iota^j$. If the roots of $\Gamma_N(\iota) = 0$ are such that $|\iota| \leq 1$ and those for which $|\iota| = 1$ are simple, then the N-step method/formula is zero-stable. In addition, the zero-stability is sometimes called Dahlquist stability or root stability.*

Definition 3 *An N-step method/formula is said to be consistent if its truncation error is $\mathcal{O}(g^p)$, with $p > 0$ for the smooth exact solution.*

Definition 4 *An N-step method/formula is convergent, i.e.,* $x_{[(t-t_{\text{ini}})/g]} \to x^*(t)$, *for all* $t \in [t_{\text{ini}}, t_{\text{fin}}]$, *as* $g \to 0$, *if and only if the method/formula is zero-stable and consistent. In other words, zero-stability plus consistency leads to convergence. In particular, a zero-stable and consistent method/formula converges with the order of its truncation error.*

On the basis of the above three definitions, we have the following theoretical results about the ZT-DTZNN-K algorithm (1.5) and the ZT-DTZNN-U algorithm (1.7).

Theorem 2 *Suppose that* $A_k \in \mathbb{R}^{m\times n}$ *is of full row rank. With the sufficiently small sampling gap* $g \in (0,1)$, *the ZT-DTZNN-K algorithm (1.5) is zero-stable.*

Proof. According to Definition 2, the characteristic polynomial of the ZT-DTZNN-K algorithm (1.5) is derived as

$$\Gamma_3(\iota) = \iota^3 - 1.5\iota^2 + \iota - 0.5,$$

which has three roots on or inside the unit circle/disk, i.e., $\iota_1 = 1$, $\iota_2 = 0.25 + 0.6614\mathrm{i}$, and $\iota_3 = 0.25 - 0.6614\mathrm{i}$, with i denoting the imaginary unit. Therefore, the ZT-DTZNN-K algorithm (1.5) is zero-stable. The proof is therefore completed. □

Theorem 3 *Suppose that* $A_k \in \mathbb{R}^{m\times n}$ *is of full row rank. With the sufficiently small sampling gap* $g \in (0,1)$, *let* $\mathbf{O}(g^3)$ *denote the error (especially, the truncation error) with each element being* $\mathcal{O}(g^3)$. *The ZT-DTZNN-K algorithm (1.5) is consistent and convergent, which converges with the order of truncation error being* $\mathbf{O}(g^3)$ *for all* $t_k \in [t_{\text{ini}}, t_{\text{fin}}]$.

Proof. In view of (1.4), we have the following equation:

$$X_{k+1} = -gX_k\dot{A}_kX_k - \hbar X_k(A_kX_k - I_{m\times m}) + \frac{3}{2}X_k - X_{k-1} + \frac{1}{2}X_{k-2} + \mathbf{O}(g^3), \quad (1.8)$$

where $I_{m\times m}$ denotes an $m\times m$ identity matrix. Note that dropping $\mathbf{O}(g^3)$ of (1.8) yields exactly the ZT-DTZNN-K algorithm (1.5), and thus the truncation error of the ZT-DTZNN-K algorithm (1.5) is $\mathbf{O}(g^3)$. Therefore, according to Definition 3, the ZT-DTZNN-K algorithm (1.5) is consistent. In view of Theorem 2, the ZT-DTZNN-K algorithm (1.5) is both zero-stable and consistent. Finally, on the basis of Definition 4, it is concluded that the ZT-DTZNN-K algorithm (1.5) is consistent and convergent, which converges with the order of truncation error being $\mathbf{O}(g^3)$ for all $t_k \in [t_{\text{ini}}, t_{\text{fin}}]$. The proof is therefore completed. □

Note that the residual error is defined as $\hat{e}_{k+1} = \|X_{k+1}A_{k+1}A_{k+1}^{\mathrm{T}} - A_{k+1}^{\mathrm{T}}\|_{\mathrm{F}}$ for solving the FMRP problem (1.2) in this chapter [22], where $\|\cdot\|_{\mathrm{F}}$ denotes the Frobenius norm of a matrix.

Theorem 4 *Consider the FMRP problem (1.2) with* $A_k \in \mathbb{R}^{m\times n}$ *being of full row rank and uniformly norm bounded. With the sufficiently small sampling gap* $g \in (0,1)$, *the maximal steady-state residual error (MSSRE)* $\lim_{k\to\infty}\sup \hat{e}_{k+1}$ *synthesized by the ZT-DTZNN-K algorithm (1.5) is* $\mathcal{O}(g^3)$.

Proof. In view of Definition 3 as well as Theorems 2 and 3, it can be concluded that $A_{k+1}^{\dagger} = X_{k+1} + \mathbf{O}(g^3)$ with k large enough. Then, we obtain

$$\|X_{k+1}A_{k+1}A_{k+1}^{\mathrm{T}} - A_{k+1}^{\mathrm{T}}\|_{\mathrm{F}} = \|A_{k+1}^{\dagger}A_{k+1}A_{k+1}^{\mathrm{T}} - A_{k+1}^{\mathrm{T}} + \mathbf{O}(g^3)A_{k+1}A_{k+1}^{\mathrm{T}}\|_{\mathrm{F}}. \quad (1.9)$$

From Lemma 1, we get $A_{k+1}^{\dagger}A_{k+1}A_{k+1}^{\mathrm{T}} - A_{k+1}^{\mathrm{T}} = O_{n\times m}$, with $O_{n\times m}$ denoting an $n\times m$ zero matrix. Note that with $A_{k+1}A_{k+1}^{\mathrm{T}}$ being a constant matrix at a certain time instant, the term $\mathbf{O}(g^3)A_{k+1}A_{k+1}^{\mathrm{T}}$ changes in an $\mathbf{O}(g^3)$ pattern; i.e., with g decreasing to one-tenth of its original value, $\|\mathbf{O}(g^3)A_{k+1}A_{k+1}^{\mathrm{T}}\|_{\mathrm{F}}$ decreases to one-thousandth of its original value. Therefore, we have $\|\mathbf{O}(g^3)A_{k+1}A_{k+1}^{\mathrm{T}}\|_{\mathrm{F}} = \|\mathbf{O}(g^3)\|_{\mathrm{F}}$ and further have

$$\|X_{k+1}A_{k+1}A_{k+1}^{\mathrm{T}} - A_{k+1}^{\mathrm{T}}\|_{\mathrm{F}} = \|\mathbf{O}(g^3)A_{k+1}A_{k+1}^{\mathrm{T}}\|_{\mathrm{F}} = \|\mathbf{O}(g^3)\|_{\mathrm{F}} = \mathcal{O}(g^3).$$

The proof is therefore completed. □

Theorem 5 *Consider the FMRP problem (1.2) with $A_k \in \mathbb{R}^{m\times n}$ being of full row rank and uniformly norm bounded. With the sufficiently small sampling gap $g \in (0,1)$, the MSSRE $\lim_{k\to\infty}\sup \hat{e}_{k+1}$ synthesized by the ZT-DTZNN-U algorithm (1.7) is $\mathscr{O}(g^3)$.*

Proof. In view of (1.6) and (1.9), we have the following equation for the ZT-DTZNN-U algorithm (1.7):

$$\begin{aligned} X_{k+1} &= -gX_k(\dot{A}_k + \mathbf{O}(g^3))X_k - \hbar X_k(A_kX_k - I_{m\times m}) + \frac{3}{2}X_k - X_{k-1} + \frac{1}{2}X_{k-2} + \mathbf{O}(g^3) \\ &= -gX_k\dot{A}_kX_k - \hbar X_k(A_kX_k - I_{m\times m}) + \frac{3}{2}X_k - X_{k-1} + \frac{1}{2}X_{k-2} - gX_k(\mathbf{O}(g^3))X_k + \mathbf{O}(g^3) \\ &= -gX_k\dot{A}_kX_k - \hbar X_k(A_kX_k - I_{m\times m}) + \frac{3}{2}X_k - X_{k-1} + \frac{1}{2}X_{k-2} + \mathbf{O}(g^3). \end{aligned} \tag{1.10}$$

Note that dropping $\mathbf{O}(g^3)$ of (1.10) yields exactly the ZT-DTZNN-K algorithm (1.5), and thus the truncation error of the ZT-DTZNN-U algorithm (1.7) is $\mathbf{O}(g^3)$. Therefore, according to Definition 3, the ZT-DTZNN-U algorithm (1.7) is consistent. By following Theorems 3 and 4, it can be readily generalized and similarly proved that the MSSRE $\lim_{k\to\infty}\sup \hat{e}_{k+1}$ synthesized by the ZT-DTZNN-U algorithm (1.7) is $\mathscr{O}(g^3)$. The proof is therefore completed. □

1.4 Euler-Type ZNN Discretization and NI

In this section, for comparison purposes, ET-DTZNN algorithms and the NI algorithm are presented and analyzed to solve the FMRP problem (1.2).

1.4.1 ET-DTZNN-K and ET-DTZNN-U algorithms

By following the similar steps given in Subsection 1.3.2, the ET-DTZNN-K algorithm is obtained via Euler forward formula (i.e., $\dot{\zeta}_k = (\zeta_{k+1} - \zeta_k)/g + \mathscr{O}(g)$) and directly given as

$$X_{k+1} \doteq -gX_k\dot{A}_kX_k - \hbar(X_kA_kX_k - X_k) + X_k. \tag{1.11}$$

By approximating $\dot{A}_k$ with Euler backward formula (i.e., $\dot{\zeta}_k = (\zeta_k - \zeta_{k-1})/g + \mathscr{O}(g)$), the ET-DTZNN-U algorithm is obtained as

$$X_{k+1} \doteq -X_k(A_k - A_{k-1})X_k - \hbar(X_kA_kX_k - X_k) + X_k. \tag{1.12}$$

Theorem 6 *Suppose that $A_k \in \mathbb{R}^{m\times n}$ is of full row rank. With the sufficiently small sampling gap $g \in (0,1)$, the ET-DTZNN-K algorithm (1.11) is zero-stable.*

Proof. According to Definition 2, the characteristic polynomial of the ET-DTZNN-K algorithm (1.11) is derived as

$$\Gamma_1(\iota) = \iota - 1,$$

which has only one root (i.e., $\iota = 1$) on the unit circle. Hence, the ET-DTZNN-K algorithm (1.11) is zero-stable. The proof is therefore completed. □

Theorem 7 *Consider the FMRP problem (1.2) with $A_k \in \mathbb{R}^{m\times n}$ being of full row rank and uniformly norm bounded. With the sufficiently small sampling gap $g \in (0,1)$, both the MSSREs $\lim_{k\to\infty}\sup \hat{e}_{k+1}$ synthesized by the ET-DTZNN-K algorithm (1.11) and the ET-DTZNN-U algorithm (1.12) are $\mathscr{O}(g^2)$.*

Proof. In light of Theorem 6, by following Theorems 3–5, it is readily generalized and similarly proved that both the MSSREs $\lim_{k\to\infty}\sup\hat{e}_{k+1}$ synthesized by the ET-DTZNN-K algorithm (1.11) and the ET-DTZNN-U algorithm (1.12) are $\mathscr{O}(g^2)$. The proof is therefore completed. □

1.4.2 NI algorithm

The classical NI algorithm is generalized and developed to solve (1.2), which is formulated as [6]:

$$X_{k+1} \doteq -(X_kA_kX_k - X_k) + X_k. \tag{1.13}$$

Evidently, the above NI algorithm is actually a special case of the presented ET-DTZNN-K algorithm (1.11) by taking the step length $\hbar = 1$ and omitting the time-derivative matrix $\dot{A}_k$. In other words, in addition to differences, we discover the connections between the ET-DTZNN-K algorithm (1.11) and the NI algorithm (1.13). That is, a more general form of the NI algorithm (1.13) for solving (1.2) is the ET-DTZNN-K algorithm (1.11); a simplified form of the ET-DTZNN-K algorithm (1.11) is the NI algorithm (1.13); the methods of the DTZNN and the NI are closely related. This discovery is also a contribution of this chapter [22]. By following the similar steps, one can prove that the MSSRE synthesized by the NI algorithm (1.13) is theorectically $\mathscr{O}(g)$. In addition, we have the following theorem to reveal that the MSSREs synthesized by any method designed intrinsically for time-independent matrix right pseudoinversion when employed for future one is $\mathscr{O}(g)$.

Theorem 8 *Suppose that a method designed intrinsically for time-independent matrix right pseudoinversion converges to the optimal solution to a time-independent matrix right pseudoinversion within computational time g. If the method is employed for solving the FMRP problem (1.2) and with the sufficiently small sampling gap $g \in (0,1)$, then the MSSRE synthesized by the method is $\mathscr{O}(g)$.*

Proof. As supposed, the time derivative of $X(t)$ exists, i.e., $\mathrm{d}x_{ij,k}/\mathrm{d}t = p_{ij}$ at time instant $t = kg$ with $x_{ij}(t)$ being the ijth element of matrix $X(t)$ and p_{ij} being a constant. Then, it can be readily derived that $\lim_{g\to 0}\Delta x_{ij,k}/g = \mathrm{d}x_{ij,k}/\mathrm{d}t = p_{ij}$ and $\Delta x_{ij,k} \approx p_{ij}g$. Therefore, $\Delta x_{ij,k}$ changes in an $\mathscr{O}(g)$ pattern, i.e., $\Delta x_{ij,k} = \mathscr{O}(g)$ and $\Delta X_k = \mathbf{O}(g)$. Note that, at each computational time interval $[kg,(k+1)g)$, the method converges to the optimal solution X_k^* to the FMRP problem at time instant $t = kg$ and $X_{k+1}^* = X_k^* + \Delta X_k$. Thus, at time instant $t = (k+1)g$, the difference between the solution generated by the method and the optimal solution is ΔX_k, i.e., $X_{k+1}^* = X_k^* + \mathbf{O}(g) = X_{k+1} + \mathbf{O}(g)$. Then, we obtain

$$\|X_{k+1}A_{k+1}A_{k+1}^{\mathrm{T}} - A_{k+1}^{\mathrm{T}}\|_{\mathrm{F}} = \|A_{k+1}^{\dagger}A_{k+1}A_{k+1}^{\mathrm{T}} - A_{k+1}^{\mathrm{T}} + \mathbf{O}(g)A_{k+1}A_{k+1}^{\mathrm{T}}\|_{\mathrm{F}}.$$

From Lemma 1, we get $A_{k+1}^{\dagger}A_{k+1}A_{k+1}^{\mathrm{T}} - A_{k+1}^{\mathrm{T}} = O_{n\times m}$. Then, we further have

$$\|X_{k+1}A_{k+1}A_{k+1}^{\mathrm{T}} - A_{k+1}^{\mathrm{T}}\|_{\mathrm{F}} = \|\mathbf{O}(g^3)A_{k+1}A_{k+1}^{\mathrm{T}}\|_{\mathrm{F}} = \|\mathbf{O}(g)\|_{\mathrm{F}} = \mathscr{O}(g).$$

The proof is therefore completed. □

Thus, supported by Theorem 8, it can be concluded that the MSSREs synthesized by the methods in [5–8] have $\mathscr{O}(g)$ patterns for solving the FMRP problem (1.2).

In conclusion, we have constructed five different algorithms, i.e., the ZT-DTZNN-K algorithm (1.5), the ZT-DTZNN-U algorithm (1.7), the ET-DTZNN-K algorithm (1.11), the ET-DTZNN-U algorithm (1.12), and the NI algorithm (1.13) for solving the FMRP problem (1.2).

It is noted that, three initial states X_0, X_1, and X_2 are needed for the initialization of the ZT-DTZNN-K algorithm (1.5). Besides, from (1.6), we cannot obtain $\dot{A}_0$ since t starts from 0 s and thus A_{-1} is undefined. Therefore, in the ensuing numerical experiments as well as the application to motion generation, in view of the NI algorithm (1.13) has the simplest structure, we exploit the NI

TABLE 1.1: Problem, scheme, model, and algorithms in this chapter.

Problem	$A_{k+1} - X_{k+1}^{\dagger} = O_{m\times n}$.
Scheme	*Step 1*: Define ZF as $Z(t) = A(t) - X^{\dagger}(t)$. *Step 2*: Adopt ZNN design formula as $\dot{Z}(t) = -\eta Z(t)$. *Step 3*: Discretize CTZNN model (1.3).
Model	$\dot{X}(t) = -X(t)\dot{A}(t)X(t) - \eta(X(t)A(t)X(t) - X(t))$.
Algorithms	$X_{k+1} \doteq -gX_k\dot{A}_kX_k - \hbar(X_kA_kX_k - X_k) + \frac{3}{2}X_k - X_{k-1} + \frac{1}{2}X_{k-2}$, $X_{k+1} \doteq -X_k(\frac{11}{6}A_k - 3A_{k-1} + \frac{3}{2}A_{k-2} - \frac{1}{3}A_{k-3})X_k$ $-\hbar(X_kA_kX_k - X_k) + \frac{3}{2}X_k - X_{k-1} + \frac{1}{2}X_{k-2}$, $X_{k+1} \doteq -gX_k\dot{A}_kX_k - \hbar(X_kA_kX_k - X_k) + X_k$, $X_{k+1} \doteq -X_k(A_k - A_{k-1})X_k - \hbar(X_kA_kX_k - X_k) + X_k$, $X_{k+1} \doteq -(X_kA_kX_k - X_k) + X_k$.

algorithm (1.13) for the initializations of the ZT-DTZNN-K algorithm (1.5), the ZT-DTZNN-U algorithm (1.7), and the ET-DTZNN-U algorithm (1.12). Besides, in the ensuing section, the MSSREs are based on the following criterion: $(\hat{e}_{k+1} - \hat{e}_k)/\hat{e}_k < 0.01$, where $\hat{e}_{k+1} = \|X_{k+1}A_{k+1}A_{k+1}^{\mathrm{T}} - A_{k+1}^{\mathrm{T}}\|_{\mathrm{F}}$ and $\hat{e}_k = \|X_kA_kA_k^{\mathrm{T}} - A_k^{\mathrm{T}}\|_{\mathrm{F}}$. When the criterion is satisfied for the first time during the solving process, we have $k_{\mathrm{m}} = k+1$ and MSSRE $= \max\{\hat{e}_j\}$ with $j = k_{\mathrm{m}}, k_{\mathrm{m}}+1, \cdots$.

For a more intuitive understanding of the main content of this chapter [22], Table 1.1 lists the problem, scheme, model, and algorithms.

1.5 Numerical Experiments

In this section, numerical experiments based on two time-dependent matrices are provided to verify the efficacy of the presented DTZNN algorithms for the FMRP.

Example 1.1 Let us consider the following FMRP problem with X_{k+1} to be computed at each computational time interval $[kg, (k+1)g) \subset [0, 10]$ s:

$$A_k = \begin{bmatrix} \sin(t_k) & \cos(t_k) & -\sin(t_k) \\ -\cos(t_k) & \sin(t_k) & \cos(t_k) \end{bmatrix}. \tag{1.14}$$

To check the solution correctness of the presented DTZNN algorithms, from (1.1), we can obtain the theoretical right pseudoinverse of matrix A_k as

$$A_k^{\dagger} = \begin{bmatrix} 0.5\sin(t_k) & -0.5\cos(t_k) \\ \cos(t_k) & \sin(t_k) \\ -0.5\sin(t_k) & 0.5\cos(t_k) \end{bmatrix}.$$

Starting with $X_0 = [0, -2/3; 2/3, 0; 0, 2/3]$ in MATLAB notation, the corresponding numerical experimental results are shown in Figure 1.1. Specifically, the element trajectories of the state X_{k+1} are shown in Figure 1.1(a), from which we could observe that the solution of the ZT-DTZNN-K algorithm (1.5) converges to the theoretical right pseudoinverse. In addition, as shown in Figure 1.1(b), the residual error (i.e., $\hat{e}_{k+1}$) synthesized by the ZT-DTZNN-K algorithm (1.5) converges to near zero rapidly. Therefore, the efficacy of the presented ZT-DTZNN-K algorithm (1.5) for the FMRP is illustrated primarily. Note that the figures generated by other DTZNN algorithms and the NI algorithm (1.13) are similar to Figure 1.1 and are thus omitted.

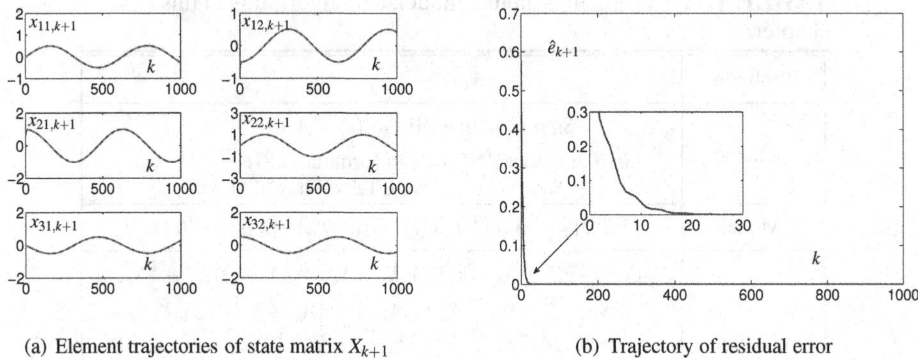

(a) Element trajectories of state matrix X_{k+1}

(b) Trajectory of residual error

FIGURE 1.1: Convergence performance of ZT-DTZNN-K algorithm (1.5) for FMRP in Example 1.1. In panel (a), solid curves correspond to neural-network solutions and dash curves correspond to theoretical solutions.

To evidently compare the ZT-DTZNN-K algorithm (1.5) and the ZT-DTZNN-U algorithm (1.7) with the ET-DTZNN-K algorithm (1.11), the ET-DTZNN-U algorithm (1.12), and the NI algorithm (1.13) for the FMRP, the further numerical experimental results are visualized in Figure 1.2. As seen from Figure 1.2(a), with the same initial state $X_0 = [0, -2/3; 2/3, 0; 0, 2/3]$, $\hbar = 0.3$, and $g = 0.1$ s, the residual errors synthesized by DTZNN algorithms converge to near zero rapidly, whereas the

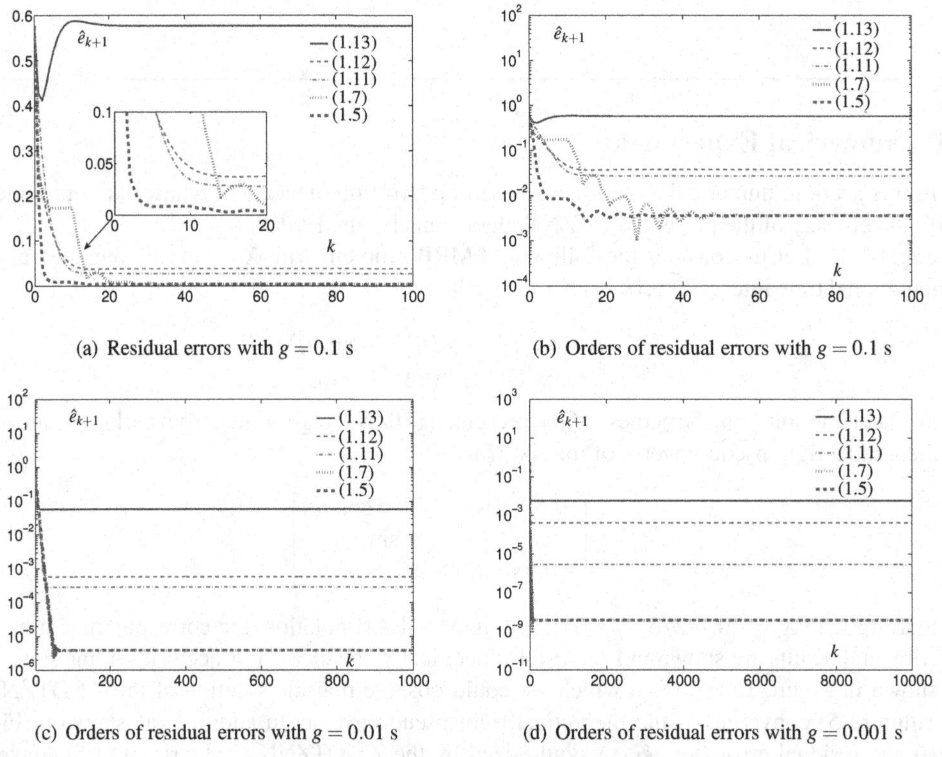

(a) Residual errors with $g = 0.1$ s

(b) Orders of residual errors with $g = 0.1$ s

(c) Orders of residual errors with $g = 0.01$ s

(d) Orders of residual errors with $g = 0.001$ s

FIGURE 1.2: Trajectories of residual errors $\hat{e}_{k+1}$ synthesized by five different algorithms for FMRP in Example 1.1.

residual error synthesized by the NI algorithm (1.13) has an obvious lagging error. As shown in Figure 1.2(b), the MSSREs synthesized by the ZT-DTZNN-K algorithm (1.5) and the ZT-DTZNN-U algorithm (1.7) are of orders 10^{-3} and the MSSREs synthesized by the ET-DTZNN-K algorithm (1.11) and the ET-DTZNN-U algorithm (1.12) are of orders 10^{-2}. By contrast, the MSSRE synthesized by the NI algorithm (1.13) is of order 10^{-1}. Besides, the residual errors synthesized by these five different algorithms with sampling gap g being 0.01 s and 0.001 s are displayed in Figure 1.2(c) and (d), respectively. These comparative results substantiate the higher accuracy of the presented ZT-DTZNN-K algorithm (1.5) and ZT-DTZNN-U algorithm (1.7) (compared with the ET-DTZNN-K algorithm (1.11), the ET-DTZNN-U algorithm (1.12), and the NI algorithm (1.13)) as well as the important role of the time-derivative information in obtaining the higher solution accuracy.

Example 1.2 In this example, we consider a more complicated situation of the FMRP problem with X_{k+1} to be computed at each computational time interval $[kg,(k+1)g) \subset [0,10]$ s:

$$A_k = \begin{bmatrix} a_{11,k} & a_{12,k} & a_{13,k} & \cdots & a_{1n,k} \\ a_{21,k} & a_{22,k} & a_{23,k} & \cdots & a_{2n,k} \\ a_{31,k} & a_{32,k} & a_{33,k} & \cdots & a_{3n,k} \\ \vdots & \vdots & \vdots & \ddots & \vdots \\ a_{m1,k} & a_{m2,k} & a_{m3,k} & \cdots & a_{mn,k} \end{bmatrix} \in \mathbb{R}^{m\times n}. \tag{1.15}$$

Thereinto, the ijth element of A_k (with $i = 1,2,\cdots,m$ and $j = 1,2,\cdots,n$) is expressed as

$$a_{ij,k} = \begin{cases} i+\sin(5t_k), & i=j, \\ \cos(5t_k)/(i-j), & i>j, \\ \sin(5t_k)/(j-i), & i<j. \end{cases}$$

Without loss of generality, we set $m = 8$ and $n = 9$ in this example. Due to the complexity of matrix (1.15), the analytical solution of theoretical right pseudoinverse is difficult to be obtained. Therefore, we only present the residual errors $\hat{e}_{k+1}$ synthesized by five different algorithms, which are shown in Figure 1.3. Besides, more detailed MSSREs and the average computing time per updating (ACTPU) data synthesized by five different algorithms are shown in Table 1.2 with respect to different values of sampling gap g. From Figure 1.3 as well as Table 1.2, the following important facts are summarized, which further substantiate the theoretical results very well.

1. The MSSRE synthesized by the NI algorithm (1.13) without utilizing time derivative of time-dependent coefficient changes in an $\mathscr{O}(g)$ pattern. For example, it follows from Table 1.2 that the MSSRE synthesized by the NI algorithm (1.13) is of order 10^0, 10^{-1}, or 10^{-2}, corresponding to $g = 0.1, 0.01$, or 0.001 s, respectively.

2. The MSSREs synthesized by the ET-DTZNN-K algorithm (1.11) and the ET-DTZNN-U algorithm (1.12), which utilize time derivative of time-dependent coefficient and are discretized via the Euler forward formula, change in $\mathscr{O}(g^2)$ patterns. This fact is evidently shown in Table 1.2.

3. The MSSREs synthesized by the ZT-DTZNN-K algorithm (1.5) and the ZT-DTZNN-U algorithm (1.7), which utilize time derivative of time-dependent coefficient and are discretized via the presented Zhang–Taylor discretization formula (1.4), change in $\mathscr{O}(g^3)$ patterns. For example, as displayed in Table 1.2, the MSSREs synthesized by the ZT-DTZNN-K algorithm (1.5) and the ZT-DTZNN-U algorithm (1.7) are of orders 10^0, 10^{-3}, or 10^{-6}, corresponding to $g = 0.1, 0.01$, or 0.001 s, respectively.

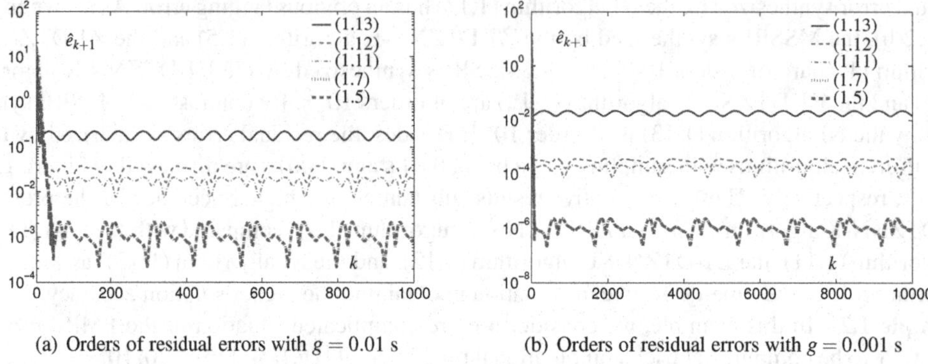

(a) Orders of residual errors with $g = 0.01$ s

(b) Orders of residual errors with $g = 0.001$ s

FIGURE 1.3: Trajectories of residual errors $\hat{e}_{k+1}$ synthesized by five different algorithms for FMRP in Example 1.2.

4. Even for a small sampling gap g, such as 0.001 s (i.e., 1 ms), the five different algorithms all have a small ACTPU (i.e., around of order 10^{-4}), thereby satisfying well the requirement of real-time computation.

1.6 Application to Motion Generation

In this section, the ZT-DTZNN-U algorithm (1.7) and the NI algorithm (1.13) are applied to the motion generation of a five-link redundant manipulator. For such a manipulator operating with task duration T, at time instant $t_k \in [0, T]$ s, the relation between the end-effector position vector

TABLE 1.2: MSSREs and ACTPU data synthesized by five different algorithms when $\hbar = 0.3$ for FMRP in Example 1.2.

g (s)	Algorithm	MSSRE	ACTPU (s)
0.1	ZT-DTZNN-K algorithm (1.5)	2.7350	4.6212×10^{-4}
	ZT-DTZNN-U algorithm (1.7)	2.6852	4.6151×10^{-4}
	ET-DTZNN-K algorithm (1.11)	2.1311	4.4386×10^{-4}
	ET-DTZNN-U algorithm (1.12)	2.1461	4.3773×10^{-4}
	NI algorithm (1.13)	2.2268	3.9950×10^{-4}
0.01	ZT-DTZNN-K algorithm (1.5)	2.1465×10^{-3}	4.6599×10^{-4}
	ZT-DTZNN-U algorithm (1.7)	2.1616×10^{-3}	4.6342×10^{-4}
	ET-DTZNN-K algorithm (1.11)	2.0953×10^{-2}	4.6054×10^{-4}
	ET-DTZNN-U algorithm (1.12)	3.7839×10^{-2}	4.5768×10^{-4}
	NI algorithm (1.13)	2.2107×10^{-1}	4.0379×10^{-4}
0.001	ZT-DTZNN-K algorithm (1.5)	2.3170×10^{-6}	4.6634×10^{-4}
	ZT-DTZNN-U algorithm (1.7)	2.3185×10^{-6}	4.6183×10^{-4}
	ET-DTZNN-K algorithm (1.11)	2.1273×10^{-4}	4.5747×10^{-4}
	ET-DTZNN-U algorithm (1.12)	3.8356×10^{-4}	4.5922×10^{-4}
	NI algorithm (1.13)	2.2120×10^{-2}	4.1326×10^{-4}

$\mathbf{r}_{\mathrm{a},k} \in \mathbb{R}^2$ and the joint-angle vector $\vartheta_k \in \mathbb{R}^5$ is [16, 17]:

$$\mathbf{f}(\vartheta_k) = \mathbf{r}_{\mathrm{a},k}, \tag{1.16}$$

where $\mathbf{f}(\cdot)$ denotes a forward-kinematics mapping function with known structure and parameters for a given manipulator. The inverse-kinematic problem (i.e., given $\mathbf{r}_{\mathrm{a},k}$, to solve for ϑ_k) is usually solved at the joint-velocity level. Then, the following relation among the actual end-effector velocity vector $\dot{\mathbf{r}}_{\mathrm{a},k}$ and the joint velocity vector $\dot{\vartheta}_k$ can be derived:

$$J(\vartheta_k)\dot{\vartheta}_k = \dot{\mathbf{r}}_{\mathrm{a},k}, \tag{1.17}$$

where the Jacobi matrix $J(\vartheta_k) = \partial\mathbf{f}(\vartheta_k)/\partial\vartheta_k$. Evidently, the analytical solution to the inverse-kinematic problem is $\dot{\vartheta}_k = J^{\dagger}(\vartheta_k)\dot{\mathbf{r}}_{\mathrm{a},k}$, where $J^{\dagger}(\vartheta_k)$ is the right pseudoinverse of time-dependent Jacobi matrix. We need to obtain $J^{\dagger}(\vartheta_k)$ in real time for the control of the manipulator. Defining $A_k = J(\vartheta_k)$, we could exploit the aforementioned algorithms to solve $J^{\dagger}(\vartheta_{k+1})$ as well as to expedite the computation process and achieve better control precision. For simplicity and illustration, with each link length being 1 m, the five-link redundant manipulator is investigated to track a square path with the side length being 2.4 m, where the task duration $T = 20$ s and the initial joint-angle vector $\vartheta_0 = [\pi/4, \pi/12, \pi/4, \pi/12, \pi/4]^{\mathrm{T}}$ rad. Observing that the ACTPU is smaller than 1 ms in Example 1.2, we choose the sampling gap $g = 1$ ms and the step length $\hbar = 0.3$.

The numerical experimental results synthesized by the ZT-DTZNN-U algorithm (1.7) and the NI algorithm (1.13) are shown in Figures 1.4 and 1.5. Note that similar to Figure 1.4 synthesized by the ZT-DTZNN-U algorithm (1.7), the joint angle, joint velocity, and motion trajectories generated by the NI algorithm (1.13) are omitted due to space limitation.

The X-axis and Y-axis tracking errors (i.e., $\tilde{e}_{\mathrm{X},k+1}$ and $\tilde{e}_{\mathrm{Y},k+1}$) are shown in Figure 1.5. As seen in Figure 1.5(a), the maximal steady-state tracking error (MSSTE) synthesized by the ZT-DTZNN-U algorithm (1.7) is of order 10^{-5} m, which is roughly 10 times smaller than that synthesized by the NI algorithm (1.13) in Figure 1.5(b). This application to the motion generation of the five-link redundant manipulator further illustrates the superiority of the presented ZT-DTZNN-U algorithm (1.7) for the FMRP.

1.7 Chapter Summary

In this chapter, in order to achieve higher computational accuracy in approximating the first-order derivative and discretize effectively the CTZNN model, the Zhang–Taylor discretization formula (1.4) has been presented and investigated. Afterward, on the basis of the formula, the ZT-DTZNN-K algorithm (1.5) and the ZT-DTZNN-U algorithm (1.7) have been presented for solving the FMRP problem (1.2). For comparison, the ET-DTZNN-K algorithm (1.11), the ET-DTZNN-U algorithm (1.12), and the NI algorithm (1.13) have been presented for the same solution task. Meanwhile, interesting connections between the ET-DTZNN-K algorithm (1.11) and the NI algorithm (1.13) have been discovered. Moreover, the stability and convergence of the five different algorithms have been investigated in detail. The theoretical analyses have shown that MSSREs synthesized by the ZT-DTZNN-K algorithm (1.5) and the ZT-DTZNN-U algorithm (1.7) have $\mathscr{O}(g^3)$ patterns; the ET-DTZNN-K algorithm (1.11) and the ET-DTZNN-U algorithm (1.12) have $\mathscr{O}(g^2)$ patterns; the NI algorithm (1.13) has an $\mathscr{O}(g)$ pattern. The numerical experimental results of three illustrative examples (including one application example) have further illustrated the efficacy and superiority of the presented ZT-DTZNN-K algorithm (1.5) and ZT-DTZNN-U algorithm (1.7) (compared with the ET-DTZNN-K algorithm (1.11), the ET-DTZNN-U algorithm (1.12), and the NI algorithm (1.13).

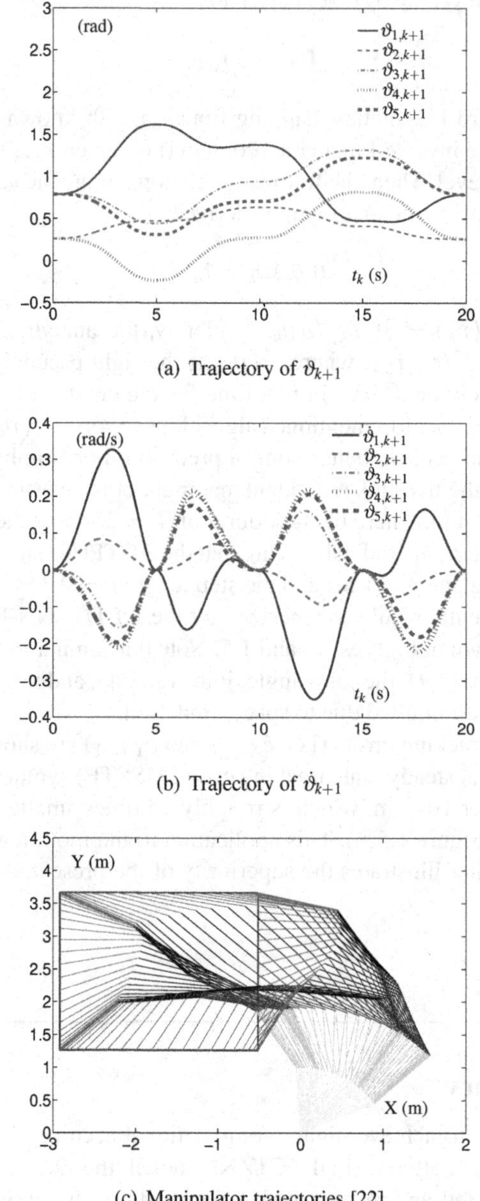

(a) Trajectory of ϑ_{k+1}

(b) Trajectory of $\dot{\vartheta}_{k+1}$

(c) Manipulator trajectories [22]

FIGURE 1.4: Motion generation of five-link redundant manipulator synthesized by ZT-DTZNN-U algorithm (1.7) with its end-effector tracking square path.

Appendix A: Proof of Theorem 1

According to Taylor expansion [20], we have the following equation:

$$\zeta_{k+1} = \zeta_k + g\dot{\zeta}_k + \frac{g^2}{2!}\ddot{\zeta}_k + \frac{g^3}{3!}\dddot{\zeta}(c_1),$$

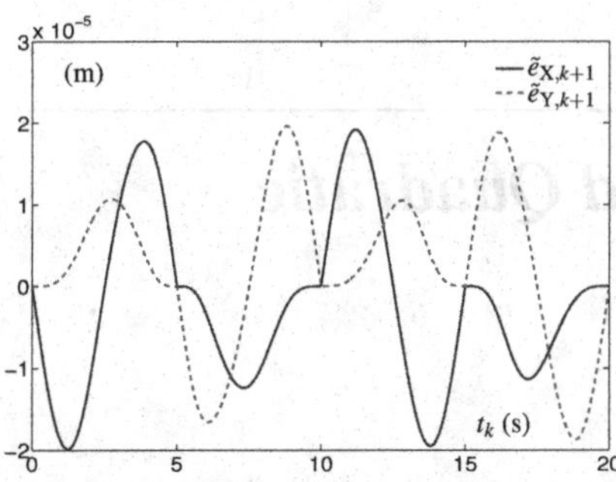

(a) X-axis and Y-axis tracking errors synthesized by algorithm (1.7)

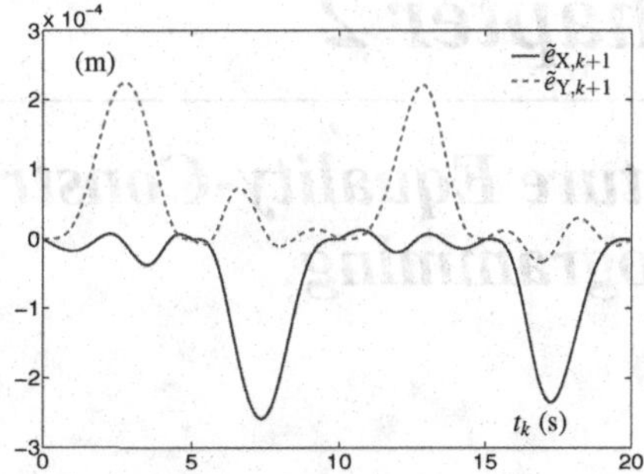

(b) X-axis and Y-axis tracking errors synthesized by algorithm (1.13)

FIGURE 1.5: Trajectories of tracking errors $\tilde{e}_{k+1}$ synthesized by ZT-DTZNN-U algorithm (1.7) and NI algorithm (1.13).

where $n!$ denotes the factorial of n, and c_1 lies between kg and $(k+1)g$. It is rewritten as

$$\dot{\zeta}_k = \frac{\zeta_{k+1} - \zeta_k}{g} - \frac{g}{2!}\ddot{\zeta}_k - \frac{g^2}{3!}\dddot{\zeta}(c_1). \tag{1.18}$$

In a similar way, one obtains

$$\zeta_{k-1} = \zeta_k - g\dot{\zeta}_k + \frac{g^2}{2!}\ddot{\zeta}_k - \frac{g^3}{3!}\dddot{\zeta}(c_2)$$

and

$$\zeta_{k-2} = \zeta_k - 2g\dot{\zeta}_k + \frac{4g^2}{2!}\ddot{\zeta}_k - \frac{8g^3}{3!}\dddot{\zeta}(c_3),$$

with c_2 and c_3 lying in the intervals $((k-1)g, kg)$ and $((k-2), kg)$, respectively. Then, the above two equations are rewritten as

$$\dot{\zeta}_k = \frac{\zeta_k - \zeta_{k-1}}{g} + \frac{g}{2!}\ddot{\zeta}_k - \frac{g^2}{3!}\dddot{\zeta}(c_2) \tag{1.19}$$

and

$$\dot{\zeta}_k = \frac{\zeta_k - \zeta_{k-2}}{2g} + g\ddot{\zeta}_k - \frac{2g^2}{3}\dddot{\zeta}(c_3). \tag{1.20}$$

Let (1.18) add (1.20), and then subtract (1.19). Thus, we obtain the following numerical-differentiation formula:

$$\dot{\zeta}_k = \frac{2\zeta_{k+1} - 3\zeta_k + 2\zeta_{k-1} - \zeta_{k-2}}{2g} + g^2\left(-\frac{1}{3!}\dddot{\zeta}(c_1) + \frac{1}{3!}\dddot{\zeta}(c_2) - \frac{2}{3}\dddot{\zeta}(c_3)\right).$$

The above equation is further rewritten as

$$\dot{\zeta}_k = \frac{2\zeta_{k+1} - 3\zeta_k + 2\zeta_{k-1} - \zeta_{k-2}}{2g} + \mathscr{O}(g^2),$$

which is just the Zhang–Taylor discretization formula (1.4). The proof is therefore completed. □

Chapter 2

Future Equality-Constrained Quadratic Programming

Abstract

In this chapter, a problem called future equality-constrained quadratic programming (FECQP) is developed and discussed. For the FECQP solving, the corresponding continuous time-dependent equality-constrained quadratic programming (CTDECQP) is presented and its continuous-time zeroing neural network (CTZNN) model is obtained. Then, the Zhang–Taylor discretization formula is presented to discretize the CTZNN model and obtain higher computational accuracy. On the basis of the Zhang–Taylor discretization formula, two Zhang–Taylor discrete-time zeroing neural network (ZT-DTZNN) algorithms are presented and discussed to perform the FECQP. For comparison, Euler-type DTZNN (ET-DTZNN) algorithms and Newton iteration (NI) algorithm, with interesting links being found, are also presented. It is proven that maximal steady-state residual errors (MSSREs) synthesized by the presented ZT-DTZNN algorithms, ET-DTZNN algorithms, and NI algorithm have patterns of $\mathcal{O}(g^3)$, $\mathcal{O}(g^2)$, and $\mathcal{O}(g)$, respectively, with g denoting the sampling gap. Numerical experiments (including the application examples) are carried out, of which the results further substantiate the theoretical findings and the efficacy of the ZT-DTZNN algorithms. Finally, the comparisons with Zhang–Taylor discrete-time derivative dynamics (ZT-DTDD) algorithm and Lagrange-type DTZNN (LT-DTZNN) algorithms for the FECQP solving substantiate the superiority of the presented ZT-DTZNN algorithms once again.

2.1 Introduction

The problems of equality-constrained quadratic programming are widely encountered in scientific and engineering fields, such as robotics [26, 27], fast model predictive control [28], and signal processing [29]. Because neural algorithms are specifically designed to be readily implemented in hardware and possess the characteristics of parallelism and adaptivity, a large number of recurrent neural networks (RNNs) have been presented for solving constrained optimization problems in real time [30, 31]. Generally, these neural networks can be divided into two classes: the continuous-time RNNs and the discrete-time RNNs. Hopfield and Tank first proposed a neural network for solving quadratic optimization [32]. After that, numerous continuous-time neural networks were presented owing to the seminal work. Xia and Wang presented a single-layer structure neural network for solving nonlinear convex programming problems with linear constraints [33]. Liu and Wang presented a simplified dual neural network which was proven to be globally convergent to the exact optimal solution, and it can be utilized to solve convex quadratic programming problems with equality and

DOI: 10.1201/9781003497783-2

inequality constraints [34]. Hosseini *et al* presented a penalty-based RNN for solving a class of constrained optimization problems with generalized convex objective functions [13]. Barbarosou and Maratos presented a nonfeasible gradient projection neural network of which the analog circuit realizations were given, and it can be used to solve both convex and nonconvex equality-constrained optimization problems [35].

On the other hand, there are much fewer discrete-time neural algorithms to solve constrained optimization problems, because their stability and convergence are generally more difficult to assure. In [36], a discrete-time RNN was presented to perform the strictly convex quadratic real optimization with bound constraints. A general discrete-time recurrent network was presented for performing quadratic optimizations with hybrid constraints in [37]. Liu and Cao presented a discrete-time RNN, of which the global exponential stability was proved, for solving linear constrained quadratic programming problems [38]. In [39], using Wolfe's dual theory, a simple discrete-time RNN was presented to solve quadratic optimization with general linear constraints.

It is worth noting that most of the aforementioned neural networks, regardless of continuous-time or discrete-time ones, were designed intrinsically for solving static (or called, time-independent) constrained optimization problems. However, many problems are inherently dynamic (or called, time-dependent), i.e., the parameters of the problems are time-dependent [34, 40]. When encountering time-dependent problems, these neural algorithms may be less favorable. Recently, a special class of continuous-time RNNs, called zeroing neural network (ZNN), was presented as a systematic approach to solve such problems [41, 42]; ZNN differs from conventional gradient-based RNNs in terms of problems to be solved, error function, design formula, dynamic equation, and the utilization of time derivatives [19, 43–45]. On the one hand, the ZNN possesses the superiority in solving various time-dependent problems. On the other hand, compared with continuous-time RNNs, discrete-time RNNs present advantages for computer implementations and are particularly advantageous in time-dependent applications. Therefore, with the corresponding continuous time-dependent equality-constrained quadratic programming (CTDECQP) and its continuous-time ZNN (CTZNN) model, it is desirable to design the discrete-time ZNN (DTZNN) algorithms, which can be generated from the discretization of CTZNN model, for the future equality-constrained quadratic programming (FECQP) solving.

To approximate the first-order derivative and then discretize the CTZNN model, there are numerous numerical-differentiation formulas that we can consider. However, in consideration of the facts [20]: (1) that the backward numerical-differentiation formulas may not accommodate to the fast variational rate of the first-order derivative of the target point; (2) that the central numerical-differentiation formulas cannot approximate the first-order derivative of the target point without enough number of data points on either side; (3) that a numerical-differentiation formula does not necessarily generate a stable and convergent DTZNN algorithm, not to mention a high-accuracy one, a numerical-differentiation formula is urgently needed. Following this analysis, we present Zhang–Taylor discretization formula for approximating the first-order derivative. Moreover, by employing the formula, two Zhang–Taylor DTZNN (ZT-DTZNN) algorithms are presented for the FECQP problem solving. To be more specific, the ZT-DTZNN with $\dot{C}_k$ and $\dot{\mathbf{d}}_k$ known (ZT-DTZNN-K) and the ZT-DTZNN with $\dot{C}_k$ and $\dot{\mathbf{d}}_k$ unknown (ZT-DTZNN-U) algorithms are derived from the CTZNN model with time-derivative information known and with time-derivative information unknown, respectively. Such two ZT-DTZNN algorithms are theoretically proven to be convergent to the time-dependent theoretical solution with $\mathscr{O}(g^3)$ residual error pattern. In addition, for comparison, two Euler-type DTZNN (ET-DTZNN) algorithms (i.e., the ET-DTZNN with $\dot{C}_k$ and $\dot{\mathbf{d}}_k$ known (ET-DTZNN-K) and the ET-DTZNN with $\dot{C}_k$ and $\dot{\mathbf{d}}_k$ unknown (ET-DTZNN-U) algorithms) and the conventional Newton iteration (NI) algorithm, together with their stability and convergence analyses, are also presented. Finally, the numerical experimental results further verify the theoretical findings and the efficacy of ZT-DTZNN algorithms presented herein for solving the FECQP.

2.2 Problem Formulation and CTZNN Model

In this section, the problem formulation for the FECQP solving is given. Then, the design procedure of CTZNN model for solving this problem is presented.

2.2.1 Problem formulation

The FECQP, which is to be solved at each computational time interval $[t_k, t_{k+1}) \subset [t_{\text{ini}}, t_{\text{fin}}] \subset [0, +\infty)$, can be stated as

$$\begin{aligned} \min\ & \varphi(\mathbf{x}_{k+1}, t_{k+1}) = \frac{1}{2}\mathbf{x}_{k+1}^{\mathrm{T}} Q_{k+1}\mathbf{x}_{k+1} + \mathbf{p}_{k+1}^{\mathrm{T}}\mathbf{x}_{k+1} \\ \text{s. t.}\ & A_{k+1}\mathbf{x}_{k+1} = \mathbf{b}_{k+1}, \end{aligned} \tag{2.1}$$

where t_{ini} and t_{fin} represent the initial and final time instants, respectively. Besides, the superscript ^{T} denotes the transpose of a vector or matrix. What is more, $\varphi(\cdot,\cdot): \mathbb{R}^n \to \mathbb{R}$ is time-dependent; $\mathbf{x}_{k+1} \in \mathbb{R}^n$ (being unknown), $Q_{k+1} \in \mathbb{R}^{n\times n}$, $\mathbf{p}_{k+1} \in \mathbb{R}^n$, $A_{k+1} \in \mathbb{R}^{m\times n}$ (being of full row rank), and $\mathbf{b}_{k+1} \in \mathbb{R}^m$ are supposed to be generated or measured from smoothly time-dependent $\mathbf{x}(t)$, $Q(t)$, $\mathbf{p}(t)$, $A(t)$, and $\mathbf{b}(t)$ by sampling at time instant $t = (k+1)g$ (denoted by t_{k+1}), respectively. Besides, $g > 0$ represents the sampling gap, and $k = 0, 1, 2, \cdots$ represents the updating index. It is worth pointing out here that, in the online solution process of the FECQP (2.1), the operation has to be executed based on the present or previous data. For instance, during the computational time interval $[t_k, t_{k+1})$, only known information such as $\mathbf{x}_k$, Q_k, $\mathbf{p}_k$, A_k, and $\mathbf{b}_k$, instead of unknown information such as Q_{k+1}, $\mathbf{p}_{k+1}$, A_{k+1}, and $\mathbf{b}_{k+1}$, can be used to compute the unknown vector $\mathbf{x}_{k+1}$. Therefore, the objective of this chapter [46] is, through the present or previous data, to find the unknown vector $\mathbf{x}_{k+1}$ during $[t_k, t_{k+1})$, which achieves the FECQP (2.1) at each time instant.

Then, the corresponding CTDECQP problem can be expressed as

$$\begin{aligned} \min\ & \varphi(\mathbf{x}(t), t) = \frac{1}{2}\mathbf{x}^{\mathrm{T}}(t) Q(t)\mathbf{x}(t) + \mathbf{p}^{\mathrm{T}}(t)\mathbf{x}(t) \\ \text{s. t.}\ & A(t)\mathbf{x}(t) = \mathbf{b}(t), \end{aligned} \tag{2.2}$$

where $Q(t)$ is a positive definite and symmetric matrix such that the CTDECQP (2.2) is strictly convex at every time instant t.

2.2.2 CTZNN model

To effectively develop the DTZNN algorithms to achieve the FECQP (2.1), which is actually a future optimization problem, the CTZNN model can be constructed.

For the CTDECQP (2.2), we define a Lagrange function as below:

$$L(\mathbf{x}(t), \mathbf{l}(t), t) = \varphi(\mathbf{x}(t), t) + \mathbf{l}^{\mathrm{T}}(t)(A(t)\mathbf{x}(t) - \mathbf{b}(t)),$$

where $\mathbf{l}(t) \in \mathbb{R}^m$ is referred to as the Lagrange-multiplier vector. Then, we have

$$\begin{bmatrix} \frac{\partial L}{\partial \mathbf{x}} \\ \frac{\partial L}{\partial \mathbf{l}} \end{bmatrix} = C(t)\mathbf{y}(t) + \mathbf{d}(t), \tag{2.3}$$

where

$$C(t) = \begin{bmatrix} Q(t) & A^{\mathrm{T}}(t) \\ A(t) & \mathbf{0} \end{bmatrix} \in \mathbb{R}^{(n+m)\times(n+m)},$$

$$\mathbf{y}(t) = \begin{bmatrix} \mathbf{x}(t) \\ \mathbf{l}(t) \end{bmatrix} \in \mathbb{R}^{n+m}, \text{ and } \mathbf{d}(t) = \begin{bmatrix} \mathbf{p}(t) \\ -\mathbf{b}(t) \end{bmatrix} \in \mathbb{R}^{n+m}.$$

On the basis of the previous results on equality-constrained optimization problems [47, 48], the CTDECQP (2.2) can be solved by zeroing out (2.3) at any time instant $t \in [t_{\text{ini}}, t_{\text{fin}})$. It also means, for the theoretical solution $\mathbf{y}^*(t) \in \mathbb{R}^{n+m}$, the following equation always holds true at every time instant:

$$C(t)\mathbf{y}^*(t) + \mathbf{d}(t) = \mathbf{0}. \tag{2.4}$$

Given that $Q(t)$ is positive definite and $A(t)$ is of full row rank at any time instant $t \in [t_{\text{ini}}, t_{\text{fin}})$, the augmented matrix $C(t)$ is nonsingular at any time instant $t \in [t_{\text{ini}}, t_{\text{fin}})$, which guarantees the solution uniqueness of (2.4) [47, 48].

By following the ZNN method [19, 43–45], a vector-valued zeroing function (ZF) $\mathbf{z}(t) = C(t)\mathbf{y}(t) + \mathbf{d}(t)$ can be defined. Then, utilizing the ZNN design formula $\dot{\mathbf{z}}(t) = \mathrm{d}\mathbf{z}(t)/\mathrm{d}t = -\eta\mathbf{z}(t)$, we obtain the following dynamical equation of the CTZNN model:

$$\dot{\mathbf{y}}(t) = -C^{-1}(t)\big(\dot{C}(t)\mathbf{y}(t) + \eta(C(t)\mathbf{y}(t) + \mathbf{d}(t)) + \dot{\mathbf{d}}(t)\big), \tag{2.5}$$

where $\mathbf{y}(t)$, starting from a randomly generated initial condition $\mathbf{y}(0) \in \mathbb{R}^{n+m}$, denotes the neural state corresponding to the theoretical solution $\mathbf{y}^*(t)$ in (2.4), of which the first n elements are the ZNN solutions achieving the CTDECQP (2.2). Note that the ZNN design parameter $\eta > 0 \in \mathbb{R}$ is used to scale the convergence rate of the CTZNN model (2.5).

In the solution process of the CTDECQP (2.2), a real-time solver receives the specific data at one single time instant; then, the solver does computations based on the present or the stored previous data; finally, it outputs the result to the user. In view of the fact that computation consumes time inevitably, we cannot solve directly the CTDECQP (2.2) at every time instant t by the CTZNN model (2.5) running on a digital computer. That is, after the computation, the problem to be solved is no longer the same as that before the computation due to the time variation of the CTDECQP (2.2). Note that, in the solution process, the solver cannot use the future data because they are unknown and have not come yet at the present time instant. Thus, what we need to do is through the present or previous data to find the future vector $\mathbf{x}_{k+1}$ during $[t_k, t_{k+1})$, which achieves the FECQP (2.1) at next time instant.

2.3 Zhang–Taylor ZNN Discretization

In order to achieve higher computational accuracy in approximating the first-order derivative of the target point and conduct ZNN discretization successfully, the Zhang–Taylor discretization formula is presented first in this section. Afterwards, two ZT-DTZNN algorithms are presented for solving the FECQP (2.1), which are derived from (2.5). Moreover, the theoretical analyses about the convergence and the stability of ZT-DTZNN algorithms are also presented.

2.3.1 Effective $\mathscr{O}(g^2)$ formula

A Taylor series is an infinite sum of terms that are computed from the values of derivatives of a function at a single point. In scientific and engineering fields, the partial sums can be accumulated until an approximation to the function achieves an acceptable accuracy. Thus, by eliminating the second-order derivative, the Zhang–Taylor discretization formula can be exploited for the first-order derivative approximation, which possesses higher computational accuracy to discretize the ZNN.

Theorem 9 *With the sufficiently small sampling gap $g \in (0,1)$, let $\mathscr{O}(g^2)$ denote the error (especially, the truncation error) positively or negatively proportional to g^2, i.e., of the order of g^2. Suppose that $\zeta(t)$ is sufficiently smooth. With $\zeta_{k+1} = \zeta(t_{k+1}) = \zeta((k+1)g)$, the Zhang–Taylor discretization formula is formulated as*

$$\dot{\zeta}_k = \frac{2\zeta_{k+1} - 3\zeta_k + 2\zeta_{k-1} - \zeta_{k-2}}{2g} + \mathscr{O}(g^2). \tag{2.6}$$

Proof. The proof is presented in Appendix A in Chapter 1. □

On the basis of Theorem 9, an effective $\mathscr{O}(g^2)$ formula is obtained for the first-order derivative approximation, which is expected to be applied for ZNN discretization for a higher accuracy in comparison with the ET-DTZNN-K algorithm, the ET-DTZNN-U algorithm, and the NI algorithm. In the next subsection, the ZT-DTZNN-K algorithm and the ZT-DTZNN-U algorithm are presented.

2.3.2 ZT-DTZNN-K and ZT-DTZNN-U algorithms

By adopting the Zhang–Taylor discretization formula (2.6) presented herein, two ZT-DTZNN algorithms are constructed and discussed in this subsection for performing the FECQP (2.1).

Afterwards, by applying the Zhang–Taylor discretization formula (2.6) to discretize the CTZNN model (2.5), a ZT-DTZNN-K algorithm is obtained as

$$\mathbf{y}_{k+1} \doteq 1.5\mathbf{y}_k - \mathbf{y}_{k-1} + 0.5\mathbf{y}_{k-2} - C_k^{-1}\left(g\dot{C}_k\mathbf{y}_k + \hbar(C_k\mathbf{y}_k + \mathbf{d}_k) + g\dot{\mathbf{d}}_k\right), \tag{2.7}$$

where $\doteq$ denotes the computational assignment operator, and $\hbar = g\eta > 0$ denotes the step length. Considering that the time-derivative information (i.e., $\dot{C}_k$ and $\dot{\mathbf{d}}_k$) is known and used in the preceding model, (2.7) is thus referred to as the ZT-DTZNN-K algorithm for presentation convenience.

Note that, in some real-world applications, it may be difficult to know or obtain the value of $\dot{C}_k$ and $\dot{\mathbf{d}}_k$ directly. Therefore, it is imperative to investigate the ZT-DTZNN algorithm with $\dot{C}_k$ and $\dot{\mathbf{d}}_k$ unknown. In this situation, $\dot{C}_k$ and $\dot{\mathbf{d}}_k$ can be approximated by utilizing the Lagrange numerical-differentiation formula of order $\mathscr{O}(g^2)$ [20]:

$$\dot{\zeta}_k = \frac{3\zeta_k - 4\zeta_{k-1} + \zeta_{k-2}}{2g} + \mathscr{O}(g^2). \tag{2.8}$$

Accordingly, another DTZNN algorithm with time-derivative information unknown, named ZT-DTZNN-U algorithm, is expressed as

$$\mathbf{y}_{k+1} \doteq 1.5\mathbf{y}_k - \mathbf{y}_{k-1} + 0.5\mathbf{y}_{k-2} - C_k^{-1}(\Delta C_k\mathbf{y}_k + \hbar(C_k\mathbf{y}_k + \mathbf{d}_k) + \Delta\mathbf{d}_k), \tag{2.9}$$

where $\Delta C_k = (3C_k - 4C_{k-1} + C_{k-2})/2$ and $\Delta\mathbf{d}_k = (3\mathbf{d}_k - 4\mathbf{d}_{k-1} + \mathbf{d}_{k-2})/2$.

2.3.3 Theoretical analyses

To provide a basis for further discussion, three definitions (i.e., Definitions 2–4) are given in Chapter 1. On the basis of these definitions, the following theoretical results about the ZT-DTZNN-K algorithm (2.7) and the ZT-DTZNN-U algorithm (2.9) can be readily generalized.

Theorem 10 *Consider the FECQP (2.1). Suppose that Q_k is positive definite and A_k is of full row rank. With the sufficiently small sampling gap $g \in (0,1)$, the ZT-DTZNN-K algorithm (2.7) is zero-stable.*

Proof. According to Definition 2 in Chapter 1, the characteristic polynomial of the ZT-DTZNN-K algorithm (2.7) is

$$\Gamma_3(\iota) = \iota^3 - 1.5\iota^2 + \iota - 0.5,$$

which has three roots on/in the unit circle, i.e., $\iota_1 = 1$, $\iota_2 = 0.25 + 0.6614\mathrm{i}$, and $\iota_3 = 0.25 - 0.6614\mathrm{i}$, with i denoting the imaginary unit. Therefore, the ZT-DTZNN-K algorithm (2.7) is zero-stable. The proof is therefore completed. □

Theorem 11 *Consider the FECQP (2.1). Suppose that Q_k is positive definite and A_k is of full row rank. With the sufficiently small sampling gap $g \in (0,1)$, let $\mathbf{O}(g^3)$ denote the error (especially, the truncation error) with each element being $\mathscr{O}(g^3)$. The ZT-DTZNN-K algorithm (2.7) is consistent and convergent, which converges with the order of truncation error being $\mathbf{O}(g^3)$ for all $t_k \in [t_{\text{ini}}, t_{\text{fin}})$.*

Proof. On the basis of (2.6), the following equation is obtained:

$$\mathbf{y}_{k+1} = 1.5\mathbf{y}_k - \mathbf{y}_{k-1} + 0.5\mathbf{y}_{k-2} - C_k^{-1}\big(g\dot{C}_k\mathbf{y}_k + \hbar(C_k\mathbf{y}_k + \mathbf{d}_k) + g\dot{\mathbf{d}}_k\big) + \mathbf{O}(g^3). \tag{2.10}$$

Note that dropping $\mathbf{O}(g^3)$ of (2.10) yields exactly the ZT-DTZNN-K algorithm (2.7), and thus the truncation error of the ZT-DTZNN-K algorithm (2.7) is $\mathbf{O}(g^3)$. Thus, according to Definition 3 in Chapter 1, the ZT-DTZNN-K algorithm (2.7) is consistent. Combining with Theorem 10 in Chapter 1, the ZT-DTZNN-K algorithm (2.7) is both zero-stable and consistent. Considering Definition 4 in Chapter 1, it can be concluded that the ZT-DTZNN-K algorithm (2.7) is consistent and convergent, which converges with the order of truncation error being $\mathbf{O}(g^3)$ for all $t_k \in [t_{\text{ini}}, t_{\text{fin}})$. The proof is therefore completed. □

Note that the residual error is defined as $\hat{e}_{k+1} = \|C_{k+1}\mathbf{y}_{k+1} + \mathbf{d}_{k+1}\|_2$ for the FECQP (2.1) in this chapter [46], where $\|\cdot\|_2$ denotes the 2-norm of a vector.

Theorem 12 *Consider the FECQP (2.1) with C_k being uniformly norm bounded. Suppose that Q_k is positive definite and A_k is of full row rank. With the sufficiently small sampling gap $g \in (0,1)$, the maximal steady-state residual error (MSSRE) $\lim_{k\to\infty}\sup\hat{e}_{k+1}$ synthesized by the ZT-DTZNN-K algorithm (2.7) is $\mathscr{O}(g^3)$.*

Proof. Let $\mathbf{y}_{k+1}^* \in \mathbb{R}^{n+m}$ denote the theoretical solution of (2.1). Following from (2.4), we know that $C_{k+1}\mathbf{y}_{k+1}^* + \mathbf{d}_{k+1} = \mathbf{0}$. In addition, in consideration of Definition 3 in Chapter 1, Theorems 10 and 11, it can be concluded that $\mathbf{y}_{k+1} = \mathbf{y}_{k+1}^* + \mathbf{O}(g^3)$ with the sufficiently large k. Therefore, we obtain

$$\lim_{k\to\infty}\|C_{k+1}\mathbf{y}_{k+1} + \mathbf{d}_{k+1}\|_2 = \lim_{k\to\infty}\|C_{k+1}\mathbf{y}_{k+1}^* + \mathbf{d}_{k+1} + C_{k+1}\mathbf{O}(g^3)\|_2 = \lim_{k\to\infty}\|C_{k+1}\mathbf{O}(g^3)\|_2.$$

Taking into account that C_{k+1} is a constant matrix at a certain time instant, we further have

$$\lim_{k\to\infty}\|C_{k+1}\mathbf{y}_{k+1} + \mathbf{d}_{k+1}\|_2 = \lim_{k\to\infty}\|C_{k+1}\mathbf{O}(g^3)\|_2 = \mathscr{O}(g^3).$$

The proof is therefore completed. □

Theorem 13 *Consider the FECQP (2.1) with C_k being uniformly norm bounded. Suppose that Q_k is positive definite and A_k is of full row rank. With the sufficiently small sampling gap $g \in (0,1)$, the MSSRE $\lim_{k\to\infty}\sup\hat{e}_{k+1}$ synthesized by the ZT-DTZNN-U algorithm (2.9) is $\mathscr{O}(g^3)$.*

Proof. According to (2.6) and (2.8), we have the equation below for the ZT-DTZNN-U algorithm (2.9):

$$\mathbf{y}_{k+1} = 1.5\mathbf{y}_k - \mathbf{y}_{k-1} + 0.5\mathbf{y}_{k-2} - C_k^{-1}\big(g(\dot{C}_k + \mathbf{O}(g^2))\mathbf{y}_k + \hbar(C_k\mathbf{y}_k + \mathbf{d}_k) + g(\dot{\mathbf{d}}_k + \mathbf{O}(g^2))\big) + \mathbf{O}(g^3).$$

It is further rewritten as

$$\begin{aligned}\mathbf{y}_{k+1} &= 1.5\mathbf{y}_k - \mathbf{y}_{k-1} + 0.5\mathbf{y}_{k-2} - C_k^{-1}\big(g\dot{C}_k\mathbf{y}_k + \hbar(C_k\mathbf{y}_k + \mathbf{d}_k) + g\dot{\mathbf{d}}_k\big) - C_k^{-1}\mathbf{O}(g^3)\mathbf{y}_k + \mathbf{O}(g^3)\\ &= 1.5\mathbf{y}_k - \mathbf{y}_{k-1} + 0.5\mathbf{y}_{k-2} - C_k^{-1}\big(g\dot{C}_k\mathbf{y}_k + \hbar(C_k\mathbf{y}_k + \mathbf{d}_k) + g\dot{\mathbf{d}}_k\big) + \mathbf{O}(g^3).\end{aligned}$$

Evidently, the ZT-DTZNN-K algorithm (2.7) is obtained by dropping $\mathbf{O}(g^3)$ from the above equation. Therefore, the truncation error of the ZT-DTZNN-U algorithm (2.9) is also $\mathbf{O}(g^3)$. That is to say, the ZT-DTZNN-U algorithm (2.9) is consistent. Similar to the proof of Theorem 12, it can be readily proved that the MSSRE $\lim_{k\to\infty}\sup\hat{e}_{k+1}$ synthesized by the ZT-DTZNN-U algorithm (2.9) is $\mathscr{O}(g^3)$. The proof is therefore completed. □

2.4 Euler-Type ZNN Discretization and NI

In this section, for comparison purposes, two ET-DTZNN algorithms and the NI algorithm [20, 45] are presented and discussed for solving the FECQP (2.1).

2.4.1 ET-DTZNN-K and ET-DTZNN-U algorithms

For the CTZNN model (2.5), via the Euler forward formula [20,45], we obtain an ET-DTZNN-K algorithm as

$$\mathbf{y}_{k+1} \doteq \mathbf{y}_k - C_k^{-1}\big(g\dot{C}_k\mathbf{y}_k + \hbar(C_k\mathbf{y}_k + \mathbf{d}_k) + g\dot{\mathbf{d}}_k\big), \tag{2.11}$$

considering that the derivative information (i.e., $\dot{C}_k$ and $\dot{\mathbf{d}}_k$) is known. When the derivative information is unknown, $\dot{C}_k$ and $\dot{\mathbf{d}}_k$ can be approximated by the simple Euler backward formula of order $\mathscr{O}(g)$ (i.e., $\dot{\zeta}_k = (\zeta_k - \zeta_{k-1})/g + \mathscr{O}(g)$). Then, the ET-DTZNN-U algorithm can be obtained as

$$\mathbf{y}_{k+1} \doteq \mathbf{y}_k - C_k^{-1}\big(\tilde{\Delta}C_k\mathbf{y}_k + \hbar(C_k\mathbf{y}_k + \mathbf{d}_k) + \tilde{\Delta}\mathbf{d}_k\big), \tag{2.12}$$

where $\tilde{\Delta}C_k = C_k - C_{k-1}$ and $\tilde{\Delta}\mathbf{d}_k = \mathbf{d}_k - \mathbf{d}_{k-1}$.

Moreover, with regard to the ET-DTZNN algorithms, we have the following theoretical analyses.

Theorem 14 *Consider the FECQP (2.1). Suppose that Q_k is positive definite and A_k is of full row rank. With the sufficiently small sampling gap $g \in (0,1)$, the ET-DTZNN-K algorithm (2.11) is zero-stable.*

Proof. According to Definition 2 in Chapter 1, the characteristic polynomial of the ET-DTZNN-K algorithm (2.11) can be stated as

$$\Gamma_1(\iota) = \iota - 1,$$

which has only one root (i.e., $\iota = 1$) on the unit circle. As a result, the ET-DTZNN-K algorithm (2.11) is zero-stable. The proof is therefore completed. □

Theorem 15 *Consider the FECQP (2.1). Suppose that Q_k is positive definite and A_k is of full row rank. With the sufficiently small sampling gap $g \in (0,1)$, the ET-DTZNN-K algorithm (2.11) is consistent and convergent, which converges with the order of truncation error being $\mathbf{O}(g^2)$ for all $t_k \in [t_{\text{ini}}, t_{\text{fin}})$.*

Proof. Using (2.6), one can obtain

$$\mathbf{y}_{k+1} = \mathbf{y}_k - C_k^{-1}\big(g\dot{C}_k\mathbf{y}_k + \hbar(C_k\mathbf{y}_k + \mathbf{d}_k) + g\dot{\mathbf{d}}_k\big) + \mathbf{O}(g^2). \tag{2.13}$$

Dropping $\mathbf{O}(g^2)$ from (2.13) yields exactly the ET-DTZNN-K algorithm (2.11). Then, the truncation error of the ET-DTZNN-K algorithm (2.11) is $\mathbf{O}(g^2)$. According to Definition 3 in Chapter 1, the ET-DTZNN-K algorithm (2.11) is consistent. That is, the ET-DTZNN-K algorithm (2.11) is zero-stable and consistent. Finally, in view of Definition 4 in Chapter 1, we know that the ET-DTZNN-K algorithm (2.11) is consistent and convergent, which converges with the order of truncation error being $\mathbf{O}(g^2)$ for all $t_k \in [t_{\text{ini}}, t_{\text{fin}})$. The proof is therefore completed. □

Theorem 16 *Consider the FECQP (2.1) with C_k being uniformly norm bounded. Suppose that Q_k is positive definite and A_k is of full row rank. With the sufficiently small sampling gap $g \in (0,1)$, both the MSSREs $\lim_{k\to\infty}\sup \hat{e}_{k+1}$ synthesized by the ET-DTZNN-K algorithm (2.11) and the ET-DTZNN-U algorithm (2.12) are $\mathscr{O}(g^2)$.*

TABLE 2.1: Different DTZNN algorithms and NI algorithm for solving FECQP (2.1).

Algorithm	Expression
(2.7)	$\mathbf{y}_{k+1} \doteq 1.5\mathbf{y}_k - \mathbf{y}_{k-1} + 0.5\mathbf{y}_{k-2} - C_k^{-1}(g\dot{C}_k\mathbf{y}_k + \hbar(C_k\mathbf{y}_k + \mathbf{d}_k) + g\dot{\mathbf{d}}_k)$
(2.9)	$\mathbf{y}_{k+1} \doteq 1.5\mathbf{y}_k - \mathbf{y}_{k-1} + 0.5\mathbf{y}_{k-2} - C_k^{-1}(\Delta C_k\mathbf{y}_k + \hbar(C_k\mathbf{y}_k + \mathbf{d}_k) + \Delta\mathbf{d}_k)$
(2.11)	$\mathbf{y}_{k+1} \doteq \mathbf{y}_k - C_k^{-1}(g\dot{C}_k\mathbf{y}_k + \hbar(C_k\mathbf{y}_k + \mathbf{d}_k) + g\dot{\mathbf{d}}_k)$
(2.12)	$\mathbf{y}_{k+1} \doteq \mathbf{y}_k - C_k^{-1}(\tilde{\Delta} C_k\mathbf{y}_k + \hbar(C_k\mathbf{y}_k + \mathbf{d}_k) + \tilde{\Delta}\mathbf{d}_k)$
(2.14)	$\mathbf{y}_{k+1} \doteq -C_k^{-1}\mathbf{d}_k$

Proof. Similar to the proof of Theorems 12 and 13, it can be readily proved that the MSSREs $\lim_{k\to\infty}\sup\hat{e}_{k+1}$ synthesized by the ET-DTZNN-K algorithm (2.11) and the ET-DTZNN-U algorithm (2.12) are $\mathscr{O}(g^2)$ by taking into account Theorems 14 and 15. The proof is therefore completed. □

2.4.2 NI algorithm

From the numerical-algorithm viewpoint [20,45,49,50], to solve the FECQP (2.1), we have the conventional NI algorithm:

$$\mathbf{y}_{k+1} \doteq -C_k^{-1}\mathbf{d}_k. \tag{2.14}$$

Evidently, the NI algorithm (2.14) is actually a special case of the presented ET-DTZNN-K algorithm (2.11) by setting the step length $\hbar = 1$ and omitting the time-derivative terms (i.e., $\dot{C}_k$ and $\dot{\mathbf{d}}_k$). In other words, apart from differences, the links between the ET-DTZNN algorithm and the NI algorithm are discovered. To be more specific, the NI algorithm (2.14) for the FECQP (2.1) is a special case of the ET-DTZNN-K algorithm (2.11); the methods of the DTZNN and the NI are closely related.

By following Theorems 10–16, it can be readily generalized and similarly proved that the NI algorithm (2.14) is consistent and convergent, which converges with the order of truncation error being $\mathbf{O}(g)$. Moreover, the MSSREs $\lim_{k\to\infty}\sup\hat{e}_{k+1}$ synthesized by the NI algorithm (2.14) is theorectically $\mathscr{O}(g)$.

In summary, four DTZNN algorithms (i.e., the ZT-DTZNN-K algorithm (2.7), the ZT-DTZNN-U algorithm (2.9), the ET-DTZNN-K algorithm (2.11), and the ET-DTZNN-U algorithm (2.12)) and the NI algorithm (2.14) have been developed and analyzed for solving the FECQP (2.1). For readers' convenience and also for comparison, these DTZNN algorithms and the NI algorithm are listed comparatively in Table 2.1.

For a more intuitive understanding of the main content of this chapter [46], Table 2.2 lists the problem, scheme, model, and algorithms.

2.5 Numerical Experiments

In this section, numerical experiments are conducted for making comparisons among these different algorithms to solve the FECQP (2.1). Through the numerical experiments, the efficacy and superiority of the ZT-DTZNN algorithms presented herein are illustrated.

It is important to note that, for the ZT-DTZNN-K algorithm (2.7) and the ZT-DTZNN-U algorithm (2.9), three initial state vectors (i.e., $\mathbf{y}_0$, $\mathbf{y}_1$, and $\mathbf{y}_2$) are needed to be set. Hereafter, $\mathbf{y}_0$ is chosen to be a randomly generated value. Meanwhile, given that the NI algorithm (2.14) has the simplest structure, we thus make use of (2.14) to obtain the two other initial state vectors, i.e., $\mathbf{y}_1$ and $\mathbf{y}_2$.

TABLE 2.2: Problem, scheme, model, and algorithms in this chapter.

Problem	$\min\ \varphi(\mathbf{x}_{k+1},t_{k+1})=\frac{1}{2}\mathbf{x}_{k+1}^{\mathrm{T}}Q_{k+1}\mathbf{x}_{k+1}+\mathbf{p}_{k+1}^{\mathrm{T}}\mathbf{x}_{k+1}$ s. t. $A_{k+1}\mathbf{x}_{k+1}=\mathbf{b}_{k+1}$.
Scheme	*Step 1*: Define ZF as $\mathbf{z}(t)=C(t)\mathbf{y}(t)+\mathbf{d}(t)$. *Step 2*: Adopt ZNN design formula as $\dot{\mathbf{z}}(t)=-\eta\mathbf{z}(t)$. *Step 3*: Discretize CTZNN model (2.5).
Model	$\dot{\mathbf{y}}(t)=-C^{-1}(t)(\dot{C}(t)\mathbf{y}(t)+\eta(C(t)\mathbf{y}(t)+\mathbf{d}(t))+\dot{\mathbf{d}}(t))$.
Algorithms	$\mathbf{y}_{k+1}\doteq 1.5\mathbf{y}_k-\mathbf{y}_{k-1}+0.5\mathbf{y}_{k-2}-C_k^{-1}(g\dot{C}_k\mathbf{y}_k+\hbar(C_k\mathbf{y}_k+\mathbf{d}_k)+g\dot{\mathbf{d}}_k)$, $\mathbf{y}_{k+1}\doteq 1.5\mathbf{y}_k-\mathbf{y}_{k-1}+0.5\mathbf{y}_{k-2}-C_k^{-1}(\Delta C_k\mathbf{y}_k+\hbar(C_k\mathbf{y}_k+\mathbf{d}_k)+\Delta\mathbf{d}_k)$, $\mathbf{y}_{k+1}\doteq\mathbf{y}_k-C_k^{-1}(g\dot{C}_k\mathbf{y}_k+\hbar(C_k\mathbf{y}_k+\mathbf{d}_k)+g\dot{\mathbf{d}}_k)$, $\mathbf{y}_{k+1}\doteq\mathbf{y}_k-C_k^{-1}(\tilde{\Delta}C_k\mathbf{y}_k+\hbar(C_k\mathbf{y}_k+\mathbf{d}_k)+\tilde{\Delta}\mathbf{d}_k)$, $\mathbf{y}_{k+1}\doteq -C_k^{-1}\mathbf{d}_k$.

Example 2.1 Consider a special case of the FECQP (2.1). More specifically, $\mathbf{y}_{k+1}$ is computed at each computational time interval $[kg,(k+1)g)\subset[0,10]$ s, with the following time-dependent coefficients:

$$Q_k=\begin{bmatrix}2\sin(t_k)+4 & \cos(t_k)\\ \cos(t_k) & \cos(t_k)+2\end{bmatrix}\ \text{and}\ \mathbf{p}_k=\begin{bmatrix}\sin(3t_k)\\ \cos(3t_k)\end{bmatrix}. \tag{2.15}$$

Evidently, $\mathbf{y}_k=\mathbf{x}_k$, $C_k=Q_k$, and $\mathbf{d}_k=\mathbf{p}_k$ in this case. The corresponding numerical experimental results are displayed in Figures 2.1 and 2.2. As seen from Figure 2.1(a), starting with a randomly generated $\mathbf{x}_0\in[-0.5,0.5]^2$, the state vector $\mathbf{x}_{k+1}$ of the ZT-DTZNN-K algorithm (2.7) with $\hbar=0.3$ and $g=0.01$ s converges to the theoretical solution $\mathbf{x}_{k+1}^*$ rapidly. Besides, it follows from Figure 2.1(b) that the residual error $\hat{e}_{k+1}$ synthesized by the ZT-DTZNN-K algorithm (2.7) diminishes to near zero within 20 iterations. Therefore, the effectiveness of the presented ZT-DTZNN-K algorithm (2.7) for solving the FECQP (2.1) is substantiated primarily. Note that the figures yielded by the other DTZNN algorithms and the NI algorithm (2.14) are similar to Figure 2.1, and thus are omitted here.

To clearly compare the ZT-DTZNN-K algorithm (2.7) and the ZT-DTZNN-U algorithm (2.9) with the ET-DTZNN-K algorithm (2.11), the ET-DTZNN-U algorithm (2.12), and the NI algorithm (2.14) for solving (2.1), the trajectories of residual errors synthesized by these five different al-

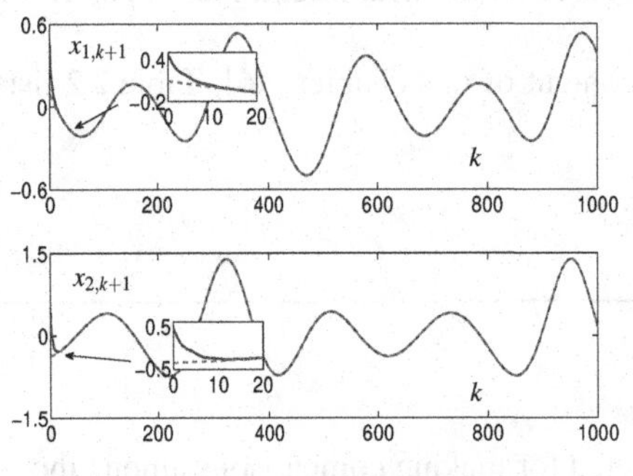

(a) Element trajectories of state vector $\mathbf{x}_{k+1}$

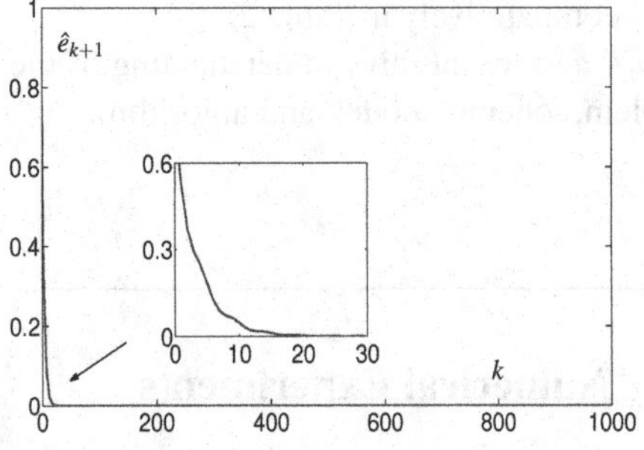

(b) Trajectory of residual error $\hat{e}_{k+1}$

FIGURE 2.1: Convergence performance of ZT-DTZNN-K algorithm (2.7) with $\hbar=0.3$, $g=0.01$ s, and $\mathbf{x}_0\in[-0.5,0.5]^2$ in Example 2.1. In panel (a), solid curves correspond to neural-network solutions and dash curves correspond to theoretical solutions.

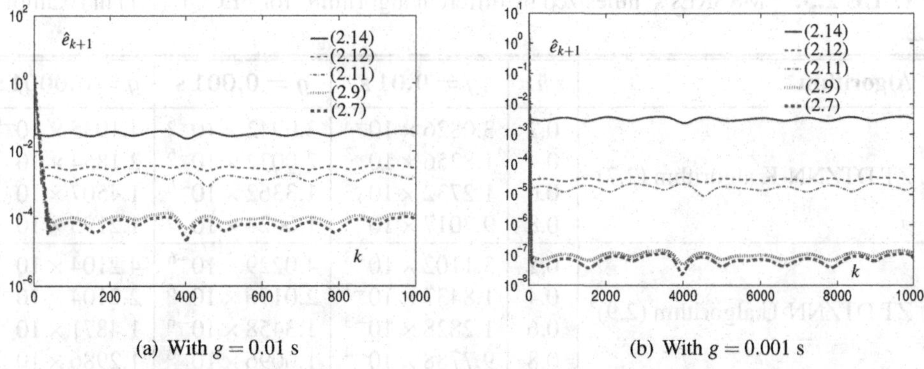

(a) With $g = 0.01$ s

(b) With $g = 0.001$ s

FIGURE 2.2: Trajectories of residual errors $\hat{e}_{k+1}$ synthesized by DTZNN algorithms with $\hbar = 0.3$ and NI algorithm in Example 2.1.

gorithms with $g = 0.01$ and 0.001 s are depicted in Figure 2.2. As shown in Figure 2.2(a), with $g = 0.01$ s, MSSREs, i.e., the maximal steady-state $\hat{e}_{k+1}$ with g large enough, synthesized by the ZT-DTZNN-K algorithm (2.7) and the ZT-DTZNN-U algorithm (2.9), are of orders 10^{-4}. By contrast, the MSSREs synthesized by the ET-DTZNN-K algorithm (2.11) and the ET-DTZNN-U algorithm (2.12) are of orders 10^{-3}, and the MSSRE synthesized by the NI algorithm (2.14) is of order 10^{-2}. When $g = 0.001$ s, it can be seen from Figure 2.2(b) that the MSSREs synthesized by the ZT-DTZNN algorithms, the ET-DTZNN algorithms, and the NI algorithm (2.14) are of orders 10^{-7}, 10^{-5}, and 10^{-3}, respectively. These experimental results further validate the higher accuracy of the presented ZT-DTZNN-K algorithm (2.7) and ZT-DTZNN-U algorithm (2.9) (compared with the ET-DTZNN-K algorithm (2.11), the ET-DTZNN-U algorithm (2.12), and the NI algorithm (2.14)) as well as the important role of the time-derivative information for solving the FECQP problem.

Example 2.2 Consider a more general case of the FECQP (2.1). To be more specific, the following equality constraint is considered for (2.15):

$$A_k = \begin{bmatrix}\cos(2t_k) & \sin(2t_k)\end{bmatrix} \text{ and } \mathbf{b}_k = \cos(t_k).$$

It follows from (2.3) that

$$C_k = \begin{bmatrix} 2\sin(t_k)+4 & \cos(t_k) & \cos(2t_k) \\ \cos(t_k) & \cos(t_k)+2 & \sin(2t_k) \\ \cos(2t_k) & \sin(2t_k) & 0 \end{bmatrix}, \quad \mathbf{d}_k = \begin{bmatrix} \sin(3t_k) \\ \cos(3t_k) \\ -\cos(t_k) \end{bmatrix}, \quad \text{and } \mathbf{y}_k = \begin{bmatrix} x_{1,k} \\ x_{2,k} \\ l_{1,k} \end{bmatrix}.$$

Specifically, Figure 2.3(a) illustrates the element trajectories of the state vector $\mathbf{y}_{k+1}$ of the ZT-DTZNN-K algorithm (2.7) by using $\hbar = 0.3$ and $g = 0.01$ s, with the trajectories of the residual error $\hat{e}_{k+1}$ shown in Figure 2.3(b). Note that similar figures associated with the other algorithms are omitted for space reasons. As observed from Figure 2.3(a), the state vector $\mathbf{y}_{k+1}$ of the ZT-DTZNN-K algorithm (2.7) converges to the theoretical solution $\mathbf{y}^*_{k+1}$ accurately. In addition, from Figure 2.3(b), we may find that $\hat{e}_{k+1}$ converges to zero quickly. Thus, the efficacy of the ZT-DTZNN-K algorithm is validated once more. For further investigation, more detailed MSSREs data synthesized by these five different algorithms are listed in Table 2.3 with respect to different values of $\hbar$ and g. From Table 2.3 as well as Figures 2.1–2.3, we may obtain the following important facts which coincide well with the theoretical results.

1. The MSSRE synthesized by the NI algorithm (2.14) without utilizing the time derivative of time-dependent coefficients changes in an $\mathscr{O}(g)$ pattern. For instance, as seen from Table 2.3, the MSSREs synthesized by the NI algorithm (2.14) are of orders 10^{-1}, 10^{-2}, and 10^{-3}, corresponding to the sampling gap $g = 0.01, 0.001$, and 0.0001 s, respectively.

TABLE 2.3: MSSREs synthesized by different algorithms for FECQP (2.1) in Example 2.2.

Algorithm	$\hbar$	$g = 0.01$ s	$g = 0.001$ s	$g = 0.0001$ s
ZT-DTZNN-K algorithm (2.7)	0.2	3.0826×10^{-3}	3.9942×10^{-6}	4.1035×10^{-9}
	0.4	1.8256×10^{-3}	2.0032×10^{-6}	2.1854×10^{-9}
	0.6	1.2732×10^{-3}	1.3362×10^{-6}	1.4507×10^{-9}
	0.8	9.7017×10^{-4}	1.0024×10^{-6}	1.2195×10^{-9}
ZT-DTZNN-U algorithm (2.9)	0.2	3.1102×10^{-3}	4.0229×10^{-6}	4.2104×10^{-9}
	0.4	1.8437×10^{-3}	2.0176×10^{-6}	2.2104×10^{-9}
	0.6	1.2828×10^{-3}	1.3458×10^{-6}	1.4871×10^{-9}
	0.8	9.7788×10^{-4}	1.0096×10^{-6}	1.2986×10^{-9}
ET-DTZNN-K algorithm (2.11)	0.2	1.7772×10^{-2}	1.9206×10^{-4}	1.8621×10^{-6}
	0.4	9.5157×10^{-3}	9.6136×10^{-5}	9.6065×10^{-7}
	0.6	6.4271×10^{-3}	6.4100×10^{-5}	6.4251×10^{-7}
	0.8	4.8346×10^{-3}	4.8077×10^{-5}	4.8253×10^{-7}
ET-DTZNN-U algorithm (2.12)	0.2	2.0165×10^{-2}	2.1602×10^{-4}	2.1625×10^{-6}
	0.4	1.0704×10^{-2}	1.0812×10^{-4}	1.0894×10^{-6}
	0.6	7.2208×10^{-3}	7.2086×10^{-5}	7.2015×10^{-7}
	0.8	5.4285×10^{-3}	5.4067×10^{-5}	5.4108×10^{-7}
NI algorithm (2.14)	N/A	1.5632×10^{-1}	1.5615×10^{-2}	1.5613×10^{-3}

2. The MSSREs synthesized by the ET-DTZNN algorithms which utilize the time derivative and are discretized through the Euler forward formula, change in $\mathcal{O}(g^2)$ patterns. This fact is clearly illustrated in Table 2.3.

3. The MSSREs synthesized by the ZT-DTZNN algorithms which make use of the time derivative and are discretized via the Zhang–Taylor discretization formula (2.6), change in $\mathcal{O}(g^3)$ patterns. For instance, it follows from Table 2.3 that the MSSREs synthesized by the ZT-DTZNN-K algorithm (2.7) and the ZT-DTZNN-U algorithm (2.9) are of orders 10^{-3}, 10^{-6}, and 10^{-9}, corresponding to $g = 0.01, 0.001$, and 0.0001 s, respectively.

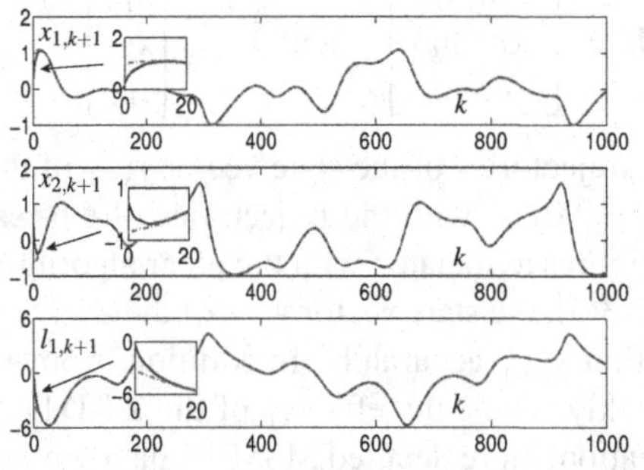

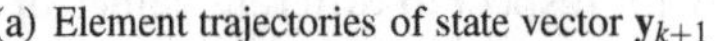

(a) Element trajectories of state vector $\mathbf{y}_{k+1}$

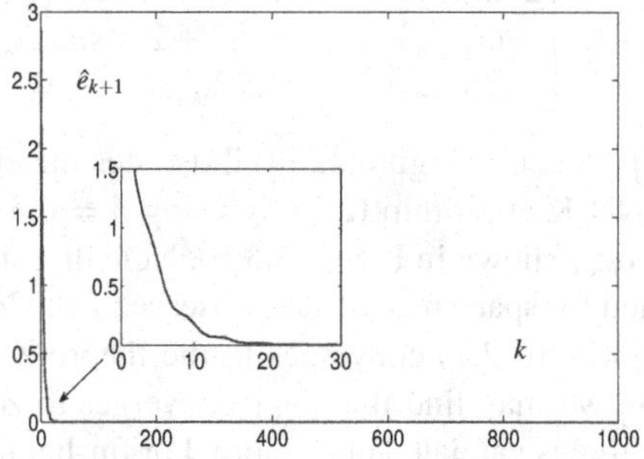

(b) Trajectory of residual error $\hat{e}_{k+1}$

FIGURE 2.3: Convergence performance of ZT-DTZNN-K algorithm (2.7) with $\hbar = 0.3$, $g = 0.01$ s, and $\mathbf{y}_0 \in [-0.5, 0.5]^3$ in Example 2.2. In panel (a), solid curves correspond to neural-network solutions and dash curves correspond to theoretical solutions.

4. With $\hbar$ and g fixed, the ZT-DTZNN-K algorithm (2.7) is the best one in terms of solution accuracy, followed by the ZT-DTZNN-U algorithm (2.9), the ET-DTZNN-K algorithm (2.11), the ET-DTZNN-U algorithm (2.12), and the NI algorithm (2.14).

Remark 2 *It is worth noting that the different values of step length $\hbar$ have an important effect on the MSSREs synthesized by the presented algorithms. For illustrating the facts, Figure 2.4 is given with respect to different values of $\hbar$. It can be seen that a good choice of the $\hbar$ value is needed in achieving high solution precision. Specifically, $\hbar = 0.8$ is the best choice for the ZT-DTZNN-K algorithm (2.7) and the ZT-DTZNN-U algorithm (2.9).*

Example 2.3 Consider motion generation in manipulators making use of the presented the ZT-DTZNN algorithms. On the basis of the authors' previous research result [27], the motion generation problem of manipulators can be described as the FECQP problem, i.e., (2.1), with $\mathbf{x}_k$ corresponding to $\dot{\vartheta}_k$, $Q_k = I_{n\times n} \in \mathbb{R}^{n\times n}$, $\mathbf{p}_k = \kappa(\vartheta_k - \vartheta_0)$, $A_k = J(\vartheta_k)$, and $\mathbf{b}_k = \dot{\mathbf{r}}_{\mathrm{d},k} + \rho(\mathbf{r}_{\mathrm{d},k} - \mathbf{r}_{\mathrm{a},k})$. In addition, $\vartheta_k \in \mathbb{R}^n$ denotes the joint-angle vector, $J(\vartheta_k) \in \mathbb{R}^{m\times n}$ denotes the Jacobi matrix of the manipulator, $\mathbf{r}_{\mathrm{d},k} \in \mathbb{R}^m$ denotes the end-effector desired path, $\mathbf{r}_{\mathrm{a},k} \in \mathbb{R}^m$ denotes the actual end-effector position vector, $\kappa > 0 \in \mathbb{R}$ is a design parameter used to scale the magnitude of the manipulator response to joint displacements, and $\rho > 0 \in \mathbb{R}$ is a feedback gain. As a consequence, on the basis of (2.3), C_k and $\mathbf{d}_k$ can be generated from the following time-dependent matrix and vector, respectively:

$$C_k = \begin{bmatrix} I_{n\times n} & J^{\mathrm{T}}(\vartheta_k) \\ J(\vartheta_k) & O_{m\times m} \end{bmatrix} \in \mathbb{R}^{(n+m)\times(n+m)} \text{ and } \mathbf{d}_k = \begin{bmatrix} \kappa(\vartheta_k - \vartheta_0) \\ -\dot{\mathbf{r}}_{\mathrm{d},k} - \rho(\mathbf{r}_{\mathrm{d},k} - \mathbf{r}_{\mathrm{a},k}) \end{bmatrix} \in \mathbb{R}^{n+m},$$

where $I_{n\times n}$ denotes an $n \times n$ identity matrix, and $O_{m\times m}$ denotes an $m \times m$ zero matrix. Generally, for a given manipulator, $\dot{J}(\vartheta_k)$ (being an element of $\dot{C}_k$) and $\ddot{\mathbf{r}}_{\mathrm{d},k}$ (being an element of $\dot{\mathbf{d}}_k$) cannot be obtained directly. Hence, the ZT-DTZNN-U algorithm (2.9) and the ET-DTZNN-U algorithm (2.12) are employed in this example.

For illustration, a three-link redundant manipulator is considered to track a Lissajous-figure path. The amplitudes of the Lissajous-figure path at the X-axis and Y-axis are set as 0.5 m, and the frequency at the X-axis is twice that at the Y-axis. The task duration $T = 10$ s, the initial joint-angle vector $\vartheta_0 = [\pi/4, \pi/5, -\pi/3]^{\mathrm{T}}$ rad, $\kappa = 10$, and ρ is set to be 15. Moreover, we choose $\hbar = 0.5$ and $g = 8$ ms. The corresponding numerical experimental results synthesized by the ZT-DTZNN-U algorithm (2.9), the ET-DTZNN-U algorithm (2.12), and the NI algorithm (2.14) are reported in Figures 2.5 and 2.6.

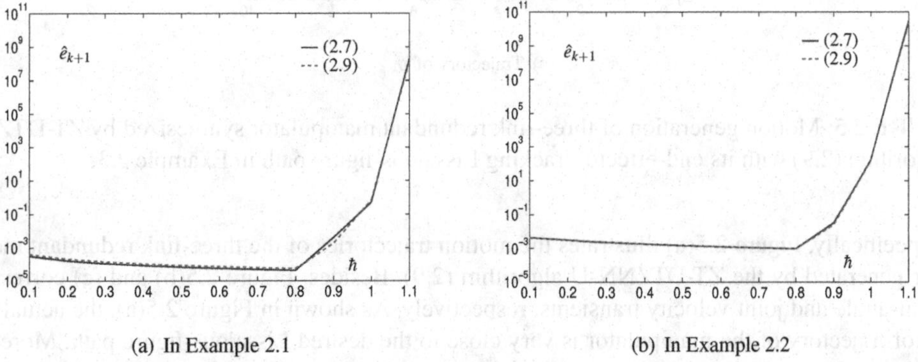

FIGURE 2.4: MSSREs synthesized by ZT-DTZNN-K algorithm (2.7) and ZT-DTZNN-U algorithm (2.9) for solving FECQP problems with $g = 0.01$ s and with different $\hbar$.

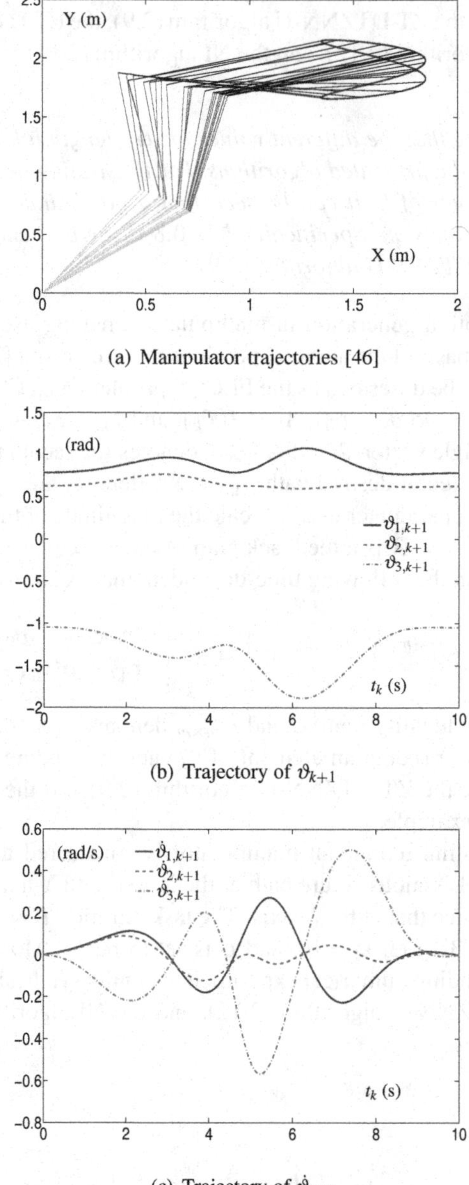

(a) Manipulator trajectories [46]

(b) Trajectory of ϑ_{k+1}

(c) Trajectory of $\dot{\vartheta}_{k+1}$

FIGURE 2.5: Motion generation of three-link redundant manipulator synthesized by ZT-DTZNN-U algorithm (2.9) with its end-effector tracking Lissajous-figure path in Example 2.3.

Specifically, Figure 2.5(a) illustrates the motion trajectories of the three-link redundant manipulator generated by the ZT-DTZNN-U algorithm (2.9). Besides, Figure 2.5(b) and (c) correspond to joint-angle and joint velocity transients, respectively. As shown in Figure 2.5(a), the actual end-effector trajectory of the manipulator is very close to the desired Lissajous-figure path. Moreover, the joint variables (i.e., the joint-angle vector ϑ_{k+1} and the joint velocity vector $\dot{\vartheta}_{k+1}$) shown in Figure 2.5(b) and (c) are smooth and have not undergone abrupt changes, which is suitable for engineering applications. For comparison, the tracking errors $\tilde{e}_{k+1} = \|\mathbf{r}_{\mathrm{a},k+1} - \mathbf{r}_{\mathrm{d},k+1}\|_2$ synthesized

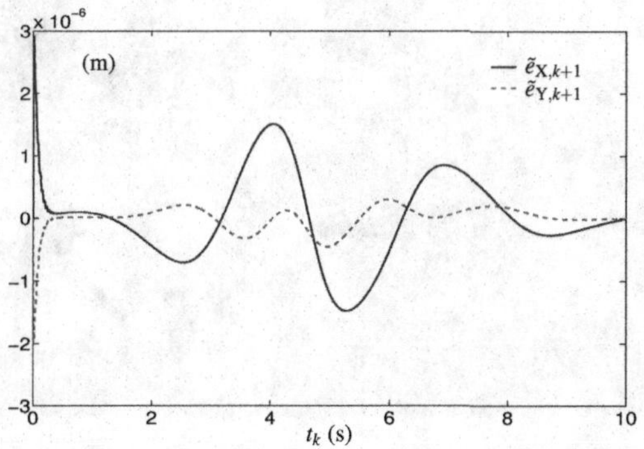

(a) X-axis and Y-axis tracking errors synthesized by algorithm (2.9)

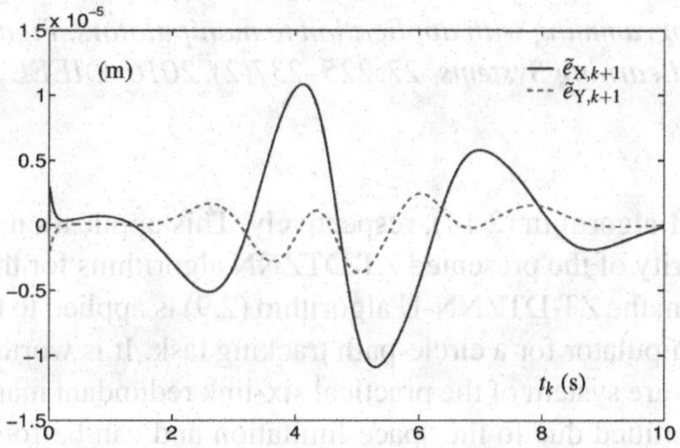

(b) X-axis and Y-axis tracking errors synthesized by algorithm (2.12)

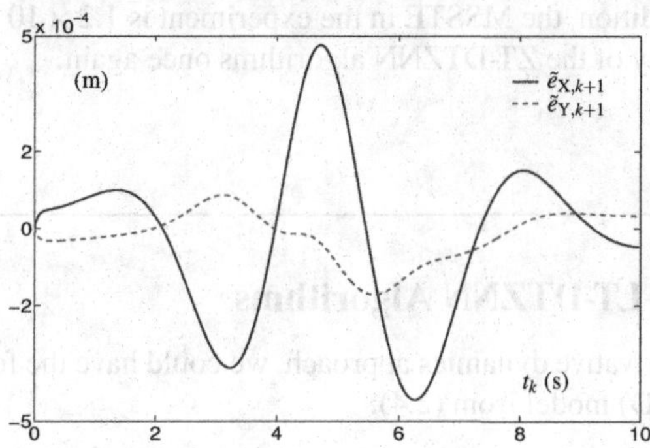

(c) X-axis and Y-axis tracking errors synthesized by algorithm (2.14)

FIGURE 2.6: Trajectories of tracking errors $\tilde{e}_{k+1}$ synthesized by ZT-DTZNN-U algorithm (2.9), ET-DTZNN-U algorithm (2.12), and NI algorithm (2.14) in Example 2.3.

by the ZT-DTZNN-U algorithm (2.9), the ET-DTZNN-U algorithm (2.12), and the NI algorithm (2.14), are displayed in Figure 2.6. As seen from Figure 2.6(a), the maximal steady-state tracking error (MSSTE) $\lim_{k\to+\infty}\sup\tilde{e}_{k+1}$ synthesized by the ZT-DTZNN-U algorithm (2.9) is of order 10^{-6} m, which is roughly 10 times and 100 times smaller than that synthesized by the ET-DTZNN-U al-

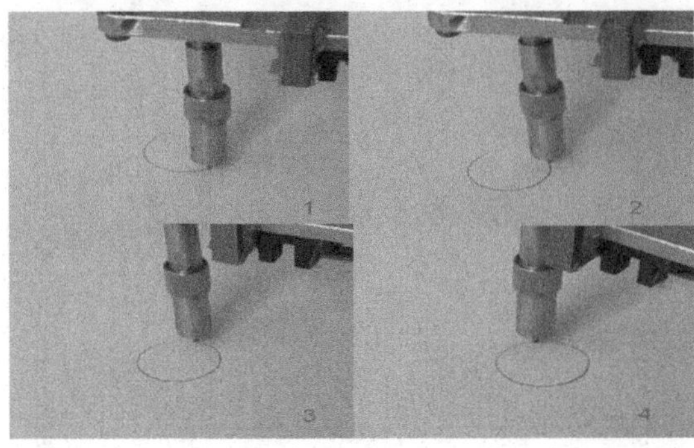

FIGURE 2.7: Snapshots for actual task execution of six-link redundant manipulator. *Reproduced from B. Liao, Y. Zhang, and L. Jin, Taylor $O(h^3)$ discretization of ZNN models for dynamic equality-constrained quadratic programming with application to manipulators, Figure 7, IEEE Transactions on Neural Networks and Learning Systems, 27:225–237(2), 2016. ©IEEE 2015. With kind permission of IEEE.*

gorithm (2.12) and the NI algorithm (2.14), respectively. This application further substantiates the effectiveness and superiority of the presented ZT-DTZNN algorithms for the FECQP solving.

For further verification, the ZT-DTZNN-U algorithm (2.9) is applied to the motion generation of a practical redundant manipulator for a circle-path tracking task. It is worth noting that the detailed descriptions for the hardware system of the practical six-link redundant manipulator used for experimental application are omitted due to the space limitation and can be found in [27]. Specifically, Figure 2.7 shows the corresponding experimental results of the physical system. As shown in the figure, the snapshots at different time instants of the task execution show that the end-effector tracks the circle path well. In addition, the MSSTE in the experiment is 1.2×10^{-4} m, which substantiates the efficacy and superiority of the ZT-DTZNN algorithms once again.

2.6 ZT-DTDD and LT-DTZNN Algorithms

On the basis of the derivative dynamics approach, we could have the following continuous-time derivative dynamic (CTDD) model from (2.4):

$$\dot{\mathbf{y}}(t) = -C^{-1}(t)\big(\dot{C}(t)\mathbf{y}(t) + \dot{\mathbf{d}}(t)\big), \text{ with } \mathbf{y}(0) = \mathbf{y}^*(0),$$

of which the discrete form via the Zhang–Taylor discretization formula (2.6) is further obtained as

$$\mathbf{y}_{k+1} \doteq 1.5\mathbf{y}_k - \mathbf{y}_{k-1} + 0.5\mathbf{y}_{k-2} - C_k^{-1}\big(g\dot{C}_k\mathbf{y}_k + g\dot{\mathbf{d}}_k\big), \text{ with } \mathbf{y}_0 = \mathbf{y}_0^*. \tag{2.16}$$

For convenience, we name (2.16) as Zhang–Taylor discrete-time derivative dynamics (ZT-DTDD) algorithm. It is worth noting that the corresponding comparisons between the algorithms with time-derivative information (i.e., $\dot{C}_k$ and $\dot{\mathbf{d}}_k$) unknown are omitted due to the similarity to those between the algorithms with time-derivative information known. Comparing the ZT-DTZNN-K algorithm (2.7) with the ZT-DTDD algorithm (2.16), we find that the former exploits the error-feedback information (i.e., $C_k\mathbf{y}_k + \mathbf{d}_k$) during the real-time solution process, while the latter does not exploit such important information. Theoretically speaking, the ZT-DTZNN-K algorithm (2.7) reduces to the ZT-DTDD algorithm (2.16) with $C_k\mathbf{y}_k + \mathbf{d}_k = \mathbf{0}$, and thus the ZT-DTDD algorithm (2.16) can be viewed as a special case of the ZT-DTZNN-K algorithm (2.7). However, by considering the facts that the initial state $\mathbf{y}_0^*$ may not be obtained in advance and that the computational errors (e.g., resulting from truncation errors and round-off errors) are inevitable between the obtained solution and the theoretical solution, the error-feedback information is an indispensable term for achieving a more robust and accurate solution for solving the FECQP (2.1). For further investigation and comparison, the ZT-DTZNN-K algorithm (2.7) and the ZT-DTDD algorithm (2.16) are exploited to solve the FECQP (2.1) depicted in Example 2.1. The corresponding numerical experimental results are shown in Figure 2.8. Specifically, as seen from Figure 2.8(a), starting with $\mathbf{y}_0^*$, the MSSREs synthesized by the ZT-DTZNN-K algorithm (2.7) and the ZT-DTDD algorithm (2.16) are both relatively small. It can be clearly seen from the figure that the MSSREs synthesized by the ZT-DTDD algorithm (2.16) are larger than those synthesized by the ZT-DTZNN-K algorithm (2.7), and this is evidently due to the lack of error feedback in the ZT-DTDD algorithm (2.16). It is observed from Figure 2.8(b) that, with initial state $\mathbf{y}_0 \neq \mathbf{y}_0^*$, the residual error synthesized by the ZT-DTDD algorithm (2.16) does not converge to zero, while residual error synthesized by the ZT-DTZNN-K algorithm (2.7) converges to zero rapidly, which means that the ZT-DTDD algorithm (2.16) is highly sensitive to the initial value thereby limiting its application in practice. In summary, these comparative results have illustrated once again the efficacy and superiority of the presented ZT-DTZNN-K algorithm (2.7) for solving the FECQP (2.1).

Moreover, a basic requirement for a discretization formula to discretize ZNN is that it should have and only have one data point ahead of the target point. That is, with the numerical-differentiation formula applied to the ZNN discretization, the counterpart DTZNN algorithm should have one and only one unknown $\mathbf{y}_{k+1}$ to be computed via the known data (e.g., $\mathbf{y}_k$ and $\mathbf{y}_{k-1}$). Thus, the backward and central numerical-differentiation formulas cannot be applied to the ZNN discretization, no matter how small the truncation error of each formula is. In addition, only the forward numerical-differentiation formulas with one step ahead can be considered for the discretization of ZNN.

As stated in Section 2.1, a discretization formula does not necessarily generate a stable and convergent DTZNN algorithm. For further investigation and comparison, a group of one-step-ahead Lagrange numerical-differentiation formulas are provided in Table 2.4 [51]. These formulas not only achieve higher computational precision but also can be considered for the possible discretization of ZNN. The counterpart Lagrange-type DTZNN (LT-DTZNN) algorithms generated by one-step-ahead Lagrange numerical-differentiation formulas are shown in Table 2.5. Note that these LT-DTZNN algorithms cannot be guaranteed to be zero-stable due to the existence of the root of the

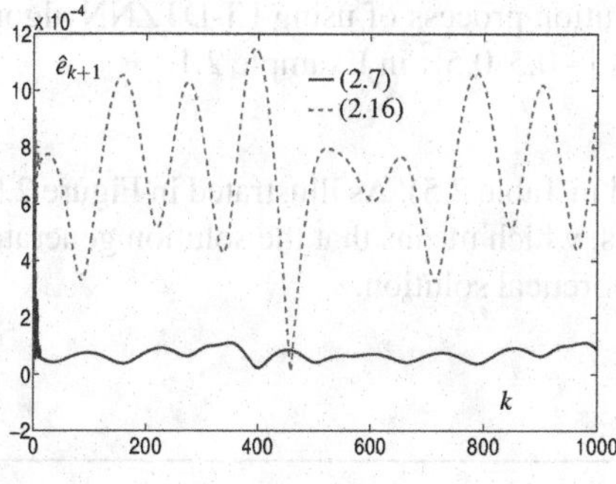

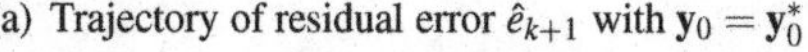

(a) Trajectory of residual error $\hat{e}_{k+1}$ with $\mathbf{y}_0 = \mathbf{y}_0^*$

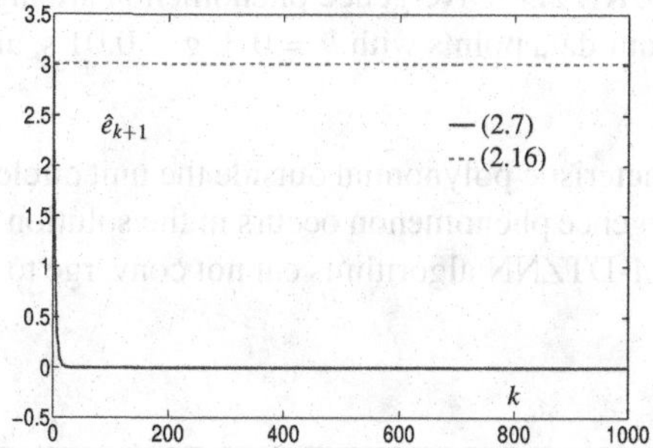

(b) Trajectory of residual error $\hat{e}_{k+1}$ with $\mathbf{y}_0 \neq \mathbf{y}_0^*$

FIGURE 2.8: Convergence performance of ZT-DTZNN-K algorithm (2.7) and ZT-DTDD algorithm (2.16) with $\hbar = 0.3$ and $g = 0.01$ s in Example 2.1.

TABLE 2.4: One-step-ahead Lagrange numerical-differentiation formulas using four through eight data points presented in [51].

Data point number	One-step-ahead Lagrange numerical-differentiation formula
Four	$\dot{\zeta}_k=(2\zeta_{k+1}+3\zeta_k-6\zeta_{k-1}+\zeta_{k-2})/(6g)+\mathscr{O}(g^3)$
Five	$\dot{\zeta}_k=(3\zeta_{k+1}+10\zeta_k-18\zeta_{k-1}+6\zeta_{k-2}-\zeta_{k-3})/(12g)+\mathscr{O}(g^4)$
Six	$\dot{\zeta}_k=(12\zeta_{k+1}+65\zeta_k-120\zeta_{k-1}+60\zeta_{k-2}-20\zeta_{k-3}+3\zeta_{k-4})/(60g)+\mathscr{O}(g^5)$
Seven	$\dot{\zeta}_k=(10\zeta_{k+1}+77\zeta_k-150\zeta_{k-1}+100\zeta_{k-2}-50\zeta_{k-3}$ $+15\zeta_{k-4}-2\zeta_{k-5})/(60g)+\mathscr{O}(g^6)$
Eight	$\dot{\zeta}_k=(60\zeta_{k+1}+609\zeta_k-1260\zeta_{k-1}+1050\zeta_{k-2}-700\zeta_{k-3}$ $+315\zeta_{k-4}-84\zeta_{k-5}+10\zeta_{k-6})/(420g)+\mathscr{O}(g^7)$

TABLE 2.5: LT-DTZNN algorithms based on one-step-ahead Lagrange numerical-differentiation formulas in Table 2.4 (with ROUD denoting root outside unit circle).

Data point number	LT-DTZNN algorithm	ROUD
Four	$\mathbf{y}_{k+1}\doteq-3/2\mathbf{y}_k+3\mathbf{y}_{k-1}-1/2\mathbf{y}_{k-2}-3C_k^{-1}(g\dot{C}_k\mathbf{y}_k+\hbar(C_k\mathbf{y}_k+\mathbf{d}_k)+g\dot{\mathbf{d}}_k)$	−2.6861
Five	$\mathbf{y}_{k+1}\doteq-10/3\mathbf{y}_k+6\mathbf{y}_{k-1}-2\mathbf{y}_{k-2}+1/3\mathbf{y}_{k-3}-4C_k^{-1}(g\dot{C}_k\mathbf{y}_k+\hbar(C_k\mathbf{y}_k+\mathbf{d}_k)+g\dot{\mathbf{d}}_k)$	−4.6979
Six	$\mathbf{y}_{k+1}\doteq-65/12\mathbf{y}_k+10\mathbf{y}_{k-1}-5\mathbf{y}_{k-2}+5/3\mathbf{y}_{k-3}-1/4\mathbf{y}_{k-4}$ $-5C_k^{-1}(g\dot{C}_k\mathbf{y}_k+\hbar(C_k\mathbf{y}_k+\mathbf{d}_k)+g\dot{\mathbf{d}}_k)$	−6.9614
Seven	$\mathbf{y}_{k+1}\doteq-77/10\mathbf{y}_k+15\mathbf{y}_{k-1}-10\mathbf{y}_{k-2}+5\mathbf{y}_{k-3}-3/2\mathbf{y}_{k-4}+1/5\mathbf{y}_{k-5}$ $-6C_k^{-1}(g\dot{C}_k\mathbf{y}_k+\hbar(C_k\mathbf{y}_k+\mathbf{d}_k)+g\dot{\mathbf{d}}_k)$	−9.4127
Eight	$\mathbf{y}_{k+1}\doteq-203/20\mathbf{y}_k+21\mathbf{y}_{k-1}-35/2\mathbf{y}_{k-2}+35/3\mathbf{y}_{k-3}-21/4\mathbf{y}_{k-4}+7/5\mathbf{y}_{k-5}$ $-1/6\mathbf{y}_{k-6}-7C_k^{-1}(g\dot{C}_k\mathbf{y}_k+\hbar(C_k\mathbf{y}_k+\mathbf{d}_k)+g\dot{\mathbf{d}}_k)$	−12.0244

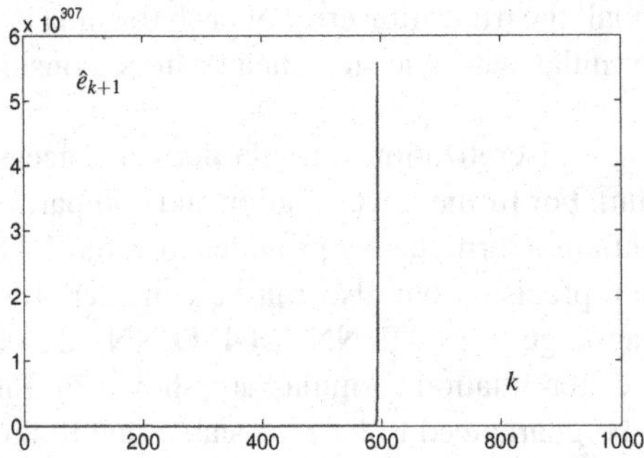

FIGURE 2.9: Divergence phenomenon arising in solution process of using LT-DTZNN algorithm via four data points with $\hbar=0.3$, $g=0.01$ s, and $\mathbf{y}_0\in[-0.5,0.5]^2$ in Example 2.1.

characteristic polynomial outside the unit circle (listed in Table 2.5). As illustrated in Figure 2.9, the divergence phenomenon occurs in the solution process, which means that the solution generated by the LT-DTZNN algorithms cannot converge to the theoretical solution.

2.7 Chapter Summary

In this chapter, we have presented the Zhang–Taylor discretization formula (2.6) to achieve higher computational accuracy in approximating the first-order derivative and to discretize

(2.7) and the ZT-DTZNN-U algorithm (2.9) have been presented for solving the FECQP (2.1). For comparison, the ET-DTZNN-K algorithm (2.11), the ET-DTZNN-U algorithm (2.12), and the NI algorithm (2.14) have been presented for solving the same problem. In addition, the detailed theoretical analyses about the performance of these five different algorithms have been provided. It has shown that the presented ZT-DTZNN algorithms, ET-DTZNN algorithms, and NI algorithm (2.14) converge toward the theoretical solution of the FECQP (2.1), with $\mathcal{O}(g^3)$ residual errors, $\mathcal{O}(g^2)$ residual errors, and $\mathcal{O}(g)$ residual errors, respectively. Besides, the numerical experimental results including the applications to manipulators have further demonstrated the efficacy and superiority of the ZT-DTZNN-K algorithm (2.7) and the ZT-DTZNN-U algorithm (2.9) for the FECQP solving. Finally, the comparisons with the ZT-DTDD algorithm (2.16) and other LT-DTZNN algorithms for the FECQP have substantiated the superiority of the presented ZT-DTZNN algorithms once again.

Part II

ZTD 6321 Formula and Applications

Chapter 3

Future Matrix Inversion with Noises

Abstract

Inevitable noises and limited computational time are major issues for future matrix inversion (FMI) in practice. When designing an algorithm, it is highly demanded to suppress noises without violating the performance of real-time computation. However, most existing algorithms only consider a nominal system in the absence of noises and may suffer from a great computational error when noises are taken into account. Some other algorithms suppose that denoising has been conducted before computation, which may consume extra time and may not be suitable in practice. By considering the above situation, in this chapter, a discrete-time enhanced zeroing neural network (DTEZNN) algorithm is presented, analyzed, and investigated for the FMI. For comparison, a discrete-time conventional zeroing neural network (DTCZNN) algorithm is presented. Note that the DTEZNN algorithm is superior to the DTCZNN algorithm in suppressing various kinds of bias noises. Moreover, theoretical analyses show the convergence of the presented DTEZNN algorithm under various kinds of bias noises. In addition, numerical experiments including an application to manipulator motion planning are provided to substantiate the efficacy and superiority of the presented DTEZNN algorithm for the FMI.

3.1 Introduction

Matrix inversion is considered to be one fundamental problem widely encountered in science and engineering fields [52–56], such as optimization [52], manipulator control [53], and image processing [54]. In practice, the ability to invert a matrix quickly and accurately determines the effectiveness of a computational tool [57]. Therefore, a lot of research efforts have been devoted to such a problem solving [58, 59]. The matrix inversion, especially for large-scale cases, has been significantly advanced and its time complexity has been much reduced in past years [57–60].

As a variant of the time-independent matrix inversion, time-dependent matrix inversion has become increasingly popular in recent years [16, 61–63]. Generally speaking, the time-dependent matrix inversion is more complicated than the time-independent matrix inversion, and the models for the time-dependent matrix inversion must satisfy the urgent requirement of real-time computation. Note that conventional methods for the time-independent matrix inversion may not satisfy the real-time computational requirement of the time-dependent matrix inversion [64, 65]. Specifically, the object matrix varies with time, while time is inevitably consumed by each computational method. After the inverse of a time-dependent matrix at a time instant is obtained, the matrix is not the conventional one.

DOI: 10.1201/9781003497783-3

With the characteristics of high-speed parallel processing and superiority in large scale online processing, neural networks have been widely employed in scientific computation and optimization [11, 66, 67]. Especially, recurrent neural networks (RNNs) have been presented and investigated as powerful alternatives to online scientific problems solving [12, 14, 68]. For solving online time-dependent problems, including the time-dependent matrix inversion, zeroing neural network (ZNN), a special class of RNNs, was proposed [42]. The continuous-time conventional ZNN (CTCZNN) model is able to perfectly track time-dependent solution for the time-dependent matrix inversion with the condition that the solving process is free of noises [16]. However, by considering that noises always exist and denoising may consume extra time, the pre-denoising method may not adapt well for the online time-dependent matrix inversion due to the urgent requirement of real-time computation in practice.

By considering the above situation, a continuous-time enhanced ZNN (CTEZNN) model is presented for the continuous time-dependent matrix inversion (CTDMI) [69]. Note that the CTEZNN model perfectly tracks time-dependent solution and suppresses various kinds of bias noises, such as constant bias noise, bounded random bias noise, and even (unbounded) linear-increasing bias noise, in one unified framework. Besides, as discrete-time algorithms are convenient for numerical implementation on digital computers, the CTEZNN model and the CTCZNN model, which are continuous-time ZNN (CTZNN) models, need to be discretized for practical realization [22, 70, 71]. Different from the CTCZNN model, the CTEZNN model contains an integral term. Thus, we may not obtain a convergent algorithm by discretizing the integral term directly. To solve this problem, in this chapter [72], mathematical manipulations are employed to avoid discretizing the integral term directly. Then a discrete-time enhanced ZNN (DTEZNN) algorithm is obtained for future matrix inversion (FMI). Note that the DTEZNN algorithm not only inherits the superiority of discrete-time conventional ZNN (DTCZNN) algorithm [71] (i.e., the DTCZNN algorithm predicts the inverse of time-dependent matrix with high accuracy, or say, the inverse of time-dependent matrix at a time instant can be obtained before or at that time instant) but also has the ability of suppressing various kinds of bias noises.

This chapter [72] first presents the CTZNN models for the CTDMI, including the CTEZNN model and the CTCZNN model. Then, by employing a three-step Zhang time discretization (3S-ZTD) formula, termed as ZTD 6321 formula, to discretize the CTEZNN model, the DTEZNN algorithm is developed. Moreover, the DTCZNN algorithm is presented for comparison, and the stability and convergence of the DTEZNN algorithm are analyzed. We analyze and investigate the DTEZNN algorithm for the FMI under constant bias noise, bounded random bias noise, and even linear-increasing bias noise. Finally, an application to manipulator motion planning is presented for further substantiating the efficacy of the DTEZNN algorithm.

3.2 Problem Formulation

In this section, the problem formulation of the FMI is presented.

Let us consider the following FMI problem with the computational time interval $[t_k, t_{k+1}) \subset [t_{\text{ini}}, t_{\text{fin}}] \subset [0, +\infty)$:

$$A_{k+1}X_{k+1} = I_{n\times n} \in \mathbb{R}^{n\times n}, \tag{3.1}$$

where t_{ini} and t_{fin} represent the initial and final time instants, respectively. Besides, $I_{n\times n}$ denotes an $n \times n$ identity matrix, and $A_{k+1} \in \mathbb{R}^{n\times n}$ is supposed to be generated or measured from $A(t)$ by sampling at time instant $t = (k+1)g$ (denoted as t_{k+1}). Here, $k = 0, 1, \cdots$ is the updating index, and g denotes the sampling gap. The reason why (3.1) is referred to as the FMI problem is explained as follows. In the solving process of (3.1), all computations have to be executed from present or previous data. For example, at time instant t_k, only the present and previous information, such as A_i for $i \leq k$, is known. The future unknown information, such as A_{k+1} and its derivatives, has not been sampled or computed yet and cannot be used to compute the future unknown matrix $X_{k+1} \in \mathbb{R}^{n\times n}$ during the computational time interval $[t_k, t_{k+1})$. The objective of this study is to find the future unknown matrix X_{k+1} during $[t_k, t_{k+1})$ from present or previous data so that (3.1) holds true at the next discrete time instant (i.e., t_{k+1}).

3.3 CTCZNN and CTEZNN Models

To solve the FMI problem (3.1), the CTDMI problem is considered firstly:

$$A(t)X(t) = I_{n\times n}, \text{with } t \geq 0, \tag{3.2}$$

where $A(t) \in \mathbb{R}^{n\times n}$ is a nonsingular time-dependent matrix, and $X(t) \in \mathbb{R}^{n\times n}$ is the unknown matrix to be obtained. We suppose that $A(t)$ and its time derivative are uniformly norm bounded.

To monitor and control the solving process of (3.2), we define the following matrix-valued indefinite zeroing function (ZF):

$$Z(t) = A(t)X(t) - I_{n\times n} \in \mathbb{R}^{n\times n}. \tag{3.3}$$

Each element of $Z(t)$ should be convergent to zero. On the basis of the ZF (3.3) and the conventional ZNN design formula $\dot{Z}(t) = -\eta Z(t)$, where $\dot{Z}(t)$ denotes the first-order time derivative of $Z(t)$, we obtain the implicit CTCZNN model under bias noises as below [16]:

$$A(t)\dot{X}(t) = -\dot{A}(t)X(t) - \eta(A(t)X(t) - I_{n\times n}) + B(t), \tag{3.4}$$

where the design parameter $\eta > 0$, and $B(t) \in \mathbb{R}^{n\times n}$ denotes matrix-valued noises, such as constant bias noise, bounded random bias noise, and linear-increasing bias noise. If $B(t) = \mathbf{0}$ (i.e., under no bias noise), the implicit CTCZNN model (3.4) is evidently convergent [22]. Thus, we approximately have $X(t) = A^{-1}(t)$. Then, the implicit CTCZNN model (3.4) can be rewritten in explicit form as below:

$$\dot{X}(t) = -X(t)\dot{A}(t)X(t) - \eta X(t)(A(t)X(t) - I_{n\times n}) + X(t)B(t). \tag{3.5}$$

Note that the explicit CTCZNN model (3.5) is also Getz–Marsden dynamic system (but with different origins) [16,73,74]. If $B(t) = \mathbf{0}$, we obtain a CTCZNN model under no bias noise. Comparing the explicit (3.5) with the implicit (3.4), it is noted that the implicit (3.4) is convergent globally, while the explicit (3.5) is convergent locally due to the approximation $X(t) = A^{-1}(t)$ [73]. Besides, the CTCZNN model (3.5), or say, Getz–Marsden dynamic system, cannot converge to the theoretical solution of the problem (3.2) under bias noises.

To suppress bias noises, the enhanced ZNN design formula

$$\dot{Z}(t) = -\eta_1 Z(t) - \eta_2 \int_0^t Z(\tau)\mathrm{d}\tau \tag{3.6}$$

is employed [69], where the design parameters $\eta_1 > 0$ and $\eta_2 > 0$. On the basis of the design formula (3.6) and the ZF (3.3), the following implicit CTEZNN model under bias noises is obtained:

$$A(t)\dot{X}(t) = -\dot{A}(t)X(t) - \eta_1(A(t)X(t) - I_{n\times n}) - \eta_2 \int_0^t (A(\tau)X(\tau) - I_{n\times n})\mathrm{d}\tau + B(t). \tag{3.7}$$

Note that the implicit CTEZNN model (3.7) can suppress various kinds of noises and compute the time-dependent matrix inverse simultaneously. Besides, the following lemmas guarantee the convergence of the implicit CTEZNN model (3.7).

Lemma 2 *Consider the CTDMI problem (3.2) with $A(t)$ being always nonsingular. Suppose that $A(t)$ and its time derivative are uniformly norm bounded. Under no bias noise, the implicit CTEZNN model (3.7) converges to the theoretical solution of (3.2) with the continuous-time steady-state residual error (CTSSRE) $\lim_{t\to+\infty}\|A(t)X(t)-I_{n\times n}\|_{\mathrm{F}}=0$, where $\|\cdot\|_{\mathrm{F}}$ denotes the Frobenius norm of a matrix.*

Proof. See Appendix B for details. □

Lemma 3 *Consider the CTDMI problem (3.2) with $A(t)$ being always nonsingular. Suppose that $A(t)$ and its time derivative are uniformly norm bounded. Under constant bias noise, the implicit CTEZNN model (3.7) converges to the theoretical solution of (3.2) with the CTSSRE being 0.*

Proof. See Appendix C for details. □

Lemma 4 *Consider the CTDMI problem (3.2) with $A(t)$ being always nonsingular. Suppose that $A(t)$ and its time derivative are uniformly norm bounded. Under continuous-time bounded random bias noise, the implicit CTEZNN model (3.7) converges to the theoretical solution of (3.2) with the CTSSRE being bounded and approximately in inverse proportion to η_1.*

Proof. See Appendix D for details. □

Lemma 5 *Consider the CTDMI problem (3.2) with $A(t)$ being always nonsingular. Suppose that $A(t)$ and its time derivative are uniformly norm bounded. Under continuous-time (unbounded) linear-increasing bias noise, the implicit CTEZNN model (3.7) converges to the theoretical solution of (3.2) with the CTSSRE being bounded and in inverse proportion to η_2.*

Proof. See Appendix E for details. □

On the basis of the above lemmas, we know that the implicit model (3.7) is convergent, even under various kinds of bias noises. Thus, we approximately have $X(t)=A^{-1}(t)$. Then, the implicit CTEZNN model (3.7) can be rewritten as explicit form as below:

$$\dot{X}(t)=-X(t)\dot{A}(t)X(t)-\eta_1X(t)(A(t)X(t)-I_{n\times n})-\eta_2X(t)\int_0^t(A(\tau)X(\tau)-I_{n\times n})\mathrm{d}\tau+X(t)B(t). \tag{3.8}$$

Note that, similar to the explicit CTCZNN model (3.5), the explicit CTEZNN model (3.8) is convergent locally due to the approximation $X(t)=A^{-1}(t)$. In addition, if $B(t)=\mathbf{0}$ is employed, we obtain the CTEZNN model under no bias noise.

3.4 DTCZNN and DTEZNN Algorithms

As aforementioned, the DTEZNN algorithm and the DTCZNN algorithm are easier to develop into numerical algorithms [22]. In this section, a ZTD 6321 formula is presented to approximate the first-order time derivative with the truncation error being $\mathscr{O}(g^2)$. Then, the ZTD 6321 formula is employed to discretize the CTCZNN model (3.5) and the CTEZNN model (3.8), and thus two algorithms are obtained for the FMI under bias noises.

On the basis of Taylor expansion [20], the ZTD 6321 formula, which uses four continuous sampling instants, approximates the first-order time derivative with high computational precision and with truncation error being $\mathscr{O}(g^2)$ [20,71]. Specifically, the ZTD 6321 formula is presented by the following theorem.

Theorem 17 *With the sufficiently small sampling gap $g \in (0,1)$, let $\mathcal{O}(g^2)$ denote the error (especially, the truncation error) positively or negatively proportional to g^2, i.e., of the order of g^2. Suppose that $\zeta(t)$ is sufficiently smooth. With $\zeta_{k+1} = \zeta(t_{k+1}) = \zeta((k+1)g)$, the ZTD 6321 formula is formulated as follows:*

$$\dot{\zeta}_k = \frac{6\zeta_{k+1} - 3\zeta_k - 2\zeta_{k-1} - \zeta_{k-2}}{10g} + \mathcal{O}(g^2). \tag{3.9}$$

Proof. See Appendix F for details. □

In view of the integral term $\int_0^t (A(\tau)X(\tau) - I_{n\times n})\mathrm{d}\tau$ of (3.8), the ZTD 6321 formula (3.9) cannot be used directly for discretization. In addition, if the integral term $\int_0^t (A(\tau)X(\tau) - I_{n\times n})\mathrm{d}\tau$ and the time derivative term $\dot{X}(t)$ are discretized by different ways, we may not obtain a convergent DTEZNN algorithm. To avoid the above situation, we define $Y(t) = \int_0^t (A(\tau)X(\tau) - I_{n\times n})\mathrm{d}\tau$, and then (3.8) is rewritten as

$$\begin{bmatrix}\dot{X}(t)\\ \dot{Y}(t)\end{bmatrix} = \begin{bmatrix}Q(t) - \eta_2 X(t)Y(t) + X(t)B(t)\\ A(t)X(t) - I_{n\times n}\end{bmatrix}, \tag{3.10}$$

where $Q(t)$ denotes $-X(t)\dot{A}(t)X(t) - \eta_1 X(t)(A(t)X(t) - I_{n\times n})$.

On the basis of the ZTD 6321 formula (3.9), (3.10) is discretized as

$$\begin{bmatrix}X_{k+1}\\ Y_{k+1}\end{bmatrix} \doteq \frac{5}{3}\begin{bmatrix}\hat{Q}_k - \hbar_2 X_k Y_k + gX_k B_k\\ g(A_k X_k - I_{n\times n})\end{bmatrix} + \frac{1}{2}\begin{bmatrix}X_k\\ Y_k\end{bmatrix} + \frac{1}{3}\begin{bmatrix}X_{k-1}\\ Y_{k-1}\end{bmatrix} + \frac{1}{6}\begin{bmatrix}X_{k-2}\\ Y_{k-2}\end{bmatrix}, \tag{3.11}$$

where $\doteq$ denotes the computational assignment operator. Besides, $\hat{Q}_k$ denotes $-gX_k\dot{A}_kX_k - \hbar_1 X_k(A_kX_k - I_{n\times n})$, $\hbar_1 = g\eta_1$, and $\hbar_2 = g\eta_2$, which is called DTEZNN algorithm. Note that the DTEZNN algorithm (3.11) is generated by discretizing the explicit CTEZNN model (3.8). Thus, the DTEZNN algorithm (3.11) is also convergent locally. That is, the initial state X_0 should sufficiently reach the theoretical initial solution X_0^*.

For comparison, the DTCZNN algorithm generated by the ZTD 6321 formula (3.9) is presented. Specifically, we use the ZTD 6321 formula (3.9) to discretize the explicit CTCZNN model (3.5) directly. Notedly, there is no integral term in the CTCZNN model (3.5), and thus we can use the ZTD 6321 formula (3.9) directly for discretization. The DTCZNN algorithm is obtained as [71]:

$$X_{k+1} \doteq \frac{5}{3}\big(-gX_k\dot{A}_kX_k - \hbar X_k(A_kX_k - I_{n\times n}) + gX_kB_k\big) + \frac{1}{2}X_k + \frac{1}{3}X_{k-1} + \frac{1}{6}X_{k-2}, \tag{3.12}$$

where the step length $\hbar = g\eta$.

Focusing on the DTEZNN algorithm (3.11) and the DTCZNN algorithm (3.12), one can observe that, for obtaining X_{k+1}, we just need X_k, X_{k-1}, X_{k-2}, A_k, and $\dot{A}_k$ instead of the unknown A_{k+1}. In other words, X_{k+1} can be obtained at each computational time interval $[t_k, t_{k+1})$ and be used then (i.e., before or at time instant t_{k+1}), which evidently satisfies the urgent requirement of real-time computing. Moreover, compared with the DTCZNN algorithm (3.12), the DTEZNN algorithm (3.11) has the ability of suppressing various kinds of bias noises.

In terms of the DTEZNN algorithm (3.11) and the DTCZNN algorithm (3.12), if $B_k = \mathbf{0}$ is employed, the two algorithms reduce to simpler forms under no bias noise. To substantiate the efficacy of the presented DTEZNN algorithm (3.11) under no bias noise, the following proposition is presented on the basis of Definitions 2–4 in Chapter 1. Note that the residual error is defined as $\hat{e}_{k+1} = \|A_{k+1}X_{k+1} - I_{n\times n}\|_\mathrm{F}$ for solving the FMI problem (3.1) in this chapter [72].

Proposition 1 *Consider the FMI problem (3.1) with A_k being always nonsingular. Suppose that A_k and its time derivative are uniformly norm bounded. With the sufficiently small sampling period $g \in (0,1)$, the DTEZNN algorithm under no bias noise*

$$\begin{bmatrix} X_{k+1} \\ Y_{k+1} \end{bmatrix} \doteq \frac{5}{3}\begin{bmatrix} \hat{Q}_k - \hbar_2 X_k Y_k \\ g(A_k X_k - I_{n\times n}) \end{bmatrix} + \frac{1}{2}\begin{bmatrix} X_k \\ Y_k \end{bmatrix} + \frac{1}{3}\begin{bmatrix} X_{k-1} \\ Y_{k-1} \end{bmatrix} + \frac{1}{6}\begin{bmatrix} X_{k-2} \\ Y_{k-2} \end{bmatrix}$$

is convergent to the theoretical solution of (3.2) with the maximal steady-state residual error (MSSRE) $\lim_{k\to\infty}\sup \hat{e}_{k+1}$ being $\mathscr{O}(g^3)$.

Proof. According to Definition 2 in Chapter 1, the characteristic polynomial of the DTEZNN algorithm (3.11) can be derived as

$$\Gamma_3(\iota) = \iota^3 - \frac{1}{2}\iota^2 - \frac{1}{3}\iota - \frac{1}{6}, \tag{3.13}$$

which has three roots, i.e., $\iota_1 = 1$, $\iota_2 = 0.25 + 0.3227\mathrm{i}$, and $\iota_3 = 0.25 - 0.3227\mathrm{i}$, where i denotes imaginary unit. Evidently, these roots are on or in the unit circle, and thus the DTEZNN algorithm (3.11) under no bias noise is zero-stable. In addition, we know that the CTSSRE synthesized by the model (3.8) is 0 from Lemma 2 and that the truncation error of the ZTD 6321 formula (3.9) is $\mathscr{O}(g^2)$ from Theorem 17. Therefore, we have the following equation:

$$\begin{bmatrix} X_{k+1} \\ Y_{k+1} \end{bmatrix} = \frac{5}{3}\begin{bmatrix} \hat{Q}_k - \hbar_2 X_k Y_k \\ g(A_k X_k - I_{n\times n}) \end{bmatrix} + \frac{1}{2}\begin{bmatrix} X_k \\ Y_k \end{bmatrix} + \frac{1}{3}\begin{bmatrix} X_{k-1} \\ Y_{k-1} \end{bmatrix} + \frac{1}{6}\begin{bmatrix} X_{k-2} \\ Y_{k-2} \end{bmatrix} + \mathbf{O}(g^3),$$

where $\mathbf{O}(g^3)$ denotes a matrix with each element being $\mathscr{O}(g^3)$. Then, according to Definitions 3 and 4 in Chapter 1, it can be derived that the DTEZNN algorithm (3.11) is consistent and convergent, which converges with the order of truncation error being $\mathbf{O}(g^3)$. From the above analysis, it can be concluded that $X_{k+1} = X^*_{k+1} + \mathbf{O}(g^3)$ with k large enough. Therefore,

$$\begin{aligned} &\lim_{k\to\infty}\sup \|A_{k+1}X_{k+1} - I_{n\times n}\|_\mathrm{F} \\ &= \lim_{k\to\infty}\sup \|A_{k+1}X^*_{k+1} - I_{n\times n} + A_{k+1}\mathbf{O}(g^3)\|_\mathrm{F} \\ &= \lim_{k\to\infty}\sup \|A_{k+1}\mathbf{O}(g^3)\|_\mathrm{F}. \end{aligned}$$

The proof is thus completed. □

To further substantiate the efficacy of the DTEZNN algorithm (3.11) under no bias noise for the FMI, numerical experiments are conducted, and the corresponding numerical experimental results are presented. Specifically, we consider the following nonsingular time-dependent matrix:

$$\begin{bmatrix} 0.1\sin(t_k) + 0.4 & 0.1\cos(t_k) \\ -0.1\cos(t_k) & 0.1\sin(t_k) + 0.4 \end{bmatrix}, \text{with } t_k \in [0, 50] \text{ s}. \tag{3.14}$$

The numerical experiments start with the initial state $X_0 = aA_0^\mathrm{T}$ to make sure the convergence of the DTEZNN algorithm (3.11), where A_0 is the initial state of time-dependent matrix A_k, A_0^T is the transposition of A_0, and $a = 2/\mathrm{tr}(A_0 A_0^\mathrm{T})$ [45]. In addition, $\hbar_1 = 0.1$, $\hbar_2 = 1$, and $g = 0.1$, 0.01, or 0.001 s are employed. The corresponding numerical experimental results are displayed in Figure 3.1. In Figure 3.1(a), for displaying the convergent phenomenon visually, the theoretical inverse of the discrete-time matrix (3.14), together with the solution generated by the DTEZNN algorithm (3.11), is plotted in the same figure, where the solid curves correspond to the solution elements generated by the DTEZNN algorithm (3.11), and the dash curves correspond to the theoretical solution elements. Evidently, with g being 0.1 s, all the elements of X_k converge to the theoretical

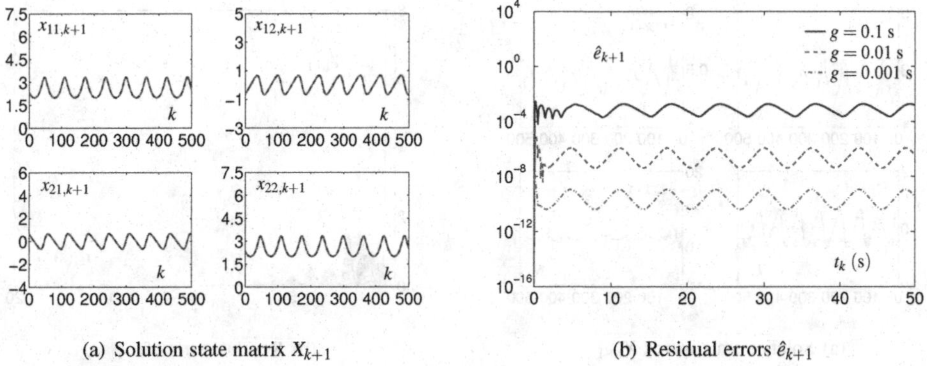

(a) Solution state matrix X_{k+1}

(b) Residual errors $\hat{e}_{k+1}$

FIGURE 3.1: Trajectories of solution state matrix and residual errors synthesized by DTEZNN algorithm (3.11) under no bias noise.

ones rapidly, and the trajectories generated by the DTEZNN algorithm (3.11) almost completely overlap with those of theoretical solutions. In Figure 3.1(b), with g being 0.1, 0.01, or 0.001 s, the MSSRE is of order 10^{-3}, 10^{-6}, or 10^{-9}, respectively. Thus, Figure 3.1(b) substantiates that the MSSRE synthesized by the DTEZNN algorithm (3.11) is $\mathcal{O}(g^3)$ under no bias noise. In other words, the numerical experimental results presented in Figure (3.1) show the efficacy of the presented DTEZNN algorithm (3.11) under no bias noise for the FMI.

Remark 3 *In this chapter [72], we relatively freely select the values of $\hbar_1$ and $\hbar_2$ in appropriate ranges. As we know, $\hbar_1 = \eta_1 g$ and $\hbar_2 = \eta_2 g$. Besides, η_1 and η_2 are parts of the enhanced ZNN design formula (3.6). Thus, we may investigate the enhanced ZNN design formula (3.6) to discuss the selection of parameters. Firstly, for solving the problem $A(t)X(t) = I_{n\times n}$, we design $Z(t) = A(t)X(t) - I_{n\times n}$ and $Z_1(t) = \int_0^t Z(\tau)\mathrm{d}\tau$, and we use the conventional ZNN design formula $\dot{Z}_1(t) = -\eta_1 Z_1(t)$. Then, we obtain that $Z(t) = -\eta_1 \int_0^t Z(\tau)\mathrm{d}\tau$. Secondly, we design $Z_2 = Z(t) + \eta_1 \int_0^t Z(\tau)\mathrm{d}\tau$ and use the conventional ZNN design formula $\dot{Z}_2(t) = -\eta_2 Z_2(t)$ again. Then, we obtain*

$$\dot{Z}(t) = -\eta_1 Z(t) - \eta_2 Z(t) - \eta_1\eta_2 \int_0^t Z(\tau)\mathrm{d}\tau.$$

For the consistency of the conventional ZNN design formula, it is better to set $\eta_1 = \eta_2$, and thus, we obtain that

$$\dot{Z}(t) = -2\eta_1 Z(t) - \eta_1^2 \int_0^t Z(\tau)\mathrm{d}\tau. \tag{3.15}$$

Comparing (3.6) with (3.15), we find that $\eta_1^2 = 4\eta_2$ may be a good and acceptable choice.

From the viewpoint of convergence, as equation (3.6) is a second-order linear dynamical system, the characteristics of the system can be analyzed via its characteristic roots. The convergence speed of the system is determined by the locations of its characteristic roots. Note that the two characteristic roots for the equation are $\iota_1 = \left(-\eta_1 + \sqrt{\eta_1^2 - 4\eta_2}\right)/2$ and $\iota_2 = \left(-\eta_1 - \sqrt{\eta_1^2 - 4\eta_2}\right)/2$, where $\eta_1 > 0$ and $\eta_2 > 0$. If $\eta_1^2 - 4\eta_2 \leq 0$, the two characteristic roots are a couple of conjugate complex roots located on the left half-plane and the convergence speed is then determined by η_1. That is to say, in this situation, the integration term would not affect the convergence speed. Therefore, it is better to set $\eta_1^2 - 4\eta_2 \leq 0$.

By considering that the initial state may affect the numerical experimental results, different values of initial state X_0 are employed. Specifically, in terms of discrete-time matrix (3.14), 20 different initial states are employed and the numerical experimental results are shown in Figure 3.2.

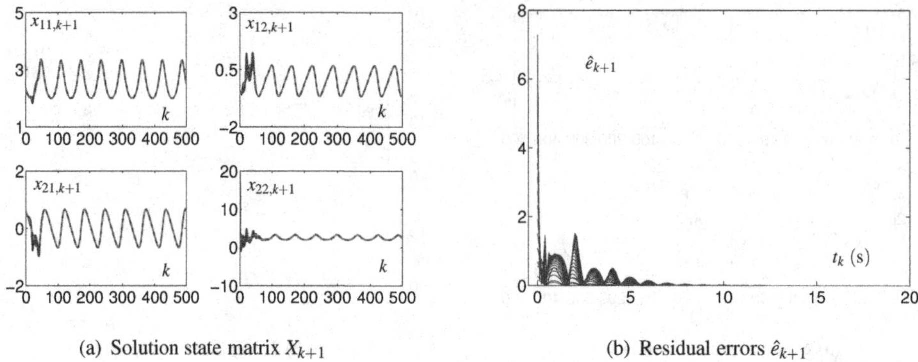

(a) Solution state matrix X_{k+1}

(b) Residual errors $\hat{e}_{k+1}$

FIGURE 3.2: Trajectories of solution state matrix and residual errors synthesized by DTEZNN algorithm (3.11) with different initial states.

Specifically, Figure 3.2(a) shows that, from different initial states, all solution elements generated by the DTEZNN algorithm (3.11) are convergent to the theoretical solution elements. Moreover, from Figure 3.2(b), one observes that even though the initial state is rather bad (the initial error Z_0 is rather big), the DTEZNN algorithm (3.11) performs quite well.

For a more intuitive understanding of the main content of this chapter [72], Table 3.1 lists the problem, scheme, model, and algorithms.

3.5 DTEZNN Algorithm under Bias Noises

There always exist noises in practice. In this section, the DTEZNN algorithm (3.11) under different kinds of discrete-time bias noises is analyzed for the FMI, such as constant bias noise, discrete-time bounded random bias noise, and even discrete-time linear-increasing bias noise. To further substantiate the efficacy and superiority of the DTEZNN algorithm (3.11) under bias noises, numerical experiments are conducted. Moreover, the numerical experimental results generated by the DTCZNN algorithm (3.12) under bias noises are presented for comparison. In the numerical experiments, $\hbar_1 = 0.1$ and $\hbar_2 = 1$ are employed for good convergent performances, and $\hbar = 0.1$ is employed for comparison. Note that if $\hbar = 0.1$ is employed, the DTCZNN algorithm (3.12) under no bias noise will be convergent to the theoretical solution of (3.2).

3.5.1 Constant bias noise

Under constant bias noise $B_k = C \in \mathbb{R}^{n\times n}$, where C denotes a constant or time-independent matrix, the DTEZNN algorithm (3.11) is analyzed and investigated for the FMI. Specifically, we have a proposition as below to guarantee the efficacy of the DTEZNN algorithm (3.11) under constant bias noise.

Proposition 2 *Consider the FMI problem (3.1) with A_k being always nonsingular. Suppose that A_k and its time derivative are uniformly norm bounded. With the sufficiently small sampling period $g \in (0,1)$, the DTEZNN algorithm under constant bias noise*

$$\begin{bmatrix} X_{k+1} \\ Y_{k+1} \end{bmatrix} \doteq \frac{5}{3}\begin{bmatrix} \hat{Q}_k - \hbar_2 X_k Y_k + g X_k C \\ g(A_k X_k - I_{n\times n}) \end{bmatrix} + \frac{1}{2}\begin{bmatrix} X_k \\ Y_k \end{bmatrix} + \frac{1}{3}\begin{bmatrix} X_{k-1} \\ Y_{k-1} \end{bmatrix} + \frac{1}{6}\begin{bmatrix} X_{k-2} \\ Y_{k-2} \end{bmatrix}$$

is convergent to the theoretical solution of (3.2) with the MSSRE being $\mathcal{O}(g^3)$.

TABLE 3.1: Problem, schemes, models, and algorithms in this chapter.

Problem	$A_{k+1}X_{k+1} = I_{n\times n}$.
Schemes	*Step 1*: Define ZF as $Z(t) = A(t)X(t) - I_{n\times n}$. *Step 2*: Adopt conventional ZNN design formula as $\dot{Z}(t) = -\eta Z(t)$. *Step 3*: Adopt ZTD 6321 formula (3.9) to discretize CTCZNN model (3.5).
	Step 1: Define ZF as $Z(t) = A(t)X(t) - I_{n\times n}$. *Step 2*: Adopt enhanced ZNN design formula as $\dot{Z}(t) = -\eta_1 Z(t) - \eta_2 \int_0^t Z(\tau)\mathrm{d}\tau$. *Step 3*: Adopt ZTD 6321 formula (3.9) to discretize CTEZNN model (3.10).
Models	$\dot{X}(t) = -X(t)\dot{A}(t)X(t) - \eta X(t)(A(t)X(t) - I_{n\times n}) + X(t)B(t)$, $\begin{bmatrix}\dot{X}(t)\\ \dot{Y}(t)\end{bmatrix} = \begin{bmatrix}Q(t) - \eta_2 X(t)Y(t) + X(t)B(t)\\ A(t)X(t) - I_{n\times n}\end{bmatrix}$.
Algorithms	$X_{k+1} \doteq \frac{5}{3}(-gX_k\dot{A}_kX_k - \hbar X_k(A_kX_k - I_{n\times n}) + gX_kB_k) + \frac{1}{2}X_k + \frac{1}{3}X_{k-1} + \frac{1}{6}X_{k-2}$, $\begin{bmatrix}X_{k+1}\\ Y_{k+1}\end{bmatrix} \doteq \frac{5}{3}\begin{bmatrix}\hat{Q}_k - \hbar_2 X_kY_k + gX_kB_k\\ g(A_kX_k - I_{n\times n})\end{bmatrix} + \frac{1}{2}\begin{bmatrix}X_k\\ Y_k\end{bmatrix} + \frac{1}{3}\begin{bmatrix}X_{k-1}\\ Y_{k-1}\end{bmatrix} + \frac{1}{6}\begin{bmatrix}X_{k-2}\\ Y_{k-2}\end{bmatrix}$.

Proof. The proof procedure is similar to Proposition 1 and is omitted due to space limitation. □

To further substantiate the efficacy and superiority of the DTEZNN algorithm (3.11) under constant bias noise C for the FMI, numerical experiments are conducted and the corresponding numerical experimental results are presented in Figures 3.3 and 3.4. Specifically, by considering the aforementioned discrete-time matrix (3.14) and constant bias noise $B_k = C = [4,4;4,4]$ (which is MATLAB notation [20]), the numerical experimental results generated by the DTEZNN algorithm (3.11) are presented in Figures 3.3(a) and 3.4(a), and the numerical experimental results generated by the DTCZNN algorithm (3.12) are presented in Figures 3.3(b) and 3.4(b) for comparison. From Figures 3.3(a) and 3.4(a), one can observe that all the elements of X_k generated by the DTEZNN algorithm (3.11) converge to the theoretical ones rapidly and that any element of X_k generated by the DTCZNN algorithm (3.12) does not. From Figure 3.4(a), one can observe that with g being 0.1, 0.01, or 0.001 s, the MSSRE synthesized by the DTEZNN algorithm (3.11) is of order 10^{-3}, 10^{-6}, or 10^{-9}, respectively. However, as shown in Figure 3.4(b), the DTCZNN algorithm (3.12) performs not well. Specifically, with g being 0.1 s, the value of the MSSRE is between 10 and 100. Besides, although the value of the MSSRE is smaller with g being smaller, the relatively big value of the MSSRE may not satisfy the requirement of computational precision.

3.5.2 Bounded random bias noise

It is worth analyzing and investigating the DTEZNN algorithm (3.11) under discrete-time bounded random bias noise $B_k = R_k \in \mathbb{R}^{n\times n}$, all elements of which are bounded and random at any time instant. Specifically, the following proposition is presented to guarantee the efficacy of the DTEZNN algorithm (3.11) under discrete-time bounded random bias noise.

Proposition 3 *Consider the FMI problem (3.1) with A_k being always nonsingular. Suppose that A_k and its time derivative are uniformly norm bounded. With the sufficiently small sampling period $g \in (0,1)$, the DTEZNN algorithm under discrete-time bounded random bias noise*

$$\begin{bmatrix}X_{k+1}\\ Y_{k+1}\end{bmatrix} \doteq \frac{5}{3}\begin{bmatrix}\hat{Q}_k - \hbar_2 X_kY_k + gX_kR_k\\ g(A_kX_k - I_{n\times n})\end{bmatrix} + \frac{1}{2}\begin{bmatrix}X_k\\ Y_k\end{bmatrix} + \frac{1}{3}\begin{bmatrix}X_{k-1}\\ Y_{k-1}\end{bmatrix} + \frac{1}{6}\begin{bmatrix}X_{k-2}\\ Y_{k-2}\end{bmatrix}$$

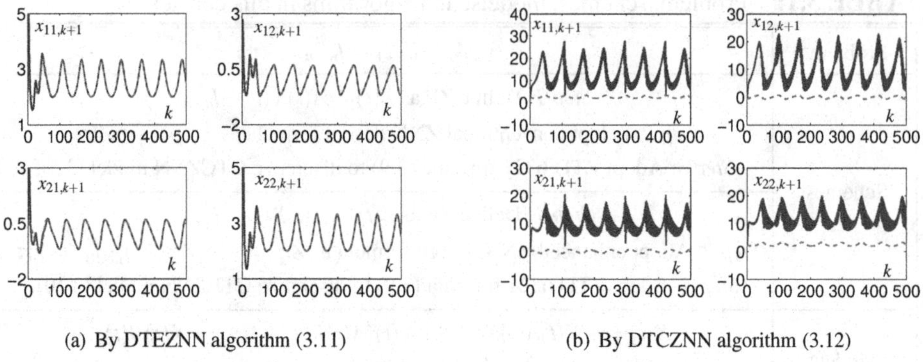

(a) By DTEZNN algorithm (3.11) (b) By DTCZNN algorithm (3.12)

FIGURE 3.3: Trajectories of solution state matrix X_{k+1} generated by DTEZNN algorithm (3.11) and DTCZNN algorithm (3.12) under constant bias noise C with $g = 0.1$ s.

converges to the theoretical solution of (3.2) with the MSSRE being approximately $\mathscr{O}(g)$ if the value of $\hbar_1$ is unaltered.

Proof. According to Definition 2 in Chapter 1, we know that the DTEZNN algorithm (3.11) under discrete-time bounded random bias noise R_k is zero-stable. From Lemma 4, we know that the CTEZNN model (3.8) converges to the theoretical solution of (3.2) with the CTSSRE being approximately in inverse proportion to η_1, i.e., the CTSSRE is approximately $\mathscr{O}(1/\eta_1)$. In addition, we know that $\hbar_1 = g\eta_1$ in the DTEZNN algorithm (3.11). Thus, if the value of $\hbar_1$ is unaltered, g is in inverse proportion to η_1, i.e., $g = \hbar_1/\eta_1$. Besides, the computational precision of the ZTD 6321 formula (3.9) is $\mathscr{O}(g^2)$. Thus, if the value of $\hbar_1$ is unaltered, we have

$$\begin{bmatrix} X_{k+1} \\ Y_{k+1} \end{bmatrix} = \frac{5}{3}\begin{bmatrix} \hat{Q}_k - \hbar_2 X_k Y_k + g X_k R_k \\ g(A_k X_k - I_{n\times n}) \end{bmatrix} + \frac{1}{2}\begin{bmatrix} X_k \\ Y_k \end{bmatrix} + \frac{1}{3}\begin{bmatrix} X_{k-1} \\ Y_{k-1} \end{bmatrix} + \frac{1}{6}\begin{bmatrix} X_{k-2} \\ Y_{k-2} \end{bmatrix} + \mathbf{O}(g) + \mathbf{O}(g^3).$$

Then, according to Definitions 3 and 4 in Chapter 1, the convergence of the DTEZNN algorithm (3.11) is ensured. From the above analysis, we have $X_{k+1} = X^*_{k+1} + \mathbf{O}(g)$ with k large enough.

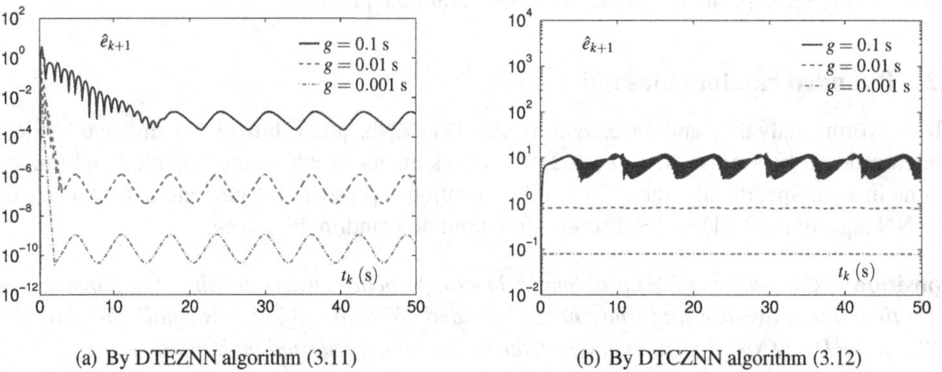

(a) By DTEZNN algorithm (3.11) (b) By DTCZNN algorithm (3.12)

FIGURE 3.4: Trajectories of residual errors $\hat{e}_{k+1}$ synthesized by DTEZNN algorithm (3.11) and DTCZNN algorithm (3.12) under constant bias noise C with different values of g.

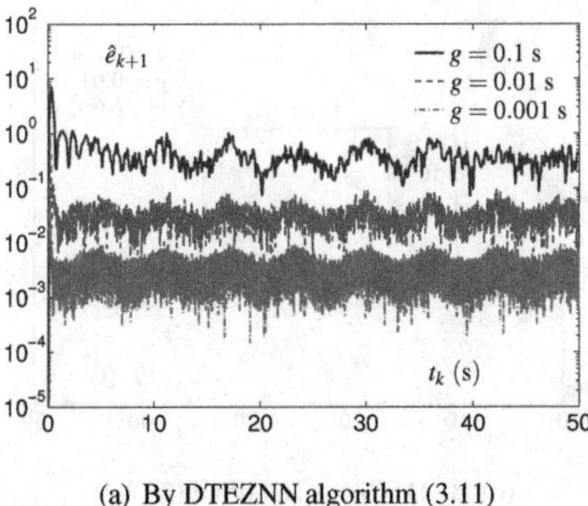

(a) By DTEZNN algorithm (3.11)

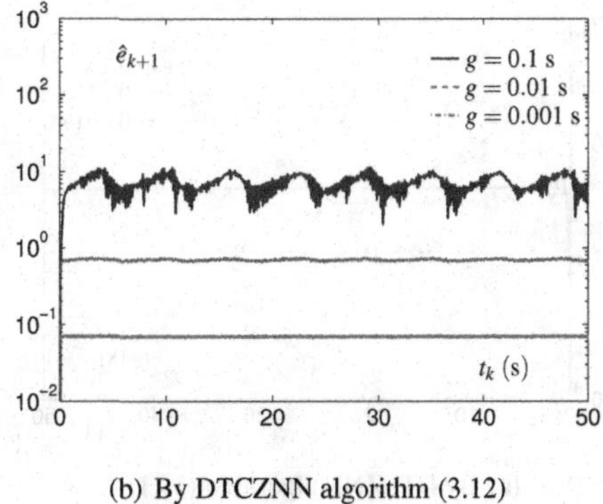

(b) By DTCZNN algorithm (3.12)

FIGURE 3.5: Trajectories of residual errors $\hat{e}_{k+1}$ synthesized by DTEZNN algorithm (3.11) and DTCZNN algorithm (3.12) under discrete-time bounded random bias noise R_k with different values of g.

Therefore,

$$\begin{aligned}
&\lim_{k\to\infty}\sup \|A_{k+1}X_{k+1} - I_{n\times n}\|_{\mathrm{F}} \\
&= \lim_{k\to\infty}\sup \|A_{k+1}X^*_{k+1} - I_{n\times n} + A_{k+1}\mathbf{O}(g)\|_{\mathrm{F}} \\
&= \lim_{k\to\infty}\sup \|A_{k+1}\mathbf{O}(g)\|_{\mathrm{F}}.
\end{aligned}$$

Finally, we obtain that the DTEZNN algorithm (3.11) converges to the theoretical solution of (3.2) with the MSSRE being approximately $\mathscr{O}(g)$. The proof is thus completed. □

To further substantiate the efficacy and superiority of the DTEZNN algorithm (3.11) under discrete-time bounded random bias noise R_k for the FMI, numerical experiments are conducted and the corresponding numerical experimental results are presented in Figure 3.5. Specifically, the aforementioned discrete-time matrix (3.14) and discrete-time bounded random bias noise σ_k, which is constituted of four random elements ranging from 3 to 5 at any time instant, are considered. From Figure 3.5(a), one can observe that with g being 0.1, 0.01, or 0.001 s, the MSSRE synthesized by the DTEZNN algorithm (3.11) is of order 10^{-1}, 10^{-2}, or 10^{-3}, respectively. However, in Figure 3.5(b), even when the value of g is 0.001 s, the MSSRE synthesized by the DTCZNN algorithm (3.12) is ranging from 0.1 to 1, which may not satisfy the requirement of computational precision.

3.5.3 Linear-increasing bias noise

Under discrete-time linear-increasing bias noise $B_k = Lt_k \in \mathbb{R}^{n\times n}$, where L is constituted by the time-dependent ratios of the linear-increasing bias noise, the DTEZNN algorithm (3.11) is analyzed and investigated for the FMI in this subsection. Specifically, a proposition is presented to show the efficacy of the DTEZNN algorithm (3.11). In addition, numerical experiments are conducted to further substantiate the efficacy and superiority for the FMI.

Proposition 4 *Consider the FMI problem (3.1) with A_k being always nonsingular. Suppose that A_k and its time derivative are uniformly norm bounded. With the sufficiently small sampling period $g \in (0,1)$, the DTEZNN algorithm under discrete-time linear-increasing bias noise*

$$\begin{bmatrix} X_{k+1} \\ Y_{k+1} \end{bmatrix} \doteq \frac{5}{3}\begin{bmatrix} \hat{Q}_k - \hbar_2 X_k Y_k + gX_k L_k \\ g(A_k X_k - I_{n\times n}) \end{bmatrix} + \frac{1}{2}\begin{bmatrix} X_k \\ Y_k \end{bmatrix} + \frac{1}{3}\begin{bmatrix} X_{k-1} \\ Y_{k-1} \end{bmatrix} + \frac{1}{6}\begin{bmatrix} X_{k-2} \\ Y_{k-2} \end{bmatrix}$$

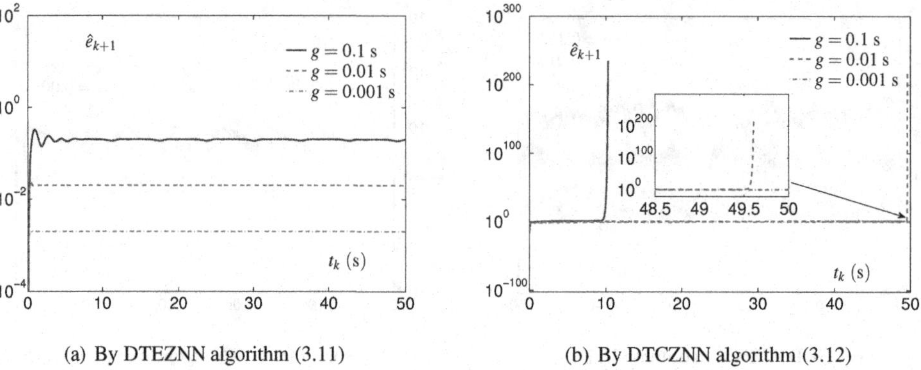

(a) By DTEZNN algorithm (3.11)

(b) By DTCZNN algorithm (3.12)

FIGURE 3.6: Trajectories of residual errors $\hat{e}_{k+1}$ synthesized by DTEZNN algorithm (3.11) and DTCZNN algorithm (3.12) under discrete-time linear-increasing bias noise L_k with different values of g.

converges to the theoretical solution of (3.2) with the MSSRE being $\mathscr{O}(g)$ if the value of $\hbar_2$ is unaltered.

Proof. The proof procedure is similar to Proposition 3 and is omitted due to space limitation. □

To further substantiate the efficacy and superiority of the DTEZNN algorithm (3.11) under discrete-time linear-increasing bias noise for the FMI, the discrete-time matrix (3.14) and discrete-time linear-increasing bias noise $B_k = [kg, kg; kg, kg]$ are considered. The numerical experimental results are presented in Figure 3.6. Specifically, in Figure 3.6(a), with g being 0.1, 0.01, or 0.001 s, the MSSRE synthesized by the DTEZNN algorithm (3.11) is of order 10^{-1}, 10^{-2}, or 10^{-3}, respectively. Note that although the discrete-time linear-increasing bias noise becomes larger and larger with time increasing, the residual error synthesized by the DTEZNN algorithm (3.11) does not increase. However, in Figure 3.6(b), the MSSRE synthesized by the DTCZNN algorithm (3.12) tends to infinity, which substantiate that the DTCZNN algorithm (3.12) is not convergent under discrete-time linear-increasing bias noise.

3.5.4 Complicated time-dependent matrix

The complexity of time-dependent matrix can be interpreted as the expression complexity and the dimension complexity (i.e., higher dimension). With respect to the expression complexity of A_k, for obtaining X_{k+1}, we just need some numerical values before the time instant t_{k+1}, instead of the analytical expression. Thus, the expression complexity does not affect the great performance of the DTEZNN algorithm (3.11). With respect to the dimension complexity, if the DTEZNN algorithm (3.11) is realized by a computer, higher dimension may lead to more time cost. However, the problem can be solved by parallel computing. Besides, higher dimension does not affect the computational accuracy. In this subsection, we consider a more complicated time-dependent matrix $A_k \in \mathbb{R}^{10\times 10}$ with each element

$$a_{ij,k} = \begin{cases} 10+\sin(5t_k), & \text{if } i=j, \\ \cos(5t_k)/(i-j), & \text{if } i>j, \\ \sin(5t_k)/(j-i), & \text{if } i<j, \end{cases} \quad \text{with } i,j=1,2,\cdots,10. \tag{3.16}$$

In numerical experiments, we consider the constant bias noise, discrete-time bounded random bias noise, and discrete-time linear-increasing bias noise. As seen in Figures 3.7 and 3.8, the DTEZNN algorithm (3.11) performs much better than the DTCZNN algorithm (3.12).

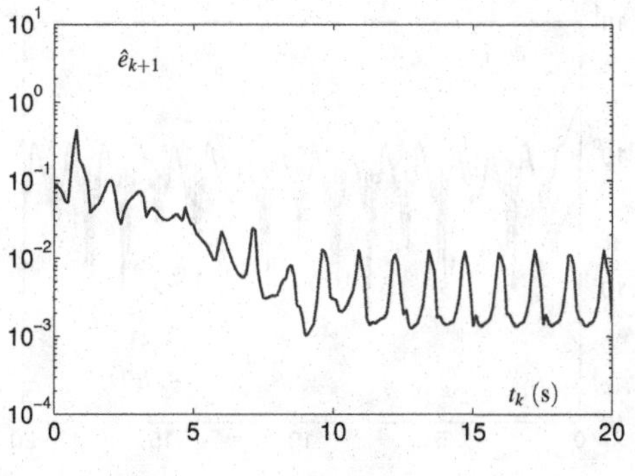

(a) Under constant bias noise

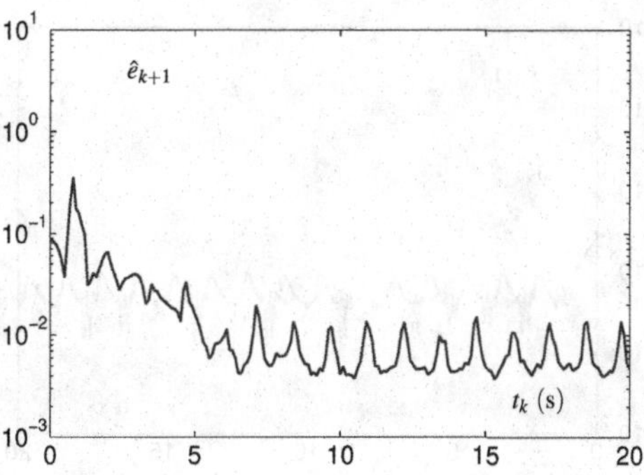

(b) Under discrete-time bounded random bias noise

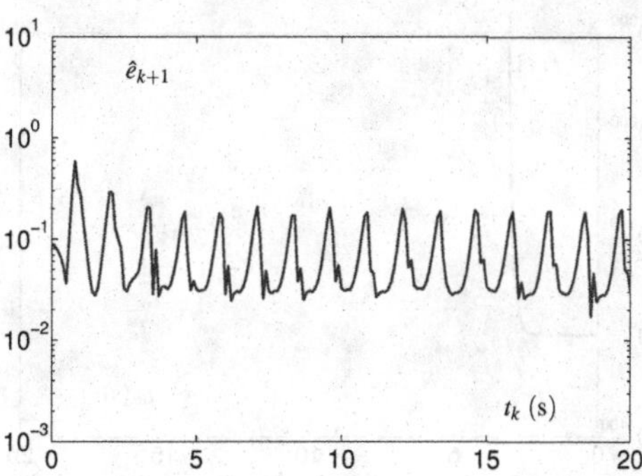

(c) Under discrete-time linear-increasing bias noise

FIGURE 3.7: Trajectories of residual errors $\hat{e}_{k+1}$ synthesized by DTEZNN algorithm (3.11) under different kinds of discrete-time bias noises with $g = 0.1$ s.

3.6 Application to Manipulator Motion Planning

In this section, the DTEZNN algorithm (3.11) is applied to the manipulator motion planning under various kinds of discrete-time bias noises. For comparison, the DTCZNN algorithm (3.12) is also applied to such a task.

To be specific, a two-link manipulator is used, and the following equation is obtained:

$$\mathbf{f}(\vartheta_k) = \mathbf{r}_{\mathrm{a},k}, \text{ with } t_k \in [0, T] \text{ s}, \tag{3.17}$$

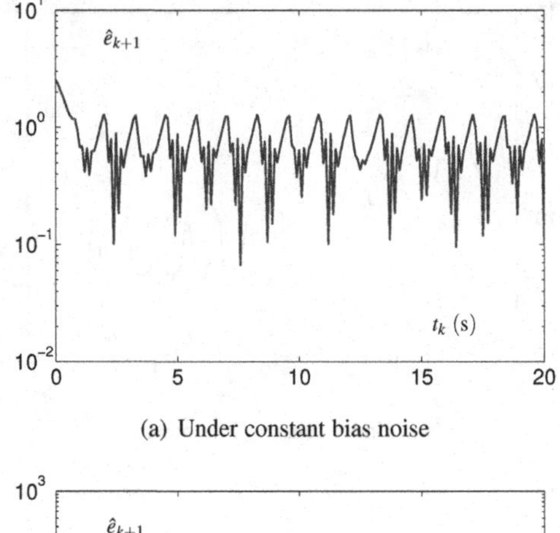

(a) Under constant bias noise

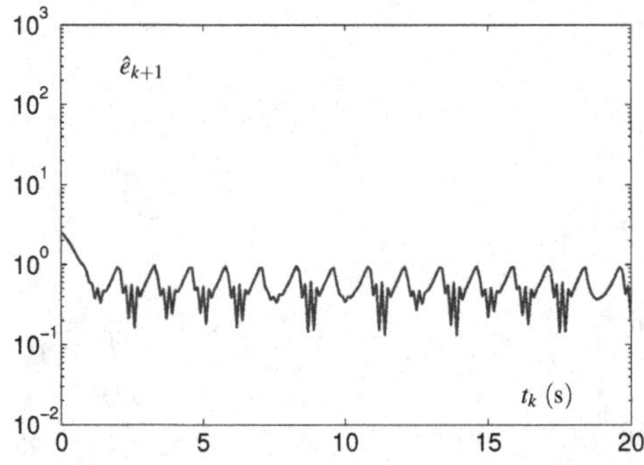

(b) Under discrete-time bounded random bias noise

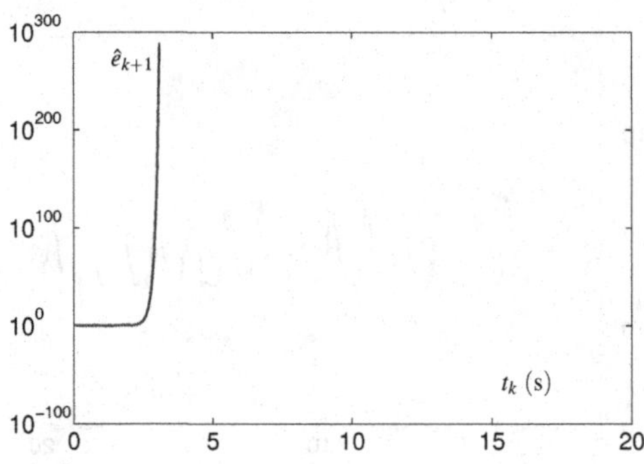

(c) Under discrete-time linear-increasing bias noise

FIGURE 3.8: Trajectories of residual errors $\hat{e}_{k+1}$ synthesized by DTCZNN algorithm (3.12) under different kinds of discrete-time bias noises with $g = 0.1$ s.

where $\mathbf{f}(\cdot)$ is the continuous forward-kinematics mapping function with known structure and parameters for a given manipulator [16, 22, 75]. In addition, $\vartheta_k \in \mathbb{R}^2$ and $\mathbf{r}_{\text{a},k} \in \mathbb{R}^2$ denote the joint-angle vector and the end-effector Cartesian position vector, respectively, and T denotes the task duration. By differentiating both sides of (3.17), the following relation between the actual end-effector velocity vector $\dot{\mathbf{r}}_{\text{a},k}$ and the joint velocity vector $\dot{\vartheta}_k$ is obtained:

$$J(\vartheta_k)\dot{\vartheta}_k = \dot{\mathbf{r}}_{\text{a},k}, \quad (3.18)$$

where the Jacobi matrix $J(\vartheta_k) = \partial\mathbf{f}(\vartheta_k)/\partial\vartheta_k \in \mathbb{R}^{2\times 2}$. The inverse-kinematic problem (i.e., given $\mathbf{r}_{\text{a},k}$, to solve for ϑ_k) can be solved by this way. Evidently, for obtaining $\dot{\vartheta}_k$, the inverse of $J(\vartheta_k)$ needs

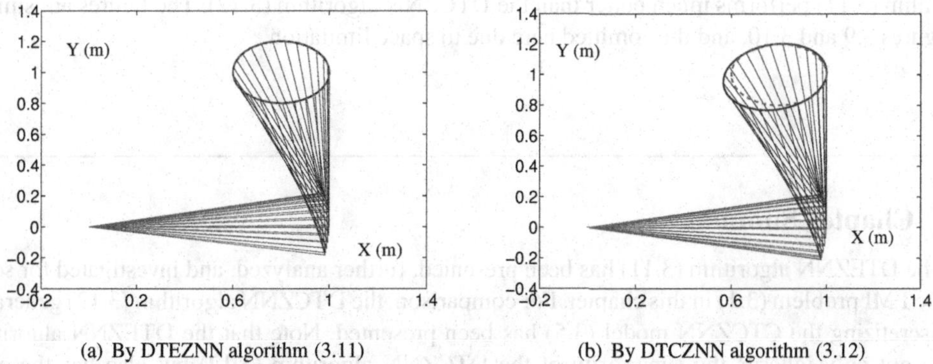

(a) By DTEZNN algorithm (3.11)
(b) By DTCZNN algorithm (3.12)

FIGURE 3.9: Motion trajectories synthesized by DTEZNN algorithm (3.11) and DTCZNN algorithm (3.12) under discrete-time bounded random bias noise R_k with its end-effector tracking circle path, where solid curves correspond to actual trajectories and dash curves correspond to desired paths [72].

to be computed in real time. Moreover, noises are inevitable in practice. Therefore, the DTEZNN algorithm (3.11) is employed for such a task. Specifically, we define $A_k = J(\vartheta_k)$, and A_{k+1}^{-1} (i.e., the inverse of A_{k+1}) can be computed during the computational time interval $[kg, (k+1)g)$, and various kinds of discrete-time bias noises can be suppressed at the same time. For simplicity and illustration, the manipulator is investigated to track a circle path with the radius being 0.2 m under various kinds of discrete-time bias noises, where the task duration $T = 2\pi$ s, each link length being 1 m, and the initial joint state $\vartheta_0 = [0, \pi/2]^{\mathrm{T}}$ rad.

In this application, we set the parameters $\hbar_1 = 0.5$ and $\hbar_2 = 3$. In addition, the discrete-time bounded random bias noise σ_k, which is constituted of four random elements ranging from 2 to 3 at any time instant, is employed. For comparison, the DTCZNN algorithm (3.12) is employed with the parameter $\hbar = 0.3$. The numerical experimental results are presented in Figures 3.9 and 3.10. From Figure 3.9, one can observe that the discrete-time bound random bias noise is suppressed successfully by using the DTEZNN algorithm (3.11), and the trajectory of the end-effector generated by the DTCZNN algorithm (3.12) is evidently not a circle. Besides, Figure 3.10 shows the profiles of ϑ_{k+1} and $\dot{\vartheta}_{k+1}$ generated by the DTEZNN algorithm (3.11) under discrete-time bound random bias noise. Under constant bias noise or discrete-time linear-increasing bias noise, the DTEZNN

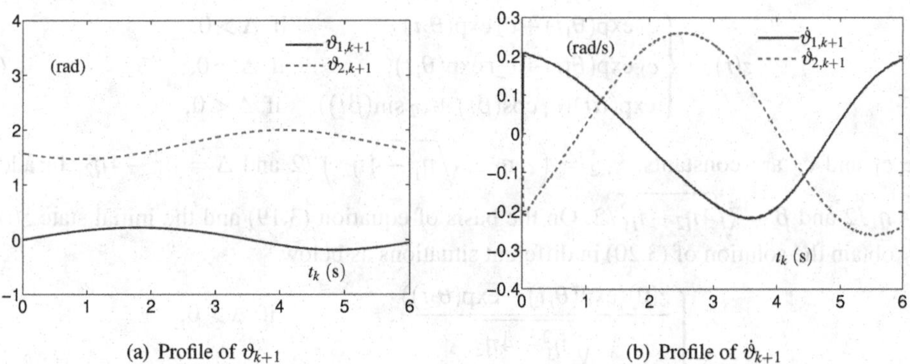

(a) Profile of ϑ_{k+1}
(b) Profile of $\dot{\vartheta}_{k+1}$

FIGURE 3.10: Profiles of ϑ_{k+1} and $\dot{\vartheta}_{k+1}$ generated by DTEZNN algorithm (3.11) under discrete-time bounded random bias noise R_k.

algorithm (3.11) performs much better than the DTCZNN algorithm (3.12). The figures are similar to Figures 3.9 and 3.10, and thus omitted here due to space limitation.

3.7 Chapter Summary

The DTEZNN algorithm (3.11) has been presented, further analyzed, and investigated for solving the FMI problem (3.1) in this chapter. For comparison, the DTCZNN algorithm (3.12) generated by discretizing the CTCZNN model (3.5) has been presented. Note that the DTEZNN algorithm (3.11) not only inherits the superiority of the DTCZNN algorithm (3.12) but also has the ability of suppressing various kinds of bias noises. For obtaining the DTEZNN algorithm (3.11), the CTEZNN model (3.8) and the ZTD 6321 formula (3.9) have been presented. Moreover, the theoretical analyses have shown the stability and convergence of the presented DTEZNN algorithm (3.11). In addition, the DTEZNN algorithm (3.11) has been analyzed and investigated for solving the FMI problem (3.1) under constant bias noise, discrete-time bounded random bias noise, and even discrete-time linear-increasing bias noise. Besides, the application to manipulator motion planning has been presented to further substantiate the efficacy of the DTEZNN algorithm (3.11).

Appendix B: Proof of Lemma 2

For analyzing the convergence and obtaining the CTSSRE synthesized by model (3.7), we consider the following subsystem:

$$\dot{z}(t)+\eta_1 z(t)+\eta_2\int_0^t \dot{z}(\tau)\mathrm{d}\tau=0, \tag{3.19}$$

which is any one of the $n\times n$ subsystems of (3.6). Then, we differentiate both sides of the equation (3.19) in terms of time t, and the following equation is obtained:

$$\ddot{z}(t)+\eta_1\dot{z}(t)+\eta_2 z(t)=0, \tag{3.20}$$

which is a second-order linear homogeneous differential equation. On the basis of different values of η_1 and η_2, there are three situations as below.

$$z(t)=\begin{cases} c_1\exp(\theta_1 t)+c_2\exp(\theta_2 t), & \text{if } \Delta>0,\\ c_1\exp(\theta_1 t)+c_2 t\exp(\theta_1 t), & \text{if } \Delta=0,\\ \exp(\alpha t)(c_1\cos(\beta t)+c_2\sin(\beta t)), & \text{if } \Delta<0, \end{cases} \tag{3.21}$$

where c_1 and c_2 are constants, $\theta_{1,2}=\left(-\eta_1\pm\sqrt{\eta_1^2-4\eta_2}\right)/2$ and $\Delta=\eta_1^2-4\eta_2$. In addition, $\alpha=-\eta_1/2$ and $\beta=\sqrt{4\eta_2-\eta_1^2}/2$. On the basis of equation (3.19) and the initial state $z(0)$, we finally obtain the solution of (3.20) in different situations as below.

$$z(t)=\begin{cases} \dfrac{z(0)(\exp(\theta_1 t)-\exp(\theta_2 t))}{\sqrt{\eta_1^2-4\eta_2}}, & \text{if } \Delta>0,\\ z(0)(\exp(\theta_1 t)+\theta_1 t\exp(\theta_1 t)), & \text{if } \Delta=0,\\ z(0)\exp(\alpha t)\left(\dfrac{\alpha\sin(\beta t)}{\beta}+\cos(\beta t)\right), & \text{if } \Delta<0. \end{cases} \tag{3.22}$$

We know that $\theta_{1,2} < 0$ and $\alpha < 0$. Thus, we obtain that $\lim_{t\to\infty} z(t) = 0$. Finally, the CTSSRE $\lim_{t\to\infty} \|Z(t)\|_{\mathrm{F}} = 0$ is obtained. The proof is thus completed. □

Appendix C: Proof of Lemma 3

For analyzing the convergence and obtaining the CTSSRE synthesized by model (3.7) under constant noise, we consider the subsystem

$$\dot{z}(t) + \eta_1 z(t) + \eta_2 \int_0^t z(\tau)\mathrm{d}\tau = c, \tag{3.23}$$

where c denotes any element of matrix-form constant bias noise. Then, we differentiate both sides of equation (3.23) in terms of time t, and the following equation is obtained:

$$\ddot{z}(t) + \eta_1 \dot{z}(t) + \eta_2 z(t) = 0,$$

which is the same as equation (3.20). Then, the following process is similar with the process of Lemma 2 and is omitted due to space limitation. □

Appendix D: Proof of Lemma 4

For analyzing the convergence and obtaining the CTSSRE synthesized by model (3.7) under bounded random bias noise, we consider the subsystem

$$\dot{z}(t) = -\eta_1 z(t) - \eta_2 \int_0^t z(\tau)\mathrm{d}\tau + r(t), \tag{3.24}$$

where $r(t)$ denotes any element of the unknown matrix-form bounded random bias noise. According to the values of η_1 and η_2, the analyses can be divided into the following three situations.

(1) For $\eta_1^2 > 4\eta_2$, the solution to the subsystem (3.24) is obtained as

$$\begin{aligned} z(t) = &\frac{z(0)(\theta_1 \exp(\theta_1 t) - \theta_2 \exp(\theta_2 t))}{\theta_1 - \theta_2} \\ &+ \left(\int_0^t (\theta_1 \exp(\theta_1 (t-\tau)) - \theta_2 \exp(\theta_2 (t-\tau))) r(\tau)\mathrm{d}\tau \right) \frac{1}{\theta_1 - \theta_2}. \end{aligned}$$

From the triangle inequality, we have

$$\begin{aligned} |z(t)| \leq &\frac{|z(0)(\theta_1 \exp(\theta_1 t) - \theta_2 \exp(\theta_2 t))|}{\theta_1 - \theta_2} \\ &+ \frac{\int_0^t |\theta_1 \exp(\theta_1 (t-\tau))||r(\tau)|\mathrm{d}\tau}{\theta_1 - \theta_2} + \frac{\int_0^t |\theta_2 \exp(\theta_2 (t-\tau))||r(\tau)|\mathrm{d}\tau}{\theta_1 - \theta_2}. \end{aligned}$$

We further have

$$|z(t)| \leq \frac{|z(0)(\theta_1 \exp(\theta_1 t) - \theta_2 \exp(\theta_2 t))|}{\theta_1 - \theta_2} + \frac{2}{\theta_1 - \theta_2} \max_{0\leq\tau\leq t} |r(\tau)|$$
$$= \frac{|z(0)(\theta_1 \exp(\theta_1 t) - \theta_2 \exp(\theta_2 t))|}{\theta_1 - \theta_2} + \frac{2}{\sqrt{\eta_1^2 - 4\eta_2}} \max_{0\leq\tau\leq t} |r(\tau)|.$$

Finally, we have

$$\lim_{t\to\infty} \sup \|Z(t)\|_{\mathrm{F}} \leq \frac{2n}{\sqrt{\eta_1^2 - 4\eta_2}} \sup_{0\leq\tau\leq t} |r(\tau)|.$$

(2) For $\eta_1^2 = 4\eta_2$, the solution to the subsystem (3.24) can be obtained as

$$z(t) = z(0)t\theta_1 \exp(\theta_1 t) + z(0)\exp(\theta_1 t)$$
$$+ \int_0^t ((t-\tau)\theta_1 \exp(\theta_1(t-\tau)))r(\tau)\mathrm{d}\tau + \int_0^t \exp(\theta_1(t-\tau))r(\tau)\mathrm{d}\tau,$$

where $\theta_1 = \left(-\eta_1 + \sqrt{\eta_1^2 - 4\eta_2}\right)/2 = -\gamma/2$. From Theorem 1 in [76], we know that there exist $\mu > 0$ and $v > 0$, such that

$$|\theta_1|t\exp(\theta_1 t) \leq \mu \exp(-vt).$$

Thus, according to the above inequality as well as the triangle inequality, we have

$$|z(t)| \leq |z(0)(\theta_1 t \exp(\theta_1 t) + \exp(\theta_1 t))|$$
$$+ \int_0^t |\mu \exp(-v(t-\tau))||r(\tau)|\mathrm{d}\tau + \int_0^t |\exp(\theta_1(t-\tau))||r(\tau)|\mathrm{d}\tau.$$

We further have

$$|z(t)| \leq |z(0)(\theta_1 t \exp(\theta_1 t) + \exp(\theta_1 t))| + \left(\frac{\mu}{v} - \frac{1}{\theta_1}\right) \max_{0\leq\tau\leq t} |r(\tau)|.$$

Finally, we have

$$\lim_{t\to\infty} \sup \|Z(t)\|_{\mathrm{F}} \leq \left(\frac{\mu}{v} - \frac{1}{\theta_1}\right) n \sup_{0\leq\tau\leq t} |r(\tau)|.$$

(3) For $\eta_1^2 < 4\eta_2$, the solution to the subsystem (3.24) can be obtained as

$$z(t) = z(0)\exp(\alpha t)(\alpha \sin(\beta t)/\beta + \cos(\beta t))$$
$$+ \int_0^t (\alpha \sin(\beta(t-\tau))\exp(\alpha(t-\tau))/\beta + \cos(\beta(t-\tau))\exp(\alpha(t-\tau)))r(\tau)\mathrm{d}\tau,$$

where $\alpha = -\gamma/2$ and $\beta = \sqrt{4\eta_2 - \eta_1^2}/2$. Thus, according to triangle inequality, we can similarly have

$$|z(t)| \leq |z(0)\exp(\alpha t)(\alpha \sin(\beta t)/\beta + \cos(\beta t)))| - \frac{\sqrt{\alpha^2 + \beta^2}}{\alpha\beta} \max_{0\leq\tau\leq t} |r(\tau)|$$
$$= |z(0)\exp(\alpha t)(\alpha \sin(\beta t)/\beta + \cos(\beta t))| + \frac{4\eta_2}{\eta_1\sqrt{4\eta_2 - \eta_1^2}} \max_{0\leq\tau\leq t} |r(\tau)|.$$

Finally, we have

$$\lim_{t\to\infty}\sup\|Z(t)\|_{\mathrm{F}} \leq \frac{4\eta_2 n}{\eta_1\sqrt{4\eta_2-\eta_1^2}}\sup_{0\leq\tau\leq t}|r(\tau)|.$$

The above analysis of the three situations shows that, under the unknown matrix-form bounded random bias noise, the CTSSRE synthesized by the CTEZNN model (3.7) is bounded by $2n\sup_{0\leq\tau\leq t}|r(\tau)|/\sqrt{\eta_1^2-4\eta_2}$ for $\eta_1^2>4\eta_2$, or $4n\eta_2\sup_{0\leq\tau\leq t}|r(\tau)|/\left(\eta_1\sqrt{4\eta_2-\eta_1^2}\right)$ for $\eta_1^2<4\eta_2$. That is, the upper bound of $\lim_{t\to\infty}\|Z(t)\|_{\mathrm{F}}$ is approximately in inverse proportion to η_1. The proof is thus completed. □

Appendix E: Proof of Lemma 5

For analyzing the convergence and obtaining the CTSSRE synthesized by model (3.7) under linear-increasing bias noise, we consider the subsystem

$$\dot{z}(t)+\eta_1 z(t)+\eta_2\int_0^t z(\tau)\mathrm{d}\tau = lt, \tag{3.25}$$

where lt denotes an element of matrix-form linear-increasing bias noise. Then, we differentiate both sides of equation (3.25) in terms of time t, and the following equation is obtained:

$$\ddot{z}(t)+\eta_1\dot{z}(t)+\eta_2 z(t) = l, \tag{3.26}$$

which is a second-order linear nonhomogeneous differential equation. From Lemma 2, we know that the result of corresponding second-order linear homogeneous differential equation is (3.21). In addition, l/η_2 is a particular solution of (3.26). Then, the general solution of (3.26) is obtained as below:

$$z(t)=\begin{cases} c_1\exp(\theta_1 t)+c_2\exp(\theta_2 t)+\dfrac{l}{\eta_2}, & \text{if } \Delta>0,\\ c_1\exp(\theta_1 t)+c_2 t\exp(\theta_1 t)+\dfrac{l}{\eta_2}, & \text{if } \Delta=0,\\ \exp(\alpha t)(c_1\cos(\beta t)+c_2\sin(\beta t))+\dfrac{l}{\eta_2}, & \text{if } \Delta<0.\end{cases}$$

Note that c_1 and c_2 are constants and can be specified by the initial residual error $z(0)$ and the subsystem (3.25). Considering the above situations, we obtain that $\lim_{t\to\infty} z(t) = l/\eta_2$. Finally, we obtain that the CTSSRE $\lim_{t\to\infty}\|Z(t)\|_{\mathrm{F}}$ synthesized by model (3.7) is in inverse proportion to η_2 under linear-increasing bias noise. The proof is thus completed. □

Appendix F: Proof of Theorem 17

According to Taylor expansion [20], we have the following equations:

$$\zeta_{k+1} = \zeta_k + g\dot{\zeta}_k + \frac{g^2}{2}\ddot{\zeta}_k + \mathscr{O}(g^3), \tag{3.27}$$

$$\zeta_{k-1} = \zeta_k - g\dot{\zeta}_k + \frac{g^2}{2}\ddot{\zeta}_k + \mathscr{O}(g^3), \tag{3.28}$$

and

$$\zeta_{k-2} = \zeta_k - 2g\dot{\zeta}_k + 2g^2\ddot{\zeta}_k + \mathscr{O}(g^3), \tag{3.29}$$

where $\ddot{\zeta}_k$ denotes the second-order time derivative of $\zeta(t)$ at time instant t_k.

Let (3.27) multiply 3, (3.28) multiply −1, and (3.29) multiply −0.5. Add together these results. Thus, the ZTD 6321 formula is obtained as

$$\dot{\zeta}_k = \frac{3}{5g}\zeta_{k+1} - \frac{3}{10g}\zeta_k - \frac{1}{5g}\zeta_{k-1} - \frac{1}{10g}\zeta_{k-2} + \mathscr{O}(g^2).$$

The proof is thus completed. □

Chapter 4

Future Matrix Pseudoinversion

Abstract

In this chapter, a three-step Zhang time discretization (3S-ZTD) formula, termed as the ZTD 6321 formula, is presented, which obtains higher computational precision in approximating the first-order derivative. Then, the ZTD 6321 formula is used for the discretization of the continuous-time zeroing neural network (CTZNN) model and it can greatly overcome the limitation of conventional formulas in the CTZNN discretization. On the basis of the ZTD 6321 formula, a discrete-time ZNN (DTZNN) 6321 algorithm is presented and investigated for future matrix pseudoinversion (FMP), which is further divided into future matrix left pseudoinversion (FMLP) and future matrix right pseudoinversion (FMRP). Numerical experimental results further validate the feasibility, effectiveness, and superiority of the presented DTZNN 6321 algorithm for the FMLP. Moreover, the presented DTZNN 6321 algorithm is applied to the manipulator control, which involves an FMRP problem. The physical experimental results based on a four-link redundant manipulator substantiate the realizability and effectiveness of the presented DTZNN 6321 algorithm.

4.1 Introduction

Numerical differentiation is commonly used to solve ordinary differential equations and partial differential equations in natural and engineering science fields [77], such as electromagnetism [78], control [79], and computer science [80]. In terms of the problem of the first-order derivative approximation, there is much effort spent by previous researchers [81, 82], which has been devoted to find effective algorithms that have advantages over traditional algorithms. For example, in [81], the linear combinations of Taylor expansions were used to develop three-point numerical-differentiation formulas for the first-order and second-order derivatives of a function at a given node; in [82], Khan and Ohba presented closed-form expressions of the numerical-differentiation approximations of arbitrary order for the first-order and higher-order derivatives.

In recent decades, neural networks have been widely investigated and employed in control and optimization [83–85]. For example, in [83], Liu *et al* studied the problem of H_∞ state estimation for static neural networks with time-dependent delay. Besides, in [85], Yang *et al* showed a new neural network for solving quadratic programming problems with equality and inequality constraints. Besides, with the rapid development of very large-scale integration (VLSI), the hardware implementation of neural networks becomes feasible [86–88]. For example, in [86], Ortega-Zamorano *et al* showed that a novel neural network algorithm could be implemented in a field programmable gate array. A neural network-based automatic optical inspection system for the diagnosis of solder joint defects in industrial surface mounting technology was presented in [87]. An artificial neural network-based adaptive estimator was presented for the estimation of rotor speed in a sensorless vector-controlled induction motor drive in [88]. Among them, recurrent neural network (RNN) has

DOI: 10.1201/9781003497783-4

attracted attention from researchers [89, 90], because it is a powerful tool for solving mathematical and engineering problems [91]. For instance, in many industrial application fields, the manipulator has played an increasingly important role. Note that the redundant manipulator is the manipulator having more degrees of freedom than required to perform a given end-effector primary task, and RNN can be used to operate such redundant manipulator systems.

Zeroing neural network (ZNN) is a special class of RNNs, which derives from the research of Hopfield neural network [92]. It is proposed as a systematic approach for solving time-dependent problems. Note that ZNN is different from the conventional gradient-based RNN in terms of error function, design formula, dynamic equation, and the utilization of time derivatives [92].

More importantly, hardware implementations of continuous-time models are always developed on analogue VLSI, which have some typical weaknesses, such as accuracy, design time, and cost. To overcome those weaknesses, it is necessary to investigate the discretization of the continuous-time model. In addition, the discrete-time algorithm is easier to implement industrially in current hardware (e.g., digital VLSI or digital computer) than the continuous-time model. Thus, it is very important for the discretization of continuous-time ZNN (CTZNN) models to obtain discrete-time ZNN (DTZNN) algorithms.

There are lots of numerical-differentiation formulas that could obtain the first-order derivative approximation. In this chapter [93], we show several conventional numerical-differentiation formulas, including the Euler forward formula, Newton iteration (NI) method, and another developed Zhang–Taylor discretization formula [22], which are generally used in discretization. However, those formulas have less satisfactory precision. Therefore, we need to use a high-precision one-step-ahead numerical-differentiation formula.

Specifically speaking, firstly, in light of the above analyses, a three-step Zhang time discretization (3S-ZTD) formula, termed as the ZTD 6321 formula, is presented for the first-order derivative approximation, of which the precision is $\mathscr{O}(g^2)$ with g denoting the sampling gap. Note that such a ZTD 6321 formula, in the area of ultra-precision motion control, can effectively replace the widely used Euler forward formula, especially in solving various time-dependent problems. Secondly, we present a DTZNN 6321 algorithm based on the ZTD 6321 formula, and the DTZNN 6321 algorithm is zero-stable and convergent. Compared with similar DTZNN algorithms in the previous research works [22, 70], the DTZNN 6321 algorithm not only possesses superior performance but also can be implemented in a real-world application (i.e., a four-link redundant manipulator inverse-kinematics control problem). The presented physical experimental results further validate the usefulness and superiority of the presented DTZNN 6321 algorithm for solving the inverse kinematics problem, and such an algorithm can also be widely used in the related area of ultra-precision motion control.

4.2 Problem Formulation and CTZNN Model

In this section, the problem formulation of the FMP and the design procedure of the CTZNN model are presented.

4.2.1 Problem formulation

Let us consider the following FMP problem with X_{k+1} to be computed at each computational time interval $[t_k, t_{k+1}) = [kg, (k+1)g) \subset [t_{\text{ini}}, t_{\text{fin}}] \subset [0, +\infty)$:

$$A_{k+1} - X_{k+1}^{\dagger} = O_{m\times n} \in \mathbb{R}^{m\times n}, \tag{4.1}$$

where t_{ini} and t_{fin} represent the initial and final time instants, respectively. Besides, $O_{m\times n}$ denotes an $m\times n$ zero matrix; $A_{k+1}\in\mathbb{R}^{m\times n}$ being of full rank is generated or measured from the smoothly time-dependent matrix $A(t)\in\mathbb{R}^{m\times n}$ by sampling at time instant $t_{k+1}=(k+1)g$; $X_{k+1}\in\mathbb{R}^{n\times m}$ is the unknown matrix obtained during $[t_k,\ t_{k+1})$. Note that $k=0,1,2,\cdots$ denotes the updating index. It is worth mentioning that, according to Definition 1 and Lemma 1 in Chapter 1, the FMP is further divided into future matrix left pseudoinversion (FMLP) and future matrix right pseudoinversion (FMRP).

4.2.2 CTZNN model

Being a special class of RNNs, ZNN has been proposed for solving various time-dependent problems (e.g., time-dependent matrix pseudoinversion [19]). To develop DTZNN algorithms effectively, the CTZNN model can be obtained by exploiting the ZNN method [92]. Consider the following continuous time-dependent matrix pseudoinversion (CTDMP) problem as the continuation of (4.1):

$$A(t)-X^{\dagger}(t)=O_{m\times n},$$

where $A(t)\in\mathbb{R}^{m\times n}$ denotes a smoothly time-dependent coefficient matrix; $X(t)\in\mathbb{R}^{n\times m}$ is the unknown time-dependent matrix to be solved, and $X^{\dagger}(t)$ denotes the pseudoinverse of $X(t)$. To lay a basis for further discussion, we suppose that $A(t)$ is of full rank at any time instant $t\in[t_{\text{ini}},t_{\text{fin}})$, and thus the pseudoinverse of $A(t)$ exists and is obtained.

We define a zeroing function (ZF) that can monitor and control the solving process:

$$Z(t)=A(t)-X^{\dagger}(t),$$

where $Z(t)\in\mathbb{R}^{m\times n}$, and t denotes the ever-increasing time with $t\in[t_{\text{ini}},t_{\text{fin}})$. Then, by adopting the ZNN design formula $\dot{Z}(t)=-\eta Z(t)$, where $\eta>0$ is used to control the convergence rate of the neural network, we obtain $\dot{A}(t)-\dot{X}^{\dagger}(t)=-\eta\left(A(t)-X^{\dagger}(t)\right)$. Besides, by employing Lemma 3 in [19], the above equation can be further modified as $X^{\dagger}(t)\dot{X}(t)X^{\dagger}(t)=-\dot{A}(t)-\eta\left(A(t)-X^{\dagger}(t)\right)$. Thus, we have

$$\dot{X}(t)=-X(t)\dot{A}(t)X(t)-\eta\left(X(t)A(t)X(t)-X(t)\right),\tag{4.2}$$

which is the explicit CTZNN model for solving the CTDMP problem. Note that (4.2) is also the Getz–Marsden dynamic system (but with different origins) [16, 94]. From the previous studies [23, 24, 95–97], the Getz–Marsden dynamic system is not always effective on the CTDMP problems. Those that cannot be solved by the Getz–Marsden dynamic system are classified and named as Zhang matrix pseudoinversion problem, while those that can be well solved are named as Getz–Masden matrix pseudoinversion problem. We only consider the Getz–Masden matrix pseudoinversion problem.

4.3 Conventional Algorithms and DTZNN 6321 Algorithm

In reality, with the discrete-time algorithm being easier to digital circuit or digital computer realization than the continuous-time model, the CTZNN model (4.2) needs to be discretized. In this section, an Euler-type DTZNN (ET-DTZNN) algorithm, an NI algorithm, and a Zhang–Taylor DTZNN (ZT-DTZNN) algorithm are presented. More importantly, we present the ZTD 6321 formula and the DTZNN 6321 algorithm.

4.3.1 Conventional algorithms

Before presenting DTZNN algorithms, the unique characteristics of a method for solving the time-dependent problem, which are different from time-independent case, are given as follows. On the one hand, how to develop a discrete-time algorithm without using future data is a key point. On the other hand, computation consumes time unavoidably during each computational period. In other words, the discrete-time algorithm should satisfy the requirement of real-time computation.

In order to discretize the CTZNN model (4.2), firstly, we refer to the following two conventional discretization methods: the Euler forward formula and NI method.

On the basis of the Euler forward formula [16], we have the following ET-DTZNN algorithm:

$$X_{k+1} \doteq -gX_k\dot{A}_kX_k - \hbar X_k(A_kX_k - I_{n\times n}) + X_k, \tag{4.3}$$

with $\doteq$ denoting the computational assignment operator and $\hbar = g\eta$ representing the step length. Besides, $I_{n\times n}$ denotes an $n\times n$ identity matrix. Note that the ET-DTZNN algorithm (4.3) traditionally starts from theoretical initial pseudoinverse or its neighboring value [16, 70, 94].

As seen from (4.3), with $gX_k\dot{A}_kX_k$ being omitted and $\hbar = 1$ [70], the ET-DTZNN algorithm (4.3) reduces to the NI algorithm as follows:

$$X_{k+1} \doteq -X_k(A_kX_k - I_{n\times n}) + X_k. \tag{4.4}$$

Evidently, the NI algorithm (4.4) is a special case of the ET-DTZNN algorithm (4.3) for solving the FMP problem (4.1). In other words, in addition to differences, the links between the ET-DTZNN algorithm (4.3) and the NI algorithm (4.4) are presented in [70].

4.3.2 DTZNN 6321 algorithm

First of all, the ZTD 6321 formula is presented by the following theorem.

Theorem 18 *With the sufficiently small sampling gap $g \in (0,1)$, let $\mathscr{O}(g^2)$ denote the error (especially, the truncation error) positively or negatively proportional to g^2, i.e., of the order of g^2. Suppose that $\zeta(t)$ is sufficiently smooth. With $\zeta_{k+1} = \zeta(t_{k+1}) = \zeta((k+1)g)$, the ZTD 6321 formula is formulated as follows:*

$$\dot{\zeta}_k = \frac{6\zeta_{k+1} - 3\zeta_k - 2\zeta_{k-1} - \zeta_{k-2}}{10g} + \mathscr{O}(g^2). \tag{4.5}$$

Proof. The proof is presented in Appendix F in Chapter 3. □

Secondly, by exploiting the presented ZTD 6321 formula (4.5) to discretize (4.2), the following equation is obtained:

$$X_{k+1} = -\frac{5}{3}gX_k\dot{A}_kX_k - \frac{5}{3}\hbar X_k(A_kX_k - I_{n\times n}) + \frac{1}{2}X_k + \frac{1}{3}X_{k-1} + \frac{1}{6}X_{k-2} + \mathbf{O}(g^3)$$

where $\mathbf{O}(g^3)$ denotes the truncation error matrix with each element being $\mathscr{O}(g^3)$. Ignoring the term $\mathbf{O}(g^3)$, we obtain the DTZNN 6321 algorithm as follows:

$$X_{k+1} \doteq -\frac{5}{3}gX_k\dot{A}_kX_k - \frac{5}{3}\hbar X_k(A_kX_k - I_{n\times n}) + \frac{1}{2}X_k + \frac{1}{3}X_{k-1} + \frac{1}{6}X_{k-2}. \tag{4.6}$$

Remark 4 *The truncation error of the presented DTZNN 6321 algorithm (4.6) is $\mathbf{O}(g^3)$, and the truncation errors of the ET-DTZNN algorithm (4.3) and the NI algorithm (4.4) are $\mathbf{O}(g^2)$ and $\mathbf{O}(g)$, respectively. In addition, as a similar algorithm, in [22], Jin and Zhang presented a ZT-DTZNN algorithm as*

$$X_{k+1} \doteq -gX_k\dot{A}_kX_k - \hbar X_k(A_kX_k - I_{n\times n}) + \frac{3}{2}X_k - X_{k-1} + \frac{1}{2}X_{k-2}. \tag{4.7}$$

TABLE 4.1: Four different algorithms for solving FMP problem (4.1).

Algorithm	Expression
NI algorithm (4.4)	$X_{k+1} \doteq -X_k(A_kX_k - I_{n\times n}) + X_k$
ET-DTZNN algorithm (4.3)	$X_{k+1} \doteq -gX_k\dot{A}_kX_k - \hbar X_k(A_kX_k - I_{n\times n}) + X_k$
ZT-DTZNN algorithm (4.7)	$X_{k+1} \doteq -gX_k\dot{A}_kX_k - \hbar X_k(A_kX_k - I_{n\times n}) + 3X_k/2 - X_{k-1} + X_{k-2}/2$
DTZNN 6321 algorithm (4.6)	$X_{k+1} \doteq -5gX_k\dot{A}_kX_k/3 - 5\hbar X_k(A_kX_k - I_{n\times n})/3 + X_k/2 + X_{k-1}/3 + X_{k-2}/6$

For convenience and also for comparison purposes, we list comparatively the aforementioned algorithms in Table 4.1. It is worth pointing out, that, although the truncation error of the ZT-DTZNN algorithm (4.7) is also $\mathbf{O}(g^3)$*, the computational precision of the presented DTZNN 6321 algorithm (4.6) is approximately enhanced by two times compared with the ZT-DTZNN algorithm (4.7). For details, please see Appendix G.*

For a more intuitive understanding of the main content of this chapter [93], Table 4.2 lists the problem, scheme, model, and algorithms.

4.4 Numerical Experiments

In this section, we conduct two numerical experiments to verify the feasibility, effectiveness, and superiority of the presented DTZNN 6321 algorithm (4.6) using different values of g.

Example 4.1 For illustration, let us consider the following FMLP problem with X_{k+1} to be computed at each computational time interval $[t_k, t_{k+1}) \subset [0, 10]$ s, where

$$A_k = \begin{bmatrix} \sin(t_k) & \cos(t_k) \\ -\cos(t_k) & \sin(t_k) \\ \sin(t_k) & \cos(t_k) \end{bmatrix}.$$

To check the correctness of the solution computed by the presented DTZNN algorithm, the theoretical time-dependent pseudoinverse of matrix A_{k+1} is given as

$$A^{\dagger}_{k+1} = \begin{bmatrix} 0.5\sin(t_{k+1}) & -\cos(t_{k+1}) & 0.5\sin(t_{k+1}) \\ 0.5\cos(t_{k+1}) & \sin(t_{k+1}) & 0.5\cos(t_{k+1}) \end{bmatrix}.$$

For comparison and illustration, we define two errors, i.e., the solution error $\check{e}_{k+1} = \|X_{k+1} - A^{\dagger}_{k+1}\|_{\mathrm{F}}$ and the residual error $\hat{e}_{k+1} = \|X_{k+1}A_{k+1}A^{\mathrm{T}}_{k+1} - A^{\mathrm{T}}_{k+1}\|_{\mathrm{F}}$, where $\|\cdot\|_{\mathrm{F}}$ and ^{T} denote the Frobenius norm and the transpose operator of a matrix or vector, respectively. As seen

TABLE 4.2: Problem, scheme, model, and algorithms in this chapter.

Problem	$A_{k+1} - X^{\dagger}_{k+1} = O_{m\times n}$.
Scheme	*Step 1*: Define ZF as $Z(t) = A(t) - X^{\dagger}(t)$. *Step 2*: Adopt ZNN design formula as $\dot{Z}(t) = -\eta Z(t)$. *Step 3*: Discretize CTZNN model (1.3).
Model	$\dot{X}(t) = -X(t)\dot{A}(t)X(t) - \eta(X(t)A(t)X(t) - X(t))$.
Algorithms	$X_{k+1} \doteq -X_k(A_kX_k - I_{n\times n}) + X_k$, $X_{k+1} \doteq -gX_k\dot{A}_kX_k - \hbar X_k(A_kX_k - I_{n\times n}) + X_k$, $X_{k+1} \doteq -gX_k\dot{A}_kX_k - \hbar X_k(A_kX_k - I_{n\times n}) + 3X_k/2 - X_{k-1} + X_{k-2}/2$, $X_{k+1} \doteq -5gX_k\dot{A}_kX_k/3 - 5\hbar X_k(A_kX_k - I_{n\times n})/3 + X_k/2 + X_{k-1}/3 + X_{k-2}/6$.

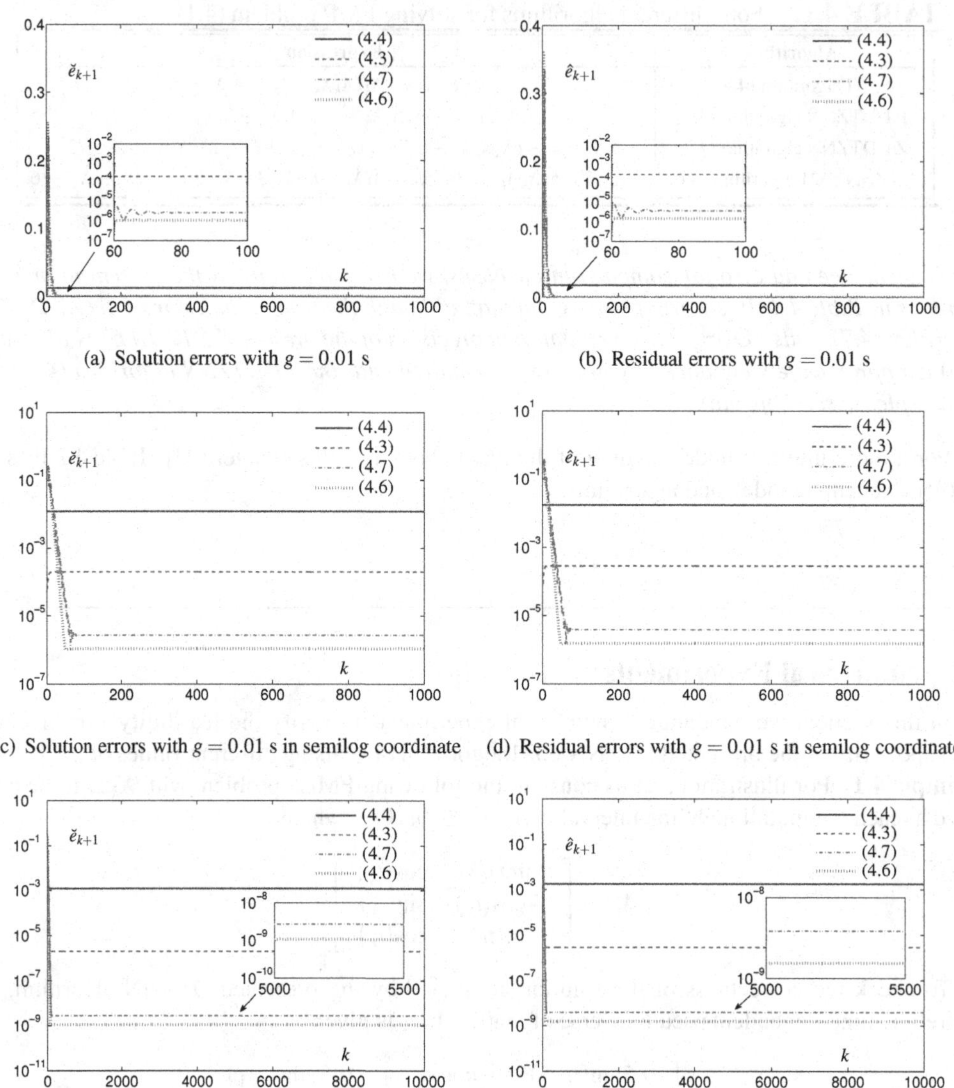

(a) Solution errors with $g = 0.01$ s

(b) Residual errors with $g = 0.01$ s

(c) Solution errors with $g = 0.01$ s in semilog coordinate

(d) Residual errors with $g = 0.01$ s in semilog coordinate

(e) Solution errors with $g = 0.001$ s in semilog coordinate

(f) Residual errors with $g = 0.001$ s in semilog coordinate

FIGURE 4.1: Trajectories of solution errors and residual errors synthesized by four different algorithms with $\hbar = 0.3$ for FMLP in Example 4.1.

from Figure 4.1, we compare the corresponding solution errors and residual errors synthesized by four different algorithms for solving the above FMLP problem with the same initial state, i.e., $A_0^{\dagger} = [0, -1, 0; 0.5, 0, 0.5]$. Specifically, Figure 4.1(a) shows the trajectories of solution errors in standard coordinate, and Figure 4.1(b) shows the trajectories of residual errors in standard coordinate. As illustrated in Figure 4.1(a) and (b), the solution errors and residual errors synthesized by four different algorithms all converge to zero rapidly, whereas the errors synthesized by the NI algorithm (4.4) are larger.

For further investigation, more details are shown in semilog coordinate. Specifically, Figure 4.1(c) and (d) shows the trajectories of the solution errors and residual errors synthesized by four different algorithms with $g = 0.01$ s. Moreover, the trajectories of the solution errors and

TABLE 4.3: Comparisons among four different algorithms in terms of MSSSEs and MSSREs as well as ACTPU data with $\hbar = 0.3$ for FMLP in Example 4.1.

g (s)	Algorithm	MSSSE	MSSRE	ACTPU (ms)
0.1	NI algorithm (4.4)	1.2243×10^{-1}	1.7313×10^{-1}	0.0202
	ET-DTZNN algorithm (4.3)	1.9359×10^{-2}	2.7382×10^{-2}	0.0338
	ZT-DTZNN algorithm (4.7)	2.3774×10^{-2}	3.3621×10^{-2}	0.0365
	DTZNN 6321 algorithm (4.6)	1.0317×10^{-3}	1.4594×10^{-3}	0.0385
0.05	NI algorithm (4.4)	6.1231×10^{-2}	8.6594×10^{-2}	0.0189
	ET-DTZNN algorithm (4.3)	5.0333×10^{-3}	7.1182×10^{-3}	0.0316
	ZT-DTZNN algorithm (4.7)	3.8279×10^{-4}	5.4134×10^{-4}	0.0359
	DTZNN 6321 algorithm (4.6)	1.3419×10^{-4}	1.8978×10^{-4}	0.0375
0.01	NI algorithm (4.4)	1.2241×10^{-2}	1.7320×10^{-2}	0.0183
	ET-DTZNN algorithm (4.3)	2.0401×10^{-4}	2.8851×10^{-4}	0.0318
	ZT-DTZNN algorithm (4.7)	2.7201×10^{-6}	3.8468×10^{-6}	0.0361
	DTZNN 6321 algorithm (4.6)	1.0800×10^{-6}	1.5387×10^{-6}	0.0372
0.005	NI algorithm (4.4)	6.1237×10^{-3}	8.6602×10^{-3}	0.0202
	ET-DTZNN algorithm (4.3)	5.1024×10^{-5}	7.2159×10^{-5}	0.0322
	ZT-DTZNN algorithm (4.7)	3.4016×10^{-7}	4.8106×10^{-7}	0.0375
	DTZNN 6321 algorithm (4.6)	1.3606×10^{-7}	1.9242×10^{-7}	0.0388
0.001	NI algorithm (4.4)	1.2247×10^{-3}	1.7320×10^{-3}	0.0179
	ET-DTZNN algorithm (4.3)	2.0412×10^{-6}	2.8867×10^{-6}	0.0302
	ZT-DTZNN algorithm (4.7)	2.7216×10^{-9}	3.8190×10^{-9}	0.0357
	DTZNN 6321 algorithm (4.6)	1.0887×10^{-9}	1.5396×10^{-9}	0.0372
0.0005	NI algorithm (4.4)	6.1237×10^{-4}	8.6603×10^{-4}	0.0178
	ET-DTZNN algorithm (4.3)	5.1031×10^{-7}	7.2169×10^{-7}	0.0303
	ZT-DTZNN algorithm (4.7)	3.4021×10^{-10}	4.8113×10^{-10}	0.0360
	DTZNN 6321 algorithm (4.6)	1.3608×10^{-10}	1.9245×10^{-10}	0.0371

residual errors synthesized by these four algorithms with $g = 0.001$ s are shown in Figure 4.1(e) and (f). Besides, more details that include maximal steady-state solution errors (MSSSEs), maximal steady-state residual errors (MSSREs), and average computing time per updating (ACTPU) data with respect to different values of sampling gap g are shown in Table 4.3.

Example 4.2 Let us consider a more complicated FMLP problem with X_{k+1} to be computed at each computational time interval $[t_k, t_{k+1}) \subset [0, 10]$ s, where

$$A_k = \begin{bmatrix} 2\sin(3t_k) & -\cos(3t_k) \\ \cos(3t_k) & 2\sin(3t_k) \\ 0.5\cos(3t_k) & \sin(3t_k) \\ \sin(3t_k) & -0.5\cos(3t_k) \end{bmatrix}.$$

The trajectories of the solution errors and residual errors synthesized by the aforementioned four different algorithms for the FMLP are displayed in Figure 4.2. As seen from Figure 4.2(a) and (b), with $g = 0.01$ s, the trajectories of the solution errors and residual errors are shown in standard coordinate, respectively. To facilitate observation and comparison of the numerical experimental results, the semilog coordinate needs to be used, and more details are shown in Figure 4.2(c)–(f). The effectiveness and superiority of the presented DTZNN 6321 algorithm (4.6) are validated again. Besides, more detailed MSSSEs, MSSREs, and ACTPU data are shown in Table 4.4.

From these numerical experimental results, we summarize the following important points, which further substantiate the theoretical results completely.

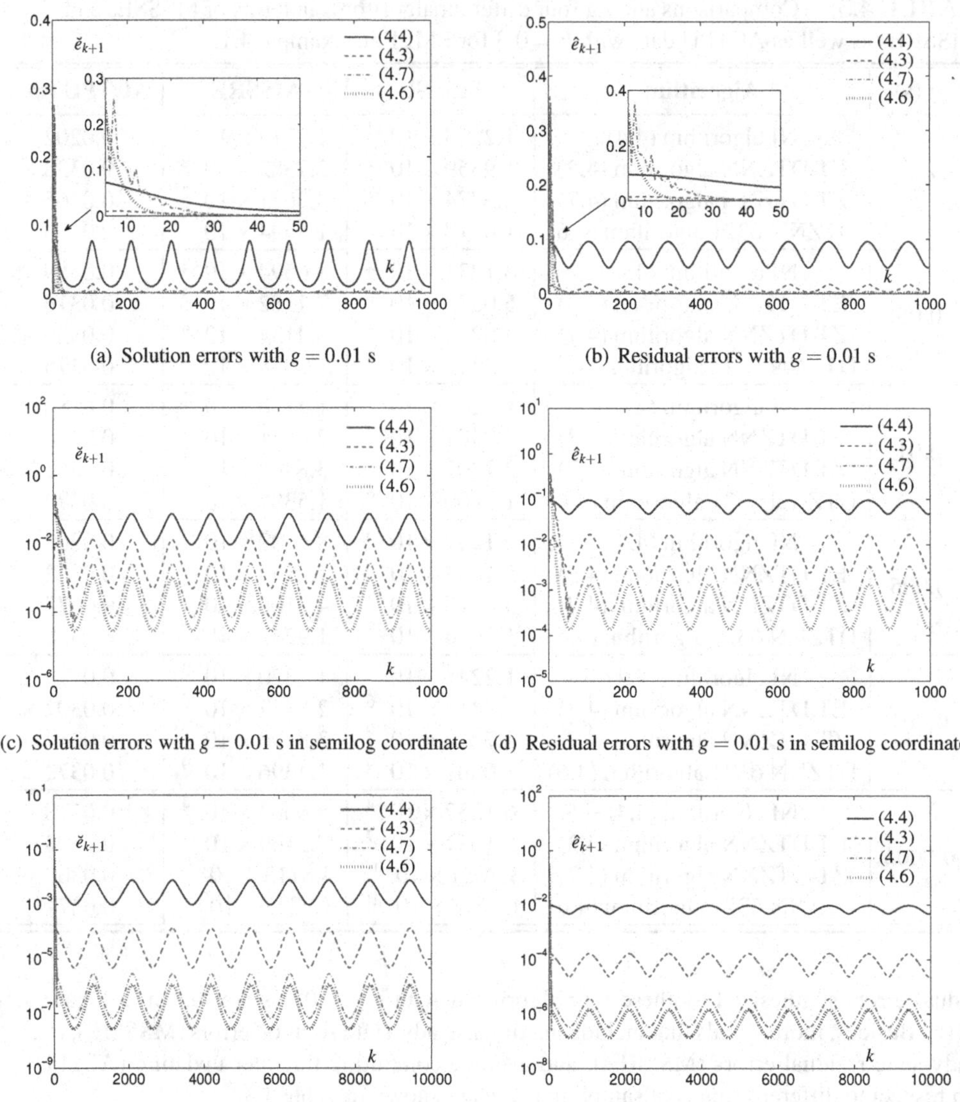

(a) Solution errors with $g = 0.01$ s

(b) Residual errors with $g = 0.01$ s

(c) Solution errors with $g = 0.01$ s in semilog coordinate

(d) Residual errors with $g = 0.01$ s in semilog coordinate

(e) Solution errors with $g = 0.001$ s in semilog coordinate

(f) Residual errors with $g = 0.001$ s in semilog coordinate

FIGURE 4.2: Trajectories of solution errors and residual errors synthesized by four different algorithms with $\hbar = 0.3$ for FMLP in Example 4.2.

1. The NI algorithm (4.4) does not use the time derivative information and its MSSSE and MSSRE change in $\mathscr{O}(g)$ patterns. For example, as shown in Table 4.3, the MSSSE and MSSRE synthesized by the NI algorithm (4.4) are of orders 10^{-2} and 10^{-3}, corresponding to 0.01 and 0.001, respectively.

2. Compared with the NI algorithm (4.4), the MSSSE and MSSRE synthesized by the ET-DTZNN algorithm (4.3) change in $\mathscr{O}(g^2)$ patterns. Note that the ET-DTZNN algorithm (4.3) utilizes time derivatives of time-dependent coefficients.

3. As a similar DTZNN algorithm, the ZT-DTZNN algorithm (4.7) utilizes time derivatives of time-dependent coefficients, and the MSSSE and MSSRE synthesized by the ZT-DTZNN algorithm (4.7) change in $\mathscr{O}(g^3)$ patterns. However, note that the MSSSE and MSSRE

TABLE 4.4: Comparisons among four different algorithms in terms of MSSSEs and MSSREs as well as ACTPU data with $\hbar = 0.3$ for FMLP in Example 4.2.

g (s)	Algorithm	MSSSE	MSSRE	ACTPU (ms)
0.05	NI algorithm (4.4)	4.5532×10^{-1}	5.9076×10^{-1}	0.0206
	ET-DTZNN algorithm (4.3)	4.3949×10^{-1}	6.7640×10^{-1}	0.0316
	ZT-DTZNN algorithm (4.7)	4.6388×10^{-1}	1.4412×10^{0}	0.0400
	DTZNN 6321 algorithm (4.6)	1.4077×10^{-1}	1.9328×10^{-1}	0.0431
0.01	NI algorithm(4.4)	7.6303×10^{-2}	9.5387×10^{-2}	0.0197
	ET-DTZNN algorithm (4.3)	1.3427×10^{-2}	1.6900×10^{-2}	0.0307
	ZT-DTZNN algorithm (4.7)	2.6820×10^{-3}	3.3898×10^{-3}	0.0368
	DTZNN 6321 algorithm (4.6)	1.0645×10^{-3}	1.3453×10^{-3}	0.0379
0.005	NI algorithm(4.4)	3.7998×10^{-2}	4.7498×10^{-2}	0.0184
	ET-DTZNN algorithm (4.3)	3.3295×10^{-3}	4.1691×10^{-3}	0.0309
	ZT-DTZNN algorithm (4.7)	3.5140×10^{-4}	4.4129×10^{-4}	0.0363
	DTZNN 6321 algorithm (4.6)	1.4055×10^{-4}	1.7640×10^{-4}	0.0376
0.001	NI algorithm(4.4)	7.5899×10^{-3}	9.4873×10^{-3}	0.0183
	ET-DTZNN algorithm (4.3)	1.3283×10^{-4}	1.6605×10^{-4}	0.0312
	ZT-DTZNN algorithm (4.7)	2.8805×10^{-6}	3.6015×10^{-6}	0.0361
	DTZNN 6321 algorithm (4.6)	1.1523×10^{-6}	1.4406×10^{-6}	0.0376
0.0005	NI algorithm(4.4)	3.7948×10^{-3}	4.7435×10^{-3}	0.0185
	ET-DTZNN algorithm (4.3)	3.3205×10^{-5}	4.1507×10^{-5}	0.0312
	ZT-DTZNN algorithm (4.7)	3.6039×10^{-7}	4.5052×10^{-7}	0.0366
	DTZNN 6321 algorithm (4.6)	1.4416×10^{-7}	1.8021×10^{-7}	0.0375

synthesized by the ZT-DTZNN algorithm (4.7) are approximately two times larger than those synthesized by the DTZNN 6321 algorithm (4.6).

4. As shown in numerical experimental results, the MSSSE and MSSRE synthesized by the DTZNN 6321 algorithm (4.6) change in $\mathscr{O}(g^3)$ patterns. Note that the DTZNN 6321 algorithm (4.6) also utilizes time derivatives of time-dependent coefficients. Under same conditions, this algorithm has much better performance compared with other algorithms. For example, as seen from Table 4.4, the MSSSE and MSSRE synthesized by the DTZNN 6321 algorithm (4.6) are of orders 10^{-1}, 10^{-4}, and 10^{-7}, corresponding to the values of g being 0.05, 0.005, and 0.0005 s, respectively. That is, the MSSSE or MSSRE synthesized by the DTZNN 6321 algorithm (4.6) reduces by 1000 times when the value of g decreases by ten times. Besides, the ACTPU data synthesized by the DTZNN 6321 algorithm (4.6) are just slightly larger than those synthesized by other DTZNN algorithms. In general, compared with the other algorithms, the DTZNN 6321 algorithm (4.6) achieves the most excellent computational precision.

4.5 Application to Manipulator

In this section, the presented DTZNN 6321 algorithm is implemented on a practical four-link redundant manipulator to further verify its physical realizability and effectiveness.

The hardware system of the practical four-link redundant manipulator is shown in Figure 4.3. Specifically speaking, Figure 4.3(a) shows the simplified model of the four-link redundant

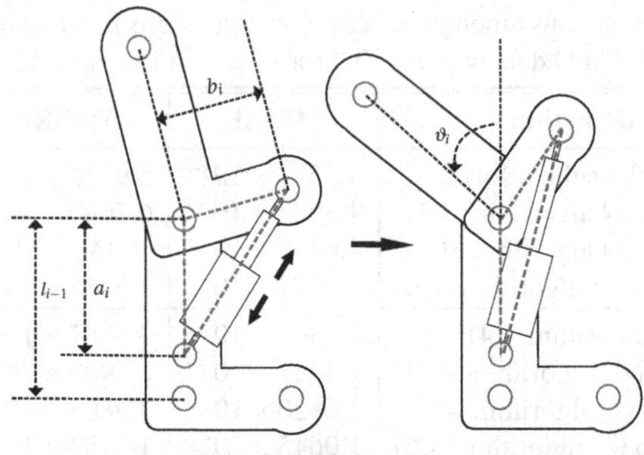

(a) Simplified model

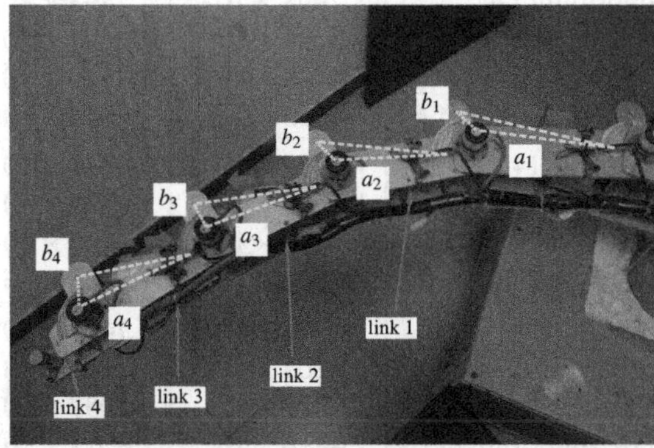

(b) Practical manipulator

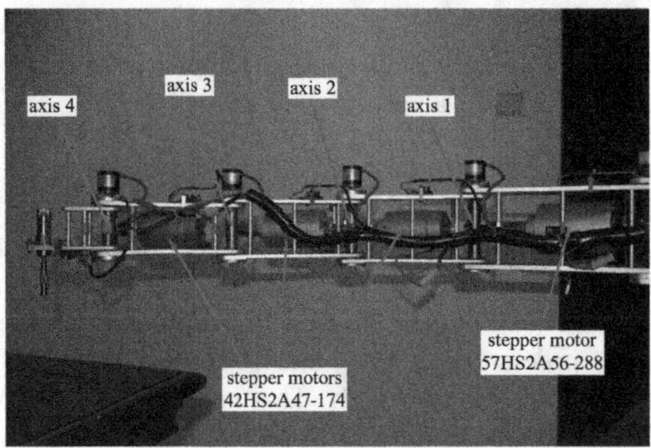

(c) Practical manipulator

FIGURE 4.3: Hardware system of four-link redundant manipulator. *Reproduced from Y. Shi, B. Qiu, D. Chen, J. Li, and Y. Zhang, Proposing and validation of a new four-point finite-difference formula with manipulator application, Figure 3, IEEE Transactions on Industrial Informatics, 14:1323–1333(4), 2018. ©IEEE 2017. With kind permission of IEEE.*

manipulator; Figure 4.3(b) and (c) shows the practical manipulator. Furthermore, for the convenience of theoretical analysis and presentation, the barycenter of each link can be seen in the physical midpoint of each link, and the detailed specifications of the four-link redundant manipulator and stepper motors are shown in Tables 4.5 and 4.6, respectively. Note that, in order to simply and effectively present the physical realizability and effectiveness of the DTZNN 6321 algorithm (4.6), although the four-link redundant manipulator has equipped encoders, in this chapter [93], these

TABLE 4.5: Physical specifications of four-link redundant manipulator.

Parameter	Meaning	Value	Parameter	Meaning	Value
a_1	Length of a_1	0.250 m	b_3	Length of b_3	0.080 m
a_2	Length of a_2	0.190 m	b_4	Length of b_4	0.080 m
a_3	Length of a_3	0.185 m	m_1	Mass of link 1	3.116 kg
a_4	Length of a_4	0.174 m	m_2	Mass of link 2	2.965 kg
l_1	Length of link 1	0.230 m	m_3	Mass of link 3	2.773 kg
l_2	Length of link 2	0.225 m	m_4	Mass of link 4	0.337 kg
l_3	Length of link 3	0.214 m	I_1	Inertia of link 1	0.041 kg·m^2
l_4	Length of link 4	0.103 m	I_2	Inertia of link 2	0.038 kg·m^2
b_1	Length of b_1	0.080 m	I_3	Inertia of link 3	0.032 kg·m^2
b_2	Length of b_2	0.080 m	I_4	Inertia of link 4	8.938×10^{-4} kg·m^2

encoders are not used in the presented control system. That is, the whole control system is an open-loop control system, and more in-depth research works (e.g., closed-loop control system) would be future research directions.

For such a manipulator control with the task duration T, at time instant $t_k \in [0,T]$, there is a corresponding relationship between the joint-angle vector $\vartheta_k = \left[\vartheta_{1,k}, \vartheta_{2,k}, \vartheta_{3,k}, \vartheta_{4,k}\right]^{\mathrm{T}} \in \mathbb{R}^4$ and the actual end-effector position vector $\mathbf{r}_{\mathrm{a},k} = \left[r_{\mathrm{X},k}, r_{\mathrm{Y},k}\right]^{\mathrm{T}} \in \mathbb{R}^2$. Then, we define this relationship as follows: $\mathbf{f}(\vartheta_k) = \mathbf{r}_{\mathrm{a},k}$, where $\mathbf{f}(\cdot)$ denotes the forward-kinematics mapping function with known structure and parameters for a given manipulator. Thus, guided by [27,98], the relationship between the joint-velocity vector $\dot{\vartheta}_k$ and the end-effector velocity vector $\dot{\mathbf{r}}_{\mathrm{a},k}$ can be obtained as $J(\vartheta_k)\dot{\vartheta}_k = \dot{\mathbf{r}}_{\mathrm{a},k}$, where the Jacobi matrix $J(\vartheta_k) = \partial\mathbf{f}(\vartheta_k)/\partial\vartheta_k$. In this chapter [93], we only consider the Jacobi matrix is of full row rank for all $t_k \in [0,T]$, which implies an FMRP problem. To track the end-effector desired path $\mathbf{r}_{\mathrm{d},k} \in \mathbb{R}^2$, we have $\dot{\vartheta}_k = J^{\dagger}(\vartheta_k)\dot{\mathbf{r}}_{\mathrm{d},k}$ by pseudoinverse-based method, where $J^{\dagger}(\vartheta_k)$ denotes the pseudoinverse of the time-dependent Jacobi matrix $J(\vartheta_k)$. Evidently, for the presented inverse-kinematics motion control problem, we need to obtain $J^{\dagger}(\vartheta_k)$ in real time. In addition, the disturbance and computational round-off errors always exist in practical application.

TABLE 4.6: Physical specifications of stepper motors.

Stepper motor	42HS2A47-174	57HS2A56-288
Holding torque	0.45 N·m	1.0 N·m
Rated current	1.7 A	2.8 A
Inductance	1.68 mH	1.2 mH
Resistance	2.5 Ohm	0.8 Ohm
Rotor inertia	68 g·cm^2	280 g·cm^2
Motor length	47 mm	56 mm
Motor weight	0.35 kg	0.68 kg

Algorithm 1: Conversion from ϑ and $\dot{\vartheta}$ to PPS
1. For all joints, set parameter $\sigma = 0.01\pi$, $\xi = 32$, and $s_i = 2.5 \times 10^{-3}$.
2. For $i = 1,2,3,4$ per sampling gap, compute $\mathrm{PPS}_i = (2\pi/(\sigma/\xi))v_i = 6400a_ib_i\dot{\vartheta}_i\cos\vartheta_i/\left(s_i\sqrt{a_i^2+b_i^2+2a_ib_i\sin\vartheta_i}\right)$.

Algorithm 2: Control procedure of four-link redundant manipulator
1. Initialize variables.
2. Set end-effector desired path $\mathbf{r}_{\mathrm{d},k}$.
3. Compute Jacobi matrix $J(\vartheta_k)$.
4. Compute $J^{\dagger}(\vartheta_{k+1})$ via DTZNN 6321 algorithm (4.6).
5. Compute $\dot{\vartheta}_k$ via $\dot{\vartheta}_k = J^{\dagger}(\vartheta_k)(\dot{\mathbf{r}}_{\mathrm{d},k} + \lambda(\mathbf{r}_{\mathrm{d},k} - \mathbf{f}(\vartheta_k)))$.
6. Compute ϑ_{k+1} via ZTD 6321 formula (4.5).
7. Compute PPS via Algorithm 1.
8. Send PPS and control motors.

To obtain a better tracking behavior, one approach [46] is to add a simple position error term $\lambda(\mathbf{r}_{\mathrm{d},k} - \mathbf{f}(\vartheta_k))$, where $\lambda = \rho/g > 0 \in \mathbb{R}$ denotes a gain parameter.

Therefore, we exploit the presented DTZNN 6321 algorithm (4.6) for solving $J^{\dagger}(\vartheta_{k+1})$ during the computational time interval $[t_k, t_{k+1}) \subset [0, T]$ s, and $J(\vartheta_k)$ is known. It means that, at every single time instant, we, on the basis of the present and previous data, compute the future or next result to control the four-link redundant manipulator.

Moreover, the stepper motors of the manipulator joints are driven by pulse commands transmitted from the host computer. Then, the computational joint variables (i.e., ϑ_k and $\dot{\vartheta}_k$) should be converted into the pulses per second (PPS) control signal. Inspired by [27], the corresponding algorithm description about conversion equations is shown in Algorithm 1. Specifically, the parameter σ denotes the stepping angle of each stepper motor; parameter ξ denotes the subdivision multiple; parameter s_i denotes the elongation rate of the ith push-rod (i.e., the elongation length when the motor moves a full turn); variable v_i denotes the rotation rate of the ith motor, which is computed as $v_i = a_ib_i\dot{\vartheta}_i\cos\vartheta_i/(s_i\sqrt{a_i^2+b_i^2+2a_ib_i\sin\vartheta_i}\,)$ with $i = 1,2,3,4$. In this chapter [93], for our manipulator, $\sigma = 0.01\pi$ rad/pulse, $\xi = 32$, $s_i = 2.5 \times 10^{-3}$ m/rot, the reduction gear ratio of all motors is 1, and a_i and b_i are shown in Table 4.5. In addition, the main control procedure of the four-link redundant manipulator is shown in Algorithm 2.

For simplicity and better understanding, firstly, the physical computation of the four-link redundant manipulator is carried out in MATLAB version 7.0 environment implemented on a personal computer equipped with Pentium E5300 at 2.6 GHz, 4.0-GB memory, and Microsoft Windows XP Professional operating system. For convenience and also for consistency, we choose the task duration $T = 20$ s, the sampling gap $g = 0.01$ s, the step length $\hbar = 0.3$, $\rho = 0.3$, and the initial joint-angle vector $\vartheta_0 = [\pi/12, \pi/12, \pi/12, \pi/12]^{\mathrm{T}}$ rad. The practical computational results are illustrated in Figures 4.4 and 4.5. As seen from Figure 4.4, when the end-effector tracking the square path, the joint-angle vector ϑ_{k+1} and the joint-velocity vector $\dot{\vartheta}_{k+1}$ are presented in Figure 4.4(a) and (b), respectively. In addition, the PPS of the four-link redundant manipulator, which can be used to drive the corresponding stepper motors, are presented in Figure 4.4(c). For a clearer presentation, the end-effector velocity and acceleration are denoted as $\dot{\mathbf{r}}_{\mathrm{a},k+1} = [\dot{r}_{\mathrm{X},k+1}, \dot{r}_{\mathrm{Y},k+1}]^{\mathrm{T}}$ and $\ddot{\mathbf{r}}_{\mathrm{a},k+1} = [\ddot{r}_{\mathrm{X},k+1}, \ddot{r}_{\mathrm{Y},k+1}]^{\mathrm{T}}$, respectively. The tracking error of the end-effector velocity is defined as

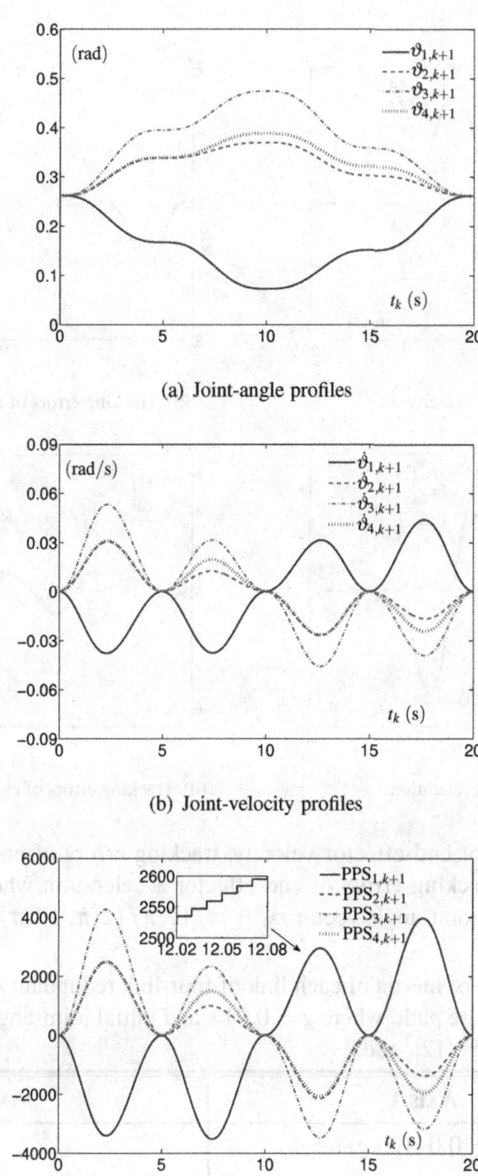

(a) Joint-angle profiles

(b) Joint-velocity profiles

(c) PPS for experiment

FIGURE 4.4: Motion generation of four-link redundant manipulator when end-effector tracking square path, where $g = 0.01$ s and initial joint-angle vector $\vartheta_0 = [\pi/12, \pi/12, \pi/12, \pi/12]^{\mathrm{T}}$ rad.

$\dot{\mathbf{e}}_{k+1} = \dot{\mathbf{r}}_{\mathrm{a},k+1} - \dot{\mathbf{r}}_{\mathrm{d},k+1}$. Furthermore, $\dot{e}_{\mathrm{X},k+1}$ and $\dot{e}_{\mathrm{Y},k+1}$ are the tracking errors of the end-effector velocity in the X-axis and Y-axis, respectively. Similarly, the tracking errors of the end-effector acceleration in the X-axis and Y-axis are defined as $\ddot{e}_{\mathrm{X},k+1}$ and $\ddot{e}_{\mathrm{Y},k+1}$, respectively. The tracking profiles are shown in Figure 4.5, and the detailed moment of inertia of the ith link relative to the jth axis of rotation is also presented in Table 4.7, with $i = 1,2,3,4$ and $j = 1,2,3,4$.

Secondly, the physics experiment is performed on a four-link redundant manipulator. The corresponding experimental result is shown in Figure 4.6. As shown in Figure 4.6(a), the snapshots at

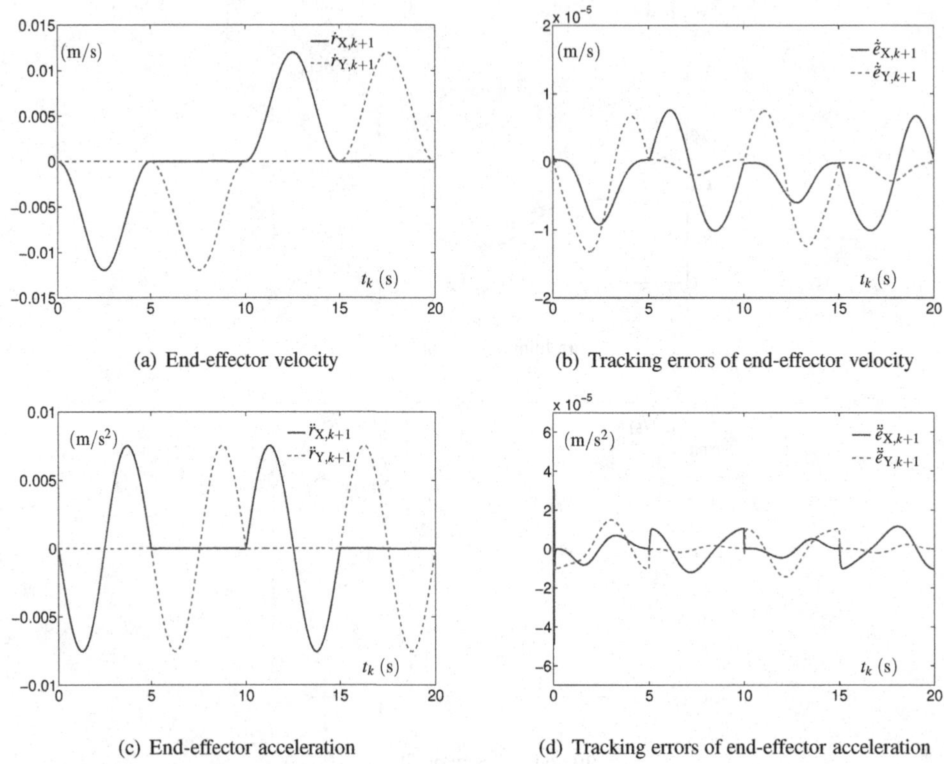

FIGURE 4.5: Trajectories of end-effector velocity, tracking errors of end-effector velocity, end-effector acceleration, and tracking errors of end-effector acceleration when tracking square path, where $g = 0.01$ s and initial joint-angle vector $\vartheta_0 = [\pi/12, \pi/12, \pi/12, \pi/12]^{\mathrm{T}}$ rad.

TABLE 4.7: Moment of inertia of each link of four-link redundant manipulator when end-effector tracking square path, where $g = 0.01$ s and initial joint-angle vector $\vartheta_0 = [\pi/12, \pi/12, \pi/12, \pi/12]^{\mathrm{T}}$ rad.

	Axis 1	**Axis 2**
Link 1	$I_{11,k} = 0.0412\ \mathrm{kg}\cdot\mathrm{m}^2$	–
Link 2	$0.5931\ \mathrm{kg}\cdot\mathrm{m}^2 \leqslant I_{21,k} \leqslant 0.6034\ \mathrm{kg}\cdot\mathrm{m}^2$	$I_{22,k} = 0.0375\ \mathrm{kg}\cdot\mathrm{m}^2$
Link 3	$1.1007\ \mathrm{kg}\cdot\mathrm{m}^2 \leqslant I_{31,k} \leqslant 1.1856\ \mathrm{kg}\cdot\mathrm{m}^2$	$0.2909\ \mathrm{kg}\cdot\mathrm{m}^2 \leqslant I_{32,k} \leqslant 0.3011\ \mathrm{kg}\cdot\mathrm{m}^2$
Link 4	$0.1666\ \mathrm{kg}\cdot\mathrm{m}^2 \leqslant I_{41,k} \leqslant 0.1868\ \mathrm{kg}\cdot\mathrm{m}^2$	$0.0742\ \mathrm{kg}\cdot\mathrm{m}^2 \leqslant I_{42,k} \leqslant 0.0787\ \mathrm{kg}\cdot\mathrm{m}^2$
	Axis 3	**Axis 4**
Link 1	–	–
Link 2	–	–
Link 3	$I_{33,k} = 0.0317\ \mathrm{kg}\cdot\mathrm{m}^2$	–
Link 4	$0.0232\ \mathrm{kg}\cdot\mathrm{m}^2 \leqslant I_{43,k} \leqslant 0.0235\ \mathrm{kg}\cdot\mathrm{m}^2$	$I_{44,k} = 8.9380 \times 10^{-4}\ \mathrm{kg}\cdot\mathrm{m}^2$

Note that "–" means that the item does not apply to the four-link redundant manipulator.

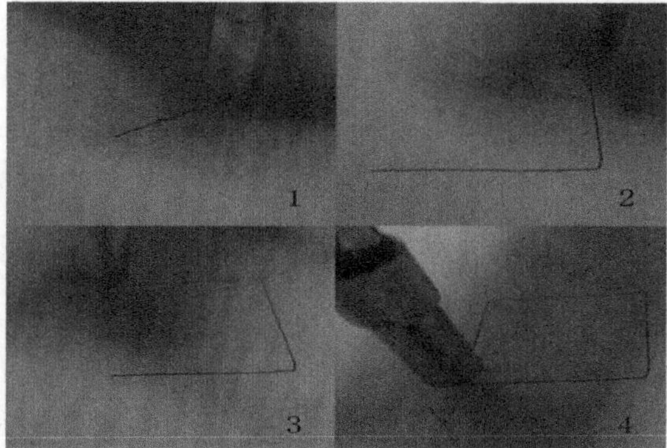

(a) Snapshots for square path tracking

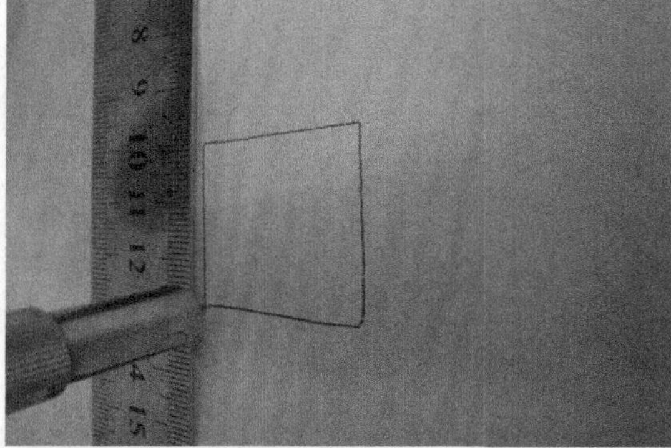

(b) Actual end-effector trajectory

(c) Actual end-effector trajectory

FIGURE 4.6: Snapshots of task execution and actual end-effector trajectory of planar four-link redundant manipulator. *Reproduced from Y. Shi, B. Qiu, D. Chen, J. Li, and Y. Zhang, Proposing and validation of a new four-point finite-difference formula with manipulator application, Figure 6, IEEE Transactions on Industrial Informatics, 14:1323–1333(4), 2018. ©IEEE 2017. With kind permission of IEEE.*

different time instant show that the end-effector tracks the square well. In addition, Figure 4.6(b) and (c) shows that the square is satisfactory.

In addition, for better showing the superiority of the presented DTZNN 6321 algorithm (4.6), guided by [22, 46], the ZT-DTZNN algorithm (4.7) is also applied to the control of the four-link re-

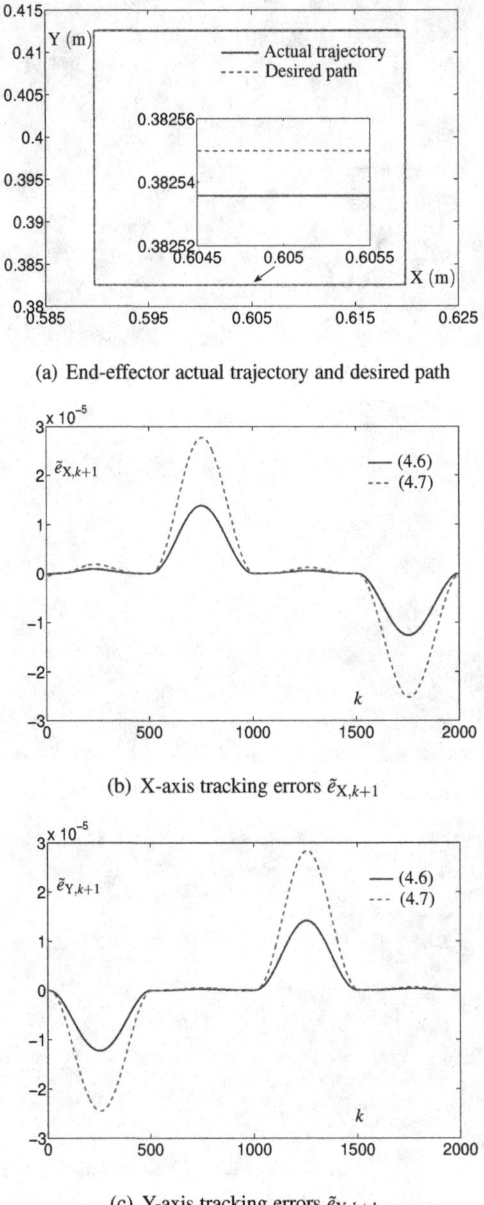

(a) End-effector actual trajectory and desired path

(b) X-axis tracking errors $\tilde{e}_{\mathrm{X},k+1}$

(c) Y-axis tracking errors $\tilde{e}_{\mathrm{Y},k+1}$

FIGURE 4.7: Trajectories of end-effector and tracking errors of end-effector positions when tracking square path, where $g = 0.01$ s and initial joint-angle vector $\vartheta_0 = [\pi/12, \pi/12, \pi/12, \pi/12]^{\mathrm{T}}$ rad.

dundant manipulator. On the basis of the above-mentioned parameters settings and guided by [46], the comparisons of practical computational results between the presented DTZNN 6321 algorithm (4.6) and the ZT-DTZNN algorithm (4.7) are shown in Figures 4.7 and 4.8. As seen from the figures, the tracking errors of end-effector positions, $\tilde{e}_{\mathrm{X},k+1}$ and $\tilde{e}_{\mathrm{Y},k+1}$, which are defined in a similar way to the velocity and acceleration, are all small enough, thereby implying that the end-effector trajectories of the four-link redundant manipulator are sufficiently close to the corresponding desired paths. However, evidently, the computational precision of the presented DTZNN 6321 algorithm

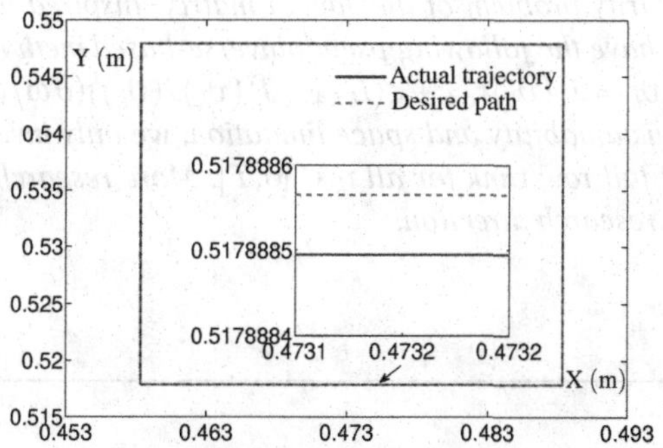

(a) End-effector actual trajectory and desired path

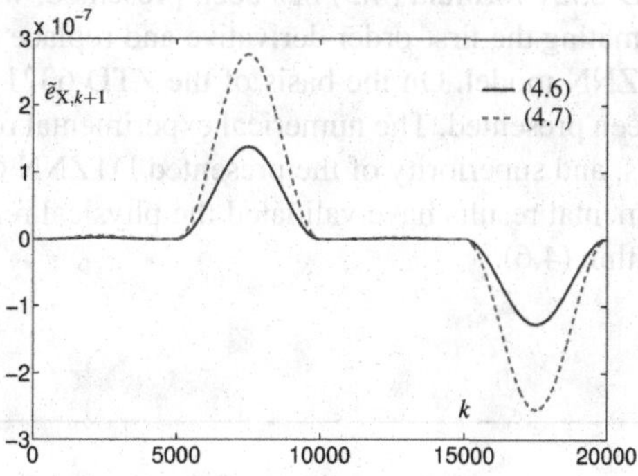

(b) X-axis tracking errors $\tilde{e}_{X,k+1}$

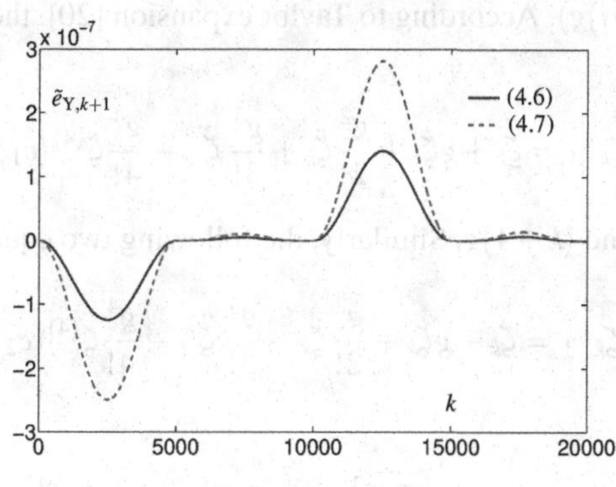

(c) Y-axis tracking errors $\tilde{e}_{Y,k+1}$

FIGURE 4.8: Trajectories of end-effector and tracking errors of end-effector positions when tracking square path, where $g = 0.001$ s and initial joint-angle vector $\vartheta_0 = [\pi/6, \pi/15, \pi/12, \pi/6]^{\mathrm{T}}$ rad.

(4.6) is higher than that of the ZT-DTZNN algorithm (4.7). That is, the presented DTZNN 6321 algorithm (4.6) achieves better computational performance than the ZT-DTZNN algorithm (4.7).

Remark 5 *When the Jacobi matrix is rank-deficient, the manipulator is in a singular state. Such a singular state is not desirable because the end-effector position vector cannot move in a certain direction, meaning that the manipulability is seriously deteriorated [99]. To effectively analyze the singularity problem, inspired by [99] and [100], the manipulability measure* ω *is given as* $\omega = \det\big(J(\vartheta_k)J^{\mathrm{T}}(\vartheta_k)\big)$, *where* $\det(\cdot)$ *denotes the determinant of a matrix. Therefore,* ω *can be* *used to monitor the singularity problem of the Jacobi matrix. Inspired by the gradient method in optimization [65, 101], we have the following pseudoinverse-based method for maximizing the manipulability measure* ω *as* $\dot{\vartheta}_k = J^{\dagger}(\vartheta_k)\dot{\mathbf{r}}_{\mathrm{d},k} + \varsigma(I_{4\times4} - J^{\dagger}(\vartheta_k)J(\vartheta_k))(\partial\omega/\partial\vartheta)$. *In this chapter [93], considering the research sustainability and space limitation, we only investigate the situation with the Jacobi matrix being of full row rank for all* $t_k \in [0,T]$. *More research works about singularity problem would be a future research direction.*

4.6 Chapter Summary

In this chapter, the ZTD 6321 formula (4.5) has been presented, which can enhance computational precision in approximating the first-order derivative and replace conventional formulas used in discretization of the CTZNN model. On the basis of the ZTD 6321 formula (4.5), the DTZNN 6321 algorithm (4.6) has been presented. The numerical experimental results have further validated the feasibility, effectiveness, and superiority of the presented DTZNN 6321 algorithm (4.6). In addition, the physical experimental results have validated the physical realizability and effectiveness of the DTZNN 6321 algorithm (4.6).

Appendix G: Analysis of DTZNN 6321 Algorithm (4.6)

Let ζ_{k+i} denote $\zeta((k+i)g)$. According to Taylor expansion [20], the following equation is further derived:

$$\zeta_{k+1} = \zeta_k + g\dot{\zeta}_k + \frac{g^2}{2!}\ddot{\zeta}_k + \frac{g^3}{3!}\dddot{\zeta}_k + \frac{g^4}{4!}\zeta^{(4)}(c_1), \tag{4.8}$$

where c_1 lies between kg and $(k+1)g$. Similarly, the following two equations are obtained:

$$\zeta_{k-1} = \zeta_k - g\dot{\zeta}_k + \frac{g^2}{2!}\ddot{\zeta}_k - \frac{g^3}{3!}\dddot{\zeta}_k + \frac{g^4}{4!}\zeta^{(4)}(c_2) \tag{4.9}$$

and

$$\zeta_{k-2} = \zeta_k - 2g\dot{\zeta}_k + \frac{(2g)^2}{2!}\ddot{\zeta}_k - \frac{(2g)^3}{3!}\dddot{\zeta}_k + \frac{(2g)^4}{4!}\zeta^{(4)}(c_3), \tag{4.10}$$

with c_2 and c_3 lying in the intervals $((k-1)g, kg)$ and $((k-2)g, kg)$, respectively. Besides, $\dot{\zeta}_k$, $\ddot{\zeta}_k$, $\dddot{\zeta}_k$, and $\zeta_k^{(4)}$ denote the first-order, second-order, third-order, and forth-order time derivatives. Let (4.8) multiply 3, let (4.9) multiply -1, and let (4.10) multiply $-1/2$. Then, add these results together. The following equation is thus obtained:

$$\dot{\zeta}_k = \frac{3}{5g}\zeta_{k+1} - \frac{3}{10g}\zeta_k - \frac{1}{5g}\zeta_{k-1} - \frac{1}{10g}\zeta_{k-2} + \varepsilon_1, \tag{4.11}$$

where ε_1 denotes the truncation error of (4.11), and we have

$$\varepsilon_1 \leq |\varepsilon_1| = \left|-\frac{4}{15}g^2\dddot{\zeta}_k + \mathcal{O}(g^3)\right| \leq \frac{4}{15}g^2 p + |\mathcal{O}(g^3)|$$

with $p = \left|\dddot{\zeta}_k\right|$ denoting a positive constant and $\mathscr{O}(g^3)$ absorbing the terms $(1/40)g^3\zeta^{(4)}(c_1)$, $(1/120)g^3\zeta^{(4)}(c_2)$, and $(1/15)g^3\zeta^{(4)}(c_3)$.

In addition, in [22], Jin and Zhang presented the Zhang–Taylor discretization formula as

$$\dot{\zeta}_k = \frac{1}{g}\zeta_{k+1} - \frac{3}{2g}\zeta_k + \frac{1}{g}\zeta_{k-1} - \frac{1}{2g}\zeta_{k-2} + \varepsilon_2. \tag{4.12}$$

Thus, we have

$$\varepsilon_2 \leq |\varepsilon_2| = \left|-\frac{2}{3}g^2\dddot{\zeta}_k + \mathscr{O}(g^3)\right| \leq \frac{2}{3}g^2 p + |\mathscr{O}(g^3)|$$

with $\mathscr{O}(g^3)$ absorbing the terms $(1/12)g^3\zeta^{(4)}(c_1)$, $(1/12)g^3\zeta^{(4)}(c_2)$, and $-(2/3)g^3\zeta^{(4)}(c_3)$.

As presented above, the term ε_1 denotes the truncation error of (4.11), and the term ε_2 denotes the truncation error of (4.12). In view of p denoting a positive constant, it is well-known that $(4/15)g^2p + |\mathscr{O}(g^3)|$ is the upper bound of the truncation error ε_1, and $(2/3)g^2p + |\mathscr{O}(g^3)|$ is the upper bound of the truncation error ε_2, and we have $\sup|\varepsilon_1| < \sup|\varepsilon_2|$. Specifically, the value of $\sup|\varepsilon_1|$ is approximately 40% of the value of $\sup|\varepsilon_2|$.

Moreover, considering the discretization of the CTZNN model, the presented numerical-differentiation formula (4.11) is adopted as a discretization tool. Then, the following equation is obtained:

$$X_{k+1} = -\frac{5}{3}gX_k\dot{A}_kX_k - \frac{5}{3}\hbar X_k(A_kX_k - I_{n\times n}) + \frac{1}{2}X_k + \frac{1}{3}X_{k-1} + \frac{1}{6}X_{k-2} + E_1,$$

where E_1 denotes the truncation error of the DTZNN 6321 algorithm. Therefore, we have $\sup\|E_1\|_{\mathrm{F}} = (4/9)g^3\|M\|_{\mathrm{F}} + \mathscr{O}(g^4)$, where M denotes a constant matrix. Besides, in [22], Jin and Zhang presented the ZT-DTZNN algorithm as

$$X_{k+1} = -gX_k\dot{A}_kX_k - \hbar X_k(A_kX_k - I_{n\times n}) + \frac{3}{2}X_k - X_{k-1} + \frac{1}{2}X_{k-2} + E_2,$$

where E_2 denotes the truncation error of the ZT-DTZNN algorithm. Therefore, we have $\sup\|E_2\|_{\mathrm{F}} = (2/3)g^3\|M\|_{\mathrm{F}} + \mathscr{O}(g^4)$. Evidently, $\sup\|E_1\|_{\mathrm{F}} < \sup\|E_2\|_{\mathrm{F}}$. It means that the computational precision of the presented DTZNN 6321 algorithm (4.6) is approximately enhanced by two times compared with the one presented in [22].

Part III

General Formulas and Applications of ZTD

Chapter 5

Future Constrained Nonlinear Optimization with $\mathscr{O}(g^3)$

Abstract

Previous works provide a few effective discretization formulas for continuous-time zeroing neural network (CTZNN), of which the precision is a square pattern. However, those formulas are separately developed via many relatively blind attempts. In this chapter, general Zhang time discretization (ZTD) formulas are developed via the idea of the second-order derivative elimination (SODE). All existing ZTD formulas in the previous works are included in the framework of the general ZTD formulas. The connections and differences of various general formulas are also discussed. Furthermore, the general ZTD formulas are used to solve future constrained nonlinear optimization (FCNO), and corresponding general discrete-time zeroing neural network (DTZNN) algorithms are developed. The general DTZNN algorithms have at least one parameter to adjust, thereby determining their zero-stability. Thus, the parameter domains are obtained by restricting the zero-stability. Finally, numerous comparative numerical experiments, including the motion control of PUMA560 manipulator, are provided to substantiate theoretical results and their superiority to conventional Euler forward formula.

5.1 Introduction

Time-dependent problem solving is increasingly desired with the development of industry [102–105], and increasing practical engineering problems should be viewed as discrete time-dependent problems, such as discrete time-dependent optimization [106, 107]. Most researchers focus on solving time-independent problems [20, 108] partially due to the low requirement of real-time computation. For example, many classical and effective methods, such as Gaussian elimination [109] and triangular factorization [110], were developed to solve time-independent linear systems. The problem of time-independent nonlinear systems can be perfectly solved by Newton–Raphson, bracketing, and secant methods [20].

Time-dependent problems could be considered the composition of infinite correlative time-independent problems compared with pure time-independent problems, and they have time-stream solutions. If conventional methods for time-independent problems are directly used to solve time-dependent problems, then the relevancy of solutions with time cannot be considered, leading to low precision denoted as $\mathscr{O}(g)$ [22, 111], where g denotes the sampling gap.

Recently, time-dependent problems have attracted the increasing attention of researchers, and many methods used for solving time-dependent problems have been developed [46, 112–115]. For example, interesting prediction-correction algorithms were developed in [112] to track the solutions of time-dependent constrained optimization problems. Specifically, a prediction step is first

DOI: 10.1201/9781003497783-5

TABLE 5.1: Existing effective ZTD formulas for derivative approximation.

Paper	Formula expression
[106]	$\dot{\zeta}_k = \frac{5}{8g}\zeta_{k+1} - \frac{3}{8g}\zeta_k - \frac{1}{8g}\zeta_{k-1} - \frac{1}{8g}\zeta_{k-2} + \mathcal{O}(g^2)$
[107]	$\dot{\zeta}_k = \frac{26}{30g}\zeta_{k+1} - \frac{33}{30g}\zeta_k + \frac{18}{30g}\zeta_{k-1} - \frac{11}{30g}\zeta_{k-2} + \mathcal{O}(g^2)$
[70]	$\dot{\zeta}_k = \frac{1}{g}\zeta_{k+1} - \frac{3}{2g}\zeta_k + \frac{1}{g}\zeta_{k-1} - \frac{1}{2g}\zeta_{k-2} + \mathcal{O}(g^2)$
[72]	$\dot{\zeta}_k = \frac{3}{5g}\zeta_{k+1} - \frac{3}{10g}\zeta_k - \frac{1}{5g}\zeta_{k-1} - \frac{1}{10g}\zeta_{k-2} + \mathcal{O}(g^2)$
[127]	$\dot{\zeta}_k = \frac{22}{30g}\zeta_{k+1} - \frac{21}{30g}\zeta_k + \frac{6}{30g}\zeta_{k-1} - \frac{7}{30g}\zeta_{k-2} + \mathcal{O}(g^2)$

conducted to obtain a predictive result and solution at a specific time instant, and then the result is corrected to find the theoretical solution by at least one correction step. In [114], the asymptotic stability of discrete-time linear time-dependent systems was analyzed with the difference between nonuniform exponential stability and uniform exponential stability being revealed and illustrated by numerical experiments.

Zeroing neural network (ZNN) is a great alternative to solve time-dependent problems [43]. It is a special class of recurrent neural networks (RNNs) [46, 116–118], which originates from Hopfield neural network [119, 120]. ZNN is developed to solve time-dependent problems and fully utilizes the information of time derivative and correlation of solutions of adjacent moments. ZNN has been used to solve various problems in science and engineering fields, such as manipulators [98, 121–123], control [124, 125], and time-dependent mathematical operations [22, 46, 106], ever since its development.

ZNN has the capability of predicting future solutions on the basis of current and past information compared with other methods for time-dependent problems. This characteristic of ZNN satisfies the requirement of strictly real-time computation for time-dependent problems. That is, the solution at this instant should already be obtained when a time instant arrives; thus, practical tasks can be completed in real time. This superior performance of strictly real-time computation originates from an effective discretization of continuous-time ZNN (CTZNN). Therefore, discretization formulas are the key points to the solution of discrete time-dependent problems (also termed as future problems).

Effective discretization formulas are different from common numerical-differentiation formulas existing in numerical ordinary differential equation (ODE) literature, and these discretization formulas must satisfy strict conditions. First, these formulas must be one-step-ahead, i.e., discretizing $\dot{\zeta}_k$ by ζ_{k+1}, ζ_k, ζ_{k-1}, and $\zeta_{k-2}\cdots$, where k denotes the updating index. Second, one-step-ahead formulas do not necessarily lead to zero-stable algorithms. In [51], a series of one-step-ahead Lagrange numerical-differentiation formulas that do not lead to stable algorithms were presented. To the best of the authors' knowledge, only a few discretization formulas [70, 72, 106, 107, 126, 127] are available. Specifically, the Euler forward formula is the first operational formula and also the simplest one that has been developed and widely applied for decades [126]. The formula is

$$\dot{\zeta}_k = \frac{\zeta_{k+1} - \zeta_k}{g} + \mathcal{O}(g). \tag{5.1}$$

Zhang–Taylor discretization formula, which is a special Zhang time discretization (ZTD) formula, is considered the second operational formula that has been developed and applied by Zhang *et al* [70]. Then, a series of ZTD formulas were developed; these ZTD formulas are listed in Table 5.1.

These ZTD formulas are isolated and developed via many relatively blind attempts. Before this work, it was difficult to know how many ZTD formulas exist, not to mention the optimal formula with respect to stability. Besides, all existing ZTD formulas have utilized four instants, and how to develop ZTD formulas with more instants was unknown. In this work, general ZTD formulas, including general three-step ZTD (3S-ZTD) and general four-step ZTD (4S-ZTD) formulas, are developed for CTZNN via the idea of the second-order derivative elimination (SODE). On the basis of the developed general ZTD formulas, we find infinite ZTD formulas. Among infinite ZTD formulas, we can select different formulas in different situations. For example, formulas with lower truncation errors can be employed in situations where high precision is much desired. The ZTD formulas in Table 5.1 are included in the framework of the general ZTD formulas. Besides, the optimal ZTD formulas with respect to the stability and ZTD formulas with more instants are also found. The study of the general ZTD formulas makes the discetization topic more convincing and complete. Furthermore, the general ZTD formulas are used to solve future constrained nonlinear optimization (FCNO), and the corresponding general discrete-time ZNN (DTZNN) algorithms are developed.

5.2 Problem Formulation and CTZNN Model

The problem of FCNO [106] is formulated as below with $\mathbf{x}_{k+1}$ to be obtained at each computational time interval $[t_k, t_{k+1}) = [kg, (k+1)g) \subset [t_{\text{ini}}, t_{\text{fin}}] \subset [0, +\infty)$:

$$\begin{aligned} &\min \ \varphi(\mathbf{x}_{k+1}, t_{k+1}) \\ &\text{s. t. } A_{k+1}\mathbf{x}_{k+1} = \mathbf{b}_{k+1}, \end{aligned} \tag{5.2}$$

where t_{ini} and t_{fin} represent the initial and final time instants, respectively. Besides, $\mathbf{x}_{k+1} \in \mathbb{R}^n$, $A_{k+1} \in \mathbb{R}^{m\times n}$, and $\mathbf{b}_{k+1} \in \mathbb{R}^m$ are supposed to be generated from corresponding smoothly time-dependent signals by sampling at time instant $t_{k+1} = (k+1)g$. The object function $\varphi(\cdot,\cdot): \mathbb{R}^n \times [0,+\infty) \to \mathbb{R}$ is time-dependent, nonlinear, and convex with respect to $\mathbf{x}$, and the rank of $A_{k+1} \in \mathbb{R}^{m\times n}$ is constantly equal to m with $m < n$. In addition, the matrix A and the vector $\mathbf{b}$ are supposed to have the bounded third-order derivatives, and the function φ is supposed to have the bounded fourth-order partial derivative. Thus, the problem (5.2) is a discrete time-dependent convex problem, and any local optimum of this convex problem is constantly global.

The future information of optimization is unknown; thus, the future solution $\mathbf{x}_{k+1}$ must be predicted before the time instant t_{k+1} to satisfy the strictly real-time computation. On the basis of the previous work [106], the problem (5.2) is converted into a continuous-time form, and the corresponding CTZNN model is obtained as

$$\dot{\mathbf{y}}(t) = -H^{-1}(\mathbf{y}(t),t)\left(\eta \mathbf{h}(\mathbf{y}(t),t) + \dot{\mathbf{h}}_t(\mathbf{y}(t),t)\right), \tag{5.3}$$

with $\mathbf{y}(t) = \left[\mathbf{x}^{\mathrm{T}}(t), \mathbf{l}^{\mathrm{T}}(t)\right]^{\mathrm{T}} \in \mathbb{R}^{n+m}$. Moreover, $\mathbf{l}^{\mathrm{T}}(t) \in \mathbb{R}^m$ is the Lagrange-multiplier vector, and $\mathbf{h}(\mathbf{y}(t),t)$ is defined as

$$\mathbf{h}(\mathbf{y}(t),t) = \begin{bmatrix} \dfrac{\partial \varphi(\mathbf{x}(t),t)}{\partial \mathbf{x}} + A^{\mathrm{T}}(t)\mathbf{l}(t) \\ A(t)\mathbf{x}(t) - \mathbf{b}(t) \end{bmatrix} \in \mathbb{R}^{n+m}.$$

$H(\mathbf{y}(t),t)$ is defined as

$$H(\mathbf{y}(t),t) = \begin{bmatrix} \dfrac{\partial \varphi^2(\mathbf{x}(t),t)}{\partial \mathbf{x}\partial \mathbf{x}^{\mathrm{T}}} & A^{\mathrm{T}}(t) \\ A(t) & \mathbf{0} \end{bmatrix}.$$

$\dot{\mathbf{h}}_t(\mathbf{y}(t),t)$ is the partial derivative of $\mathbf{h}(\mathbf{y}(t),t)$ with respect to t, which is defined as

$$\dot{\mathbf{h}}_t(\mathbf{y}(t),t) = \frac{\partial \mathbf{h}(\mathbf{y}(t),t)}{\partial t}.$$

The ZNN design parameter $\eta > 0$ should be set as large as the hardware permits or set appropriately for simulative or experimental purposes.

5.3 General ZTD Formulas

In this section, general ZTD formulas are developed for the first-order derivative approximation. Specifically, the general 3S-ZTD formula is developed via the idea of the SODE with Taylor expansions of three instants. Similarly, the general 3S-ZTD formula is developed via the idea of the SODE with Taylor expansions of four instants. Moreover, the general ZTD formulas with additional parameters can be developed by using the Taylor expansions of further instants.

5.3.1 General 3S-ZTD formula

The general 3S-ZTD formula, which uses four instants, is developed by the following theorem.

Theorem 19 *With the sufficiently small sampling gap $g \in (0,1)$, let $\mathscr{O}(g^2)$ denote the error (especially, the truncation error) positively or negatively proportional to g^2, i.e., of the order of g^2. Suppose that $\zeta(t)$ is sufficiently smooth. With $\zeta_{k+1} = \zeta(t_{k+1}) = \zeta((k+1)g)$, the general 3S-ZTD formula is developed as below:*

$$\dot{\zeta}_k = \frac{2a}{(3a-1)g}\zeta_{k+1} - \frac{3a+3}{2(3a-1)g}\zeta_k + \frac{2}{(3a-1)g}\zeta_{k-1} + \frac{-1-a}{2(3a-1)g}\zeta_{k-2} + \mathscr{O}(g^2), \tag{5.4}$$

where the parameter a is not equal to 0 or 1/3.

Proof. According to Taylor expansion [20], the following equations are obtained:

$$\zeta_{k+1} = \zeta_k + g\dot{\zeta}_k + \frac{g^2}{2}\ddot{\zeta}_k + \frac{g^3}{6}\dddot{\zeta}(c_1), \tag{5.5}$$

$$\zeta_{k-1} = \zeta_k - g\dot{\zeta}_k + \frac{g^2}{2}\ddot{\zeta}_k - \frac{g^3}{6}\dddot{\zeta}(c_2), \tag{5.6}$$

and

$$\zeta_{k-2} = \zeta_k - 2g\dot{\zeta}_k + 2g^2\ddot{\zeta}_k - \frac{4g^3}{3}\dddot{\zeta}(c_2), \tag{5.7}$$

where $\ddot{\zeta}_k$ and $\dddot{\zeta}_k$ denote the second-order and third-order time derivatives of $\zeta(t)$ with respect to t at time instant t_k, respectively; c_1, c_2, and c_3 lie in (t_k, t_{k+1}), (t_{k-1}, t_k), and (t_{k-2}, t_k), correspondingly. To obtain the first-order derivative approximation, we aim to eliminate the second-order derivative. Thus, the above equations are rewritten as

$$\ddot{\zeta}_k = \frac{2}{g^2}\zeta_{k+1} - \frac{2}{g^2}\zeta_k - \frac{2}{g}\dot{\zeta}_k - \frac{g}{3}\dddot{\zeta}(c_1), \tag{5.8}$$

$$\ddot{\zeta}_k = \frac{2}{g^2}\zeta_{k-1} - \frac{2}{g^2}\zeta_k + \frac{2}{g}\dot{\zeta}_k + \frac{g}{3}\dddot{\zeta}(c_2), \tag{5.9}$$

and

$$\ddot{\zeta}_k = \frac{1}{2g^2}\zeta_{k-2} - \frac{1}{2g^2}\zeta_k + \frac{1}{g}\dot{\zeta}_k + \frac{2g}{3}\dddot{\zeta}(c_3). \tag{5.10}$$

To obtain a general form, (5.8) is multiplied by an arbitrary constant $a \neq 0$. To eliminate the terms of the second-order derivative, let (5.10) multiply $(-1-a)$ and add these results together. Then, we obtain

$$\frac{2a}{g^2}\zeta_{k+1} - \frac{3a+3}{2g^2}\zeta_k + \frac{2}{g^2}\zeta_{k-1} + \frac{-1-a}{2g^2}\zeta_{k-2} + \frac{-3a+1}{g}\dot{\zeta}_k - \frac{ag}{3}\dddot{\zeta}(c_1) + \frac{g}{3}\dddot{\zeta}(c_2) + \frac{2(-1-a)g}{3}\dddot{\zeta}(c_3) = 0, \tag{5.11}$$

and then the following equation with $a \neq 1/3$ is obtained:

$$\dot{\zeta}_k = \frac{2a}{(3a-1)g}\zeta_{k+1} - \frac{3a+3}{2(3a-1)g}\zeta_k + \frac{2}{(3a-1)g}\zeta_{k-1} + \frac{-1-a}{2(3a-1)g}\zeta_{k-2} - \frac{ag^2}{3(3a-1)}\dddot{\zeta}(c_1) + \frac{g^2}{3(3a-1)}\dddot{\zeta}(c_2) + \frac{2(-1-a)g^2}{3(3a-1)}\dddot{\zeta}(c_3).$$

The terms of $-(ag^2)/(3(3a-1))\dddot{\zeta}(c_1) + (g^2)/(3(3a-1))\dddot{\zeta}(c_2) + (2(-1-a)g^2)/(3(3a-1))\dddot{\zeta}(c_3)$ are absorbed into $\mathscr{O}(g^2)$, which is the truncation error. Then, the general 3S-ZTD formula (5.4) is obtained. The proof is thus completed. □

Note that the form of the general 3S-ZTD formula is not unique. For example, if we make (5.8) multiply the constant 1 and make (5.9) multiply an arbitrary constant a, another form of general 3S-ZTD formula will be obtained. However, different forms of the general 3S-ZTD formula are the same essentially because they can be obtained interchangeably by adjusting the parameter a.

5.3.2 General 4S-ZTD formula

The Taylor expansion of ζ_{k-3} is utilized to obtain the general 4S-ZTD formula, which is developed by the following theorem.

Theorem 20 *With the sufficiently small sampling gap $g \in (0,1)$, let $\mathscr{O}(g^2)$ denote the error (especially, the truncation error) positively or negatively proportional to g^2, i.e., of the order of g^2. Suppose that $\zeta(t)$ is sufficiently smooth. With $\zeta_{k+1} = \zeta(t_{k+1}) = \zeta((k+1)g)$, the general 4S-ZTD formula is developed as below:*

$$\dot{\zeta}_k = \frac{-6}{(4b_1+b_2-8)g}\zeta_{k+1} + \frac{32b_1+32+5b_2}{6(4b_1+b_2-8)g}\zeta_k - \frac{6b_1}{(4b_1+b_2-8)g}\zeta_{k-1} - \frac{3b_2}{2(4b_1+b_2-8)g}\zeta_{k-2} + \frac{2(1+b_1+b_2)}{3(4b_1+b_2-8)g}\zeta_{k-3} + \mathscr{O}(g^2), \tag{5.12}$$

where $4b_1+b_2-8 \neq 0$.

Proof. On the basis of the Taylor expansions [20] of ζ_{k+1}, ζ_{k-1}, and ζ_{k-2}, the equations (5.5), (5.6), and (5.7) are obtained. Similarly, the Taylor expansion of ζ_{k-3} is

$$\zeta_{k-3} = \zeta_k - 3g\dot{\zeta}_k + \frac{9g^2}{2}\ddot{\zeta}_k - \frac{9g^3}{2}\dddot{\zeta}(c_4),$$

which is rewritten as

$$\ddot{\zeta}_k = \frac{2}{9g^2}\zeta_{k-3} - \frac{2}{9g^2}\zeta_k + \frac{2}{3g}\dot{\zeta}_k + g\dddot{\zeta}(c_4), \tag{5.13}$$

where c_4 lies in (t_{k-3}, t_k). Let (5.9) multiply an arbitrary constant b_1, and let (5.10) multiply an arbitrary constant b_2. Via the idea of the SODE, let (5.13) multiply $(-1-b_1-b_2)$ and add these results together. Then, the following equation is obtained:

$$\frac{2}{g^2}\zeta_{k+1} - \frac{32b_1+32+5b_2}{18g^2}\zeta_k + \frac{2b_1}{g^2}\zeta_{k-1} + \frac{b_2}{2g^2}\zeta_{k-2} - \frac{2(1+b_1+b_2)}{9g^2}\zeta_{k-3} + \frac{4b_1+b_2-8}{3g}\dot{\zeta}_k - \frac{g}{3}\dddot{\zeta}(c_1) + \frac{b_1 g}{3}\dddot{\zeta}(c_2) + \frac{2b_2 g}{3}\dddot{\zeta}(c_3) - (1+b_1+b_2)g\dddot{\zeta}(c_4) = 0,$$

which is rewritten as below with $4b_1+b_2-8\neq 0$:

$$\frac{6}{(4b_1+b_2-8)g}\zeta_{k+1}-\frac{32b_1+32+5b_2}{6(4b_1+b_2-8)g}\zeta_k+\frac{6b_1}{(4b_1+b_2-8)g}\zeta_{k-1}+\frac{3b_2}{2(4b_1+b_2-8)g}\zeta_{k-2}$$
$$-\frac{2(1+b_1+b_2)}{3(4b_1+b_2-8)g}\zeta_{k-3}+\dot{\zeta}_k-\frac{g^2}{4b_1+b_2-8}\dddot{\zeta}(c_1)+\frac{b_1g^2}{4b_1+b_2-8}\dddot{\zeta}(c_2)+\frac{2b_2g^2}{4b_1+b_2-8}\dddot{\zeta}(c_3)$$
$$-\frac{3(1+b_1+b_2)g^2}{4b_1+b_2-8}\dddot{\zeta}(c_4)=0.$$

By absorbing the truncation error into $\mathscr{O}(g^2)$, the general 4S-ZTD formula (5.12) is obtained. The proof is thus completed. □

The SODE with Taylor expansions of three instants leads to the general 3S-ZTD formula (5.4), and the SODE with Taylor expansions of four instants leads to the general 4S-ZTD formula (5.12) from the proof processes of Theorems 19 and 20. Similarly, the SODE with Taylor expansions of additional instants leads to the general ZTD formula with additional parameters. Moreover, the connections and differences of these general ZTD formulas are discussed in the following remark.

Remark 6 *We focus on the general ZTD formulas (5.4) and (5.12). If $b_1+b_2+1=0$ holds, then the term $2\zeta_{k-3}(1+b_1+b_2)/(3(4b_1+b_2-8)g)$ in (5.12) becomes 0 and the general 4S-ZTD formula (5.12) is simplified as*

$$\dot{\zeta}_k=\frac{-2}{(b_1-3)g}\zeta_{k+1}+\frac{3b_1+3}{2(b_1-3)g}\zeta_k-\frac{2b_1}{(b_1-3)g}\zeta_{k-1}+\frac{b_1+1}{2(b_1-3)g}\zeta_{k-2}+\mathscr{O}(g^2).$$

Then, the parameter a is defined as $1/b_1$, and the following formula is obtained:

$$\dot{\zeta}_k=\frac{2a}{(3a-1)g}\zeta_{k+1}-\frac{3a+3}{2(3a-1)g}\zeta_k+\frac{2}{(3a-1)g}\zeta_{k-1}+\frac{-1-a}{2(3a-1)g}\zeta_{k-2}+\mathscr{O}(g^2),$$

which is exactly the general 3S-ZTD formula (5.4). From the above discussion, the general 3S-ZTD formula (5.4) is a special case of the general 4S-ZTD formula (5.12). Similarly, the general 4S-ZTD formula (5.12) is a special case of the general ZTD formula with additional parameters. However, Taylor expansions of additional instants lead to large upper bounds of truncation errors. Thus, the general 3S-ZTD formula is generally superior to formulas with at least two parameters. Moreover, general ZTD formulas with one (generally using four instants), two (generally using five instants), and more parameters have the truncation error with a square pattern, i.e., the precision of all mentioned general formulas is $\mathscr{O}(g^2)$. This finding indicates that the utilization of additional instants does not necessarily lead to high-precision formulas, which may be inconsistent with intuitional guessing.

5.4 DTZNN Algorithms

In this section, the general ZTD formulas are used for discretizing the CTZNN model (5.3) and thus the corresponding general DTZNN algorithms are developed for solving the FCNO (5.2).

5.4.1 General 3S-DTZNN algorithm

Let (5.4) discretize the CTZNN model (5.3). Then, the following equation is obtained:

$$\mathbf{y}_{k+1}=-\frac{3a-1}{2a}(H^{-1}(\mathbf{y}_k,t_k)(\hbar\mathbf{h}(\mathbf{y}_k,t_k)+g\dot{\mathbf{h}}_t(\mathbf{y}_k,t_k)))+\frac{3a+3}{4a}\mathbf{y}_k-\frac{1}{a}\mathbf{y}_{k-1}+\frac{a+1}{4a}\mathbf{y}_{k-2}+\mathbf{O}(g^3),$$

where $\hbar = g\eta$ represents the step length. Omitting the truncation error term yields the general three-step DTZNN (3S-DTZNN) algorithm as below:

$$\mathbf{y}_{k+1} \doteq -\frac{3a-1}{2a}\left(H^{-1}(\mathbf{y}_k,t_k)\left(\hbar\mathbf{h}(\mathbf{y}_k,t_k)+g\dot{\mathbf{h}}_t(\mathbf{y}_k,t_k)\right)\right)+\frac{3a+3}{4a}\mathbf{y}_k-\frac{1}{a}\mathbf{y}_{k-1}+\frac{a+1}{4a}\mathbf{y}_{k-2}, \quad (5.14)$$

where $\doteq$ denotes the computational assignment operator.

The effective domain of the parameter a in the general 3S-DTZNN algorithm (5.14) is analyzed and obtained by the following theorem to guarantee the effectiveness of the general 3S-DTZNN algorithm (5.14).

Theorem 21 *Suppose that the matrix $H(\mathbf{y}_k,t_k)$ is always nonsingular. With the sufficiently small sampling gap $g \in (0,1)$, let $\mathbf{O}(g^3)$ denote the error (especially, the truncation error) with each element being $\mathscr{O}^3$. The general 3S-DTZNN algorithm (5.14) is zero-stable, consistent, and convergent, which converges with the order of truncation error being $\mathbf{O}(g^3)$, when $a > 1/3$ or $a < -1$.*

Proof. According to Definition 2 in Chapter 1, the characteristic polynomial of the general 3S-DTZNN algorithm (5.14) is expressed as

$$\Gamma_3(\iota) = 2a\iota^3 - \frac{3a+3}{2}\iota^2 + 2\iota + \frac{-1-a}{2} = \frac{\iota-1}{2}(4a\iota^2+(a-3)\iota+a+1).$$

Let $\Gamma_3(\iota) = 0$ and three roots exist, i.e.,

$$\iota_1 = 1 \text{ and } \iota_{2,3} = \frac{3-a\pm\sqrt{(-3a+1)(5a+9)}}{8a}.$$

Let $|\iota_2| < 1$ and $|\iota_3| < 1$ with $|\cdot|$ denoting the modular arithmetic. The effective domain for the zero-stability is obtained as $a < -1$ or $a > 1/3$.

Besides, the truncation error of the general 3S-DTZNN algorithm (5.14) is $\mathbf{O}(g^3)$ from the algorithm derive process. Thus, the general 3S-DTZNN algorithm (5.14) is consistent. On the basis of Definitions 3 and 4 in Chapter 1, the general 3S-DTZNN algorithm (5.14) converges with the order of truncation error being $\mathbf{O}(g^3)$. The proof is thus completed. □

Furthermore, the maximal steady-state residual error (MSSRE) synthesized by the general 3S-DTZNN algorithm (5.14) for solving the FCNO (5.2) is analyzed by the ensuing theorem. Note that the residual error is defined as $\hat{e}_{k+1} = \|\mathbf{h}(\mathbf{y}_{k+1},t_{k+1})\|_2$ for the FCNO (5.2) in this chapter [128], where $\|\cdot\|_2$ denotes the 2-norm of a vector.

Theorem 22 *Consider the FCNO (5.2). Suppose that the matrix $H(\mathbf{y}_k,t_k)$ is always nonsingular and uniformly norm bounded. With the sufficiently small sampling gap $g \in (0,1)$, the MSSRE $\lim_{k\to+\infty}\sup\hat{e}_{k+1}$ synthesized by the general 3S-DTZNN algorithm (5.14) with an effective parameter a is $\mathscr{O}(g^3)$.*

Proof. Let $\mathbf{y}^*_{k+1}$ be the theoretical solution, and we have $\mathbf{y}_{k+1} = \mathbf{y}^*_{k+1} + \mathbf{O}(g^3)$ from Definition 3 in Chapter 1 and Theorem 21 when k is sufficiently large. Thus, the following is derived with $H(\mathbf{y}^*_{k+1},t_{k+1}) = \partial\mathbf{h}(\mathbf{y}^*_{k+1},t_{k+1})/\partial\mathbf{y}^*_{k+1}$:

$$\begin{aligned}
&\lim_{k\to+\infty}\|\mathbf{h}(\mathbf{y}_{k+1},t_{k+1})\|_2\\
&=\lim_{k\to+\infty}\|\mathbf{h}(\mathbf{y}^*_{k+1}+\mathbf{O}(g^3),t_{k+1})\|_2\\
&=\lim_{k\to+\infty}\|\mathbf{h}(\mathbf{y}^*_{k+1})+H(\mathbf{y}^*_{k+1},t_{k+1})\mathbf{O}(g^3)+\mathbf{O}(g^6)\|_2\\
&=\lim_{k\to+\infty}\|H(\mathbf{y}^*_{k+1},t_{k+1})\mathbf{O}(g^3)\|_2\\
&=\mathscr{O}(g^3).
\end{aligned}$$

According to the assumptions in the problem formulation, $H(\mathbf{y}^*_{k+1}, t_{k+1})$ is uniformly norm bounded. The MSSRE synthesized by the general 3S-DTZNN algorithm (5.14) is $\mathscr{O}(g^3)$. The proof is thus completed. □

For the convenience of readers and researchers, the general 3S-ZTD formula (5.4) and the general 3S-DTZNN algorithm (5.14) with different effective values of a (i.e., $a < -1$ or $a > 1/3$) are listed in Table 5.2.

Then, the optimal parameter for the optimal zero-stability is obtained by the following theorem.

Theorem 23 *Suppose that the matrix $H(\mathbf{y}_k, t_k)$ is always nonsingular. With the sufficiently small sampling gap $g \in (0,1)$, the effective domain of the parameter a is $a > 1/3$ or $a < -1$. From the perspective of zero-stability, the parameter $a = -9/5$ is optimal for the general 3S-DTZNN algorithm (5.14).*

Proof. The effective domain of the parameter a from Theorem 21 in the general 3S-DTZNN algorithm (5.14) is $a > 1/3$ or $a < -1$. We know $\iota_{2,3} = (3 - a \pm \sqrt{(-3a+1)(5a+9)})/(8a)$. The following problem is solved to obtain the optimal value of a from the perspective of the zero-stability:

$$\underset{a>1/3 \text{ or } a<-1}{\operatorname{argmin}} \quad \max\{|\iota_2|, |\iota_3|\}. \tag{5.15}$$

The term $(-3a+1)(5a+9)$ is defined as Δ to solve (5.15), and the effective domain of the parameter a is divided into three parts (i.e., $a < -9/5$, $-9/5 \leqslant a < -1$, and $a > 1/3$).

First, we obtain $\Delta < 0$ when $a < -9/5$ or $a > 1/3$, and

$$|\iota_2| = |\iota_3| = \sqrt{\frac{(3-a)^2 + (3a-1)(5a+9)}{64a^2}} = \sqrt{\frac{1}{4} + \frac{1}{4a}}.$$

Thus, the ranges of $|\iota_2|$ and $|\iota_3|$ are obtained as $(1/3, 1/2)$ or $(1/2, 1)$ for $a < -9/5$ or $a > 1/3$. Then, we have $\Delta \geqslant 0$ when $-9/5 \leqslant a < -1$, and

$$|\iota_2| = \left|\frac{3 - a + \sqrt{\Delta}}{8a}\right| \geqslant |\iota_3| = \left|\frac{3 - a - \sqrt{\Delta}}{8a}\right|.$$

Thus, the following problem is solved:

$$\underset{-9/5 \leqslant a < -1}{\operatorname{argmin}} \left|\frac{3 - a + \sqrt{\Delta}}{8a}\right|.$$

The range of $|\iota_2|$ is $[1/3, 1)$ for $-9/5 \leqslant a < -1$. Moreover, $|\iota_2| = 1/3$ when $a = -9/5$.

The solution of (5.15) is obtained as $a = -9/5$ considering the two situations of $\Delta < 0$ and $\Delta \geqslant 0$. Thus, the parameter $a = -9/5$ from the perspective of the zero-stability is optimal for the general 3S-DTZNN algorithm (5.14). The proof is thus completed. □

The theoretical analysis on the parameter a from the perspective of the truncation error is further provided by the following theorem.

Theorem 24 *Suppose that the matrix $H(\mathbf{y}_k, t_k)$ is always nonsingular. With the sufficiently small sampling gap $g \in (0,1)$, the effective domain of the parameter a is $a > 1/3$ or $a < -1$. From the perspective of the truncation error, the situation is better with $a < -1$ than with $a > 1/3$ for the general 3S-DTZNN algorithm (5.14).*

Proof. According to the equation (5.11), the truncation error term of the general 3S-ZTD formula (5.4) is exactly

$$\frac{3 - 9a^2}{g} \dddot{\zeta}(c_1) - \frac{1}{3 - 9a} g^2 \dddot{\zeta}(c_2) + \frac{2a + 2}{3 - 9a} g^2 \dddot{\zeta}(c_3).$$

TABLE 5.2: Expressions of general 3S-ZTD formula and general 3S-DTZNN algorithm with different effective values of parameter a, i.e., $a < -1$ or $a > 1/3$.

a	Formula expression	Algorithm expression
3	$\dot{\zeta}_k = \frac{3}{4g}\zeta_{k+1} - \frac{3}{4g}\zeta_k + \frac{1}{4g}\zeta_{k-1} - \frac{1}{4g}\zeta_{k-2} + \mathcal{O}(g^2)$	$\mathbf{y}_{k+1} \doteq -\frac{4}{3}\tilde{H}(\mathbf{y}_k,t_k) + \mathbf{y}_k - \frac{1}{3}\mathbf{y}_{k-1} + \frac{1}{3}\mathbf{y}_{k-2}$
2	$\dot{\zeta}_k = \frac{4}{5g}\zeta_{k+1} - \frac{9}{10g}\zeta_k + \frac{2}{5g}\zeta_{k-1} - \frac{3}{10g}\zeta_{k-2} + \mathcal{O}(g^2)$	$\mathbf{y}_{k+1} \doteq -\frac{5}{4}\tilde{H}(\mathbf{y}_k,t_k) + \frac{9}{8}\mathbf{y}_k - \frac{1}{2}\mathbf{y}_{k-1} + \frac{3}{8}\mathbf{y}_{k-2}$
1	$\dot{\zeta}_k = \frac{1}{g}\zeta_{k+1} - \frac{3}{2g}\zeta_k + \frac{1}{g}\zeta_{k-1} - \frac{1}{2g}\zeta_{k-2} + \mathcal{O}(g^2)$	$\mathbf{y}_{k+1} \doteq -\tilde{H}(\mathbf{y}_k,t_k) + \frac{3}{2}\mathbf{y}_k - \mathbf{y}_{k-1} + \frac{1}{2}\mathbf{y}_{k-2}$
$-\frac{9}{5}$	$\dot{\zeta}_k = \frac{9}{16g}\zeta_{k+1} - \frac{3}{16g}\zeta_k - \frac{5}{16g}\zeta_{k-1} - \frac{1}{16g}\zeta_{k-2} + \mathcal{O}(g^2)$	$\mathbf{y}_{k+1} \doteq -\frac{16}{9}\tilde{H}(\mathbf{y}_k,t_k) + \frac{1}{3}\mathbf{y}_k + \frac{5}{9}\mathbf{y}_{k-1} + \frac{1}{9}\mathbf{y}_{k-2}$
-2	$\dot{\zeta}_k = \frac{4}{7g}\zeta_{k+1} - \frac{3}{14g}\zeta_k - \frac{2}{7g}\zeta_{k-1} - \frac{1}{14g}\zeta_{k-2} + \mathcal{O}(g^2)$	$\mathbf{y}_{k+1} \doteq -\frac{7}{4}\tilde{H}(\mathbf{y}_k,t_k) + \frac{3}{8}\mathbf{y}_k + \frac{1}{2}\mathbf{y}_{k-1} + \frac{1}{8}\mathbf{y}_{k-2}$
-3	$\dot{\zeta}_k = \frac{3}{5g}\zeta_{k+1} - \frac{3}{10g}\zeta_k - \frac{1}{5g}\zeta_{k-1} - \frac{1}{10g}\zeta_{k-2} + \mathcal{O}(g^2)$	$\mathbf{y}_{k+1} \doteq -\frac{5}{3}\tilde{H}(\mathbf{y}_k,t_k) + \frac{1}{2}\mathbf{y}_k + \frac{1}{3}\mathbf{y}_{k-1} + \frac{1}{6}\mathbf{y}_{k-2}$
-4	$\dot{\zeta}_k = \frac{8}{13g}\zeta_{k+1} - \frac{9}{26g}\zeta_k - \frac{2}{13g}\zeta_{k-1} - \frac{3}{26g}\zeta_{k-2} + \mathcal{O}(g^2)$	$\mathbf{y}_{k+1} \doteq -\frac{13}{8}\tilde{H}(\mathbf{y}_k,t_k) + \frac{9}{16}\mathbf{y}_k + \frac{1}{4}\mathbf{y}_{k-1} + \frac{3}{16}\mathbf{y}_{k-2}$

Note that $\tilde{H}(\mathbf{y}_k,t_k) = H^{-1}(\mathbf{y}_k,t_k)\left(\hbar\mathbf{h}(\mathbf{y}_k,t_k) + g\dot{\mathbf{h}}_t(\mathbf{y}_k,t_k)\right)$.

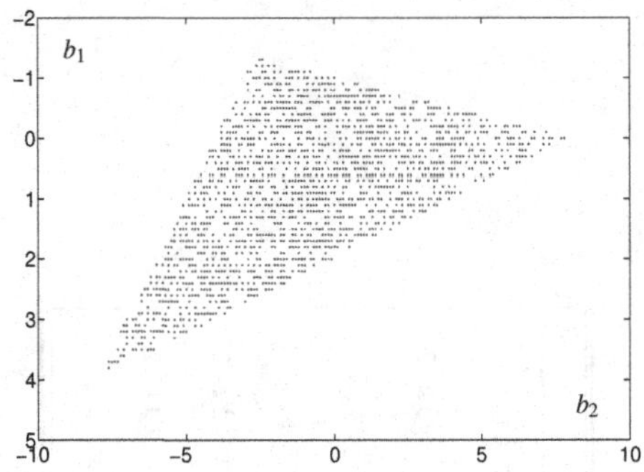

FIGURE 5.1: Effective domain composed of parameters b_1 and b_2 in general 4S-ZTD formula (5.12).

The general 3S-DTZNN algorithm (5.14) is based on the general 3S-ZTD formula (5.4) and has a truncation error term as follows:

$$-\frac{1}{6}g^3\,\dddot{\mathbf{y}}(c_1)+\frac{1}{6a}g^3\,\dddot{\mathbf{y}}(c_2)-\frac{a+1}{3a}g^3\,\dddot{\mathbf{y}}(c_3).$$

On the basis of the CTZNN model (5.3), the boundedness of $\|\dot{\mathbf{y}}(t)\|_2$ for all time t is guaranteed. Furthermore, on the basis of the assumptions that the matrix $A(t)$ and the vector $\mathbf{b}(t)$ have the bounded third-order derivatives at least and that the function $\varphi(\cdot,\cdot)$ has the bounded fourth-order partial derivatives at least, the boundedness of $\|\dddot{\mathbf{y}}(t)\|_2$ for all time t is guaranteed. Thus, the values of $\|\dddot{\mathbf{y}}(c_i)\|_2$ (with $i=1,2,3$) are bounded for all time instant t_k. We define their maximal value as κ and obtain

$$\begin{aligned}&\left\|-\frac{1}{6}g^3\,\dddot{\mathbf{y}}(c_1)+\frac{1}{6a}g^3\,\dddot{\mathbf{y}}(c_2)-\frac{a+1}{3a}g^3\,\dddot{\mathbf{y}}(c_3)\right\|_2\\ &\leqslant\left\|\frac{1}{6}g^3\,\dddot{\mathbf{y}}(c_1)\right\|_2+\left\|\frac{1}{6a}g^3\,\dddot{\mathbf{y}}(c_2)\right\|_2+\left\|\frac{a+1}{3a}g^3\,\dddot{\mathbf{y}}(c_3)\right\|_2\\ &\leqslant\left(\frac{1}{6}+\left|\frac{1}{6a}\right|+\left|\frac{a+1}{3a}\right|\right)\kappa g^3.\end{aligned}$$

The term $1/6+|1/(6a)|+|(a+1)/(3a)|$ is defined as $f_{\mathrm{e}}(a)$, and $\varphi_{\mathrm{e}}(a)\in(1/3,1/2)$ when $a<-1$, whereas $\varphi_{\mathrm{e}}(a)\in(1/2,4/3)$ when $a>1/3$. Thus, the situation is better with $a<-1$ than with $a>1/3$ for the general 3S-DTZNN algorithm (5.14) from the perspective of the truncation error. The proof is thus completed. □

5.4.2 General 4S-DTZNN algorithm

Let the general 4S-ZTD formula (5.12) discretize the CTZNN model (5.3), and the following general four-step DTZNN (4S-DTZNN) algorithm is obtained with its truncation error omitted:

$$\begin{aligned}\mathbf{y}_{k+1}\doteq{}&\frac{4b_1+b_2-8}{6}\left(H^{-1}(\mathbf{y}_k,t_k)(\hbar\mathbf{h}(\mathbf{y}_k,t_k)+g\dot{\mathbf{h}}_t(\mathbf{y}_k,t_k))\right)+\frac{32b_1+32+5b_2}{36}\mathbf{y}_k-b_1\mathbf{y}_{k-1}\\ &-\frac{b_2}{4}\mathbf{y}_{k-2}+\frac{1+b_1+b_2}{9}\mathbf{y}_{k-3}.\end{aligned}\tag{5.16}$$

As mentioned above, if $1+b_1+b_2=0$ holds, then the general 4S-ZTD formula (5.12) will be simplified as the general 3S-ZTD formula (5.4); thus, the general 4S-DTZNN algorithm (5.16) will also be simplified as the general 3S-DTZNN algorithm (5.14). The effective domain composed of b_1 and b_2 is investigated by a numerical experiment, of which the result is presented in

Figure 5.1 to ensure the zero-stability of the general 4S-DTZNN algorithm (5.16). The shadow area of Figure 5.1 is the effective domain. Moreover, several effective 4S-ZTD formulas with different values of b_1 and b_2 are summarized in Table 5.3.

The precision of the general 4S-DTZNN algorithm (5.16) is guaranteed by the following theorem.

Theorem 25 *Consider the FCNO (5.2). Suppose that the matrix $H(\mathbf{y}_k, t_k)$ is always nonsingular and uniformly norm bounded. With the sufficiently small sampling gap $g \in (0,1)$, the MSSRE synthesized by the general 4S-DTZNN algorithm (5.16) with effective parameters b_1 and b_2 is $\mathscr{O}(g^3)$.*

Proof. The proof process is similar to that of Theorem 22, and thus is omitted here. □

Remark 7 *The derivative information about $\mathbf{h}(\mathbf{y}_k, t_k)$, i.e., $\dot{\mathbf{h}}_t(\mathbf{y}_k, t_k)$, by focusing on the general DTZNN algorithms (5.14) and (5.16), is necessary but may be unknown in some applications. The following backward numerical-differentiation formula is used to approximate the value of $\dot{\mathbf{h}}_t(\mathbf{y}_k, t_k)$ to solve this problem [20, 106]:*

$$\dot{\zeta}_k = \frac{3\zeta_k - 4\zeta_{k-1} + \zeta_{k-2}}{2g} + \mathscr{O}(g^2). \tag{5.17}$$

The above approximation only uses current and past information, but not future information; thus, the general DTZNN algorithms (5.14) and (5.16) remain capable of prediction. Moreover, the approximation has minimal effect on the general DTZNN algorithms (5.14) and (5.16) with respect to the precision because the backward numerical-differentiation formula (5.17) has a truncation error of $\mathscr{O}(g^2)$, which is similar to that of the general ZTD formulas.

For a more intuitive understanding of the main content of this chapter [128], Table 5.4 lists the problem, scheme, model, and algorithms.

5.5 Numerical Experiments

In this section, several numerical experiments are conducted to verify the effectiveness and precision of the general ZTD formulas and corresponding general DTZNN algorithms. Numerous comparative numerical experimental results are presented to substantiate the theoretical results provided in the previous sections.

5.5.1 Derivative approximation

Example 5.1 In this subsection, the general 3S-ZTD formula (5.4) and the general 4S-ZTD formula (5.12) as well as the Euler forward formula (5.1) are used to approximate the first-order derivative of

$$f_k = f(t_k) = \sin(2t_k). \tag{5.18}$$

The numerical experimental results are presented in Figures 5.2 and 5.3. The approximation errors $\check{e}_k = |\dot{f}_k - \dot{f}_k^*|$ synthesized by the general 3S-ZTD formula (5.4) with different a values decrease by a factor of 100 when the sampling gap g decreases by a factor of 10 (i.e., from 0.1 s to 0.01 s), as illustrated in Figure 5.2, where $\dot{f}_k^*$ denotes the theoretical value. Thus, the precision of the general 3S-ZTD formula (5.4) is $\mathscr{O}(g^2)$, which is consistent with Theorem 19. Similarly, the precision of the general 4S-ZTD formula (5.12), which is also $\mathscr{O}(g^2)$, is substantiated by the numerical experimental results presented in Figure 5.3. However, the approximation error synthesized by the Euler forward

TABLE 5.3: Expressions of general 4S-ZTD formula and general 4S-DTZNN algorithm with different effective values of parameters b_1 and b_2.

b_1	b_2	Formula expression	Algorithm expression
2	−4	$\dot{\zeta}_k = \frac{3}{2g}\zeta_{k+1} - \frac{19}{6g}\zeta_k + \frac{3}{g}\zeta_{k-1} - \frac{3}{2g}\zeta_{k-2} + \frac{1}{6g}\zeta_{k-3} + \mathcal{O}(g^2)$	$\mathbf{y}_{k+1} \doteq -\frac{2}{3}\tilde{H}(\mathbf{y}_k,t_k) + \frac{19}{9}\mathbf{y}_k - 2\mathbf{y}_{k-1} + \mathbf{y}_{k-2} - \frac{1}{9}\mathbf{y}_{k-3}$
1	−4	$\dot{\zeta}_k = \frac{3}{4g}\zeta_{k+1} - \frac{11}{12g}\zeta_k + \frac{3}{4g}\zeta_{k-1} - \frac{3}{4g}\zeta_{k-2} + \frac{1}{6g}\zeta_{k-3} + \mathcal{O}(g^2)$	$\mathbf{y}_{k+1} \doteq -\frac{4}{3}\tilde{H}(\mathbf{y}_k,t_k) + \frac{11}{9}\mathbf{y}_k - \mathbf{y}_{k-1} + \mathbf{y}_{k-2} - \frac{2}{9}\mathbf{y}_{k-3}$
1	−3	$\dot{\zeta}_k = \frac{6}{7g}\zeta_{k+1} - \frac{7}{6g}\zeta_k + \frac{6}{7g}\zeta_{k-1} - \frac{9}{14g}\zeta_{k-2} + \frac{2}{21g}\zeta_{k-3} + \mathcal{O}(g^2)$	$\mathbf{y}_{k+1} \doteq -\frac{7}{6}\tilde{H}(\mathbf{y}_k,t_k) + \frac{49}{36}\mathbf{y}_k - \mathbf{y}_{k-1} + \frac{3}{4}\mathbf{y}_{k-2} - \frac{1}{9}\mathbf{y}_{k-3}$
1	−1	$\dot{\zeta}_k = \frac{6}{5g}\zeta_{k+1} - \frac{59}{30g}\zeta_k + \frac{6}{5g}\zeta_{k-1} - \frac{3}{10g}\zeta_{k-2} - \frac{2}{15g}\zeta_{k-3} + \mathcal{O}(g^2)$	$\mathbf{y}_{k+1} \doteq -\frac{5}{6}\tilde{H}(\mathbf{y}_k,t_k) + \frac{59}{36}\mathbf{y}_k - \mathbf{y}_{k-1} + \frac{1}{4}\mathbf{y}_{k-2} + \frac{1}{9}\mathbf{y}_{k-3}$
1	0	$\dot{\zeta}_k = \frac{3}{2g}\zeta_{k+1} - \frac{8}{3g}\zeta_k + \frac{3}{2g}\zeta_{k-1} - \frac{1}{3g}x_{k-3} + \mathcal{O}(g^2)$	$\mathbf{y}_{k+1} \doteq -\frac{2}{3}\tilde{H}(\mathbf{y}_k,t_k) + \frac{16}{9}\mathbf{y}_k - \mathbf{y}_{k-1} + \frac{2}{9}\mathbf{y}_{k-3}$
0	−2	$\dot{\zeta}_k = \frac{3}{5g}\zeta_{k+1} - \frac{11}{30g}\zeta_k - \frac{3}{10g}\zeta_{k-2} + \frac{1}{15g}\zeta_{k-3} + \mathcal{O}(g^2)$	$\mathbf{y}_{k+1} \doteq -\frac{5}{3}\tilde{H}(\mathbf{y}_k,t_k) + \frac{11}{18}\mathbf{y}_k + \frac{1}{2}\mathbf{y}_{k-2} - \frac{1}{9}\mathbf{y}_{k-3}$

Note that $\tilde{H}(\mathbf{y}_k,t_k) = H^{-1}(\mathbf{y}_k,t_k)\left(\hbar\mathbf{h}(\mathbf{y}_k,t_k) + g\dot{\mathbf{h}}_t(\mathbf{y}_k,t_k)\right)$.

TABLE 5.4: Problem, scheme, model, and algorithms in this chapter.

Problem	$\min\ \varphi(\mathbf{x}_{k+1},t_{k+1})$ s. t. $A_{k+1}\mathbf{x}_{k+1}=\mathbf{b}_{k+1}$.
Scheme	Adopt ZTD formulas to discretize CTZNN model (5.3).
Model	$\dot{\mathbf{y}}(t)=-H^{-1}(\mathbf{y}(t),t)(\eta\mathbf{h}(\mathbf{y}(t),t)+\dot{\mathbf{h}}_t(\mathbf{y}(t),t))$.
Algorithms	$\mathbf{y}_{k+1}\doteq-\frac{3a-1}{2a}(H^{-1}(\mathbf{y}_k,t_k)(\hbar\mathbf{h}(\mathbf{y}_k,t_k)+g\dot{\mathbf{h}}_t(\mathbf{y}_k,t_k)))+\frac{3a+3}{4a}\mathbf{y}_k-\frac{1}{a}\mathbf{y}_{k-1}+\frac{a+1}{4a}\mathbf{y}_{k-2}$, $\mathbf{y}_{k+1}\doteq\frac{4b_1+b_2-8}{6}(H^{-1}(\mathbf{y}_k,t_k)(\hbar\mathbf{h}(\mathbf{y}_k,t_k)+g\dot{\mathbf{h}}_t(\mathbf{y}_k,t_k)))+\frac{32b_1+32+5b_2}{36}\mathbf{y}_k$ $-b_1\mathbf{y}_{k-1}-\frac{b_2}{4}\mathbf{y}_{k-2}+\frac{1+b_1+b_2}{9}\mathbf{y}_{k-3}$.

formula (5.1) decreases by a factor of 10 when the sampling gap g decreases by a factor of 10, which means that it has a lower precision being $\mathscr{O}(g)$. Besides, the comparison of Figures 5.2 and 5.3 indicates that the approximation errors are generally smaller for the general 3S-ZTD formula (5.4) than for the general 4S-ZTD formula (5.12), although these formulas all have the precision patterns of $\mathscr{O}(g^2)$.

5.5.2 FCNO solving

In this subsection, a specific problem of the FCNO is considered to substantiate the efficacy and superiority of the general 3S-DTZNN algorithm (5.14) and the general 4S-DTZNN algorithm (5.16) with effective parameters.

Example 5.2 The following FCNO is considered and solved at each computational time interval $[t_k,t_{k+1})=[kg,(k+1)g)\subset[0,20]$ s:

$$\begin{aligned}\min\ &\frac{1}{4}(\sin(0.1t_{k+1})+1)x_{1,k+1}^4+\frac{1}{4}(\cos(0.1t_{k+1})+1)x_{2,k+1}^4+\frac{1}{2}x_{1,k+1}^2+\frac{1}{2}x_{2,k+1}^2\\ \text{s. t. }&\sin(0.2t_{k+1})x_{1,k+1}+\cos(0.2t_{k+1})x_{2,k+1}=\cos(0.5t_{k+1}).\end{aligned}\tag{5.19}$$

The general 3S-DTZNN algorithm (5.14) with $a=-9/5$ is used to solve this problem, of which the algorithm expression is shown as below:

$$\mathbf{y}_{k+1}\doteq-\frac{16}{9}(H^{-1}(\mathbf{y}_k,t_k)(\hbar\mathbf{h}(\mathbf{y}_k,t_k)+g\dot{\mathbf{h}}_t(\mathbf{y}_k,t_k)))+\frac{1}{3}\mathbf{y}_k+\frac{5}{9}\mathbf{y}_{k-1}+\frac{1}{9}\mathbf{y}_{k-2}.\tag{5.20}$$

For comparison, the conventional Newton iteration (NI) algorithm and the Euler-type DTZNN (ET-DTZNN) algorithm are considered and investigated [46, 126], of which the algorithm expressions

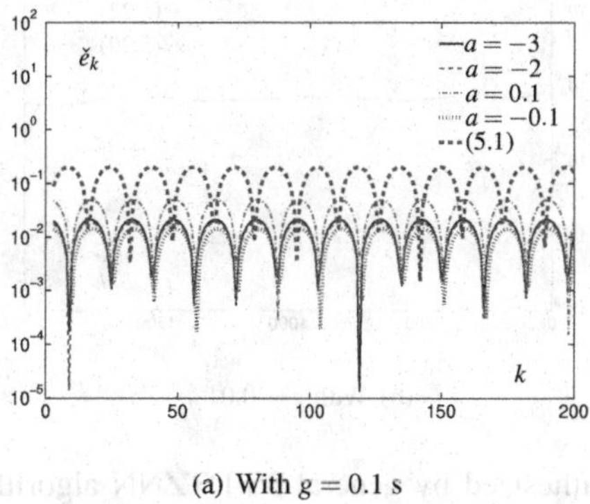

(a) With $g=0.1$ s

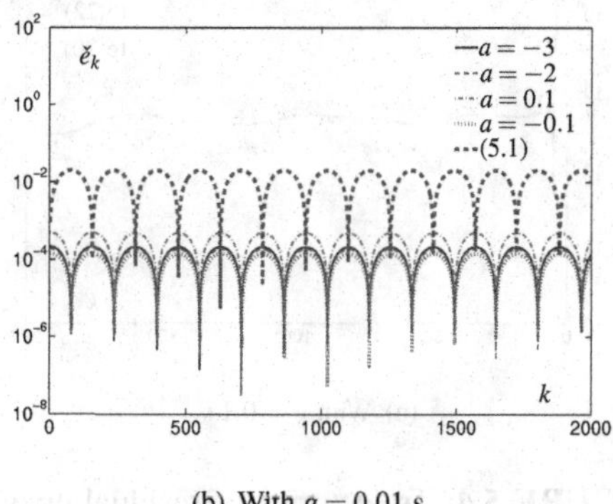

(b) With $g=0.01$ s

FIGURE 5.2: Trajectories of approximation errors $\check{e}_k$ synthesized by general 3S-ZTD formula (5.4) and Euler forward formula (5.1) with different a and g values in Example 5.1.

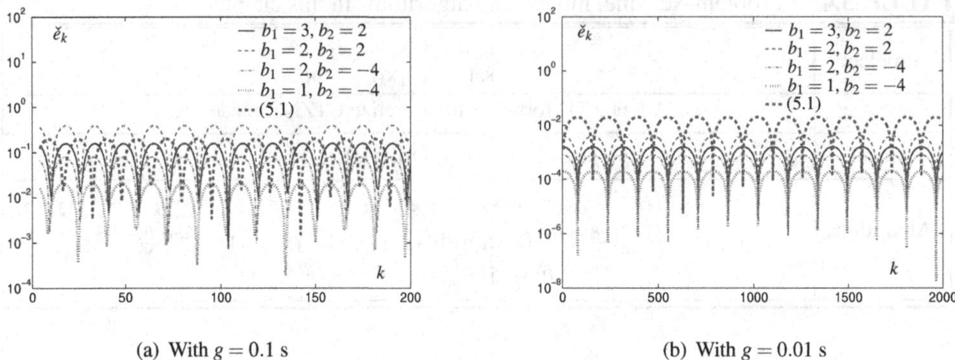

FIGURE 5.3: Trajectories of approximation errors $\check{e}_k$ synthesized by general 4S-ZTD formula (5.12) and Euler forward formula (5.1) with different b_1, b_2, and g values in Example 5.1.

are shown as below:

$$\mathbf{y}_{k+1} \doteq -H^{-1}(\mathbf{y}_k, t_k)\mathbf{h}(\mathbf{y}_k, t_k) + \mathbf{y}_k \tag{5.21}$$

and

$$\mathbf{y}_{k+1} \doteq -\big(H^{-1}(\mathbf{y}_k, t_k)\big(\hbar\mathbf{h}(\mathbf{y}_k, t_k) + g\dot{\mathbf{h}}_t(\mathbf{y}_k, t_k)\big)\big) + \mathbf{y}_k. \tag{5.22}$$

The numerical experimental results are presented in Figure 5.4. Specifically, the residual error $\hat{e}_{k+1}$ synthesized by the 3S-DTZNN algorithm (5.20) is of order 10^{-3} with the sampling gap $g = 0.1$ s from Figure 5.4(a), and the residual error decreases by a factor of 10^3 with the sampling gap g decreasing by a factor of 10 from Figure 5.4(b). Thus, the precision of the general 3S-DTZNN algorithm (5.14) is substantiated. In comparison, the residual errors synthesized by the NI algorithm (5.21) and the ET-DTZNN algorithm (5.22) decrease by factors of 10 and 10^2, respectively, with g decreasing by a factor of 10, which shows the superiority of the general 3S-DTZNN algorithm (5.14) in terms of the precision.

Note that, to satisfy the requirement of real-time computation, the values of average computing time per updating (ACTPU) for these algorithms should be smaller than the sampling gap. In these

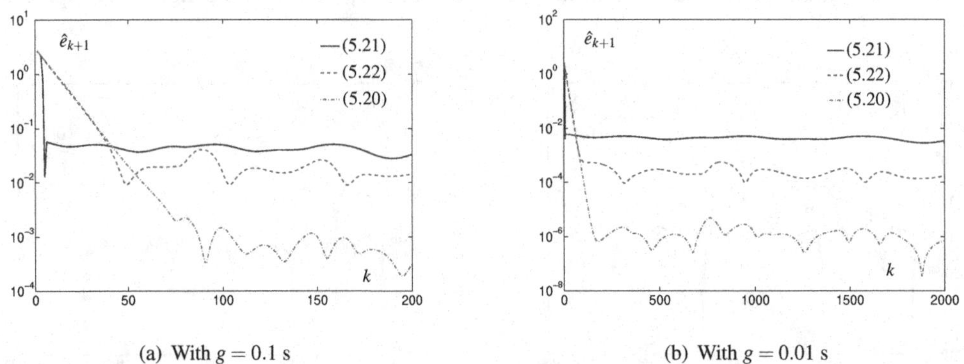

FIGURE 5.4: Trajectories of residual errors $\hat{e}_{k+1}$ synthesized by general 3S-DTZNN algorithm (5.14) with $a = -9/5$, i.e., algorithm (5.20), compared with NI algorithm (1.21) and ET-DTZNN algorithm (1.22) with different values of sampling gap g in Example 5.2.

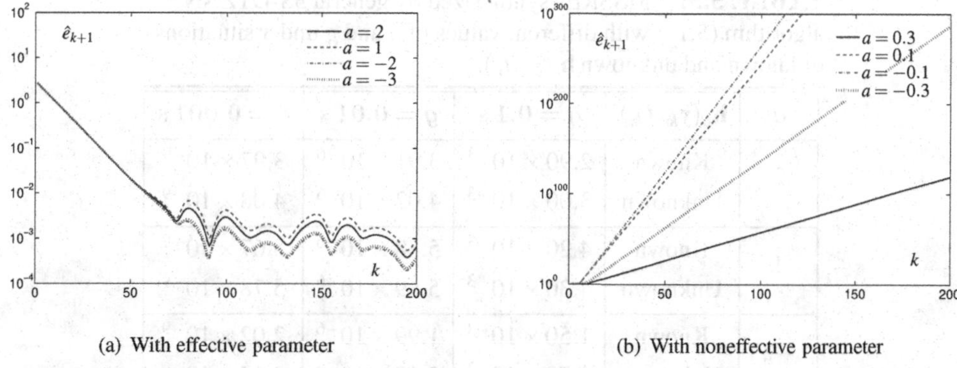

(a) With effective parameter (b) With noneffective parameter

FIGURE 5.5: Trajectories of residual errors $\hat{e}_{k+1}$ synthesized by general 3S-DTZNN algorithm (5.14) with different values of parameter a in Example 5.2.

numerical experiments, the ACTPU data are all less than 0.1 ms and they all satisfy the requirement of real-time computation.

For further investigations of the FCNO problem, the general 3S-DTZNN algorithm (5.14) and the general 4S-DTZNN algorithm (5.16) with different values of their parameters are employed to solve this problem. The numerical experimental results are presented in Figures 5.5 and 5.6. Specifically, from Figure 5.5(a), the residual errors synthesized by the general 3S-DTZNN algorithm (5.14) with different effective parameter a are convergent. From Figure 5.5(b), the residual errors synthesized by the general 3S-DTZNN algorithm (5.14) with different noneffective parameter a are divergent. The numerical experimental results are consistent with the theoretical results in Theorem 21. Besides, from Figure 5.6, the numerical experimental results for the general 4S-DTZNN algorithm (5.16) are consistent with theoretical results in Subsection 5.4.2. Focusing on Figure 5.5(a), although the residual errors synthesized by the general 3S-DTZNN algorithm (5.14) with different effective parameter a are of orders 10^{-3}, they are relatively smaller for $a = -2$ and $a = -3$ $(a < -1)$ than for $a = 2$ and $a = 1$ $(a > 1/3)$. It means that the situation is better with $a < -1$ than with $a > 1/3$ in terms of the precision, which is consistent with the theoretical result in Theorem 24.

Furthermore, we consider the two situations with $\mathbf{h}_t(\mathbf{y}_k, t_k)$ known and unknown, and the corresponding MSSREs are summarized in Tables 5.5 and 5.6. The MSSREs synthesized by the general DTZNN algorithms (5.14) and (5.16) with effective parameters are reduced by factors of 10^3 or 10^6 (i.e., from 10^{-3} to 10^{-6} or 10^{-9}), whether $\mathbf{h}_t(\mathbf{y}_k, t_k)$ is known or not, when the sampling gap g decreases by a factor of 10 or 100 (i.e., from 0.1 to 0.01 or 0.001 s). Thus, the situation with unknown $\dot{\mathbf{h}}_t(\mathbf{y}_k, t_k)$ has minimal effect on the two algorithms, of which the precision is still $\mathscr{O}(g^3)$.

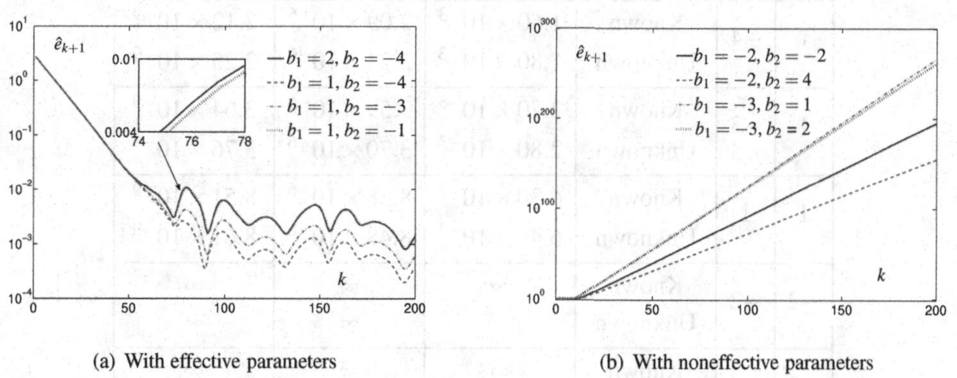

(a) With effective parameters (b) With noneffective parameters

FIGURE 5.6: Trajectories of residual errors $\hat{e}_{k+1}$ synthesized by general 4S-DTZNN algorithm (5.16) with different values of parameters b_1 and b_2 in Example 5.2.

TABLE 5.5: MSSREs synthesized by general 3S-DTZNN algorithm (5.14) with different values of a and g under situations of known and unknown $\dot{\mathbf{h}}_t(\mathbf{y}_k,t_k)$.

a	$\dot{\mathbf{h}}_t(\mathbf{y}_k,t_k)$	$g=0.1$ s	$g=0.01$ s	$g=0.001$ s
2	Known	2.90×10^{-3}	3.91×10^{-6}	3.97×10^{-9}
	Unknown	3.00×10^{-3}	4.02×10^{-6}	4.08×10^{-9}
1	Known	4.20×10^{-3}	5.58×10^{-6}	5.67×10^{-9}
	Unknown	4.30×10^{-3}	5.69×10^{-6}	5.78×10^{-9}
−2	Known	1.50×10^{-3}	1.99×10^{-6}	2.02×10^{-9}
	Unknown	1.70×10^{-3}	2.12×10^{-6}	2.15×10^{-9}
−3	Known	1.70×10^{-3}	2.23×10^{-6}	2.27×10^{-9}
	Unknown	1.80×10^{-3}	2.36×10^{-6}	2.39×10^{-9}
−0.3	Known	∞	∞	∞
	Unknown	∞	∞	∞
0.3	Known	∞	∞	∞
	Unknown	∞	∞	∞

5.5.3 Manipulator control

In this subsection, the real-time motion control of PUMA560 manipulator [129, 130], which is a three-dimensional manipulator, is investigated and solved by the abovementioned general DTZNN algorithms. First, the kinematic equation of the PUMA560 manipulator at position level is given as $\mathbf{f}(\vartheta_k)=\mathbf{r}_{\mathrm{a},k}$, where $\mathbf{f}(\cdot)$ is a forward-kinematics mapping function with known structure and parameters. In addition, $\vartheta_k\in\mathbb{R}^6$ is the joint-angle vector and $\mathbf{r}_{\mathrm{a},k}\in\mathbb{R}^3$ is the end-effector position

TABLE 5.6: MSSREs synthesized by general 4S-DTZNN algorithm (5.16) with different values of b_1, b_2, and g under situations of known and unknown $\dot{\mathbf{h}}_t(\mathbf{y}_k,t_k)$.

b_1	b_2	$\dot{\mathbf{h}}_t(\mathbf{y}_k,t_k)$	$g=0.1$ s	$g=0.01$ s	$g=0.001$ s
2	−4	Known	6.30×10^{-3}	8.38×10^{-6}	8.51×10^{-9}
		Unknown	6.40×10^{-3}	8.48×10^{-6}	8.61×10^{-9}
1	−4	Known	1.60×10^{-3}	2.09×10^{-6}	2.12×10^{-9}
		Unknown	1.80×10^{-3}	2.22×10^{-6}	2.25×10^{-9}
1	−3	Known	2.70×10^{-3}	3.59×10^{-6}	3.64×10^{-9}
		Unknown	2.80×10^{-3}	3.70×10^{-6}	3.76×10^{-9}
1	1	Known	6.30×10^{-3}	8.38×10^{-6}	8.51×10^{-9}
		Unknown	6.40×10^{-3}	8.48×10^{-6}	8.61×10^{-9}
−2	−2	Known	∞	∞	∞
		Unknown	∞	∞	∞
−2	−4	Known	∞	∞	∞
		Unknown	∞	∞	∞

vector. The equation at velocity level is obtained as $J(\vartheta_k)\dot{\vartheta}_k = \dot{\mathbf{r}}_{\mathrm{a},k}$, where $J(\vartheta_k) \in \mathbb{R}^{3\times 6}$ is the Jacobi matrix of PUMA560 manipulator.

Example 5.3 The following problem is solved at each computational time interval $[t_k, t_{k+1}) = [kg, (k+1)g) \subset [0, 10]$ s on the basis of the previous works [129, 131]:

$$\begin{aligned} &\min \ \|\dot{\vartheta}_{k+1} + \rho(\vartheta_{k+1} - \vartheta_0)\|_2^2/2 \\ &\text{s. t. } \ J(\vartheta_{k+1})\dot{\vartheta}_{k+1} = \dot{\mathbf{r}}_{\mathrm{a},k+1}, \end{aligned} \tag{5.23}$$

where ρ is a positive design parameter used to scale the magnitude of the joint-angle displacements. The end effector is controlled to track a circular spiral, which is expressed as

$$\mathbf{r}_{\mathrm{d},k} = \begin{bmatrix} (0.5 + 0.01\sin(3\pi t_k))\cos(0.2\pi t_k) \\ (0.5 + 0.01\sin(3\pi t_k))\sin(0.2\pi t_k) \\ 0.01\cos(3\pi t_k) \end{bmatrix}. \tag{5.24}$$

The general 3S-DTZNN algorithm (5.14) with $a = -9/5$, i.e., the 3S-DTZNN algorithm (5.20), is used to solve this problem. This algorithm is optimal with respect to stability. For comparison, the ET-DTZNN algorithm (5.22) is also investigated to solve the same problem. For the 3S-DTZNN algorithm (5.20) and the ET-DTZNN algorithm (5.22), the initial joint-angle vector is set as $\vartheta_0 = [0, -\pi/4, 0, \pi/2, 0, -\pi/4]^{\mathrm{T}}$; the parameter $\rho = 0.1$; the parameter $\hbar = 0.1$; the sampling gap $g = 0.001$ s; the task duration $T = 10$ s. The numerical experimental results are presented in Figure 5.7. Specifically, Figure 5.7(a) displays the trajectories of the joint angles generated by the 3S-DTZNN algorithm(5.20). Besides, Figure 5.7(b) and (c) display the manipulator trajectories and end-effector

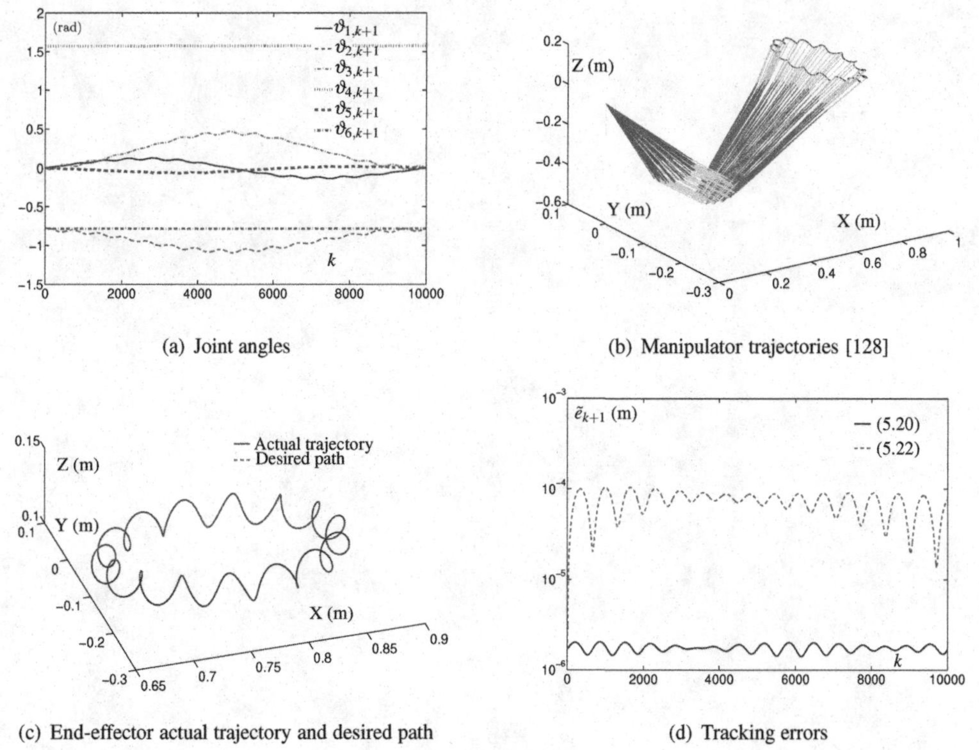

(a) Joint angles

(b) Manipulator trajectories [128]

(c) End-effector actual trajectory and desired path

(d) Tracking errors

FIGURE 5.7: Trajectories of joint angles, redundant manipulator, and end-effector generated by 3S-DTZNN algorithm (5.20), as well as tracking errors $\tilde{e}_{k+1}$ synthesized by 3S-DTZNN algorithm (5.20) and ET-DTZNN algorithm (5.22) in Example 5.3.

trajectories. In addiction, Figure 5.7(d) depicts the trajectories of the tracking errors (i.e., $\tilde{e}_{k+1} = \|\mathbf{r}_{\mathrm{a},k+1} - \mathbf{r}_{\mathrm{d},k+1}\|_2$) synthesized by the 3S-DTZNN algorithm (5.20) and the ET-DTZNN algorithm (5.22). Evidently, the 3S-DTZNN algorithm (5.20) completes the task successfully and is superior to the ET-DTZNN algorithm (5.22). Besides, the ACTPU data for the 3S-DTZNN algorithm (5.20) and the ET-DTZNN algorithm (5.22) are 0.3 ms and 0.25 ms, respectively, which are smaller than the sampling gap g and satisfy the real-time motion control requirement.

5.6 Chapter Summary

In this chapter, the general ZTD formulas have been developed for the first-order derivative approximation via the idea of the SODE. The general DTZNN algorithms have been developed to solve the FCNO (5.2) on the basis of the developed general ZTD formulas and previous works. The different values of parameters for the general DTZNN algorithms lead to the different discrete-time algorithms. Their stability has been analyzed and corresponding effective domains of parameters in the general DTZNN algorithms have been investigated to guarantee the effectiveness of the general DTZNN algorithms. Moreover, the precision of the general ZTD formulas and corresponding general DTZNN algorithms has been analyzed and guaranteed. The numerical experiments, including the real-time motion control of PUMA560 manipulator, have been conducted to substantiate the theoretical results of the general ZTD formulas and corresponding general DTZNN algorithms.

Chapter 6

Future Unconstrained Nonlinear Optimization with $\mathscr{O}(g^4)$

Abstract

Unconstrained nonlinear optimization (UNO) problems are considered important issues in various scientific disciplines and industrial applications. In this chapter, a continuous-time derivative dynamics (CTDD) model is developed for solving continuous time-dependent UNO (CTDUNO) problem. Furthermore, aiming to remedy the weaknesses of the CTDD model, a continuous-time zeroing neural network (CTZNN) model is presented and investigated. For potential digital hardware realization, by using bilinear transformation, a general four-step Zhang time discretization (4S-ZTD) formula is presented and applied to the discretization of both the CTDD and CTZNN models. For solving future UNO (FUNO) problem, a general four-step discrete-time derivative dynamics (4S-DTDD) algorithm and a general four-step discrete-time zeroing neural network (4S-DTZNN) algorithm are presented on the basis of the general 4S-ZTD formula. Further theoretical analyses indicate that the general 4S-DTZNN algorithm is zero-stable, consistent, and convergent with the truncation error of $\mathbf{O}(g^4)$, which denotes a vector with elements being $\mathscr{O}(g^4)$ (g denoting the sampling gap). Theoretical analyses also indicate that the maximal steady-state residual error (MSSRE) synthesized by the general 4S-DTZNN algorithm has an $\mathscr{O}(g^4)$ pattern confirmedly. The efficacy and accuracy of the general 4S-DTDD algorithm and the general 4S-DTZNN algorithm are further verified by numerical experimental results.

6.1 Introduction

In numerous scientific disciplines and industrial applications, time-dependent optimization problems have been widely encountered, and such problems are fundamental and essential [106, 111, 132–140]. Since nonlinear optimization is an important subtopic of optimization problems, research works on this are abundant, and many of which have been applied in the engineering fields such as system control [141–143] and signal processing [112, 144–146]. Various algorithms have been presented and analyzed for nonlinear optimization problems solving [112, 140–156]. For example, in [141], a decomposition scheme was presented to solve parametric non-convex programs. Such a scheme consisted of a fixed number of proximal linearized alternating minimizations and a dual updating per time step. The presented approach was attractive in a real-time distributed context and the performance of the optimality-tracking scheme could be enhanced via a continuation technique. In [143], a self-triggered algorithm was presented to solve a class of convex optimization problems with time-dependent objective functions. The algorithm predicted the temporal evolution of the gradient by using known upper bounds on the higher-order derivatives of the objective function. The method guaranteed convergence to an arbitrarily small neighborhood of the optimal

DOI: 10.1201/9781003497783-6

trajectory in finite time and without incurring Zeno behavior. In [146], based on prediction and correction steps, Simonetto *et al* presented two algorithms with a discrete time-sampling scheme. Considering the correction step consisted either of one or multiple gradient steps or Newton steps, the two algorithms were termed as gradient trajectory tracking and Newton trajectory tracking algorithms. The two algorithms behaved as $\mathbf{O}(g^2)$ and in some cases as $\mathbf{O}(g^4)$ with g denoting the sampling gap. Furthermore, in [112], online algorithms were developed to track solutions of time-dependent constrained optimization problems. Resembling workhorse Kalman filtering-based approaches for dynamical systems, the presented methods involved prediction correction steps to provably track the trajectory of the optimal solutions of time-dependent convex problems and improved the convergence speed of existing prediction-correction methods when applied to unconstrained problems. However, most of these algorithms and methods are dedicated to solving time-independent/static nonlinear optimization problems, which means that they may not possess the capability of handling time-dependent nonlinear optimization problems [149–151]. In this chapter [157], the continuous time-dependent unconstrained nonlinear optimization (CTDUNO) problem is first investigated. The main difference between the CTDUNO problems and continuous time-independent unconstrained nonlinear optimization problems is evidently that the CTDUNO problems change with time. This difference makes the time derivative play an important role in obtaining accurate real-time solutions for the CTDUNO problems.

Traditional numerical algorithms such as the Newton iteration (NI) and other methods [140, 147–149] are designed intrinsically for time-independent optimization. Generally speaking, these methods are under the assumption that the optimization problems do not change during the computational time. Thus, the computed solutions are directly used in the optimization problems after the computation. Compared to the traditional numerical algorithms, the neural network approaches are superior because of the potential real-time application advantages such as self-adaption, parallel processing, distributed storage, and hardware applications [35, 75, 95, 158, 159]. For example, in [75], finite-time Zhang neural networks (or say, zeroing neural networks, ZNNs) were designed to solve time-dependent quadratic programming (QP) problems and applied to manipulator tracking. In [158], a class of recurrent neural networks (RNNs) was presented to solve QP problems. In [159], the finite-time RNNs with continuous but non-smooth activation functions were presented to solve nonlinearly constrained optimization problems. In this chapter [157], the derivative dynamics approach is exploited as an intuitive one, while the ZNN method is exploited for potential predictive power [51, 64]. More specifically speaking, a continuous-time derivative dynamics (CTDD) model and a continuous-time ZNN (CTZNN) model are generalized, developed, and investigated for the CTDUNO problems.

For potential digital hardware realization, i.e., solving future unconstrained nonlinear optimization (FUNO) problem, it is necessary to discretize the continuous-time models. Fortunately, a class of finite-difference methods and formulas termed as Zhang time discretization (ZTD) is developed, named, and applied by Zhang *et al* since 2014 after nearly 8-year search and preparation [70]. It is worth pointing out that ZTD formulas can be used for stable, convergent, and accurate discretization of neural network/dynamics (e.g., derivative dynamics and ZNN) and other continuous time-dependent ordinary differential equation systems [70]. It is worth noting that, in [75, 158, 159], the optimal solutions of some time-dependent nonlinear optimization problems can be achieved in finite-time interval.

6.2 Problem Formulation

In this section, the problem formulation of the FUNO is presented.

Let us consider the following FUNO problem with the computational time interval $[t_k, t_{k+1}) \subset [t_{\text{ini}}, t_{\text{fin}}] \subset [0, +\infty)$:

$$\min_{\mathbf{x}_{k+1} \in \mathbb{R}^n} \varphi(\mathbf{x}_{k+1}, t_{k+1}) \in \mathbb{R}, \tag{6.1}$$

where t_{ini} and t_{fin} represent the initial and final time instants, respectively. Besides, $\varphi(\mathbf{x}_{k+1}, t_{k+1})$ is generated or measured from the smoothly time-dependent signal $\varphi(\mathbf{x}(t), t)$ by sampling at time instant $t = (k+1)g$ (which is denoted as t_{k+1}).

In the real-time solution process of the FUNO (6.1), computation has to be performed based on the present or previous data. For example, at time instant t_k, during the computational time interval $[t_k, t_{k+1})$, we could only use known information such as $\mathbf{x}(t_k)$, $\varphi(\mathbf{x}(t_k), t_k)$, and its derivatives, instead of unknown information such as $\varphi(\mathbf{x}_{k+1}, t_{k+1})$ and its derivatives. Thus, the objective is by utilizing the present or previous data to find the unknown vector $\mathbf{x}_{k+1}$ of the unknown function $\varphi(\mathbf{x}_{k+1}, t_{k+1})$ during $[t_k, t_{k+1})$, such that (6.1) achieves its minimal value at each time instant. Note that, at the start of the computation with $t_0 = 0$, we could not compute $\mathbf{x}_0$ based on previous data; thus $\mathbf{x}_0$ can be randomly generated or directly set as $\mathbf{x}_0^*$, where $\mathbf{x}_0^*$ denotes the theoretical solution of (6.1) at time instant t_0.

6.3 Continuous-Time Models

To solve the FUNO (6.1), the corresponding CTDUNO problem needs to be first investigated. On the basis of the CTDUNO problem, the CTDD model and the CTZNN model are developed. The problem formulation of the CTDUNO is as follows:

$$\min_{\mathbf{x}(t) \in \mathbb{R}^n} \varphi(\mathbf{x}(t), t) \in \mathbb{R}, \text{with } t \in [t_{\text{ini}}, t_{\text{fin}}], \tag{6.2}$$

where the time-dependent nonlinear mapping function $\varphi(\cdot,\cdot) : \mathbb{R}^n \times [t_{\text{ini}}, t_{\text{fin}}] \to \mathbb{R}$ should be second-order differentiable and bounded. The real-time optimization solution is denoted by $\mathbf{x}(t) \in \mathbb{R}^n$. Such a solution ought to be found in real time and guarantees that the CTDUNO (6.2) achieves its minimum value for all time t.

In order to obtain the real-time solution of the CTDUNO (6.2), we define a differentiable nonlinear mapping function as

$$\begin{aligned}\mathbf{\Psi}(\mathbf{x}(t), t) = \frac{\partial \varphi(\mathbf{x}(t), t)}{\partial \mathbf{x}(t)} &= \left[\frac{\partial \varphi}{\partial x_1}, \frac{\partial \varphi}{\partial x_2}, \cdots, \frac{\partial \varphi}{\partial x_n}\right]^{\mathrm{T}} \\ &= [\psi_1(\mathbf{x}(t), t), \psi_2(\mathbf{x}(t), t), \cdots, \psi_n(\mathbf{x}(t), t)]^{\mathrm{T}} \in \mathbb{R}^n,\end{aligned}$$

where $\partial\varphi/\partial x_i = \partial\varphi(\mathbf{x}(t), t)/\partial x_i(t) = \psi_i(\mathbf{x}(t), t)$, with $i = 1, 2, \cdots, n$, and the superscript ^{T} denotes the transpose operator of a matrix/vector. Furthermore, we define the time-dependent set:

$$\Omega^* = \{\mathbf{x}^*(t) \mid \partial\varphi(\mathbf{x}^*(t), t)/\partial \mathbf{x}^*(t) = \mathbf{0}\},$$

for time $t \in [t_{\text{ini}}, t_{\text{fin}}]$. It is worth pointing out that, in order to obtain the theoretical solution $\mathbf{x}^*(t)$, which can guarantee the minimization of the CTDUNO (6.2), $\mathbf{\Psi}(\mathbf{x}(t), t)$ should be set to zero.

6.3.1 CTDD model

To obtain the real-time solution of the CTDUNO (6.2), the derivative dynamics approach is an intuitive attempt. More specifically speaking, in order to achieve the theoretical solution $\mathbf{x}^*(t)$ that can maintain $\boldsymbol{\Psi}(\mathbf{x}(t),t)=\mathbf{0}$, for time $t\in[t_{\text{ini}},t_{\text{fin}}]$, the derivative of the gradient function $\boldsymbol{\Psi}(\mathbf{x}(t),t)$ with respect to time t should be zero, and we have

$$\frac{\mathrm{d}\boldsymbol{\Psi}(\mathbf{x}(t),t)}{\mathrm{d}t}=\frac{\partial\boldsymbol{\Psi}(\mathbf{x}(t),t)}{\partial t}+\frac{\partial\boldsymbol{\Psi}(\mathbf{x}(t),t)}{\partial\mathbf{x}(t)}\frac{\mathrm{d}\mathbf{x}(t)}{\mathrm{d}t}=\dot{\boldsymbol{\Psi}}_t(\mathbf{x}(t),t)+H(\mathbf{x}(t),t)\frac{\mathrm{d}\mathbf{x}(t)}{\mathrm{d}t}=\mathbf{0},\tag{6.3}$$

where the Hessian matrix $H(\mathbf{x}(t),t)$ and the time-derivative vector $\dot{\boldsymbol{\Psi}}_t(\mathbf{x}(t),t)$ are defined respectively as follows:

$$H(\mathbf{x}(t),t)=\begin{bmatrix}\frac{\partial\psi_1}{\partial x_1} & \frac{\partial\psi_1}{\partial x_2} & \cdots & \frac{\partial\psi_1}{\partial x_n}\\ \frac{\partial\psi_2}{\partial x_1} & \frac{\partial\psi_2}{\partial x_2} & \cdots & \frac{\partial\psi_2}{\partial x_n}\\ \vdots & \vdots & \ddots & \vdots\\ \frac{\partial\psi_n}{\partial x_1} & \frac{\partial\psi_n}{\partial x_2} & \cdots & \frac{\partial\psi_n}{\partial x_n}\end{bmatrix}=\begin{bmatrix}\frac{\partial^2\varphi}{\partial x_1\partial x_1} & \frac{\partial^2\varphi}{\partial x_1\partial x_2} & \cdots & \frac{\partial^2\varphi}{\partial x_1\partial x_n}\\ \frac{\partial^2\varphi}{\partial x_2\partial x_1} & \frac{\partial^2\varphi}{\partial x_2\partial x_2} & \cdots & \frac{\partial^2\varphi}{\partial x_2\partial x_n}\\ \vdots & \vdots & \ddots & \vdots\\ \frac{\partial^2\varphi}{\partial x_n\partial x_1} & \frac{\partial^2\varphi}{\partial x_n\partial x_2} & \cdots & \frac{\partial^2\varphi}{\partial x_n\partial x_n}\end{bmatrix}\in\mathbb{R}^{n\times n}$$

and

$$\dot{\boldsymbol{\Psi}}_t(\mathbf{x}(t),t)=\frac{\partial\boldsymbol{\Psi}(\mathbf{x}(t),t)}{\partial t}=\frac{\partial^2\varphi(\mathbf{x}(t),t)}{\partial\mathbf{x}(t)\partial t}\in\mathbb{R}^n.$$

Note that ψ_i and x_i denote the ith element of $\boldsymbol{\Psi}(\mathbf{x}(t),t)$ and $\mathbf{x}(t)$, respectively. Suppose that Hessian matrix $H(\mathbf{x}(t),t)$ is nonsingular for any $t\in[t_{\text{ini}},t_{\text{fin}}]$. The CTDD model for the CTDUNO (6.2) is formulated as [111, 134, 137–139]:

$$\dot{\mathbf{x}}(t)=-H^{-1}(\mathbf{x}(t),t)\frac{\partial^2\varphi(\mathbf{x}(t),t)}{\partial\mathbf{x}(t)\partial t},\ \text{with}\ \mathbf{x}_0=\mathbf{x}_0^*.\tag{6.4}$$

According to Lemma 1 in [111], suppose that the Hessian matrix $H(\mathbf{x}(t),t)$ is positive definite, and the solution of (6.4) corresponds to the real-time theoretical solution of the CTDUNO (6.2).

Lemma 6 *With* $\mathbf{x}(t)\in\mathbb{R}^n$ *and* $n\geqslant 2$, *suppose that the n-variable bounded function* $\varphi(\mathbf{x}(t),t)$ *has the second-order continuous partial derivatives in the neighborhood of point* $\mathrm{p}^*=\mathbf{x}^*(t_{\mathrm{p}})=[x_1^*(t_{\mathrm{p}}),\cdots,x_n^*(t_{\mathrm{p}})]^{\mathrm{T}}$ *at time instant* t_{p}, *which satisfies* $\partial\varphi(\mathbf{x}(t),t)/\partial x_i(t)|_{t=t_{\mathrm{p}},\,\mathbf{x}(t_{\mathrm{p}})=\mathrm{p}^*}=0$, *with* $i=1,2,\cdots,n$. *If the corresponding Hessian matrix* $H(\mathrm{p}^*,t_{\mathrm{p}})$ *is positive definite, then* $\varphi(\mathbf{x}(t),t)$ *achieves its minimum at point* p^* *of time instant* t_{p}.

Note that the CTDD model does not possess the nature of exploiting the error-feedback information throughout the real-time solution process. Moreover, supposing that the initial state $\mathbf{x}_0$ is not selected appropriately, more specifically speaking if $\boldsymbol{\Psi}(\mathbf{x}_0,0)\neq\mathbf{0}$, $\boldsymbol{\Psi}(\mathbf{x}(t),t)$ would remain nonzero during the whole computing process. Furthermore, even if $\mathbf{x}_0$ is accurately found, potential perturbations or computational errors may lead to a result that $\boldsymbol{\Psi}(\mathbf{x}(t),t)\neq\mathbf{0}$ for all $t\geq 0$. Thus, in viewpoint of control, this nature of not utilizing error-feedback information may cost the CTDD model (6.4) its robustness over perturbations and computational errors [111]. Therefore, a method utilizing both derivative information and error-feedback information simultaneously is required.

6.3.2 CTZNN model

In this subsection, the formulation of the CTZNN model is presented. It is worth pointing out that, according to previous works [51, 64, 70, 161], when comparing with derivative dynamics models, ZNN models not only have higher accuracy but also have better robustness for obtaining the real-time solution for the CTDUNO (6.2), because it exploits error-feedback information as well as the time-derivative information [111].

For monitoring and controlling purposes during the solving process of the CTDUNO (6.2), we first define a vector-valued indefinite zeroing function (ZF):

$$\mathbf{z}(t) = [z_1(t), z_2(t), \cdots, z_n(t)]^{\mathrm{T}} = \Psi(\mathbf{x}(t), t), \tag{6.5}$$

where $z_i(t) = \psi_i(\mathbf{x}(t), t)$, with $i = 1, 2, \cdots, n$, denotes the ith element of $\mathbf{z}(t)$. It is evident that the convergence of solution $\mathbf{x}(t)$ toward the theoretical solution $\mathbf{x}^*(t)$ can be achieved when the ZF (i.e., $\mathbf{z}(t)$) converges to zero. In order to make every element of $\mathbf{z}(t)$ converge to zero, on the basis of previous work on ZNN, the ZNN design formula is obtained as follows:

$$\frac{\mathrm{d}\mathbf{z}(t)}{\mathrm{d}t} = -\eta\Phi(\mathbf{z}(t)), \text{ i.e., } \frac{\mathrm{d}\Psi(\mathbf{x}(t),t)}{\mathrm{d}t} = -\eta\Phi(\Psi(\mathbf{x}(t),t)), \tag{6.6}$$

where the value of design parameter $\eta > 0$ should be selected accordingly for numerical stability, since it is used to scale the convergence rate. Besides, $\Phi(\cdot): \mathbb{R}^n \to \mathbb{R}^n$ denotes a vector activation function array and $\phi(\cdot)$ is used to denote the element of $\Phi(\cdot)$. It is worth mentioning that the ZNN design formula (6.6) is asymptotically stable (specifically, exponentially stable), which is proven in our previous work [51, 64, 70]. Besides, generally speaking, any monotonically increasing odd activation function $\phi(\cdot)$ can be used for constructing the neural network and different choices of activation function $\phi(\cdot)$ may lead to different convergence performances. In this chapter [157], the activation function applied to construct the CTZNN model is the simple linear activation function:

$$\phi_{\text{lin}}(u) = u. \tag{6.7}$$

After expanding the ZNN design formula (6.6) and considering (6.7), the following differential equation is obtained:

$$H(\mathbf{x}(t),t)\dot{\mathbf{x}}(t) = -\eta\Psi(\mathbf{x}(t),t) - \dot{\Psi}_t(\mathbf{x}(t),t). \tag{6.8}$$

Then, in view of $H(\mathbf{x}(t),t)$ being nonsingular in (6.8), the CTZNN model is obtained as below [111, 134, 137–139]:

$$\begin{aligned} \dot{\mathbf{x}}(t) &= -H^{-1}(\mathbf{x}(t),t)\left(\eta\Psi(\mathbf{x}(t),t) + \dot{\Psi}_t(\mathbf{x}(t),t)\right) \\ &= -H^{-1}(\mathbf{x}(t),t)\left(\eta\frac{\partial\varphi(\mathbf{x}(t),t)}{\partial\mathbf{x}(t)} + \frac{\partial^2\varphi(\mathbf{x}(t),t)}{\partial\mathbf{x}(t)\partial t}\right), \end{aligned} \tag{6.9}$$

where $\mathbf{x}(t)$ denotes the state of the neural network and starts with randomly generated initial condition $\mathbf{x}_0 \in \mathbb{R}^n$.

6.4 General 4S-ZTD Formula and Discrete-Time Algorithms

For potential digital hardware realization, it is necessary to discretize the CTDD model and the CTZNN model. In this section, the general four-step ZTD (4S-ZTD) formula is designed, and the general four-step DTDD (4S-DTDD) algorithm and the general four-step DTZNN (4S-DTZNN) algorithm are presented.

6.4.1 General *N*S-ZTD formula

The general *N*-step ZTD (*N*S-ZTD) formula is presented to lay the foundation of the general 4S-ZTD formula. On the basis of previous work [70], the general *N*S-ZTD formula is presented as

$$\dot{\zeta}_k = \frac{1}{g}\left(\sum_{i=1}^{N+1} a_i\zeta_{k-N+i}\right) + \mathscr{O}(g^p), \tag{6.10}$$

where N represents the amount of the steps of the ZTD formula (6.10); a_i denotes the coefficients, with $i = 1, 2, \cdots, N+1$; g denotes the sampling gap; $\mathscr{O}(g^p)$ denotes the truncation error; ζ_k denotes the value of $\zeta(t)$ at time instant $t_k = kg$, i.e., $\zeta_k = \zeta(t_k)$; $\dot{\zeta}_k = \dot{\zeta}(t_k)$ for simplicity; k denotes the updating index. For example, the general 4S-ZTD formula is presented as

$$\dot{\zeta}_k = \frac{a_5\zeta_{k+1} + a_4\zeta_k + a_3\zeta_{k-1} + a_2\zeta_{k-2} + a_1\zeta_{k-3}}{g} + \mathscr{O}(g^p). \tag{6.11}$$

However, the coefficients are remaining to be determined in Section 6.4.2.

6.4.2 General 4S-ZTD formula

For the readability of this chapter [157] and the integrity of the structure, the important achievements during the design procedure of the general 4S-ZTD formula are presented in the following theorem and corollary.

Theorem 26 *With the sufficiently small sampling gap $g \in (0,1)$, let $\mathscr{O}(g^3)$ denote the error (especially, the truncation error) positively or negatively proportional to g^3, i.e., of the order of g^3. Suppose that $\zeta(t)$ is sufficiently smooth. With $\zeta_{k+1} = \zeta(t_{k+1}) = \zeta((k+1)g)$, the general 4S-ZTD formula is presented as follows:*

$$\dot{\zeta}_k = \frac{(6a_1+2)\zeta_{k+1} - (24a_1-3)\zeta_k + (36a_1-6)\zeta_{k-1} - (24a_1-1)\zeta_{k-2} + 6a_1\zeta_{k-3}}{6g} + \mathscr{O}(g^3), \tag{6.12}$$

where the effective domain of a_1 is $1/12 < a_1 < 1/6$. This general 4S-ZTD formula is convergent with the truncation error of $\mathscr{O}(g^3)$.

Proof. According to Definitions 2–4 in Chapter 1, we conclude that as an N-step method, (6.12) is convergent if it is both consistent and zero-stable. The design procedure of (6.12) is illustrated in the remaining part of this subsection. First, the mth-order Taylor expansion [161] is presented as

$$\zeta_{k+1} = \zeta_k + g\dot{\zeta}_k + \frac{g^2}{2}\ddot{\zeta}_k + \cdots + \frac{g^m}{m!}\zeta_k^{(m)} + \mathscr{O}(g^{m+1}). \tag{6.13}$$

In order to obtain the general 4S-ZTD formula (6.11) with the truncation error of $\mathscr{O}(g^4)$, the following Taylor expansions of ζ_{k+1}, ζ_{k-1}, ζ_{k-2}, and ζ_{k-3} are given as

$$\zeta_{k+1} = \zeta_k + g\dot{\zeta}_k + \frac{g^2}{2}\ddot{\zeta}_k - \frac{g^3}{6}\dddot{\zeta}_k + \frac{g^4}{24}\zeta_k^{(4)} + \mathscr{O}(g^5), \tag{6.14}$$

$$\zeta_{k-1} = \zeta_k - g\dot{\zeta}_k + \frac{g^2}{2}\ddot{\zeta}_k - \frac{g^3}{6}\dddot{\zeta}_k + \frac{g^4}{24}\zeta_k^{(4)} + \mathscr{O}(g^5), \tag{6.15}$$

$$\zeta_{k-2} = \zeta_k - 2g\dot{\zeta}_k + 2g^2\ddot{\zeta}_k - \frac{4g^3}{3}\dddot{\zeta}_k + \frac{2g^4}{3}\zeta_k^{(4)} + \mathscr{O}(g^5), \tag{6.16}$$

and

$$\zeta_{k-3} = \zeta_k - 3g\dot{\zeta}_k + \frac{9g^2}{2}\ddot{\zeta}_k - \frac{9g^3}{2}\dddot{\zeta}_k + \frac{27g^4}{8}\zeta_k^{(4)} + \mathscr{O}(g^5). \tag{6.17}$$

By substituting (6.14)–(6.17) into (6.11), the following equation is obtained:

$$b_0\zeta_k + b_1g\dot{\zeta}_k + b_2g^2\ddot{\zeta}_k + b_3g^3\dddot{\zeta}_k + b_4g^4\zeta_k^{(4)} + \mathscr{O}(g^5) = \mathscr{O}(g^{p+1}), \tag{6.18}$$

where $b_0 = a_5 + a_4 + a_3 + a_2 + a_1$, $b_1 = a_5 - a_3 - 2a_2 - 3a_1 - 1$, $b_2 = a_5/2 + a_3/2 + 2a_2 + 9a_1/2$, $b_3 = a_5/6 - a_3/6 - 4a_2/3 - 9a_1/2$, and $b_4 = a_5/24 + a_3/24 + 2a_2/3 + 27a_1/8$. If $p = 4$ and the general 4S-ZTD formula (6.11) is consistent and has a truncation error of $\mathscr{O}(g^4)$, the conditions below must be satisfied:

$$\begin{cases} b_0 = a_5 + a_4 + a_3 + a_2 + a_1 = 0, \\ b_1 = a_5 - a_3 - 2a_2 - 3a_1 - 1 = 0, \\ b_2 = a_5/2 + a_3/2 + 2a_2 + 9a_1/2 = 0, \\ b_3 = a_5/6 - a_3/6 - 4a_2/3 - 9a_1/2 = 0, \\ b_4 = a_5/24 + a_3/24 + 2a_2/3 + 27a_1/8 = 0. \end{cases} \tag{6.19}$$

By solving (6.19), we obtain the solution as

$$\begin{cases} a_1 = -\dfrac{1}{12}, \\ a_2 = \dfrac{1}{2}, \\ a_3 = -\dfrac{3}{2}, \\ a_4 = \dfrac{5}{6}, \\ a_5 = \dfrac{1}{4}. \end{cases} \tag{6.20}$$

Therefore, we obtain the characteristic polynomial of (6.11) as follows:

$$\Gamma_4(\iota) = 3\iota^4 + 10\iota^3 - 18\iota^2 + 6\iota - 1, \tag{6.21}$$

of which the roots are -4.7028, 1, $0.1847+0.1917$i, and $0.1847-0.1917$i with i denoting imaginary unit. It does not satisfy the zero-stability since one root lies outside of the unit circle. Thus, there are no coefficients that can guarantee $p=4$ and the general 4S-ZTD formula (6.11) has a truncation error of $\mathscr{O}(g^4)$.

If $p=3$ and the general 4S-ZTD formula (6.11) has a truncation error of $\mathscr{O}(g^3)$, the conditions below must be satisfied:

$$\begin{cases} b_0 = a_5 + a_4 + a_3 + a_2 + a_1 = 0, \\ b_1 = a_5 - a_3 - 2a_2 - 3a_1 - 1 = 0, \\ b_2 = a_5/2 + a_3/2 + 2a_2 + 9a_1/2 = 0, \\ b_3 = a_5/6 - a_3/6 - 4a_2/3 - 9a_1/2 = 0. \end{cases} \tag{6.22}$$

By computing the solution of (6.22), we obtain

$$\begin{cases} a_5 = a_1 + 3, \\ a_4 = -4a_1 + \dfrac{1}{2}, \\ a_3 = 6a_1 - 1, \\ a_2 = -4a_1 + \dfrac{1}{6}. \end{cases} \tag{6.23}$$

Besides, from the above computation process, we obtain $b_4 = a_1 + 1/12$. Then, (6.18) is formulated as

$$\left(a_1 + \frac{1}{12}\right) g^4 \zeta_k^{(4)} + \mathscr{O}(g^5) = \mathscr{O}(g^4). \tag{6.24}$$

Evidently, (6.24) holds true. Thus, according to Definition 3 in Chapter 1, we obtain the general 4S-ZTD formula (6.11) which is consistent and with the truncation error of $\mathscr{O}(g^3)$.

Furthermore, according to Definition 4 in Chapter 1, we need to further investigate the zero-stability of the general 4S-ZTD formula (6.11) to have a better understanding of its convergency. With $\doteq$ denoting the computational assignment operator, the general 4S-ZTD formula (6.11) is rewritten as

$$a_5\zeta_{k+1}+a_4\zeta_k+a_3\zeta_{k-1}+a_2\zeta_{k-2}+a_1\zeta_{k-3}\doteq g\dot{\zeta}_k, \tag{6.25}$$

which gives us the characteristic polynomial of (6.25) as below according to Definition 2 in Chapter 1:

$$\Gamma_4(\iota)=a_5\iota^4+a_4\iota^3+a_3\iota^2+a_2\iota+a_1. \tag{6.26}$$

In order to investigate the roots of (6.26), by adopting bilinear transformation (also termed as Tustin transformation [162, 163]) $\iota=(\omega+1)/(\omega-1)$, the following equation is obtained:

$$c_4\omega^4+c_3\omega^3+c_2\omega^2+c_1\omega+c_0=0. \tag{6.27}$$

After substituting solution (6.23) to (6.27), we obtain $c_0=0$, $c_1=2$, $c_2=4$, $c_3=2/3$, and $c_4=16a_1-4/3$, which means (6.27) is reformulated as

$$\left(16a_1-\frac{4}{3}\right)\omega^4+\frac{2}{3}\omega^3+4\omega^2+2\omega+0=0.$$

According to the Routh stability criterion [164], we have

$$\frac{1}{12}<a_1<\frac{1}{6}.$$

On the basis of the solution (6.23) and Taylor expansions (6.14)–(6.17), we have

$$\begin{aligned}&\frac{(6a_1+2)\zeta_{k+1}-(24a_1-3)\zeta_k+(36a_1-6)\zeta_{k-1}-(24a_1-1)\zeta_{k-2}+6a_1\zeta_{k-3}}{6g}\\&=\dot{\zeta}_k+\left(a_1+\frac{1}{12}\right)g^3\zeta_k^{(4)}+\mathscr{O}(g^4).\end{aligned} \tag{6.28}$$

After rearranging (6.28), the general 4S-ZTD formula is presented as

$$\begin{aligned}\dot{\zeta}_k=&\frac{(6a_1+2)\zeta_{k+1}-(24a_1-3)\zeta_k+(36a_1-6)\zeta_{k-1}-(24a_1-1)\zeta_{k-2}+6a_1\zeta_{k-3}}{6g}\\&-\left(a_1+\frac{1}{12}\right)g^3\zeta_k^{(4)}+\mathscr{O}(g^4)\end{aligned} \tag{6.29}$$

or

$$\dot{\zeta}_k=\frac{(6a_1+2)\zeta_{k+1}-(24a_1-3)\zeta_k+(36a_1-6)\zeta_{k-1}-(24a_1-1)\zeta_{k-2}+6a_1\zeta_{k-3}}{6g}+\mathscr{O}(g^3),$$

where $1/12<a_1<1/6$. Apparently, we see that the truncation error of (6.29) is $-(a_1+1/12)g^3\zeta_k^{(4)}=\mathscr{O}(g^3)$. In addition, the collection of the general 4S-ZTD formula (6.12) with different values of a_1 is shown in Table 6.1. The proof is therefore completed. □

Corollary 1 *With the sufficiently small sampling gap $g\in(0,1)$, the truncation error of the general 4S-ZTD formula (6.12) becomes smaller when a_1 approaches toward* $1/12$.

Proof. From (6.29), we see that the expression of truncation error is $-(a_1+1/12)g^3\zeta_k^{(4)}$. Since the effective domain of parameter a_1 is $1/12<a_1<1/6$, it is evident that when the value of a_1 approaches toward $1/12$, the truncation error of the general 4S-ZTD formula (6.12) becomes smaller. The proof is therefore completed. □

TABLE 6.1: Collection of 4S-ZTD formulas with various values of a_1.

a_1	Formula expression
$1/12 < a_1 < 1/6$	$\dot{\zeta}_k = \frac{(6a_1+2)\zeta_{k+1}-(24a_1-3)\zeta_k+(36a_1-6)\zeta_{k-1}-(24a_1-1)\zeta_{k-2}+6a_1\zeta_{k-3}}{6g}+\mathscr{O}(g^3)$
$1/11$	$\dot{\zeta}_k = \frac{28\zeta_{k+1}+9\zeta_k-30\zeta_{k-1}-13\zeta_{k-2}+6\zeta_{k-3}}{66g}+\mathscr{O}(g^3)$
$1/10$	$\dot{\zeta}_k = \frac{13\zeta_{k+1}+3\zeta_k-12\zeta_{k-1}-7\zeta_{k-2}+3\zeta_{k-3}}{30g}+\mathscr{O}(g^3)$
$1/9$	$\dot{\zeta}_k = \frac{8\zeta_{k+1}+\zeta_k-6\zeta_{k-1}-5\zeta_{k-2}+2\zeta_{k-3}}{18g}+\mathscr{O}(g^3)$
$1/8$	$\dot{\zeta}_k = \frac{11\zeta_{k+1}-6\zeta_{k-1}-8\zeta_{k-2}+3\zeta_{k-3}}{24g}+\mathscr{O}(g^3)$
$1/7$	$\dot{\zeta}_k = \frac{20\zeta_{k+1}-3\zeta_k-6\zeta_{k-1}-17\zeta_{k-2}+6\zeta_{k-3}}{42g}+\mathscr{O}(g^3)$

6.4.3 General discrete-time algorithms

Due to potential digital hardware realization such as digital computer and digital circuit realization, the development of discrete-time algorithms is necessary. In this subsection, on the basis of the CTDD model and CTZNN model, both the general 4S-DTDD algorithm and the general 4S-DTZNN algorithm are presented by adopting the general 4S-ZTD formula (6.12).

6.4.3.1 General 4S-DTDD algorithm

After adopting the formula (6.12) to discretize the CTDD model (6.4), we obtain

$$\begin{aligned}&\frac{(6a_1+2)\mathbf{x}_{k+1}-(24a_1-3)\mathbf{x}_k+(36a_1-6)\mathbf{x}_{k-1}-(24a_1-1)\mathbf{x}_{k-2}+6a_1\mathbf{x}_{k-3}}{6g}+\mathbf{O}(g^3)\\&=-H^{-1}(\mathbf{x}_k,t_k)\frac{\partial^2\varphi(\mathbf{x}_k,t_k)}{\partial\mathbf{x}_k\partial t_k},\end{aligned}\tag{6.30}$$

which is formulated as

$$\begin{aligned}\mathbf{x}_{k+1}\doteq&-\frac{6}{6a_1+2}gH^{-1}(\mathbf{x}_k,t_k)\,\mathbf{\Psi}_t(\mathbf{x}_k,t_k)\\&+\frac{24a_1-3}{6a_1+2}\mathbf{x}_k-\frac{36a_1-6}{6a_1+2}\mathbf{x}_{k-1}+\frac{24a_1-1}{6a_1+2}\mathbf{x}_{k-2}-\frac{6a_1}{6a_1+2}\mathbf{x}_{k-3}.\end{aligned}\tag{6.31}$$

Thus, the design procedure of the general 4S-DTDD algorithm is completed.

6.4.3.2 General 4S-DTZNN algorithm

In order to obtain the accurate discretization, the general 4S-ZTD formula (6.12) is adopted to discretize the CTZNN model (6.9). Therefore, we have

$$\begin{aligned}&\frac{(6a_1+2)\mathbf{x}_{k+1}-(24a_1-3)\mathbf{x}_k+(36a_1-6)\mathbf{x}_{k-1}-(24a_1-1)\mathbf{x}_{k-2}+6a_1\mathbf{x}_{k-3}}{6g}+\mathbf{O}(g^3)\\&=-H^{-1}(\mathbf{x}_k,t_k)\left(\eta\frac{\partial\varphi(\mathbf{x}_k,t_k)}{\partial\mathbf{x}_k}+\frac{\partial^2\varphi(\mathbf{x}_k,t_k)}{\partial\mathbf{x}_k\partial t_k}\right),\end{aligned}\tag{6.32}$$

which is formulated as

$$\begin{aligned}\mathbf{x}_{k+1}\doteq&-\frac{6}{6a_1+2}H^{-1}(\mathbf{x}_k,t_k)\left(\hbar\mathbf{\Psi}(\mathbf{x}_k,t_k)+g\dot{\mathbf{\Psi}}_t(\mathbf{x}_k,t_k)\right)\\&+\frac{24a_1-3}{6a_1+2}\mathbf{x}_k-\frac{36a_1-6}{6a_1+2}\mathbf{x}_{k-1}+\frac{24a_1-1}{6a_1+2}\mathbf{x}_{k-2}-\frac{6a_1}{6a_1+2}\mathbf{x}_{k-3},\end{aligned}\tag{6.33}$$

where the step length $\hbar = g\eta$. Thus, the design procedure of the general 4S-DTZNN algorithm is completed.

6.5 Theoretical Analyses

On the basis of Definitions 2–4 in Chapter 1, we have the following theoretical analyses about the general 4S-DTZNN algorithm (6.33).

Theorem 27 *Suppose that $H(\mathbf{x}_k,t_k)$ is always nonsingular. With the sufficiently small sampling gap $g\in(0,1)$, let $\mathbf{O}(g^4)$ denote the error (especially, the truncation error) with each element being $\mathscr{O}(g^4)$. The general 4S-DTZNN algorithm (6.33) is zero-stable, consistent, and convergent with the truncation error of $\mathbf{O}(g^4)$ when $1/12<a_1<1/6$.*

Proof. According to Section 6.4.3.2, the general 4S-DTZNN algorithm (6.33) is rewritten as

$$\begin{aligned}\mathbf{x}_{k+1}=&-\frac{6}{6a_1+2}H^{-1}(\mathbf{x}_k,t_k)\left(\hbar\boldsymbol{\Psi}(\mathbf{x}_k,t_k)+g\dot{\boldsymbol{\Psi}}_t(\mathbf{x}_k,t_k)\right)\\&+\frac{24a_1-3}{6a_1+2}\mathbf{x}_k-\frac{36a_1-6}{6a_1+2}\mathbf{x}_{k-1}+\frac{24a_1-1}{6a_1+2}\mathbf{x}_{k-2}-\frac{6a_1}{6a_1+2}\mathbf{x}_{k-3}+\mathbf{O}(g^4),\end{aligned}$$

where apparently the truncation error is $\mathbf{O}(g^4)$. In addition, according to Definitions 2 and 3 in Chapter 1, based on the design procedure of the general 4S-ZTD formula (6.11) and the general 4S-DTZNN algorithm (6.33), it is known that the general 4S-DTZNN algorithm (6.33) is zero-stable and consistent with the truncation error of $\mathbf{O}(g^4)$ when $1/12<a_1<1/6$. Therefore, according to Definition 4 in Chapter 1, we know that the general 4S-DTZNN algorithm (6.33) is zero-stable, consistent, and convergent with the truncation error of $\mathbf{O}(g^4)$ when $1/12<a_1<1/6$. The proof is therefore completed. □

Note that the residual error is defined as $\hat{e}_{k+1}=\|\partial\varphi(\mathbf{x}_{k+1},t_{k+1})/\partial\mathbf{x}_{k+1}\|_2=\|\boldsymbol{\Psi}(\mathbf{x}_{k+1},t_{k+1})\|_2$ for the FUNO (6.1) in this chapter [157], where $\|\cdot\|_2$ denotes the 2-norm of a vector.

Theorem 28 *Consider the FUNO (6.1) with $\varphi(\cdot,\cdot)$ being second-order differentiable and bounded. Suppose that $H(\mathbf{x}_k,t_k)$ is always nonsingular and uniformly norm bounded. With the sufficiently small sampling gap $g\in(0,1)$, the maximal steady-state residual error (MSSRE) $\lim_{k\to+\infty}\sup\hat{e}_{k+1}$ synthesized by the general 4S-DTZNN algorithm (6.33) is $\mathscr{O}(g^4)$.*

Proof. Let $\mathbf{x}^*_{k+1}\in\mathbb{R}^n$ denote the theoretical solution of the FUNO (6.1). According to Lemma 1 in [111], we know that $\boldsymbol{\Psi}(\mathbf{x}^*_{k+1},t_{k+1})=\mathbf{0}$. Furthermore, from Theorem 27, it is obtained that $\mathbf{x}_{k+1}=\mathbf{x}^*_{k+1}+\mathbf{O}(g^4)$ when k is large enough. Therefore, the following result is obtained:

$$\lim_{k\to\infty}\sup\|\boldsymbol{\Psi}(\mathbf{x}_{k+1},t_{k+1})\|_2=\lim_{k\to\infty}\sup\|\boldsymbol{\Psi}(\mathbf{x}^*_{k+1}+\mathbf{O}(g^4),t_{k+1})\|_2.$$

By using Taylor expansion [20], we obtain

$$\begin{aligned}\lim_{k\to\infty}\sup\|\boldsymbol{\Psi}(\mathbf{x}_{k+1},t_{k+1})\|_2&=\lim_{k\to\infty}\sup\|\boldsymbol{\Psi}(\mathbf{x}^*_{k+1},t_{k+1})+H(\mathbf{x}^*_{k+1},t_{k+1})\mathbf{O}(g^4)+\mathbf{O}(g^8)\|_2\\&=\lim_{k\to\infty}\sup\|H(\mathbf{x}^*_{k+1},t_{k+1})\mathbf{O}(g^4)+\mathbf{O}(g^8)\|_2.\end{aligned}$$

Considering that $H(\mathbf{x}^*_{t_{k+1}},t_{k+1})$ is a constant matrix at a certain time instant, we further have

$$\lim_{k\to\infty}\sup\|\boldsymbol{\Psi}(\mathbf{x}_{k+1},t_{k+1})\|_2=\mathscr{O}(g^4).$$

The proof is therefore completed. □

For a more intuitive understanding of the main content of this chapter [157], Table 6.2 lists the problem, scheme, models, and algorithms.

TABLE 6.2: Problem, scheme, models, and algorithms in this chapter.

Problem	$\min_{\mathbf{x}_{k+1}\in\mathbb{R}^n} \varphi(\mathbf{x}_{k+1},t_{k+1})\in\mathbb{R}.$
Scheme	*Step 1*: For CTDD model, define gradient function as $\boldsymbol{\Psi}(\mathbf{x}(t),t)=\partial\varphi(\mathbf{x}(t),t)/\partial\mathbf{x}(t)$, and adopt derivative dynamics approach as $\mathrm{d}\boldsymbol{\Psi}(\mathbf{x}(t),t)/\mathrm{d}t=\mathbf{0}$. *Step 2*: For CTZNN model, define ZF as $\mathbf{z}(t)=\boldsymbol{\Psi}(\mathbf{x}(t),t)$, and adopt ZNN design formula as $\dot{\mathbf{z}}(t)=-\eta\mathbf{z}(t)$. *Step 3*: Adopt ZTD formula to discretize CTDD model (6.4) and CTZNN model (6.9).
Models	$\dot{\mathbf{x}}(t)=-H^{-1}(\mathbf{x}(t),t)\frac{\partial^2\varphi(\mathbf{x}(t),t)}{\partial\mathbf{x}(t)\partial t}$, $\dot{\mathbf{x}}(t)=-H^{-1}(\mathbf{x}(t),t)\left(\eta\frac{\partial\varphi(\mathbf{x}(t),t)}{\partial\mathbf{x}(t)}+\frac{\partial^2\varphi(\mathbf{x}(t),t)}{\partial\mathbf{x}(t)\partial t}\right)$.
Algorithms	$\mathbf{x}_{k+1}\doteq-\frac{6}{6a_1+2}gH^{-1}(\mathbf{x}_k,t_k)\,\boldsymbol{\Psi}_t(\mathbf{x}_k,t_k)+\frac{24a_1-3}{6a_1+2}\mathbf{x}_k-\frac{36a_1-6}{6a_1+2}\mathbf{x}_{k-1}+\frac{24a_1-1}{6a_1+2}\mathbf{x}_{k-2}-\frac{6a_1}{6a_1+2}\mathbf{x}_{k-3}$, $\mathbf{x}_{k+1}\doteq-\frac{6}{6a_1+2}H^{-1}(\mathbf{x}_k,t_k)\left(\hbar\boldsymbol{\Psi}(\mathbf{x}_k,t_k)+g\dot{\boldsymbol{\Psi}}_t(\mathbf{x}_k,t_k)\right)+\frac{24a_1-3}{6a_1+2}\mathbf{x}_k-\frac{36a_1-6}{6a_1+2}\mathbf{x}_{k-1}+\frac{24a_1-1}{6a_1+2}\mathbf{x}_{k-2}-\frac{6a_1}{6a_1+2}\mathbf{x}_{k-3}.$

6.6 Numerical Experiments

In order to verify the efficacy and accuracy of the general 4S-DTDD algorithm (6.31) and the general 4S-DTZNN algorithm (6.33), numerical experiments are conducted. Without loss of generality, these experiments are carried out in MATLAB version 7.6.0 environment with a personal digital computer [161].

6.6.1 FUNO problem solving by general 4S-DTDD algorithm (6.31) and general 4S-DTZNN algorithm (6.33)

In this subsection, for illustrative and comparative purposes, one same example of the FUNO (6.1) is synthesized by the general 4S-DTDD algorithm (6.31) and the general 4S-DTZNN algorithm (6.33) simultaneously. Furthermore, in order to investigate the robustness of these algorithms, several experiments are started with various initial states.

Example 6.1 Let us consider a specific FUNO problem, which is expressed as

$$\begin{aligned}\min_{\mathbf{x}_k\in\mathbb{R}^4}\varphi(\mathbf{x}_k,t_k)=&\left(x_{1,k}+10\sin\left(\frac{\pi t_k}{40}\right)\right)^2+\left(x_{2,k}+\frac{t_k}{4}\right)^2+\left(x_{3,k}-\exp\left(-\frac{t_k}{4}\right)\right)^2\\&+\frac{1}{40}(t_k-1)x_{3,k}x_{4,k}+\left(x_{1,k}+\ln\left(\sin\left(\frac{\pi t_k}{40}\right)+1\right)\right)\left(x_{2,k}+\sin\left(\frac{t_k}{8}\right)+\cos\left(\frac{t_k}{8}\right)\right)\\&-(x_{1,k}+(x_{1,k}+\sin(t_k))x_{3,k}+\left(x_{4,k}+\exp\left(-\frac{t_k}{4}\right)\right)^2.\end{aligned}\tag{6.34}$$

First, the general 4S-DTDD algorithm (6.31) and the general 4S-DTZNN algorithm (6.33) are applied to solve the FUNO (6.34) with $g=0.05$ s, $\hbar=0.05$, and $a_1=1/9$. The corresponding numerical experimental results are presented in Figure 6.1.

In Figure 6.1(a), the dash curve and the solid curve denote the values of $\varphi(\mathbf{x}_{k+1},t_{k+1})$ corresponding to the solutions of the FUNO (6.34) generated by the general 4S-DTDD algorithm (6.31) and the general 4S-DTZNN algorithm (6.33), respectively. Note that the numerical experiments generated by the general 4S-DTDD algorithm (6.31) and the general 4S-DTZNN algorithm (6.33) start with the same initial state vector $\mathbf{x}_0=[1,2,3,4]^\mathrm{T}$ with the task duration T being 30 s. Then according to our previous work [70, 111], the state vectors of the second and the third sampling nodes

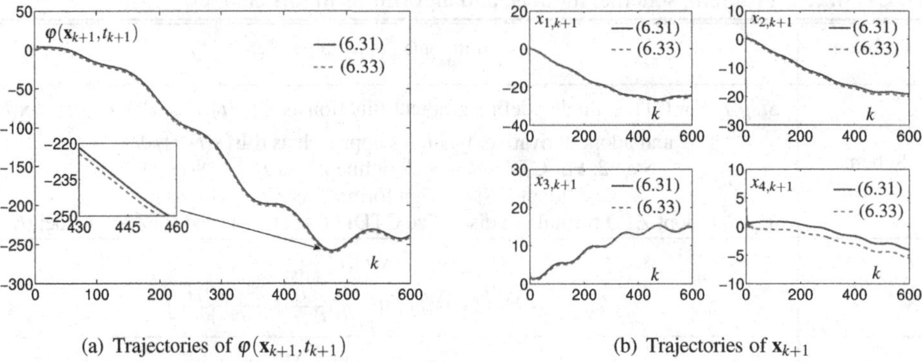

(a) Trajectories of $\varphi(\mathbf{x}_{k+1}, t_{k+1})$ (b) Trajectories of $\mathbf{x}_{k+1}$

FIGURE 6.1: Trajectories of $\varphi(\mathbf{x}_{k+1}, t_{k+1})$ and $\mathbf{x}_{k+1}$ generated by general 4S-DTDD algorithm (6.31) and general 4S-DTZNN algorithm (6.33) with $a_1 = 1/9$ and $\hbar = 0.05$ in Example 6.1.

are computed by using the Euler-type discrete-time algorithm since the algorithm requires just the state vector of one preceding sampling node. After the state vectors of the first four sampling nodes are acquired, the general 4S-DTDD algorithm (6.31) and the general 4S-DTZNN algorithm (6.33) are both adopted to solve the FUNO (6.34).

From Figure 6.1, it is easy for us to obtain an intuitive understanding that: when the initial state $\mathbf{x}_0$ does not satisfy $\mathbf{x}_0 = \mathbf{x}_0^*$, although both the general 4S-DTDD algorithm (6.31) and the general 4S-DTZNN algorithm (6.33) are adequate for solving the FUNO (6.34), the general 4S-DTZNN algorithm (6.33) is more accurate. More specifically speaking, as shown in Figure 6.1(a), the value of $\varphi(\mathbf{x}_{k+1}, t_{k+1})$ generated by the general 4S-DTZNN algorithm (6.33) remains to be smaller than the value of $\varphi(\mathbf{x}_{k+1}, t_{k+1})$ generated by the general 4S-DTDD algorithm (6.31).

In order to have a better understanding of the real-time convergence of the general 4S-DTDD algorithm (6.31) and the general 4S-DTZNN algorithm (6.33), we investigate the residual error $\hat{e}_{k+1} = \|\Psi(\mathbf{x}_{k+1}, t_{k+1})\|_2$, as the optimization of the FUNO (6.34) can be achieved when $\hat{e}_{k+1}$ is convergent to zero.

The trajectories of residual error $\hat{e}_{k+1}$ when the initial state $\mathbf{x}_0$ does not satisfy $\mathbf{x}_0 = \mathbf{x}_0^*$ are illustrated in Figure 6.2.

As seen from Figure 6.2(a), when $g = 0.05$ s, the residual error synthesized by the general 4S-DTZNN algorithm (6.33) converges to near zero, while the residual error synthesized by the general 4S-DTDD algorithm (6.31) does not converge to zero and remains relatively large, which is around

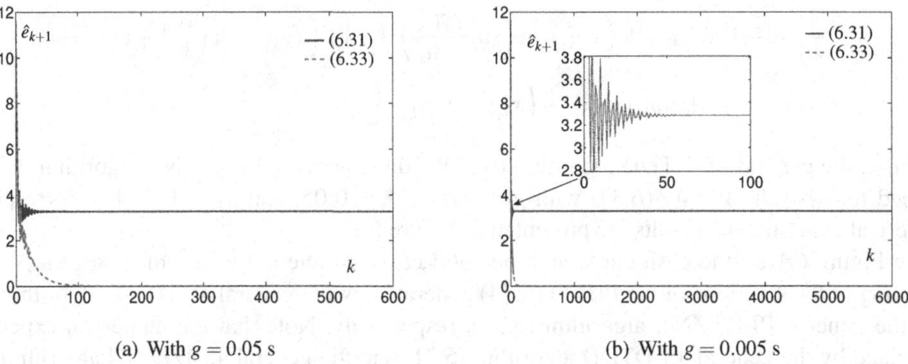

(a) With $g = 0.05$ s (b) With $g = 0.005$ s

FIGURE 6.2: Trajectories of residual errors $\hat{e}_{k+1}$ synthesized by general 4S-DTDD algorithm (6.31) and general 4S-DTZNN algorithm (6.33) with $a_1 = 1/9$ and $\hbar = 0.05$ in Example 6.1.

TABLE 6.3: MSSREs synthesized by general 4S-DTDD algorithm (6.31) and general 4S-DTZNN algorithm (6.33) when initial states satisfying $\mathbf{x}_0 = \mathbf{x}_0^*$ with $a_1 = 1/9$ and $\hbar = 0.05$ in Example 6.1.

Discrete-time algorithm	$g = 0.05$ s	$g = 0.005$ s	$g = 0.0005$ s
4S-DTDD algorithm (6.31)	6.9452×10^{-4}	4.8745×10^{-6}	6.6863×10^{-8}
4S-DTZNN algorithm (6.33)	1.6144×10^{-5}	2.2714×10^{-9}	2.5334×10^{-13}

3.28. Moreover, from Figure 6.2(b), we see that when $g = 0.005$ s there is an evident enhancement of the performance of the general 4S-DTZNN algorithm (6.33), while the residual error synthesized by the general 4S-DTDD algorithm (6.31) still does not converge to zero.

Second, to further investigate the performance of both discrete-time algorithms when $\mathbf{x}_0 = \mathbf{x}_0^*$, a few more experiments are conducted and the corresponding numerical experimental results are presented in Figure 6.3 and Table 6.3. Specifically, Table 6.3 presents the corresponding MSSREs. From Figure 6.3, when the initial state is delicately selected to satisfy $\mathbf{x}_0 = \mathbf{x}_0^*$, the residual error $\hat{e}_{k+1}$ synthesized by the general 4S-DTDD algorithm (6.31) converges to near zero after a short time of oscillation, but the general 4S-DTZNN algorithm (6.33) shows to be more accurate. More specifically speaking, as seen from Figure 6.3(a), the residual error $\hat{e}_{k+1}$ synthesized by the general 4S-DTDD algorithm (6.31) is of order 10^{-4} when the sampling gap being $g = 0.05$ s, and in Figure 6.3(b), the residual error is of order 10^{-6} when the sampling gap $g = 0.005$ s. It is shown that the residual error $\hat{e}_{k+1}$ synthesized by the general 4S-DTDD algorithm (6.31) is of order $\mathscr{O}(g^2)$ when the initial state $\mathbf{x}_0$ satisfies $\mathbf{x}_0 = \mathbf{x}_0^*$.

As to the performance of the general 4S-DTZNN algorithm (6.33), from Table 6.3 we see it evidently that the MSSRE synthesized by the general 4S-DTZNN algorithm (6.33) is of order 10^{-5} when $g = 0.05$ s, of order 10^{-9} when $g = 0.005$ s, and of order 10^{-13} when $g = 0.0005$ s. We draw the conclusion that the MSSRE synthesized by the general 4S-DTZNN algorithm (6.33) is of order $\mathscr{O}(g^4)$, and this conclusion collaborates with Theorem 28 in Section 6.5. It is also seen from Table 6.3 that the MSSRE synthesized by the general 4S-DTDD algorithm (6.31) shows a pattern of $\mathscr{O}(g^2)$.

Furthermore, from Figures 6.1 and 6.2, it is evident that the general 4S-DTDD algorithm (6.31) is sensitive to the initial state, while the general 4S-DTZNN algorithm (6.33) is robust.

Finally, to further investigate the influence of parameter a_1 over the performance of the general 4S-DTZNN algorithm (6.31), the general 4S-DTZNN algorithm is exploited to solve the FUNO

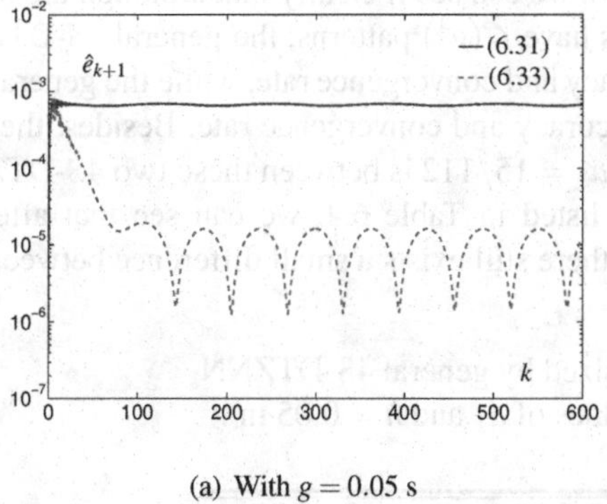

(a) With $g = 0.05$ s

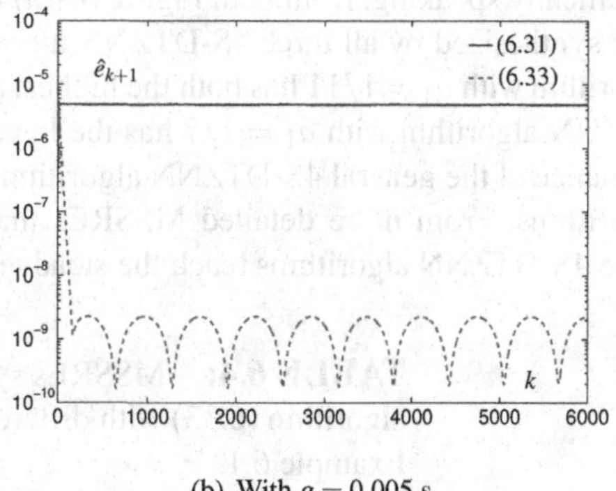

(b) With $g = 0.005$ s

FIGURE 6.3: Trajectories of residual errors $\hat{e}_{k+1}$ synthesized by general 4S-DTDD algorithm (6.31) and general 4S-DTZNN algorithm (6.33) when $\mathbf{x}_0 = \mathbf{x}_0^*$ with $a_1 = 1/9$ and $\hbar = 0.05$ in Example 6.1.

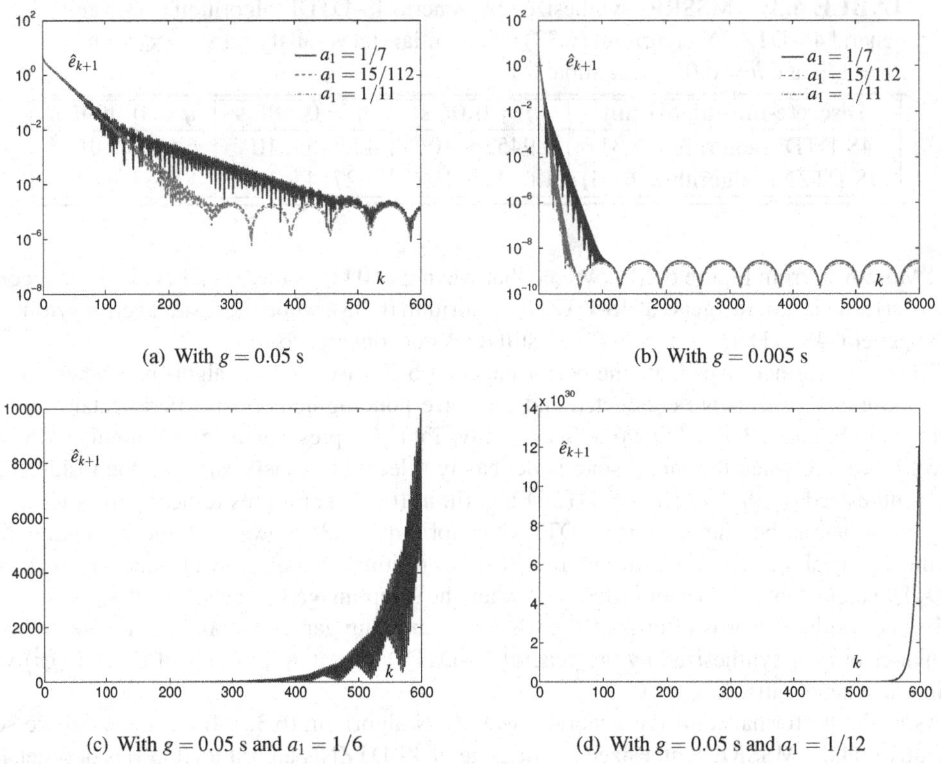

(a) With $g = 0.05$ s

(b) With $g = 0.005$ s

(c) With $g = 0.05$ s and $a_1 = 1/6$

(d) With $g = 0.05$ s and $a_1 = 1/12$

FIGURE 6.4: Trajectories of residual errors $\hat{e}_{k+1}$ synthesized by general 4S-DTZNN algorithm (6.33) with $\hbar = 0.05$ and different values of a_1 in Example 6.1.

(6.34) with the values of a_1 being $a_1 = 1/6$, $a_1 = 1/7$, $a_1 = 15/112$, $a_1 = 1/11$, and $a_1 = 1/12$. Without loss of generality, the numerical experiments begin with the same randomly generated initial state. The corresponding numerical experimental results are presented in Figure 6.4 and Table 6.4.

From Figure 6.4(a) and (b), we obtain an intuitive conclusion that there exist notable enhancements of the performance of the general 4S-DTZNN algorithm (6.33) as a_1 approaches $1/12$. More specifically speaking, from both Figure 6.4(a) and (b), we can see it clearly that although the MSSREs synthesized by all three 4S-DTZNN algorithms have $\mathscr{O}(g^4)$ patterns, the general 4S-DTZNN algorithm with $a_1 = 1/11$ has both the highest accuracy and convergence rate, while the general 4S-DTZNN algorithm with $a_1 = 1/7$ has the lowest accuracy and convergence rate. Besides, the performance of the general 4S-DTZNN algorithm with $a_1 = 15/112$ is between these two 4S-DTZNN algorithms. From more detailed MSSREs that are listed in Table 6.4, we can see that after all three 4S-DTZNN algorithms reach the steady state, there still exists a small difference between the

TABLE 6.4: MSSREs synthesized by general 4S-DTZNN algorithm (6.33) with different values of a_1 and $\hbar = 0.05$ in Example 6.1.

a_1	$g = 0.05$ s	$g = 0.005$ s	$g = 0.0005$ s
1/7	3.6688×10^{-5}	2.8024×10^{-9}	3.0990×10^{-13}
15/112	1.9130×10^{-5}	2.6918×10^{-9}	3.0326×10^{-13}
1/11	1.5343×10^{-5}	2.1588×10^{-9}	2.6126×10^{-13}

TABLE 6.5: ACTPU data of ET-DTZNN algorithm (6.35), general 4S-DTDD algorithm (6.31), and general 4S-DTZNN algorithm (6.33) with $a_0 = 1/9$ and different g in Example 6.1.

Algorithm	$g = 0.01$ s	$g = 0.02$ s	$g = 0.03$ s	$g = 0.04$ s	$g = 0.05$ s
(6.35)	9.55×10^{-5} s	9.75×10^{-5} s	9.49×10^{-5} s	9.84×10^{-5} s	9.80×10^{-5} s
(6.31)	9.88×10^{-5} s	1.02×10^{-4} s	1.02×10^{-4} s	1.02×10^{-4} s	1.03×10^{-4} s
(6.33)	1.00×10^{-4} s	1.03×10^{-4} s	1.05×10^{-4} s	1.06×10^{-4} s	1.05×10^{-4} s

MSSREs synthesized by these three 4S-DTZNN algorithms. From Table 6.4, we draw the conclusion that all three 4S-DTZNN algorithms have MSSREs being the orders of $\mathscr{O}(g^4)$, and the general 4S-DTZNN algorithm (6.33) has a smaller MSSRE as a_1 approaches toward $1/12$. This conclusion coincides with both Theorem 28 and Corollary 1. Furthermore, as shown in Figure 6.4(c) and (d), the general 4S-DTZNN algorithm (6.33) does not converge when $a_1 = 1/6$ and $a_1 = 1/12$, which is consistent with Theorem 26 that the effective domain of parameter a_1 is $1/12 < a_1 < 1/6$.

6.6.2 Computational complexity

In this subsection, we present the computational complexity of the general 4S-DTDD algorithm (6.31) and the general 4S-DTZNN algorithm (6.33) for solving the FUNO (6.34), including computational complexity analyses and numerical comparisons. For the convenience of comparisons on the performance of computational complexity, we present the classical Euler-type DTZNN (ET-DTZNN) algorithm for solving the FUNO (6.1) [111, 134] as

$$\mathbf{x}_{k+1} \doteq \mathbf{x}_k - H^{-1}(\mathbf{x}_k,t_k)(\hbar\boldsymbol{\Psi}(\mathbf{x}_k,t_k) + g\dot{\boldsymbol{\Psi}}_t(\mathbf{x}_k,t_k)), \tag{6.35}$$

which is convergent with the truncation error of $\mathbf{O}(g^2)$. For the n-dimension FUNO problem, $\mathbf{x}_k$, $\boldsymbol{\Psi}(\mathbf{x}_k,t_k)$, and $\dot{\boldsymbol{\Psi}}_t(\mathbf{x}_k,t_k)$ are n-dimension vectors, and $H(\mathbf{x}_k,t_k)$ is an n-dimension square matrix. Excluding the same matrix-inverse operation, the multiplications of the ET-DTZNN algorithm (6.35), the general 4S-DTDD algorithm (6.31), and the general 4S-DTZNN algorithm (6.33) are n^2+2n, n^2+6n, and n^2+7n per updating, respectively. The additions of the ET-DTZNN algorithm (6.35), the general 4S-DTDD algorithm (6.31), and the general 4S-DTZNN algorithm (6.33) are n^2+n, n^2+3n, and n^2+4n per updating, respectively. Besides, the main multiplications and additions come from the same matrix operation of the above three algorithms for a high dimensional FUNO problem, which are n^2 and n^2-n, respectively. It means that the main computational complexity of these algorithms originates from the problem itself. In this sense, the slightly more multiplications and additions of the general 4S-DTDD algorithm (6.31) and the 4S-DTZNN algorithm (6.33) can be ignored.

To substantiate the above analyses, we apply the ET-DTZNN algorithm (6.35), the general 4S-DTDD algorithm (6.31), and the general 4S-DTZNN algorithm (6.33) for solving the FUNO (6.34). Average computing time per updating (ACTPU) data of the three algorithms are considered in numerical experiments, which are presented in Table 6.5. In order to guarantee the accuracy of the results, we run the program in the same environments of hardware and software and take average testing values. The numerical experimental results are presented as Table 6.5. We observe from Table 6.5 that the ACTPU data of the three algorithms are similar, coinciding with the above analyses.

According to the computational complexity analyses and numerical comparisons, we know that the proposed general 4S-DTDD algorithm (6.31) and the general 4S-DTZNN algorithm (6.33) are similar to the ET-DTZNN algorithm (6.35) in terms of computational complexity for solving the FUNO problem, but the first two algorithms have higher computational precision than the ET-DTZNN algorithm (6.35).

6.6.3 Real-time motion control of manipulator

In this subsection, the real-time motion control of a two-link manipulator is investigated and solved by the above-mentioned general 4S-DTZNN algorithm (6.33). First, the actual discrete-time kinematics equation of two-link manipulator at the position level is given as $\mathbf{f}(\vartheta_k)=\mathbf{r}_{\mathrm{a},k}$, where $\mathbf{f}(\cdot)$ is a forward-kinematics mapping function with known structure and parameters. Besides, $\vartheta_k=\vartheta(t_k)\in\mathbb{R}^2$ is the joint-angle vector and $\mathbf{r}_{\mathrm{a},k}\in\mathbb{R}^2$ is the end-effector position vector.

Example 6.2 In view of manipulator control, the following problem is to be solved at each computational time interval $[t_k,t_{k+1})=[kg,(k+1)g)\subset[0,T]$ s:

$$\min_{\vartheta_k\in\mathbb{R}^2}\|\mathbf{r}_{\mathrm{a},k}-\mathbf{r}_{\mathrm{d},k}\|_2^2,$$

where $\mathbf{r}_{\mathrm{d},k}$ denotes the desired path vector at time instant t_k. Besides, the above FUNO problem can be rewritten as

$$\min_{\vartheta_k\in\mathbb{R}^2}\frac{\mathbf{r}_{\mathrm{a},k}^{\mathrm{T}}\mathbf{r}_{\mathrm{a},k}}{2}-\mathbf{r}_{\mathrm{a},k}^{\mathrm{T}}\mathbf{r}_{\mathrm{d},k}. \tag{6.36}$$

Moreover, the real-time optimization solution of the FUNO problem (6.36) at time instant t_k is denoted by $\vartheta_k^*\in\mathbb{R}^2$. Such a solution ought to be found at each computational time interval and guarantees that the FUNO problem (6.36) achieves its minimum value for each time instant t_k.

Furthermore, according to the general 4S-DTZNN algorithm (6.33) and in view of kinematics, we have the following algorithm, which can solve the FUNO problem successfully.

$$\begin{aligned}\vartheta_{k+1}\doteq&-\frac{6}{6a_1+2}\left(J_k^{\mathrm{T}}J_k\right)^{-1}\left(\hbar J_k^{\mathrm{T}}(\mathbf{r}_{\mathrm{a},k}-\mathbf{r}_{\mathrm{d},k})+gJ_k^{\mathrm{T}}\dot{\mathbf{r}}_{\mathrm{d},k}\right)\\&+\frac{24a_1-3}{6a_1+2}\vartheta_k-\frac{36a_1-6}{6a_1+2}\vartheta_{k-1}+\frac{24a_1-1}{6a_1+2}\vartheta_{k-2}-\frac{6a_1}{6a_1+2}\vartheta_{k-3},\end{aligned}\tag{6.37}$$

where the truncation error of (6.37) is $\mathbf{O}(g^4)$. Besides, J_k stands for $J(\vartheta_k)$ for convenience purposes and $J(\vartheta_k)\in\mathbb{R}^{2\times2}$ denotes the Jacobi matrix of the two-link manipulator at time instant t_k.

The end-effector is controlled to track a Lissajous curve, which is expressed as

$$\mathbf{r}_{\mathrm{d},k}=\begin{bmatrix}1.5+0.2\sin\left(\frac{\pi t_k}{5}\right)\\ \frac{\sqrt{3}}{2}+0.2\sin\left(\frac{2\pi t_k}{5}+\frac{\pi}{3}\right)\end{bmatrix}. \tag{6.38}$$

Moreover, since $\partial(\mathbf{r}_{\mathrm{a},k}^{\mathrm{T}}\mathbf{r}_{\mathrm{a},k}/2-\mathbf{r}_{\mathrm{a},k}^{\mathrm{T}}\mathbf{r}_{\mathrm{d},k})/\partial\vartheta=J_k^{\mathrm{T}}(\mathbf{r}_{\mathrm{a},k}-\mathbf{r}_{\mathrm{d},k})$, we define the residual error $\bar{e}_{k+1}$ as $\bar{e}_{k+1}=\|J_{k+1}^{\mathrm{T}}(\mathbf{r}_{\mathrm{a},k+1}-\mathbf{r}_{\mathrm{d},k+1})\|_2$. Apparently, the joint-angle vector ϑ_{k+1} converges to the real-time optimal solution ϑ_{k+1}^* when residual error $\bar{e}_{k+1}$ converges to zero.

Discrete-time algorithm (6.37) with $a_1=1/9$ is employed to solve this problem, and the corresponding numerical experimental results are presented in Figure 6.5. The initial joint-angle vector is set as $\vartheta_0=[0,\pi/3]^{\mathrm{T}}$, the parameter $\hbar=0.05$, and the task duration $T=40$ s. Specifically, Figure 6.5(a) shows manipulator trajectories generated by the algorithm (6.37). Besides, Figure 6.5(b), (c), and (d) shows the trajectories of residual errors $\bar{e}_{k+1}$ synthesized by the algorithm (6.37) with different g. From Figure 6.5(a), we can see that it is evident that the algorithm (6.37) completes the task successfully. Furthermore, the residual error $\bar{e}_{k+1}$ is of order 10^{-5} when $g=0.05$ s, of order 10^{-9} when $g=0.005$ s, and of order 10^{-13} when $g=0.0005$ s, respectively. Apparently, the residual error $\bar{e}_{k+1}$ has a pattern of $\mathscr{O}(g^4)$ as well.

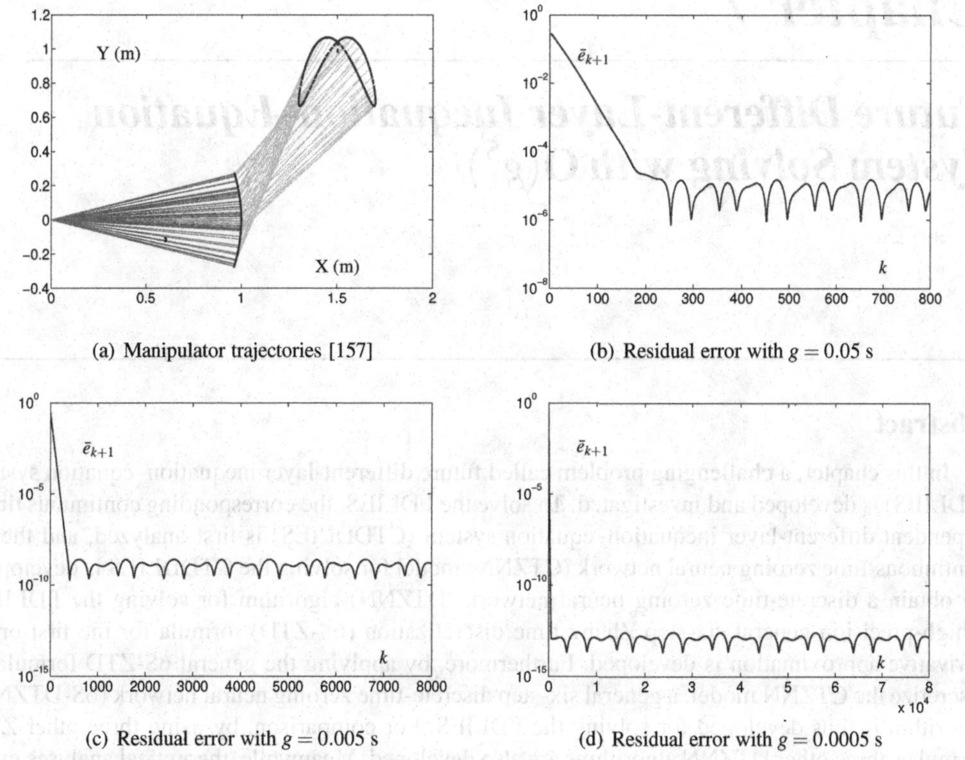

(a) Manipulator trajectories [157]

(b) Residual error with $g = 0.05$ s

(c) Residual error with $g = 0.005$ s

(d) Residual error with $g = 0.0005$ s

FIGURE 6.5: Manipulator trajectories and residual errors $\bar{e}_{k+1}$ synthesized by algorithm (6.37) with $\hbar = 0.05$ and different values of g in Example 6.2.

6.7 Chapter Summary

In this chapter, for solving the FUNO problem (6.1), the CTDD model (6.4) and the CTZNN model (6.9) have been developed and presented. Then, the general 4S-ZTD formula (6.11) using bilinear transformation has been presented and investigated. On the basis of the general 4S-ZTD formula (6.11), the discrete-time algorithms have been developed and investigated for potential digital hardware realization. Through the theoretical analyses, the fact that the MSSRE synthesized by the general 4S-DTZNN algorithm (6.33) has a pattern of $\mathscr{O}(g^4)$ has been theoretically proved. Moreover, the efficacy and accuracy of the general 4S-DTDD algorithm (6.31) and the general 4S-DTZNN algorithm (6.33) when solving the FUNO problem have been illustrated through the numerical experimental results. Note that the general 4S-DTDD algorithm (6.31) is sensitive to the initial states and its MSSRE shows a pattern of $\mathscr{O}(g^2)$, and the general 4S-DTZNN algorithm (6.33) is robust with the MSSRE having a pattern of $\mathscr{O}(g^4)$.

Chapter 7

Future Different-Layer Inequation–Equation System Solving with $\mathbf{O}(g^5)$

Abstract

In this chapter, a challenging problem called future different-layer inequation–equation system (FDLIES) is developed and investigated. To solve the FDLIES, the corresponding continuous time-dependent different-layer inequation–equation system (CTDDLIES) is first analyzed, and then a continuous-time zeroing neural network (CTZNN) model for solving the CTDDLIES is developed. To obtain a discrete-time zeroing neural network (DTZNN) algorithm for solving the FDLIES, a high-precision general six-step Zhang time discretization (6S-ZTD) formula for the first-order derivative approximation is developed. Furthermore, by applying the general 6S-ZTD formula to discretize the CTZNN model, a general six-step discrete-time zeroing neural network (6S-DTZNN) algorithm is thus developed for solving the FDLIES. For comparison, by using three other ZTD formulas, three other DTZNN algorithms are also developed. Meanwhile, theoretical analyses guarantee the efficacy and superiority of the general 6S-DTZNN algorithm compared with the three other DTZNN algorithms for solving the FDLIES. Finally, several comparative numerical experiments, including the motion control of a five-link redundant manipulator, are provided to substantiate the efficacy and superiority of the general 6S-ZTD formula and the corresponding 6S-DTZNN algorithm.

7.1 Introduction

Linear equation plays an important role in mathematics and engineering. This equation is formulated as $A\mathbf{x} = \mathbf{b}$ [20]. Given $A \in \mathbb{R}^{n\times n}$ and $\mathbf{b} \in \mathbb{R}^n$, the objective is to obtain an appropriate solution $\mathbf{x} \in \mathbb{R}^n$, satisfying the linear equation. Different from linear inequation [165], nonlinear inequation formulated as $\varphi(\mathbf{x}) \leq \mathbf{0}$ is widely encountered in science and engineering fields [166]. Given a nonlinear function $\varphi(\cdot) : \mathbb{R}^n \to \mathbb{R}^m$, the objective is to find an appropriate solution $\mathbf{x} \in \mathbb{R}^n$, satisfying the nonlinear inequation.

Many methods have been developed for solving linear equation [167–169] and nonlinear inequation [170–172]. For example, the symmetric successive overrelaxation methods for finding the solution of the linear system were developed as shown in [168]. The accelerated overrelaxation methods for solving linear system were proposed in [169]. Mayne *et al* proposed a modified Newton algorithm for solving nonlinear inequation in [172]. However, in recent years, real-time performance has been increasingly desired because of the fast-changing conditions [43,46,173]. The problems should be formulated as mathematical ones in the time-dependent perspective [43, 102, 115]. Therefore, linear equation and nonlinear inequation are generalized as time-dependent linear equa-

DOI: 10.1201/9781003497783-7

tion [174] and time-dependent nonlinear inequation [175], which are formulated as $A(t)\mathbf{x}(t) = \mathbf{b}(t)$ and $\varphi(\mathbf{x}(t),t) \leq \mathbf{0}$, respectively.

As a special class of recurrent neural networks (RNNs) [176–179], originating and extending from the research of Hopfield neural network [180], zeroing neural network (also termed as Zhang neural network, ZNN) was proposed by Zhang *et al* [64, 160]. ZNN has been developed and investigated as a systematic and efficient method to solve various time-dependent problems in real time, and it differs from conventional gradient-based RNNs in terms of the problem to be solved, error function, design formula, dynamic equation, and the utilization of derivative information [43, 128, 181–186]. ZNN can perfectly track the time-dependent solution by fully exploiting the derivative information of time-dependent parameters [43, 128, 181–186]. Time-dependent linear equation and time-dependent nonlinear inequation were successfully solved by using the ZNN method [166, 174, 175, 187]. Specifically, Jin *et al* [174] proposed a noise-suppressing ZNN algorithm for solving time-dependent linear equation. Qiu *et al* proposed ZNN models to obtain the least-squares solution of the time-dependent linear equation with a rank-deficient coefficient in [187]. For solving time-dependent nonlinear inequation, two types of modified ZNN models were proposed by Xiao *et al* [166, 175]. Moreover, for convenient digital hardware implementation and numerical algorithm development, the discrete time-dependent problems and discrete-time ZNN algorithms were further investigated as outlined in [166, 188, 189].

Previous time-dependent linear equation and time-dependent nonlinear inequation are generally solved at the same layer, i.e., the problem is only connected with $\mathbf{x}(t)$. In this chapter [190], an interesting problem is investigated, which consists of a discrete time-dependent nonlinear inequation connected with $\mathbf{x}_{k+1}$ and a discrete time-dependent linear equation connected with $\dot{\mathbf{x}}_{k+1}$. In a real-time computational process, the future unknown solution should be obtained on the basis of present or previous data. Hence, the problem is termed as future different-layer inequation–equation system (FDLIES). The problem formulation of the FDLIES is specified in the following section.

To solve the FDLIES, the corresponding continuous time-dependent different-layer inequation–equation system (CTDDLIES) is first investigated. By using the ZNN method, the different-layer problem is transformed into a same-layer problem, and a continuous-time ZNN (CTZNN) model is thus developed for solving the CTDDLIES. To obtain a discrete-time ZNN (DTZNN) algorithm, an effective discretization formula is the key [70, 189, 191]. By applying the discretization formula to discretize the CTZNN model, the DTZNN algorithm is obtained for solving the FDLIES. Effective discretization formulas are different from those numerical-differentiation formulas existing in numerical ordinary differential equation (ODE) literature. Effective discretization formulas must be one-step-ahead, i.e., approximating $\dot{\zeta}(t_k)$ by $\zeta(t_{k+1})$, $\zeta(t_k)$, $\zeta(t_{k-1})$, $\zeta(t_{k-2})$, $\cdots$, where k denotes the updating index. In addition, effective discretization formulas must lead to zero-stable algorithms. That is, effective discretization formulas must satisfy strict conditions, which are difficult to be found. Recently, a class of effective discretization formulas has been proposed and termed as Zhang time discretization (ZTD) [70, 93, 189, 191, 192], which can be used for the discretization of the continuous-time models. However, those ZTD formulas are isolated and developed via many relatively blind attempts. In this chapter [190], a general six-step ZTD (6S-ZTD) formula is developed and investigated, which has higher precision than previous ZTD formulas. Furthermore, by applying the general 6S-ZTD formula, a general six-step DTZNN (6S-DTZNN) algorithm is thus developed for solving the FDLIES. Note that the different choices of parameters in the general 6S-ZTD formula lead to different 6S-ZTD formulas and 6S-DTZNN algorithms.

7.2 Problem Formulation and CTZNN Model

This section presents the problem formulation and the corresponding CTZNN model.

7.2.1 Problem formulation

The FDLIES, with $\mathbf{x}_{k+1} = \mathbf{x}(t_{k+1}) \in \mathbb{R}^n$ to be obtained at each computational time interval $[t_k, t_{k+1}) = [kg, (k+1)g) \subset [t_{\text{ini}}, t_{\text{fin}}] \subset [0, +\infty)$, is formulated as

$$\begin{cases} \varphi(\mathbf{x}_{k+1}, t_{k+1}) \leq \mathbf{0}, & (7.1) \\ A_{k+1}\dot{\mathbf{x}}_{k+1} = \mathbf{b}_{k+1}, & (7.2) \end{cases}$$

where t_{ini} and t_{fin} represent the initial and final time instants, respectively. Besides, $\varphi(\cdot,\cdot) : \mathbb{R}^n \to \mathbb{R}^m$ is time-dependent and nonlinear; the coefficient matrix $A_{k+1} \in \mathbb{R}^{l\times n}$ and the coefficient vector $\mathbf{b}_{k+1} \in \mathbb{R}^l$ are supposed to be generated from corresponding smoothly time-dependent signals by sampling at time instant $t_{k+1} = (k+1)g$, with $k \in \mathbb{N}$ and $g \in \mathbb{R}^+$ denoting the updating index and the sampling gap, respectively. Note that $m + l = n$. In addition, $\dot{\mathbf{x}}_{k+1} \in \mathbb{R}^n$ denotes the first-order derivative of $\mathbf{x}_{k+1}$ at time instant t_{k+1}. Evidently, (7.1) is connected with $\mathbf{x}_{k+1}$, and (7.2) is connected with $\dot{\mathbf{x}}_{k+1}$. Therefore, the FDLIES (7.1) and (7.2) are of different levels, making the system interesting and complicated. To satisfy the real-time computation requirement, the future unknown solution $\mathbf{x}_{k+1}$ must be obtained during the computational time interval $[t_k, t_{k+1})$ on the basis of known data, such as $\mathbf{x}_j$, $\varphi(\mathbf{x}_j, t_j)$, A_j, $\mathbf{b}_j$, and their derivatives with $j \leq k$ [93, 192, 193].

To solve the FDLIES (7.1) and (7.2), the CTDDLIES is first investigated, which is formulated as

$$\begin{cases} \varphi(\mathbf{x}(t), t) \leq \mathbf{0}, & (7.3) \\ A(t)\dot{\mathbf{x}}(t) = \mathbf{b}(t), & (7.4) \end{cases}$$

where $\mathbf{x}(t) \in \mathbb{R}^n$ denotes the unknown time-dependent solution to be obtained in real time t, such that the CTDDLIES (7.3) and (7.4) hold true.

7.2.2 CTZNN model

For solving the CTDDLIES (7.3) and (7.4), a vector-valued zeroing function (ZF) is defined as [166, 175]:

$$\mathbf{z}(\mathbf{x}(t), t) = [z_1(\mathbf{x}(t), t), z_2(\mathbf{x}(t), t), \cdots, z_m(\mathbf{x}(t), t)]^{\mathrm{T}} \in \mathbb{R}^m,$$

in which $z_i(\mathbf{x}(t), t) = (\max\{0, \varphi_i(\mathbf{x}(t), t)\})^2/2$, with $i = 1, 2, \cdots, m$. Applying the ZNN design formula as $\dot{\mathbf{z}}(\mathbf{x}(t), t) = -\eta\mathbf{z}(\mathbf{x}(t), t)$, one has the following lemma about (7.3) based on the previous work [166, 175].

Lemma 7 *Let the Jacobi matrix $J(\mathbf{x}(t), t) \in \mathbb{R}^{m\times n}$ be defined as $\partial\varphi(\mathbf{x}(t), t)/\partial\mathbf{x}(t)$ and let the partial derivative $\dot{\varphi}_t(\mathbf{x}(t), t) \in \mathbb{R}^m$ be defined as $\partial\varphi(\mathbf{x}(t), t)/t$. With the ZNN design parameter $\eta \gg 0$ and the time instant $t \gg 0$, (7.3) is equivalent to*

$$J(\mathbf{x}(t), t)\dot{\mathbf{x}}(t) = -\frac{1}{2}\eta \max\{\mathbf{0}, \varphi(\mathbf{x}(t), t)\} - \dot{\varphi}_t(\mathbf{x}(t), t), \tag{7.5}$$

where

$$J(\mathbf{x}(t), t) = \begin{bmatrix} \frac{\partial\varphi_1}{\partial x_1} & \frac{\partial\varphi_1}{\partial x_2} & \cdots & \frac{\partial\varphi_1}{\partial x_n} \\ \frac{\partial\varphi_2}{\partial x_1} & \frac{\partial\varphi_2}{\partial x_2} & \cdots & \frac{\partial\varphi_2}{\partial x_n} \\ \vdots & \vdots & \ddots & \vdots \\ \frac{\partial\varphi_m}{\partial x_1} & \frac{\partial\varphi_m}{\partial x_2} & \cdots & \frac{\partial\varphi_m}{\partial x_n} \end{bmatrix} \in \mathbb{R}^{m\times n}$$

and

$$\dot{\varphi}_t(\mathbf{x}(t), t) = \left[\frac{\partial\varphi_1}{\partial t}, \frac{\partial\varphi_2}{\partial t}, \cdots, \frac{\partial\varphi_m}{\partial t}\right]^{\mathrm{T}} \in \mathbb{R}^m.$$

Note that the ZNN design parameter η, whose international unit is Hz, corresponds to the reciprocal of the product of a resistance parameter and a capacitance parameter [43,187,194]. Evidently, from Lemma 7, (7.5) is connected with $\mathbf{x}(t)$ and $\dot{\mathbf{x}}(t)$, which is at the same layer as (7.4). The different-layer problem is thus transformed into a same-layer problem. Combining (7.5) and (7.4), one can easily obtain the following result:

$$C(\mathbf{x}(t),t)\dot{\mathbf{x}}(t) = \mathbf{d}(\mathbf{x}(t),t),$$

where

$$C(\mathbf{x}(t),t) = \begin{bmatrix} J(\mathbf{x}(t),t) \\ A(t) \end{bmatrix} \in \mathbb{R}^{n\times n}$$

and

$$\mathbf{d}(\mathbf{x}(t),t) = \begin{bmatrix} -\frac{1}{2}\eta \max\{\mathbf{0},\varphi(\mathbf{x}(t),t)\} - \dot{\varphi}_t(\mathbf{x}(t),t) \\ \mathbf{b}(t) \end{bmatrix} \in \mathbb{R}^n.$$

To guarantee that the CTDDLIES (7.3) and (7.4) can be solved, $C(\mathbf{x}(t),t)$ is supposed to be nonsingular. Thus, the following CTZNN model is developed to solve the CTDDLIES (7.3) and (7.4):

$$\dot{\mathbf{x}}(t) = C^{-1}(\mathbf{x}(t),t)\mathbf{d}(\mathbf{x}(t),t). \tag{7.6}$$

Furthermore, one has the following lemma [64, 166, 175] about the CTZNN model (7.6) for solving the CTDDLIES (7.3) and (7.4).

Lemma 8 *As* $t \to +\infty$, *each element of* $\max\{\mathbf{0},\varphi(\mathbf{x}(t),t)\}$ *globally converges to 0. In addition,* $\dot{\mathbf{x}}(t)$ *satisfies (7.4) and (7.6), i.e.,* $\|A(t)\dot{\mathbf{x}}(t) - \mathbf{b}(t)\|_2 = 0$, *where* $\|\cdot\|_2$ *denotes the 2-norm of a vector.*

7.3 General 6S-ZTD Formula

To develop an effective discrete-time algorithm, an effective discretization formula is necessary [70,189,191]. In recent years, many ZTD formulas have been proposed and applied [70,93,189,191, 192]. To provide a general and effective method to find ZTD formulas, rather than blind attempts, the derivation process of a general 6S-ZTD formula with higher precision than previous ZTD formulas is presented in this section.

The general 6S-ZTD formula, which involves seven instants, is developed by the following theorem.

Theorem 29 *With the parameters* $p_1, p_2 \in \mathbb{R}$ *and the sufficiently small sampling gap* $g \in (0,1)$, *let* $\mathscr{O}(g^4)$ *denote the error (especially, the truncation error) positively or negatively proportional to* g^4, *i.e., of the order of* g^4. *Suppose that* $\zeta(t)$ *is sufficiently smooth. With* $\zeta_{k+1} = \zeta(t_{k+1}) = \zeta((k+1)g)$, *the general 6S-ZTD formula is presented as follows:*

$$\begin{aligned}\dot{\zeta}_k =& \frac{-5}{(2p_1+p_2-10)g}\zeta_{k+1} + \frac{(214p_1+77p_2+130)}{60(2p_1+p_2-10)g}\zeta_k - \frac{5p_1}{(2p_1+p_2-10)g}\zeta_{k-1} \\ &- \frac{5p_2}{(2p_1+p_2-10)g}\zeta_{k-2} + \frac{5(2p_1+4p_2+5)}{3(2p_1+p_2-10)g}\zeta_{k-3} - \frac{5(2p_1+3p_2+6)}{4(2p_1+p_2-10)g}\zeta_{k-4} \\ &+ \frac{(3p_1+4p_2+10)}{5(2p_1+p_2-10)g}\zeta_{k-5} + \mathscr{O}(g^4).\end{aligned} \tag{7.7}$$

Proof. According to Taylor expansion [20], one can obtain the following six equations:

$$\zeta_{k+1} = \zeta_k + g\dot{\zeta}_k + \frac{g^2}{2!}\ddot{\zeta}_k + \frac{g^3}{3!}\dddot{\zeta}_k + \frac{g^4}{4!}\zeta_k^{(4)} + \mathscr{O}(g^5), \tag{7.8}$$

$$\zeta_{k-1} = \zeta_k - g\dot{\zeta}_k + \frac{g^2}{2!}\ddot{\zeta}_k - \frac{g^3}{3!}\dddot{\zeta}_k + \frac{g^4}{4!}\zeta_k^{(4)} + \mathscr{O}(g^5), \tag{7.9}$$

$$\zeta_{k-2} = \zeta_k - 2g\dot{\zeta}_k + \frac{(2g)^2}{2!}\ddot{\zeta}_k - \frac{(2g)^3}{3!}\dddot{\zeta}_k + \frac{(2g)^4}{4!}\zeta_k^{(4)} + \mathscr{O}(g^5), \tag{7.10}$$

$$\zeta_{k-3} = \zeta_k - 3g\dot{\zeta}_k + \frac{(3g)^2}{2!}\ddot{\zeta}_k - \frac{(3g)^3}{3!}\dddot{\zeta}_k + \frac{(3g)^4}{4!}\zeta_k^{(4)} + \mathscr{O}(g^5), \tag{7.11}$$

$$\zeta_{k-4} = \zeta_k - 4g\dot{\zeta}_k + \frac{(4g)^2}{2!}\ddot{\zeta}_k - \frac{(4g)^3}{3!}\dddot{\zeta}_k + \frac{(4g)^4}{4!}\zeta_k^{(4)} + \mathscr{O}(g^5), \tag{7.12}$$

and

$$\zeta_{k-5} = \zeta_k - 5g\dot{\zeta}_k + \frac{(5g)^2}{2!}\ddot{\zeta}_k - \frac{(5g)^3}{3!}\dddot{\zeta}_k + \frac{(5g)^4}{4!}\zeta_k^{(4)} + \mathscr{O}(g^5), \tag{7.13}$$

where $\ddot{\zeta}_k$, $\dddot{\zeta}_k$, and $\zeta_k^{(4)}$ denote the second-order, third-order, and fourth-order time derivatives of $\zeta(t)$ at time instant t_k, respectively; the symbol ! denotes the factorial operator. By using an algebraic operation "(7.8) + $p_1 \times$ (7.9) + $p_2 \times$ (7.10) + $p_3 \times$ (7.11) + $p_4 \times$ (7.12) + $p_5 \times$ (7.13)", the general expression with five parameters is obtained, which is omitted here due to the page limitation.

To eliminate $\ddot{\zeta}_k$, $\dddot{\zeta}_k$, and $\zeta_k^{(4)}$ in the general expression, one has

$$\begin{cases} 1 + p_1 + 4p_2 + 9p_3 + 16p_4 + 25p_5 = 0, \\ 1 - p_1 - 8p_2 - 27p_3 - 64p_4 - 125p_5 = 0, \\ 1 + p_1 + 16p_2 + 81p_3 + 256p_4 + 625p_5 = 0. \end{cases}$$

Hence, one obtains

$$\begin{cases} p_3 = -\dfrac{2p_1 + 4p_2 + 5}{3}, \\ p_4 = \dfrac{2p_1 + 3p_2 + 6}{4}, \\ p_5 = -\dfrac{3p_1 + 4p_2 + 10}{25}. \end{cases} \tag{7.14}$$

Replacing p_3, p_4, and p_5 with p_1 and p_2 according to (7.14) in the general expression, one can finally obtain the general 6S-ZTD formula (7.7). The proof is thus completed. □

To generate a zero-stable discrete-time algorithm, the following conditions for p_1 and p_2 should be satisfied.

Theorem 30 *To guarantee the efficacy of the general 6S-ZTD formula (7.7), the effective domain composed of the parameters p_1 and p_2 is determined by a line and the upper-left branch of a hyperbola, shown as*

$$\begin{cases} p_1 - 7p_2 - 5 > 0, \\ 204p_1^2 + 196p_2^2 + 419p_1p_2 + 800p_1 + 525p_2 + 500 < 0, \\ p_1 < 0. \end{cases} \tag{7.15}$$

Proof. The characteristic equation of the general 6S-ZTD formula (7.7) is

$$\iota^6 - \frac{214p_1 + 77p_2 + 130}{300}\iota^5 + p_1\iota^4 + p_2\iota^3 - \frac{2p_1 + 4p_2 + 5}{3}\iota^2 + \frac{2p_1 + 3p_2 + 6}{4}\iota - \frac{3p_1 + 4p_2 + 10}{25} = 0.$$

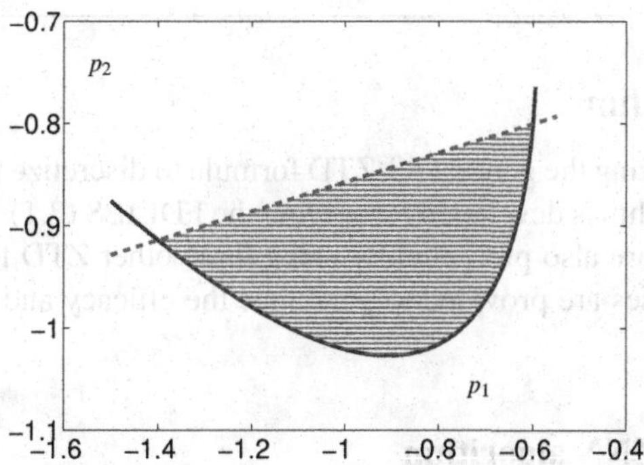

FIGURE 7.1: Effective domain composed of parameters p_1 and p_2 in general 6S-ZTD formula (7.7).

Using bilinear transformation (also termed as Tustin transformation) $\iota = (\omega+1)/(\omega-1)$ [25,162–164,195], one obtains

$$(30p_1+15p_2-150)\omega^5+(120p_1+60p_2-600)\omega^4+(160p_1+80p_2-800)\omega^3$$
$$+(40p_1+20p_2-200)\omega^2-(334p_1+287p_2+730)\omega-(16p_1-112p_2-80)=0.$$

According to the Routh stability criterion [164, 195], one obtains

$$\begin{cases} 2p_1+p_2-10<0, \\ 19p_1+17p_2+25<0, \\ 334p_1+287p_2+730>0, \\ p_1-7p_2-5>0, \\ 204p_1^2+196p_2^2+419p_1p_2+800p_1+525p_2+500<0, \end{cases}$$

which can be simplified as the domain surrounded by a line and the upper-left branch of a hyperbola:

$$\begin{cases} p_1-7p_2-5>0, \\ 204p_1^2+196p_2^2+419p_1p_2+800p_1+525p_2+500<0, \\ p_1<0. \end{cases}$$

Note that $p_1<0$ is used to denote the upper-left branch of the hyperbola. Moreover, $2p_1+p_2-10\neq 0$ is necessary but is also absorbed by the above domain. Thus, the effective domain composed of the parameters p_1 and p_2 is obtained. The proof is thus completed. □

For the convenience of readers and researchers, the effective domain composed of the parameters p_1 and p_2 is shown as the shadow area in Figure 7.1. By selecting different parameters p_1 and p_2 in the effective domain, different effective 6S-ZTD formulas with $\mathscr{O}(g^4)$ truncation error can be obtained for the first-order derivative approximation and discretization. If p_1 or p_2 is not in the effective domain, the six-step formula obtained is also useful for the first-order derivative approximation, but it cannot generate a zero-stable discrete-time algorithm, which is not a ZTD formula.

7.4 DTZNN Algorithms

In this section, by applying the general 6S-ZTD formula to discretize the CTZNN model (7.6), a general 6S-DTZNN algorithm is developed for solving the FDLIES (7.1) and (7.2). For comparison, three DTZNN algorithms are also presented by using three other ZTD formulas [70, 166, 188]. In addition, theoretical analyses are provided to guarantee the efficacy and superiority of the general 6S-DTZNN algorithm.

7.4.1 General 6S-DTZNN algorithm

Using the general 6S-ZTD formula (7.7) to discretize the CTZNN model (7.6), one obtains

$$\begin{aligned}\mathbf{x}_{k+1}=&\frac{214p_1+77p_2+130}{300}\mathbf{x}_k-p_1\mathbf{x}_{k-1}-p_2\mathbf{x}_{k-2}+\frac{2p_1+4p_2+5}{3}\mathbf{x}_{k-3}\\&-\frac{2p_1+3p_2+6}{4}\mathbf{x}_{k-4}+\frac{3p_1+4p_2+10}{25}\mathbf{x}_{k-5}-\frac{2p_1+p_2-10}{5}C_k^{-1}\hat{\mathbf{d}}_k+\mathbf{O}(g^5),\end{aligned}\tag{7.16}$$

where

$$\hat{\mathbf{d}}_k=\begin{bmatrix}-\frac{1}{2}\hbar\max\{\mathbf{0},\varphi(\mathbf{x}_k,t_k)\}-g\dot{\varphi}_t(\mathbf{x}_k,t_k)\\ g\mathbf{b}_k\end{bmatrix},$$

with the step length $\hbar=g\eta$ and $C_k=C(\mathbf{x}_k,t_k)$ for simplification. In addition, $\mathbf{O}(g^5)$ denotes a vector with every element being $\mathscr{O}(g^5)$. Thus, the general 6S-DTZNN algorithm is developed as

$$\begin{aligned}\mathbf{x}_{k+1}\doteq&\frac{214p_1+77p_2+130}{300}\mathbf{x}_k-p_1\mathbf{x}_{k-1}-p_2\mathbf{x}_{k-2}+\frac{2p_1+4p_2+5}{3}\mathbf{x}_{k-3}\\&-\frac{2p_1+3p_2+6}{4}\mathbf{x}_{k-4}+\frac{3p_1+4p_2+10}{25}\mathbf{x}_{k-5}-\frac{2p_1+p_2-10}{5}C_k^{-1}\hat{\mathbf{d}}_k,\end{aligned}\tag{7.17}$$

where $\doteq$ denotes the computational assignment operator.

For the convenience of readers and researchers, the expressions of the 6S-ZTD formulas and corresponding 6S-DTZNN algorithms with different effective values of the parameters p_1 and p_2 are listed in Table 7.1. Moreover, the initial value of a 6S-DTZNN algorithm at time $t=0$ s is randomly generated, and the other initial values can be obtained by using the following one-step DTZNN (1S-DTZNN) algorithm.

7.4.2 Other DTZNN algorithms

The conventional Euler forward formula [166], which can be considered the first and the simplest one of the ZTD formulas, is termed as one-step ZTD (1S-ZTD) formula and presented as

$$\dot{\zeta}_k=\frac{\zeta_{k+1}}{g}-\frac{\zeta_k}{g}+\mathscr{O}(g).\tag{7.18}$$

By using the 1S-ZTD formula (7.18) to discretize the CTZNN model (7.6), the following equation is obtained:

$$\mathbf{x}_{k+1}=\mathbf{x}_k+C_k^{-1}\hat{\mathbf{d}}_k+\mathbf{O}(g^2).$$

TABLE 7.1: Expressions of 6S-ZTD formulas and 6S-DTZNN algorithms with different effective values of parameters p_1 and p_2.

p_1	p_2	Formula and algorithm expressions
$-\frac{49}{44}$	$-\frac{21}{22}$	$\dot{\zeta}_k=\frac{11}{29g}\zeta_{k+1}+\frac{20}{87g}\zeta_k-\frac{49}{116g}\zeta_{k-1}-\frac{21}{58g}\zeta_{k-2}+\frac{23}{174g}\zeta_{k-3}+\frac{5}{58g}\zeta_{k-4}-\frac{5}{116g}\zeta_{k-5}+\mathscr{O}(g^4)$ $\mathbf{x}_{k+1}\doteq-\frac{20}{33}\mathbf{x}_k+\frac{49}{44}\mathbf{x}_{k-1}+\frac{21}{22}\mathbf{x}_{k-2}-\frac{23}{66}\mathbf{x}_{k-3}-\frac{5}{22}\mathbf{x}_{k-4}+\frac{5}{44}\mathbf{x}_{k-5}+\frac{29}{11}C_k^{-1}\hat{\mathbf{d}}_k$
$-\frac{95}{102}$	$-\frac{15}{17}$	$\dot{\zeta}_k=\frac{51}{130g}\zeta_{k+1}+\frac{7}{39g}\zeta_k-\frac{19}{52g}\zeta_{k-1}-\frac{9}{26g}\zeta_{k-2}+\frac{2}{39g}\zeta_{k-3}+\frac{19}{130g}\zeta_{k-4}-\frac{3}{52g}\zeta_{k-5}+\mathscr{O}(g^4)$ $\mathbf{x}_{k+1}\doteq-\frac{70}{153}\mathbf{x}_k+\frac{95}{102}\mathbf{x}_{k-1}+\frac{15}{17}\mathbf{x}_{k-2}-\frac{20}{153}\mathbf{x}_{k-3}-\frac{19}{51}\mathbf{x}_{k-4}+\frac{5}{34}\mathbf{x}_{k-5}+\frac{130}{51}C_k^{-1}\hat{\mathbf{d}}_k$
$-\frac{24}{23}$	$-\frac{22}{23}$	$\dot{\zeta}_k=\frac{23}{60g}\zeta_{k+1}+\frac{16}{75g}\zeta_k-\frac{2}{5g}\zeta_{k-1}-\frac{11}{30g}\zeta_{k-2}+\frac{7}{60g}\zeta_{k-3}+\frac{1}{10g}\zeta_{k-4}-\frac{7}{150g}\zeta_{k-5}+\mathscr{O}(g^4)$ $\mathbf{x}_{k+1}\doteq-\frac{64}{115}\mathbf{x}_k+\frac{24}{23}\mathbf{x}_{k-1}+\frac{22}{23}\mathbf{x}_{k-2}-\frac{7}{23}\mathbf{x}_{k-3}-\frac{6}{23}\mathbf{x}_{k-4}+\frac{14}{115}\mathbf{x}_{k-5}+\frac{60}{23}C_k^{-1}\hat{\mathbf{d}}_k$
$-\frac{11}{12}$	$-\frac{17}{18}$	$\dot{\zeta}_k=\frac{9}{23g}\zeta_{k+1}+\frac{25}{138g}\zeta_k-\frac{33}{92g}\zeta_{k-1}-\frac{17}{46g}\zeta_{k-2}+\frac{11}{138g}\zeta_{k-3}+\frac{3}{23g}\zeta_{k-4}-\frac{5}{92g}\zeta_{k-5}+\mathscr{O}(g^4)$ $\mathbf{x}_{k+1}\doteq-\frac{25}{54}\mathbf{x}_k+\frac{11}{12}\mathbf{x}_{k-1}+\frac{17}{18}\mathbf{x}_{k-2}-\frac{11}{54}\mathbf{x}_{k-3}-\frac{1}{3}\mathbf{x}_{k-4}+\frac{5}{36}\mathbf{x}_{k-5}+\frac{23}{9}C_k^{-1}\hat{\mathbf{d}}_k$
$-\frac{46}{41}$	$-\frac{38}{41}$	$\dot{\zeta}_k=\frac{41}{108g}\zeta_{k+1}+\frac{31}{135g}\zeta_k-\frac{23}{54g}\zeta_{k-1}-\frac{19}{54g}\zeta_{k-2}+\frac{13}{108g}\zeta_{k-3}+\frac{5}{54g}\zeta_{k-4}-\frac{2}{45g}\zeta_{k-5}+\mathscr{O}(g^4)$ $\mathbf{x}_{k+1}\doteq-\frac{124}{205}\mathbf{x}_k+\frac{46}{41}\mathbf{x}_{k-1}+\frac{38}{41}\mathbf{x}_{k-2}-\frac{13}{41}\mathbf{x}_{k-3}-\frac{10}{41}\mathbf{x}_{k-4}+\frac{24}{205}\mathbf{x}_{k-5}+\frac{108}{41}C_k^{-1}\hat{\mathbf{d}}_k$

Hence, the 1S-DTZNN algorithm is presented as

$$\mathbf{x}_{k+1}\doteq\mathbf{x}_k+C_k^{-1}\hat{\mathbf{d}}_k. \tag{7.19}$$

The three-step ZTD (3S-ZTD) formula [70] is presented as follows:

$$\dot{\zeta}_k=\frac{1}{g}\zeta_{k+1}-\frac{3}{2g}\zeta_k+\frac{1}{g}\zeta_{k-1}-\frac{1}{2g}\zeta_{k-2}+\mathscr{O}(g^2). \tag{7.20}$$

Applying the 3S-ZTD formula (7.20) to discretize the CTZNN model (7.6), one obtains

$$\mathbf{x}_{k+1}=\frac{3}{2}\mathbf{x}_k-\mathbf{x}_{k-1}+\frac{1}{2}\mathbf{x}_{k-2}+C_k^{-1}\hat{\mathbf{d}}_k+\mathbf{O}(g^3).$$

Correspondingly, the three-step DTZNN (3S-DTZNN) algorithm is presented as below:

$$\mathbf{x}_{k+1}\doteq\frac{3}{2}\mathbf{x}_k-\mathbf{x}_{k-1}+\frac{1}{2}\mathbf{x}_{k-2}+C_k^{-1}\hat{\mathbf{d}}_k. \tag{7.21}$$

Guo *et al* [188] proposed the five-step ZTD (5S-ZTD) formula:

$$\dot{\zeta}_k=\frac{1}{2g}\zeta_{k+1}-\frac{5}{48g}\zeta_k-\frac{1}{4g}\zeta_{k-1}-\frac{1}{8g}\zeta_{k-2}-\frac{1}{12g}\zeta_{k-3}+\frac{1}{16g}\zeta_{k-4}+\mathscr{O}(g^3). \tag{7.22}$$

Using the 5S-ZTD formula (7.22) to discretize the CTZNN model (7.6), one obtains

$$\mathbf{x}_{k+1}=\frac{5}{24}\mathbf{x}_k+\frac{1}{2}\mathbf{x}_{k-1}+\frac{1}{4}\mathbf{x}_{k-2}+\frac{1}{6}\mathbf{x}_{k-3}-\frac{1}{8}\mathbf{x}_{k-4}+2C_k^{-1}\hat{\mathbf{d}}_k+\mathbf{O}(g^4).$$

Then, the five-step DTZNN (5S-DTZNN) algorithm is presented as below:

$$\mathbf{x}_{k+1}\doteq\frac{5}{24}\mathbf{x}_k+\frac{1}{2}\mathbf{x}_{k-1}+\frac{1}{4}\mathbf{x}_{k-2}+\frac{1}{6}\mathbf{x}_{k-3}-\frac{1}{8}\mathbf{x}_{k-4}+2C_k^{-1}\hat{\mathbf{d}}_k. \tag{7.23}$$

7.4.3 Theoretical analyses

On the basis of the three definitions in Chapter 1, the following theoretical analyses about the DTZNN algorithms for solving the FDLIES (7.1) and (7.2) are provided.

Theorem 31 *Suppose that C_k is always nonsingular. With the sufficiently small sampling gap $g \in (0,1)$, let $\mathbf{O}(g^5)$ denote the error (especially, the truncation error) with each element being $\mathscr{O}(g^5)$. The general 6S-DTZNN algorithm (7.17) is zero-stable, consistent, and convergent, which converges with the order of truncation error being $\mathbf{O}(g^5)$.*

Proof. According to Definition 2 in Chapter 1 and Theorem 30, the general 6S-DTZNN algorithm discretized by the general 6S-ZTD formula (7.7) in the effective domain is zero-stable. According to (7.16), one obtains that the general 6S-DTZNN algorithm (7.17) is consistent and its truncation error is $\mathbf{O}(g^5)$. Thus, according to Definitions 3 and 4 in Chapter 1, the general 6S-DTZNN algorithm (7.17) converges with the order of its truncation error being $\mathbf{O}(g^5)$. The proof is thus completed. □

Note that the residual error is defined as $\hat{e}_{k+1} = \|\max\{\mathbf{0}, \varphi(\mathbf{x}_k, t_k)\}\|_2 + \|A_k\dot{\mathbf{x}}_k - \mathbf{b}_k\|_2$ for the FDLIES (7.1) and (7.2) in this chapter [190], where $\|\cdot\|_2$ denotes the 2-norm of a vector.

Theorem 32 *Consider the FDLIES (7.1) and (7.2) with $\varphi(\cdot,\cdot)$ being first-order differentiable and bounded. Suppose that C_k is always nonsingular. With the sufficiently small sampling gap $g \in (0,1)$, the maximal steady-state residual error (MSSRE) $\lim_{k\to+\infty}\sup\hat{e}_{k+1}$ synthesized by the general 6S-DTZNN algorithm (7.17) is $\mathscr{O}(g^5)$.*

Proof. Evidently, when $\varphi(\mathbf{x}_k, t_k) \leq \mathbf{0}$, one has

$$\begin{aligned}
&\lim_{k\to+\infty}\sup(\|\max\{\mathbf{0}, \varphi(\mathbf{x}_k, t_k)\}\|_2 + \|A_k\dot{\mathbf{x}}_k - \mathbf{b}_k\|_2)\\
&= \lim_{k\to+\infty}\sup\|A_k\dot{\mathbf{x}}_k - \mathbf{b}_k\|_2\\
&= 0.
\end{aligned}$$

Otherwise, let $\varphi_\nabla(\mathbf{x}_k, t_k)$ denote the positive part of $\varphi(\mathbf{x}_k, t_k)$, and $\mathbf{x}_k$ can converge to theoretical solution $\mathbf{x}_k^*$ with $\varphi_\nabla(\mathbf{x}_k^*, t_k) = \mathbf{0}$. According to Theorem 31, one has $\mathbf{x}_k = \mathbf{x}_k^* + \mathbf{O}(g^5)$. By using Taylor expansion [20], the following result is obtained:

$$\begin{aligned}
\varphi_\nabla(\mathbf{x}_k, t_k) &= \varphi_\nabla(\mathbf{x}_k^* + \mathbf{O}(g^5), t_k)\\
&= \varphi_\nabla(\mathbf{x}_k^*, t_k) + J_\nabla(\mathbf{x}_k^*, t_k)\mathbf{O}(g^5) + \mathbf{O}(g^{10})\\
&= J_\nabla(\mathbf{x}_k^*, t_k)\mathbf{O}(g^5),
\end{aligned}$$

where $J_\nabla(\mathbf{x}, t) = \partial\varphi_\nabla(\mathbf{x}, t)/\partial\mathbf{x}^{\mathrm{T}}$. Therefore, one has

$$\begin{aligned}
&\lim_{k\to+\infty}\sup(\|\max\{\mathbf{0}, \varphi(\mathbf{x}_k, t_k)\}\|_2 + \|A_k\dot{\mathbf{x}}_k - \mathbf{b}_k\|_2)\\
&= \lim_{k\to+\infty}\sup\|\max\{\mathbf{0}, \varphi_\nabla(\mathbf{x}_k, t_k)\}\|_2\\
&= \lim_{k\to+\infty}\sup\|\varphi_\nabla(\mathbf{x}_k, t_k)\|_2\\
&\leq \lim_{k\to+\infty}\sup\|J_\nabla(\mathbf{x}_k^*, t_k)\|_{\mathrm{F}}\mathscr{O}(g^5),
\end{aligned}$$

where $\|\cdot\|_{\mathrm{F}}$ denotes the Frobenius norm of a matrix. Suppose that the sequence $J_\nabla(\mathbf{x}_k^*, t_k)$ is uniformly norm bounded, and then it can be concluded that the MSSRE synthesized by the general 6S-DTZNN algorithm (7.17) is $\mathscr{O}(g^5)$. The proof is thus completed. □

Moreover, one obtains the following three corollaries about the 1S-DTZNN algorithm (7.19), the 3S-DTZNN algorithm (7.21), and the 5S-DTZNN algorithm (7.23) for solving the FDLIES (7.1) and (7.2), which are similarly provable.

Corollary 2 *Consider the FDLIES (7.1) and (7.2) with $\varphi(\cdot,\cdot)$ being first-order differentiable and bounded. Suppose that C_k is always nonsingular. With the sufficiently small sampling gap $g \in (0,1)$,*

TABLE 7.2: Problem, scheme, model, and algorithms in this chapter.

Problem	$\begin{cases} \varphi(\mathbf{x}_{k+1}, t_{k+1}) \leq \mathbf{0}, \\ A_{k+1}\dot{\mathbf{x}}_{k+1} = \mathbf{b}_{k+1}. \end{cases}$
Scheme	*Step 1*: Define ZF as $\mathbf{z}(\mathbf{x}(t),t) = [(\max\{0, \varphi_1(\mathbf{x}(t),t)\})^2/2, (\max\{0, \varphi_2(\mathbf{x}(t),t)\})^2/2, \cdots, (\max\{0, \varphi_m(\mathbf{x}(t),t)\})^2/2]^{\mathrm{T}}$. *Step 2*: Adopt ZNN design formula as $\dot{\mathbf{z}}(\mathbf{x}(t),t) = -\eta\mathbf{z}(\mathbf{x}(t),t)$. *Step 3*: Adopt ZTD formulas to discretize CTZNN model (7.6).
Model	$\dot{\mathbf{x}}(t) = C^{-1}(\mathbf{x}(t),t)\mathbf{d}(\mathbf{x}(t),t)$.
Algorithms	$\mathbf{x}_{k+1} \doteq -\frac{20}{33}\mathbf{x}_k + \frac{49}{44}\mathbf{x}_{k-1} + \frac{21}{22}\mathbf{x}_{k-2} - \frac{23}{66}\mathbf{x}_{k-3} - \frac{5}{22}\mathbf{x}_{k-4} + \frac{5}{44}\mathbf{x}_{k-5} + \frac{29}{11}C_k^{-1}\hat{\mathbf{d}}_k,$ $\mathbf{x}_{k+1} \doteq \frac{5}{24}\mathbf{x}_k + \frac{1}{2}\mathbf{x}_{k-1} + \frac{1}{4}\mathbf{x}_{k-2} + \frac{1}{6}\mathbf{x}_{k-3} - \frac{1}{8}\mathbf{x}_{k-4} + 2C_k^{-1}\hat{\mathbf{d}}_k,$ $\mathbf{x}_{k+1} \doteq \frac{3}{2}\mathbf{x}_k - \mathbf{x}_{k-1} + \frac{1}{2}\mathbf{x}_{k-2} + C_k^{-1}\hat{\mathbf{d}}_k,$ $\mathbf{x}_{k+1} \doteq \mathbf{x}_k + C_k^{-1}\hat{\mathbf{d}}_k.$

let $\mathbf{O}(g^2)$ *denote the error (especially, the truncation error) with each element being* $\mathscr{O}(g^2)$*. The 1S-DTZNN algorithm (7.19) is zero-stable, consistent, and convergent, which converges with the order of truncation error being* $\mathbf{O}(g^5)$*. In addition, the MSSRE synthesized by the 1S-DTZNN algorithm (7.19) is* $\mathscr{O}(g^2)$*.*

Corollary 3 *Consider the FDLIES (7.1) and (7.2) with* $\varphi(\cdot,\cdot)$ *being first-order differentiable and bounded. Suppose that* C_k *is always nonsingular. With the sufficiently small sampling gap* $g \in (0,1)$*, let* $\mathbf{O}(g^3)$ *denote the error (especially, the truncation error) with each element being* $\mathscr{O}(g^3)$*. The 3S-DTZNN algorithm (7.21) is zero-stable, consistent, and convergent, which converges with the order of truncation error being* $\mathbf{O}(g^3)$*. Moreover, the MSSRE synthesized by the 3S-DTZNN algorithm (7.21) is* $\mathscr{O}(g^3)$*.*

Corollary 4 *Consider the FDLIES (7.1) and (7.2) with* $\varphi(\cdot,\cdot)$ *being first-order differentiable and bounded. Suppose that* C_k *is always nonsingular. With the sufficiently small sampling gap* $g \in (0,1)$*, let* $\mathbf{O}(g^4)$ *denote the error (especially, the truncation error) with each element being* $\mathscr{O}(g^4)$*. The 5S-DTZNN algorithm (7.23) is zero-stable, consistent, and convergent, which converges with the order of truncation error being* $\mathbf{O}(g^4)$*. Furthermore, the MSSRE synthesized by the 5S-DTZNN algorithm (7.23) is* $\mathscr{O}(g^4)$*.*

Remark 8 *Excluding the inverse operation, the general 6S-DTZNN algorithm (7.17) contains* $mn+m$ *differentiation operations,* m *comparison operations,* n^2+8n+m *multiplication/division operations, and* n^2+5n+m *addition/subtraction operations per updating. Generally, the computing complexity of inverse operation is* $O(n^3)$*. Hence, the computing complexity of the general 6S-DTZNN algorithm (7.17) is* $O(n^3)$*. The computing complexities of the 1S-DTZNN algorithm (7.19), 3S-DTZNN algorithm (7.21), and 5S-DTZNN algorithm (7.23) are also* $O(n^3)$ *in view of the fact that they all need one inverse operation per updating, although they contain less multiplication/division and addition/subtraction operations per updating. That is, the inverse operation makes the computing complexities of these four DTZNN algorithms at the same order.*

For a more intuitive understanding of the main content of this chapter [190], Table 7.2 lists the problem, scheme, model, and algorithms.

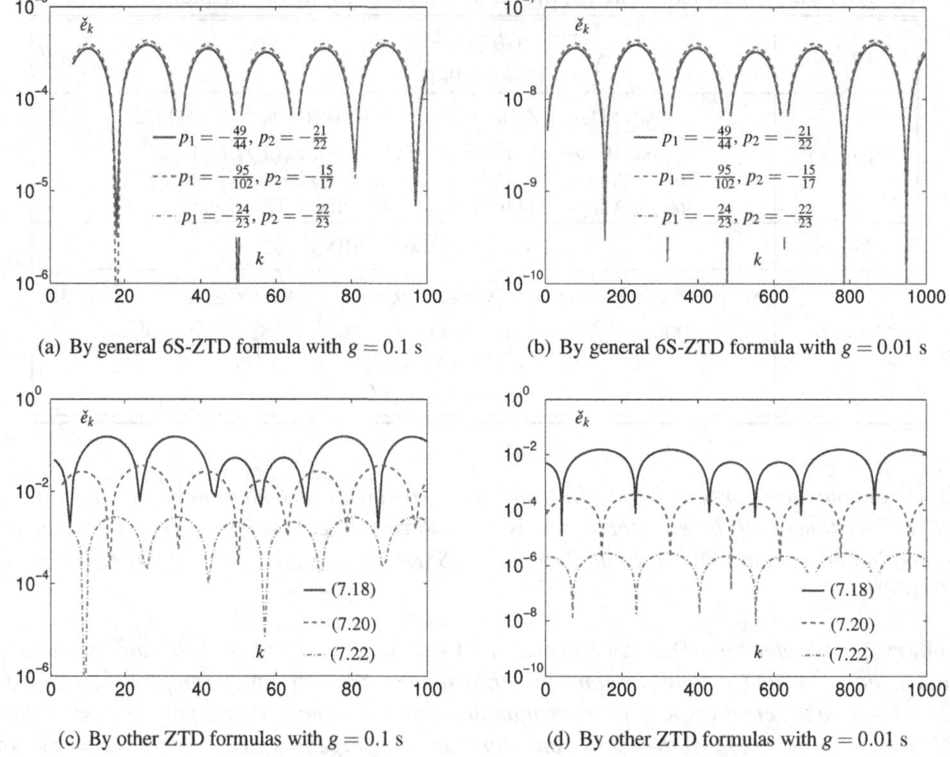

(a) By general 6S-ZTD formula with $g=0.1$ s

(b) By general 6S-ZTD formula with $g=0.01$ s

(c) By other ZTD formulas with $g=0.1$ s

(d) By other ZTD formulas with $g=0.01$ s

FIGURE 7.2: Trajectories of approximation errors $\check{e}_k$ synthesized by three 6S-ZTD formulas and three other ZTD formulas in Example 7.1.

7.5 Numerical Experiments

In this section, several numerical experiments are conducted to substantiate the efficacy and superiority of the general 6S-ZTD formula (7.7) and the general 6S-DTZNN algorithm (7.17).

7.5.1 Derivative approximation

To verify the efficacy and superiority of the general 6S-ZTD formula, the following example is considered.

Example 7.1 The general 6S-ZTD formula and other ZTD formulas are used to approximate the first-order derivative of

$$f_k = f(t_k) = \sin^2(t_k) + \sin(t_k) + \cos(t_k),$$

during the computational time interval $[0, 10]$ s.

The numerical experimental results synthesized by three 6S-ZTD formulas with effective values of the parameters p_1 and p_2 and three other ZTD formulas are presented in Figure 7.2. As illustrated in Figure 7.2(a) and (b), when $g=0.1$ and 0.01 s, the approximation errors $\check{e}_k = |\dot{f}_k - \dot{f}_k^*|$ synthesized by the general 6S-ZTD formula (7.7) with different effective values of the parameters p_1 and p_2 are of orders 10^{-4} and 10^{-8}, respectively, where $\dot{f}_k^*$ denotes the theoretical value. Evidently, the approximation error synthesized by the general 6S-ZTD formula (7.7) decreases by a factor of 10^4 when the sampling gap g decreases by a factor of 10. Thus, the precision of the general 6S-ZTD

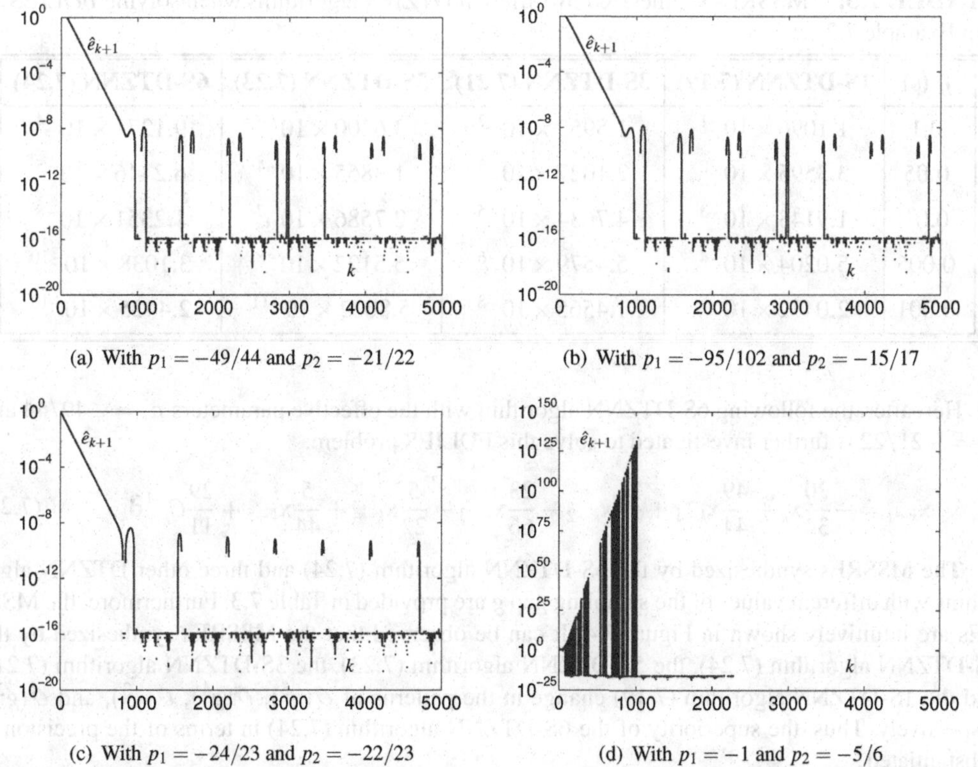

FIGURE 7.3: Trajectories of residual errors $\hat{e}_{k+1}$ synthesized by four 6S-DTZNN algorithms when solving FDLIES with $\mathbf{x}_0 = [1,1,1,1]^{\mathrm{T}}$, $\hbar = 0.05$, and $g = 0.01$ s in Example 7.2.

formula (7.7) is $\mathscr{O}(g^4)$, which is consistent with Theorem 29. Besides, Figure 7.2(c) and (d) shows the trajectories of the approximation errors synthesized by three other ZTD formulas with $g = 0.1$ and 0.01 s, respectively. Evidently, the precision of the general 6S-ZTD formula (7.7) is higher than that of the three other ZTD formulas.

7.5.2 FDLIES solving

In this subsection, a specific problem of the FDLIES is considered to substantiate the efficacy and superiority of the 6S-DTZNN algorithms with effective parameters.

Example 7.2 Consider a specific example of the FDLIES with $\mathbf{x}_{k+1}$ to be obtained at each computational time interval $[t_k, t_{k+1}) \subset [0,50]$ s:

$$\begin{cases} (\sin(t_k)+2)x_{1,k} + x_{2,k}x_{3,k} + x_{4,k}^2 + \sin(x_{3,k}) - 1/(t_k+1) \leq 0, \\ (\cos(t_k)+3)x_{2,k} + x_{3,k}x_{4,k} + \cos(x_{3,k}) - \exp(-t_k)\sin(t_k) \leq 0, \\ (\sin(t_k)+4)\dot{x}_{3,k} + \cos(t_k)\dot{x}_{4,k} = \cos(t_k), \\ (\cos(t_k)+5)\dot{x}_{4,k} = \sin(t_k). \end{cases}$$

By relatively arbitrarily setting initial state $\mathbf{x}_0 = [1,1,1,1]^{\mathrm{T}}$, the residual errors $\hat{e}_{k+1}$ synthesized by four 6S-DTZNN algorithms with $\hbar = 0.05$ and $g = 0.01$ s are presented in Figure 7.3. Evidently, the FDLIES is successfully solved by three 6S-DTZNN algorithms with the effective parameters p_1 and p_2, as illustrated in Figure 7.3(a)–(c). The other 6S-DTZNN algorithm with the noneffective parameters p_1 and p_2 fails to solve the FDLIES, as illustrated in Figure 7.3(d). Hence, the effective domain of parameters p_1 and p_2 is substantiated.

TABLE 7.3: MSSREs synthesized by different DTZNN algorithms when solving FDLIES in Example 7.2.

g (s)	1S-DTZNN (7.19)	3S-DTZNN (7.21)	5S-DTZNN (7.23)	6S-DTZNN (7.24)
0.1	1.1096×10^{-1}	1.5952×10^{-2}	3.6200×10^{-3}	9.1271×10^{-4}
0.05	3.3595×10^{-2}	2.1027×10^{-3}	1.3865×10^{-4}	6.2446×10^{-5}
0.01	1.9143×10^{-3}	4.7634×10^{-5}	2.7586×10^{-7}	1.2351×10^{-8}
0.005	5.0204×10^{-4}	5.4579×10^{-6}	5.5122×10^{-8}	3.1038×10^{-10}
0.001	2.0472×10^{-5}	1.4565×10^{-8}	5.8022×10^{-11}	2.4425×10^{-13}

Hereafter, the following 6S-DTZNN algorithm with the effective parameters $p_1=-49/44$ and $p_2=-21/22$ is further investigated to solve this FDLIES problem:

$$\mathbf{x}_{k+1}\doteq-\frac{20}{33}\mathbf{x}_k+\frac{49}{44}\mathbf{x}_{k-1}+\frac{21}{22}\mathbf{x}_{k-2}-\frac{23}{66}\mathbf{x}_{k-3}-\frac{5}{22}\mathbf{x}_{k-4}+\frac{5}{44}\mathbf{x}_{k-5}+\frac{29}{11}C_k^{-1}\hat{\mathbf{d}}_k. \quad (7.24)$$

The MSSREs synthesized by the 6S-DTZNN algorithm (7.24) and three other DTZNN algorithms with different values of the sampling gap g are provided in Table 7.3. Furthermore, the MSSREs are intuitively shown in Figure 7.4. It can be observed that the MSSREs synthesized by the 6S-DTZNN algorithm (7.24), the 5S-DTZNN algorithm (7.23), the 3S-DTZNN algorithm (7.21), and the 1S-DTZNN algorithm (7.19) change in the patterns of $\mathscr{O}(g^5)$, $\mathscr{O}(g^4)$, $\mathscr{O}(g^3)$, and $\mathscr{O}(g^2)$, respectively. Thus, the superiority of the 6S-DTZNN algorithm (7.24) in terms of the precision is substantiated.

7.5.3 Manipulator control

In recent years, manipulator control has been widely applied in the industry [122, 196–198]. In this subsection, an application to manipulator control is conducted.

Specifically, the real-time motion control of a five-link redundant manipulator is investigated at time instant $t_{k+1}\in[t_{\text{ini}},t_{\text{fin}}]$. The kinematic equation of the manipulator is $\mathbf{f}(\vartheta_{k+1})=\mathbf{r}_{\text{a},k+1}$, in which $\mathbf{f}(\cdot)$ is a nonlinear forward-kinematics mapping function [98, 199, 200]. In addition, $\vartheta_{k+1}\in\mathbb{R}^5$ is the joint angle vector, and $\mathbf{r}_{\text{a},k+1}\in\mathbb{R}^2$ denotes the end-effector position vector. Furthermore, the relationship between the joint velocity vector $\dot{\vartheta}_{k+1}$ and the end-effector velocity vector $\dot{\mathbf{r}}_{\text{a},k+1}\in\mathbb{R}^2$

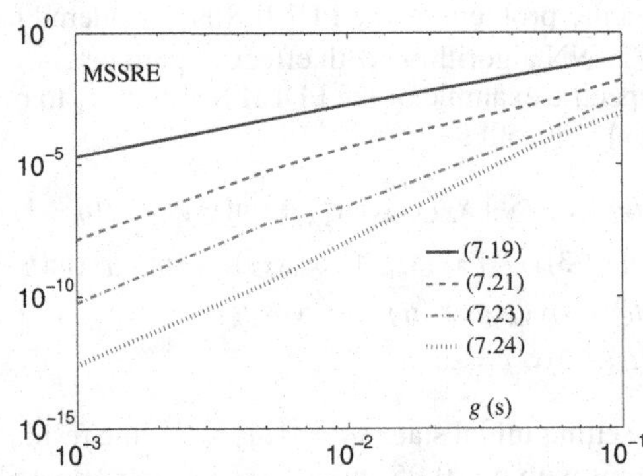

FIGURE 7.4: MSSREs synthesized by four DTZNN algorithms with different values of sampling gap g when solving FDLIES in Example 7.2.

is obtained as $J(\vartheta_{k+1})\dot{\vartheta}_{k+1} = \dot{\mathbf{r}}_{\mathrm{a},k+1}$, where $J(\vartheta_{k+1}) \in \mathbb{R}^{2\times 5}$ is the Jacobi matrix of the manipulator. To make the end-effector track the desired path $\mathbf{r}_{\mathrm{d},k+1} \in \mathbb{R}^2$, a ZF is defined as $\bar{\mathbf{z}}_{k+1} = \mathbf{r}_{\mathrm{a},k+1} - \mathbf{r}_{\mathrm{d},k+1}$. According to the previous work [198], one has

$$J(\vartheta_{k+1})\dot{\vartheta}_{k+1} = \dot{\mathbf{r}}_{\mathrm{d},k+1} - \eta(\mathbf{r}_{\mathrm{a},k+1} - \mathbf{r}_{\mathrm{d},k+1}),$$

which can be regarded as (7.2) of the FDLIES with $A_{k+1} = J(\vartheta_{k+1})$ and $\mathbf{b}_{k+1} = \dot{\mathbf{r}}_{\mathrm{d},k+1} - \eta(\mathbf{r}_{\mathrm{a},k+1} - \mathbf{r}_{\mathrm{d},k+1})$.

Example 7.3 Consider a situation where the first three joints are damaged or restricted during task execution. Specifically, the first three joint angles should not be less than 0 rad and not larger than $\pi/2$ rad. Thus, one obtains $\vartheta_{i,k+1}(\vartheta_{i,k+1} - \pi/2) \leq 0$, with $i = 1,2,3$, which can be considered as (7.1) of the FDLIES. Moreover, the end-effector of the manipulator is expected to track a flower path expressed as below:

$$\mathbf{r}_{\mathrm{d},k} = \begin{bmatrix} 0.3(\cos(t_k) - 0.5)\cos(0.8t_k) + \rho_1 \\ 0.3(\cos(t_k) - 0.5)\sin(0.8t_k) + \rho_2 \end{bmatrix},$$

where the parameters ρ_1 and ρ_2 are two constants deciding the initial position of the desired flower path.

Specifically, with $g = 0.01$ s, Figure 7.5 illustrates the trajectories of the manipulator, end-effector, and joint angles. The tracking process of the manipulator is presented in Figure 7.5(a). From Figure 7.5(b), the actual trajectory of the end-effector synthesized by the 6S-DTZNN algorithm (7.24) almost completely overlaps with the desired path, indicating that the tracking task is successfully completed. From Figure 7.5(c), the first three joint angles satisfy the condition (i.e., not less than 0 rad and not larger than $\pi/2$ rad). That is, the motion control problem with the first three damaged or restricted joints is solved successfully by using the 6S-DTZNN algorithm (7.24).

To substantiate the high precision and superiority of the general 6S-DTZNN algorithm, the tracking errors $\tilde{e}_{k+1} = \|\mathbf{r}_{\mathrm{a},k+1} - \mathbf{r}_{\mathrm{d},k+1}\|_2$ synthesized by the 6S-DTZNN algorithm (7.24), the 1S-DTZNN algorithm (7.19), the 3S-DTZNN algorithm (7.21), and the 5S-DTZNN algorithm (7.23) are presented in Figure 7.6. Evidently, as illustrated in Figure 7.6(a) and (b), one can observe that the precision of the 6S-DTZNN algorithm (7.24) is always the highest among these four DTZNN algorithms. As illustrated in Figure 7.6(c), with $g = 0.001$ s, the tracking error synthesized by the 6S-DTZNN algorithm (7.24) is of order 10^{-14}, which is quite small.

Moreover, to satisfy the real-time tracking requirement, the values of average computing time per updating (ACTPU) of these four DTZNN algorithms should be smaller than the value of the sampling gap g. In this example, the ACTPU data of these four DTZNN algorithms are approximately 0.12 ms, which satisfies the requirement.

In summary, the efficacy and superiority of the general 6S-ZTD formula (7.7) and the general 6S-DTZNN algorithm (7.17) compared with the other ZTD formulas and corresponding DTZNN algorithms are substantiated successfully.

7.6 Chapter Summary

The complicated FDLIES (7.1) and (7.2) have been developed and investigated in this chapter. By using the ZNN method, the CTZNN model (7.6) has been obtained for solving the CTDDLIES (7.3) and (7.4). Then, the general 6S-ZTD formula (7.7) has been developed for approximating the first-order derivative. Hence, the general 6S-DTZNN algorithm (7.17) has been further developed

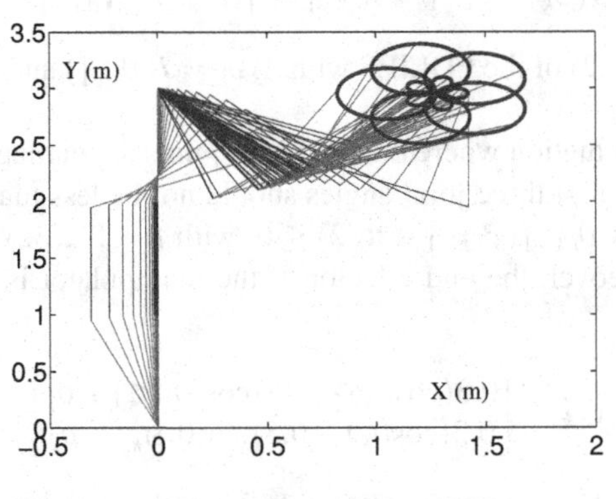

(a) Manipulator trajectories [190]

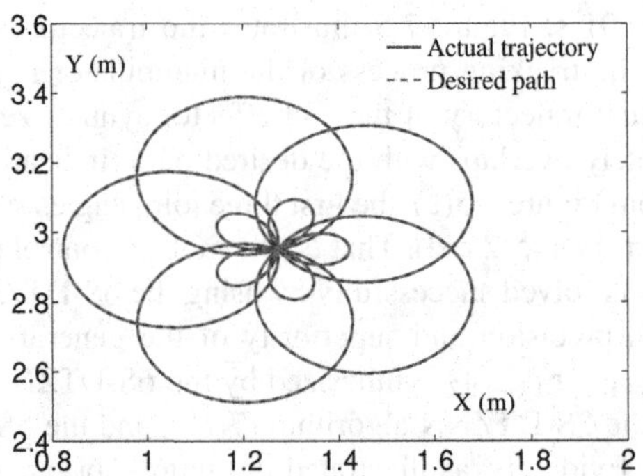

(b) End-effector actual trajectory and desired path [190]

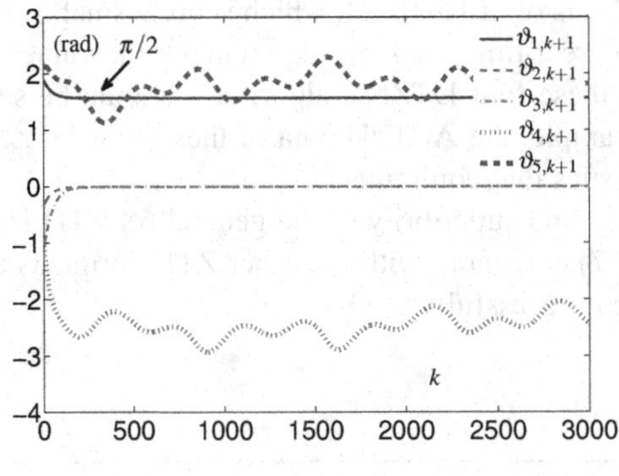

(c) Trajectories of joint angles

FIGURE 7.5: Trajectories of redundant manipulator, end-effector, and joint angles synthesized by 6S-DTZNN algorithm (7.24) with $\hbar = 0.05$ and $g = 0.01$ s in Example 7.3.

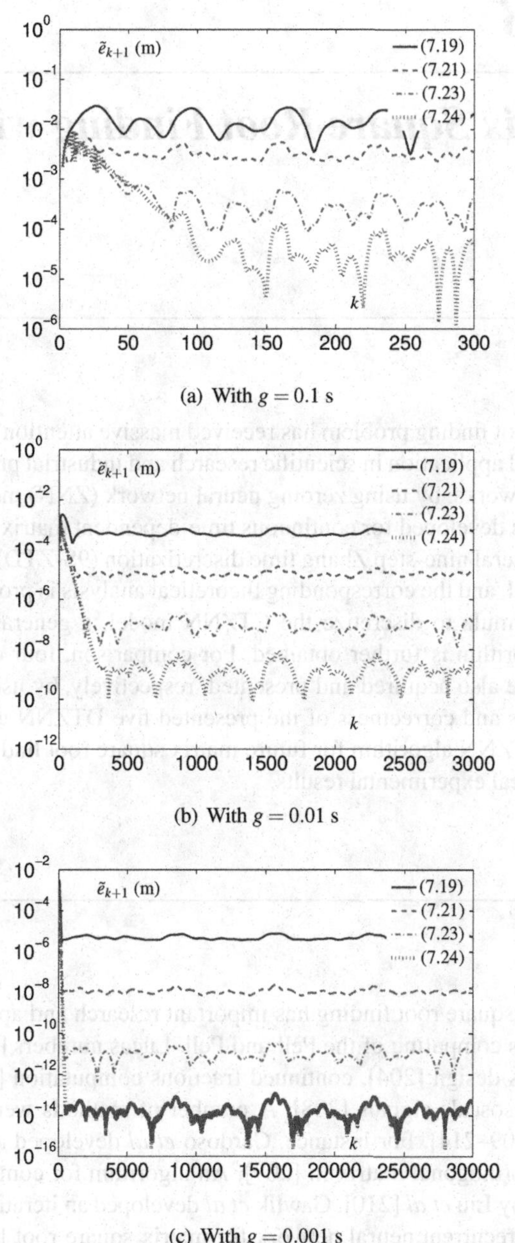

(a) With $g = 0.1$ s

(b) With $g = 0.01$ s

(c) With $g = 0.001$ s

FIGURE 7.6: Tracking errors synthesized by four DTZNN algorithms with $\hbar = 0.05$ and different values of sampling gap g in Example 7.3.

for solving the FDLIES (7.1) and (7.2). The precision of the general 6S-ZTD formula (7.7) and the general 6S-DTZNN algorithm (7.17) has been guaranteed by the theoretical analyses. For comparison, the 1S-DTZNN algorithm (7.19), the 3S-DTZNN algorithm (7.21), and the 5S-DTZNN algorithm (7.23) using three other ZTD formulas have also been developed for solving the FDLIES (7.1) and (7.2). The numerical experiments, including the real-time motion control of the five-link redundant manipulator, have been conducted to substantiate the efficacy and superiority of the general 6S-ZTD formula (7.7) and the general 6S-DTZNN algorithm (7.17).

Chapter 8

Future Matrix Square Root Finding with $\mathbf{O}(g^6)$

Abstract

The matrix square root finding problem has received massive attention and study, because of its extensive appearance and application in scientific research and industrial production. In this chapter, on the basis of previous works, by using zeroing neural network (ZNN) method, a continuous-time ZNN (CTZNN) model is developed for continuous time-dependent matrix square root finding (CT-DMSRF). Besides, a general nine-step Zhang time discretization (9S-ZTD) formula is derived, constructed, and investigated, and the corresponding theoretical analysis is provided. Next, by applying the general 9S-ZTD formula to discretize the CTZNN model, a general nine-step discrete-time ZNN (9S-DTZNN) algorithm is further obtained. For comparison, four other discrete-time ZNN (DTZNN) algorithms are also acquired and presented, respectively, by using other ZTD formulas. Finally, the effectiveness and correctness of the presented five DTZNN algorithms as well as the superiority of the 9S-DTZNN algorithm for future matrix square root finding (FMSRF) are further substantiated by numerical experimental results.

8.1 Introduction

As we know, matrix square root finding has important research and application values in many fields [201–208], such as computing of the Pell and Pell–Lucas numbers [201], GPS/SINS navigation system [203], filters design [204], continued fractions computation [207], and application to the control of ocean mesoscale signals [208]. A number of methods were presented and applied to solve this problem [209–214]. For instance, Cardoso *et al* developed a method to compute the square root of a real P-orthogonal matrix in [209]. An algorithm for complex square roots of real matrices was presented by Liu *et al* [210]. Gawlik *et al* developed an iteration method to find matrix square root in [212]. A recurrent neural network for matrix square root finding was presented by Li *et al* in [213]. Besides, in [214], Sra developed a geometric optimization for matrix square root finding.

Nowadays, with the rapid development of computer technology, neural network methods have been deeply studied and widely used [215–221]. Under such background, a new neural network method, which is termed as zeroing neural network (ZNN), has been proposed and applied to handle many types of problems, especially time-dependent ones [219, 222–229], such as quadratic optimization [222], Lyapunov equation [223], matrix pseudoinversion [227], and matrix inequality [228]. Note that, by adopting the ZNN design formula, the original problem can be transformed into a continuous-time solution model. In general, for the convenience of digital hardware calculation, we further discretize the continuous-time solution model into a discrete-time solution algorithm by using a Zhang time discretization (ZTD) formula [22, 188, 230–234]. Moreover, on the basis of

DOI: 10.1201/9781003497783-8

previous study, we know that the precision of the discrete-time solution algorithm is highly related to the accuracy of the ZTD formula. In short, high-precision ZTD formulas lead to high-precision discrete-time solution algorithms.

In this chapter [235], by following previous research [229], a continuous-time ZNN (CTZNN) model is developed for continuous time-dependent matrix square root finding (CTDMSRF). In order to obtain a high-precision discrete-time ZNN (DTZNN) algorithm, a general nine-step ZTD (9S-ZTD) formula is constructed and presented. Next, by using the 9S-ZTD formula, a general nine-step discrete-time ZNN (9S-DTZNN) algorithm is further acquired. The corresponding theoretical analyses are provided to prove the convergence performance of the 9S-DTZNN algorithm. Besides, for comparison, four other DTZNN algorithms, i.e., seven-step DTZNN (7S-DTZNN), five-step DTZNN (5S-DTZNN), three-step DTZNN (3S-DTZNN), and one-step DTZNN (1S-DTZNN) algorithms, are also derived and presented by applying other ZTD formulas. Through the numerical experiments, the validity and precision of the DTZNN algorithms for future matrix square root finding (FMSRF) are well substantiated.

8.2 Problem Formulation and CTZNN Model

Let us consider the following FMSRF problem with X_{k+1} to be computed at each computational time interval $[t_k, t_{k+1}) \subset [t_{\text{ini}}, t_{\text{fin}}] \subset [0, +\infty)$:

$$A_{k+1} = X_{k+1}X_{k+1} \in \mathbb{R}^{n\times n}, \tag{8.1}$$

where t_{ini} and t_{fin} represent the initial and final time instants, respectively; A_{k+1} being positive definite is generated from the smoothly time-dependent matrix $A(t) \in \mathbb{R}^{n\times n}$ by sampling at time instant $t_{k+1} = (k+1)g$; $X_{k+1} \in \mathbb{R}^{n\times n}$ is the unknown matrix obtained during $[t_k,\ t_{k+1})$. Note that $k = 0, 1, 2, \cdots$ denotes the updating index. On the basis of the current or previous data (e.g., A_k), the future solution X_{k+1} can be computed before the time instant t_{k+1} and then for the future or next use. In other words, the algorithm should satisfy the needs of strict real-time computation during the solution process of the FMSRF problem (8.1).

To solve the FMSRF problem (8.1), the corresponding CTDMSRF problem needs to be investigated first, which is described as

$$A(t) = X(t)X(t). \tag{8.2}$$

Thereinto, $A(t) \in \mathbb{R}^{n\times n}$ is a given time-dependent matrix, which is smooth at any time instant $t \in [t_{\text{ini}}, t_{\text{fin}}] \subset [0, +\infty)$. Besides, $X(t) \in \mathbb{R}^{n\times n}$ is the unknown time-dependent matrix that needs to be obtained, such that the CTDMSRF problem (8.2) holds true at any time instant $t \in [0, +\infty)$. It is worth mentioning that, to guarantee the existence of the solution, $A(t)$ is supposed to be positive definite at any time instant $t \in [t_{\text{ini}}, t_{\text{fin}}] \subset [0, +\infty)$ [211].

On the basis of the previous work [229], by adopting the ZNN method, the continuous-time solution model for solving the CTDMSRF problem (8.2) is formulated as

$$\text{vec}(\dot{X}(t)) = (X^{\mathrm{T}}(t) \otimes I_{n\times n} + I_{n\times n} \otimes X(t))^{-1}(\text{vec}(\dot{A}(t)) + \eta(\text{vec}(A(t)) - (X^{\mathrm{T}}(t) \otimes I_{n\times n})\text{vec}(X(t)))),$$

in which $I_{n\times n} \in \mathbb{R}^{n\times n}$ denotes an $n\times n$ identity matrix; the superscript ^{T} is the transpose operator of a matrix; the symbol $\otimes$ represents the Kronecker product; $\text{vec}(\cdot)$ generates a column vector by stacking all columns of a matrix together; $\eta \in \mathbb{R}^+$ is the ZNN design parameter. In addition, let $B(t) = (X^{\mathrm{T}}(t) \otimes I_{n\times n} + I_{n\times n} \otimes X(t))^{-1}$, $\mathbf{a}(t) = \text{vec}(X(t))$, $\dot{\mathbf{a}}(t) = \text{vec}(\dot{X}(t))$, $\mathbf{b}(t) = \text{vec}(\dot{X}(t))$, and

$\mathbf{c}(t) = \text{vec}(A(t)) - (X^{\text{T}}(t) \otimes I_{n\times n})\mathbf{a}(t)$. The above equation, i.e., the CTZNN model, is given as below:

$$\dot{\mathbf{a}}(t) = B(t)(\mathbf{b}(t) + \eta\mathbf{c}(t)). \tag{8.3}$$

8.3 General 9S-ZTD Formula and DTZNN Algorithms

In order to obtain the general 9S-DTZNN algorithm, the general 9S-ZTD formula is derived, constructed, and developed. Moreover, four other DTZNN algorithms are presented for comparison.

8.3.1 General 9S-ZTD formula

The general 9S-ZTD formula is given by the following theorem.

Theorem 33 *With the sufficiently small sampling gap $g \in (0,1)$, let $\mathscr{O}(g^5)$ denote the error (especially, the truncation error) positively or negatively proportional to g^5, i.e., of the order of g^5. Suppose that $\zeta(t)$ is sufficiently smooth. With $\zeta_{k+1} = \zeta(t_{k+1}) = \zeta((k+1)g)$, the real numbers p_1, p_2, p_3, and p_4 satisfy*

$$\begin{cases} e_1 < 0, \\ e_2 > 0, \\ e_3 < 0, \\ 5845p_1 + 9810p_2 + 7305p_3 + 2588p_4 > -19278, \\ 8365p_1 + 27330p_2 + 28225p_3 + 12604p_4 < -26334, \\ 70p_1 + 235p_2 + 205p_3 + 148p_4 < -238, \\ 1176e_1q_2 + 8232e_3q_1 > 0, \\ 28812q_3e_3^2 + 576240q_1e_3q_2 + 605052e_1e_2e_3 + 82320e_1q_2^2 > 0, \\ 609892416e_1^2e_2^2 + 58084992e_1e_2e_3q_3 - 580849920e_1e_2q_1q_2 \\ +3951360e_1q_2^2q_3 - 4065949440e_2e_3q_1^2 + 1382976e_3^2q_3^2 + 27659520e_3q_1q_2q_3 < 0, \end{cases} \tag{8.4}$$

where $e_1 = 35p_1 + 30p_2 + 15p_3 + 4p_4 - 126$, $e_2 = 985p_1 + 1530p_2 + 1565p_3 + 844p_4 + 2214$, $e_3 = 245p_1 + 150p_2 + 45p_3 + 4p_4 - 1386$, $q_1 = 35p_1 + 40p_2 + 25p_3 + 8p_4 - 42$, $q_2 = 5005p_1 + 9630p_2 + 7965p_3 + 3104p_4 + 16254$, and $q_3 = 3045p_1 + 9210p_2 + 9505p_3 + 4308p_4 + 9198$. Then, the general 9S-ZTD formula is presented as follows:

$$\begin{aligned} \dot{\zeta}_k = {} & \frac{d_0}{g}\zeta_{k+1} + \frac{d_1}{g}\zeta_k + \frac{d_2}{g}\zeta_{k-1} + \frac{d_3}{g}\zeta_{k-2} + \frac{d_4}{g}\zeta_{k-3} + \frac{d_5}{g}\zeta_{k-4} \\ & + \frac{d_6}{g}\zeta_{k-5} + \frac{d_7}{g}\zeta_{k-6} + \frac{d_8}{g}\zeta_{k-7} + \frac{d_9}{g}\zeta_{k-8} + \mathscr{O}(g^5). \end{aligned} \tag{8.5}$$

Thereinto, $d_0 = -70/e_1$, $d_1 = (48055p_1 + 28590p_2 + 12195p_3 + 2972p_4 + 38682)/(840e_1)$, $d_2 = -70p_1/e_1$, $d_3 = -70p_2/e_1$, $d_4 = -70p_3/e_1$, $d_5 = -70p_4/e_1$, $d_6 = 14(35p_1 + 80p_2 + 90p_3 + 64p_4 + 84)/(5e_1)$, $d_7 = -70(7p_1 + 15p_2 + 15p_3 + 8p_4 + 18)/(3e_1)$, $d_8 = 10(70p_1 + 144p_2 + 135p_3 + 64p_4 + 189)/(7e_1)$, and $d_9 = -35(5p_1 + 10p_2 + 9p_3 + 4p_4 + 14)/(8e_1)$.

Proof. The proof is presented in Appendix H. □

Additionally, for the convenience of readers or researchers, the coefficients of twelve 9S-ZTD formulas are provided in Table 8.1.

TABLE 8.1: Coefficients of 9S-ZTD formulas.

Number	d_0	d_1	d_2	d_3	d_4	d_5	d_6	d_7	d_8	d_9
1	$\frac{350}{841}$	$\frac{11471}{235480}$	$\frac{-140}{841}$	$\frac{-280}{841}$	$\frac{-350}{2523}$	$\frac{70}{841}$	$\frac{784}{4205}$	$\frac{-70}{2523}$	$\frac{-680}{5887}$	$\frac{315}{6728}$
2	$\frac{35}{82}$	$\frac{643}{34440}$	$\frac{-7}{41}$	$\frac{-21}{82}$	$\frac{-7}{41}$	0	$\frac{49}{205}$	$\frac{7}{246}$	$\frac{-103}{574}$	$\frac{21}{328}$
3	$\frac{175}{418}$	$\frac{7237}{175560}$	$\frac{-35}{209}$	$\frac{-35}{114}$	$\frac{-35}{209}$	$\frac{35}{418}$	$\frac{623}{3135}$	$\frac{-35}{1254}$	$\frac{-355}{2926}$	$\frac{245}{5016}$
4	$\frac{25}{59}$	$\frac{487}{49560}$	$\frac{-5}{59}$	$\frac{-25}{59}$	$\frac{-5}{59}$	$\frac{5}{59}$	$\frac{41}{295}$	$\frac{5}{177}$	$\frac{-60}{413}$	$\frac{25}{472}$
5	$\frac{525}{1273}$	$\frac{83789}{1069320}$	$\frac{-315}{1273}$	$\frac{-315}{1273}$	$\frac{-175}{1273}$	$\frac{35}{1273}$	$\frac{1127}{6365}$	$\frac{175}{3819}$	$\frac{-1490}{8911}$	$\frac{595}{10184}$
6	$\frac{700}{1773}$	$\frac{63563}{496440}$	$\frac{-140}{591}$	$\frac{-700}{1773}$	$\frac{-70}{1773}$	$\frac{70}{591}$	$\frac{952}{8865}$	$\frac{-70}{1773}$	$\frac{-290}{4137}$	$\frac{455}{14184}$
7	$\frac{350}{871}$	$\frac{89603}{731640}$	$\frac{-280}{871}$	$\frac{-140}{871}$	$\frac{-210}{871}$	$\frac{70}{871}$	$\frac{1204}{4355}$	$\frac{-350}{2613}$	$\frac{-360}{6097}$	$\frac{245}{6968}$
8	$\frac{175}{446}$	$\frac{24989}{187320}$	$\frac{-105}{446}$	$\frac{-175}{446}$	$\frac{-35}{446}$	$\frac{35}{223}$	$\frac{329}{2230}$	$\frac{-175}{1338}$	$\frac{-20}{1561}$	$\frac{35}{1784}$
9	$\frac{350}{857}$	$\frac{51901}{719880}$	$\frac{-140}{857}$	$\frac{-350}{857}$	$\frac{-70}{857}$	$\frac{140}{857}$	$\frac{168}{4285}$	$\frac{140}{2571}$	$\frac{-780}{5999}$	$\frac{315}{6856}$
10	$\frac{350}{897}$	$\frac{39107}{251160}$	$\frac{-280}{897}$	$\frac{-245}{897}$	$\frac{-140}{897}$	$\frac{140}{897}$	$\frac{56}{345}$	$\frac{-35}{299}$	$\frac{-190}{6279}$	$\frac{175}{7176}$
11	$\frac{25}{64}$	$\frac{323}{2240}$	$\frac{-25}{96}$	$\frac{-35}{96}$	$\frac{-5}{48}$	$\frac{5}{24}$	$\frac{29}{480}$	$\frac{-5}{96}$	$\frac{-65}{1344}$	$\frac{5}{192}$
12	$\frac{175}{424}$	$\frac{2629}{44520}$	$\frac{-35}{212}$	$\frac{-315}{848}$	$\frac{-35}{424}$	$\frac{35}{848}$	$\frac{119}{530}$	$\frac{-175}{2544}$	$\frac{-135}{1484}$	$\frac{35}{848}$

8.3.2 DTZNN algorithms

At the beginning, the general 9S-ZTD formula (8.5) is adopted to discretize the CTZNN model (8.3), and the corresponding general 9S-DTZNN algorithm is developed as

$$\begin{aligned}\mathbf{a}_{k+1} \doteq\ & \frac{1}{d_0}\tilde{\mathbf{a}}_k - \frac{d_1}{d_0}\mathbf{a}_k - \frac{d_2}{d_0}\mathbf{a}_{k-1} - \frac{d_3}{d_0}\mathbf{a}_{k-2} - \frac{d_4}{d_0}\mathbf{a}_{k-3} - \frac{d_5}{d_0}\mathbf{a}_{k-4}\\ & - \frac{d_6}{d_0}\mathbf{a}_{k-5} - \frac{d_7}{d_0}\mathbf{a}_{k-6} - \frac{d_8}{d_0}\mathbf{a}_{k-7} - \frac{d_9}{d_0}\mathbf{a}_{k-8},\end{aligned} \tag{8.6}$$

where $\doteq$ denotes the computational assignment operator, and $\hbar = g\eta$ represents the step length. The truncation error of (8.6) is $\mathbf{O}(g^6)$ with each element being $\mathscr{O}(g^6)$. Besides, B_k, $\mathbf{b}_k$, and $\mathbf{c}_k$ denote $B(t_k)$, $\mathbf{b}(t_k)$, and $\mathbf{c}(t_k)$, respectively; $\tilde{\mathbf{a}}_k = B_k(g\mathbf{b}_k + \hbar\mathbf{c}_k)$ and $t_k = kg$. Meanwhile, the following theorem is given to guarantee the precision and correctness of this algorithm.

Theorem 34 *With the sufficiently small sampling gap, let* $\mathbf{O}(g^6)$ *denote the error (especially, the truncation error) with each element being* $\mathscr{O}(g^6)$*. Suppose that* A_k *is positive definite. The general 9S-DTZNN algorithm (8.6) is zero-stable, consistent, and convergent, which converges with the order of truncation error being* $\mathbf{O}(g^6)$*.*

Proof. The proof is presented in Appendix I. □

Next, four other ZTD formulas (i.e.,7S-ZTD, 5S-ZTD, 3S-ZTD, and 1S-ZTD formulas) are applied to obtaining the corresponding DTZNN algorithms in this chapter [235]. The 7S-ZTD, 5S-ZTD, 3S-ZTD, and 1S-ZTD formulas are given below [22, 188, 231]:

$$\begin{aligned}\dot{\zeta}_k =\ & \frac{50}{111g}\zeta_{k+1} - \frac{17}{740g}\zeta_k - \frac{20}{111g}\zeta_{k-1} - \frac{10}{37g}\zeta_{k-2} - \frac{10}{111g}\zeta_{k-3}\\ & + \frac{35}{444g}\zeta_{k-4} + \frac{44}{555g}\zeta_{k-5} - \frac{5}{111g}\zeta_{k-6} + \mathscr{O}(g^4),\end{aligned} \tag{8.7}$$

$$\dot{\zeta}_k = \frac{1}{2g}\zeta_{k+1} - \frac{5}{48g}\zeta_k - \frac{1}{4g}\zeta_{k-1} - \frac{1}{8g}\zeta_{k-2} - \frac{1}{12g}\zeta_{k-3} + \frac{1}{16g}\zeta_{k-4} + \mathscr{O}(g^3), \tag{8.8}$$

$$\dot{\zeta}_k = \frac{1}{g}\zeta_{k+1} - \frac{3}{2g}\zeta_k + \frac{1}{g}\zeta_{k-1} - \frac{1}{2g}\zeta_{k-2} + \mathscr{O}(g^2), \tag{8.9}$$

and

$$\dot{\zeta}_k = \frac{1}{g}\zeta_{k+1} - \frac{1}{g}\zeta_k + \mathscr{O}(g). \tag{8.10}$$

Note that, by setting the parameters $\eta_1 = -1/2$, $\eta_2 = -1/5$, and $\eta_3 = -2/5$ in [231], the 7S-ZTD formula (8.7) is acquired. Besides, the 1S-ZTD formula (8.10) can be seen as the simplest ZTD formula.

By utilizing the formulas (8.7), (8.8), (8.9), and (8.10) to discretize the CTZNN model (8.3), the corresponding DTZNN algorithms, i.e., 7S-DTZNN, 5S-DTZNN, 3S-DTZNN, and 1S-DTZNN algorithms, are respectively obtained as

$$\mathbf{a}_{k+1} \doteq \frac{111}{50}\tilde{\mathbf{a}}_k + \frac{51}{1000}\mathbf{a}_k + \frac{2}{5}\mathbf{a}_{k-1} + \frac{3}{5}\mathbf{a}_{k-2} + \frac{1}{5}\mathbf{a}_{k-3} - \frac{7}{40}\mathbf{a}_{k-4} - \frac{22}{125}\mathbf{a}_{k-5} + \frac{1}{10}\mathbf{a}_{k-6}, \tag{8.11}$$

$$\mathbf{a}_{k+1} \doteq 2\tilde{\mathbf{a}}_k + \frac{5}{24}\mathbf{a}_k + \frac{1}{2}\mathbf{a}_{k-1} + \frac{1}{4}\mathbf{a}_{k-2} + \frac{1}{6}\mathbf{a}_{k-3} - \frac{1}{8}\mathbf{a}_{k-4}, \tag{8.12}$$

$$\mathbf{a}_{k+1} \doteq \tilde{\mathbf{a}}_k + \frac{3}{2}\mathbf{a}_k - \mathbf{a}_{k-1} + \frac{1}{2}\mathbf{a}_{k-2}, \tag{8.13}$$

and

$$\mathbf{a}_{k+1} \doteq \tilde{\mathbf{a}}_k + \mathbf{a}_k. \tag{8.14}$$

The truncation errors of (8.11), (8.12), (8.13), and (8.14) are $\mathbf{O}(g^5)$, $\mathbf{O}(g^4)$, $\mathbf{O}(g^3)$, and $\mathbf{O}(g^2)$ with elements being $\mathscr{O}(g^5)$, $\mathscr{O}(g^4)$, $\mathscr{O}(g^3)$, and $\mathscr{O}(g^2)$, respectively.

Similarly, we have the following corollary for the above four DTZNN algorithms.

Corollary 5 *With the sufficiently small sampling gap $g \in (0,1)$, let $\mathbf{O}(g^5)$, $\mathbf{O}(g^4)$, $\mathbf{O}(g^3)$, or $\mathbf{O}(g^2)$ denote the error (especially, the truncation error) with each element being $\mathscr{O}(g^5)$, $\mathscr{O}(g^4)$, $\mathscr{O}(g^3)$, or $\mathscr{O}(g^2)$, respectively. Suppose that A_k is positive definite. The 7S-DTZNN algorithm (8.11), the 5S-DTZNN algorithm (8.12), the 3S-DTZNN algorithm (8.13), and the 1S-DTZNN algorithm (8.14) are zero-stable, consistent, and convergent, which converge with the orders of their truncation errors being $\mathbf{O}(g^5)$, $\mathbf{O}(g^4)$, $\mathbf{O}(g^3)$, and $\mathbf{O}(g^2)$, respectively.*

Note that the residual error is defined as $\hat{e}_{k+1} = \|X_{k+1}X_{k+1} - A_{k+1}\|_\mathrm{F}$ for the FMSRF problem (8.1) in this chapter [235], where $\|\cdot\|_\mathrm{F}$ denotes the Frobenius norm of a matrix.

Theorem 35 *Consider the FMSRF problem (8.1) with A_k being positive definite and uniformly norm bounded. With the sufficiently small sampling gap $g \in (0,1)$, the maximal steady-state residual error (MSSRE) $\lim_{k\to+\infty}\sup\hat{e}_{k+1}$ synthesized by the general 9S-DTZNN algorithm (8.6) is $\mathscr{O}(g^6)$.*

Proof. The proof is presented in Appendix J. □

Corollary 6 *Consider the FMSRF problem (8.1) with A_k being positive definite and uniformly norm bounded. With the sufficiently small sampling gap $g \in (0,1)$, the MSSREs $\lim_{k\to+\infty}\sup\hat{e}_{k+1}$ synthesized by the 7S-DTZNN algorithm (8.11), the 5S-DTZNN algorithm (8.12), the 3S-DTZNN algorithm (8.13), and the 1S-DTZNN algorithm (8.14) are $\mathscr{O}(g^5)$, $\mathscr{O}(g^4)$, $\mathscr{O}(g^3)$, and $\mathscr{O}(g^2)$, respectively.*

For a more intuitive understanding of the main content of this chapter [235], Table 8.2 lists the problem, scheme, model, and algorithms.

TABLE 8.2: Problem, scheme, model, and algorithms in this chapter.

Problem	$A_{k+1} = X_{k+1}X_{k+1} \in \mathbb{R}^{n\times n}$
Scheme	Adopt ZTD formulas to discretize CTZNN model (8.3).
Model	$\dot{\mathbf{a}}(t) = B(t)(\mathbf{b}(t) + \eta\mathbf{c}(t))$.
Algorithms	$\mathbf{a}_{k+1} \doteq \frac{1}{d_0}\tilde{\mathbf{a}}_k - \frac{d_1}{d_0}\mathbf{a}_k - \frac{d_2}{d_0}\mathbf{a}_{k-1} - \frac{d_3}{d_0}\mathbf{a}_{k-2} - \frac{d_4}{d_0}\mathbf{a}_{k-3} - \frac{d_5}{d_0}\mathbf{a}_{k-4} - \frac{d_6}{d_0}\mathbf{a}_{k-5} - \frac{d_7}{d_0}\mathbf{a}_{k-6} - \frac{d_8}{d_0}\mathbf{a}_{k-7} - \frac{d_9}{d_0}\mathbf{a}_{k-8}$, $\mathbf{a}_{k+1} \doteq \frac{111}{50}\tilde{\mathbf{a}}_k + \frac{51}{1000}\mathbf{a}_k + \frac{2}{5}\mathbf{a}_{k-1} + \frac{3}{5}\mathbf{a}_{k-2} + \frac{1}{5}\mathbf{a}_{k-3} - \frac{7}{40}\mathbf{a}_{k-4} - \frac{22}{125}\mathbf{a}_{k-5} + \frac{1}{10}\mathbf{a}_{k-6}$, $\mathbf{a}_{k+1} \doteq 2\tilde{\mathbf{a}}_k + \frac{5}{24}\mathbf{a}_k + \frac{1}{2}\mathbf{a}_{k-1} + \frac{1}{4}\mathbf{a}_{k-2} + \frac{1}{6}\mathbf{a}_{k-3} - \frac{1}{8}\mathbf{a}_{k-4}$, $\mathbf{a}_{k+1} \doteq \tilde{\mathbf{a}}_k + \frac{3}{2}\mathbf{a}_k - \mathbf{a}_{k-1} + \frac{1}{2}\mathbf{a}_{k-2}$, $\mathbf{a}_{k+1} \doteq \tilde{\mathbf{a}}_k + \mathbf{a}_k$.

8.4 Numerical Experiments

To verify the feasibility, effectiveness, and accuracy of the presented DTZNN algorithms, three numerical experiments are carried out. It is worth pointing out that the values of ten coefficients, which are applied in all these numerical experiments for the general 9S-DTZNN algorithm (8.6), are shown in the first row of Table 8.1.

Example 8.1 The following FMSRF problem with X_{k+1} to be solved at each computational time interval $[t_k, t_{k+1}) \subset [0, 30]$ s is considered:

$$A_k = \begin{bmatrix} \cos(t_k)\sin(t_k) + (\cos(t_k)+3)^2 & 2\sin(t_k)(\cos(t_k)+3) \\ 2\cos(t_k)(\cos(t_k)+3) & \cos(t_k)\sin(t_k) + (\cos(t_k)+3)^2 \end{bmatrix}.$$

To check the correctness of the solution synthesized by the DTZNN algorithms, the corresponding theoretical time-dependent solution is given as

$$X_k^* = \begin{bmatrix} 3+\cos(t_k) & \sin(t_k) \\ \cos(t_k) & 3+\cos(t_k) \end{bmatrix}.$$

The initial state is arbitrarily set as $X_0 = [12.5, 2.2; 1.85, 17.6]$, and the step length $\hbar$ is uniformly set as 0.1. For comparison and illustration, we define two errors, i.e., the residual error $\hat{e}_{k+1} = \|X_{k+1}X_{k+1} - A_{k+1}\|_\text{F}$ and the solution error $\check{e}_{k+1} = \|X_{k+1} - X_{k+1}^*\|_\text{F}$, where $\|\cdot\|_\text{F}$ denotes the Frobenius norm. The corresponding numerical experimental results are presented in Figures 8.1–8.3 with different g. Specially, Figures 8.1 and 8.2 display the numerical experimental results with $g = 0.1$ s.

The element trajectories of the state matrix X_{k+1} synthesized by the general 9S-DTZNN algorithm (8.6) together with the theoretical solution X_{k+1}^* are shown in Figure 8.1. As observed from Figure 8.1, the element trajectories of the state matrix X_{k+1} nearly overlap with theoretical ones. Therefore, the general 9S-DTZNN algorithm (8.6) for solving the above FMSRF problem is effective. The trajectories of residual errors and solution errors synthesized by the five DTZNN algorithms (8.6), (8.11), (8.12), (8.13), and (8.14) with $g = 0.1$ s are displayed in Figure 8.2(a) and (b), respectively. As seen, the solution errors and residual errors synthesized by five DTZNN algorithms all converge to zero rapidly, with that synthesized by (8.6) being smaller. Therefore, the effectiveness and accuracy of the presented five DTZNN algorithms as well as the superiority of the general 9S-DTZNN algorithm (8.6) are substantiated. Note that, in practical applications, we

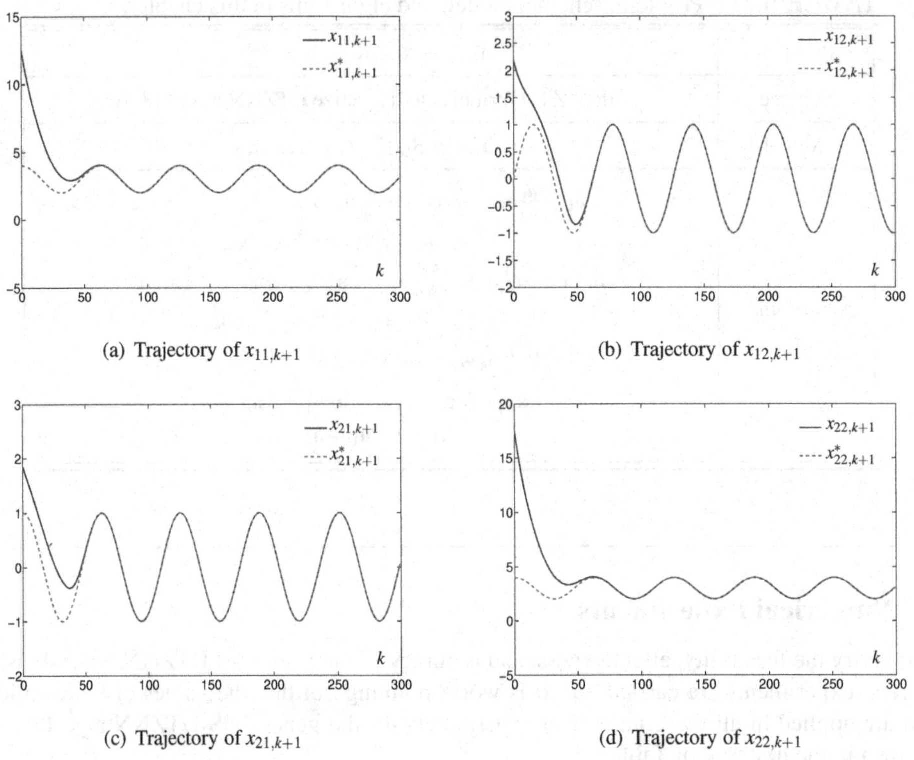

(a) Trajectory of $x_{11,k+1}$ (b) Trajectory of $x_{12,k+1}$

(c) Trajectory of $x_{21,k+1}$ (d) Trajectory of $x_{22,k+1}$

FIGURE 8.1: Element trajectories of state matrix X_{k+1} synthesized by general 9S-DTZNN algorithm (8.6) with $g = 0.1$ s for FMSRF in Example 8.1.

can obtain higher computational accuracy by simply setting the value of g a little smaller. Besides, Figure 8.3(a) and (b) shows the trajectories of residual errors and solution errors synthesized by five DTZNN algorithms with $g = 0.01$ s. As shown in Figure 8.3, with $g = 0.01$ s, the accuracy of the computational results of all the DTZNN algorithms is improved, and especially the magnitude of the MSSRE synthesized by the general 9S-DTZNN algorithm (8.6) is about 10^{-11}.

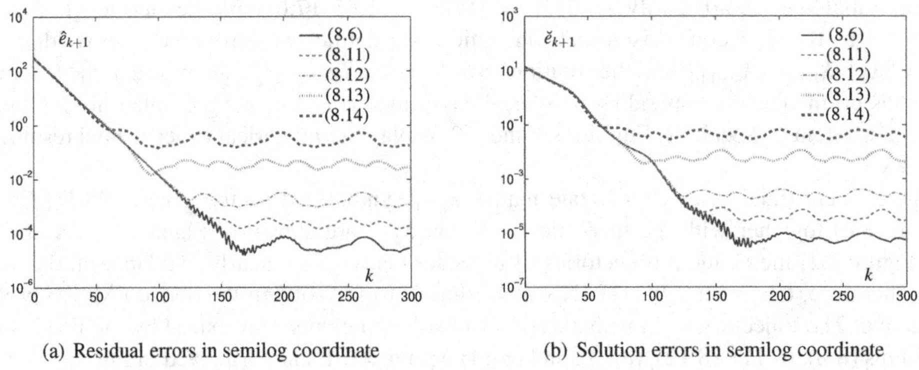

(a) Residual errors in semilog coordinate (b) Solution errors in semilog coordinate

FIGURE 8.2: Trajectories of residual errors and solution errors synthesized by five DTZNN algorithms with $g = 0.1$ s for FMSRF in Example 8.1.

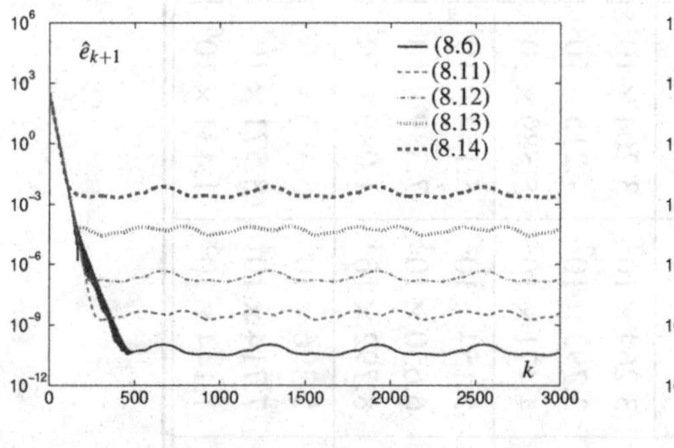

(a) Residual errors in semilog coordinate

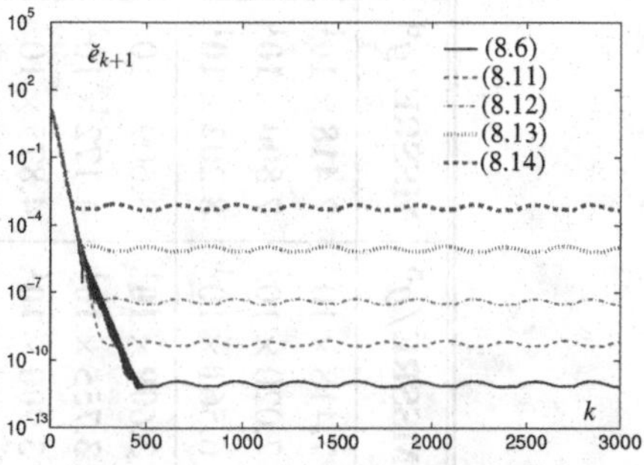

(b) Solution errors in semilog coordinate

FIGURE 8.3: Trajectories of residual errors and solution errors synthesized by five DTZNN algorithms with $g = 0.01$ s for FMSRF in Example 8.1.

In order to further observe variation patterns of the MSSRE synthesized by five DTZNN algorithms with different values of g, more numerical experiments are conducted, and the corresponding numerical experimental results are shown in Table 8.3. As seen in Table 8.3, the values of MSSRE/g^6 for the general 9S-DTZNN algorithm (8.6) are nearly equal to a constant, which means that the MSSREs synthesized by the general 9S-DTZNN algorithm (8.6) are almost directly proportional to $\mathscr{O}(g^6)$. Similarly, according to the values of MSSRE$/g^5$, MSSRE$/g^4$, MSSRE$/g^3$, and MSSRE$/g^2$ for the algorithms (8.11), (8.12), (8.13), and (8.14), one concludes that the MSSREs synthesized by the algorithms (8.11), (8.12), (8.13), and (8.14) are almost directly proportional to $\mathscr{O}(g^5)$, $\mathscr{O}(g^4)$, $\mathscr{O}(g^3)$, and $\mathscr{O}(g^2)$, respectively. Thus, the correctness of Theorems 34 and 35 is further substantiated.

Example 8.2 The following FMSRF problem with X_{k+1} to be solved at each computational time interval $[t_k, t_{k+1}) \subset [0, 30]$ s is considered:

$$A_k = \begin{bmatrix} p_{11} & p_{12} & p_{13} \\ p_{21} & p_{22} & p_{23} \\ p_{31} & p_{32} & p_{33} \end{bmatrix},$$

where $p_{11} = c^2 - cs + (c+5)^2$, $p_{12} = cs + c(c+5) + c(s+3)$, $p_{13} = cs - s(c+5) - s(s+2)$, $p_{21} = cs + c(c+5) + c(s+3)$, $p_{22} = c^2 - cs + (s+3)^2$, $p_{23} = s(s+2) - cs + s(s+3)$, $p_{31} = c(c+5) - c^2 + c(s+2)$, $p_{32} = c^2 - c(s+2) - c(s+3)$, and $p_{33} = (s+2)^2 - 2cs$, as well as $c = \cos(t_k)$ and $s = \sin(t_k)$. To check the correctness of the solution synthesized by the DTZNN algorithms, the corresponding theoretical time-dependent solution is given as

$$X_k^* = \begin{bmatrix} 5+\cos(t_k) & \cos(t_k) & -\sin(t_k) \\ \cos(t_k) & 3+\sin(t_k) & \sin(t_k) \\ \cos(t_k) & -\cos(t_k) & 2+\sin(t_k) \end{bmatrix}.$$

The initial state is arbitrarily set as $X_0 = [9.5, 0.7, 0.6; -1.1, 12, 1.3; -1.6, 0.2, 9]$, the step length $\hbar = 0.1$, and the sampling gap $g = 0.1$ s. The corresponding numerical experimental results are presented in Figures 8.4–8.7.

The element trajectories of the state matrix X_{k+1} synthesized by the general 9S-DTZNN algorithm (8.6) together with the theoretical solution X_{k+1}^* are shown in Figures 8.4–8.6. One sees from Figures 8.4–8.6 that the state matrix X_{k+1} is time-dependent, which coincides with the corresponding theoretical solution. Besides, Figure 8.7 displays the trajectories of residual errors and solution errors synthesized by the five DTZNN algorithms (8.6), (8.11), (8.12), (8.13), and (8.14). One concludes from this figure that the MSSREs synthesized by the algorithms (8.6), (8.11), (8.12), (8.13),

TABLE 8.3: MSSREs synthesized by DTZNN algorithms with different values of g in Example 8.1.

DTZNN algorithm	g (s)	MSSRE	MSSRE$/g$	MSSRE$/g^2$	MSSRE$/g^3$	MSSRE$/g^4$	MSSRE$/g^5$	MSSRE$/g^6$
9S-DTZNN algorithm (8.6)	0.1	7.418×10^{-5}	7.418×10^{-4}	7.418×10^{-3}	7.418×10^{-2}	7.418×10^{-1}	7.418×10^{0}	$\mathbf{7.418\times10^{1}}$
	0.09	4.145×10^{-5}	4.606×10^{-4}	5.117×10^{-3}	5.686×10^{-2}	6.318×10^{-1}	7.020×10^{0}	$\mathbf{7.800\times10^{1}}$
	0.08	2.150×10^{-5}	2.688×10^{-4}	3.359×10^{-3}	4.199×10^{-2}	5.249×10^{-1}	6.561×10^{0}	$\mathbf{8.202\times10^{1}}$
7S-DTZNN algorithm (8.11)	0.1	3.609×10^{-4}	3.609×10^{-3}	3.609×10^{-2}	3.609×10^{-1}	3.609×10^{0}	$\mathbf{3.609\times10^{1}}$	3.609×10^{2}
	0.09	2.217×10^{-4}	2.463×10^{-3}	2.737×10^{-2}	3.041×10^{-1}	3.379×10^{0}	$\mathbf{3.755\times10^{1}}$	4.172×10^{2}
	0.08	1.278×10^{-4}	1.598×10^{-3}	1.997×10^{-2}	2.496×10^{-1}	3.120×10^{0}	$\mathbf{3.900\times10^{1}}$	4.875×10^{2}
5S-DTZNN algorithm (8.12)	0.1	3.264×10^{-3}	3.264×10^{-2}	3.264×10^{-1}	3.264×10^{0}	$\mathbf{3.264\times10^{1}}$	3.264×10^{2}	3.264×10^{3}
	0.09	2.240×10^{-3}	2.489×10^{-2}	2.765×10^{-1}	3.073×10^{0}	$\mathbf{3.414\times10^{1}}$	3.793×10^{2}	4.215×10^{3}
	0.08	1.465×10^{-3}	1.831×10^{-2}	2.289×10^{-1}	2.861×10^{0}	$\mathbf{3.577\times10^{1}}$	4.471×10^{2}	5.589×10^{3}
3S-DTZNN algorithm (8.13)	0.1	5.154×10^{-2}	5.154×10^{-1}	5.154×10^{0}	$\mathbf{5.154\times10^{1}}$	5.154×10^{2}	5.154×10^{3}	5.154×10^{4}
	0.09	3.927×10^{-2}	4.363×10^{-1}	4.848×10^{0}	$\mathbf{5.387\times10^{1}}$	5.985×10^{2}	6.650×10^{3}	7.389×10^{4}
	0.08	2.881×10^{-2}	3.601×10^{-1}	4.502×10^{0}	$\mathbf{5.627\times10^{1}}$	7.034×10^{2}	8.792×10^{3}	1.099×10^{5}
1S-DTZNN algorithm (8.14)	0.1	5.396×10^{-1}	5.396×10^{0}	$\mathbf{5.396\times10^{1}}$	5.396×10^{2}	5.396×10^{3}	5.396×10^{4}	5.396×10^{5}
	0.09	4.555×10^{-1}	5.061×10^{0}	$\mathbf{5.623\times10^{1}}$	6.248×10^{2}	6.943×10^{3}	7.714×10^{4}	8.571×10^{5}
	0.08	3.750×10^{-1}	4.688×10^{0}	$\mathbf{5.859\times10^{1}}$	7.324×10^{2}	9.155×10^{3}	1.144×10^{5}	1.431×10^{6}

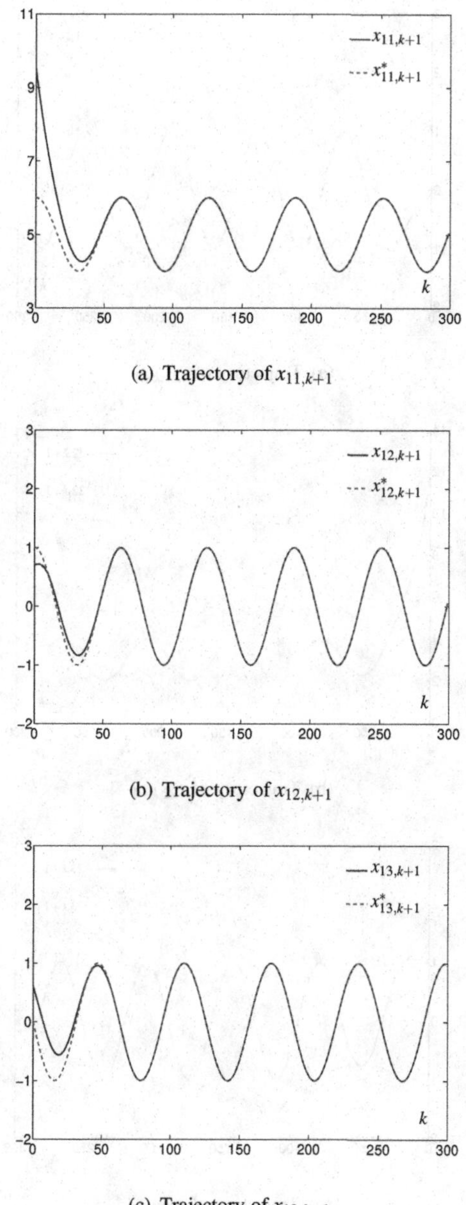

(a) Trajectory of $x_{11,k+1}$

(b) Trajectory of $x_{12,k+1}$

(c) Trajectory of $x_{13,k+1}$

FIGURE 8.4: Element trajectories of row-1 of state matrix X_{k+1} synthesized by general 9S-DTZNN algorithm (8.6) with $g = 0.1$ s for FMSRF in Example 8.2.

and (8.14) are almost directly proportional to $\mathcal{O}(g^6)$, $\mathcal{O}(g^5)$, $\mathcal{O}(g^4)$, $\mathcal{O}(g^3)$, and $\mathcal{O}(g^2)$, respectively. Moreover, the effectiveness and accuracy of the presented five DTZNN algorithms as well as the superiority of the general 9S-DTZNN algorithm (8.6) are substantiated again.

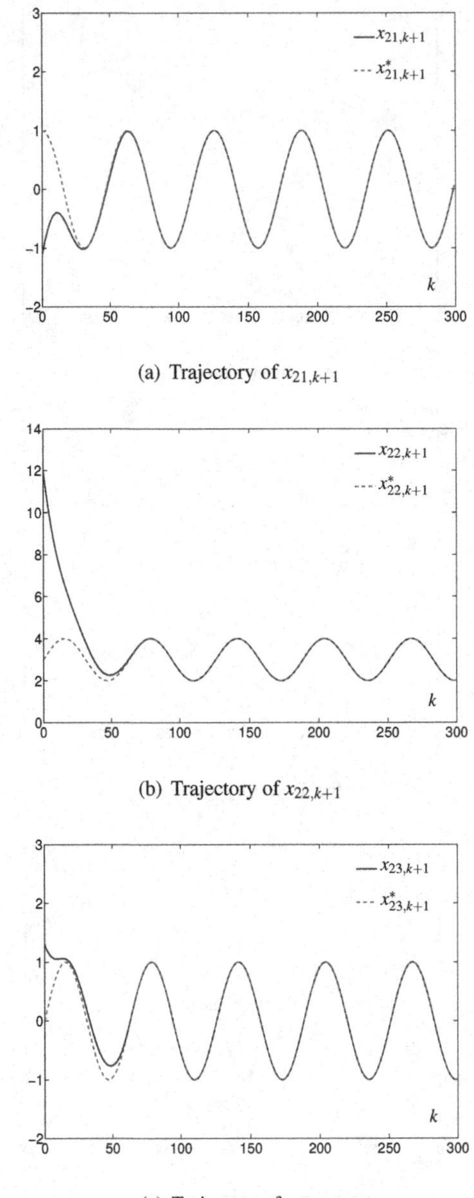

(a) Trajectory of $x_{21,k+1}$

(b) Trajectory of $x_{22,k+1}$

(c) Trajectory of $x_{23,k+1}$

FIGURE 8.5: Element trajectories of row-2 of state matrix X_{k+1} synthesized by general 9S-DTZNN algorithm (8.6) with $g = 0.1$ s for FMSRF in Example 8.2.

Example 8.3 The following FMSRF problem with X_{k+1} to be solved at each computational time interval $[t_k, t_{k+1}) \subset [0, 30]$ s is considered:

$$A_k = \begin{bmatrix} q_{11} & q_{12} & q_{13} & q_{14} \\ q_{21} & q_{22} & q_{23} & q_{24} \\ q_{31} & q_{32} & q_{33} & q_{34} \\ q_{41} & q_{42} & q_{43} & q_{44} \end{bmatrix},$$

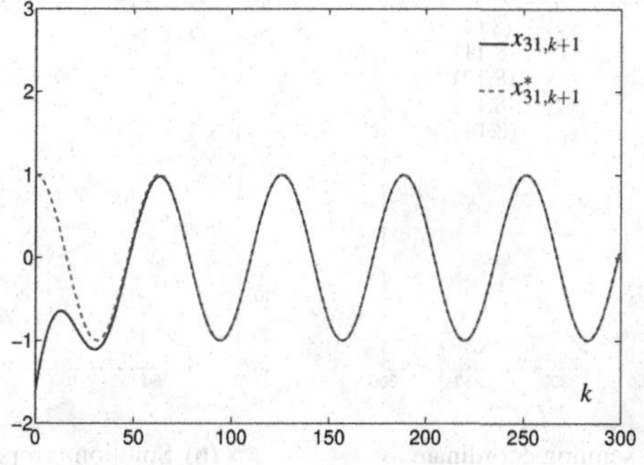

(a) Trajectory of $x_{31,k+1}$

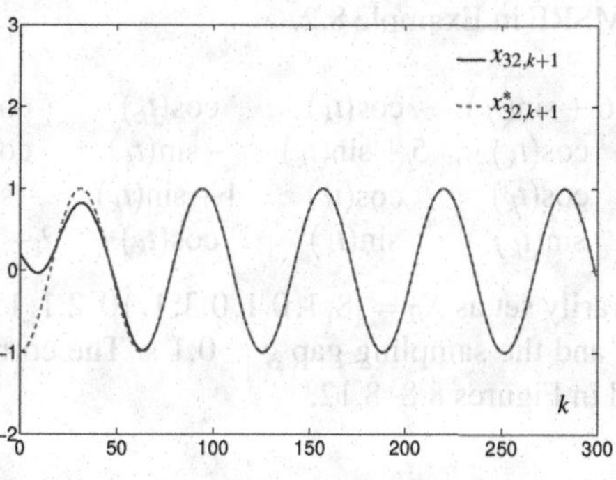

(b) Trajectory of $x_{32,k+1}$

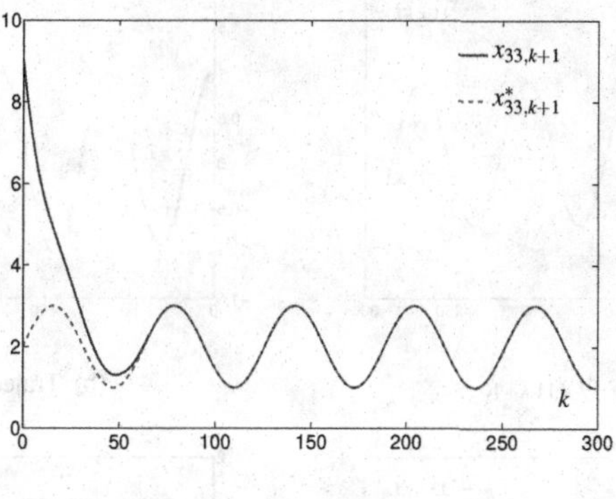

(c) Trajectory of $x_{33,k+1}$

FIGURE 8.6: Element trajectories of row-3 of state matrix X_{k+1} synthesized by general 9S-DTZNN algorithm (8.6) with $g = 0.1$ s for FMSRF in Example 8.2.

where $q_{11} = cs + 2c^2 + (s+6)^2$, $q_{12} = cs + c^2 + c(s+5) + c(s+6)$, $q_{13} = c^2 - cs + c(s+4) + c(s+6)$, $q_{14} = c^2 - cs + c(s+2) + c(s+6)$, $q_{21} = c(s+5) + c(s+6)$, $q_{22} = c^2 + (s+5)^2$, $q_{23} = 2c^2 - s(s+4) - s(s+5)$, $q_{24} = c^2 + s^2 + c(s+2) + c(s+5)$, $q_{31} = c^2 - s^2 + c(s+4) + c(s+6)$, $q_{32} = c^2 - s^2 + c(s+4) + c(s+5)$, $q_{33} = c^2 - 2cs + (s+4)^2$, $q_{34} = 2c^2 - s(s+2) - s(s+4)$, $q_{41} = c^2 + sc + s(s+2) + s(s+6)$, $q_{42} = c^2 + sc + s(s+2) + s(s+5)$, $q_{43} = cs - s^2 + c(s+2) + c(s+4)$, and $q_{44} = cs + (s+2)^2$, as well as $c = \cos(t_k)$ and $s = \sin(t_k)$. The corresponding theoretical solution is as follows:

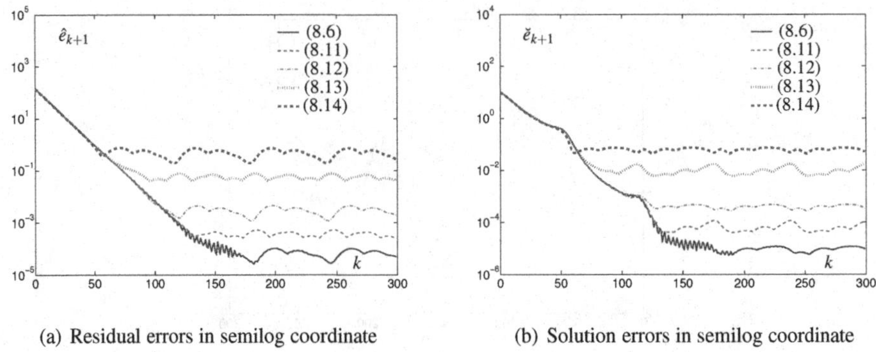

(a) Residual errors in semilog coordinate

(b) Solution errors in semilog coordinate

FIGURE 8.7: Trajectories of residual errors and solution errors synthesized by five DTZNN algorithms with $g = 0.1$ s for FMSRF in Example 8.2.

$$X_k^* = \begin{bmatrix} 6+\sin(t_k) & \cos(t_k) & \cos(t_k) & \cos(t_k) \\ \cos(t_k) & 5+\sin(t_k) & -\sin(t_k) & \cos(t_k) \\ \cos(t_k) & \cos(t_k) & 4+\sin(t_k) & -\sin(t_k) \\ \sin(t_k) & \sin(t_k) & \cos(t_k) & 2+\sin(t_k) \end{bmatrix}.$$

The initial state is arbitrarily set as $X_0 = [8, 1, 0.1, 0.3; 1, 10, 2.1, 1.5; 0.9, 0.2, 8, 3.1; 1.7, 0.5, 2.7, 7]$, the step length $\hbar = 0.1$, and the sampling gap $g = 0.1$ s. The corresponding numerical experimental results are presented in Figures 8.8–8.12.

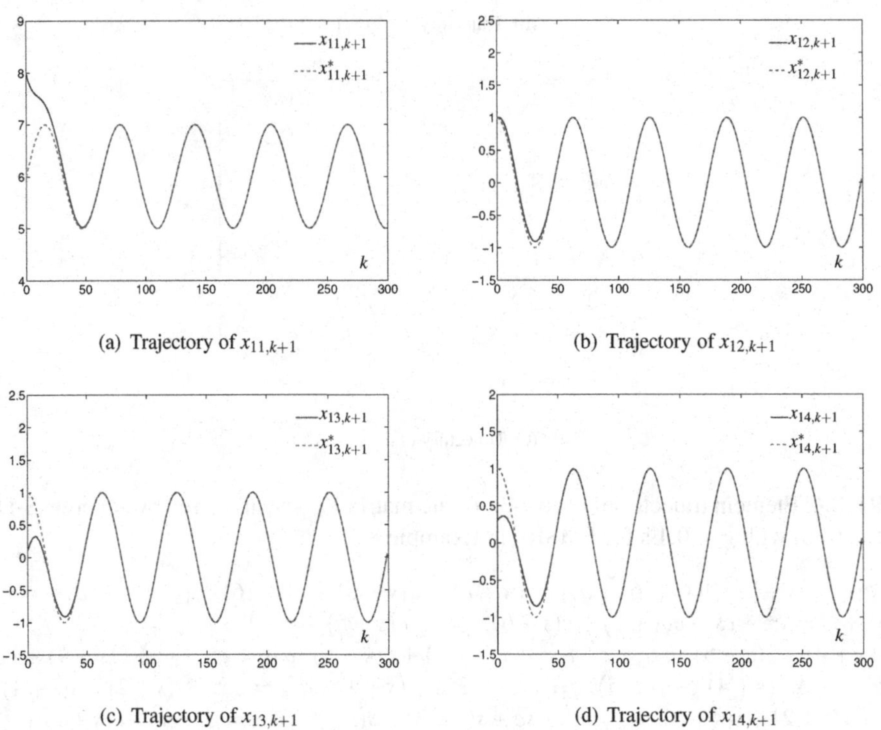

(a) Trajectory of $x_{11,k+1}$

(b) Trajectory of $x_{12,k+1}$

(c) Trajectory of $x_{13,k+1}$

(d) Trajectory of $x_{14,k+1}$

FIGURE 8.8: Element trajectories of row-1 of state matrix X_{k+1} synthesized by general 9S-DTZNN algorithm (8.6) with $g = 0.1$ s for FMSRF in Example 8.3.

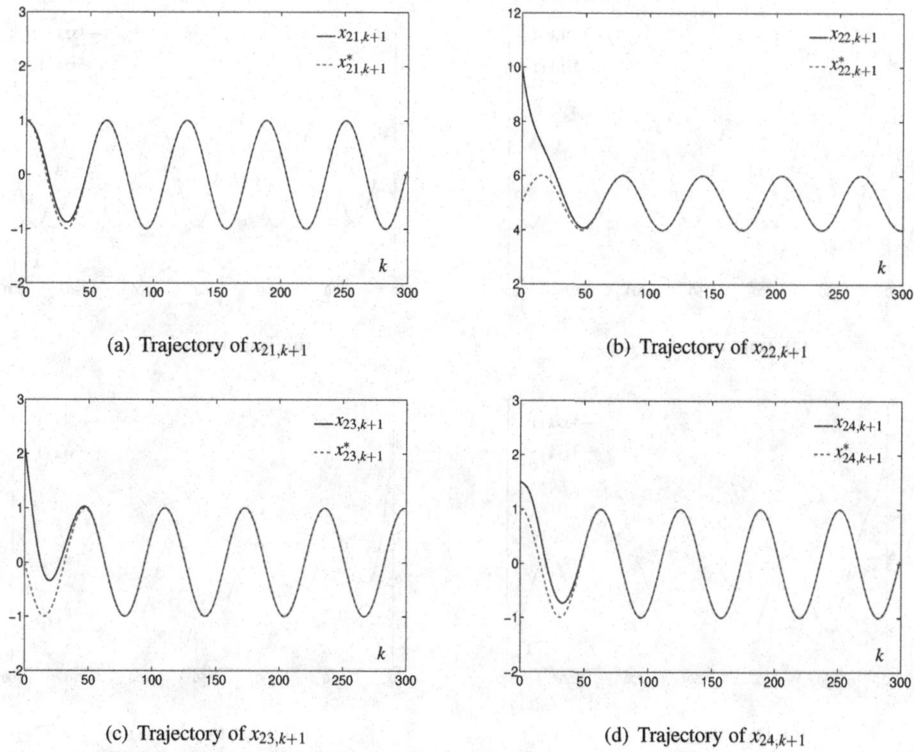

(a) Trajectory of $x_{21,k+1}$

(b) Trajectory of $x_{22,k+1}$

(c) Trajectory of $x_{23,k+1}$

(d) Trajectory of $x_{24,k+1}$

FIGURE 8.9: Element trajectories of row-2 of state matrix X_{k+1} synthesized by general 9S-DTZNN algorithm (8.6) with $g = 0.1$ s for FMSRF in Example 8.3.

Specifically, Figures 8.8–8.11 present the element trajectories of the state matrix X_{k+1} synthesized by the general 9S-DTZNN algorithm (8.6) together with the theoretical solution X^*_{k+1}. Besides, Figure 8.12 shows the trajectories of residual errors and solution errors synthesized by the five DTZNN algorithms (8.6), (8.11), (8.12), (8.13), and (8.14). Similarly to Examples 8.1 and 8.2, one can conclude that the MSSREs synthesized by the algorithms (8.6), (8.11), (8.12), (8.13), and (8.14) roughly change in the patterns of $\mathcal{O}(g^6)$, $\mathcal{O}(g^5)$, $\mathcal{O}(g^4)$, $\mathcal{O}(g^3)$, and $\mathcal{O}(g^2)$, respectively, which substantiates the effectiveness and accuracy of the DTZNN algorithms as well as the superiority of the general 9S-DTZNN algorithm (8.6) again.

8.5 Chapter Summary

To handle the FMSRF problem (8.1), the CTZNN model (8.3) has been given according to previous research. In addition, the general 9S-ZTD formula (8.5) has been constructed, developed, and investigated. Then, five DTZNN algorithms (8.6), (8.11), (8.12), (8.13), and (8.14) for solving the FMSRF problem (8.1) have been derived and presented. Ultimately, theoretical analyses and numerical experimental results have substantiated the accuracy and effectiveness of the DTZNN algorithms as well as the superiority of the general 9S-DTZNN algorithm (8.6).

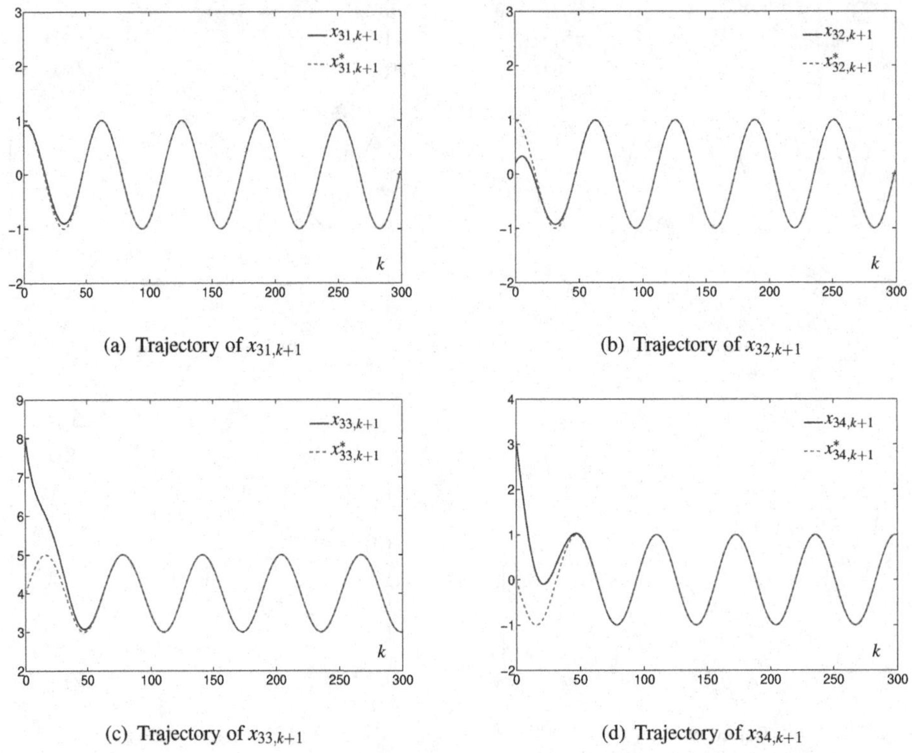

(a) Trajectory of $x_{31,k+1}$

(b) Trajectory of $x_{32,k+1}$

(c) Trajectory of $x_{33,k+1}$

(d) Trajectory of $x_{34,k+1}$

FIGURE 8.10: Element trajectories of row-3 of state matrix X_{k+1} synthesized by general 9S-DTZNN algorithm (8.6) with $g = 0.1$ s for FMSRF in Example 8.3.

Appendix H: Proof of Theorem 33

According to Taylor expansion [20], one has

$$\zeta_{k+1} = \zeta_k + g\dot{\zeta}_k + \frac{g^2}{2}\ddot{\zeta}_k + \frac{g^3}{6}\dddot{\zeta}_k + \frac{g^4}{24}\zeta_k^{(4)} + \frac{g^5}{120}\zeta_k^{(5)} + \frac{g^6}{720}\zeta^{(6)}(c_1), \tag{8.15}$$

$$\zeta_{k-1} = \zeta_k - g\dot{\zeta}_k + \frac{g^2}{2}\ddot{\zeta}_k - \frac{g^3}{6}\dddot{\zeta}_k + \frac{g^4}{24}\zeta_k^{(4)} - \frac{g^5}{120}\zeta_k^{(5)} + \frac{g^6}{720}\zeta^{(6)}(c_2), \tag{8.16}$$

$$\zeta_{k-2} = \zeta_k - 2g\dot{\zeta}_k + 2g^2\ddot{\zeta}_k - \frac{4g^3}{3}\dddot{\zeta}_k + \frac{2g^4}{3}\zeta_k^{(4)} - \frac{4g^5}{15}\zeta_k^{(5)} + \frac{4g^6}{45}\zeta^{(6)}(c_3), \tag{8.17}$$

$$\zeta_{k-3} = \zeta_k - 3g\dot{\zeta}_k + \frac{9g^2}{2}\ddot{\zeta}_k - \frac{9g^3}{2}\dddot{\zeta}_k + \frac{27g^4}{8}\zeta_k^{(4)} - \frac{81g^5}{40}\zeta_k^{(5)} + \frac{81g^6}{80}\zeta^{(6)}(c_4), \tag{8.18}$$

$$\zeta_{k-4} = \zeta_k - 4g\dot{\zeta}_k + 8g^2\ddot{\zeta}_k - \frac{32g^3}{3}\dddot{\zeta}_k + \frac{32g^4}{3}\zeta_k^{(4)} - \frac{128g^5}{15}\zeta_k^{(5)} + \frac{256g^6}{45}\zeta^{(6)}(c_5), \tag{8.19}$$

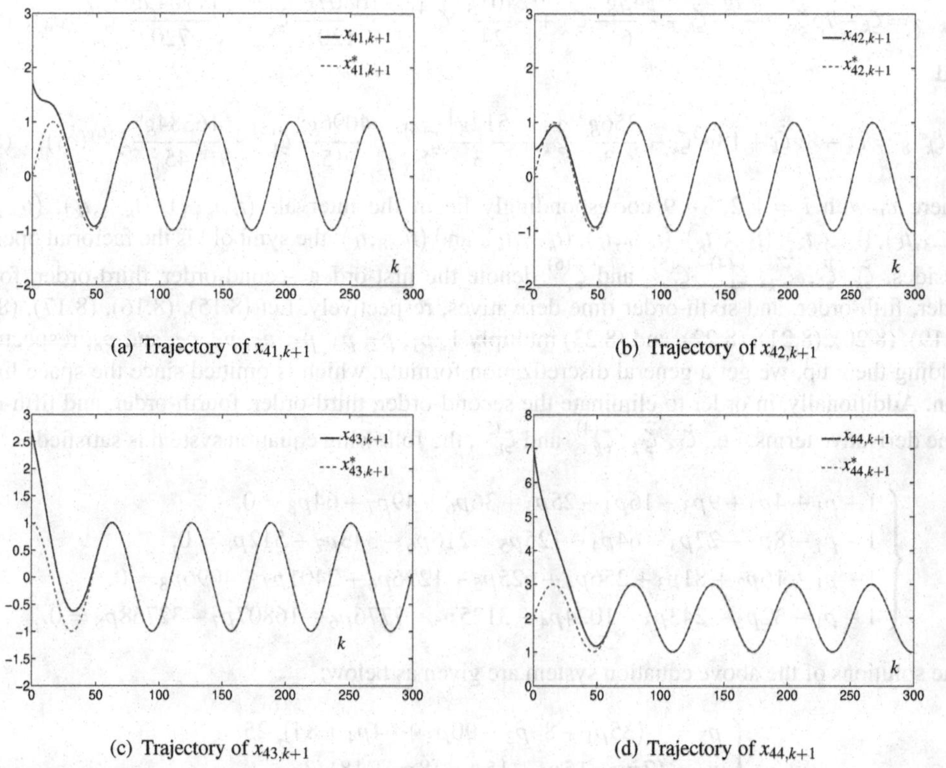

FIGURE 8.11: Element trajectories of row-4 of state matrix X_{k+1} synthesized by general 9S-DTZNN algorithm (8.6) with $g = 0.1$ s for FMSRF in Example 8.3.

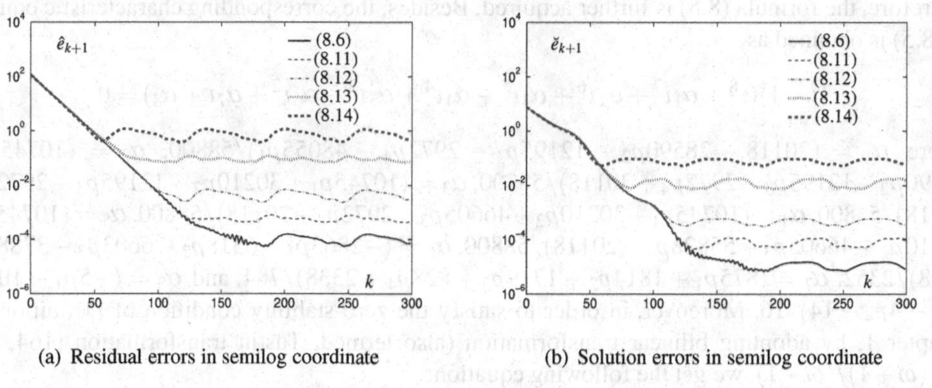

FIGURE 8.12: Trajectories of residual errors and solution errors synthesized by five DTZNN algorithms with $g = 0.1$ s for FMSRF in Example 8.3.

$$\zeta_{k-5} = \zeta_k - 5g\dot{\zeta}_k + \frac{25g^2}{2}\ddot{\zeta}_k - \frac{125g^3}{6}\dddot{\zeta}_k + \frac{625g^4}{24}\zeta_k^{(4)} - \frac{625g^5}{24}\zeta_k^{(5)} + \frac{3125g^6}{144}\zeta^{(6)}(c_6), \quad (8.20)$$

$$\zeta_{k-6} = \zeta_k - 6g\dot{\zeta}_k + 18g^2\ddot{\zeta}_k - 36\dddot{\zeta}_k + 54g^4\zeta_k^{(4)} - \frac{324g^5}{5}\zeta_k^{(5)} + \frac{324g^6}{5}\zeta^{(6)}(c_7), \quad (8.21)$$

$$\zeta_{k-7}=\zeta_k-7g\dot{\zeta}_k+\frac{49g^2}{2}\ddot{\zeta}_k-\frac{343g^3}{6}\dddot{\zeta}_k+\frac{2401g^4}{24}\zeta_k^{(4)}-\frac{16807g^5}{120}\zeta_k^{(5)}+\frac{117649g^6}{720}\zeta^{(6)}(c_8), \quad (8.22)$$

and

$$\zeta_{k-8}=\zeta_k-8g\dot{\zeta}_k+18g^2\ddot{\zeta}_k-\frac{256g^3}{3}\dddot{\zeta}_k+\frac{512g^4}{3}\zeta_k^{(4)}-\frac{4096g^5}{15}\zeta_k^{(5)}+\frac{16384g^6}{45}\zeta^{(6)}(c_9), \quad (8.23)$$

where c_i with $i=1,2,\cdots,9$ correspondingly lie in the intervals (t_k,t_{k+1}), (t_{k-1},t_k), (t_{k-2},t_k), (t_{k-3},t_k), (t_{k-4},t_k), (t_{k-5},t_k), (t_{k-6},t_k), (t_{k-7},t_k), and (t_{k-8},t_k); the symbol ! is the factorial operator. Besides, $\dot{\zeta}_k$, $\ddot{\zeta}_k$, $\dddot{\zeta}_k$, $\zeta_k^{(4)}$, $\zeta_k^{(5)}$, and $\zeta_k^{(6)}$ denote the first-order, second-order, third-order, fourth-order, fifth-order, and sixth-order time derivatives, respectively. Let (8.15), (8.16), (8.17), (8.18), (8.19), (8.20), (8.21), (8.22), and (8.23) multiply 1, p_1, p_2, p_3, p_4, p_5, p_6, p_7, and p_8, respectively. Adding them up, we get a general discretization formula, which is omitted since the space limitation. Additionally, in order to eliminate the second-order, third-order, fourth-order, and fifth-order time derivative terms, i.e., $\ddot{\zeta}_k$, $\dddot{\zeta}_k$, $\zeta_k^{(4)}$, and $\zeta_k^{(5)}$, the following equation system is satisfied:

$$\begin{cases}1+p_1+4p_2+9p_3+16p_4+25p_5+36p_6+49p_7+64p_8=0,\\1-p_1-8p_2-27p_3-64p_4-125p_5-216p_6-343p_7-512p_8=0,\\1+p_1+16p_2+81p_3+256p_4+625p_5+1296p_6+2401p_7+4096p_8=0,\\1-p_1-32p_2-243p_3-1024p_4-3125p_5-7776p_6-16807p_7-32768p_8=0.\end{cases}$$

The solutions of the above equation system are given as below:

$$\begin{cases}p_5=-(35p_1+80p_2+90p_3+64p_4+84)/25,\\p_6=(7p_1+15p_2+15p_3+8p_4+18)/3,\\p_7=-(70p_1+144p_2+135p_3+64p_4+189)/49,\\p_8=(5p_1+10p_2+9p_3+4p_4+14)/16.\end{cases}$$

Therefore, the formula (8.5) is further acquired. Besides, the corresponding characteristic equation of (8.5) is obtained as

$$(\iota-1)(\iota^8+\alpha_1\iota^7+\alpha_2\iota^6+\alpha_3\iota^5+\alpha_4\iota^4+\alpha_5\iota^3+\alpha_6\iota^2+\alpha_7\iota+\alpha_8)=0,$$

where $\alpha_1=(20118-28590p_2-12195p_3-2972p_4-48055p_1)/58800$, $\alpha_2=(10745p_1-28590p_2-12195p_3-2972p_4+20118)/58800$, $\alpha_3=(10745p_1+30210p_2-12195p_3-2972p_4+20118)/58800$, $\alpha_4=(10745p_1+30210p_2+46605p_3-2972p_4+20118)/58800$, $\alpha_5=(10745p_1+30210p_2+46605p_3+55828p_4+20118)/58800$, $\alpha_6=(-2863p_1-6318p_2-6603p_3-3788p_4-7098)/2352$, $\alpha_7=(875p_1+1814p_2+1719p_3+828p_4+2338)/784$, and $\alpha_8=(-5p_1-10p_2-9p_3-4p_4-14)/16$. Moreover, in order to satisfy the zero-stability condition of Definition 2 in Chapter 1, by adopting bilinear transformation (also termed, Tustin transformation [164, 195]) $\iota=(\omega+1)/(\omega-1)$, we get the following equation:

$$\beta_0\omega^8+\beta_1\omega^7+\beta_2\omega^6+\beta_3\omega^5+\beta_4\omega^4+\beta_5\omega^3+\beta_6\omega^2+\beta_7\omega+\beta_8=0,$$

in which $\beta_0=13230-3150p_2-1575p_3-420p_4-3675p_1$, $\beta_1=92610-22050p_2-11025p_3-2940p_4-25725p_1$, $\beta_2=269010-64050p_2-32025p_3-8540p_4-74725p_1$, $\beta_3=401310-95550p_2-47775p_3-12740p_4-111475p_1$, $\beta_4=276066-65730p_2-32865p_3-8764p_4-76685p_1$, $\beta_5=286405p_1+480690p_2+357945p_3+126812p_4+944622$, $\beta_6=-125475p_1-409950p_2-423375p_3-189060p_4-395010$, $\beta_7=144795p_1+224910p_2+230055p_3+124068p_4+325458$, and $\beta_8=-13440p_1-45120p_2-39360p_3-28416p_4-45696$. Finally, on the basis of Routh stability criterion [164, 195], (8.4) is obtained. The proof is therefore completed. □

Appendix I: Proof of Theorem 34

According to Appendix H, one knows that the characteristic polynomial of the general 9S-DTZNN algorithm (8.6) is formulated as

$$\Gamma_9(\iota) = (\iota - 1)(\iota^8 + \alpha_1\iota^7 + \alpha_2\iota^6 + \alpha_3\iota^5 + \alpha_4\iota^4 + \alpha_5\iota^3 + \alpha_6\iota^2 + \alpha_7\iota + \alpha_8),$$

and the roots of $\Gamma_9(\iota)$ satisfy the root condition of Definition 2 in Chapter 1. Therefore, according to Definition 2 in Chapter 1, the general 9S-DTZNN algorithm (8.6) is zero-stable.

According to (8.3) and (8.6), one has

$$\begin{aligned}\mathbf{a}_{k+1} = {}& \frac{1}{d_0}\tilde{\mathbf{a}}_k - \frac{d_1}{d_0}\mathbf{a}_k - \frac{d_2}{d_0}\mathbf{a}_{k-1} - \frac{d_3}{d_0}\mathbf{a}_{k-2} - \frac{d_4}{d_0}\mathbf{a}_{k-3} - \frac{d_5}{d_0}\mathbf{a}_{k-4}\\ & - \frac{d_6}{d_0}\mathbf{a}_{k-5} - \frac{d_7}{d_0}\mathbf{a}_{k-6} - \frac{d_8}{d_0}\mathbf{a}_{k-7} - \frac{d_9}{d_0}\mathbf{a}_{k-8} + \mathbf{O}(g^6).\end{aligned}$$

The truncation error of the general 9S-DTZNN algorithm (8.6) is $\mathbf{O}(g^6)$. According to Definitions 3 and 4 in Chapter 1, the general 9S-DTZNN algorithm (8.6) is consistent and converges with the order of truncation error being $\mathbf{O}(g^6)$. The proof is therefore completed. □

Appendix J: Proof of Theorem 35

Suppose that X_{k+1}^* is the theoretical solution of $X_{k+1}X_{k+1} - A_{k+1} = O_{n\times n}$ with $O_{n\times n}$ denoting an $n \times n$ zero matrix. According to the general 9S-DTZNN algorithm (8.6), one has $X_{k+1} = X_{k+1}^* + \mathbf{O}(g^6)$ with $k \to +\infty$, and further has

$$\begin{aligned}&\lim_{k\to+\infty} \sup \|X_{k+1}X_{k+1} - A_{k+1}\|_{\mathrm{F}}\\ &= \lim_{k\to+\infty} \sup \|(X_{k+1}^* + \mathbf{O}(g^6))(X_{k+1}^* + \mathbf{O}(g^6)) - A_{k+1}\|_{\mathrm{F}}\\ &= \lim_{k\to+\infty} \sup \|X_{k+1}^*\mathbf{O}(g^6) + \mathbf{O}(g^6)X_{k+1}^* + \mathbf{O}(g^{12})\|_{\mathrm{F}} = \mathcal{O}(g^6).\end{aligned}$$

The proof is therefore completed. □

Part IV

$\mathscr{O}(g^3)$ ZTD Formulas and Applications

Chapter 9

Tracking Control of Serial and Parallel Manipulators

Abstract

It is increasingly desirable to improve the performance of tracking control. It is a routine for most conventional algorithms to track the current desired output by the control input at current time instant. However, lagging errors resulting from computing time and the fluctuation of the desired output exist in the tracking control. In this chapter, different from conventional algorithms, a look-ahead scheme of zeroing neural network (ZNN) is established to achieve the real-time tracking control of both serial and parallel manipulators. With the exploitation of current and previous data, the control inputs generated by discrete-time ZNN (DTZNN) algorithms never lead to lagging errors caused by the inevitable computing time. To reduce prediction errors synthesized by DTZNN algorithms, a high-precision discretization formula, as an essential part of DTZNN algorithms, is presented to confine the prediction error in an ignorable range compared with lagging errors.

9.1 Introduction

Real-time tracking has been a fundamental research topic in the control field [117,236]. Various methods have been developed as found in the literature [118,237,238]. Tracking control of manipulators has been widely applied in industry [239,240]. In [241], the state feedback linearization was applied to the control of nonholonomic wheeled mobile manipulators. Furthermore, in [242], a modified input–output linearization method using the generalized inverse of decoupling matrices was presented for the tracking control of two-wheeled mobile manipulators. In [243], a robust motion controller based on neural networks and backstepping was developed for a two-degrees-of-freedom low-quality mobile manipulator, which guaranteed that the mobile manipulator followed the desired path. Sliding mode control is also a classical method for tracking control problems [244–246]. The literature [246] studied the practical tracking control design of manipulators with continuous fractional-order nonsingular terminal sliding mode based on time-delay estimation, which required no detailed information about the manipulator dynamics. Many other advanced methods exist, e.g., adaptive learning control [247] and neural networks [122, 123].

Conventional methods established in continuous time usually degrade when implemented in discrete time due to the one-step delay. It is a common practice to track the current desired output by the control input at current time instant. It is known that computation takes time, while the desired output varies with time, which causes the existence of lagging errors during the tracking control. When conventional methods are utilized for the real-time tracking problems, the obtained control

DOI: 10.1201/9781003497783-9

input at current time instant is supposed to be a one-step delay. Due to this fact, the actual precision of conventional methods is usually in proportion to the sampling gap [22,111].

Zeroing neural network (ZNN) is a powerful method for time-dependent problems in real time [43,72,129,248,249], and it is in part driven by the evolution of recurrent neural networks (RNNs) [181,196,250]. In practice, time-dependent problems are solved by digital computation sometimes, and in this case, the discrete-time ZNN (DTZNN) was developed in [22]. On the basis of a one-step-ahead discretization formula, the DTZNN has the ability to predict the future solution at the next time instant. The ZNN method is presented in the ensuing section. Note that one-step-ahead DTZNN algorithms have been widely applied to solve various time-dependent problems [75,189,249]. For example, in [189], a three-step discrete-time algorithm based on the ZNN method was developed to solve time-dependent nonlinear systems. In [75], the time-dependent quadratic programming was solved by utilizing the ZNN method.

Considering the superiority of the ZNN method to predict future solutions, this chapter [130] applies ZNN to the real-time tracking control of both serial and parallel manipulators. The corresponding DTZNN algorithms are developed to predict the future control input at the next time instant by using current and past information. As a unique feature of the ZNN method, the time consumption for computation does not lead to lagging errors. Considering the existence of prediction errors, a high-precision one-step-ahead discretization formula, i.e., four-step Zhang time discretization (4S-ZTD) formula, is presented and analyzed to obtain much smaller prediction errors than lagging errors. It should be pointed out that the 4S-ZTD formula has a truncation error being $\mathscr{O}(g^3)$, where g represents the sampling gap, and the precision of the corresponding DTZNN algorithms is $\mathscr{O}(g^4)$, which is significantly better than that synthesized by conventional methods. It is noted that, on the basis of the theorems in [111], the precision of conventional methods is $\mathscr{O}(g)$ for the real-time tracking control. The ZNN method has been applied to manipulator motion control in the literature [22,191]. For example, in [191], a two-link serial manipulator was controlled to draw a four-leaf clover. It is worth mentioning that those existing algorithms are derived on the basis of an equation at velocity level at the beginning, and then the idea of ZNN is employed to solve that equation. Because of the indirect use of ZNN, the initial errors of those algorithms must be sufficiently small, which is less practical in real applications. Different from existing algorithms, the presented DTZNN algorithms in this chapter [130] directly employ the idea of ZNN to force the actual trajectory to converge to the desired path, and therefore, the initial errors are allowed to be arbitrarily large for the presented DTZNN algorithms. Moreover, considering the same discretization formula, DTZNN algorithms in this chapter [130] outperform existing ones in terms of precision.

The notations used in this chapter [130] are summarized in Table 9.1.

TABLE 9.1: Notations in this chapter.

Notation	Meaning
$\varphi(\mathbf{x}(t),t)$	Nonlinear time-dependent function vector
$J(\mathbf{x}(t),t)$	Jacobi matrix of $\varphi(\mathbf{x}(t),t)$
$\varphi_t'(\mathbf{x}(t),t)$	Partial derivative of $\varphi(\mathbf{x}(t),t)$ with respect to t
$\boldsymbol{\vartheta}$	Joint-angle vector of serial manipulator
$\mathbf{f}(\boldsymbol{\vartheta})$	Forward-kinematics mapping function of serial manipulator
$J(\boldsymbol{\vartheta}(t))$	Jacobi matrix of serial manipulator
$\mathbf{l}$	Vector containing lengths of six legs of Stewart platform
$\mathbf{d}_j$	Position vector of leg j of Stewart platform
$\mathbf{r}_{\mathrm{a}}$	Actual position vector of manipulator end-effector
$\mathbf{r}_{\mathrm{d}}$	Desired path for serial manipulator or Stewart platform

9.2 FNES Solving

In this section, ZNN (specifically, DTZNN) is introduced for further investigation. It is worth mentioning that ZNN has solved various discrete time-dependent problems effectively [22,111,189], and particularly, the problem of future nonlinear equation system (FNES) is taken as an example [189]. Specifically, the following problem is considered, which is to be solved at each computational time interval $[t_k, t_{k+1}) \subset [t_{\text{ini}}, t_{\text{fin}}] \subset [0, +\infty)$:

$$\arg_{\mathbf{x}_{k+1} \in \mathbb{R}^n} \left(\varphi(\mathbf{x}_{k+1}, t_{k+1}) = \mathbf{0} \in \mathbb{R}^n\right), \tag{9.1}$$

where t_{ini} and t_{fin} represent the initial and final time instants, respectively. Besides, $\varphi(\cdot,\cdot): \mathbb{R}^n \times [t_{\text{ini}}, t_{\text{fin}}) \to \mathbb{R}^n$ is time-dependent, differentiable, and nonlinear for all $t_k > 0$ with the updating index $k = 0, 1, \cdots$, and $\mathbf{x}_{k+1} = \mathbf{x}(t_{k+1}) = \mathbf{x}((k+1)g)$ with g denoting the sampling gap. During the computational time interval $[t_k, t_{k+1})$, only the current and past information, e.g., $\varphi(\mathbf{x}_k, t_k)$, $\varphi(\mathbf{x}_{k-1}, t_{k-1})$, $\mathbf{x}_k$, and $\mathbf{x}_{k-1}$, are available, and the future information, e.g., $\varphi(\mathbf{x}_{k+1}, t_{k+1})$, is unknown, which means that we need to predict the future solution $\mathbf{x}_{k+1}$ at each computational time interval $[t_k, t_{k+1})$.

To solve the FNES (9.1), it is first converted into a continuous-time form as below:

$$\arg_{\mathbf{x}(t) \in \mathbb{R}^n} \left(\varphi(\mathbf{x}(t), t) = \mathbf{0} \in \mathbb{R}^n\right). \tag{9.2}$$

To zero out $\varphi(\mathbf{x}(t), t)$, the following ZNN design formula is employed [43,75,189]:

$$\dot{\varphi}(\mathbf{x}(t), t) = -\eta \varphi(\mathbf{x}(t), t),$$

where $\dot{\varphi}(\mathbf{x}(t), t)$ represents the first-order time derivative of $\varphi(\mathbf{x}(t), t)$, and η denotes the ZNN design parameter. Then, a continuous-time ZNN (CTZNN) model for the problem (9.2) is obtained as below:

$$\dot{\mathbf{x}}(t) = -J^{-1}(\mathbf{x}(t), t)\left(\eta \varphi(\mathbf{x}(t), t) + \varphi_t'(\mathbf{x}(t), t)\right), \tag{9.3}$$

where

$$\varphi_t'(\mathbf{x}(t), t) = \frac{\partial \varphi(\mathbf{x}(t), t)}{\partial t} \in \mathbb{R}^n \text{ and } J(\mathbf{x}(t), t) = \frac{\partial \varphi(\mathbf{x}(t), t)}{\partial \mathbf{x}^{\mathrm{T}}} \in \mathbb{R}^{n \times n},$$

with the superscript ^{T} denoting the transpose operator of a vector or matrix. To solve the FNES (9.1), a usable one-step-ahead discretization formula is necessary to discretize the CTZNN model (9.3). There have been only a few usable discretization formulas so far [51], including Euler forward formula [161]:

$$\dot{\zeta}_k = \frac{\zeta_{k+1} - \zeta_k}{g} + \mathscr{O}(g), \tag{9.4}$$

and Zhang–Taylor discretization formula [70]:

$$\dot{\zeta}_k = \frac{2\zeta_{k+1} - 3\zeta_k + 2\zeta_{k-1} - \zeta_{k-2}}{2g} + \mathscr{O}(g^2), \tag{9.5}$$

which was proposed by Zhang *et al* [70] by using Taylor expansion iteratively for many times. By employing the above two discretization formulas to discretize the CTZNN model (9.3), two DTZNN algorithms are obtained as follows:

$$\mathbf{x}_{k+1} \doteq -J^{-1}(\mathbf{x}_k, t_k)\left(\hbar \varphi(\mathbf{x}_k, t_k) + g\varphi_t'(\mathbf{x}_k, t_k)\right) + \mathbf{x}_k, \tag{9.6}$$

and

$$\mathbf{x}_{k+1} \doteq -J^{-1}(\mathbf{x}_k,t_k)\left(\hbar\varphi(\mathbf{x}_k,t_k)+g\varphi_t'(\mathbf{x}_k,t_k)\right)+\frac{3}{2}\mathbf{x}_k-\mathbf{x}_{k-1}+\frac{1}{2}\mathbf{x}_{k-2}, \tag{9.7}$$

where $\doteq$ denotes the computational assignment operator, and $\hbar = g\eta$ represents the step length. From the above algorithms, it is found that the solution at time instant t_{k+1} is predicted and obtained by current and previous information without using $\varphi(\mathbf{x}_{k+1},t_{k+1})$, which means that the FNES (9.1) is solved in real time. Besides, it is provable that the truncation errors of the algorithms (9.6) and (9.7) are $\mathbf{O}(g^2)$ and $\mathbf{O}(g^3)$, respectively, where $\mathbf{O}(g^2)$ denotes a vector with every element being $\mathcal{O}(g^2)$.

9.3 ZNN for Tracking Control of Serial Manipulator

From the above section, it is concluded that ZNN has the ability of prediction to solve time-dependent problems, and thus, it solves them in real time. In this section, the tracking control of the serial manipulator is considered a time-dependent problem, and ZNN is employed to solve this problem. Moreover, a 4S-ZTD formula is presented, which has higher precision than the Euler forward formula (9.4) and the Zhang–Taylor discretization formula (9.5). On the basis of the 4S-ZTD formula, two four-step DTZNN (4S-DTZNN) algorithms are presented to solve the tracking control problem in real time with higher precision.

9.3.1 Problem formulation and CTZNN model

The kinematic equation for the serial manipulator is depicted as follows [91, 191]:

$$\mathbf{f}(\vartheta_k) = \mathbf{r}_{\mathrm{a},k}, \tag{9.8}$$

where $\mathbf{f}(\cdot): \mathbb{R}^n \to \mathbb{R}^m$ denotes a continuous nonlinear forward-kinematics mapping function of the serial manipulator, $\vartheta_k = \vartheta(t_k) \in \mathbb{R}^n$ denotes the joint-angle vector at time instant t_k, and $\mathbf{r}_{\mathrm{a},k} \in \mathbb{R}^m$ denotes the actual position vector of its end-effector at time instant t_k. The real-time tracking control of the serial manipulator is aimed to predict and obtain ϑ_{k+1} at each computational time interval $[t_k,t_{k+1}) \subset [t_{\mathrm{ini}},t_{\mathrm{fin}}]$ so that

$$\mathbf{r}_{\mathrm{a},k+1} \to \mathbf{r}_{\mathrm{d},k+1},$$

where $\mathbf{r}_{\mathrm{d},k+1}$ (the value of a desired path at time instant t_{k+1}) is unknown during $[t_k,t_{k+1})$. Note that obtaining ϑ_{k+1} before t_{k+1} gives the manipulator time to control and move, and when t_{k+1} comes, the end-effector has moved to $\mathbf{r}_{\mathrm{a},k+1}$. Thus, the tracking control is real-time. This problem is mathematically formulated as the form of the FNES (9.1) as below:

$$\underset{\vartheta_{k+1}\in\mathbb{R}^n}{\arg}\ \left(\mathbf{r}_{\mathrm{a},k+1}-\mathbf{r}_{\mathrm{d},k+1}=\mathbf{0}\right). \tag{9.9}$$

Then, the ZNN method is employed to solve the real-time tracking control problem (9.9). The problem (9.9) is first converted into a continuous-time form as below:

$$\underset{\vartheta(t)\in\mathbb{R}^n}{\arg}\ \left(\mathbf{r}_{\mathrm{a}}(t)-\mathbf{r}_{\mathrm{d}}(t)=\mathbf{0}\right).$$

Next, a vector-form zeroing function (ZF) is defined as below:

$$\mathbf{z}(t) = \mathbf{r}_{\mathrm{a}}(t)-\mathbf{r}_{\mathrm{d}}(t), \tag{9.10}$$

and we employ the ZNN design formula [43, 189]:

$$\dot{\mathbf{z}}(t) = -\eta \mathbf{z}(t) \tag{9.11}$$

to zero out $\mathbf{z}(t)$ with $t \to +\infty$, and by combining (9.8), (9.10), and (9.11), a CTZNN model is obtained as below:

$$\dot{\vartheta}(t) = J^{\dagger}(\vartheta(t))\left(\dot{\mathbf{r}}_{\mathrm{d}}(t) - \eta\left(\mathbf{f}(\vartheta(t)) - \mathbf{r}_{\mathrm{d}}(t)\right)\right), \tag{9.12}$$

where $J(\vartheta(t)) = \partial \mathbf{f}(\vartheta(t))/\partial \vartheta(t) \in \mathbb{R}^{m\times n}$ denotes a Jacobi matrix of the serial manipulator, the superscript † denotes the pseudoinverse operator of a matrix, and $\dot{\mathbf{r}}_{\mathrm{d}}(t)$ denotes a desired velocity of the end-effector.

9.3.2 4S-ZTD formula and 4S-DTZNN algorithms

Discretization formulas play a significant role in the performance of DTZNN algorithms, and it is always a challenging task to find a new discretization formula [51, 70]. First, to satisfy the requirement of real-time control, a usable discretization formula must be one-step-ahead (i.e., approximating $\dot{\zeta}_k$ by $\zeta_{k+1}, \zeta_k, \zeta_{k-1}, \cdots$). Second, for the effectiveness of control, DTZNN algorithms should be stable, while many discretization formulas generate unstable algorithms, which are useless in practice. Moreover, the precision of a discretization formula determines the precision of the corresponding DTZNN algorithm.

In this subsection, a one-step-ahead discretization formula, i.e., the 4S-ZTD formula, with a truncation error being $\mathscr{O}(g^3)$, is presented, which leads to a stable 4S-DTZNN algorithm. The 4S-ZTD formula is presented by the following theorem.

Theorem 36 *With the sufficiently small sampling gap $g \in (0,1)$, let $\mathscr{O}(g^3)$ denote the error (especially, the truncation error) positively or negatively proportional to g^3, i.e., of the order of g^3. Suppose that $\zeta(t)$ is sufficiently smooth. With $\zeta_{k+1} = \zeta(t_{k+1}) = \zeta((k+1)g)$, the 4S-ZTD formula is formulated as below:*

$$\dot{\zeta}_k = \frac{4}{9g}\zeta_{k+1} + \frac{1}{18g}\zeta_k - \frac{1}{3g}\zeta_{k-1} - \frac{5}{18g}\zeta_{k-2} + \frac{1}{9g}\zeta_{k-3} + \mathscr{O}(g^3). \tag{9.13}$$

Proof. The proof is presented in Appendix K. □

By adopting the 4S-ZTD formula (9.13) to discretize the CTZNN model (9.12), a 4S-DTZNN algorithm is presented as below:

$$\vartheta_{k+1} \doteq \frac{9}{4}J^{\dagger}(\vartheta_k)\left(g\dot{\mathbf{r}}_{\mathrm{d},k} - \hbar\left(\mathbf{f}(\vartheta_k) - \mathbf{r}_{\mathrm{d},k}\right)\right) - \frac{1}{8}\vartheta_k + \frac{3}{4}\vartheta_{k-1} + \frac{5}{8}\vartheta_{k-2} - \frac{1}{4}\vartheta_{k-3}. \tag{9.14}$$

For convenience and consistency, the above algorithm is named 4S-DTZNN with $\dot{\mathbf{r}}_{\mathrm{d},k}$ known for the serial manipulator (4S-DTZNN-KSM) algorithm. It is worth mentioning that the truncation error of the 4S-DTZNN-KSM algorithm (9.14) is $\mathbf{O}(g^4)$, as to be proved theoretically later. During the control process, the control input is ϑ, which is converted to pulses per second signal to control the manipulator. It is feasible to track the desired path at time instant t_{k+1} by controlling ϑ_{k+1}. The computation of ϑ_{k+1} does not need the information at time instant t_{k+1} for the 4S-DTZNN-KSM algorithm (9.14). On the condition that the sampling gap g is larger than the computing time per updating, the 4S-DTZNN-KSM algorithm (9.14) can be implemented at each computational time interval $[t_k, t_{k+1})$, and the end-effector can track the desired path at time instant t_{k+1} by the obtained ϑ_{k+1} when t_{k+1} arrives. Therefore, the whole control process is real time.

However, it may be difficult to know the time derivative of the desired path (i.e., the value of $\dot{\mathbf{r}}_{\mathrm{d},k}$) in some practical applications. Considering this situation, the backward numerical-differentiation formula can be used to approximate the value of $\dot{\mathbf{r}}_{\mathrm{d},k}$. To achieve both precision and simplicity, the truncation error of the backward numerical-differentiation formula should be equal to that of the one-step-ahead discretization formula. With the same truncation error as the 4S-ZTD formula (9.13), a backward numerical-differentiation formula is expressed as follows [161]:

$$\dot{\zeta}_k = \frac{11\zeta_k - 18\zeta_{k-1} + 9\zeta_{k-2} - 2\zeta_{k-3}}{6g} + \mathscr{O}(g^3). \tag{9.15}$$

By utilizing (9.15) to approximate the value of $\dot{\mathbf{r}}_{\mathrm{d},k}$, a 4S-DTZNN with $\dot{\mathbf{r}}_{\mathrm{d},k}$ unknown for the serial manipulator (4S-DTZNN-USM) algorithm is further expressed as below:

$$\vartheta_{k+1} \doteq \frac{9}{4}J^{\dagger}(\vartheta_k)\left(\tilde{\mathbf{r}}_{\mathrm{d},k} - \hbar\mathbf{f}(\vartheta_k)\right) - \frac{1}{8}\vartheta_k + \frac{3}{4}\vartheta_{k-1} + \frac{5}{8}\vartheta_{k-2} - \frac{1}{4}\vartheta_{k-3}, \tag{9.16}$$

where $\tilde{\mathbf{r}}_{\mathrm{d},k} = (11/6 + \hbar)\mathbf{r}_{\mathrm{d},k} - 3\mathbf{r}_{\mathrm{d},k-1} + 3\mathbf{r}_{\mathrm{d},k-2}/2 - \mathbf{r}_{\mathrm{d},k-3}/3$.

On the basis of three fundamental definitions about the zero-stability, consistency, and convergence of an N-step formula [25, 251, 252], which has been presented in Chapter 1, theoretical analyses on the 4S-DTZNN-KSM algorithm (9.14) and the 4S-DTZNN-USM algorithm (9.16) are provided.

Theorem 37 *Suppose that the Jacobi matrix $J(\vartheta_k)$ is always of full row rank. With the sufficiently small sampling gap $g \in (0,1)$, the 4S-DTZNN-KSM algorithm (9.14) and the 4S-DTZNN-USM algorithm (9.16) are zero-stable.*

Proof. According to Definition 2 in Chapter 1, the characteristic polynomial of the 4S-DTZNN-KSM algorithm (9.14) is the same as that of the 4S-DTZNN-USM algorithm (9.16), which is formulated as

$$\Gamma_4(\iota) = \iota^4 + \frac{1}{8}\iota^3 - \frac{3}{4}\iota^2 - \frac{5}{8}\iota + \frac{1}{4}.$$

It has four roots (i.e., $\iota_{1,2} = -0.7160 \pm 0.5495\mathrm{i}$, $\iota_3 = 0.3069$, and $\iota_4 = 1$). It is evident that $|\iota_{1,2,3}| < 1$ and $\iota_4 = 1$. Thus, it is proved that the 4S-DTZNN-KSM algorithm (9.14) and the 4S-DTZNN-USM algorithm (9.16) are zero-stable. The proof is thus completed. □

Theorem 38 *With the sufficiently small sampling gap $g \in (0,1)$, let $\mathbf{O}(g^4)$ denote the error (especially, the truncation error) with each element being $\mathscr{O}(g^4)$. Suppose that the Jacobi matrix $J(\vartheta_k)$ is always of full row rank. The 4S-DTZNN-KSM algorithm (9.14) and the 4S-DTZNN-USM algorithm (9.16) are consistent and convergent, which converge with the orders of truncation errors being* $\mathbf{O}(g^4)$.

Proof. The proof is divided into two parts, i.e., one part for the 4S-DTZNN-KSM algorithm (9.14) and the other one for the 4S-DTZNN-USM algorithm (9.16).

(1) The 4S-DTZNN-KSM algorithm (9.14): By using (9.13) to discretize the CTZNN model (9.12), the equation

$$\vartheta_{k+1} = \frac{9}{4}J^{\dagger}(\vartheta_k)\left(g\dot{\mathbf{r}}_{\mathrm{d},k} - \hbar\left(\mathbf{f}(\vartheta_k) - \mathbf{r}_{\mathrm{d},k}\right)\right) - \frac{1}{8}\vartheta_k + \frac{3}{4}\vartheta_{k-1} + \frac{5}{8}\vartheta_{k-2} - \frac{1}{4}\vartheta_{k-3} + \mathbf{O}(g^4) \tag{9.17}$$

is obtained. Thus, the truncation error of the 4S-DTZNN-KSM algorithm (9.14) is $\mathbf{O}(g^4)$, which means that the algorithm is consistent. Moreover, according to Theorem 37, it is zero-stable. On the basis of Definitions 3 and 4 in Chapter 1, the 4S-DTZNN-KSM algorithm (9.14) converges with the order of truncation error being $\mathbf{O}(g^4)$.

(2) The 4S-DTZNN-USM algorithm (9.16): By using (9.15) to approximate $\dot{\mathbf{r}}_{\mathrm{d},k}$ in (9.17), the equation

$$\begin{aligned}\vartheta_{k+1} &= \frac{9}{4}J^{\dagger}(\vartheta_k)\left(\tilde{\mathbf{r}}_{\mathrm{d},k} - \hbar\mathbf{f}(\vartheta_k) + \mathbf{O}(g^4)\right) - \frac{1}{8}\vartheta_k + \frac{3}{4}\vartheta_{k-1} + \frac{5}{8}\vartheta_{k-2} - \frac{1}{4}\vartheta_{k-3} + \mathbf{O}(g^4)\\ &= \frac{9}{4}J^{\dagger}(\vartheta_k)\left(\tilde{\mathbf{r}}_{\mathrm{d},k} - \hbar\mathbf{f}(\vartheta_k)\right) - \frac{1}{8}\vartheta_k + \frac{3}{4}\vartheta_{k-1} + \frac{5}{8}\vartheta_{k-2} - \frac{1}{4}\vartheta_{k-3} + \mathbf{O}(g^4)\end{aligned}$$

is obtained. Thus, the truncation error of the 4S-DTZNN-USM algorithm (9.16) is $\mathbf{O}(g^4)$, which indicates that the algorithm is consistent. Similarly, according to Theorem 37 as well as Definitions 3 and 4 in Chapter 1, the 4S-DTZNN-USM algorithm (9.16) converges with the order of truncation error being $\mathbf{O}(g^4)$. The proof is thus completed. □

Theorem 39 *Suppose that the Jacobian matrix $J(\vartheta_k)$ is always of full row rank and uniformly norm bounded. With the sufficiently small sampling gap $g \in (0,1)$, the maximal steady-state tracking errors (MSSTEs) $\lim_{k\to+\infty}\sup\|\mathbf{r}_{\mathrm{a},k+1}-\mathbf{r}_{\mathrm{d},k+1}\|_2$ synthesized by the 4S-DTZNN-KSM algorithm (9.14) and the 4S-DTZNN-USM algorithm (9.16) are $\mathscr{O}(g^4)$, where $\|\cdot\|_2$ denotes the two-norm of a vector.*

Proof. Let ϑ^*_{k+1} be an exact solution of the problem (9.9). We have $\mathbf{f}(\vartheta^*_{k+1}) = \mathbf{r}_{\mathrm{d},k+1}$ for all k values. Thus,

$$\lim_{k\to+\infty}\|\mathbf{r}_{\mathrm{a},k+1}-\mathbf{r}_{\mathrm{d},k+1}\|_2 = \lim_{k\to+\infty}\|\mathbf{f}(\vartheta_{k+1})-\mathbf{f}(\vartheta^*_{k+1})\|_2.$$

From Definition 4 in Chapter 1 as well as Theorems 37 and 38, it is concluded that $\vartheta_{k+1} = \vartheta^*_{k+1} + \mathbf{O}(g^4)$ when k is large enough. Thus, with $J(\vartheta^*_{k+1}) = \partial\mathbf{f}(\vartheta^*_{k+1})/\partial\vartheta^*_{k+1}$, it is derived that

$$\begin{aligned}
&\lim_{k\to+\infty}\|\mathbf{f}(\vartheta_{k+1})-\mathbf{f}(\vartheta^*_{k+1})\|_2\\
&= \lim_{k\to+\infty}\|\mathbf{f}(\vartheta^*_{k+1}+\mathbf{O}(g^4))-\mathbf{f}(\vartheta^*_{k+1})\|_2\\
&= \lim_{k\to+\infty}\|\mathbf{f}(\vartheta^*_{k+1})+J(\vartheta^*_{k+1})\mathbf{O}(g^4)+\mathbf{O}(g^8)-\mathbf{f}(\vartheta^*_{k+1})\|_2\\
&= \lim_{k\to+\infty}\|J(\vartheta^*_{k+1})\mathbf{O}(g^4)\|_2\\
&= \mathscr{O}(g^4),
\end{aligned}$$

with $J(\vartheta^*_{k+1})$ being uniformly norm bounded. Thus, the MSSTEs synthesized by the 4S-DTZNN-KSM algorithm (9.14) and the 4S-DTZNN-USM algorithm (9.16) are $\mathscr{O}(g^4)$. The proof is thus completed. □

9.3.3 Zhang–Taylor discretization formula and ZT-DTZNN algorithms

By adopting the Zhang–Taylor discretization formula (9.5) for discretization, a Zhang–Taylor DTZNN with $\dot{\mathbf{r}}_{\mathrm{d},k}$ known for the serial manipulator (ZT-DTZNN-KSM) algorithm is obtained as follows:

$$\vartheta_{k+1} \doteq J^\dagger(\vartheta_k)\left(g\dot{\mathbf{r}}_{\mathrm{d},k}-\hbar\left(\mathbf{f}(\vartheta_k)-\mathbf{r}_{\mathrm{d},k}\right)\right)+\frac{3}{2}\vartheta_k-\vartheta_{k-1}+\frac{1}{2}\vartheta_{k-2}. \tag{9.18}$$

With the same truncation error as the Zhang–Taylor discretization formula (9.5), another backward numerical-differentiation formula is formulated as follows [161]:

$$\dot{\zeta}_k = \frac{3\zeta_k-4\zeta_{k-1}+\zeta_{k-2}}{2g}+\mathscr{O}(g^2). \tag{9.19}$$

By using (9.19) for approximation, a Zhang–Taylor DTZNN with $\dot{\mathbf{r}}_{\mathrm{d},k}$ unknown for the serial manipulator (ZT-DTZNN-USM) algorithm is further expressed as below [161]:

$$\vartheta_{k+1} \doteq J^\dagger(\vartheta_k)\left(\left(\frac{3}{2}+\hbar\right)\mathbf{r}_{\mathrm{d},k}-2\mathbf{r}_{\mathrm{d},k-1}+\frac{1}{2}\mathbf{r}_{\mathrm{d},k-2}-\hbar\mathbf{f}(\vartheta_k)\right)+\frac{3}{2}\vartheta_k-\vartheta_{k-1}+\frac{1}{2}\vartheta_{k-2}. \tag{9.20}$$

9.3.4 Euler forward formula and ET-DTZNN algorithms

Similarly, an Euler-type DTZNN with $\dot{\mathbf{r}}_{\mathrm{d},k}$ known for the serial manipulator (ET-DTZNN-KSM) algorithm, which is attained by the combination of the CTZNN model (9.12) and the Euler forward formula (9.4), is expressed as follows:

$$\vartheta_{k+1} \doteq J^{\dagger}(\vartheta_k)\left(g\dot{\mathbf{r}}_{\mathrm{d},k} - \hbar\left(\mathbf{f}(\vartheta_k) - \mathbf{r}_{\mathrm{d},k}\right)\right) + \vartheta_k. \tag{9.21}$$

With the same truncation error as the Euler forward formula (9.4), the Euler backward formula is formulated as follows [161]:

$$\dot{\zeta}_k = \frac{\zeta_k - \zeta_{k-1}}{g} + \mathscr{O}(g). \tag{9.22}$$

By utilizing (9.22) for approximation, an Euler-type DTZNN with $\dot{\mathbf{r}}_{\mathrm{d},k}$ unknown for the serial manipulator (ET-DTZNN-USM) algorithm is further expressed as below:

$$\vartheta_{k+1} \doteq J^{\dagger}(\vartheta_k)\left((1+\hbar)\mathbf{r}_{\mathrm{d},k} - \mathbf{r}_{\mathrm{d},k-1} - \hbar\mathbf{f}(\vartheta_k)\right) + \vartheta_k. \tag{9.23}$$

9.3.5 NI method and algorithm

For comparison, one classical method, termed as Newton iteration (NI) method [161], is considered, and the corresponding NI for the serial manipulator (NI-SM) algorithm is presented as below:

$$\vartheta_{k+1} \doteq -J^{\dagger}(\vartheta_k)\left(\mathbf{f}(\vartheta_k) - \mathbf{r}_{\mathrm{d},k}\right) + \vartheta_k. \tag{9.24}$$

As mentioned in the Introduction part, the NI-SM algorithm (9.24), which is a conventional method, has a truncation error being $\mathbf{O}(g)$, of which each element is in proportion to the sampling gap, i.e., $\mathscr{O}(g)$ [22, 111].

9.4 ZNN for Tracking Control of Parallel Manipulator

In this section, the ZNN method is employed for the real-time tracking control of Stewart platform [253], which is a typical parallel manipulator.

9.4.1 Problem formulation and CTZNN model

Stewart platform contains a mobile platform and a fixed base connected by six independent prismatic legs together. The effector is set on the center of the mobile platform. The effector of Stewart platform is controlled by the lengths of six legs. The real-time tracking control of Stewart platform is aimed to predict and obtain $\mathbf{l}_{k+1} \in \mathbb{R}^6$ at each computational time interval $[t_k, t_{k+1}) \subset [t_{\mathrm{ini}}, t_{\mathrm{fin}}]$ so that

$$\mathbf{r}_{\mathrm{a},k+1} \to \mathbf{r}_{\mathrm{d},k+1},$$

where $\mathbf{l}_k = [l_{1,k}, l_{2,k}, l_{3,k}, l_{4,k}, l_{5,k}, l_{6,k}]^{\mathrm{T}}$ is a vector containing the lengths of six legs at time instant t_k, $\mathbf{r}_{\mathrm{a},k+1} \in \mathbb{R}^3$ is the actual position vector of the effector, and $\mathbf{r}_{\mathrm{d},k+1} \in \mathbb{R}^3$ is a desired path to be tracked, which is unknown at each computational time interval $[t_k, t_{k+1})$. This problem is also mathematically formulated as the form of the FNES (9.1) as

$$\underset{\mathbf{l}_{k+1} \in \mathbb{R}^6}{\arg} \left(\mathbf{r}_{\mathrm{a},k+1} - \mathbf{r}_{\mathrm{d},k+1} = \mathbf{0}\right). \tag{9.25}$$

Before employing the ZNN method, the problem (9.25) is first converted into a continuous-time form as below:

$$\underset{\mathbf{l}(t) \in \mathbb{R}^6}{\arg} \left(\mathbf{r}_{\mathrm{a}}(t) - \mathbf{r}_{\mathrm{d}}(t) = \mathbf{0}\right). \tag{9.26}$$

A vector-form ZF is defined as below:

$$\mathbf{z}(t) = \mathbf{r}_{\mathrm{a}}(t) - \mathbf{r}_{\mathrm{d}}(t), \tag{9.27}$$

and the ZNN design formula

$$\dot{\mathbf{z}}(t) = -\eta \mathbf{z}(t)$$

makes the ZF (9.27) tend to zero with $t \to +\infty$. Thus, the equation

$$\dot{\mathbf{r}}_{\mathrm{a}}(t) - \dot{\mathbf{r}}_{\mathrm{d}}(t) = -\eta(\mathbf{r}_{\mathrm{a}}(t) - \mathbf{r}_{\mathrm{d}}(t)) \tag{9.28}$$

is obtained. On the basis of the manipulator kinematic modeling of Stewart platform, the kinematic equation of the manipulator system at the velocity level is depicted as below [253]:

$$\dot{\mathbf{l}}(t) = C(\mathbf{l}(t), D(t))\dot{\mathbf{r}}_{\mathrm{a}}(t), \tag{9.29}$$

where $C(\mathbf{l}(t), D(t)) \in \mathbb{R}^{6\times 3}$ is a matrix related to the lengths of six legs (i.e., $\mathbf{l}(t)$) and the position matrix in global coordinate (i.e., $D(t)$), $D(t) = [\mathbf{d}_1(t), \mathbf{d}_2(t), \mathbf{d}_3(t), \mathbf{d}_4(t), \mathbf{d}_5(t), \mathbf{d}_6(t)] \in \mathbb{R}^{3\times 6}$, with $\mathbf{d}_j(t) \in \mathbb{R}^3$ $(j = 1, 2, \cdots, 6)$ denoting the position of the jth leg, $\dot{\mathbf{l}}(t)$ is the velocity vector of six legs, and $\dot{\mathbf{r}}_{\mathrm{a}}(t)$ is the actual velocity vector of the effector on the mobile platform. Substituting (9.28) into (9.29) yields a CTZNN model for the problem (9.26) as below:

$$\dot{\mathbf{l}}(t) = C(\mathbf{l}(t), D(t))(\dot{\mathbf{r}}_{\mathrm{d}}(t) - \eta(\mathbf{r}_{\mathrm{a}}(t) - \mathbf{r}_{\mathrm{d}}(t))). \tag{9.30}$$

9.4.2 DTZNN algorithms

Adopting the 4S-ZTD formula (9.13), the Euler forward formula (9.4), and the Zhang–Taylor discretization formula (9.5), we can get a 4S-DTZNN with $\dot{\mathbf{r}}_{\mathrm{d},k}$ known for the parallel manipulator (4S-DTZNN-KPM) algorithm:

$$\mathbf{l}_{k+1} \doteq \frac{9}{4}C(\mathbf{l}_k, D_k)(g\dot{\mathbf{r}}_{\mathrm{d},k} - \hbar(\mathbf{r}_{\mathrm{a},k} - \mathbf{r}_{\mathrm{d},k})) - \frac{1}{8}\mathbf{l}_k + \frac{3}{4}\mathbf{l}_{k-1} + \frac{5}{8}\mathbf{l}_{k-2} - \frac{1}{4}\mathbf{l}_{k-3}, \tag{9.31}$$

a Zhang–Taylor DTZNN with $\dot{\mathbf{r}}_{\mathrm{d},k}$ known for the parallel manipulator (ZT-DTZNN-KPM) algorithm:

$$\mathbf{l}_{k+1} \doteq C(\mathbf{l}_k, D_k)(g\dot{\mathbf{r}}_{\mathrm{d},k} - \hbar(\mathbf{r}_{\mathrm{a},k} - \mathbf{r}_{\mathrm{d},k})) + \frac{3}{2}\mathbf{l}_k - \mathbf{l}_{k-1} + \frac{1}{2}\mathbf{l}_{k-2}, \tag{9.32}$$

and an Euler-type DTZNN with $\dot{\mathbf{r}}_{\mathrm{d},k}$ known for the parallel manipulator (ET-DTZNN-KPM) algorithm:

$$\mathbf{l}_{k+1} \doteq C(\mathbf{l}_k, D_k)(g\dot{\mathbf{r}}_{\mathrm{d},k} - \hbar(\mathbf{r}_{\mathrm{a},k} - \mathbf{r}_{\mathrm{d},k})) + \mathbf{l}_k. \tag{9.33}$$

Like serial manipulators, it may be tricky to get the value of $\dot{\mathbf{r}}_{\mathrm{d},k}$. Therefore, in this situation, the backward numerical-differentiation formulas (9.15), (9.22), and (9.19) can also be used to approximate the value of $\dot{\mathbf{r}}_{\mathrm{d},k}$. On the basis of (9.15), a 4S-DTZNN with $\dot{\mathbf{r}}_{\mathrm{d},k}$ unknown for the parallel manipulator (4S-DTZNN-UPM) algorithm is presented as

$$\mathbf{l}_{k+1} \doteq \frac{9}{4}C(\mathbf{l}_k, D_k)(\tilde{\mathbf{r}}_{\mathrm{d},k} - \hbar\mathbf{r}_{\mathrm{a},k}) - \frac{1}{8}\mathbf{l}_k + \frac{3}{4}\mathbf{l}_{k-1} + \frac{5}{8}\mathbf{l}_{k-2} - \frac{1}{4}\mathbf{l}_{k-3}, \tag{9.34}$$

where $\tilde{\mathbf{r}}_{\mathrm{d},k} = (11/6 + \hbar)\,\mathbf{r}_{\mathrm{d},k} - 3\mathbf{r}_{\mathrm{d},k-1} + 3\mathbf{r}_{\mathrm{d},k-2}/2 - \mathbf{r}_{\mathrm{d},k-3}/3$. On the basis of (9.19), a Zhang–Taylor DTZNN with $\dot{\mathbf{r}}_{\mathrm{d},k}$ unknown for the parallel manipulator (ZT-DTZNN-UPM) algorithm is expressed as

$$\mathbf{l}_{k+1} \doteq C(\mathbf{l}_k, D_k)\left(\left(\frac{3}{2} + \hbar\right)\mathbf{r}_{\mathrm{d},k} - 2\mathbf{r}_{\mathrm{d},k-1} + \frac{1}{2}\mathbf{r}_{\mathrm{d},k-2} - \hbar\mathbf{r}_{\mathrm{a},k}\right) + \frac{3}{2}\mathbf{l}_k - \mathbf{l}_{k-1} + \frac{1}{2}\mathbf{l}_{k-2}. \tag{9.35}$$

TABLE 9.2: Problem, scheme, model, and algorithms for serial manipulator in this chapter.

Problem	$\arg_{\vartheta_{k+1}\in\mathbb{R}^n} (\mathbf{r}_{\mathrm{a},k+1} - \mathbf{r}_{\mathrm{d},k+1} = \mathbf{0})$.
Scheme	*Step 1*: Define ZF as $\mathbf{z}(t) = \mathbf{r}_\mathrm{a}(t) - \mathbf{r}_\mathrm{d}(t)$. *Step 2*: Adopt ZNN design formula as $\dot{\mathbf{z}}(t) = -\eta\mathbf{z}(t)$. *Step 3*: Adopt discretization formulas to discretize CTZNN model (9.12).
Model	$\dot{\vartheta}(t) = J^\dagger(\vartheta(t))(\dot{\mathbf{r}}_\mathrm{d}(t) - \eta(\mathbf{f}(\vartheta(t)) - \mathbf{r}_\mathrm{d}(t)))$.
Algorithms	$\vartheta_{k+1} \doteq \frac{9}{4}J^\dagger(\vartheta_k)\left(g\dot{\mathbf{r}}_{\mathrm{d},k} - \hbar\left(\mathbf{f}(\vartheta_k) - \mathbf{r}_{\mathrm{d},k}\right)\right) - \frac{1}{8}\vartheta_k + \frac{3}{4}\vartheta_{k-1} + \frac{5}{8}\vartheta_{k-2} - \frac{1}{4}\vartheta_{k-3}$, $\vartheta_{k+1} \doteq \frac{9}{4}J^\dagger(\vartheta_k)\left(\tilde{\mathbf{r}}_{\mathrm{d},k} - \hbar\mathbf{f}(\vartheta_k)\right) - \frac{1}{8}\vartheta_k + \frac{3}{4}\vartheta_{k-1} + \frac{5}{8}\vartheta_{k-2} - \frac{1}{4}\vartheta_{k-3}$, $\vartheta_{k+1} \doteq J^\dagger(\vartheta_k)\left(g\dot{\mathbf{r}}_{\mathrm{d},k} - \hbar\left(\mathbf{f}(\vartheta_k) - \mathbf{r}_{\mathrm{d},k}\right)\right) + \frac{3}{2}\vartheta_k - \vartheta_{k-1} + \frac{1}{2}\vartheta_{k-2}$, $\vartheta_{k+1} \doteq J^\dagger(\vartheta_k)\left(\left(\frac{3}{2} + \hbar\right)\mathbf{r}_{\mathrm{d},k} - 2\mathbf{r}_{\mathrm{d},k-1} + \frac{1}{2}\mathbf{r}_{\mathrm{d},k-2} - \hbar\mathbf{f}(\vartheta_k)\right) + \frac{3}{2}\vartheta_k - \vartheta_{k-1} + \frac{1}{2}\vartheta_{k-2}$, $\vartheta_{k+1} \doteq J^\dagger(\vartheta_k)\left(g\dot{\mathbf{r}}_{\mathrm{d},k} - \hbar\left(\mathbf{f}(\vartheta_k) - \mathbf{r}_{\mathrm{d},k}\right)\right) + \vartheta_k$, $\vartheta_{k+1} \doteq J^\dagger(\vartheta_k)\left((1+\hbar)\mathbf{r}_{\mathrm{d},k} - \mathbf{r}_{\mathrm{d},k-1} - \hbar\mathbf{f}(\vartheta_k)\right) + \vartheta_k$, $\vartheta_{k+1} \doteq -J^\dagger(\vartheta_k)\left(\mathbf{f}(\vartheta_k) - \mathbf{r}_{\mathrm{d},k}\right) + \vartheta_k$.

On the basis of (9.22), an Euler-type DTZNN with $\dot{\mathbf{r}}_{\mathrm{d},k}$ unknown for the parallel manipulator (ET-DTZNN-UPM) algorithm is formulated as

$$\mathbf{l}_{k+1} \doteq C(\mathbf{l}_k, D_k)\left((1+\hbar)\mathbf{r}_{\mathrm{d},k} - \mathbf{r}_{\mathrm{d},k-1} - \hbar\mathbf{r}_{\mathrm{a},k}\right) + \mathbf{l}_k. \tag{9.36}$$

Theoretical analyses on the 4S-DTZNN-KPM algorithm (9.31) and the 4S-DTZNN-UPM algorithm (9.34) are presented by the following corollaries.

Corollary 7 *With the sufficiently small sampling gap $g \in (0,1)$, the 4S-DTZNN-KPM algorithm (9.31) and the 4S-DTZNN-UPM algorithm (9.34) are zero-stable.*

Proof. The proof is similar to that of Theorem 37, and thus is omitted here. □

Corollary 8 *With the sufficiently small sampling gap $g \in (0,1)$, let $\mathbf{O}(g^4)$ denote the error (especially, the truncation error) with each element being $\mathscr{O}(g^4)$. The 4S-DTZNN-KPM algorithm (9.31) and the 4S-DTZNN-UPM algorithm (9.34) are consistent and convergent, which converge with the orders of truncation errors being $\mathbf{O}(g^4)$ for all $t_k \in [t_\mathrm{ini}, t_\mathrm{fin})$.*

Proof. The proof is similar to that of Theorem 38, and thus is omitted here. □

Corollary 9 *With the sufficiently small sampling gap $g \in (0,1)$, the MSSTEs $\lim_{k\to+\infty}\sup\|\mathbf{r}_{\mathrm{a},k+1} - \mathbf{r}_{\mathrm{d},k+1}\|_2$ synthesized by the 4S-DTZNN-KPM algorithm (9.31) and the 4S-DTZNN-UPM algorithm (9.34) are $\mathscr{O}(g^4)$.*

Proof. The proof is similar to that of Theorem 39, and thus is omitted here. □

For a more intuitive understanding of the main content of this chapter [130], Tables 9.2 and 9.3 list the problems, schemes, models, and algorithms.

9.5 Numerical Experiments

In this section, two examples are provided to show the effectiveness and the superiority of the presented DTZNN algorithms. The first example is to show the real-time tracking control of the

TABLE 9.3: Problem, scheme, model, and algorithms for parallel manipulator in this chapter.

Problem	$\arg_{\mathbf{l}_{k+1}\in\mathbb{R}^6} \left(\mathbf{r}_{\mathrm{a},k+1}-\mathbf{r}_{\mathrm{d},k+1}=\mathbf{0}\right).$
Scheme	*Step 1*: Define ZF as $\mathbf{z}(t)=\mathbf{r}_{\mathrm{a}}(t)-\mathbf{r}_{\mathrm{d}}(t)$. *Step 2*: Adopt ZNN design formula as $\dot{\mathbf{z}}(t)=-\eta\mathbf{z}(t)$. *Step 3*: Adopt discretization formulas to discretize CTZNN model (9.30).
Model	$\dot{\mathbf{l}}(t)=C(\mathbf{l}(t),D(t))(\dot{\mathbf{r}}_{\mathrm{d}}(t)-\eta(\mathbf{r}_{\mathrm{a}}(t)-\mathbf{r}_{\mathrm{d}}(t))).$
Algorithms	$\mathbf{l}_{k+1}\doteq\frac{9}{4}C(\mathbf{l}_k,D_k)(g\dot{\mathbf{r}}_{\mathrm{d},k}-\hbar(\mathbf{r}_{\mathrm{a},k}-\mathbf{r}_{\mathrm{d},k}))-\frac{1}{8}\mathbf{l}_k+\frac{3}{4}\mathbf{l}_{k-1}+\frac{5}{8}\mathbf{l}_{k-2}-\frac{1}{4}\mathbf{l}_{k-3},$ $\mathbf{l}_{k+1}\doteq\frac{9}{4}C(\mathbf{l}_k,D_k)(\tilde{\mathbf{r}}_{\mathrm{d},k}-\hbar\mathbf{r}_{\mathrm{a},k})-\frac{1}{8}\mathbf{l}_k+\frac{3}{4}\mathbf{l}_{k-1}+\frac{5}{8}\mathbf{l}_{k-2}-\frac{1}{4}\mathbf{l}_{k-3},$ $\mathbf{l}_{k+1}\doteq C(\mathbf{l}_k,D_k)(g\dot{\mathbf{r}}_{\mathrm{d},k}-\hbar(\mathbf{r}_{\mathrm{a},k}-\mathbf{r}_{\mathrm{d},k}))+\frac{3}{2}\mathbf{l}_k-\mathbf{l}_{k-1}+\frac{1}{2}\mathbf{l}_{k-2},$ $\mathbf{l}_{k+1}\doteq C(\mathbf{l}_k,D_k)\left((\frac{3}{2}+\hbar)\mathbf{r}_{\mathrm{d},k}-2\mathbf{r}_{\mathrm{d},k-1}+\frac{1}{2}\mathbf{r}_{\mathrm{d},k-2}-\hbar\mathbf{r}_{\mathrm{a},k}\right)+\frac{3}{2}\mathbf{l}_k-\mathbf{l}_{k-1}+\frac{1}{2}\mathbf{l}_{k-2},$ $\mathbf{l}_{k+1}\doteq C(\mathbf{l}_k,D_k)(g\dot{\mathbf{r}}_{\mathrm{d},k}-\hbar(\mathbf{r}_{\mathrm{a},k}-\mathbf{r}_{\mathrm{d},k}))+\mathbf{l}_k,$ $\mathbf{l}_{k+1}\doteq C(\mathbf{l}_k,D_k)\left((1+\hbar)\mathbf{r}_{\mathrm{d},k}-\mathbf{r}_{\mathrm{d},k-1}-\hbar\mathbf{r}_{\mathrm{a},k}\right)+\mathbf{l}_k.$

serial manipulator, and the other one is to show the real-time tracking control of the parallel manipulator. They substantiate the theoretical results displayed for the real-time tracking control of serial and parallel manipulators in above sections.

Example 9.1 A five-link serial manipulator is considered, and its geometry is shown in Figure 9.1(a). For simplicity and illustration, the length of each link is 1 m, and the forward-kinematics mapping function of the serial manipulator is formulated as $\mathbf{f}(\boldsymbol{\vartheta}_k)\in\mathbb{R}^2$, where $\boldsymbol{\vartheta}_k=[\vartheta_{1,k},\vartheta_{2,k},\vartheta_{3,k},\vartheta_{4,k},\vartheta_{5,k}]^{\mathrm{T}}\in\mathbb{R}^5$. It is investigated that the serial manipulator tracks the desired path at time instant t_{k+1}, which is expressed as below:

$$\mathbf{r}_{\mathrm{d},k+1}=\mathbf{r}_{\mathrm{d}}(t_{k+1})=\begin{bmatrix}0.5\sin^3(\pi t_{k+1}/5)+1.5\\ 0.5\cos^3(\pi t_{k+1}/5)+2.5\end{bmatrix},$$

during the computational time interval $[t_k,t_{k+1})$ via the information at time instant t_k. Note that the expression of the desired path is given just for the convenience of comparison, and the future information $\mathbf{r}_{\mathrm{d},k+1}$ cannot be used during $[t_k,t_{k+1})$. The 4S-DTZNN-KSM algorithm (9.14) and the 4S-DTZNN-USM algorithm (9.16) are employed to solve this problem. The initial joint angles $\boldsymbol{\vartheta}_0$ are arbitrarily set as $[3\pi/4,-\pi/2,-\pi/4,\pi/6,\pi/3]^{\mathrm{T}}$ rad, the task duration T is set as 20 s, and the step length $\hbar$ is set as 0.1.

With $\dot{\mathbf{r}}_{\mathrm{d}}(t)$ known and $g=0.1$ s, numerical experimental results synthesized by the 4S-DTZNN-KSM algorithm (9.14) are presented in Figure 9.1(b) and (c). Specifically, Figure 9.1(b) shows the trajectories of the serial manipulator, and Figure 9.1(c) shows the actual trajectory of the end-effector corresponding to the solid line, which almost overlaps with the desired path corresponding to the dash line in a short time. Thus, the effectiveness of the 4S-DTZNN-KSM algorithm (9.14) is substantiated to solve the real-time tracking control problem of the serial manipulator.

To substantiate Theorem 39, which illustrates the MSSTEs synthesized by the 4S-DTZNN-KSM algorithm (9.14) and the 4S-DTZNN-USM algorithm (9.16) are $\mathscr{O}(g^4)$, some numerical experiments are conducted by employing the 4S-DTZNN-KSM algorithm (9.14) and the 4S-DTZNN-USM algorithm (9.16) with different g values. For comparison, the ZT-DTZNN-KSM algorithm (9.18), the ZT-DTZNN-USM algorithm (9.20), the ET-DTZNN-KSM algorithm (9.21), the ET-DTZNN-USM algorithm (9.23), and the NI-SM algorithm (9.24) are also employed to solve the above real-time tracking control problem. Numerical experimental results are displayed in Tables 9.4 and 9.5.

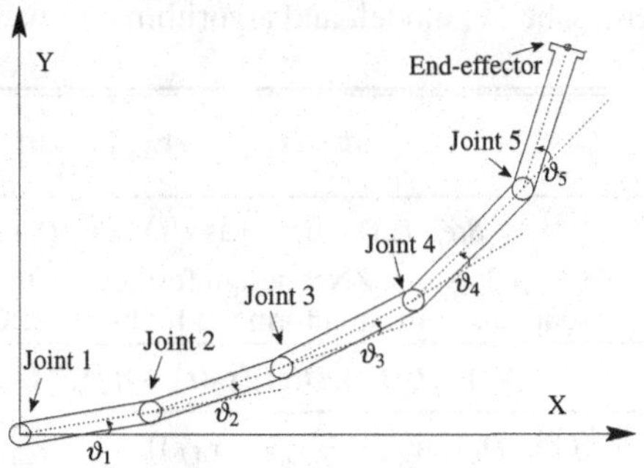

(a) Manipulator geometry [130]

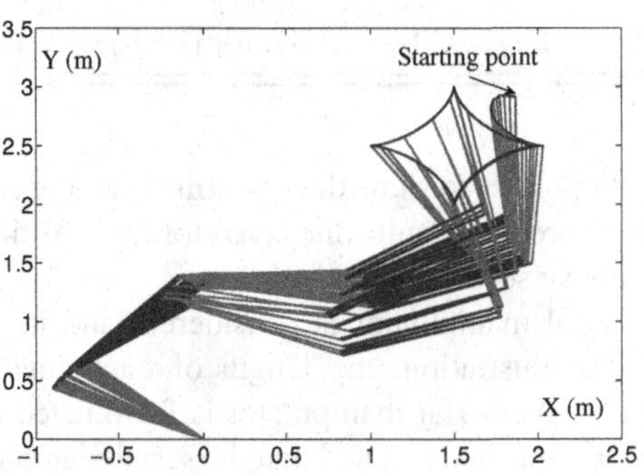

(b) Manipulator trajectories [130]

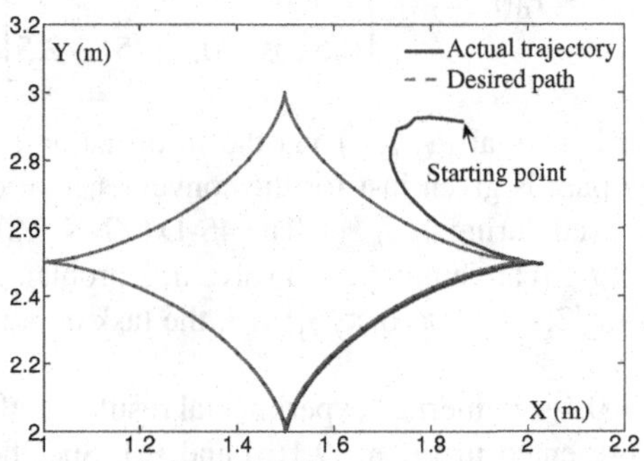

(c) End-effector actual trajectory and desired path

FIGURE 9.1: Geometry of five-link serial manipulator, and trajectories of manipulator and end-effector generated by 4S-DTZNN-KSM algorithm (9.14) with $\hbar = 0.1$ and $g = 0.1$ s.

Specifically, from Table 9.4, with $\dot{\mathbf{r}}_{\mathrm{d},k}$ known and $g = 0.1$ s, the MSSTEs synthesized by the 4S-DTZNN-KSM algorithm (9.14), the ZT-DTZNN-KSM algorithm (9.18), the ET-DTZNN-KSM algorithm (9.21), and the NI-SM algorithm (9.24) are of orders 10^{-4} m, 10^{-3} m, 10^{-2} m, and 10^{-2} m, respectively. With g reduced by a factor of 10 to be 0.01 s, their MSSTEs decrease by factors of 10^4, 10^3, 10^2, and 10, respectively. Similarly, with g reduced by a factor of 100 to be 0.001 s, their MSSTEs decrease by factors of 10^8, 10^6, 10^4, and 10^2, respectively. With $\dot{\mathbf{r}}_{\mathrm{d},k}$ unknown, the

TABLE 9.4: MSSTEs and ACTPU data synthesized by different algorithms for serial manipulator with $\dot{\mathbf{r}}_{\mathrm{d},k}$ known and with different g values.

g (ms)	Algorithm	MSSTE (m)	ACTPU (ms)
100	4S-DTZNN-KSM algorithm (9.14)	1.869×10^{-4}	0.1238
	ZT-DTZNN-KSM algorithm (9.18)	1.349×10^{-3}	0.1157
	ET-DTZNN-KSM algorithm (9.21)	1.768×10^{-2}	0.1285
	NI-SM algorithm (9.24)	4.725×10^{-2}	0.1090
50	4S-DTZNN-KSM algorithm (9.14)	1.846×10^{-5}	0.1106
	ZT-DTZNN-KSM algorithm (9.18)	2.490×10^{-4}	0.1075
	ET-DTZNN-KSM algorithm (9.21)	5.960×10^{-3}	0.1163
	NI-SM algorithm (9.24)	2.359×10^{-2}	0.1039
10	4S-DTZNN-KSM algorithm (9.14)	4.328×10^{-8}	0.1204
	ZT-DTZNN-KSM algorithm (9.18)	2.670×10^{-6}	0.1044
	ET-DTZNN-KSM algorithm (9.21)	2.924×10^{-4}	0.1047
	NI-SM algorithm (9.24)	4.714×10^{-3}	0.1017
5	4S-DTZNN-KSM algorithm (9.14)	2.763×10^{-9}	0.1163
	ZT-DTZNN-KSM algorithm (9.18)	3.383×10^{-7}	0.1175
	ET-DTZNN-KSM algorithm (9.21)	7.379×10^{-5}	0.1066
	NI-SM algorithm (9.24)	2.356×10^{-3}	0.1043
1	4S-DTZNN-KSM algorithm (9.14)	4.454×10^{-12}	0.1044
	ZT-DTZNN-KSM algorithm (9.18)	2.718×10^{-9}	0.1057
	ET-DTZNN-KSM algorithm (9.21)	2.960×10^{-6}	0.1058
	NI-SM algorithm (9.24)	4.712×10^{-4}	0.1027
0.5	4S-DTZNN-KSM algorithm (9.14)	2.824×10^{-13}	0.1053
	ZT-DTZNN-KSM algorithm (9.18)	3.398×10^{-10}	0.1055
	ET-DTZNN-KSM algorithm (9.21)	7.402×10^{-7}	0.1042
	NI-SM algorithm (9.24)	2.356×10^{-4}	0.1030

4S-DTZNN-USM algorithm (9.16), the ZT-DTZNN-USM algorithm (9.20), and the ET-DTZNN-USM algorithm (9.23) also perform well as observed from Table 9.5. Moreover, according to the average computing time per updating (ACTPU) data in Tables 9.4 and 9.5, they are around 0.1 ms under different situations, which means that the control process is real-time even when the sampling gap g is reduced to 0.5 ms.

Example 9.2 In this example, the Stewart platform, which is a six DOF parallel manipulator, is considered, and its geometry is shown in Figure 9.2(a). We aim to predict and obtain $\mathbf{l}_{k+1}\in\mathbb{R}^6$ at each computational time interval $[t_k,t_{k+1})\subset[0,T]$ s so that the effector tracks the desired path, which is expressed under cylindrical coordinates as below:

$$\begin{cases}\varepsilon = 0.6t_k,\\ r = 0.2-(0.2\sin(2.5\varepsilon))^2,\\ z = (r\sin(2.5\varepsilon))^2+1.\end{cases}$$

Similarly, the future information $\mathbf{r}_{\mathrm{d},k+1}$ is unknown and cannot be used during the computational time interval $[t_k,t_{k+1})$. The expression of the desired path is given just for the convenience of comparison. The 4S-DTZNN-KPM algorithm (9.31) is employed to solve this problem with the task duration $T=15$ s, $\hbar=0.1$, and $g=0.01$ s. The numerical experimental results synthesized by the 4S-DTZNN-KPM algorithm (9.31) are presented in Figure 9.2(b), which shows the actual trajectory corresponding to the solid line, which tracks the desired path corresponding to the dash line successfully in a short time. To substantiate theoretical results of Corollary 9 and show the superiority

TABLE 9.5: MSSTEs and ACTPU data synthesized by different algorithms for serial manipulator with $\dot{\mathbf{r}}_{\mathrm{d},k}$ unknown and with different g values.

g (ms)	Algorithm	MSSTE (m)	ACTPU (ms)
100	4S-DTZNN-USM algorithm (9.16)	3.659×10^{-4}	0.1239
	ZT-DTZNN-USM algorithm (9.20)	2.909×10^{-3}	0.1204
	ET-DTZNN-USM algorithm (9.23)	3.486×10^{-2}	0.1303
	NI-SM algorithm (9.24)	4.725×10^{-2}	0.1090
50	4S-DTZNN-USM algorithm (9.16)	3.577×10^{-5}	0.1262
	ZT-DTZNN-USM algorithm (9.20)	5.342×10^{-4}	0.1189
	ET-DTZNN-USM algorithm (9.23)	1.186×10^{-2}	0.1213
	NI-SM algorithm (9.24)	2.359×10^{-2}	0.1039
10	4S-DTZNN-USM algorithm (9.16)	8.077×10^{-8}	0.1332
	ZT-DTZNN-USM algorithm (9.20)	5.631×10^{-6}	0.1273
	ET-DTZNN-USM algorithm (9.23)	5.850×10^{-4}	0.1132
	NI-SM algorithm (9.24)	4.714×10^{-3}	0.1017
5	4S-DTZNN-USM algorithm (9.16)	5.137×10^{-9}	0.1253
	ZT-DTZNN-USM algorithm (9.20)	7.128×10^{-7}	0.1216
	ET-DTZNN-USM algorithm (9.23)	1.476×10^{-4}	0.1224
	NI-SM algorithm (9.24)	2.357×10^{-3}	0.1043
1	4S-DTZNN-USM algorithm (9.16)	8.283×10^{-12}	0.1371
	ZT-DTZNN-USM algorithm (9.20)	5.726×10^{-9}	0.1211
	ET-DTZNN-USM algorithm (9.23)	5.921×10^{-6}	0.1145
	NI-SM algorithm (9.24)	4.713×10^{-4}	0.1027
0.5	4S-DTZNN-USM algorithm (9.16)	5.199×10^{-13}	0.1212
	ZT-DTZNN-USM algorithm (9.20)	7.158×10^{-10}	0.1183
	ET-DTZNN-USM algorithm (9.23)	1.480×10^{-6}	0.1141
	NI-SM algorithm (9.24)	2.356×10^{-4}	0.1030

of the presented DTZNN algorithms, all the DTZNN algorithms for the parallel manipulator are employed to solve the real-time tracking control problem, and the corresponding numerical experimental results are shown in Tables 9.6 and 9.7. It is evident that they verify the theoretical results.

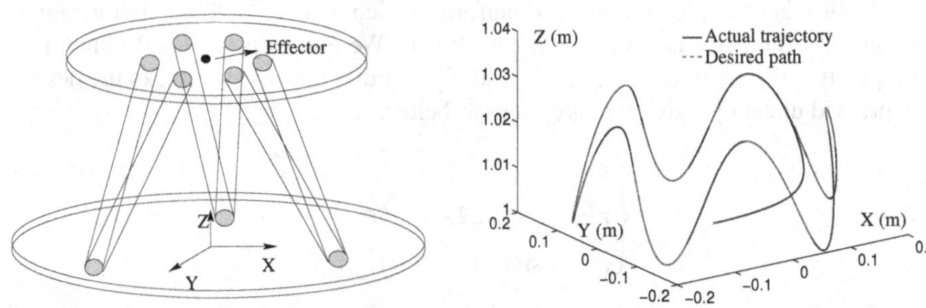

(a) Stewart platform geometry [130]

(b) Effector actual trajectory and desired path

FIGURE 9.2: Geometry of Stewart platform, and trajectory of effector generated by 4S-DTZNN-KPM algorithm (9.31) with $\hbar = 0.1$ and $g = 0.01$ s.

TABLE 9.6: MSSTEs synthesized by DTZNN algorithms for Stewart platform with $\dot{\mathbf{r}}_{\mathrm{d},k}$ known and with different g values.

g (ms)	DTZNN algorithm	MSSTE (m)
100	4S-DTZNN-KPM algorithm (9.31)	1.6493×10^{-4}
	ZT-DTZNN-KPM algorithm (9.32)	1.8000×10^{-3}
	ET-DTZNN-KPM algorithm (9.33)	6.0000×10^{-3}
50	4S-DTZNN-KPM algorithm (9.31)	1.9823×10^{-5}
	ZT-DTZNN-KPM algorithm (9.32)	3.7057×10^{-4}
	ET-DTZNN-KPM algorithm (9.33)	2.3000×10^{-3}
10	4S-DTZNN-KPM algorithm (9.31)	7.1282×10^{-8}
	ZT-DTZNN-KPM algorithm (9.32)	5.1949×10^{-6}
	ET-DTZNN-KPM algorithm (9.33)	1.4751×10^{-4}
5	4S-DTZNN-KPM algorithm (9.31)	4.8289×10^{-9}
	ZT-DTZNN-KPM algorithm (9.32)	6.8359×10^{-7}
	ET-DTZNN-KPM algorithm (9.33)	3.8206×10^{-5}
1	4S-DTZNN-KPM algorithm (9.31)	7.9693×10^{-12}
	ZT-DTZNN-KPM algorithm (9.32)	5.5814×10^{-9}
	ET-DTZNN-KPM algorithm (9.33)	1.5476×10^{-6}
0.5	4S-DTZNN-KPM algorithm (9.31)	4.9917×10^{-13}
	ZT-DTZNN-KPM algorithm (9.32)	6.9817×10^{-10}
	ET-DTZNN-KPM algorithm (9.33)	3.8705×10^{-7}

TABLE 9.7: MSSTEs synthesized by DTZNN algorithms for Stewart platform with $\dot{\mathbf{r}}_{\mathrm{d},k}$ unknown and with different g values.

g (ms)	DTZNN algorithm	MSSTE (m)
100	4S-DTZNN-UPM algorithm (9.34)	3.7284×10^{-4}
	ZT-DTZNN-UPM algorithm (9.35)	2.8000×10^{-3}
	ET-DTZNN-UPM algorithm (9.36)	1.2000×10^{-2}
50	4S-DTZNN-UPM algorithm (9.34)	4.5393×10^{-5}
	ZT-DTZNN-UPM algorithm (9.35)	5.5584×10^{-4}
	ET-DTZNN-UPM algorithm (9.36)	4.6000×10^{-3}
10	4S-DTZNN-UPM algorithm (9.34)	1.6294×10^{-7}
	ZT-DTZNN-UPM algorithm (9.35)	7.7925×10^{-6}
	ET-DTZNN-UPM algorithm (9.36)	2.9501×10^{-4}
5	4S-DTZNN-UPM algorithm (9.34)	1.1038×10^{-8}
	ZT-DTZNN-UPM algorithm (9.35)	1.0254×10^{-6}
	ET-DTZNN-UPM algorithm (9.36)	7.6410×10^{-5}
1	4S-DTZNN-UPM algorithm (9.34)	1.8217×10^{-11}
	ZT-DTZNN-UPM algorithm (9.35)	8.3721×10^{-9}
	ET-DTZNN-UPM algorithm (9.36)	3.0952×10^{-6}
0.5	4S-DTZNN-UPM algorithm (9.34)	1.1429×10^{-12}
	ZT-DTZNN-UPM algorithm (9.35)	1.0473×10^{-9}
	ET-DTZNN-UPM algorithm (9.36)	7.7410×10^{-7}

9.6 Chapter Summary

In this chapter, the ZNN scheme has been established for the real-time tracking control of serial and parallel manipulators. For the control of the serial manipulator, two 4S-DTZNN algorithms (i.e., (9.14) and (9.16)), two ZT-DTZNN algorithms (i.e., (9.18) and (9.20)), and two ET-DTZNN algorithms (i.e., (9.21) and (9.23)) have been developed. Both theoretical analyses and numerical experiments have shown that the MSSTEs synthesized by the 4S-DTZNN-KSM algorithm (9.14) and the 4S-DTZNN-USM algorithm (9.16), the ZT-DTZNN-KSM algorithm (9.18) and the ZT-DTZNN-USM algorithm (9.20), and the ET-DTZNN-KSM algorithm (9.21) and the ET-DTZNN-USM algorithm (9.23) are $\mathscr{O}(g^4)$, $\mathscr{O}(g^3)$, and $\mathscr{O}(g^2)$, respectively. For the control of the parallel manipulator, two 4S-DTZNN algorithms (i.e., (9.31) and (9.34)) with the MSSTEs being $\mathscr{O}(g^4)$, two ZT-DTZNN algorithms (i.e., (9.32) and (9.35)) with the MSSTEs being $\mathscr{O}(g^3)$, and two ET-DTZNN algorithms (i.e., (9.33) and (9.36)) with the MSSTEs being $\mathscr{O}(g^2)$ have also been developed in this chapter.

Appendix K: Proof of Theorem 36

According to Taylor expansion [161], the following equations are obtained:

$$\zeta_{k+1} = \zeta_k + g\dot{\zeta}_k + \frac{g^2}{2}\ddot{\zeta}_k + \frac{g^3}{6}\dddot{\zeta}_k + \mathscr{O}(g^4), \tag{9.37}$$

$$\zeta_{k-1} = \zeta_k - g\dot{\zeta}_k + \frac{g^2}{2}\ddot{\zeta}_k - \frac{g^3}{6}\dddot{\zeta}_k + \mathscr{O}(g^4), \tag{9.38}$$

$$\zeta_{k-2} = \zeta_k - 2g\dot{\zeta}_k + 2g^2\ddot{\zeta}_k - \frac{4}{3}g^3\dddot{\zeta}_k + \mathscr{O}(g^4), \tag{9.39}$$

and

$$\zeta_{k-3} = \zeta_k - 3g\dot{\zeta}_k + \frac{9}{2}g^2\ddot{\zeta}_k - \frac{9}{2}g^3\dddot{\zeta}_k + \mathscr{O}(g^4), \tag{9.40}$$

where $\ddot{\zeta}(t_k)$ and $\dddot{\zeta}(t_k)$ represent the second-order and third-order time derivatives of $\zeta(t)$ at time instant t_k, respectively. Let (9.37) multiply 8, let (9.38) multiply -3, let (9.39) multiply -5, and let (9.40) multiply 2. Adding them together, we finally obtain

$$\dot{\zeta}_k = \frac{4}{9g}\zeta_{k+1} + \frac{1}{18g}\zeta_k - \frac{1}{3g}\zeta_{k-1} - \frac{5}{18g}\zeta_{k-2} + \frac{1}{9g}\zeta_{k-3} + \mathscr{O}(g^3),$$

which is just the 4S-ZTD formula (9.13). The proof is thus completed. □

Chapter 10

Future Matrix Inversion with Sometimes-Singular Coefficient Matrix

Abstract

In this chapter, a five-step Zhang time discretization (5S-ZTD) formula with high precision is presented to approximate the first-order derivative. Then, such a formula is studied to discretize two continuous-time neural network models, i.e., a continuous-time zeroing neural network (CTZNN) model and a continuous-time gradient neural network (CTGNN) model. Subsequently, two discrete-time neural network algorithms, i.e., a five-step discrete-time zeroing neural network (5S-DTZNN) algorithm and a five-step discrete-time gradient neural network (5S-DTGNN) algorithm, are developed and investigated for future matrix inversion (FMI). In addition to analyzing a usual situation that the coefficient matrix is always nonsingular, this chapter investigates another situation that the coefficient matrix is sometimes singular for the FMI. Finally, two illustrative numerical examples, including an application to the inverse-kinematic control of PUMA560 manipulator, are provided to show the respective characteristics and advantages of the 5S-DTZNN algorithm and the 5S-DTGNN algorithm for the FMI in different situations, where the coefficient matrix to be inverted is always nonsingular or sometimes singular during time evolution.

10.1 Introduction

Matrix inversion is often considered as an essential step of many solutions in mathematics and cybernetics, which is also involved in numerous engineering applications, e.g., optimization [233, 254], signal processing [255], machine learning [256], and manipulator kinematics [181, 200]. In view of its fundamental roles, much effort has been devoted to the fast and high-accuracy solution of the matrix inversion problem, and many numerical algorithms or methods have been developed and investigated [57, 257–260]. It is known that most of numerical algorithms or methods are designed intrinsically for time-independent (also termed as static, constant) matrix inversion problem, which is formulated as $AX = I_{n\times n}$, where the coefficient matrix $A \in \mathbb{R}^{n\times n}$ and the identity matrix $I_{n\times n} \in \mathbb{R}^{n\times n}$ are constant matrices, and $X \in \mathbb{R}^{n\times n}$ denotes an unknown matrix to be obtained. Differing from the time-independent matrix inversion problem, the continuous time-dependent matrix inversion (CTDMI) problem is presented as

$$A(t)X(t) = I_{n\times n}, \text{with } t \in [t_{\text{ini}}, t_{\text{fin}}) \subset [0, +\infty), \tag{10.1}$$

where t_{ini} and t_{fin} represent the initial and final time instants, respectively. Besides, $A(t) \in \mathbb{R}^{n\times n}$ denotes a smoothly time-dependent coefficient matrix, and $X(t) \in \mathbb{R}^{n\times n}$ denotes a time-dependent unknown matrix to be obtained. When applied to solving the CTDMI problem (10.1), the

DOI: 10.1201/9781003497783-10

conventional static numerical algorithms or methods only adapt to the changing coefficient matrix $A(t)$ in a posteriori passive manner, and a large lagging error may thus be generated [42, 65, 196]. As a consequence, the conventional static numerical algorithms or methods may be less effective or less accurate for solving the CTDMI problem (10.1).

Over the past few decades, neural network approaches have been extensively investigated and successfully applied to solving scientific and engineering problems (including the matrix inversion problem) [64, 116, 160, 253, 261–277]. A kind of explicit recurrent neural network (RNN) based on negative-gradient descent was creatively proposed by Wang [262] for computing the inverse of a static matrix. For further improving the computational performance, Chen [278] proposed a novel kind of implicit RNN for the static matrix inversion, and its robustness was studied in [279]. It is worth noting that, unlike the static matrix inversion problem, solving the time-dependent matrix inversion problem is more challenging, which needs to obtain the solution at each time instant so as to satisfy the stringent requirement of real-time computation. In [65], the gradient neural network (GNN) designed intrinsically for the static matrix inversion was generalized and studied for the time-dependent matrix inversion. In comparison with the situation of the static matrix inversion, the corresponding continuous-time GNN (CTGNN) model could only approximately approach its theoretical inverse, instead of converging exactly. To remedy the less favorable performance of the conventional GNN, Jin *et al* [181] proposed a novel CTGNN model with an adaptive parameter for computing the inverse of a time-dependent matrix from the perspective of control. In recent years, varying from the aforementioned GNN, a novel class of RNNs, called zeroing neural network (ZNN), was proposed by Zhang *et al* and designed specially for various time-dependent problems [64, 160, 280–283]. In [64], Zhang and Ge developed a continuous-time ZNN (CTZNN) model for the time-dependent matrix inversion, which achieved global exponential convergence to the exact inverse of a given time-dependent matrix by fully exploiting its time-derivative information. For further accelerating the convergence speed, Xiao [283] developed a finite-time CTZNN model for the time-dependent matrix inversion by adopting a new design formula.

Almost all of the aforementioned literatures aimed to develop continuous-time models for continuous-time problems, but it may be difficult to directly apply continuous-time models to solve the corresponding discrete-time problems. Because digital computers and technologies are widely used in practical applications, many signals are composed of discrete-time variables instead of continuous-time ones. Therefore, discrete-time problems have been attracting much attention and extensive investigations [42, 233, 269–272, 284–287], e.g., the control problems of discrete-time interconnected systems [285–287]. For example, in [285], an adaptive output feedback control was designed for nonlinear discrete-time nested interconnected systems. In view of the above-mentioned facts and also for the purposes of potential hardware (e.g., digital computers or digital circuits) realization and numerical algorithm development, it is necessary to develop and investigate the corresponding discrete-time algorithms instead of the above continuous-time models for discrete time-dependent problems.

It is known that the classical Euler forward formula is usually considered as the first and also the simplest one-step-ahead numerical-differentiation formula, which has been proposed in 1755 and widely applied for decades [25, 45, 161, 189, 288–290]. For convenience and also for consistency, the Euler forward formula is termed as one-step Zhang time discretization (1S-ZTD) formula in this chapter [291]. In [16, 45], on the basis of the 1S-ZTD formula, the corresponding one-step discrete-time ZNN (1S-DTZNN) algorithms were developed and investigated for the time-independent matrix inversion problem and time-dependent one, respectively. Besides, another one-step-ahead numerical-differentiation formula with higher precision than the 1S-ZTD one, termed as three-step ZTD (3S-ZTD) formula in this chapter [291], was recently developed in [72] to obtain an enhanced three-step DTZNN (3S-DTZNN) algorithm for the time-dependent matrix inversion with various kinds of bias noises suppressed. In [233], Guo *et al* further exploited the 3S-ZTD formula to develop a resultant 3S-DTZNN algorithm for time-dependent nonlinear minimization, where the maximal steady-state residual error (MSSRE) has an $\mathscr{O}(g^3)$ pattern, with g denoting the sampling gap. It is worth pointing out that almost all of the existing studies associated with the ZNN or GNN generally require that the coefficient matrices involved in the matrix inversion problems are nonsingular at any time instant, regardless of continuous-time models or discrete-time algorithms. However, since many problems are inherently time-dependent, i.e., their coefficient matrices vary with time, the stringent condition of nonsingularity may not be always satisfied. In other words, the coefficient matrices may sometimes become singular as time evolves. Consequently, this may restrict many possible applications of those models or algorithms. For example, when applied to the path-tracking control of a manipulator in some unknown environments, those models or algorithms may encounter an undesired problem that the Jacobi matrix becomes singular during time evolution, which may directly lead to the failure of the path-tracking task. Thus, it is imperative to find a simple and effective approach to cope with the knotty singularity problem. Moreover, in order to overcome the intrinsic precision limitation of existing discretization formulas, finding an effective discretization formula with higher precision is also imperative to meet the stricter requirement of precision.

This chapter [291] presents a five-step ZTD (5S-ZTD) formula with higher precision than the aforementioned ZTD formulas. Subsequently, two discrete-time neural network algorithms, i.e., a five-step DTZNN (5S-DTZNN) algorithm and a five-step discrete-time GNN (5S-DTGNN) algorithm, are developed, analyzed, and investigated for a problem of discrete time-dependent matrix inversion, which is actually an future matrix inversion (FMI) problem. Specifically, the FMI problem, which is to be solved at each computational time interval $[t_k, t_{k+1}) \subset [t_{\text{ini}}, t_{\text{fin}}] \subset [0, +\infty)$, is formulated as

$$A_{k+1}X_{k+1} = I_{n\times n}, \tag{10.2}$$

where A_{k+1} is supposed to be generated or measured from $A(t)$ by sampling at time instant $t = (k+1)g$ (denoted as t_{k+1}). Thereinto, $k = 0, 1, \cdots$ is the updating index. The reason why (10.2) is referred to as the FMI problem is explained as follows. In the solving process of (10.2), all computations have to be executed from present or previous data. For example, at time instant t_k, only the present and previous information, such as A_i for $i \leq k$, is known. The future unknown information, such as A_{k+1} and its derivatives, has not been sampled or computed yet, and cannot be used to compute the future unknown matrix X_{k+1} during the computational time interval $[t_k, t_{k+1})$. The objective of this study is to find the future unknown matrix X_{k+1} during $[t_k, t_{k+1})$ from present or previous data so that (10.2) holds true at the next discrete time instant (i.e., t_{k+1}).

10.2 CTZNN Model

To develop DTZNN algorithms for solving the FMI problem (10.2), a CTZNN model is presented in this section. By following the design method in [64, 281], the explicit CTZNN model for solving the CTDMI problem (10.1) is formulated as [16, 72]:

$$\dot{X}(t) = -X(t)\dot{A}(t)X(t) - \eta X(t)(A(t)X(t) - I_{n\times n}), \tag{10.3}$$

where the design parameter $\eta \in \mathbb{R}^+$ is used to scale the convergence rate of the CTZNN model (10.3), and $X(t)$ denotes a state matrix corresponding to the theoretical inverse $A^{-1}(t)$ of the CTDMI problem (10.1). Note that the explicit CTZNN model (10.3) is also the Getz–Marsden dynamic system for the CTDMI problem (10.1) (but with different origins) [16, 72, 73]. For the explicit CTZNN model (10.3), we have the following lemma on its exponential convergence performance for solving the CTDMI problem (10.1) [16, 73].

Lemma 9 *Suppose that the coefficient matrix $A(t)$ of the CTDMI problem (10.1) is always nonsingular and the state matrix $X(t)$ of the CTZNN model (10.3) starts from an initial state X_0, which is sufficiently close to A_0^{-1}. With the sufficiently large design parameter η, $X(t)$ exponentially converges to the theoretical inverse $A^{-1}(t)$.*

10.3 5S-ZTD Formula and 5S-DTZNN Algorithm

In this section, a 5S-ZTD formula is presented and investigated. On the basis of the 5S-ZTD formula, a 5S-DTZNN algorithm is developed and analyzed for solving the FMI problem (10.2). The 5S-ZTD formula is presented by the following theorem.

Theorem 40 *With the sufficient small sampling gap $g \in (0,1)$, let $\mathcal{O}(g^3)$ denote the error (especially, the truncation error) positively or negatively proportional to g^3, i.e., of the order of g^3. Suppose that $\zeta(t)$ is sufficiently smooth. With $\zeta_{k+1} = \zeta(t_{k+1}) = \zeta((k+1)g)$, the 5S-ZTD formula is formulated as follows:*

$$\dot{\zeta}_k = \frac{13}{24g}\zeta_{k+1} - \frac{1}{4g}\zeta_k - \frac{1}{12g}\zeta_{k-1} - \frac{1}{6g}\zeta_{k-2} - \frac{1}{8g}\zeta_{k-3} + \frac{1}{12g}\zeta_{k-4} + \mathcal{O}(g^3). \tag{10.4}$$

Proof. The proof is presented in Appendix L. □

By utilizing the 5S-ZTD formula (10.4) to discretize the CTZNN model (10.3), the following expression is obtained:

$$X_{k+1} \doteq \frac{6}{13}X_k + \frac{2}{13}X_{k-1} + \frac{4}{13}X_{k-2} + \frac{3}{13}X_{k-3} - \frac{2}{13}X_{k-4} - \frac{24}{13}gX_k\dot{A}_kX_k - \frac{24}{13}\hbar X_k(A_kX_k - I_{n\times n}), \tag{10.5}$$

where $\hbar = g\eta$ denotes the step length, and $\doteq$ denotes the computational assignment operator. Besides, the time-derivative term $\dot{A}_k$ in (10.5) can be approximated by using the backward numerical-differentiation formula with four data points [161], which is expressed as below:

$$\dot{\zeta}_k = \frac{11}{6g}\zeta_k - \frac{3}{g}\zeta_{k-1} + \frac{3}{2g}\zeta_{k-2} - \frac{1}{3g}\zeta_{k-3} + \mathcal{O}(g^3). \tag{10.6}$$

Thus, a 5S-DTZNN algorithm for solving the FMI problem (10.2) is obtained as

$$X_{k+1} \doteq \frac{6}{13}X_k + \frac{2}{13}X_{k-1} + \frac{4}{13}X_{k-2} + \frac{3}{13}X_{k-3} - \frac{2}{13}X_{k-4} - \frac{4}{13}X_k\tilde{A}_{1,k}X_k - \frac{24}{13}\hbar X_k(A_kX_k - I_{n\times n}), \tag{10.7}$$

where $\tilde{A}_{1,k} = 11A_k - 18A_{k-1} + 9A_{k-2} - 2A_{k-3}$.

Then, on the basis of the three definitions in Chapter 1, the following theoretical analyses on the 5S-DTZNN algorithm (10.7) for solving the FMI problem (10.2) are provided.

Theorem 41 *With the sufficiently small sampling gap $g \in (0,1)$, let $\mathbf{O}(g^4)$ denote the error (especially, the truncation error) with each element being $\mathcal{O}(g^4)$. Suppose that the coefficient matrix A_k is always nonsingular. The 5S-DTZNN algorithm (10.7) is zero-stable, consistent, and convergent, which converges with the order of truncation error being $\mathbf{O}(g^4)$.*

Proof. On the one hand, according to Definition 2 in Chapter 1, the characteristic polynomial of the 5S-DTZNN algorithm (10.7) is expressed as

$$\Gamma_5(\iota) = \iota^5 - \frac{6}{13}\iota^4 - \frac{2}{13}\iota^3 - \frac{4}{13}\iota^2 - \frac{3}{13}\iota + \frac{2}{13},$$

which has one simple root on the unit circle (i.e., $\iota_1 = 1$) and another four roots inside the unit circle (i.e., $\iota_2 = -0.1388+0.7476\text{i}$, $\iota_3 = -0.1388-0.7476\text{i}$, $\iota_4 = -0.6624$, and $\iota_5 = 0.4016$), with i denoting the imaginary unit. Thus, the 5S-DTZNN algorithm (10.7) is zero-stable.

On the other hand, with the combination of (10.3), (10.4), and (10.6), the following equation is obtained:

$$X_{k+1} = \frac{6}{13}X_k + \frac{2}{13}X_{k-1} + \frac{4}{13}X_{k-2} + \frac{3}{13}X_{k-3} - \frac{2}{13}X_{k-4} - \frac{4}{13}X_k\tilde{A}_{1,k}X_k - \frac{24}{13}\hbar X_k(A_kX_k - I_{n\times n}) + \mathbf{O}(g^4),$$

which implies that the truncation error of the 5S-DTZNN algorithm (10.7) is $\mathbf{O}(g^4)$. Following Definition 3 in Chapter 1, we know that the 5S-DTZNN algorithm (10.7) is consistent. In light of Definition 4 in Chapter 1, it is concluded that the 5S-DTZNN algorithm (10.7) is convergent, which converges with the order of truncation error being $\mathbf{O}(g^4)$. The proof is therefore completed. □

Note that the residual error is defined as $\hat{e}_{k+1} = \|A_{k+1}X_{k+1} - I_{n\times n}\|_{\text{F}}$ in this chapter [291], where $\|\cdot\|_{\text{F}}$ denotes the Frobenius norm of a matrix.

Theorem 42 *Suppose that the coefficient matrix A_k is always nonsingular and uniformly norm bounded by a positive constant c. With the sufficiently small sampling gap $g \in (0,1)$, the MSSRE* $\lim_{k\to\infty}\sup \hat{e}_{k+1}$ *synthesized by the 5S-DTZNN algorithm (10.7) is $\mathscr{O}(g^4)$.*

Proof. Let X^*_{k+1} be the theoretical inverse of the FMI problem (10.2), and we further have $A_{k+1}X^*_{k+1} = I_{n\times n}$. It follows from Theorem 41 that $X_{k+1} = X^*_{k+1} + \mathbf{O}(g^4)$ with the sufficiently large k. Thus, we have

$$\begin{aligned}
&\lim_{k\to\infty}\sup \|A_{k+1}X_{k+1} - I_{n\times n}\|_{\text{F}} \\
&= \lim_{k\to\infty}\sup \|A_{k+1}X^*_{k+1} - I_{n\times n} + A_{k+1}\mathbf{O}(g^4)\|_{\text{F}} \\
&= \lim_{k\to\infty}\sup \|A_{k+1}\mathbf{O}(g^4)\|_{\text{F}}.
\end{aligned}$$

As the sequence A_{k+1} is uniformly norm bounded by the positive constant c, we further have

$$\lim_{k\to\infty}\sup \|A_{k+1}\mathbf{O}(g^4)\|_{\text{F}} \leq \lim_{k\to\infty}\sup \|A_{k+1}\|_{\text{F}}\|\mathbf{O}(g^4)\|_{\text{F}} \leq c\|\mathbf{O}(g^4)\|_{\text{F}} = \mathscr{O}(g^4).$$

The proof is therefore completed. □

10.4 3S-DTZNN, 1S-DTZNN, and NI Algorithms

In this section, for comparison, three different algorithms are also presented for solving the FMI problem (10.2).

10.4.1 3S-ZTD formula and 3S-DTZNN algorithm

Lately, a 3S-ZTD formula was presented and studied in [233]. In mathematics, the 3S-ZTD formula is formulated as

$$\dot{\zeta}_k = \frac{3}{5g}\zeta_{k+1} - \frac{3}{10g}\zeta_k - \frac{1}{5g}\zeta_{k-1} - \frac{1}{10g}\zeta_{k-2} + \mathscr{O}(g^2). \tag{10.8}$$

By utilizing (10.8) to discretize the CTZNN model (10.3), the following expression is obtained:

$$X_{k+1} \doteq \frac{1}{2}X_k + \frac{1}{3}X_{k-1} + \frac{1}{6}X_{k-2} - \frac{5}{3}gX_k\dot{A}_kX_k - \frac{5}{3}\hbar X_k(A_kX_k - I_{n\times n}). \tag{10.9}$$

For matching with the precision of (10.8), the time-derivative term $\dot{A}_k$ in (10.9) is approximated by the backward numerical-differentiation formula with three data points [161], i.e., $\dot{\zeta}_k = (3\zeta_k - 4\zeta_{k-1} + \zeta_{k-2})/(2g) + \mathscr{O}(g^2)$. Thus, a 3S-DTZNN algorithm is derived as

$$X_{k+1} \doteq \frac{1}{2}X_k + \frac{1}{3}X_{k-1} + \frac{1}{6}X_{k-2} - \frac{5}{6}X_k\tilde{A}_{2,k}X_k - \frac{5}{3}\hbar X_k(A_kX_k - I_{n\times n}), \tag{10.10}$$

where $\tilde{A}_{2,k} = 3A_k - 4A_{k-1} + A_{k-2}$. Moreover, we have the following theoretical result on the 3S-DTZNN algorithm (10.10), and the corresponding proof can be generalized from [72] as well as Theorem 42.

Theorem 43 *Suppose that the coefficient matrix A_k is always nonsingular and uniformly norm bounded. With the sufficiently small sampling gap $g \in (0,1)$, the MSSRE $\lim_{k\to\infty}\sup\hat{e}_{k+1}$ synthesized by the 3S-DTZNN algorithm (10.10) is $\mathscr{O}(g^3)$.*

10.4.2 1S-ZTD formula and 1S-DTZNN algorithm

In mathematics, the 1S-ZTD formula (i.e., the classical Euler forward formula) [25, 45, 161, 189, 288–290] is formulated as $\dot{\zeta}_k = (\zeta_{k+1} - \zeta_k)/g + \mathscr{O}(g)$. By adopting the 1S-ZTD formula to discretize the CTZNN model (10.3), the following expression is obtained:

$$X_{k+1} \doteq X_k - gX_k\dot{A}_kX_k - \hbar X_k(A_kX_k - I_{n\times n}). \tag{10.11}$$

Similarly, the time-derivative term $\dot{A}_k$ in (10.11) can be approximated by the Euler backward formula [161], i.e., $\dot{\zeta}_k = (\zeta_k - \zeta_{k-1})/g + \mathscr{O}(g)$. Thus, a 1S-DTZNN algorithm is derived as

$$X_{k+1} \doteq X_k - X_k\tilde{A}_{3,k}X_k - \hbar X_k(A_kX_k - I_{n\times n}), \tag{10.12}$$

where $\tilde{A}_{3,k} = A_k - A_{k-1}$. In addition, we have the following theoretical result on the 1S-DTZNN algorithm (10.12), and the corresponding proof can be generalized from [22] as well as Theorem 42.

Theorem 44 *Suppose that the coefficient matrix A_k is always nonsingular and uniformly norm bounded. With the sufficiently small sampling gap $g \in (0,1)$, the MSSRE $\lim_{k\to\infty}\sup\hat{e}_{k+1}$ synthesized by the 1S-DTZNN algorithm (10.12) is $\mathscr{O}(g^2)$.*

10.4.3 NI algorithm

The Newton iteration (NI) method [6, 292] is generalized to solve the FMI problem (10.2). In mathematics, the corresponding NI algorithm is formulated as

$$X_{k+1} \doteq X_k - X_k(A_kX_k - I_{n\times n}). \tag{10.13}$$

Besides, generalized from [22], the following theoretical result on the NI algorithm (10.13) is obtained.

Proposition 5 *Suppose that the coefficient matrix A_k is always nonsingular and uniformly norm bounded. The MSSRE $\lim_{k\to\infty}\sup\hat{e}_{k+1}$ synthesized by the NI algorithm (10.13) is $\mathscr{O}(g)$.*

10.5 5S-DTGNN Algorithm

Differing from the ZNN designed especially for time-dependent problems, the conventional GNN is designed intrinsically for time-independent problems [249, 262, 278, 279]. Recently, the

GNN has been generalized to solve various time-dependent problems [65, 281–283, 293]. Specifically, the conventional CTGNN model [64, 65, 283] is directly presented for solving the CTDMI problem (10.1):

$$\dot{X}(t) = -\eta A^{\mathrm{T}}(t)(A(t)X(t) - I_{n\times n}), \tag{10.14}$$

where the superscript ^{T} denotes the transpose operator of a matrix and the design parameter $\eta \in \mathbb{R}^+$. As mentioned in [64, 65], the conventional CTGNN model (10.14) only approximately approaches the theoretical inverse with a relatively large solution error. In view of the above, by introducing a variable design parameter, the novel CTGNN model with an adaptive parameter [181] is designed as

$$\dot{X}(t) = -\eta(t)A^{\mathrm{T}}(t)(A(t)X(t) - I_{n\times n}), \tag{10.15}$$

where the time-dependent parameter $\eta(t) \in \mathbb{R}^+$. We further apply the 5S-ZTD formula (10.4) to discretize the CTGNN model (10.15), and then a 5S-DTGNN algorithm is obtained as follows:

$$X_{k+1} \doteq \frac{6}{13}X_k + \frac{2}{13}X_{k-1} + \frac{4}{13}X_{k-2} + \frac{3}{13}X_{k-3} - \frac{2}{13}X_{k-4} - \frac{24}{13}\hbar_k A_k^{\mathrm{T}}(A_k X_k - I_{n\times n}), \tag{10.16}$$

where $\hbar_k = g\eta_k \in \mathbb{R}^+$ denotes the step length for the 5S-DTGNN algorithm (10.16). For simplicity, we set $\hbar_k = 3/\left(5\mathrm{trace}(A_k^{\mathrm{T}}A_k)\right)$ in the 5S-DTGNN algorithm (10.16) [42, 294]. Then, generalized from Theorem 8 in [22], the following proposition is further provided.

Proposition 6 *Suppose that the coefficient matrix A_k is always nonsingular. With the sufficiently small sampling gap $g \in (0,1)$, the MSSRE $\lim_{k\to\infty}\sup \hat{e}_{k+1}$ synthesized by the 5S-DTGNN algorithm (10.16) is $\mathscr{O}(g)$.*

Moreover, as illustrated in the ensuing section, the 5S-DTGNN algorithm (10.16) is capable of coping with the singularity problem for solving the FMI problem (10.2) effectively and elegantly, compared with the three DTZNN algorithms and the NI algorithm. Thus, we have the following theoretical results on the 5S-DTGNN algorithm (10.16) under the condition that the coefficient matrix A_k of the FMI problem (10.2) is sometimes singular during time evolution.

Proposition 7 *Suppose that the coefficient matrix A_k is sometimes singular. With the sufficiently small sampling gap $g \in (0,1)$, the following two results on the 5S-DTGNN algorithm (10.16) are obtained.*

(1) When k lies in nonsingular time index intervals, the 5S-DTGNN algorithm (10.16) is stable and convergent, and its MSSRE $\lim_{k\to\infty}\sup \hat{e}_{k+1}$ is $\mathscr{O}(g)$.

(2) When k lies in singular time index interval(s), the 5S-DTGNN algorithm (10.16) is still stable, and its MSSRE $\lim_{k\to\infty}\sup \hat{e}_{k+1}$ is bounded.

Proof. Theoretically speaking, with the sufficiently small sampling gap $g \in (0,1)$, the 5S-DTGNN algorithm (10.16) is practically equivalent to the CTGNN model (10.15). Thus, the above two results can be proved from the perspective of the CTGNN model (10.15). For the first situation, it can be generalized from [65] by constructing a Lyapunov function candidate $v_1(t) = \|X(t) - X^*(t)\|_{\mathrm{F}}^2/2$. So can Proposition 6. For the second situation, it can be generalized from [265] by constructing another Lyapunov function candidate $v_2(t) = \|A(t)X(t) - I_{n\times n}\|_{\mathrm{F}}^2/2$. □

Remark 9 *As presented above, on the basis of the 5S-ZTD formula (10.4), the 3S-ZTD formula (10.8), and the 1S-ZTD formula (10.11), four discrete-time neural network algorithms are developed for solving the FMI problem (10.2). The computational complexity analyses of these four algorithms are provided as follows. Specifically, the 5S-DTZNN algorithm (10.7) needs to perform $4n^3 + 6n^2$ addition or subtraction operations and $4n^3 + 11n^2 + 1$ multiplication or division operations per updating; the 3S-DTZNN algorithm (10.10) needs to perform $4n^3 + 3n^2$ addition or* *subtraction operations and $4n^3+7n^2+1$ multiplication or division operations per updating; the 1S-DTZNN algorithm (10.12) needs to perform $4n^3$ addition or subtraction operations and $4n^3+n^2$ multiplication or division operations per updating; the 5S-DTGNN algorithm (10.16) needs to perform $2n^3+4n^2$ addition or subtraction operations and $2n^3+6n^2+1$ multiplication or division operations per updating. Evidently, these four algorithms have the same order of computational complexity, i.e., $\mathcal{O}(n^3)$, although the expressions of (10.7) and (10.16) are slightly more complicated. Besides, as a reflection, the average computing time per updating (ACTPU) data of these four algorithms are tested and provided in the ensuing numerical experiments to substantiate the above.*

For a more intuitive understanding of the main content of this chapter [291], Table 10.1 lists the problem, scheme, models, and algorithms.

10.6 Numerical Experiments

In this section, two illustrative numerical examples are provided to show the respective characteristics and advantages of the presented 5S-DTZNN algorithm (10.7) and the 5S-DTGNN algorithm (10.16) for solving the FMI problem (10.2).

Example 10.1 Let us consider the following FMI problem with X_{k+1} to be obtained at each computational time interval $[t_k, t_{k+1}) \subset [0, T]$ s:

$$A_{k+1}X_{k+1} = I_{3\times 3} \in \mathbb{R}^{3\times 3}, \tag{10.17}$$

with

$$A_k = \begin{bmatrix} -\sin(\pi t_k/5) & \cos(\pi t_k/5) & -\sin(\pi t_k/5) \\ \cos(\pi t_k/5) & \sin(\pi t_k/5) & \cos(\pi t_k/5) \\ \cos(\pi t_k/5) & \cos(\pi t_k/5) & \sigma(t_k) \end{bmatrix},$$

where $\sigma(t_k)$ determines the singularity of the coefficient matrix A_k. Next, we discuss these two situations.

TABLE 10.1: Problem, scheme, models, and algorithms in this chapter.

Problem	$A_{k+1}X_{k+1} = I_{n\times n}$.
Scheme	*Step 1*: Adopt ZTD formulas to discretize CTZNN model (10.3) and CTGNN model(10.15). *Step 2*: For DTZNN algorithms, adopt backward numerical-differentiation formulas to approximate $\dot{A}_k$.
Models	$\dot{X}(t) = -X(t)\dot{A}(t)X(t) - \eta X(t)(A(t)X(t) - I_{n\times n})$, $\dot{X}(t) = -\eta(t)A^{\mathrm{T}}(t)(A(t)X(t) - I_{n\times n})$.
Algorithms	$X_{k+1} \doteq \frac{6}{13}X_k + \frac{2}{13}X_{k-1} + \frac{4}{13}X_{k-2} + \frac{3}{13}X_{k-3} - \frac{2}{13}X_{k-4} - \frac{4}{13}X_k\tilde{A}_{1,k}X_k - \frac{24}{13}\hbar X_k(A_kX_k - I_{n\times n})$, $X_{k+1} \doteq \frac{1}{2}X_k + \frac{1}{3}X_{k-1} + \frac{1}{6}X_{k-2} - \frac{5}{6}X_k\tilde{A}_{2,k}X_k - \frac{5}{3}\hbar X_k(A_kX_k - I_{n\times n})$, $X_{k+1} \doteq X_k - X_k\tilde{A}_{3,k}X_k - \hbar X_k(A_kX_k - I_{n\times n})$, $X_{k+1} \doteq X_k - X_k(A_kX_k - I_{n\times n})$, $X_{k+1} \doteq \frac{6}{13}X_k + \frac{2}{13}X_{k-1} + \frac{4}{13}X_{k-2} + \frac{3}{13}X_{k-3} - \frac{2}{13}X_{k-4} - \frac{24}{13}\hbar_kA_k^{\mathrm{T}}(A_kX_k - I_{n\times n})$.

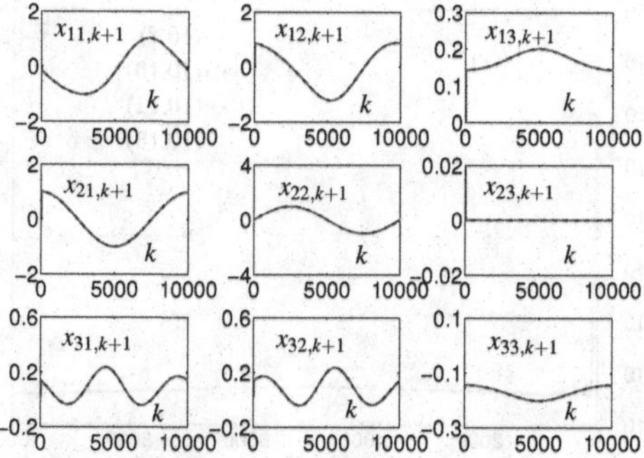

(a) Element trajectories of state matrix X_{k+1}

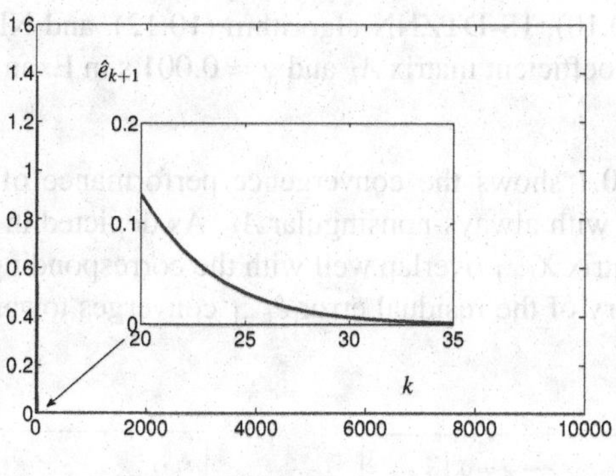

(b) Residual error

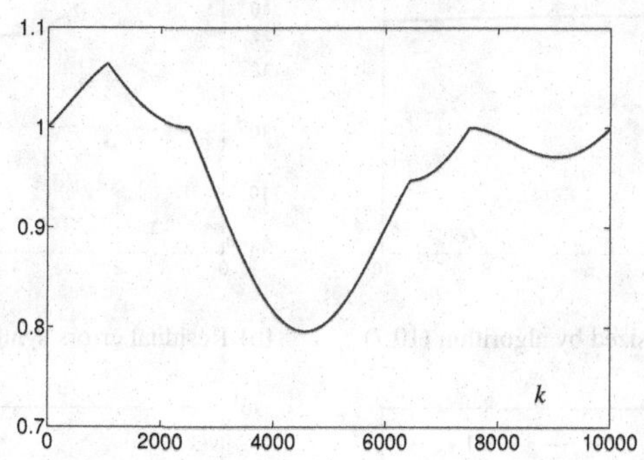

(c) Minimal absolute eigenvalue of A_k [291]

FIGURE 10.1: Convergence performance of 5S-DTZNN algorithm (10.7) for FMI with always-nonsingular coefficient matrix A_k and $g = 0.001$ s in Example 10.1. In panel (a), solid curves correspond to state matrix X_{k+1} of (10.7) and dash curves correspond to theoretical inverse X^*_{k+1}.

(a) A_k is always nonsingular: $\sigma(t_k) = -6$ in (10.17). For solving (10.17) with the always-nonsingular coefficient matrix A_k, the numerical experiments start with $X_0 = A_0/\text{trace}(A_0A_0^{\mathrm{T}})$, where A_0 is the initial state of the coefficient matrix A_k. Besides, we select the sampling gaps $g = 0.1, 0.01$, and 0.001 s, the task duration $T = 10$ s, and the step length $\hbar = 0.3$ for the three DTZNN algorithms as well as $\hbar_k = 3/\left(5\text{trace}(A_k^{\mathrm{T}}A_k)\right)$ for the 5S-DTGNN algorithm. The corresponding numerical experimental results are displayed in Figures 10.1–10.4.

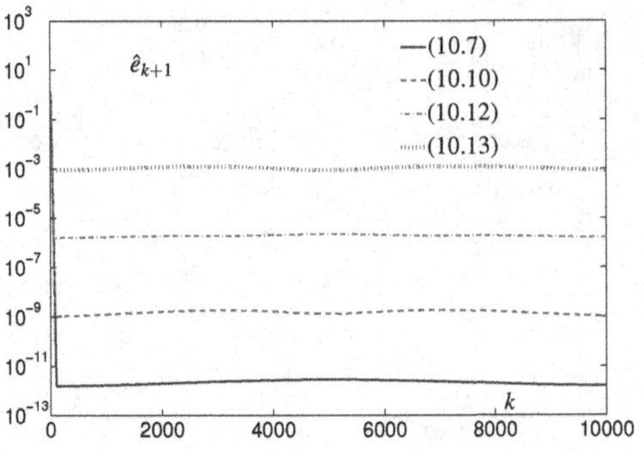

FIGURE 10.2: Trajectories of residual errors $\hat{e}_{k+1}$ synthesized by 5S-DTZNN algorithm (10.7), 3S-DTZNN algorithm (10.10), 1S-DTZNN algorithm (10.12), and NI algorithm (10.13) for FMI with always-nonsingular coefficient matrix A_k and $g = 0.001$ s in Example 10.1.

Specifically, Figure 10.1 shows the convergence performance of the 5S-DTZNN algorithm (10.7) for solving (10.17) with always-nonsingular A_k. As depicted in Figure 10.1(a), the element trajectories of the state matrix X_{k+1} overlap well with the corresponding elements of the theoretical inverse X^*_{k+1}. The trajectory of the residual error $\hat{e}_{k+1}$ converges toward zero rapidly, as shown in

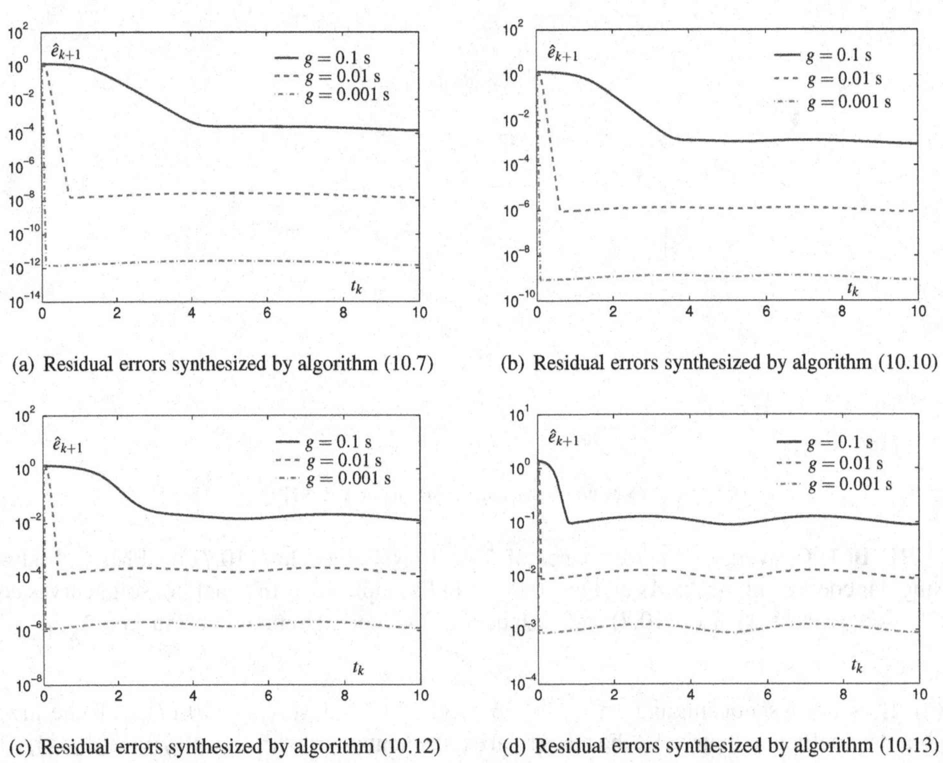

(a) Residual errors synthesized by algorithm (10.7)

(b) Residual errors synthesized by algorithm (10.10)

(c) Residual errors synthesized by algorithm (10.12)

(d) Residual errors synthesized by algorithm (10.13)

FIGURE 10.3: Trajectories of residual errors $\hat{e}_{k+1}$ synthesized by 5S-DTZNN algorithm (10.7), 3S-DTZNN algorithm (10.10), 1S-DTZNN algorithm (10.12), and NI algorithm (10.13) for FMI with always-nonsingular coefficient matrix A_k and different g values in Example 10.1.

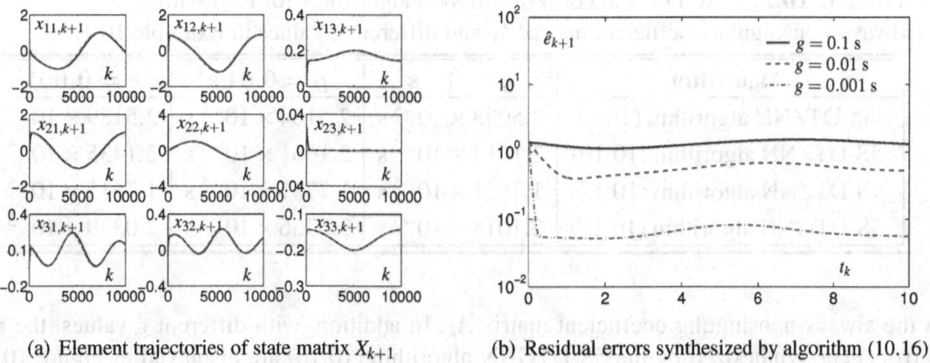

(a) Element trajectories of state matrix X_{k+1} (b) Residual errors synthesized by algorithm (10.16)

FIGURE 10.4: Convergence performance of 5S-DTGNN algorithm (10.16) for FMI with always-nonsingular coefficient matrix A_k in Example 10.1. In panel (a), solid curves correspond to state matrix X_{k+1} of (10.16) and dash curves correspond to theoretical inverse X^*_{k+1}.

Figure 10.1(b). From Figure 10.1(c), we know that the minimal absolute eigenvalue of A_k is always larger than zero, which means that the coefficient matrix A_k is nonsingular at any time instant $t_k \geq 0$. Note that the figures generated by the 3S-DTZNN algorithm (10.10), the 1S-DTZNN algorithm (10.12), and the NI algorithm (10.13) are similar to Figure 10.1(a)–(c) and are thus omitted here. Besides, the residual errors $\hat{e}_{k+1}$ synthesized by the three DTZNN algorithms and the NI algorithm with $g = 0.001$ s are displayed in Figure 10.2. As seen from this figure, the 5S-DTZNN algorithm (10.7) achieves the highest computational precision, followed by the 3S-DTZNN algorithm (10.10), the 1S-DTZNN algorithm (10.12), and finally the NI algorithm (10.13). Moreover, Figure 10.3 displays the residual errors $\hat{e}_{k+1}$ synthesized by the three DTZNN algorithms and the NI algorithm for solving (10.17) with always-nonsingular A_k and different g values, from which we observe the following facts that coincide with the presented theoretical results (i.e., Theorems 42 through 44 as well as Proposition 5).

(1) The MSSREs synthesized by the 5S-DTZNN algorithm (10.7) are of orders 10^{-4}, 10^{-8}, and 10^{-12} as the sampling gap changes from $g = 0.1$ to 0.01 and to 0.001 s, respectively; that is, the MSSRE synthesized by the 5S-DTZNN algorithm (10.7) changes in the pattern of $\mathcal{O}(g^4)$.

(2) The MSSREs synthesized by the 3S-DTZNN algorithm (10.10) are of orders 10^{-3}, 10^{-6}, and 10^{-9} as the sampling gap changes from $g = 0.1$ to 0.01, and to 0.001 s, respectively; that is, the MSSRE synthesized by the 3S-DTZNN algorithm (10.10) changes in the pattern of $\mathcal{O}(g^3)$.

(3) The MSSREs synthesized by the 1S-DTZNN algorithm (10.12) are of orders 10^{-2}, 10^{-4}, and 10^{-6} as the sampling gap changes from $g = 0.1$ to 0.01, and to 0.001 s, respectively; that is, the MSSRE synthesized by the 1S-DTZNN algorithm (10.12) changes in the pattern of $\mathcal{O}(g^2)$.

(4) The MSSREs synthesized by the NI algorithm (10.13) are of orders 10^{-1}, 10^{-2}, and 10^{-3} as the sampling gap changes from $g = 0.1$ to 0.01, and to 0.001 s, respectively; that is, the MSSRE synthesized by the NI algorithm (10.13) changes in the pattern of $\mathcal{O}(g)$.

The convergence performance of the 5S-DTGNN algorithm (10.16) for solving (10.17) with always-nonsingular A_k is displayed in Figure 10.4. As depicted in Figure 10.4(a), the element trajectories of the state matrix X_{k+1} approximately approach the corresponding elements of the theoretical inverse X^*_{k+1}. This means that the 5S-DTGNN algorithm (10.16) is also effective for solving (10.17)

TABLE 10.2: ACTPU data of four different algorithms for FMI with always-nonsingular coefficient matrix A_k and different g values in Example 10.1.

Algorithm	$g = 0.1$ s	$g = 0.01$ s	$g = 0.001$ s
5S-DTZNN algorithm (10.7)	2.5098×10^{-5} s	2.5164×10^{-5} s	2.5189×10^{-5} s
3S-DTZNN algorithm (10.10)	2.1614×10^{-5} s	2.1661×10^{-5} s	2.1435×10^{-5} s
1S-DTZNN algorithm (10.12)	1.7961×10^{-5} s	1.7731×10^{-5} s	1.7615×10^{-5} s
5S-DTGNN algorithm (10.16)	2.1018×10^{-5} s	2.0766×10^{-5} s	2.0339×10^{-5} s

with the always-nonsingular coefficient matrix A_k. In addition, with different g values, the residual errors $\hat{e}_{k+1}$ synthesized by the 5S-DTGNN algorithm (10.16) are displayed in Figure 10.4(b). As seen from this subfigure, the MSSREs synthesized by the 5S-DTGNN algorithm (10.16) are of orders 10^0, 10^{-1}, and 10^{-2} as the sampling gap changes from $g = 0.1$ to 0.01, and to 0.001 s, respectively; that is, the MSSRE synthesized by the 5S-DTGNN algorithm (10.16) changes in the pattern of $\mathscr{O}(g)$. This coincides well with the theoretical result presented in Proposition 6. Nevertheless, by further comparing with Figure 10.3, it is found that the order of the residual error $\hat{e}_{k+1}$ synthesized by the 5S-DTGNN algorithm (10.16) is larger than those of the residual errors $\hat{e}_{k+1}$ synthesized by the three DTZNN algorithms as well as the NI algorithm.

For further investigation and comparison, Table 10.2 shows the ACTPU data of the DTZNN algorithms and the DTGNN algorithm (i.e., the 5S-DTZNN algorithm (10.7), the 3S-DTZNN algorithm (10.10), the 1S-DTZNN algorithm (10.12), and the 5S-DTGNN algorithm (10.16)) with respect to different g values for solving (10.17) with always-nonsingular A_k. As seen from the table, the ACTPU data of the four different algorithms are all very small and have the same order of magnitude (i.e., 10^{-5} s), although these algorithms are discretized via three types of formulas (i.e., the 5S-ZTD formula (10.4), the 3S-ZTD formula (10.8), and the 1S-ZTD formula (10.11)). It means that the four different algorithms have similar computational complexities, which coincides well with the analyses presented in Remark 9. These ACTPU data are much smaller than the values of the corresponding sampling gap g, thereby indicating that all the four algorithms can effectively satisfy the requirement of real-time computation.

In summary, the above numerical experimental results indicate that the presented five algorithms are all effective for solving (10.17) with the always-nonsingular coefficient matrix A_k. Nevertheless, the 5S-DTZNN algorithm (10.7) possesses the highest computational precision among the presented five algorithms.

(b) A_k is sometimes singular: $\sigma(t_k) = -\cos(\pi t_k/5)$ in (10.17). In this situation, the coefficient matrix A_k becomes singular at time instants $t_s = (10j+5)/2$ with $j = 0, 1, 2, \cdots$. That is, the coefficient matrix A_k sometimes becomes singular as time evolves. In view of the task duration $T = 10$ s, there thus exist two singularity time instants during the whole computational process, i.e., $t_{s1} = 2.5$ s and $t_{s2} = 7.5$ s. For solving (10.17) with sometimes-singular A_k, the numerical experiments start with $X_0 = 12A_0/\text{trace}(A_0A_0^{\mathrm{T}})$. Note that other parameters are set to be the same as before. The corresponding numerical experimental results are shown in Figures 10.5 and 10.6.

Specifically, Figure 10.5 shows the convergence performance of the 5S-DTZNN algorithm (10.7) for solving (10.17) with the sometimes-singular coefficient matrix A_k. As illustrated in Figure 10.5(a), the element trajectories of the state matrix X_{k+1} cannot converge to the corresponding elements of the theoretical inverse X_{k+1}^* as time evolves, and their amplitudes tend to infinity. Indeed, just as displayed in Figure 10.5(b), the minimal absolute eigenvalue of A_k becomes zero at the above-mentioned two singularity time instants t_{s1} and t_{s2}. In other words, the coefficient matrix A_k becomes singular at the two singularity time instants. Besides, Figure 10.5(c) intuitively shows that the residual error $\hat{e}_{k+1}$ synthesized by the 5S-DTZNN algorithm (10.7) tends to infinity around the first singularity time instant t_{s1}. It should be noted that the figures generated by the 3S-DTZNN algorithm (10.10), the 1S-DTZNN algorithm (10.12), and the NI algorithm (10.13) are similar to

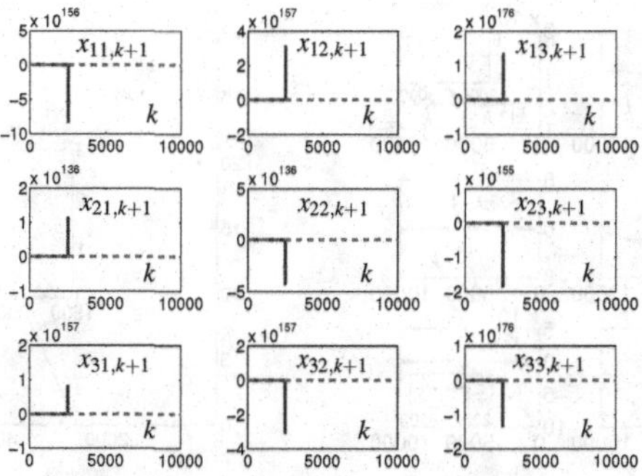

(a) Element trajectories of state matrix X_{k+1}

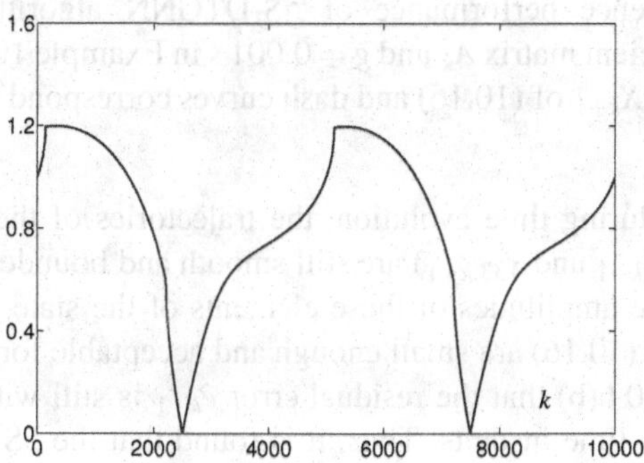

(b) Minimal absolute eigenvalue of A_k [291]

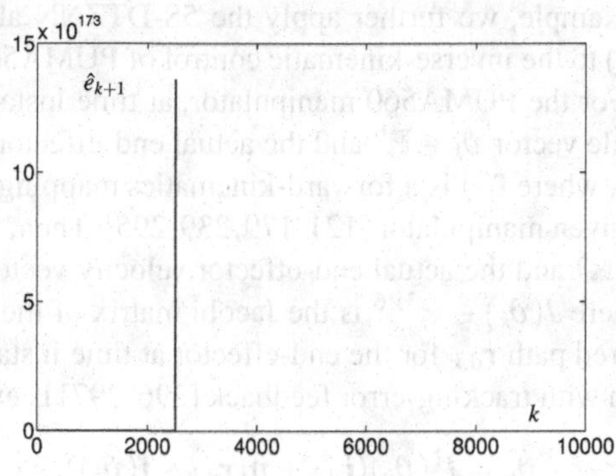

(c) Residual error [291]

FIGURE 10.5: Convergence performance of 5S-DTZNN algorithm (10.7) for FMI with sometimes-singular coefficient matrix A_k and $g = 0.001$ s in Example 10.1. In panel (a), solid curves correspond to state matrix X_{k+1} of (10.7) and dash curves correspond to theoretical inverse X^*_{k+1}.

Figure 10.5, and are thus omitted here. Thus, it is found that the three DTZNN algorithms as well as the NI algorithm are not effective for solving (10.17) with sometimes-singular A_k.

For comparison, Figure 10.6 illustrates the convergence performance of the 5S-DTGNN algorithm (10.16) for solving (10.17) with sometimes-singular A_k. As seen from Figure 10.6(a), seven element trajectories of the state matrix X_{k+1} rapidly converge to the corresponding seven-elements of the theoretical inverse X^*_{k+1} as time evolves. More importantly, although there exist the two

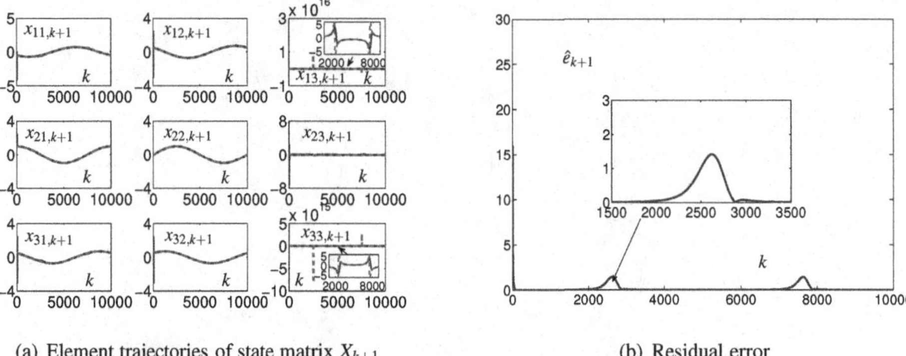

(a) Element trajectories of state matrix X_{k+1}

(b) Residual error

FIGURE 10.6: Convergence performance of 5S-DTGNN algorithm (10.16) for FMI with sometimes-singular coefficient matrix A_k and $g = 0.001$ s in Example 10.1. In panel (a), solid curves correspond to state matrix X_{k+1} of (10.16) and dash curves correspond to theoretical inverse X^*_{k+1}.

singularity time instants during time evolution, the trajectories of the two other elements of the state matrix X_{k+1} (i.e., $x_{13,k+1}$ and $x_{33,k+1}$) are still smooth and bounded within a very small range, i.e., $(-5,5)$. Evidently, the amplitudes of these elements of the state matrix X_{k+1} synthesized by the 5S-DTGNN algorithm (10.16) are small enough and acceptable for engineering applications. It is observed from Figure 10.6(b) that the residual error $\hat{e}_{k+1}$ is still within a relatively small value around the two singularity time instants. Thus, it is found that the 5S-DTGNN algorithm (10.16) is capable of coping with the singularity problem for solving (10.17) effectively and elegantly in comparison with the three DTZNN algorithms and the NI algorithm.

Example 10.2 In this example, we further apply the 5S-DTZNN algorithm (10.7) and the 5S-DTGNN algorithm (10.16) to the inverse-kinematic control of PUMA560 manipulator by means of the FMI problem (10.2). For the PUMA560 manipulator, at time instant $t_k \in [0,T]$ s, the relationship between the joint-angle vector $\vartheta_k \in \mathbb{R}^6$ and the actual end-effector position vector $\mathbf{r}_{\mathrm{a},k} \in \mathbb{R}^3$ is formulated as $\mathbf{f}(\vartheta_k) = \mathbf{r}_{\mathrm{a},k}$, where $\mathbf{f}(\cdot)$ is a forward-kinematics mapping function with known structure and parameters for a given manipulator [121, 179, 239, 295]. Then, the relationship between the joint-velocity vector $\dot{\vartheta}_k \in \mathbb{R}^6$ and the actual end-effector velocity vector $\dot{\mathbf{r}}_{\mathrm{a},k} \in \mathbb{R}^3$ is formulated as $J(\vartheta_k)\dot{\vartheta}_k = \dot{\mathbf{r}}_{\mathrm{a},k} \to \dot{\mathbf{r}}_{\mathrm{d},k}$, where $J(\vartheta_k) \in \mathbb{R}^{3\times 6}$ is the Jacobi matrix of the manipulator, and $\dot{\mathbf{r}}_{\mathrm{d},k}$ is the time derivative of the desired path $\mathbf{r}_{\mathrm{d},k}$ for the end-effector at time instant t_k. Thus, the manipulator inverse-kinematic problem with tracking-error feedback [296, 297] is expressed as

$$\dot{\vartheta}_k = J^{\dagger}(\vartheta_k)(\dot{\mathbf{r}}_{\mathrm{d},k} + \eta(\mathbf{r}_{\mathrm{d},k} - \mathbf{f}(\vartheta_k))).$$

Provided that $J(\vartheta_k)$ is of full row rank at time instant t_k, its pseudoinverse is expressed as $J^{\dagger}(\vartheta_k) = J^{\mathrm{T}}(\vartheta_k)(J(\vartheta_k)J^{\mathrm{T}}(\vartheta_k))^{-1} \in \mathbb{R}^{6\times 3}$. In order to expedite the computational process and achieve better solution precision, by defining $A_k = J(\vartheta_k)J^{\mathrm{T}}(\vartheta_k)$, the 5S-DTZNN algorithm (10.7) or the 5S-DTGNN algorithm (10.16) can be utilized to solve for $J^{\dagger}(\vartheta_{k+1})$. Specifically, $J^{\dagger}(\vartheta_{k+1}) = J^{\mathrm{T}}(\vartheta_{k+1})X_{k+1}$, where X_{k+1} is the state matrix to be computed by (10.7) or (10.16) at each computational time interval $[t_k, t_{k+1}) \subset [0,T]$ s. In this application example, the PUMA560 manipulator is expected to track a Rhodonea (also termed as four-leaf clover) path, operating with the task duration $T = 10$ s. In addition, we select the sampling gap $g = 0.001$ s and the step length $\hbar = 0.3$ in (10.7) as well as $\hbar_k = 3/\left(5\mathrm{trace}(A_k^{\mathrm{T}}A_k)\right)$ in (10.16). In what follows, we discuss two situations of the initial joint-angle vector ϑ_0 for the inverse-kinematic problem of the PUMA560 manipulator.

(i) $J(\vartheta_k)J^{\mathrm{T}}(\vartheta_k)$ is always nonsingular. Let the initial joint-angle vector $\vartheta_0 = [0, -\pi/4, 0, 2\pi/3, -\pi/4, 0]^{\mathrm{T}}$ rad. The corresponding numerical experimental results are displayed in Figure 10.7. Specifically, the manipulator trajectories generated by the 5S-DTZNN algorithm (10.7) are shown in Figure 10.7(a). It is seen from Figure 10.7(b) that the end-effector actual trajectory generated

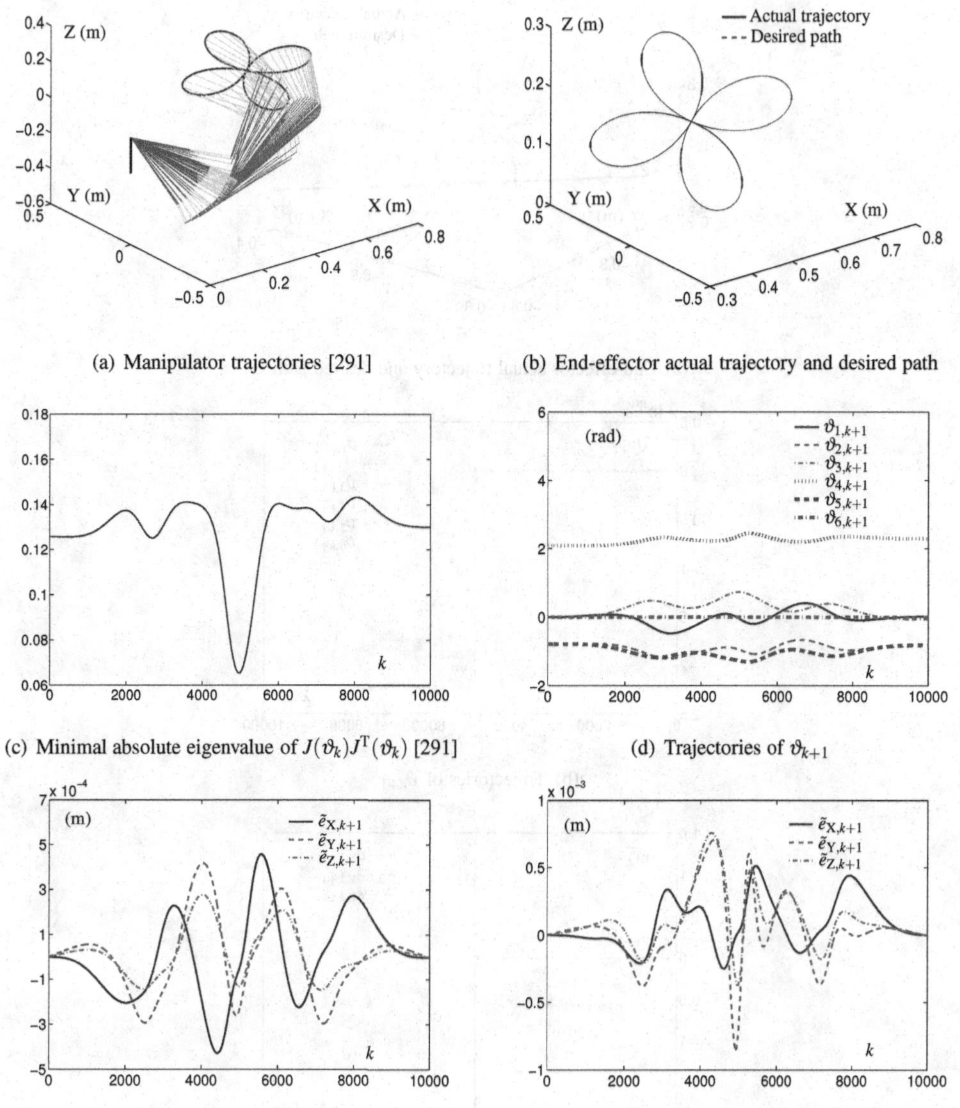

(a) Manipulator trajectories [291]

(b) End-effector actual trajectory and desired path

(c) Minimal absolute eigenvalue of $J(\vartheta_k)J^{\mathrm{T}}(\vartheta_k)$ [291]

(d) Trajectories of ϑ_{k+1}

(e) X-axis, Y-axis, and Z-axis tracking errors synthesized by (10.7)

(f) X-axis, Y-axis, and Z-axis tracking errors synthesized by (10.16)

FIGURE 10.7: Motion generation of PUMA560 manipulator synthesized by 5S-DTZNN algorithm (10.7) and 5S-DTGNN algorithm (10.16) with always-nonsingular $J(\vartheta_k)J^{\mathrm{T}}(\vartheta_k)$ and its end-effector tracking Rhodonea path in Example 10.2.

by the 5S-DTZNN algorithm (10.7) completely overlaps with the desired path, thereby implying that the Rhodonea-path tracking task is fulfilled successfully. From Figure 10.7(c), we know that the minimal absolute eigenvalue of $J(\vartheta_k)J^{\mathrm{T}}(\vartheta_k)$ is larger than zero at any time instant $t_k \geq 0$. In other words, $J(\vartheta_k)J^{\mathrm{T}}(\vartheta_k)$ is always nonsingular and the Jacobi matrix $J(\vartheta_k)$ is of full row rank during the whole task execution. Besides, as seen from Figure 10.7(d), the trajectories of the joint-angle vector ϑ_{k+1} generated by the 5S-DTZNN algorithm (10.7) are very smooth. Note that the figures generated by the 5S-DTGNN algorithm (10.16) are similar to Figure 10.7(a)–(d) and are

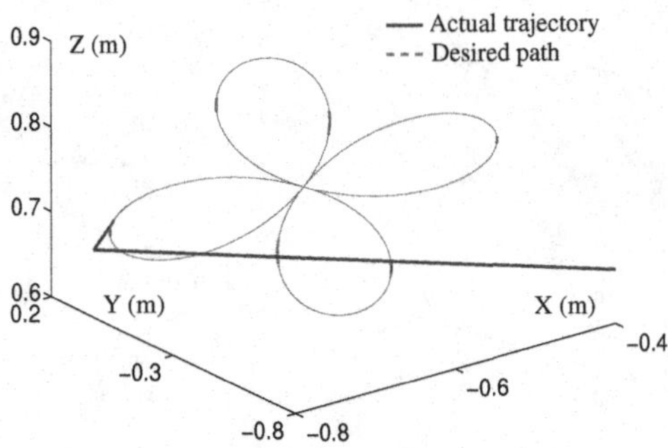

(a) End-effector actual trajectory and desired path

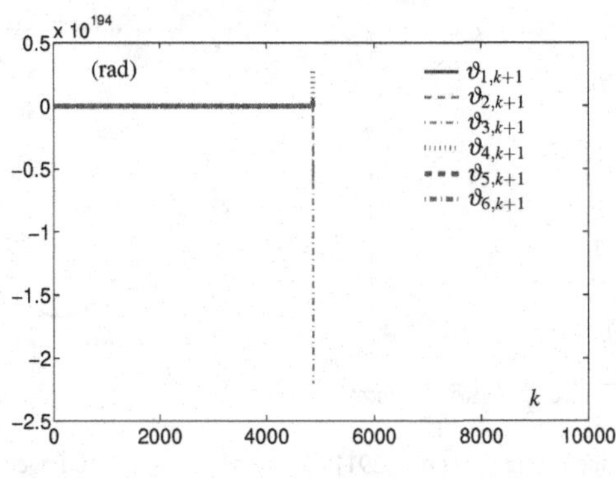

(b) Trajectories of ϑ_{k+1}

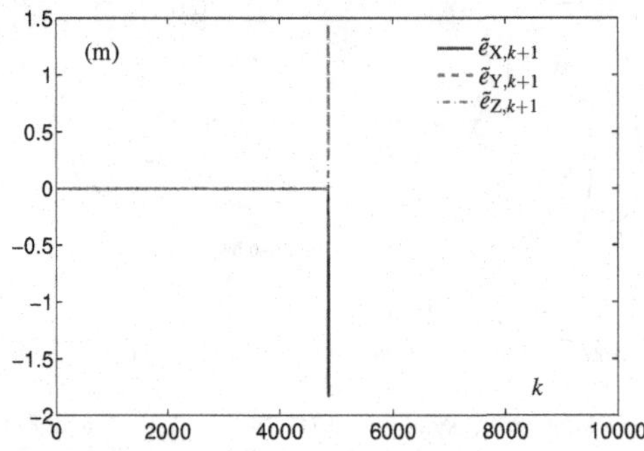

(c) X-axis, Y-axis, and Z-axis tracking errors synthesized by (10.7)

FIGURE 10.8: Motion generation of PUMA560 manipulator synthesized by 5S-DTZNN algorithm (10.7) with sometimes-singular $J(\vartheta_k)J^{\mathrm{T}}(\vartheta_k)$ and its end-effector tracking Rhodonea path in Example 10.2.

thus omitted here. In addition, the X-axis, Y-axis, and Z-axis tracking errors (i.e., $\tilde{e}_{\mathrm{X},k+1}$, $\tilde{e}_{\mathrm{Y},k+1}$, and $\tilde{e}_{\mathrm{Z},k+1}$) synthesized by the 5S-DTZNN algorithm (10.7) and the 5S-DTGNN algorithm (10.16) are shown in Figure 10.7(e) and (f). As seen from Figure 10.7(e) and (f), the maximal component of the tracking-error $\tilde{\mathbf{e}}_{k+1} = [\tilde{e}_{\mathrm{X},k+1}, \tilde{e}_{\mathrm{Y},k+1}, \tilde{e}_{\mathrm{Z},k+1}]^{\mathrm{T}}$ synthesized by the 5S-DTZNN algorithm (10.7) is about 4.5×10^{-4} m, which is nearly two times smaller than that synthesized by the 5S-DTGNN

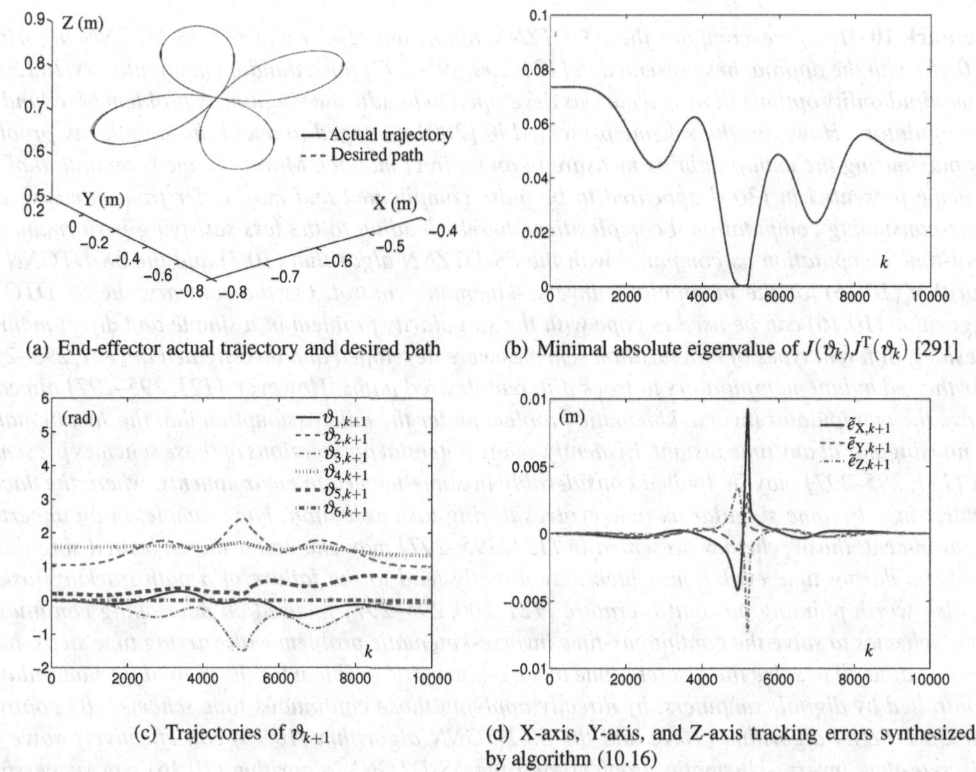

(a) End-effector actual trajectory and desired path

(b) Minimal absolute eigenvalue of $J(\vartheta_k)J^{\mathrm{T}}(\vartheta_k)$ [291]

(c) Trajectories of ϑ_{k+1}

(d) X-axis, Y-axis, and Z-axis tracking errors synthesized by algorithm (10.16)

FIGURE 10.9: Motion generation of PUMA560 manipulator synthesized by 5S-DTGNN algorithm (10.16) with sometimes-singular $J(\vartheta_k)J^{\mathrm{T}}(\vartheta_k)$ and its end-effector tracking Rhodonea path in Example 10.2.

algorithm (10.16). Therefore, the above numerical experimental results illustrate well the superiority of the 5S-DTZNN algorithm (10.7) to the 5S-DTGNN algorithm (10.16) for solving the FMI problem with a always-nonsingular coefficient matrix as well as the inverse-kinematic problem of the PUMA560 manipulator.

(ii) $J(\vartheta_k)J^{\mathrm{T}}(\vartheta_k)$ is sometimes singular. Let the initial joint-angle vector $\vartheta_0 = [0, \pi/3, 0, \pi/2, \pi/16, 0]^{\mathrm{T}}$ rad. The corresponding numerical experimental results synthesized by the 5S-DTZNN algorithm (10.7) and the 5S-DTGNN algorithm (10.16) are illustrated in Figures 10.8 and 10.9, respectively. As displayed in Figure 10.8, the Rhodonea-path tracking task equipped with the 5S-DTZNN algorithm (10.7) is interrupted around the singularity time instant $t_s \approx 5.052$ s when $J(\vartheta_k)J^{\mathrm{T}}(\vartheta_k)$ becomes singular, which is verified from Figure 10.9(b). Evidently, the 5S-DTZNN algorithm (10.7) is less applicable for solving the FMI problem with a sometimes-singular coefficient matrix as well as the inverse-kinematic control of the PUMA560 manipulator with the singularity problem. In contrast, the Rhodonea-path tracking task equipped with the 5S-DTGNN algorithm (10.16) runs uninterruptedly, which is clearly illustrated in Figure 10.9(a). Besides, as seen from Figure 10.9(c) and (d), the joint-angle trajectories are very smooth and the end-effector tracking errors are small enough (i.e., of orders 10^{-3} m), which means that the Rhodonea-path tracking task is fulfilled well by means of the 5S-DTGNN algorithm (10.16). Evidently, from Figures 10.8 and 10.9, it is found that the 5S-DTGNN algorithm (10.16) is capable of coping with the singularity problem encountered in the path-tracking control of the PUMA560 manipulator effectively and elegantly. Therefore, the advantage of the 5S-DTGNN algorithm (10.16) over the 5S-DTZNN algorithm (10.7) in handling the singularity problem is substantiated once again.

Remark 10 *Here, we compare the 5S-DTZNN algorithm (10.7) and the 5S-DTGNN algorithm (10.16) with the approaches presented in [121, 200, 295–297] for redundant manipulators. In [200], a manipulability optimization scheme was developed to handle the singularity problem of redundant manipulators. However, the scheme presented in [200] managed to avoid the singularity problem by maximizing the manipulability measure in an indirect manner. Moreover, the formulation of the scheme presented in [200] appeared to be quite complicated and may suffer from intensive and time-consuming computational complexities, thereby leading to the less satisfying performance of real-time computation as compared with the 5S-DTZNN algorithm (10.7) and the 5S-DTGNN algorithm (10.16) for the manipulator inverse-kinematic control. On the contrary, the 5S-DTGNN algorithm (10.16) can be used to cope with the singularity problem in a simple and direct manner. Besides, different types of optimization schemes were developed and investigated in [121, 295–297] for the redundant manipulators to track different desired paths. However, [121, 295–297] aimed to solve the manipulator inverse-kinematic problem under the mild assumption that the Jacobi matrix is nonsingular at any time instant. Evidently, many potential applications of those schemes presented in [121, 295–297] may be limited considerably in some uncertain environments, where the Jacobi matrix may become singular as time evolves during task execution. For example, in an uncertain environment, those schemes presented in [121, 295–297] may encounter the undesired singularity problem during time evolution, which may directly lead to the failure of a path-tracking task. It is also worth pointing out that literature [121, 200, 295–297] focused on developing continuous-time schemes to solve the continuous-time inverse-kinematic problem with varying time steps, but it may be difficult to solve the discrete-time inverse-kinematic problem for the redundant manipulators controlled by digital computers, by directly applying those continuous-time schemes. By contrast, the 5S-DTZNN algorithm (10.7) and the 5S-DTGNN algorithm (10.16) can effectively solve the discrete-time inverse-kinematic problem, and the 5S-DTGNN algorithm (10.16) can successfully cope with the singularity problem encountered in the path-tracking control of redundant manipulators in a simple, direct, and effective manner.*

10.7 Chapter Summary

This chapter has presented the 5S-ZTD formula (10.4) to approximate the first-order derivative and discretize the continuous-time neural network models with high precision. Subsequently, two discrete-time neural network algorithms, i.e., the 5S-DTZNN algorithm (10.7) and the 5S-DTGNN algorithm (10.16), have been developed and studied for solving the FMI problem (10.2). For comparison, the 3S-DTZNN algorithm (10.10), the 1S-DTZNN algorithm (10.12), and the NI algorithm (10.13) have also been developed and investigated. At last, two illustrative numerical experiments, including an application to the inverse-kinematic control of the PUMA560 manipulator, have shown the respective characteristics and advantages of the 5S-DTZNN algorithm (10.7) and the 5S-DTGNN algorithm (10.16) for solving the FMI problem (10.2) in different situations. The design methodologies of the 5S-DTZNN algorithm (10.7) and the 5S-DTGNN algorithm (10.16) displayed in this chapter can also be used and generalized to solve other discrete time-dependent (mathematical and engineering) problems by using different 5S-ZTD formulas, with their practical applications to various manipulators, especially those involving the singularity problem. Besides, the DTZNN algorithms and the DTGNN algorithms could be finally implemented on digital circuits (e.g., very large-scale integration) by researchers and engineers for solving the FMI problem

(10.2) efficiently and accurately, with the advantages of neural network (e.g., high-speed parallel-distributed processing).

Appendix L: Proof of Theorem 40

According to Taylor expansion [161], the following five equations are obtained:

$$\zeta_{k+1} = \zeta_k + g\dot{\zeta}_k + \frac{g^2}{2}\ddot{\zeta}_k + \frac{g^3}{6}\dddot{\zeta}_k + \mathscr{O}(g^4), \tag{10.18}$$

$$\zeta_{k-1} = \zeta_k - g\dot{\zeta}_k + \frac{g^2}{2}\ddot{\zeta}_k - \frac{g^3}{6}\dddot{\zeta}_k + \mathscr{O}(g^4), \tag{10.19}$$

$$\zeta_{k-2} = \zeta_k - 2g\dot{\zeta}_k + 2g^2\ddot{\zeta}_k - \frac{4g^3}{3}\dddot{\zeta}_k + \mathscr{O}(g^4), \tag{10.20}$$

$$\zeta_{k-3} = \zeta_k - 3g\dot{\zeta}_k + \frac{9g^2}{2}\ddot{\zeta}_k - \frac{9g^3}{2}\dddot{\zeta}_k + \mathscr{O}(g^4), \tag{10.21}$$

and

$$\zeta_{k-4} = \zeta_k - 4g\dot{\zeta}_k + 8g^2\ddot{\zeta}_k - \frac{32g^3}{3}\dddot{\zeta}_k + \mathscr{O}(g^4), \tag{10.22}$$

where $\ddot{\zeta}_k$ and $\dddot{\zeta}_k$ represent the second-order and third-order time derivatives of $\zeta(t)$ at time instant t_k, respectively. Let (10.18) multiply 13, let (10.19) multiply -2, let (10.20) multiply -4, let (10.21) multiply -3, and let (10.22) multiply 2. Adding them together, we finally obtain

$$\dot{\zeta}_k = \frac{13}{24g}\zeta_{k+1} - \frac{1}{4g}\zeta_k - \frac{1}{12g}\zeta_{k-1} - \frac{1}{6g}\zeta_{k-2} - \frac{1}{8g}\zeta_{k-3} + \frac{1}{12g}\zeta_{k-4} + \mathscr{O}(g^3),$$

which is just the 5S-ZTD formula (10.4). The proof is therefore completed. □

Part V

$\mathscr{O}(g^4)$ ZTD Formulas and Applications

Chapter 11

Repetitive Motion Control of Redundant Manipulators

Abstract

In this chapter, the repetitive motion control of redundant manipulators is investigated. First, a repetitive motion control problem is presented, and a continuous-time zeroing neural network (CTZNN) model is obtained for solving the problem. Meanwhile, the development of a discrete-time zeroing neural network (DTZNN) algorithm is desired for convenient computational processing. On the basis of this, this chapter presents a six-step Zhang time discretization (6S-ZTD) formula, which has high precision. By using the 6S-ZTD formula and the four-step backward numerical-differentiation formula, a six-step DTZNN (6S-DTZNN) algorithm is further developed to handle the repetitive motion control problem. Theoretical analyses verify the efficacy of the 6S-DTZNN algorithm. Additionally, some discrete-time forms of conventional models are developed for comparison. Numerical experiments based on a four-link redundant manipulator are carried out, verifying the theoretical results and showing the efficacy of the 6S-DTZNN algorithm. Finally, physical experiments based on a Kinova Jaco^2 manipulator substantiate the practicability of the 6S-DTZNN algorithm.

11.1 Introduction

In recent years, robots have played more and more significant roles in production and daily life [298–300]. On more and more occasions, robots take the place of humans, because robots do not get tired and have high efficiency. Hence, robot control has attracted much attention from researchers and engineers in various fields, and many methods have been presented and developed [301–304]. As a type of robot, the redundant manipulator is popular in industrial applications, which has been studied by numerous researchers [225, 305, 306]. For a given tracking task, there exist a number of control algorithms for the redundant manipulator because of the redundant feature, and the algorithms have their advantages as well as disadvantages. For example, the pseudoinverse-based minimal velocity scheme is a conventional approach, which has been widely adopted in industrial production [306], but it does not consider the repetitive motion.

In view of practical needs of the industry and engineering, the repetitive motion control of redundant manipulators becomes more and more important [27, 307–309]. In practical industry and engineering, the redundant manipulator is usually controlled to complete the repetitive tasks. Hence, the repetitive motion control of redundant manipulators becomes efficient and necessary. The non-repetitive motion is also called joint angle drift motion or phenomenon [310], which is less efficient in practical control. For example, on an assembly line of the machine shop, many redundant manipulators cooperate to accomplish a whole task. Each redundant manipulator is usually desired to

DOI: 10.1201/9781003497783-11

complete the same subtask (or simply saying, task) one cycle after one cycle, such as paint spraying and soldering. Under the circumstances, the repetitive motion control of redundant manipulators is necessary. The repetitive motion means the configuration of the manipulator when it accomplishes the task is equal to the configuration of the manipulator when it starts the task. In this case, the redundant manipulator just needs to start the next task rather than adjust the configuration first, which is especially meaningful. In recent years, many researchers have devoted themselves to the repetitive motion control of redundant manipulators. In [27], some fundamental principles of the repetitive motion design were introduced. In [311], some orthonormal basis functions were developed to describe the null space of the corresponding transformations. The optimal repeatable inverse strategy is thus obtained by projecting the null space onto each of these basis functions. In [312], a repeatable extended Jacobian inverse kinematics algorithm for mobile manipulators was developed based on a geometric characterization of repeatability. However, these results are relatively complicated and may not be effective enough for high-precision tracking control.

Neural networks [98, 102, 239, 313–317] play prominent roles in mathematics and computer science, which also show the abilities for the motion control of redundant manipulators. For example, in [318], the asymptotic tracking of hydraulic systems was achieved by using multilayer neural networks. Many recurrent neural network (RNN) models with good performance have been utilized for the motion control problem [179, 199, 319]. For example, three RNN models for the repetitive motion of redundant manipulators were developed in [199]. Li *et al* developed a game-theoretic RNN model for cooperative control [179]. Being a class of RNNs, zeroing neural network (ZNN) shows its abilities, especially for solving time-dependent problems [174, 320–323]. Note that the error function (also termed as zeroing function, ZF) of the ZNN can be scalar-, vector-, or matrix-valued, and the time-derivative feedback is used. Meanwhile, ZNN is useful in some specific fields, such as redundant manipulators [121, 182, 295, 324] and chaotic systems [325]. For instance, a ZNN model was developed by Jin *et al* to realize the cooperative control of manipulators in [182], and the same motion is reached by all manipulators. For mobile redundant manipulators, the repetitive motion control was realized with the help of ZNN in [324]. Note that these models are all established in continuous-time forms essentially, which are not ready for digital computer processing.

In practice, the redundant manipulator is usually controlled by a computer (also including the chip seeable as a minicomputer). As known, the computer can only process digital signals. Hence, continuous-time models cannot be directly applied to the tracking control of redundant manipulators, which should be discretized first. On the other hand, discrete-time algorithms are convenient for computer processing and program writing. Besides, the solution can be computed in advance by the discrete-time algorithm, and real-time control could be realized. When the redundant manipulator is supposed to complete a task, high precision is commonly required with the development of industry and society [130, 306, 326]. However, many conventional methods implemented in discrete-time forms cannot realize high precision because of the one-step delay [130]. In general, the precision of these methods in discrete-time forms is $\mathcal{O}(g)$, in which g denotes the sampling gap. Evidently, the precision $\mathcal{O}(g)$ is relatively low, which is incongruent with the modern industrial requirements. Therefore, a discrete-time algorithm with high precision is desired to be developed in this chapter [327].

Recently, in the field of redundant manipulators, the discrete-time ZNN (DTZNN) algorithms have not been investigated in depth. In [306], Guo *et al* developed a DTZNN algorithm for solving the pseudoinverse-based minimal velocity scheme. In [130], Li *et al* developed two DTZNN algorithms to control two kinds of redundant manipulators. However, high-precision DTZNN algorithms have not been built and studied to realize the repetitive motion control of redundant manipulators. Note that a discretization formula is necessary for developing a discrete-time algorithm. By this time, the Zhang time discretization (ZTD) formula group has been developed and supplemented for obtaining high-precision discrete-time algorithms.

Inspired by the previous work [27], a repetitive motion control problem is presented, and a continuous-time ZNN (CTZNN) model is developed to solve the problem. Further, inspired by the previous works [130, 306, 326], by applying the Taylor expansion and stability theory, an effective six-step ZTD (6S-ZTD) formula is developed in this chapter [327], which supplements the ZTD formula group. Then, a six-step DTZNN (6S-DTZNN) algorithm is established for the repetitive motion control of redundant manipulators, which is concise and effective.

11.2 Repetitive Motion Control Problem and CTZNN Model

For the redundant manipulator, the kinematic equation is depicted as $\mathbf{f}(\vartheta(t)) = \mathbf{r}_\mathrm{a}(t)$. Thereinto, $\mathbf{f}(\cdot) : \mathbb{R}^n \rightarrow \mathbb{R}^m$ is a forward-kinematics mapping function with known structure and parameters; $\vartheta(t) \in \mathbb{R}^n$ is the joint-angle vector; $\mathbf{r}_\mathrm{a}(t) \in \mathbb{R}^m$ is the actual end-effector position vector [27]. Additionally, the Jacobian matrix $\partial\mathbf{f}(\vartheta(t))/\partial\vartheta(t) \in \mathbb{R}^{m\times n}$, which is denoted as $J(\vartheta(t))$, is especially meaningful.

To track a desired path $\mathbf{r}_\mathrm{d}(t) \in \mathbb{R}^m$ for the end-effector, the objective is to obtain $\vartheta(t)$ in real-time. Hence, one has $\mathbf{f}(\vartheta(t)) = \mathbf{r}_\mathrm{a}(t) \rightarrow \mathbf{r}_\mathrm{d}(t)$ by using the synthesized $\vartheta(t)$. The pseudoinverse-based scheme is a conventional method [306]:

$$\dot{\vartheta}(t) = J^{\dagger}(\vartheta(t))\dot{\mathbf{r}}_\mathrm{d}(t), \tag{11.1}$$

in which the superscript † represents the pseudoinverse operator, and $\dot{\mathbf{r}}_\mathrm{d}(t)$ is the first-order time derivative of $\mathbf{r}_\mathrm{d}(t)$. However, (11.1) may be divergent during the tracking process because it has no feedback.

Therefore, completing a tracking task with satisfactory convergence is very important. Additionally, realizing repetitive motion is also significant [27].

Lemma 10 *For completing the tracking task and realizing repetitive motion of redundant manipulators, with the design parameter $\eta > 0$ and the superscript $^\mathrm{T}$ denoting the transpose operator, the repetitive motion control problem is described as*

$$\min \quad \frac{1}{2}\dot{\vartheta}^\mathrm{T}(t)\dot{\vartheta}(t) + \eta(\vartheta(t) - \vartheta(0))^\mathrm{T}\dot{\vartheta}(t) \tag{11.2a}$$

$$\text{s. t.} \quad J(\vartheta(t))\dot{\vartheta}(t) = \dot{\mathbf{r}}_\mathrm{d}(t) - \eta(\mathbf{r}_\mathrm{a}(t) - \mathbf{r}_\mathrm{d}(t)). \tag{11.2b}$$

Proof. To track $\mathbf{r}_\mathrm{d}(t)$, one defines the first ZF as below:

$$\mathbf{z}_1(t) = \mathbf{r}_\mathrm{a}(t) - \mathbf{r}_\mathrm{d}(t).$$

Applying the ZNN design formula $\dot{\mathbf{z}}_1(t) = -\eta\mathbf{z}_1(t)$, one instantly obtains the equality constraint (11.2b). Meanwhile, for realizing the repetitive motion, the second ZF is further defined:

$$\mathbf{z}_2(t) = \vartheta(t) - \vartheta(0).$$

By employing the ZNN design formula $\dot{\mathbf{z}}_2(t) = -\eta\mathbf{z}_2(t)$, the following result is obtained:

$$\dot{\vartheta}(t) + \eta(\vartheta(t) - \vartheta(0)) = \mathbf{0}.$$

Considering the primary tracking task, minimizing the index $\|\dot{\vartheta}(t) + \eta(\vartheta(t) - \vartheta(0))\|_2^2/2$, i.e., the optimization performance index (11.2a), is desired. On the basis of the previous works [27, 295, 324], for redundant manipulators, if (11.2) is utilized, then the tracking task is completed with the repetitive motion realized. The proof is completed. □

Remark 11 *The purpose of the ZNN design formula $\dot{\mathbf{z}}(t) = -\eta\mathbf{z}(t)$ is to make all elements of the ZF, i.e., $\mathbf{z}(t)$, globally and exponentially converge to zero. The exact solution of the ZNN design formula decreases with time, i.e., $\mathbf{z}(t) = \mathbf{z}(0)\exp(-\eta t) \to \mathbf{0}$. The design parameter η is strictly positive and should be appropriately selected for simulation and experimental purposes. Note that the equality constraint (11.2b) coming from the first ZF, i.e., $\mathbf{z}_1(t)$, should be necessarily satisfied, which guarantees that the tracking task is completed. Additionally, the optimization performance index (11.2a) coming from the second ZF, i.e., $\mathbf{z}_2(t)$, is expected to be as optimal as possible. Evidently, the joint angles are expected to change slightly during the tracking process, which also reduces the energy loss. Moreover, the desired path should be closed. When starting the tracking task, the end-effector position needs to be the same as the starting point of the desired path. In this case, the configuration of the redundant manipulator is the same as the initial configuration when the tracking task is completed. Otherwise, a restarting program is needed to drive the manipulator to the initial configuration to realize the repetitive motion.*

By defining a Lagrange multiplier vector $\mathbf{l}(t) \in \mathbb{R}^m$, the Lagrange function is defined:

$$L(\dot{\vartheta}(t),\mathbf{l}(t),t) = \frac{1}{2}\dot{\vartheta}^{\mathrm{T}}(t)\dot{\vartheta}(t) + \eta(\vartheta(t) - \vartheta(0))^{\mathrm{T}}\dot{\vartheta}(t) + \mathbf{l}^{\mathrm{T}}(t)\big(J(\vartheta(t))\dot{\vartheta}(t) \\ -\dot{\mathbf{r}}_{\mathrm{d}}(t) + \eta(\mathbf{r}_{\mathrm{a}}(t) - \mathbf{r}_{\mathrm{d}}(t))\big).$$

Then, one has

$$\begin{bmatrix} \frac{\partial L(\dot{\vartheta}(t),\mathbf{l}(t),t)}{\partial\dot{\vartheta}(t)} \\ \frac{\partial L(\dot{\vartheta}(t),\mathbf{l}(t),t)}{\partial\mathbf{l}(t)} \end{bmatrix} = A(t)\begin{bmatrix} \dot{\vartheta}(t) \\ \mathbf{l}(t) \end{bmatrix} + \mathbf{b}(t),$$

in which

$$A(t) = \begin{bmatrix} I_{n\times n} & J^{\mathrm{T}}(\vartheta(t)) \\ J(\vartheta(t)) & O_{m\times m} \end{bmatrix} \in \mathbb{R}^{(n+m)\times(n+m)} \text{ and } \mathbf{b}(t) = \begin{bmatrix} \eta(\vartheta(t) - \vartheta(0)) \\ -\dot{\mathbf{r}}_{\mathrm{d}}(t) + \eta(\mathbf{r}_{\mathrm{a}}(t) - \mathbf{r}_{\mathrm{d}}(t)) \end{bmatrix} \in \mathbb{R}^{n+m}.$$

Note that $I_{n\times n}$ denotes an $n \times n$ identity matrix, and $O_{m\times m}$ denotes an $m \times m$ zero matrix. To realize (11.2), with $\mathbf{x}(t) = [\dot{\vartheta}(t);\mathbf{l}(t)] \in \mathbb{R}^{n+m}$ in MATLAB notation [161], one defines ZF as

$$\mathbf{z}(t) = A(t)\mathbf{x}(t) + \mathbf{b}(t).$$

Applying the ZNN design formula $\dot{\mathbf{z}}(t) = -\eta\mathbf{z}(t)$, one obtains

$$A(t)\dot{\mathbf{x}}(t) + \dot{A}(t)\mathbf{x}(t) + \dot{\mathbf{b}}(t) = -\eta A(t)\mathbf{x}(t) - \eta\mathbf{b}(t),$$

in which $\dot{\mathbf{x}}(t) = [\ddot{\vartheta}(t),\dot{\mathbf{l}}(t)]^{\mathrm{T}}$. Hence, the following CTZNN model is obtained:

$$\dot{\mathbf{x}}(t) = -A^{-1}(t)\big(\dot{A}(t)\mathbf{x}(t) + \dot{\mathbf{b}}(t) + \eta A(t)\mathbf{x}(t) + \eta\mathbf{b}(t)\big). \tag{11.3}$$

From the previous works [46,75,177,328,329], one has the following lemma about the CTZNN model (11.3).

Lemma 11 *Given any initial value $\mathbf{x}(0) \in \mathbb{R}^{n+m}$, the state vector of the CTZNN model (11.3) converges to the exact solution of the repetitive motion control problem (11.2) globally and exponentially.*

Remark 12 *Evidently, the CTZNN model (11.3) is an ordinary differential equation, and $\mathbf{x}(t)$ is obtained in real time by solving the ordinary differential equation. That is, the joint velocity vector $\dot{\vartheta}(t)$ is obtained as a part of $\mathbf{x}(t)$ in real time. Hence, the joint angle vector $\vartheta(t)$ is obtained in real time. Specifically, the international unit of the design parameter η in the CTZNN model (11.3) is Hz, and the value of η should be large enough for a fast convergence speed.*

11.3 DTZNN Algorithms

In this section, the DTZNN algorithms for solving the repetitive motion control problem are developed.

For convenient computational processing, the repetitive motion control problem in a discrete-time form is presented as follows:

$$\min \frac{1}{2}\dot{\vartheta}_{k+1}^{\mathrm{T}}\dot{\vartheta}_{k+1}+\eta(\vartheta_{k+1}-\vartheta_0)^{\mathrm{T}}\dot{\vartheta}_{k+1} \tag{11.4a}$$

$$\text{s. t. } J(\vartheta_{k+1})\dot{\vartheta}_{k+1}=\dot{\mathbf{r}}_{\mathrm{d},k+1}-\eta(\mathbf{r}_{\mathrm{a},k+1}-\mathbf{r}_{\mathrm{d},k+1}), \tag{11.4b}$$

at each computational time interval $[t_k,t_{k+1})=[kg,(k+1)g)$ with $k=0,1,2,\cdots$ denoting the updating index.

11.3.1 6S-DTZNN algorithm

For developing the DTZNN algorithm, a 6S-ZTD formula is presented as shown below.

Theorem 45 *With the sufficiently small sampling gap $g\in(0,1)$, let $\mathscr{O}(g^4)$ denote the error (especially, the truncation error) positively or negatively proportional to g^4, i.e., of the order of g^4. Suppose that $\zeta(t)$ is sufficiently smooth. With $\zeta_{k+1}=\zeta(t_{k+1})=\zeta((k+1)g)$, the 6S-ZTD formula is formulated as below:*

$$\dot{\zeta}_k=\frac{31}{82g}\zeta_{k+1}+\frac{29}{123g}\zeta_k-\frac{71}{164g}\zeta_{k-1}-\frac{29}{82g}\zeta_{k-2}+\frac{16}{123g}\zeta_{k-3}+\frac{7}{82g}\zeta_{k-4}-\frac{7}{164g}\zeta_{k-5}+\mathscr{O}(g^4). \tag{11.5}$$

Proof. Please see Appendix M. □

Applying the 6S-ZTD formula (11.5) to discretize (11.3), one has

$$\begin{aligned}\mathbf{x}_{k+1}\doteq&-\frac{58}{93}\mathbf{x}_k+\frac{71}{62}\mathbf{x}_{k-1}+\frac{29}{31}\mathbf{x}_{k-2}-\frac{32}{93}\mathbf{x}_{k-3}-\frac{7}{31}\mathbf{x}_{k-4}+\frac{7}{62}\mathbf{x}_{k-5}\\&-\frac{82g}{31}A_k^{-1}(\dot{A}_k\mathbf{x}_k+\dot{\mathbf{b}}_k+\eta A_k\mathbf{x}_k+\eta\mathbf{b}_k),\end{aligned} \tag{11.6}$$

where $\mathbf{x}_{k+1}$ denotes $\mathbf{x}(t_{k+1})$. Additionally, $\doteq$ denotes the computational assignment operator. It is worth noting that some time derivatives (i.e., $\dot{A}_k$ and $\dot{\mathbf{b}}_k$) are unknown but needed in some applications. The time derivatives are approximated by using a four-step backward numerical-differentiation formula [330]:

$$\dot{\zeta}_k=\frac{25}{12g}\zeta_k-\frac{4}{g}\zeta_{k-1}+\frac{3}{g}\zeta_{k-2}-\frac{4}{3g}\zeta_{k-3}+\frac{1}{4g}\zeta_{k-4}+\mathscr{O}(g^4). \tag{11.7}$$

Hence, (11.6) is reformulated as

$$\begin{aligned}\mathbf{x}_{k+1}\doteq&-\frac{58}{93}\mathbf{x}_k+\frac{71}{62}\mathbf{x}_{k-1}+\frac{29}{31}\mathbf{x}_{k-2}-\frac{32}{93}\mathbf{x}_{k-3}-\frac{7}{31}\mathbf{x}_{k-4}+\frac{7}{62}\mathbf{x}_{k-5}\\&-\frac{82}{31}A_k^{-1}(\hat{A}_k\mathbf{x}_k+\hat{\mathbf{b}}_k+\hbar A_k\mathbf{x}_k+\hbar\mathbf{b}_k),\end{aligned} \tag{11.8a}$$

in which $\hat{A}_k=25/12A_k-4A_{k-1}+3A_{k-2}-4/3A_{k-3}+1/4A_{k-4}$, $\hat{\mathbf{b}}_k=25/12\mathbf{b}_k-4\mathbf{b}_{k-1}+3\mathbf{b}_{k-2}-4/3\mathbf{b}_{k-3}+1/4\mathbf{b}_{k-4}$, and $\hbar=g\eta$.

According to (11.8a), $\mathbf{x}_{k+1}$ is obtained; that is, $\dot{\vartheta}_{k+1}$ and $\mathbf{l}_{k+1}$ are obtained. To compute ϑ_{k+1} according to the synthesized $\dot{\vartheta}_{k+1}$, (11.7) is used again. Hence, ϑ_{k+1} is obtained as

$$\vartheta_{k+1} \doteq \frac{48}{25}\vartheta_k - \frac{36}{25}\vartheta_{k-1} + \frac{16}{25}\vartheta_{k-2} - \frac{3}{25}\vartheta_{k-3} + \frac{12g}{25}\dot{\vartheta}_{k+1}. \tag{11.8b}$$

Thus, (11.8) is termed as the 6S-DTZNN algorithm.

11.3.2 Other DTZNN algorithms

Zhang–Taylor discretization formula and a two-step backward numerical-differentiation formula are formulated as

$$\dot{\zeta}_k = \frac{1}{g}\zeta_{k+1} - \frac{3}{2g}\zeta_k + \frac{1}{g}\zeta_{k-1} - \frac{1}{2g}\zeta_{k-2} + \mathscr{O}(g^2) \tag{11.9}$$

and

$$\dot{\zeta}_k = \frac{3}{2g}\zeta_k - \frac{2}{g}\zeta_{k-1} + \frac{1}{2g}\zeta_{k-2} + \mathscr{O}(g^2). \tag{11.10}$$

By using (11.9) and (11.10), the Zhang–Taylor DTZNN (ZT-DTZNN) algorithm is obtained as follows:

$$\mathbf{x}_{k+1} \doteq \frac{3}{2}\mathbf{x}_k - \mathbf{x}_{k-1} + \frac{1}{2}\mathbf{x}_{k-2} - A_k^{-1}(\hat{A}_k\mathbf{x}_k + \hat{\mathbf{b}}_k + \hbar A_k\mathbf{x}_k + \hbar\mathbf{b}_k), \tag{11.11a}$$

in which $\hat{A}_k = 3/2A_k - 2A_{k-1} + 1/2A_{k-2}$ and $\hat{\mathbf{b}}_k = 3/2\mathbf{b}_k - 2\mathbf{b}_{k-1} + 1/2\mathbf{b}_{k-2}$, and

$$\vartheta_{k+1} \doteq \frac{4}{3}\vartheta_k - \frac{1}{3}\vartheta_{k-1} + \frac{2g}{3}\dot{\vartheta}_{k+1}. \tag{11.11b}$$

The Euler forward formula and Euler backward formula are formulated as

$$\dot{\zeta}_k = \frac{1}{g}\zeta_{k+1} - \frac{1}{g}\zeta_k + \mathscr{O}(g) \tag{11.12}$$

and

$$\dot{\zeta}_k = \frac{1}{g}\zeta_k - \frac{1}{g}\zeta_{k-1} + \mathscr{O}(g). \tag{11.13}$$

Using (11.12) and (11.13), one obtains

$$\mathbf{x}_{k+1} \doteq \mathbf{x}_k - A_k^{-1}(\hat{A}_k\mathbf{x}_k + \hat{\mathbf{b}}_k + \hbar A_k\mathbf{x}_k + \hbar\mathbf{b}_k), \tag{11.14a}$$

in which $\hat{A}_k = A_k - A_{k-1}$ and $\hat{\mathbf{b}}_k = \mathbf{b}_k - \mathbf{b}_{k-1}$, and

$$\vartheta_{k+1} \doteq \vartheta_k + g\dot{\vartheta}_{k+1}. \tag{11.14b}$$

Thus, (11.14) is termed as the Euler-type DTZNN (ET-DTZNN) algorithm.

Remark 13 *By observing the 6S-DTZNN algorithm (11.8), there are six initial values of* $\mathbf{x}_i$*, with* $i = 0, 1, \cdots, 5$*, that should be set. The first value* $\mathbf{x}_0$ *could be arbitrarily set. Then, the remaining five values could be generated based on the ET-DTZNN algorithm (11.14). The detailed implementation of the 6S-DTZNN algorithm (11.8) is presented as Algorithm 1. Additionally, the framework for repetitive motion control of redundant manipulators using the 6S-DTZNN algorithm (11.8) is presented as Figure 11.1. In the same way, several initial values of the ZT-DTZNN algorithm (11.11) can be set by using the ET-DTZNN algorithm (11.14). Moreover, the initial values do not influence the convergence precision because strict feedback is introduced in the ZNN design formula. Therefore, the method to set the initial values is simple and feasible.*

Algorithm 1: 6S-DTZNN algorithm (11.8) for redundant manipulator.

Initialize: ϑ_0, $\dot{\vartheta}_0$, $\mathbf{l}_0$, and $\mathbf{x}_0$.
Set: T, $\hbar$, g, and $\mathbf{r}_{\mathrm{d},k}$.
for $k = 0:4$
  Compute A_k, $\mathbf{b}_k$, $\hat{A}_k$, and $\hat{\mathbf{b}}_k$.
  Compute $\mathbf{x}_{k+1}$ via (11.14a).
  Compute ϑ_{k+1} via (11.14b).
end
for $k = 5:(T/g-1)$
  Compute A_k, $\mathbf{b}_k$, $\hat{A}_k$, and $\hat{\mathbf{b}}_k$.
  Compute $\mathbf{x}_{k+1}$ via (11.8a).
  Compute ϑ_{k+1} via (11.8b).
end

11.3.3 Theoretical analyses

The stability property of the 6S-DTZNN algorithm (11.8) is analyzed as follows.

Theorem 46 *Suppose that A_k is always nonsingular. With the sufficiently small sampling gap $g \in (0,1)$, the 6S-DTZNN algorithm (11.8) is zero-stable.*

Proof. According to Definition 2 in Chapter 1, the characteristic polynomial of (11.8a) is

$$\Gamma_6(\iota) = \iota^6 + \frac{58}{93}\iota^5 - \frac{71}{62}\iota^4 - \frac{29}{31}\iota^3 + \frac{32}{93}\iota^2 + \frac{7}{31}\iota - \frac{7}{62},$$

whose six roots are as follows:

$$\begin{cases} \iota_1 = 1, \\ \iota_2 = -0.8117, \\ \iota_3 = -0.7755 + 0.4339\mathrm{i}, \\ \iota_4 = -0.7755 - 0.4339\mathrm{i}, \\ \iota_5 = 0.3695 + 0.1989\mathrm{i}, \\ \iota_6 = 0.3695 - 0.1989\mathrm{i}. \end{cases}$$

One has $|\iota_1| = 1$ and $|\iota_j| < 1$ with $j = 2, \cdots, 6$. Thus, (11.8a) is zero-stable.

Additionally, the characteristic polynomial of (11.8b) is

$$\Gamma_4(\iota) = \iota^4 - \frac{48}{25}\iota^3 + \frac{36}{25}\iota^2 - \frac{16}{25}\iota + \frac{3}{25},$$

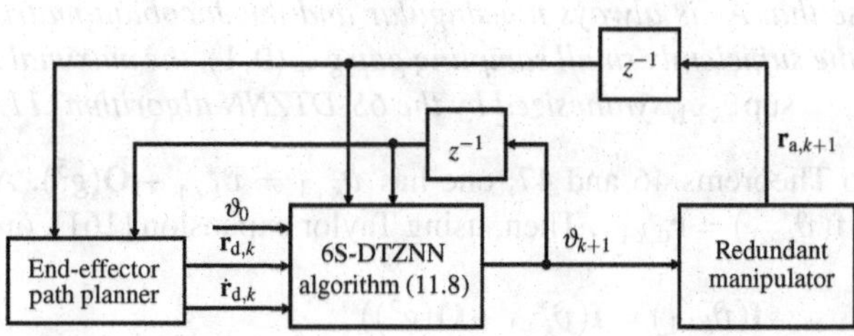

FIGURE 11.1: Framework for repetitive motion control of redundant manipulator using 6S-DTZNN algorithm (11.8).

whose four roots are as follows:

$$\begin{cases} \iota_1 = 1, \\ \iota_2 = 0.3815, \\ \iota_3 = 0.2693 + 0.4920\mathrm{i}, \\ \iota_4 = 0.2693 - 0.4920\mathrm{i}. \end{cases}$$

One has $|\iota_1| = 1$ and $|\iota_j| < 1$ with $j = 2,3,4$. Thus, (11.8b) is zero-stable. Hence, the 6S-DTZNN algorithm (11.8) is zero-stable, which completes the proof. □

Theorem 47 *Suppose that A_k is always nonsingular. With the sufficiently small sampling gap $g \in (0,1)$, let $\mathbf{O}(g^5)$ denote the error (especially, the truncation error) with each element being $\mathscr{O}(g^5)$. The 6S-DTZNN algorithm (11.8) converges with the order of truncation error being $\mathbf{O}(g^5)$.*

Proof. Applying the 6S-ZTD formula (11.5) to discretize (11.3), one obtains the following result:

$$\begin{aligned}\mathbf{x}_{k+1} = &-\frac{58}{93}\mathbf{x}_k + \frac{71}{62}\mathbf{x}_{k-1} + \frac{29}{31}\mathbf{x}_{k-2} - \frac{32}{93}\mathbf{x}_{k-3} - \frac{7}{31}\mathbf{x}_{k-4} + \frac{7}{62}\mathbf{x}_{k-5} \\ &- \frac{82}{31}A_k^{-1}(g\dot{A}_k\mathbf{x}_k + g\dot{\mathbf{b}}_k + \hbar A_k\mathbf{x}_k + \hbar\mathbf{b}_k) + \mathbf{O}(g^5).\end{aligned}$$

Additionally, according to (11.7), one has $\hat{A}_k = g\dot{A}_k + \mathbf{O}(g^5)$ and $\hat{\mathbf{b}}_k = g\dot{\mathbf{b}}_k + \mathbf{O}(g^5)$. That is, one has $g\dot{A}_k = \hat{A}_k + \mathbf{O}(g^5)$ and $g\dot{\mathbf{b}}_k = \hat{\mathbf{b}}_k + \mathbf{O}(g^5)$. Therefore, the following result is obtained:

$$\begin{aligned}\mathbf{x}_{k+1} = &-\frac{58}{93}\mathbf{x}_k + \frac{71}{62}\mathbf{x}_{k-1} + \frac{29}{31}\mathbf{x}_{k-2} - \frac{32}{93}\mathbf{x}_{k-3} - \frac{7}{31}\mathbf{x}_{k-4} + \frac{7}{62}\mathbf{x}_{k-5} \\ &- \frac{82}{31}A_k^{-1}(\hat{A}_k\mathbf{x}_k + \hat{\mathbf{b}}_k + \hbar A_k\mathbf{x}_k + \hbar\mathbf{b}_k) + \mathbf{O}(g^5).\end{aligned}$$

It is noted that removing $\mathbf{O}(g^5)$ from the above equation yields exactly (11.8a). That is, $\mathbf{x}_{k+1} = \mathbf{x}^*_{k+1} + \mathbf{O}(g^5)$, and $\dot{\vartheta}_{k+1} = \dot{\vartheta}^*_{k+1} + \mathbf{O}(g^5)$, with $\mathbf{x}^*_{k+1}$ and $\dot{\vartheta}^*_{k+1}$ being theoretical solutions. Moreover, according to (11.7), one has

$$\vartheta_{k+1} = \frac{48}{25}\vartheta_k - \frac{36}{25}\vartheta_{k-1} + \frac{16}{25}\vartheta_{k-2} - \frac{3}{25}\vartheta_{k-3} + \frac{12g}{25}\dot{\vartheta}_{k+1} + \mathbf{O}(g^5).$$

The truncation error of the algorithm (11.8b) is $\mathbf{O}(g^5)$, i.e., $\vartheta_{k+1} = \vartheta^*_{k+1} + \mathbf{O}(g^5)$, with ϑ^*_{k+1} being a theoretical solution. According to Definitions 3 and 4 in Chapter 1, the 6S-DTZNN algorithm (11.8) converges with the order of truncation error being $\mathbf{O}(g^5)$. The proof is therefore completed. □

Note that the tracking error is defined as $\tilde{e}_{k+1} = \|\mathbf{r}_{\mathrm{a},k+1} - \mathbf{r}_{\mathrm{d},k+1}\|_2$ for solving the repetitive motion control problem (11.4) in this chapter [327], where $\|\cdot\|_2$ denotes the 2-norm of a vector.

Theorem 48 *Suppose that A_k is always nonsingular and the Jacobian matrix $J(\vartheta_k)$ is uniformly norm bounded. With the sufficiently small sampling gap $g \in (0,1)$, the maximal steady-state tracking error (MSSTE) $\lim_{k\to+\infty}\sup\tilde{e}_{k+1}$ synthesized by the 6S-DTZNN algorithm (11.8) is $\mathscr{O}(g^5)$.*

Proof. According to Theorems 46 and 47, one has $\vartheta_{k+1} = \vartheta^*_{k+1} + \mathbf{O}(g^5)$. Additionally, one has $\mathbf{f}(\vartheta_{k+1}) = \mathbf{r}_{\mathrm{a},k+1}$ and $\mathbf{f}(\vartheta^*_{k+1}) = \mathbf{r}_{\mathrm{d},k+1}$. Then, using Taylor expansion [161], one has

$$\begin{aligned}\mathbf{f}(\vartheta_{k+1}) &= \mathbf{f}(\vartheta^*_{k+1} + \mathbf{O}(g^5)) \\ &= \mathbf{f}(\vartheta^*_{k+1}) + J(\vartheta^*_{k+1})\mathbf{O}(g^5) + \mathbf{O}(g^{10}) \\ &= \mathbf{f}(\vartheta^*_{k+1}) + J(\vartheta^*_{k+1})\mathbf{O}(g^5).\end{aligned}$$

Then, with $k \to +\infty$, one has

$$\begin{aligned}
&\sup \|\mathbf{r}_{\mathrm{a},k+1} - \mathbf{r}_{\mathrm{d},k+1}\|_2 \\
&= \sup \|\mathbf{f}(\vartheta_{k+1}) - \mathbf{f}(\vartheta^*_{k+1})\|_2 \\
&= \sup \|J(\vartheta^*_{k+1})\mathbf{O}(g^5)\|_2 \\
&\leq \sup \|J(\vartheta^*_{k+1})\|_{\mathrm{F}}\mathscr{O}(g^5),
\end{aligned}$$

in which $\|\cdot\|_{\mathrm{F}}$ represents the Frobenius norm. Because the Jacobian matrix $J(\vartheta^*_{k+1})$ is uniformly norm bounded, the MSSTE synthesized by the 6S-DTZNN algorithm (11.8) is $\mathscr{O}(g^5)$. The proof is completed. □

Similarly, one has the properties of the ET-DTZNN algorithm (11.14) and the ZT-DTZNN algorithm (11.11) as below.

Corollary 10 *Suppose that A_k is always nonsingular and the Jacobian matrix $J(\vartheta_k)$ is uniformly norm bounded. With the sufficiently small sampling gap $g \in (0,1)$, the ET-DTZNN algorithm (11.14) is zero-stable and convergent with the order of truncation error being $\mathbf{O}(g^2)$. Additionally, the MSSTE synthesized by the ET-DTZNN algorithm is $\mathscr{O}(g^2)$.*

Corollary 11 *Suppose that A_k is always nonsingular and the Jacobian matrix $J(\vartheta_k)$ is uniformly norm bounded. With the sufficiently small sampling gap $g \in (0,1)$, the ZT-DTZNN algorithm (11.11) is zero-stable and convergent with the order of truncation error being $\mathbf{O}(g^3)$. Additionally, the MSSTE synthesized by the ZT-DTZNN algorithm is $\mathscr{O}(g^3)$.*

Remark 14 *Note that the 6S-DTZNN algorithm (11.8) is proven to be superior to the ET-DTZNN algorithm (11.14) and the ZT-DTZNN algorithm (11.11) in terms of precision. As for the 6S-DTZNN algorithm (11.8), computing $\hat{A}_k$ requires $4(n+m)^2$ addition or subtraction operations and $5(n+m)^2$ multiplication or division operations. Computing $\hat{\mathbf{b}}_k$ requires $4(n+m)$ addition or subtraction operations and $5(n+m)$ multiplication or division operations. Excluding the commonly used inverse operation, (11.8a) requires $3(n+m)^2+6(n+m)$ addition or subtraction operations and $3(n+m)^2+9(n+m)$ multiplication or division operations. Additionally, (11.8b) requires $4n$ addition or subtraction operations and $5n$ multiplication or division operations. Thus, the 6S-DTZNN algorithm (11.8) requires $7(n+m)^2+10(n+m)+4n$ addition or subtraction operations, $8(n+m)^2+14(n+m)+5n$ multiplication or division operations, and one inverse operation per updating. Similarly, the ET-DTZNN algorithm (11.14) requires $4(n+m)^2+2(n+m)+n$ addition or subtraction operations, $3(n+m)^2+2(n+m)+n$ multiplication or division operations, and one inverse operation per updating. The ZT-DTZNN algorithm (11.11) requires $5(n+m)^2+5(n+m)+2n$ addition or subtraction operations, $6(n+m)^2+7(n+m)+3n$ multiplication or division operations, and one inverse operation per updating. Generally, the computational complexity of inverse operation (i.e., A_k^{-1}) is $O((n+m)^3)$. Although the 6S-DTZNN algorithm (11.8) seems to be more complicated than the ET-DTZNN algorithm (11.14) and the ZT-DTZNN algorithm (11.11), the computational complexity of the 6S-DTZNN algorithm (11.8) is of the same order $[O((n+m)^3)]$ as those of the ET-DTZNN algorithm (11.14) and the ZT-DTZNN algorithm (11.11), which is also verified by numerical experimental results.*

For a more intuitive understanding of the main content of this chapter [327], Table 11.1 lists the problem, scheme, model, and algorithms.

11.4 Numerical Experiments

Numerical experiments about the tracking control of the four-link redundant manipulator are conducted to show the good properties of the 6S-DTZNN algorithm (11.8) compared with the

TABLE 11.1: Problem, scheme, model, and algorithms in this chapter.

Problem	$\min\ \frac{1}{2}\dot{\vartheta}_{k+1}^{\mathrm{T}}\dot{\vartheta}+\eta(\vartheta_{k+1}-\vartheta_0)^{\mathrm{T}}\dot{\vartheta}_{k+1}$, s. t. $J(\vartheta_{k+1})\dot{\vartheta}_{k+1}=\dot{\mathbf{r}}_{\mathrm{d},k+1}-\eta(\mathbf{r}_{\mathrm{a},k+1}-\mathbf{r}_{\mathrm{d},k+1})$.
Scheme	*Step 1*: Define ZF as $\mathbf{z}(t)=A(t)\mathbf{x}(t)+\mathbf{b}(t)$. *Step 2*: Adopt ZNN design formula as $\dot{\mathbf{z}}(t)=-\eta\mathbf{z}(t)$. *Step 3*: Adopt ZTD formulas to discretize CTZNN model (11.3).
Model	$\dot{\mathbf{x}}(t)=-A^{-1}(t)(\dot{A}(t)\mathbf{x}(t)+\dot{\mathbf{b}}(t)+\eta A(t)\mathbf{x}(t)+\eta\mathbf{b}(t))$.
Algorithms	$\vartheta_{k+1}\doteq\frac{48}{25}\vartheta_k-\frac{36}{25}\vartheta_{k-1}+\frac{16}{25}\vartheta_{k-2}-\frac{3}{25}\vartheta_{k-3}+\frac{12g}{25}\dot{\vartheta}_{k+1}$, $\vartheta_{k+1}\doteq\frac{4}{3}\vartheta_k-\frac{1}{3}\vartheta_{k-1}+\frac{2g}{3}\dot{\vartheta}_{k+1}$, $\vartheta_{k+1}\doteq\vartheta_k+g\dot{\vartheta}_{k+1}$, $\vartheta_{k+1}\doteq\vartheta_k+J^{\dagger}(\vartheta_k)(\mathbf{r}_{\mathrm{d},k}-\mathbf{f}(\vartheta_k))$, $\vartheta_{k+1}\doteq\frac{33}{26}\vartheta_k-\frac{9}{13}\vartheta_{k-1}+\frac{11}{26}\vartheta_{k-2}+\frac{15}{13}J^{\dagger}(\vartheta_k)(g\dot{\mathbf{r}}_{\mathrm{d},k}+\hbar(\mathbf{r}_{\mathrm{d},k}-\mathbf{f}(\vartheta_k)))$, $\vartheta_{k+1}\doteq-\frac{1}{8}\vartheta_k+\frac{3}{4}\vartheta_{k-1}+\frac{5}{8}\vartheta_{k-2}-\frac{1}{4}\vartheta_{k-3}+\frac{9}{4}J^{\dagger}(\vartheta_k)(g\dot{\mathbf{r}}_{\mathrm{d},k}+\hbar(\mathbf{r}_{\mathrm{d},k}-\mathbf{f}(\vartheta_k)))$.

ET-DTZNN algorithm (11.14) and the ZT-DTZNN algorithm (11.11). Besides, a discrete-time gradient neural network (DTGNN) algorithm, a Newton iteration (NI) algorithm, and another two DTZNN algorithms are also developed for comparison.

For solving the repetitive motion control problem (11.2), a continuous-time gradient neural network model is developed [65]:

$$\dot{\mathbf{x}}(t)=-\eta A^{\mathrm{T}}(t)(A(t)\mathbf{x}(t)+\mathbf{b}(t)).$$

The precision of the DTGNN algorithm does not depend on the ZTD formula. Therefore, the Euler-type DTGNN (ET-DTGNN) algorithm is developed as follows:

$$\mathbf{x}_{k+1}\doteq\mathbf{x}_k-\hbar A_k^{\mathrm{T}}(A_k\mathbf{x}_k+\mathbf{b}_k) \tag{11.15a}$$

and

$$\vartheta_{k+1}\doteq\vartheta_k+g\dot{\vartheta}_{k+1}. \tag{11.15b}$$

The NI algorithm [161] is presented as

$$\vartheta_{k+1}\doteq\vartheta_k+J^{\dagger}(\vartheta_k)(\mathbf{r}_{\mathrm{d},k}-\mathbf{f}(\vartheta_k)). \tag{11.16}$$

In [306], the three-step DTZNN (3S-DTZNN) algorithm proposed by Guo *et al* is presented as

$$\vartheta_{k+1}\doteq\frac{33}{26}\vartheta_k-\frac{9}{13}\vartheta_{k-1}+\frac{11}{26}\vartheta_{k-2}+\frac{15}{13}J^{\dagger}(\vartheta_k)\big(g\dot{\mathbf{r}}_{\mathrm{d},k}+\hbar(\mathbf{r}_{\mathrm{d},k}-\mathbf{f}(\vartheta_k))\big). \tag{11.17}$$

In addition, in [130], the four-step DTZNN (4S-DTZNN) algorithm proposed by Li *et al* is presented as

$$\vartheta_{k+1}\doteq-\frac{1}{8}\vartheta_k+\frac{3}{4}\vartheta_{k-1}+\frac{5}{8}\vartheta_{k-2}-\frac{1}{4}\vartheta_{k-3}+\frac{9}{4}J^{\dagger}(\vartheta_k)\big(g\dot{\mathbf{r}}_{\mathrm{d},k}+\hbar(\mathbf{r}_{\mathrm{d},k}-\mathbf{f}(\vartheta_k))\big). \tag{11.18}$$

The following desired lung-like path is to be tracked by the four-link redundant manipulator during the computational time interval [0,20] s:

$$\mathbf{r}_{\mathrm{d},k}=\begin{bmatrix}\sin(\pi t_k/5)\cos(\sin(3\pi t_k/10))+\rho_1\\ \sin(\pi t_k/5)\sin(\sin(3\pi t_k/10))+\rho_2\end{bmatrix},$$

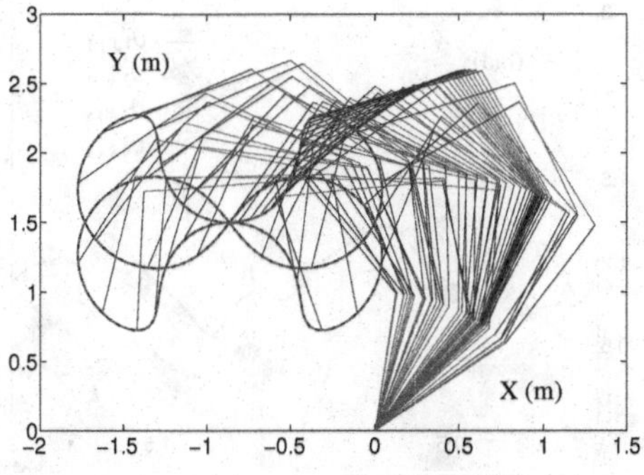

(a) Manipulator trajectories [327]

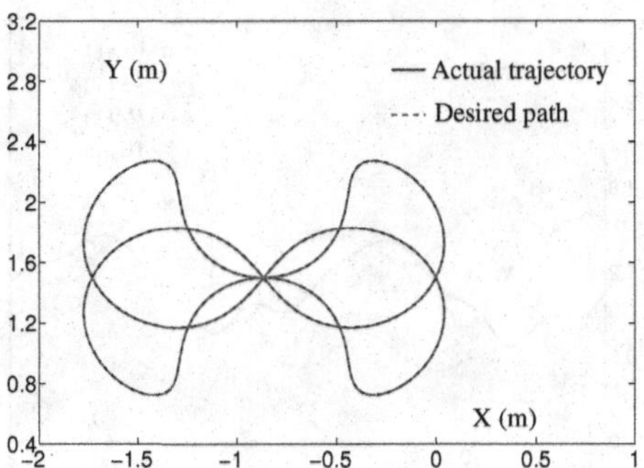

(b) End-effector actual trajectory and desired path [327]

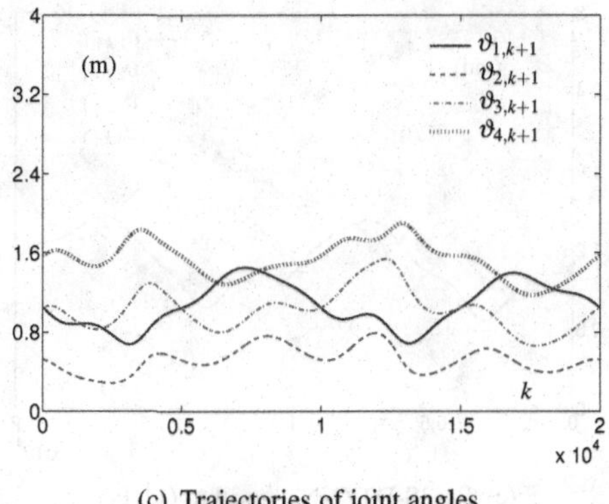

(c) Trajectories of joint angles

FIGURE 11.2: Motion generation synthesized by 6S-DTZNN algorithm (11.8) when end-effector tracking desired lung-like path with $\hbar = 0.02$ and $g = 0.001$ s.

where the parameters ρ_1 and ρ_2 are the X-axis value and Y-axis value of the initial end-effector position, respectively.

The initial joint angles are relatively casually set as $\vartheta_0 = [\pi/3, \pi/6, \pi/3, \pi/2]^{\mathrm{T}}$ rad. Specifically, Figure 11.2 shows the numerical experimental results synthesized by the 6S-DTZNN algorithm (11.8) with $\hbar = 0.02$ and $g = 0.001$ s. The motion trajectories of the redundant manipulator are presented in Figure 11.2(a). From Figure 11.2(b), one observes that the actual trajectory almost coincides with the desired path. The conclusion is preliminarily obtained that the tracking task is

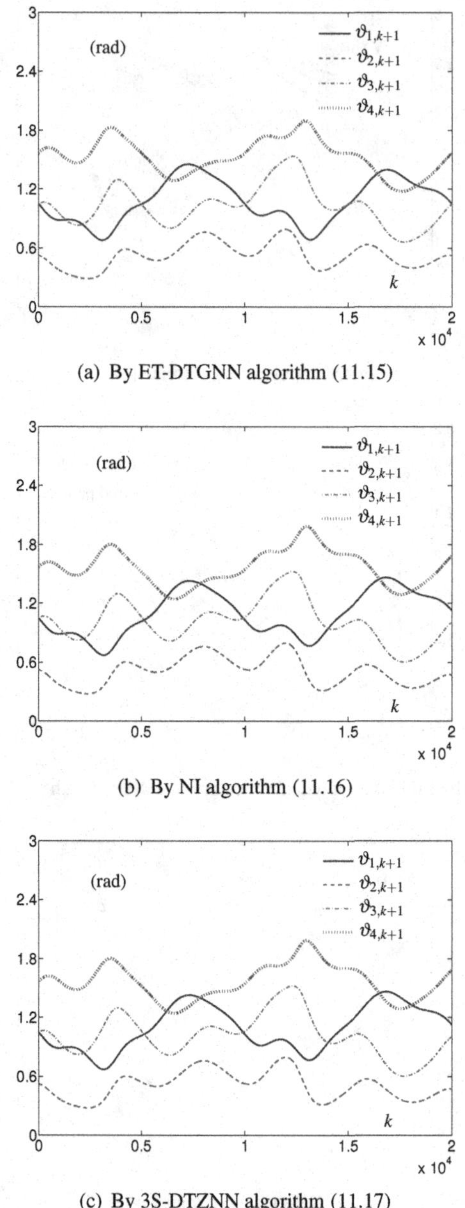

(a) By ET-DTGNN algorithm (11.15)

(b) By NI algorithm (11.16)

(c) By 3S-DTZNN algorithm (11.17)

FIGURE 11.3: Trajectories of joint angles synthesized by different algorithms when end-effector tracking desired lung-like path with $\hbar = 0.02$ and $g = 0.001$ s.

completed by the 6S-DTZNN algorithm (11.8). Besides, in Figure 11.2(c), the trajectories of joint angles are presented. Evidently, the joint angles at time $t_k = 20$ s return to the initial values. That is, one concludes that the repetitive motion is realized by the 6S-DTZNN algorithm (11.8).

Meanwhile, the ET-DTZNN algorithm (11.14), the ZT-DTZNN algorithm (11.11), the ET-DTGNN algorithm (11.15), the NI algorithm (11.16), the 3S-DTZNN algorithm (11.17), and the 4S-DTZNN algorithm (11.18) are applied to performing the tracking task for comparison. In Figure 11.3, the trajectories of the joint angles synthesized by the ET-DTGNN algorithm (11.15), the NI

TABLE 11.2: Differences between initial joint angles and final joint angles synthesized by different algorithms with sampling gap $g = 0.001$ s.

Algorithm	$\lvert\vartheta_{1,T/g} - \vartheta_{1,0}\rvert$ (rad)	$\lvert\vartheta_{2,T/g} - \vartheta_{2,0}\rvert$ (rad)	$\lvert\vartheta_{3,T/g} - \vartheta_{3,0}\rvert$ (rad)
NI algorithm (11.16)	8.0046×10^{-2}	5.0664×10^{-2}	4.1852×10^{-2}
3S-DTZNN algorithm (11.11)	7.9599×10^{-2}	5.0595×10^{-2}	4.1576×10^{-2}
4S-DTZNN algorithm (11.18)	7.9599×10^{-2}	5.0595×10^{-2}	4.1576×10^{-2}
ET-DTGNN algorithm (11.15)	1.1905×10^{-3}	8.7543×10^{-5}	9.9316×10^{-4}
ET-DTZNN algorithm (11.14)	8.9061×10^{-6}	2.5833×10^{-5}	3.7604×10^{-6}
ZT-DTZNN algorithm (11.11)	1.3700×10^{-5}	1.6692×10^{-5}	4.4704×10^{-6}
6S-DTZNN algorithm (11.8)	1.3692×10^{-5}	1.6685×10^{-5}	4.4896×10^{-6}
Algorithm	$\lvert\vartheta_{4,T/g} - \vartheta_{4,0}\rvert$ **(rad)**	$\lVert\vartheta_{T/g} - \vartheta_{0}\rVert_2$ **(rad)**	**Repetitive motion**
NI algorithm (11.16)	1.1723×10^{-1}	1.5642×10^{-1}	No
3S-DTZNN algorithm (11.11)	1.1710×10^{-1}	1.5600×10^{-1}	No
4S-DTZNN algorithm (11.18)	1.1710×10^{-1}	1.5600×10^{-1}	No
ET-DTGNN algorithm (11.15)	1.1378×10^{-3}	1.9250×10^{-3}	Yes
ET-DTZNN algorithm (11.14)	6.0770×10^{-6}	2.8245×10^{-5}	Yes
ZT-DTZNN algorithm (11.11)	9.5941×10^{-6}	2.4049×10^{-5}	Yes
6S-DTZNN algorithm (11.8)	9.6032×10^{-6}	2.4046×10^{-5}	Yes

algorithm (11.16), and the 3S-DTZNN algorithm (11.17) are shown. Specifically, Figure 11.3(a) shows that the trajectories of the joint angles synthesized by the ET-DTGNN algorithm (11.15) are similar to those shown in Figure 11.2(c). That is, the repetitive motion is also realized by the ET-DTGNN algorithm (11.15). However, as Figure 11.3(b) and (c) shows, the trajectories of the joint angles synthesized by the NI algorithm (11.16) and the 3S-DTZNN algorithm (11.17) do not return to the initial values. Note that the trajectories of joint angles synthesized by the ET-DTZNN algorithm (11.14), the ZT-DTZNN algorithm (11.11), and the ET-DTGNN algorithm (11.15) are similar to those synthesized by the 6S-DTZNN algorithm (11.8) and thus omitted.

Specifically, differences between joint angles at initial time and final time synthesized by different algorithms with sampling gap $g = 0.001$ s are displayed in Table 11.2. If the difference between each initial joint angle and each final joint angle is smaller than $\pi/180 \approx 1.7453 \times 10^{-2}$ rad, the repetitive motion is considered to be realized. As seen from Table 11.2, the repetitive motion is realized by the ET-DTGNN algorithm (11.15), the ET-DTZNN algorithm (11.14), the ZT-DTZNN algorithm (11.11), and 6S-DTZNN algorithm (11.8), while the repetitive motion is not realized by the NI algorithm (11.16), the 3S-DTZNN algorithm (11.17), and the 4S-DTZNN algorithm (11.18).

Moreover, in order to substantiate the accuracy of these algorithms for the redundant manipulator, the trajectories of tracking errors $\tilde{e}_{k+1}$ are presented in Figure 11.4. The tracking errors synthesized by the 6S-DTZNN algorithm (11.8), the ET-DTZNN algorithm (11.14), and the ZT-DTZNN algorithm (11.11) with $g = 0.01$ s are shown in Figure 11.4(a). With a large enough value of k, the tracking error synthesized by the 6S-DTZNN algorithm (11.8) is about 10^{-7} m. By contrast, tracking errors synthesized by the ET-DTZNN algorithm (11.14) and the ZT-DTZNN algorithm (11.11) are about 10^{-2} m and 10^{-4} m, respectively. Besides, Figure 11.4(b) shows the trajectories of tracking errors synthesized by the ET-DTGNN algorithm (11.15), the NI algorithm (11.16), the 3S-DTZNN algorithm (11.17), and the 4S-DTZNN algorithm (11.18) with $g = 0.01$ s. Evidently, the tracking errors synthesized by these four algorithms are all larger than the tracking error synthesized by the 6S-DTZNN algorithm (11.8). Meanwhile, the tracking errors synthesized by the 6S-DTZNN algorithm (11.8), the ZT-DTZNN algorithm (11.11), and the ET-DTZNN algorithm (11.14) with $g = 0.001$ s are presented in Figure 11.4(c). In addition, Figure 11.4(d) shows the tracking errors synthesized by the ET-DTGNN algorithm (11.15), the NI algorithm (11.16), the 3S-DTZNN algorithm (11.17), and the 4S-DTZNN algorithm (11.18) with $g = 0.001$ s. The tracking error synthesized by the 6S-DTZNN algorithm (11.8) is about 10^{-12} m, which is the smallest among these algorithms.

TABLE 11.3: MSSTE and ACTPU data synthesized by different algorithms with different values of sampling gap g.

g (s)	Algorithm	MSSTE (m)	ACTPU (s)
0.01	NI algorithm (11.16)	8.8916×10^{-3}	6.5795×10^{-5}
	3S-DTZNN algorithm (11.17)	9.4135×10^{-5}	6.0758×10^{-5}
	4S-DTZNN algorithm (11.18)	1.2782×10^{-6}	5.9936×10^{-5}
	ET-DTGNN algorithm (11.15)	3.3754×10^{-1}	5.9156×10^{-5}
	ET-DTZNN algorithm (11.14)	4.2446×10^{-3}	1.1348×10^{-4}
	ZT-DTZNN algorithm (11.11)	1.2421×10^{-4}	1.1682×10^{-4}
	6S-DTZNN algorithm (11.8)	4.8669×10^{-8}	1.2401×10^{-4}
0.005	NI algorithm (11.16)	4.4428×10^{-3}	5.8731×10^{-5}
	3S-DTZNN algorithm (11.17)	1.6077×10^{-5}	5.8039×10^{-5}
	4S-DTZNN algorithm (11.18)	1.2221×10^{-7}	5.9231×10^{-5}
	ET-DTGNN algorithm (11.15)	1.1952×10^{-1}	5.4706×10^{-5}
	ET-DTZNN algorithm (11.14)	1.1701×10^{-3}	1.0988×10^{-4}
	ZT-DTZNN algorithm (11.11)	1.6434×10^{-5}	1.1315×10^{-4}
	6S-DTZNN algorithm (11.8)	2.4719×10^{-9}	1.2278×10^{-4}
0.001	NI algorithm (11.16)	8.8809×10^{-4}	6.5357×10^{-5}
	3S-DTZNN algorithm (11.17)	1.5834×10^{-7}	5.8249×10^{-5}
	4S-DTZNN algorithm (11.18)	2.7922×10^{-10}	5.8605×10^{-5}
	ET-DTGNN algorithm (11.15)	9.4858×10^{-3}	5.4278×10^{-5}
	ET-DTZNN algorithm (11.14)	5.4547×10^{-5}	1.0880×10^{-4}
	ZT-DTZNN algorithm (11.11)	1.0686×10^{-7}	1.1038×10^{-4}
	6S-DTZNN algorithm (11.8)	1.2432×10^{-12}	1.2443×10^{-4}
0.0005	NI algorithm (11.16)	4.4401×10^{-4}	5.5818×10^{-5}
	3S-DTZNN algorithm (11.17)	2.0016×10^{-8}	5.7273×10^{-5}
	4S-DTZNN algorithm (11.18)	1.7838×10^{-11}	5.7957×10^{-5}
	ET-DTGNN algorithm (11.15)	3.9197×10^{-3}	5.4252×10^{-5}
	ET-DTZNN algorithm (11.14)	1.3719×10^{-5}	1.0781×10^{-4}
	ZT-DTZNN algorithm (11.11)	1.2813×10^{-8}	1.1006×10^{-4}
	6S-DTZNN algorithm (11.8)	4.7149×10^{-14}	1.2086×10^{-4}

Besides, Table 11.3 shows the MSSTE and average computing time per updating (ACTPU) data with different values of sampling gap g (i.e., $g = 0.01$, 0.005, 0.001, and 0.0005 s). Meanwhile, the MSSTEs synthesized by these seven algorithms with different sampling gap values are presented in Figure 11.5. From Table 11.3 and Figure 11.5, the theoretical results of the algorithm precision are verified. One finds that the MSSTE synthesized by the 6S-DTZNN algorithm (11.8) is convergent with $\mathcal{O}(g^5)$. The MSSTEs synthesized by the ZT-DTZNN algorithm (11.11) and the ET-DTZNN algorithm (11.14) converge with $\mathcal{O}(g^3)$ and $\mathcal{O}(g^2)$, respectively. Evidently, the 6S-DTZNN algorithm (11.8) has the highest precision. Moreover, in order to realize real-time tracking, the ACTPU

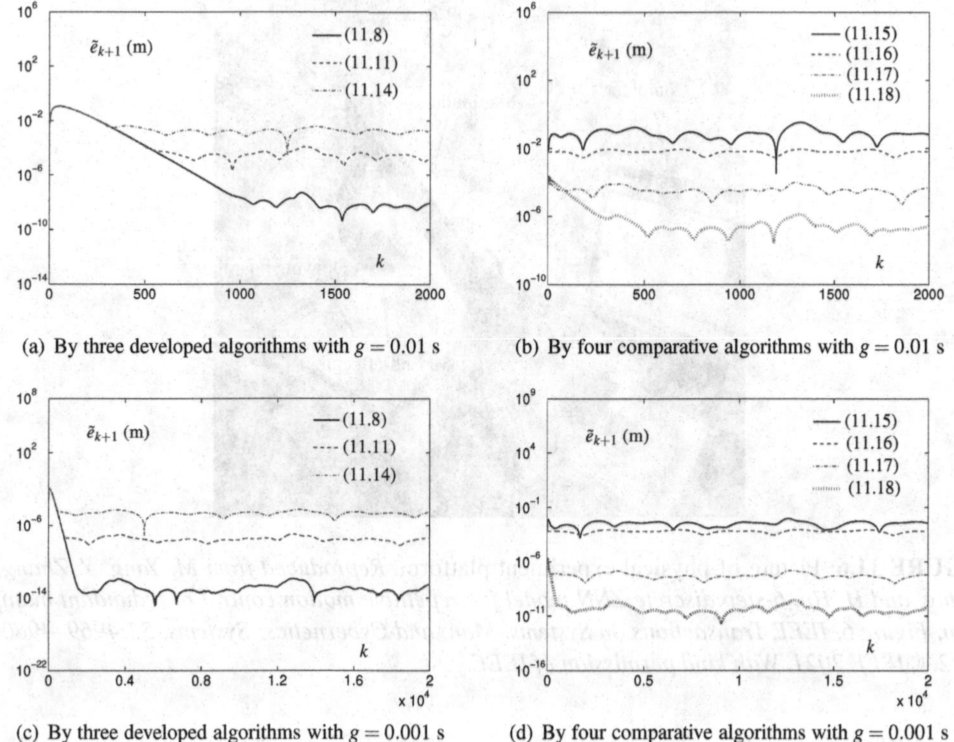

(a) By three developed algorithms with $g = 0.01$ s

(b) By four comparative algorithms with $g = 0.01$ s

(c) By three developed algorithms with $g = 0.001$ s

(d) By four comparative algorithms with $g = 0.001$ s

FIGURE 11.4: Trajectories of tracking errors synthesized by different algorithms when end-effector tracking desired lung-like path.

should be smaller than the sampling gap g. The ACTPU data of the 6S-DTZNN algorithm (11.8), the ZT-DTZNN algorithm (11.11), and the ET-DTZNN algorithm (11.14) are all around 0.1 ms, substantiating the previous analyses about computation complexities. Besides, the ACTPU data of the four other algorithms are around 0.06 ms. Hence, the tracking task is completed successfully by these algorithms, satisfying the real-time tracking requirement.

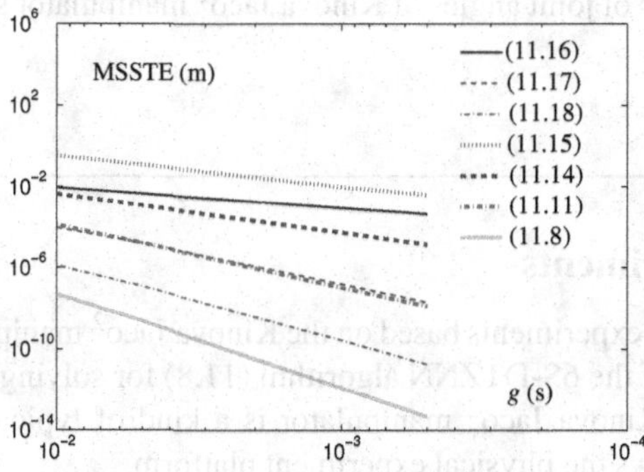

FIGURE 11.5: MSSTEs synthesized by seven algorithms with different values of sampling gap g.

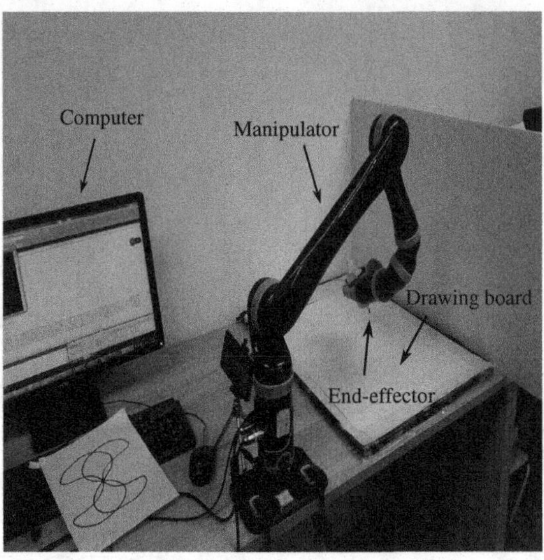

FIGURE 11.6: Picture of physical experiment platform. *Reproduced from M. Yang, Y. Zhang, Z. Zhang, and H. Hu, 6-step discrete ZNN model for repetitive motion control of redundant manipulator, Figure 6, IEEE Transactions on Systems, Man, and Cybernetics: Systems, 52:4969–4980(8), 2022. ©IEEE 2021. With kind permission of IEEE.*

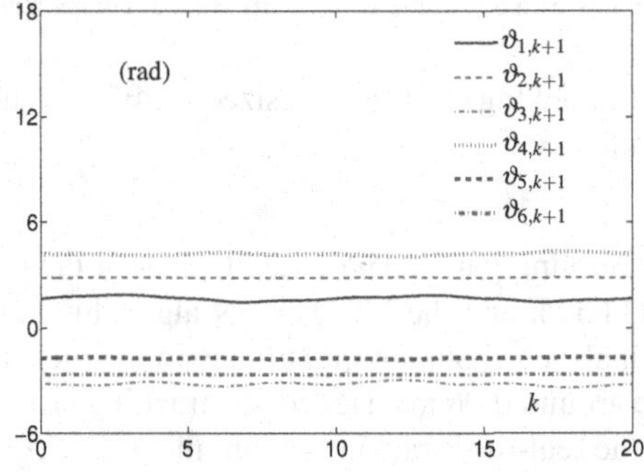

FIGURE 11.7: Trajectories of joint angles of Kinova Jaco^2 manipulator synthesized by 6S-DTZNN algorithm (11.8).

11.5 Physical Experiments

In this section, physical experiments based on the Kinova Jaco^2 manipulator [199] are performed to show the applicability of the 6S-DTZNN algorithm (11.8) for solving the repetitive motion control problem (11.4). The Kinova Jaco^2 manipulator is a kind of typical redundant manipulators. Thereinto, Figure 11.6 shows the physical experiment platform.

First, the end-effector is expected to draw the desired lung-like path on a horizontal plane for better display. The task duration is set as $T = 20$ s. Meanwhile, $\vartheta_0 = [1.675, 2.843, -3.216, 4.187, -1.710, -2.650]^{\mathrm{T}}$ rad is set. Besides, the other important parameters are set as $\hbar = 0.02$ and $g = 0.01$ s for the 6S-DTZNN algorithm (11.8). Next, the 6S-DTZNN algorithm (11.8) is utilized to perform the tracking control of the Kinova Jaco^2 manipulator.

Specifically, the trajectories of joint angles of the Kinova Jaco^2 during the tracking process are presented in Figure 11.7. Besides, Figure 11.8 presents the snapshots of the physical experimental

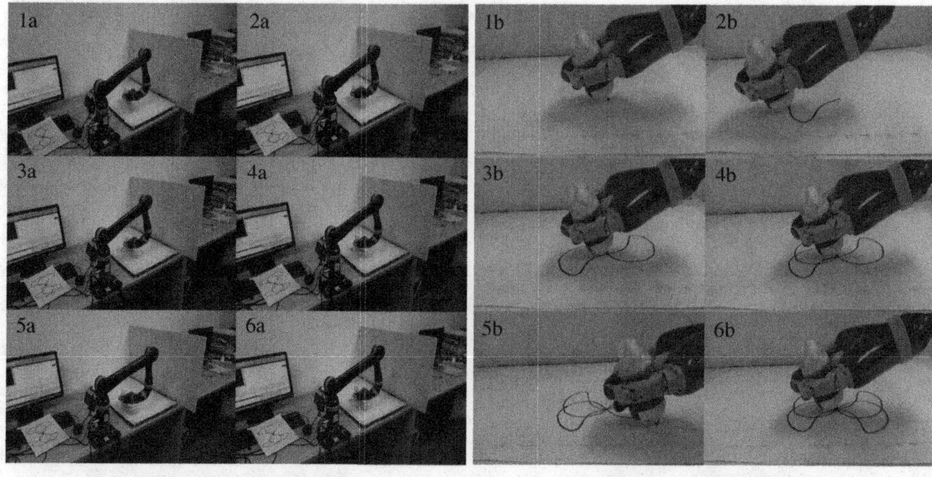

(a) Snapshots of manipulator (b) Snapshots of end-effector

FIGURE 11.8: Experimental snapshots synthesized by 6S-DTZNN algorithm (11.8) for tracking control of Kinova Jaco^2 manipulator. *Reproduced from M. Yang, Y. Zhang, Z. Zhang, and H. Hu, 6-step discrete ZNN model for repetitive motion control of redundant manipulator, Figure 8, IEEE Transactions on Systems, Man, and Cybernetics: Systems, 52:4969–4980(8), 2022. ©IEEE 2021. With kind permission of IEEE.*

results. Particularly, Figure 11.8(a) shows the overall configurations of the Kinova Jaco^2 manipulator during the tracking process. The motion of the manipulator is small during the tracking process, and the final configuration returns to the initial configuration, which means that the repetitive motion is realized. Furthermore, Figure 11.8(b) presents six snapshots of the end-effector. One finds that the tracking task is completed well. Hence, the efficacy and applicability of the 6S-DTZNN algorithm (11.8) are further substantiated by the physical experimental results.

To further substantiate the efficacy of the 6S-DTZNN algorithm (11.8) for repetitive motion control of redundant manipulators, the Kinova Jaco^2 manipulator is driven to track the same desired path for several cycles. Generally, the end-effector actual trajectories synthesized by some algorithms may not be the same because repetitive motion may not be realized. Specifically, the visible non repetitive motion usually happens when using the conventional Euler-type discrete-time pseudoinverse-based (ET-DTPB) algorithm [306]:

$$\vartheta_{k+1} \doteq \vartheta_k + gJ^{\dagger}(\vartheta_k)\dot{\mathbf{r}}_{\mathrm{d},k}. \tag{11.19}$$

By setting parameters like the previous experiment, the ET-DTPB algorithm (11.19) and the 6S-DTZNN algorithm (11.8) are applied to performing the task. First, the lung-like path is desired to be tracked for three cycles. Each cycle task duration is set as $T = 20$ s. Specifically, Figure 11.9(a) presents the experimental results by the ET-DTPB algorithm (11.19). Evidently, the movement of the end-effector is not repetitive, and the deviation is apparent, reflecting that the motion of the manipulator is also not repetitive. Meanwhile, the experimental snapshots using the 6S-DTZNN algorithm (11.8) are shown in Figure 11.9(b). One finds that the actual trajectory is coincident, which reflects the efficacy of the 6S-DTZNN algorithm (11.8).

Next, a four-leaf path is considered to be tracked for three cycles by the ET-DTPB algorithm (11.19) and the 6S-DTZNN algorithm (11.8). Similarly, the corresponding experimental results synthesized by the ET-DTPB algorithm (11.19) are illustrated in Figure 11.9(c). Correspondingly, Figure 11.9(d) shows the experimental results synthesized by the 6S-DTZNN algorithm (11.8). Undoubtedly, the superiority of the 6S-DTZNN algorithm (11.8) is verified.

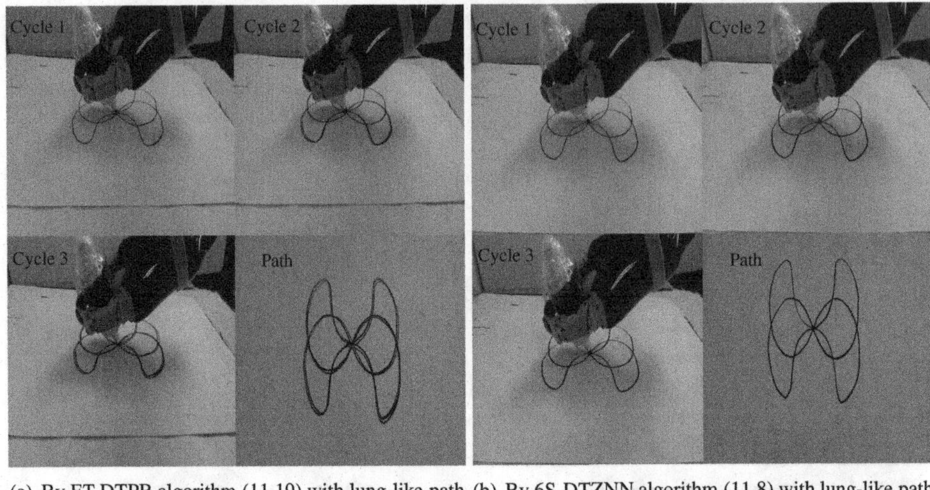

(a) By ET-DTPB algorithm (11.19) with lung-like path (b) By 6S-DTZNN algorithm (11.8) with lung-like path

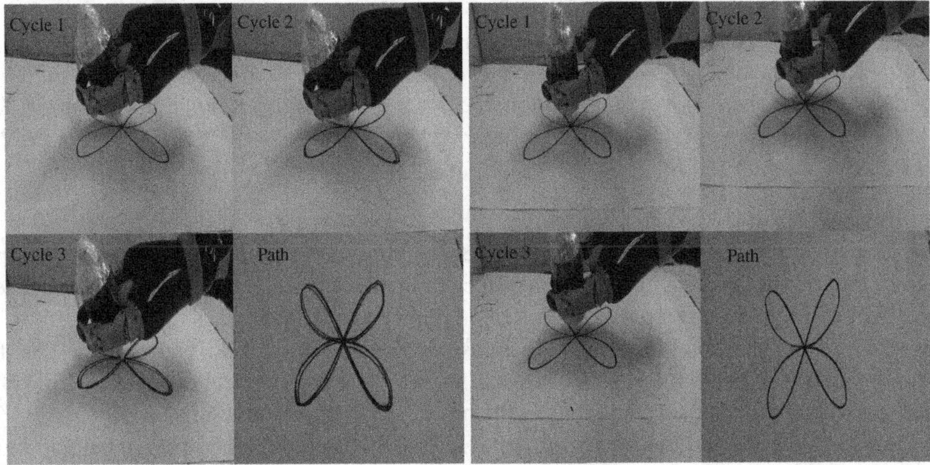

(c) By ET-DTPB algorithm (11.19) with four-leaf path (d) By 6S-DTZNN algorithm (11.8) with four-leaf path

FIGURE 11.9: Experimental snapshots when Kinova Jaco^2 manipulator tracking desired paths for three cycles. *Reproduced from M. Yang, Y. Zhang, Z. Zhang, and H. Hu, 6-step discrete ZNN model for repetitive motion control of redundant manipulator, Figure 9, IEEE Transactions on Systems, Man, and Cybernetics: Systems, 52:4969–4980(8), 2022. ©IEEE 2021. With kind permission of IEEE.*

Furthermore, the index of the joint angle drift is analyzed. Table 11.4 presents the information of approximate joint angle drifts synthesized by the ET-DTPB algorithm (11.19) and the 6S-DTZNN algorithm (11.8) for tracking the lung-like path and the four-leaf path for three cycles. Evidently, joint angle drift phenomenon happens when applying the ET-DTPB algorithm (11.19). Meanwhile, the repetitive motion is realized when applying the 6S-DTZNN algorithm (11.8). Furthermore, the index of the position error is considered to show the excellent performance of the 6S-DTZNN algorithm (11.8) compared with the ET-DTPB algorithm (11.19). Specifically, Table 11.4 shows the information of the approximate position errors synthesized by the ET-DTPB algorithm (11.19) and the 6S-DTZNN algorithm (11.8) for tracking the lung-like path and the four-leaf path for three cycles. From the snapshots and Table 11.4, one finds that the tracking task is completed successfully by the end-effector when the 6S-DTZNN algorithm (11.8) is applied. However, the repetitive

TABLE 11.4: Joint angle drifts and position errors synthesized by ET-DTPB algorithm (11.19) and 6S-DTZNN algorithm (11.8) for tracking lung-like path for and four-leaf path for three cycles.

Lung-like path	ET-DTPB algorithm (11.19)	6S-DTZNN algorithm (11.8)
$\|\vartheta_{T/g} - \vartheta_0\|_2$ (rad)	0.015	Near zero
$\|\vartheta_{2T/g} - \vartheta_0\|_2$ (rad)	0.020	Near zero
$\|\vartheta_{3T/g} - \vartheta_0\|_2$ (rad)	0.040	Near zero
$\|\mathbf{r}_{a,T/g} - \mathbf{r}_{a,0}\|_2$ (m)	0.001	Near zero
$\|\mathbf{r}_{a,2T/g} - \mathbf{r}_{a,0}\|_2$ (m)	0.003	Near zero
$\|\mathbf{r}_{a,3T/g} - \mathbf{r}_{a,0}\|_2$ (m)	0.006	Near zero
Four-leaf path	**ET-DTPB algorithm (11.19)**	**6S-DTZNN algorithm (11.8)**
$\|\vartheta_{T/g} - \vartheta_0\|_2$ (rad)	0.015	Near zero
$\|\vartheta_{2T/g} - \vartheta_0\|_2$ (rad)	0.025	Near zero
$\|\vartheta_{3T/g} - \vartheta_0\|_2$ (rad)	0.050	Near zero
$\|\mathbf{r}_{a,T/g} - \mathbf{r}_{a,0}\|_2$ (m)	0.002	Near zero
$\|\mathbf{r}_{a,2T/g} - \mathbf{r}_{a,0}\|_2$ (m)	0.004	Near zero
$\|\mathbf{r}_{a,3T/g} - \mathbf{r}_{a,0}\|_2$ (m)	0.007	Near zero

motion is not realized and the tracking task is not completed well when the ET-DTPB algorithm (11.19) is applied. In summary, the physical experimental results of the repetitive motion control of redundant manipulator further substantiate the efficacy, superiority, and practicability of the 6S-DTZNN algorithm (11.8).

11.6 Chapter Summary

The repetitive motion control problem has been presented for redundant manipulators. For solving the repetitive motion control problem (11.2), the CTZNN model (11.3) has been developed. For developing a discrete-time and high-precision algorithm, the 6S-ZTD formula (11.5) with high precision has been presented. Then, the 6S-DTZNN algorithm (11.8) has been developed for solving the repetitive motion control problem (11.4). The theoretical analyses have guaranteed that the 6S-DTZNN algorithm (11.8) has satisfying properties. Meanwhile, some other algorithms have also been developed for comparison. Finally, the illustrative numerical experiments based on the four-link redundant manipulator and physical experiments based on the Kinova Jaco^2 manipulator have been conducted to substantiate the efficacy, superiority, and applicability of the 6S-DTZNN algorithm (11.8).

Appendix M: Proof of Theorem 45

According to Taylor expansion [161], one has

$$\zeta_{k+1} = \zeta_k + g\dot{\zeta}_k + \frac{g^2}{2}\ddot{\zeta}_k + \frac{g^3}{6}\dddot{\zeta}_k + \frac{g^4}{24}\zeta_k^{(4)} + \mathscr{O}(g^5), \tag{11.20}$$

$$\zeta_{k-1}=\zeta_k-g\dot{\zeta}_k+\frac{g^2}{2}\ddot{\zeta}_k-\frac{g^3}{6}\dddot{\zeta}_k+\frac{g^4}{24}\zeta_k^{(4)}+\mathscr{O}(g^5), \tag{11.21}$$

$$\zeta_{k-2}=\zeta_k-2g\dot{\zeta}_k+2g^2\ddot{\zeta}_k-\frac{4g^3}{3}\dddot{\zeta}_k+\frac{2g^4}{3}\zeta_k^{(4)}+\mathscr{O}(g^5), \tag{11.22}$$

$$\zeta_{k-3}=\zeta_k-3g\dot{\zeta}_k+\frac{9g^2}{2}\ddot{\zeta}_k-\frac{9g^3}{2}\dddot{\zeta}_k+\frac{27g^4}{8}\zeta_k^{(4)}+\mathscr{O}(g^5), \tag{11.23}$$

$$\zeta_{k-4}=\zeta_k-4g\dot{\zeta}_k+8g^2\ddot{\zeta}_k-\frac{32g^3}{3}\dddot{\zeta}_k+\frac{32g^4}{3}\zeta_k^{(4)}+\mathscr{O}(g^5), \tag{11.24}$$

and

$$\zeta_{k-5}=\zeta_k-5g\dot{\zeta}_k+\frac{25g^2}{2}\ddot{\zeta}_k-\frac{125g^3}{6}\dddot{\zeta}_k+\frac{625g^4}{24}\zeta_k^{(4)}+\mathscr{O}(g^5), \tag{11.25}$$

where $\ddot{\zeta}_k$, $\dddot{\zeta}_k$, and $\zeta_k^{(4)}$ denote the second-order, third-order, and forth-order time derivatives, respectively. By using the algebraic operation "$186\times(11.20)-213\times(11.21)-174\times(11.22)+64\times(11.23)+42\times(11.24)-21\times(11.25)$" and simplifying the result, the following equation is obtained:

$$\dot{\zeta}_k=\frac{31}{82g}\zeta_{k+1}+\frac{29}{123g}\zeta_k-\frac{71}{164g}\zeta_{k-1}-\frac{29}{82g}\zeta_{k-2}+\frac{16}{123g}\zeta_{k-3}+\frac{7}{82g}\zeta_{k-4}-\frac{7}{164g}\zeta_{k-5}+\mathscr{O}(g^4),$$

which is just the 6S-ZTD formula (11.5). The proof is therefore completed. □

Chapter 12

Future Different-Layer Equation System Solving

Abstract

In this chapter, future different-layer equation system (FDLES) is investigated. First, on the basis of zeroing neural network (ZNN) method, a zeroing equivalency (ZE) theorem is presented. Then, a continuous-time ZNN (CTZNN) model is developed for continuous time-dependent different-layer equation system (CTDDLES) solving. Next, a seven-step Zhang time discretization (7S-ZTD) formula is presented to discretize the CTZNN model, and thus a seven-step discrete-time ZNN (7S-DTZNN) algorithm is developed for the FDLES solving. Four-step DTZNN (4S-DTZNN) and three-step DTZNN (3S-DTZNN) algorithms are also developed for the same problem solving. Besides, numerical experiments are executed to substantiate the validity and superiority of the developed 7S-DTZNN algorithm. Finally, the path-tracking control problem of a four-link redundant manipulator is formulated as a specific FDLES problem and can thus be solved by the three DTZNN algorithms. Comparative numerical experimental results further indicate the developed 7S-DTZNN algorithm is much superior to the two other DTZNN algorithms.

12.1 Introduction

The research works on equation systems have been done over the years and have already made great progress in science technology, engineering design, manipulator application, and other fields [132, 334]. Notably, the research work of equation system can be divided into two parts: one is linear equation system and the other is nonlinear equation system. A large number of attempts have been made to solve equation system, with some of them presented in [305, 334–337]. For example, in [334], a fast convergent gradient neural network model was designed for solving linear equation system. In [335], a general framework based on the dynamic repulsion technique and evolutionary algorithms was presented to effectively solve nonlinear equation system. In [336], a new algorithm for solving nonlinear equation system was presented and its semilocal convergence was proved. Since most of the known methods are inherently designed for solving time-independent equation system problems, it may be less effective to apply them to time-dependent equation system problems solving [338], e.g., real-time manipulator motion planning problem.

Solving time-dependent equation system problems is more complicated and more challenging than solving time-independent ones, which requires obtaining the solution at every time instant so as to meet the requirement of stringent real-time computation [338–340]. In the last few decades, neural network methods have been popularly developed and used to solve online science and engineering problems (including equation system) [174, 176, 179, 192, 199, 200, 266, 339–344]. For instance, in [339], aiming at solving online equality-constrained quadratic programming problem, an improved primal recurrent neural network (RNN) and its electronic implementation were presented

DOI: 10.1201/9781003497783-12

and analyzed. In [340] and [176], three RNNs were developed based on different nonlinear activation functions for solving time-dependent linear matrix equations. In [174], a noise-suppressing neural algorithm was presented for solving time-dependent linear equation system. Among them, zeroing neural network (ZNN) as a special class of RNNs is worthy of attention, which is designed specially for various time-dependent problems solving [75, 174, 188, 234, 345, 346]. For example, in [345] and [75], the time-dependent quadratic programming problems were solved by the resultant ZNN models. It is also worth mentioning that the ZNN well inherits the merits of conventional neural networks, e.g., parallel processing.

In general, the traditional single-layer research works on equation system are relatively less complicated, but they may be difficult to satisfy the demands of complex applications in reality, e.g., manipulator path-tracking control with additional restrictions. Along with the research works of time-dependent equation system, we explore a new and interesting problem, i.e., different-layer equation system. Different from the single-layer time-dependent nonlinear or linear equation system, the continuous time-dependent different-layer equation system (CTDDLES) involves one subsystem related to $\mathbf{u}(t)$ and the other subsystem related to $\dot{\mathbf{u}}(t)$, with the corresponding mathematical description as below:

$$\begin{cases} \varphi(\mathbf{u}(t),t) = \mathbf{0}, & (12.1) \\ M(t)\dot{\mathbf{u}}(t) = \mathbf{v}(t), & (12.2) \end{cases}$$

in which $\varphi(\mathbf{u}(t),t) \in \mathbb{R}^{m_1}$, $\mathbf{u}(t) \in \mathbb{R}^{m}$, as well as $\mathbf{v}(t) \in \mathbb{R}^{m_2}$ are time-dependent vectors with $m_1 + m_2 = m$, and $M(t) \in \mathbb{R}^{m_2 \times m}$ is a time-dependent row-full-rank matrix. Besides, the unknown time-dependent solution $\mathbf{u}(t)$ is to be obtained in real time, and $\dot{\mathbf{u}}(t)$ denotes the time derivative of $\mathbf{u}(t)$. Evidently, (12.1) and (12.2) are with respect to $\mathbf{u}(t)$ and $\dot{\mathbf{u}}(t)$, respectively, which can thus be regarded as one subsystem at the position layer and the other subsystem at the velocity layer.

For solving the above CTDDLES (12.1) and (12.2), a zeroing equivalency (ZE) theorem is first presented based on the ZNN method, which indicates the equivalency of solutions at different layers. Then, a continuous-time ZNN (CTZNN) model is developed on the basis of the presented ZE theorem.

Because of the sharp increase in the use of digital computers and related technologies, many signals consist of discrete-time variables rather than continuous-time ones [338, 347]. Given the aforementioned facts as well as for easier digital hardware (such as digital circuits) realization and numerical algorithm development [338], it is imperative to develop the corresponding discrete-time models/algorithms for discrete time-dependent problems solving. In recent years, Zhang time discretization (ZTD) formulas have been applied, which differ from the traditional numerical methods [161, 338]. To be more specific, the ZTD formulas are a class of one-step-ahead numerical-differentiation formulas [93, 321, 348], which can predict the future solutions of problems on the basis of present or previous data information in an effective and accurate manner [93, 321]. For convenience and also for consistency, if a ZTD formula has N steps, we might as well term it as an N-step ZTD (NS-ZTD) formula in this chapter [230]. For instance, in [93], a three-step ZTD (3S-ZTD) formula was utilized to discretize a CTZNN model for solving a discrete time-dependent matrix pseudoinversion problem. In addition, a four-step ZTD (4S-ZTD) formula with higher precision compared with the 3S-ZTD formula was recently presented in [321] to acquire a four-step discrete-time ZNN (4S-DTZNN) algorithm for different-level dynamic linear system solving. To overcome the inherent precision limitation of existing ZTD formulas, finding an effective ZTD formula with higher precision is essential to satisfy more stringent requirement of precision [321, 338].

This chapter [230] first presents a seven-step ZTD (7S-ZTD) formula with higher precision than the above-mentioned 4S-ZTD and 3S-ZTD formulas. Then, based on the CTZNN model and the 7S-ZTD formula, a seven-step DTZNN (7S-DTZNN) algorithm is developed for the future different-layer equation system (FDLES) solving. Likewise, by adopting the 4S-ZTD and 3S-ZTD formulas to discretize the CTZNN model, a 4S-DTZNN algorithm and a three-step DTZNN (3S-DTZNN) algorithm are also obtained, respectively. Note that the developed 7S-DTZNN algorithm can solve the FDLES with higher computational precision, which can satisfy more stringent precision requirement in practice. It is noteworthy that there is an important parameter termed as step length, which is closely associated with the stability of DTZNN algorithms [338]. If the value of the step length is beyond its effective interval, however small the sampling gap is, the residual errors synthesized by DTZNN algorithms cannot converge, which hence results in the failure of the FDLES solving. Considering the importance of the step length, the effective step-length interval of the 7S-DTZNN algorithm is presented and confirmed theoretically, and those of two other DTZNN algorithms are similarly obtained and directly presented. Particularly, the specific problem description of the FDLES is presented as follows, with $\mathbf{u}_{k+1}$ to be obtained at each computational time interval $[t_k, t_{k+1}) \subset [t_{\text{ini}}, t_{\text{fin}}] \subset [0, +\infty)$:

$$\begin{cases} \varphi(\mathbf{u}_{k+1}, t_{k+1}) = \mathbf{0}, & (12.3) \\ M_{k+1}\dot{\mathbf{u}}_{k+1} = \mathbf{v}_{k+1}, & (12.4) \end{cases}$$

in which t_{ini} and t_{fin} represent the initial and final time instants, respectively. Besides, $\varphi(\mathbf{u}_{k+1}, t_{k+1})$, $\mathbf{v}_{k+1}$, and M_{k+1} are generated or measured from the corresponding time-dependent vectors and matrix by sampling at time instant t_{k+1}, respectively. Thereinto, t_{k+1} denotes $t = (k+1)g$, with $k \in \mathbb{N}$ representing the updating index and $g \in \mathbb{R}^+$ denoting the sampling gap. During $[t_k, t_{k+1})$, only the present and previous data information, e.g., M_k, is known and available, whereas the future data information, e.g., M_{k+1}, is unknown. The aim is to find the future unknown solution $\mathbf{u}_{k+1}$ at each computational time interval $[t_k, t_{k+1})$ based on the present or previous data information so as to make the FDLES (12.3) and (12.4) hold true at the next discrete time instant t_{k+1}. It is evident that the FDLES (12.3) and (12.4) are of a more complicated form (i.e., discrete time-dependent and different-layer) compared with the traditional single-layer research works on nonlinear or linear equation system (e.g., solving $\varphi(\mathbf{u}(t), t) = \mathbf{0}$), which can better meet the needs of practical applications.

12.2 CTDDLES Solving

In this section, a ZE theorem is first presented as the research basis. Then, a CTZNN model is further developed for solving the CTDDLES (12.1) and (12.2). Specifically, one has the following ZE theorem.

Theorem 49 *Let the Jacobi matrix $J(\mathbf{u}(t), t) \in \mathbb{R}^{m_1 \times m}$ be defined as $\partial\varphi(\mathbf{u}(t), t)/\partial\mathbf{u}(t)$, and let the partial derivative $\dot{\varphi}_t(\mathbf{u}(t), t) \in \mathbb{R}^{m_1}$ be defined as $\partial\varphi(\mathbf{u}(t), t)/\partial t$. With the ZNN design parameter $\eta \gg 0$ and the time instant $t \gg 0$, the subsystem (12.1) at the position layer is equivalent to the following subsystem at the velocity layer:*

$$J(\mathbf{u}(t), t)\dot{\mathbf{u}}(t) = -\eta\varphi(\mathbf{u}(t), t) - \dot{\varphi}_t(\mathbf{u}(t), t). \tag{12.5}$$

Proof. In order to solve the subsystem (12.1), a zeroing function (ZF) is defined on the basis of the ZNN method [234, 338]:

$$\mathbf{z}(t) = \varphi(\mathbf{u}(t), t). \tag{12.6}$$

Then, the ZNN design formula is adopted to zero out $\mathbf{z}(t)$:

$$\dot{\mathbf{z}}(t) = -\eta\mathbf{z}(t). \tag{12.7}$$

Combining (12.6) with (12.7), we obtain

$$J(\mathbf{u}(t), t)\dot{\mathbf{u}}(t) + \dot{\varphi}_t(\mathbf{u}(t), t) = -\eta\varphi(\mathbf{u}(t), t),$$

which is actually (12.5). Evidently, finding the solution of (12.5) is equivalent to the process of solving the differential equation $\dot{\mathbf{z}}(t)+\eta\mathbf{z}(t)=\mathbf{0}$, and we obtain $\mathbf{z}(t)=\mathbf{z}(0)\exp(-\eta t)$. When $\eta \gg 0$ and $t \gg 0$, $\mathbf{z}(t)=\mathbf{0}$ physically. Hence, the solution of (12.1) is just that of (12.5) when $\eta \gg 0$ and $t \gg 0$. The proof is therefore completed. □

In accordance with the equivalency between (12.1) and (12.5), we obtain the following combined equation system by replacing (12.1) with (12.5):

$$Q(t)\dot{\mathbf{u}}(t)=\mathbf{p}(t), \tag{12.8}$$

where

$$Q(t)=\begin{bmatrix} J(\mathbf{u}(t),t) \\ M(t) \end{bmatrix} \in \mathbb{R}^{m\times m} \text{ and } \mathbf{p}(t)=\begin{bmatrix} -\eta\varphi(\mathbf{u}(t),t)-\dot{\varphi}_t(\mathbf{u}(t),t) \\ \mathbf{v}(t) \end{bmatrix} \in \mathbb{R}^{m}.$$

For solving (12.8), with $J(\mathbf{u}(t),t)$ and $M(t)$ both being of full row rank, a CTZNN model is presented as

$$\dot{\mathbf{u}}(t)=Q^{-1}(t)\mathbf{p}(t), \tag{12.9}$$

in which $Q^{-1}(t)$ is the inverse matrix of $Q(t)$. It is worth noting that the matrix $Q(t)$ consisting of $J(\mathbf{u}(t),t)$ and $M(t)$ is supposed to be nonsingular in this chapter [230].

12.3 FDLES Solving

In this section, the FDLES solving is considered. First, the seven-step formula and the corresponding 7S-DTZNN algorithm are developed. Then, for comparison purposes, another two DTZNN algorithms, i.e., 4S-DTZNN and 3S-DTZNN algorithms, are also obtained on the foundation of the CTZNN model (12.9) and two different ZTD formulas. Finally, related theoretical analyses are provided.

12.3.1 ZTD formulas and DTZNN algorithms

In this subsection, three different ZTD formulas are used for discretizing the CTZNN model (12.9), and hence the corresponding DTZNN algorithms are developed and obtained.

First, a 7S-ZTD formula with high precision is presented by the following theorem.

Theorem 50 *With the sufficiently small sampling gap $g\in(0,1)$, let $\mathscr{O}(g^4)$ denote the error (especially, the truncation error) positively or negatively proportional to g^4, i.e., of the order of g^4. Suppose that $\zeta(t)$ is sufficiently smooth. With $\zeta_{k+1}=\zeta(t_{k+1})=\zeta((k+1)g)$, the 7S-ZTD formula is presented as follows:*

$$\begin{aligned}\dot{\zeta}_k=&\frac{25}{62g}\zeta_{k+1}+\frac{131}{930g}\zeta_k-\frac{10}{31g}\zeta_{k-1}-\frac{45}{124g}\zeta_{k-2}+\frac{5}{62g}\zeta_{k-3}\\&+\frac{5}{62g}\zeta_{k-4}-\frac{1}{155g}\zeta_{k-5}-\frac{5}{372g}\zeta_{k-6}+\mathscr{O}(g^4).\end{aligned} \tag{12.10}$$

Proof. The proof is presented in Appendix N. □

Then, the 7S-ZTD formula (12.10) is adopted to discretize the CTZNN model (12.9), and hence the corresponding 7S-DTZNN algorithm is developed as

$$\mathbf{u}_{k+1}\doteq\frac{62}{25}Q_k^{-1}\tilde{\mathbf{p}}_k-\frac{131}{375}\mathbf{u}_k+\frac{4}{5}\mathbf{u}_{k-1}+\frac{9}{10}\mathbf{u}_{k-2}-\frac{1}{5}\mathbf{u}_{k-3}-\frac{1}{5}\mathbf{u}_{k-4}+\frac{2}{125}\mathbf{u}_{k-5}+\frac{1}{30}\mathbf{u}_{k-6}, \tag{12.11}$$

in which

$$\tilde{\mathbf{p}}_k = \begin{bmatrix} -\hbar\varphi(\mathbf{u}_k,t_k) - g\dot{\varphi}_t(\mathbf{u}_k,t_k) \\ g\mathbf{v}_k \end{bmatrix} \in \mathbb{R}^m,$$

with $\dot{=}$ denoting the computational assignment operator and $\hbar = g\eta$ representing the step length. The truncation error of (12.11) is $\mathbf{O}(g^5)$ with each element being $\mathscr{O}(g^5)$. Besides, Q_k^{-1} denotes the inverse matrix of $Q(t)$ at time instant $t = kg$. Fixing attention on the developed 7S-DTZNN algorithm (12.11), we need to compute $\mathbf{u}_{k+1}$ by utilizing the data information at/before time instant t_k instead of t_{k+1}, which signifies that the FDLES (12.3) and (12.4) can be solved during $[t_k, t_{k+1})$. Moreover, seven initial state vectors $\mathbf{u}_k$ with $k = 0, 1, \cdots, 6$ are necessary to start up the developed 7S-DTZNN algorithm (12.11). The first one $\mathbf{u}_0$ is relatively arbitrarily set, and the remaining initial state vectors can be generated by adopting the Euler forward formula [161] to discretize the CTZNN model (12.9), i.e., $\mathbf{u}_{k+1} \dot{=} Q_k^{-1}\tilde{\mathbf{p}}_k + \mathbf{u}_k$, with $k = 0, 1, \cdots, 5$.

It is worth pointing out that the jth neuron of the 7S-DTZNN algorithm (12.11) is expressed as

$$\begin{aligned} u_{j,k+1} \dot{=} &\sum_{l=1}^{m} q_{jl}p_l - \frac{131}{375}u_{j,k} + \frac{4}{5}u_{j,k-1} + \frac{9}{10}u_{j,k-2} \\ &- \frac{1}{5}u_{j,k-3} - \frac{1}{5}u_{j,k-4} + \frac{2}{125}u_{j,k-5} + \frac{1}{30}u_{j,k-6}, \end{aligned}$$

in which q_{jl} and p_l denote the corresponding elements of matrix $62Q_k^{-1}/25$ and vector $\tilde{\mathbf{p}}_k$, respectively. Besides, the neural network structure of the 7S-DTZNN algorithm (12.11) is presented in Figure 12.1 for the FDLES (12.3)-(12.4) solving.

For comparison, the 4S-ZTD formula [321] and the 3S-ZTD formula [93] are respectively presented as

$$\dot{\zeta}_k = \frac{7}{16g}\zeta_{k+1} + \frac{1}{12g}\zeta_k - \frac{3}{8g}\zeta_{k-1} - \frac{1}{4g}\zeta_{k-2} + \frac{5}{48g}\zeta_{k-3} + \mathscr{O}(g^3), \tag{12.12}$$

and

$$\dot{\zeta}_k = \frac{3}{5g}\zeta_{k+1} - \frac{3}{10g}\zeta_k - \frac{1}{5g}\zeta_{k-1} - \frac{1}{10g}\zeta_{k-2} + \mathscr{O}(g^2). \tag{12.13}$$

In the same manner, by utilizing the 4S-ZTD formula (12.12) and the 3S-ZTD formula (12.13) to discretize the CTZNN model (12.9), the corresponding 4S-DTZNN algorithm and 3S-DTZNN algorithm are respectively obtained as

$$\mathbf{u}_{k+1} \dot{=} \frac{16}{7}Q_k^{-1}\tilde{\mathbf{p}}_k - \frac{4}{21}\mathbf{u}_k + \frac{6}{7}\mathbf{u}_{k-1} + \frac{4}{7}\mathbf{u}_{k-2} - \frac{5}{21}\mathbf{u}_{k-3}, \tag{12.14}$$

and

$$\mathbf{u}_{k+1} \dot{=} \frac{5}{3}Q_k^{-1}\tilde{\mathbf{p}}_k + \frac{1}{2}\mathbf{u}_k + \frac{1}{3}\mathbf{u}_{k-1} + \frac{1}{6}\mathbf{u}_{k-2}, \tag{12.15}$$

where the truncation errors of (12.14) and (12.15) are $\mathbf{O}(g^4)$ and $\mathbf{O}(g^3)$, respectively. Similar to the 7S-DTZNN algorithm (12.11), four initial state vectors $\mathbf{u}_k$ with $k = 0, 1, 2, 3$ are necessary to start up the 4S-DTZNN algorithm (12.14), and three initial state vectors $\mathbf{u}_k$ with $k = 0, 1, 2$ are necessary to start up the 3S-DTZNN algorithm (12.15) by adopting the Euler forward formula to discretize the CTZNN model (12.9).

12.3.2 Effective interval of step length $\hbar$

It is important to note that there is a parameter termed as the step length in the DTZNN algorithms, which is closely involved with the stability of DTZNN algorithms. If the value of the

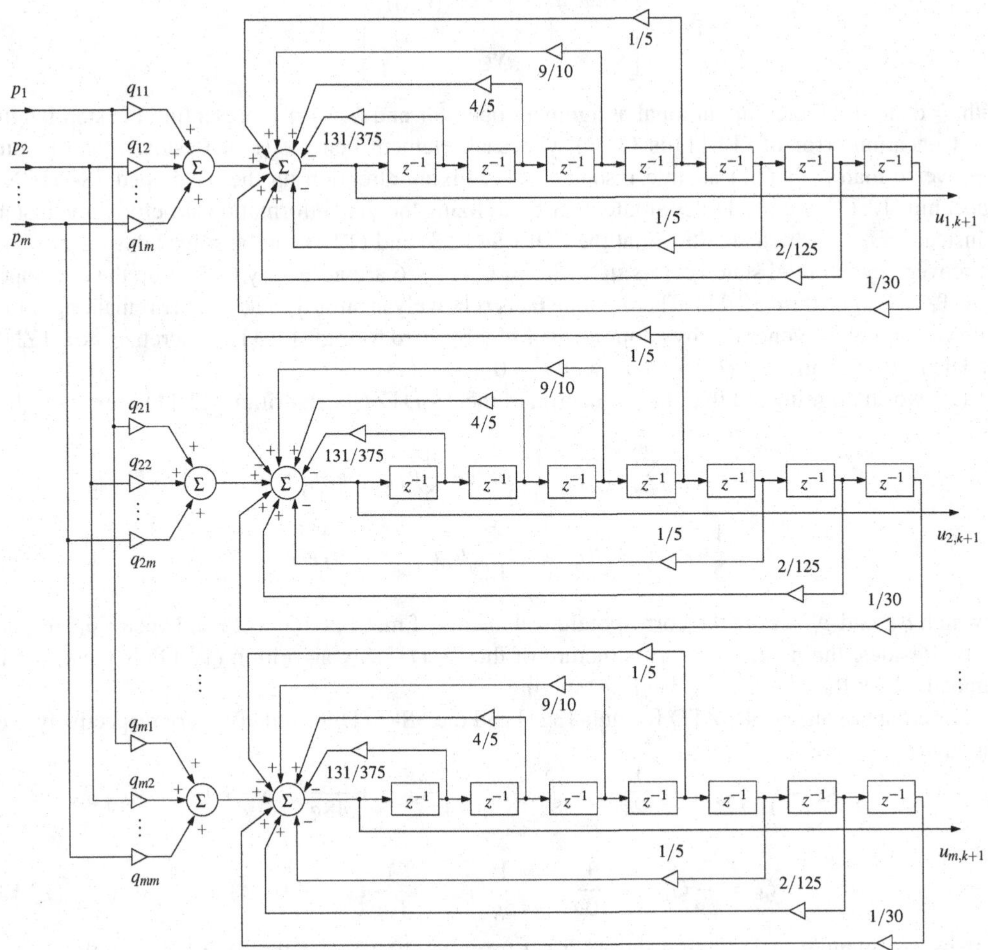

FIGURE 12.1: Neural network structure of 7S-DTZNN algorithm (12.11) for FDLES (12.3) and (12.4) solving [230].

step length is beyond its effective interval, no matter how small the sampling gap is, the DTZNN algorithms cannot achieve convergence in terms of residual errors.

Considering the importance of the step length, we further provide the following theorem.

Theorem 51 *Suppose that Q_k is always nonsingular. With the sufficiently small sampling gap $g \in (0,1)$, the effective interval of the step length $\hbar$ of the 7S-DTZNN algorithm (12.11) is* $(0, 48/155)$.

Proof. The proof is presented in Appendix O. □

For a more intuitive presentation, the effective interval of the step length $\hbar$ of the 7S-DTZNN algorithm (12.11) is shown in Figure 12.2 as well. Furthermore, the effective intervals of the step length $\hbar$ of the 4S-DTZNN algorithm (12.14) and the 3S-DTZNN algorithm (12.15) are $(0, 1/3)$ and $(0, 4/5)$, respectively, with their proofs omitted (which are similar to the proof of Theorem 51).

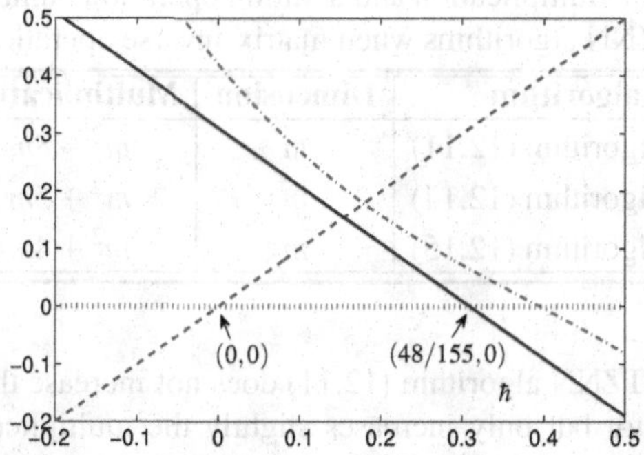

FIGURE 12.2: Effective interval of step length $\hbar$ of 7S-DTZNN algorithm (12.11).

12.3.3 Theoretical analyses

In this subsection, the specific theoretical analyses on zero-stability, consistency, and convergence, as well as the needed multiplication and addition operation numbers per updating of the three DTZNN algorithms are provided.

Firstly, we have the following theorem.

Theorem 52 *Suppose that Q_k is always nonsingular. With the sufficiently small sampling gap $g \in (0,1)$, let $\mathbf{O}(g^5)$ denote the error (especially, the truncation error) with each element being $\mathscr{O}(g^5)$. The 7S-DTZNN algorithm (12.11) is zero-stable, consistent, and convergent, which converges with the order of truncation error being $\mathbf{O}(g^5)$.*

Proof. The characteristic polynomial $\Gamma_7(\imath)$ of the 7S-DTZNN algorithm (12.11) is described as

$$\Gamma_7(\imath) = \imath^7 + \frac{131}{375}\imath^6 - \frac{4}{5}\imath^5 - \frac{9}{10}\imath^4 + \frac{1}{5}\imath^3 + \frac{1}{5}\imath^2 - \frac{2}{125}\imath - \frac{1}{30},$$

which has seven roots, i.e., $\imath_1 = 1$, $\imath_2 = -0.6996 + 0.5873\mathrm{i}$, $\imath_3 = -0.6996 - 0.5873\mathrm{i}$, $\imath_4 = 0.4048 + 0.1933\mathrm{i}$, $\imath_5 = 0.4048 - 0.1933\mathrm{i}$, $\imath_6 = -0.3799 + 0.2329\mathrm{i}$, and $\imath_7 = -0.3799 - 0.2329\mathrm{i}$. Apparently, all roots denoted by $\imath$ of the characteristic equation $\Gamma_7(\imath) = 0$ satisfy $|\imath| \leq 1$ with $|\imath| = 1$ being simple, and, as a result, the 7S-DTZNN algorithm (12.11) is zero-stable. Moreover, the truncation error of the 7S-DTZNN algorithm (12.11) is $\mathbf{O}(g^5)$. Following Definition 3 in Chapter 1, we know that the 7S-DTZNN algorithm (12.11) is consistent. Note that zero-stability plus consistency means convergence [93, 321, 338]. Thus, the 7S-DTZNN algorithm (12.11) converges with the order of truncation error being $\mathbf{O}(g^5)$. The proof is therefore completed. □

Corollary 12 *Suppose that Q_k is always nonsingular. With the sufficiently small sampling gap $g \in (0,1)$, let $\mathbf{O}(g^4)$ or $\mathbf{O}(g^3)$ denote the error (especially, the truncation error) with each element being $\mathscr{O}(g^4)$ or $\mathscr{O}(g^3)$, respectively. The 4S-DTZNN algorithm (12.14) and the 3S-DTZNN algorithm (12.15) are both zero-stable, consistent, and convergent, which converge with the orders of truncation errors being $\mathbf{O}(g^4)$ and $\mathbf{O}(g^3)$, respectively.*

Besides, Table 12.1 lists the multiplication and addition operation numbers per updating of the three DTZNN algorithms when excluding the common matrix-inverse operation. From Table 12.1, we can see that these three DTZNN algorithms have similar computational complexity, although the expression of the 7S-DTZNN algorithm (12.11) appears to be more complicated. Evidently,

TABLE 12.1: Multiplication and addition operation numbers per updating of DTZNN algorithms when matrix-inverse operation excluded.

DTZNN algorithm	Dimension	Multiplication	Addition
7S-DTZNN algorithm (12.11)	m	m^2+8m	m^2+6m
4S-DTZNN algorithm (12.14)	m	m^2+5m	m^2+3m
3S-DTZNN algorithm (12.15)	m	m^2+4m	m^2+2m

the reason is that the 7S-DTZNN algorithm (12.11) does not increase the multiplication operation number of matrix and vector but only increases slightly the multiplication operation number of scalar and vector, as well as the addition operation number of vector and vector.

In brief, the above theoretical analyses show that, with similar computational complexity, the 7S-DTZNN algorithm (12.11) has the best computational performance among the three DTZNN algorithms.

For a more intuitive understanding of the main content of this chapter [230], Table 12.2 lists the problem, scheme, model, and algorithms.

12.4 Numerical Experiments

In this section, numerical experiments are carried out with double-precision floating-point numbers used to substantiate the validity of the developed 7S-DTZNN algorithm (12.11) as well as its superiority to the 4S-DTZNN algorithm (12.14) and the 3S-DTZNN algorithm (12.15).

Example 12.1 Let us consider a specific FDLES problem with $\mathbf{u}_{k+1}$ to be computed at each computational time interval $[kg,(k+1)g) \subset [0,T]$ s, which is equipped with the following time-dependent function, matrix, and vector:

$$\varphi(\mathbf{u}_k,t_k)=\begin{bmatrix}(\sin(t_k)+6)u_{1,k}+u_{2,k}u_{3,k}+u_{4,k}+u_{5,k}\\ u_{2,k}+u_{3,k}+u_{4,k}+\sin(t_k)u_{5,k}+\cos(t_k)\\ 2u_{1,k}+(\cos(t_k)+5)u_{3,k}+u_{4,k}+u_{5,k}+u_{6,k}\end{bmatrix},$$

TABLE 12.2: Problem, scheme, model, and algorithms in this chapter.

Problem	$\begin{cases}\varphi(\mathbf{u}_{k+1},t_{k+1})=\mathbf{0},\\ M_{k+1}\dot{\mathbf{u}}_{k+1}=\mathbf{v}_{k+1}.\end{cases}$
Scheme	*Step 1*: Define ZF as $\mathbf{z}(t)=\varphi(\mathbf{u}(t),t)$. *Step 2*: Adopt ZNN design formula as $\dot{\mathbf{z}}(t)=-\eta\mathbf{z}(t)$. *Step 3*: Adopt ZTD formulas to discretize CTZNN model (12.9).
Model	$\dot{\mathbf{u}}(t)=Q^{-1}(t)\mathbf{p}(t)$.
Algorithms	$\mathbf{u}_{k+1}\doteq\frac{62}{25}Q_k^{-1}\tilde{\mathbf{p}}_k-\frac{131}{375}\mathbf{u}_k+\frac{4}{5}\mathbf{u}_{k-1}+\frac{9}{10}\mathbf{u}_{k-2}-\frac{1}{5}\mathbf{u}_{k-3}-\frac{1}{5}\mathbf{u}_{k-4}+\frac{2}{125}\mathbf{u}_{k-5}+\frac{1}{30}\mathbf{u}_{k-6}$, $\mathbf{u}_{k+1}\doteq\frac{16}{7}Q_k^{-1}\tilde{\mathbf{p}}_k-\frac{4}{21}\mathbf{u}_k+\frac{6}{7}\mathbf{u}_{k-1}+\frac{4}{7}\mathbf{u}_{k-2}-\frac{5}{21}\mathbf{u}_{k-3}$, $\mathbf{u}_{k+1}\doteq\frac{5}{3}Q_k^{-1}\tilde{\mathbf{p}}_k+\frac{1}{2}\mathbf{u}_k+\frac{1}{3}\mathbf{u}_{k-1}+\frac{1}{6}\mathbf{u}_{k-2}$.

$$M_k = \begin{bmatrix} -\sin(0.3t_k)/2 & -\sin(0.4t_k)/5 & -\sin(0.5t_k)/4 \\ -\sin(0.2t_k)/2 & -\sin(0.3t_k)/3 & -\sin(0.4t_k)/4 \\ -\sin(0.1t_k)/3 & -\sin(0.2t_k)/2 & -\sin(0.3t_k)/3 \\ \sin(0.4t_k)+9 & -\sin(0.1t_k) & -\sin(0.2t_k)/2 \\ \cos(0.1t_k) & \sin(0.5t_k)+6 & -\sin(0.1t_k) \\ \cos(0.2t_k)/2 & \cos(0.1t_k) & \sin(0.6t_k)+8 \end{bmatrix}^{\mathrm{T}},$$

and

$$\mathbf{v}_k = [2\cos(0.2t_k), 3\sin(t_k), \cos(0.3t_k)]^{\mathrm{T}}.$$

To verify the validity, the 7S-DTZNN algorithm (12.11) is adopted to solve the above FDLES. The task duration T is set as 40 s, the step length $\hbar$ is set as 0.05, and the sampling gap g is set as 0.1 s. The initial state vector $\mathbf{u}_0$ is relatively arbitrarily set as $[0.6, 0.8, 0.5, 0.7, 0.3, 0.6]^{\mathrm{T}}$. The corresponding numerical experimental results are presented in Figure 12.3. Specifically, Figure 12.3(a) describes the element trajectories of $\mathbf{u}_{k+1} = [u_{1,k+1}, u_{2,k+1}, u_{3,k+1}, u_{4,k+1}, u_{5,k+1}, u_{6,k+1}]^{\mathrm{T}}$, and Figure 12.3(b) describes the element trajectories of $\dot{\mathbf{u}}_{k+1} = [\dot{u}_{1,k+1}, \dot{u}_{2,k+1}, \dot{u}_{3,k+1}, \dot{u}_{4,k+1}, \dot{u}_{5,k+1}, \dot{u}_{6,k+1}]^{\mathrm{T}}$. In addition, the residual error is defined as $\hat{e}_{k+1} = \|\varphi(\mathbf{u}_{k+1}, t_{k+1})\|_2 + \|M_{k+1}\dot{\mathbf{u}}_{k+1} - \mathbf{v}_{k+1}\|_2$, where $\|\cdot\|_2$ denotes the 2-norm of a vector. As displayed in Figure 12.3(c), the residual error $\hat{e}_{k+1}$ converges toward zero quickly. Hence, the validity of the 7S-DTZNN algorithm (12.11) solving the FDLES is well verified.

To further substantiate the superiority of the 7S-DTZNN algorithm (12.11), we also adopt the 4S-DTZNN algorithm (12.14) and the 3S-DTZNN algorithm (12.15) to solve the FDLES in this example. The trajectories of residual errors $\hat{e}_{k+1}$ are presented in Figure 12.4, using the same initial settings but with different values of g. As seen from Figure 12.4(a), the maximal steady-state residual errors (MSSREs) $\lim_{k\to+\infty}\sup\hat{e}_{k+1}$ synthesized by (12.11), (12.14), and (12.15) are of orders 10^{-4}, 10^{-4}, and 10^{-3}, respectively, when $g = 0.1$ s. In Figure 12.4(b), the MSSREs synthesized by (12.11), (12.14), and (12.15) are of orders 10^{-9}, 10^{-8}, and 10^{-6}, respectively, when $g = 0.01$ s. In Figure 12.4(c), the MSSREs synthesized by (12.11), (12.14), and (12.15) are of orders 10^{-14}, 10^{-12}, and 10^{-9}, respectively, when $g = 0.001$ s. It can be concluded that the MSSREs synthesized by (12.11), (12.14), and (12.15) roughly change in the patterns of $\mathscr{O}(g^5)$, $\mathscr{O}(g^4)$, and $\mathscr{O}(g^3)$, respectively, which conforms with the theoretical results presented in Section 12.3. Therefore, the superiority of the 7S-DTZNN algorithm (12.11) is substantiated.

Moreover, the average computing time per updating (ACTPU) data of the three DTZNN algorithms with different values of g are shown in Table 12.3. As seen from the table, the ACTPU data of the three DTZNN algorithms are similar, although those of the 7S-DTZNN algorithm (12.11) are slightly larger. Besides, their ACTPU data are all smaller than the corresponding values of sampling gap g, and hence the validity of computational results (i.e., the requirement of stringent real-time computation) is guaranteed.

Example 12.2 Let us consider the situation that the time-dependent matrix M_k and vector $\mathbf{v}_k$ are the same as those in Example 12.1, and the time-dependent function $\varphi(\mathbf{u}_k, t_k)$ is replaced with the more complicated one as below:

$$\varphi(\mathbf{u}_k, t_k) = \begin{bmatrix} 2\ln(u_{1,k}) + u_{2,k} - u_{3,k}/(t_k+1) + 3u_{4,k} + 3u_{6,k} \\ u_{2,k}u_{3,k} + u_{4,k} - \exp(1/(t_k+1))u_{5,k} + \sin(t_k)/3 \\ u_{1,k} + u_{2,k}^2 + 2u_{3,k} + 4u_{5,k} + (\cos(t_k)+5)u_{6,k} \end{bmatrix},$$

with $\ln(\cdot)$ representing a natural logarithm.

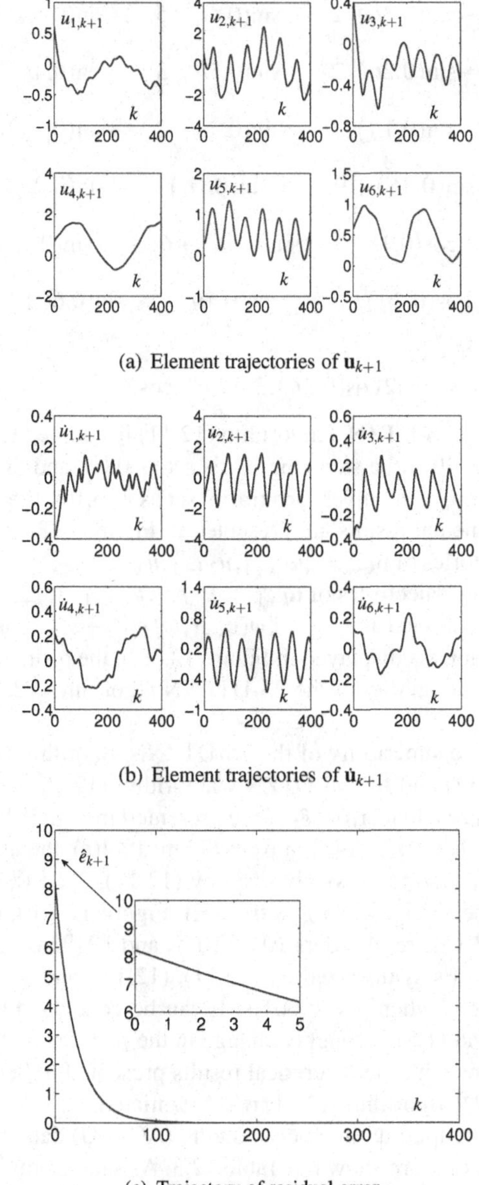

(a) Element trajectories of $\mathbf{u}_{k+1}$

(b) Element trajectories of $\dot{\mathbf{u}}_{k+1}$

(c) Trajectory of residual error

FIGURE 12.3: Trajectories of $\mathbf{u}_{k+1}$, $\dot{\mathbf{u}}_{k+1}$, and residual error $\hat{e}_{k+1}$ synthesized by 7S-DTZNN algorithm (12.11) when solving FDLES in Example 12.1.

TABLE 12.3: ACTPU data of DTZNN algorithms when $\hbar = 0.05$ in Example 12.1.

DTZNN algorithm	$g = 0.1$ s	$g = 0.01$ s	$g = 0.001$ s
7S-DTZNN algorithm (12.11)	0.08776 ms	0.03779 ms	0.03627 ms
4S-DTZNN algorithm (12.14)	0.05051 ms	0.03586 ms	0.03447 ms
3S-DTZNN algorithm (12.15)	0.04714 ms	0.03534 ms	0.03360 ms

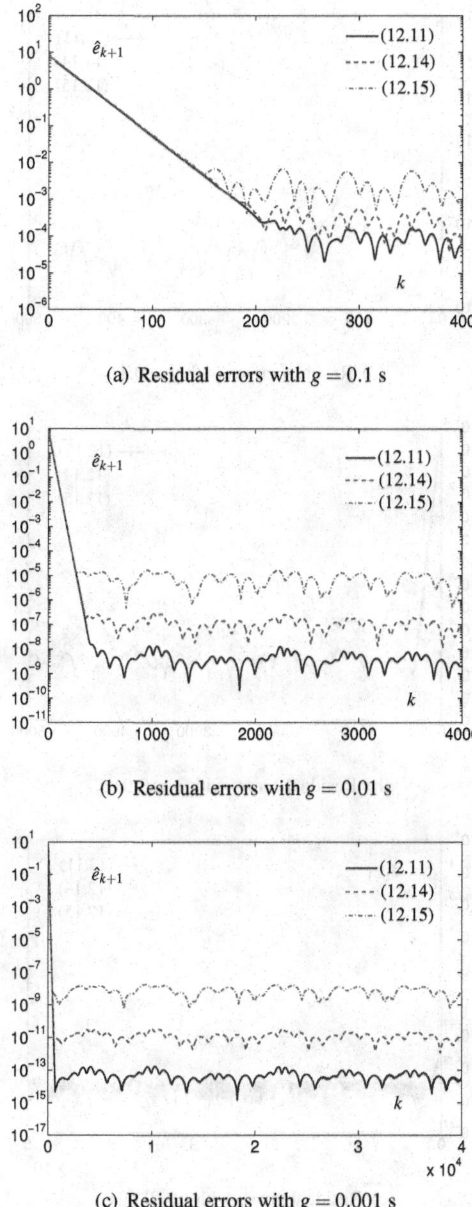

(a) Residual errors with $g = 0.1$ s

(b) Residual errors with $g = 0.01$ s

(c) Residual errors with $g = 0.001$ s

FIGURE 12.4: Trajectories of residual errors $\hat{e}_{k+1}$ synthesized by 7S-DTZNN algorithm (12.11), 4S-DTZNN algorithm (12.14), and 3S-DTZNN algorithm (12.15), respectively, when solving FDLES in Example 12.1.

The initial settings are as follows: $T = 50$ s, $\hbar = 0.08$, and $\mathbf{u}_0 = [0.3, 0.5, 0.4, 0.6, 0.7, 0.8]^{\mathrm{T}}$. The trajectories of residual errors $\hat{e}_{k+1}$ are shown in Figure 12.5 with different values of g (i.e., $g = 0.1$, 0.01, and 0.001 s) when solving the above FDLES.

Similar to Example 12.1, one can conclude that the MSSREs synthesized by (12.11), (12.14), and (12.15) roughly change in the patterns of $\mathcal{O}(g^5)$, $\mathcal{O}(g^4)$, and $\mathcal{O}(g^3)$, respectively, which substantiates the superiority of (12.11) again.

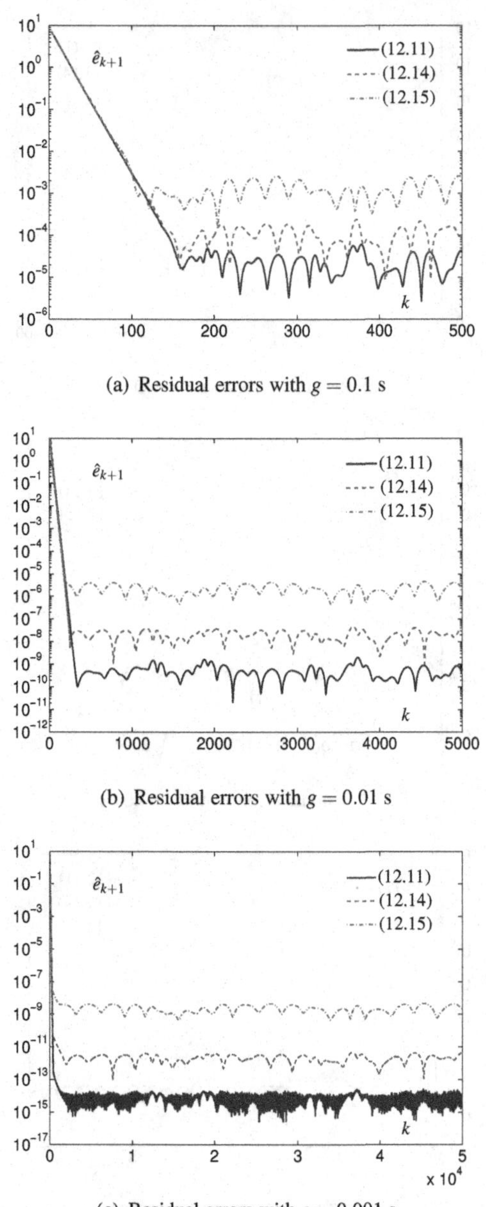

(a) Residual errors with $g = 0.1$ s

(b) Residual errors with $g = 0.01$ s

(c) Residual errors with $g = 0.001$ s

FIGURE 12.5: Trajectories of residual errors $\hat{e}_{k+1}$ synthesized by 7S-DTZNN algorithm (12.11), 4S-DTZNN algorithm (12.14), and 3S-DTZNN algorithm (12.15), respectively, when solving FDLES in Example 12.2.

Besides, Figure 12.6 presents the trajectories of residual errors $\hat{e}_{k+1}$ synthesized by (12.11), (12.14), and (12.15), respectively, with $g = 0.01$ s and various values of $\hbar$, when solving the FDLES in this example. From Figure 12.6(a), it can be observed that the residual errors $\hat{e}_{k+1}$ synthesized by (12.11) are all convergent when the values of $\hbar$ are within the effective interval of the step length (e.g., $\hbar = 0.03$, 0.06, and 0.09), whereas the residual errors $\hat{e}_{k+1}$ are divergent when the values of $\hbar$ are beyond the effective interval of the step length (e.g., $\hbar = 0.5$ and 2). Similarly, as shown in Figure 12.6(b) and (c), the residual errors $\hat{e}_{k+1}$ synthesized by (12.14) and (12.15) are convergent

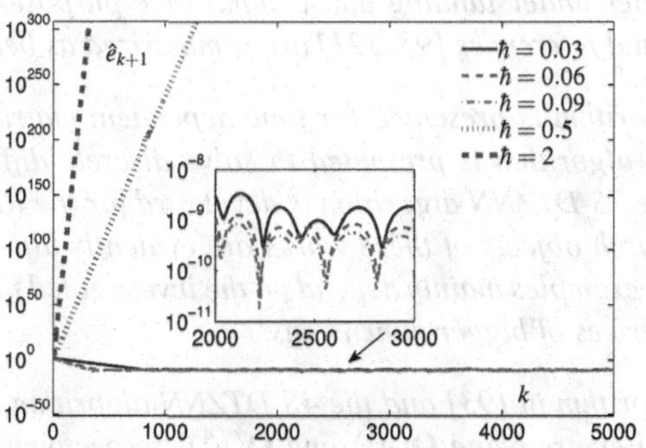

(a) Residual errors synthesized by algorithm (12.11)

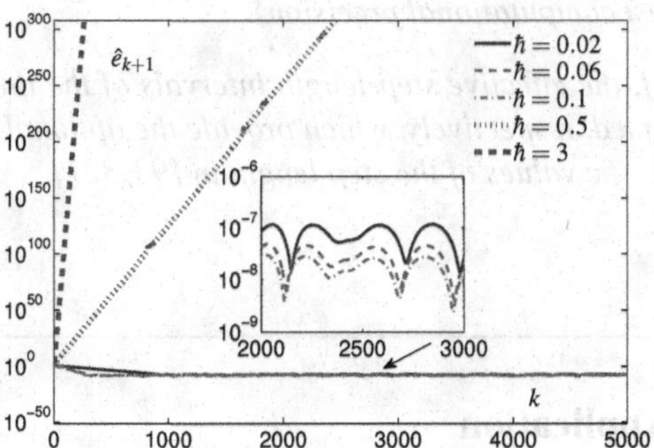

(b) Residual errors synthesized by algorithm (12.14)

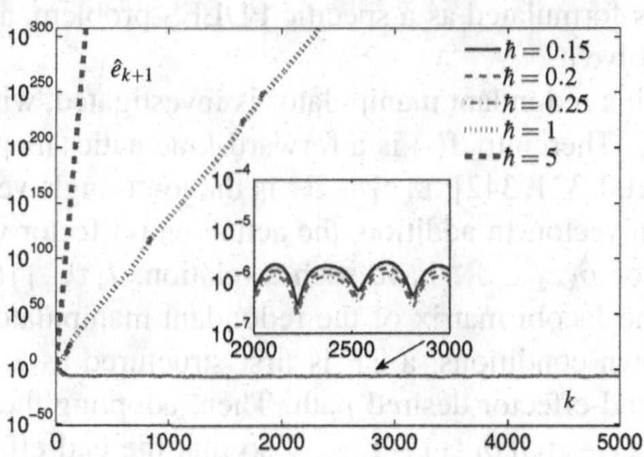

(c) Residual errors synthesized by algorithm (12.15)

FIGURE 12.6: Trajectories of residual errors $\hat{e}_{k+1}$ synthesized by 7S-DTZNN algorithm (12.11), 4S-DTZNN algorithm (12.14), and 3S-DTZNN algorithm (12.15), respectively, with $g = 0.01$ s and various values of $\hbar$, when solving FDLES in Example 12.2.

when the values of $\hbar$ are within the effective interval of the step length (e.g., $\hbar = 0.02$, 0.06, and 0.1 as well as $\hbar = 0.15$, 0.2, and 0.25). However, the residual errors $\hat{e}_{k+1}$ synthesized by (12.14) and (12.15) are divergent when the values of $\hbar$ are beyond the effective interval of the step length (e.g., $\hbar = 0.5$ and 3 as well as $\hbar = 1$ and 5). Thus, selecting an appropriate value of the step length $\hbar$ is crucial, which is closely related to the stability of DTZNN algorithms.

Remark 15 *Here, for better understanding and comparative purposes, the main differences between this chapter [230] and references [93, 321] are summarized as below.*

(1) The 3S-DTZNN algorithm is presented for time-dependent matrix pseudoinversion in [93], and the 4S-DTZNN algorithm is presented to solve discrete different-level dynamic linear system in [321]. The 7S-DTZNN algorithm is developed for the FDLES solving in this chapter [230]. The research objects of these works are evidently different, and hence the corresponding numerical examples mainly depend on the investigated problems themselves instead of just using the matrices of bigger dimensions.

(2) The 3S-DTZNN algorithm in [93] and the 4S-DTZNN algorithm in [321] converge with the orders of truncation errors being $\mathbf{O}(g^3)$ and $\mathbf{O}(g^4)$, respectively. However, the 7S-DTZNN algorithm in this chapter [230] converges with the order of truncation error being $\mathbf{O}(g^5)$. Distinctly, the 7S-DTZNN algorithm is superior to the two other DTZNN algorithms (i.e., the former has the highest computational precision).

(3) In this chapter [230], the effective step-length intervals of the three DTZNN algorithms are presented and confirmed, respectively, which provide the optional intervals of the step length rather than some specific values of the step length in [93, 321].

12.5 Manipulator Application

With the rapid development of technology, manipulators in all walks of life are a wide range of popularity and use [179, 200, 297, 344, 349, 350]. In this section, the redundant manipulator path-tracking control problem is formulated as a specific FDLES problem, and then the three DTZNN algorithms are utilized to solve it.

To be specific, a four-link redundant manipulator is investigated, with the kinematics equation defined as $\mathbf{f}(\vartheta_{k+1}) = \mathbf{r}_{\mathrm{a},k+1}$. Thereinto, $\mathbf{f}(\cdot)$ is a forward-kinematics mapping function with known structure and parameters [200, 321, 342]; $\vartheta_{k+1} \in \mathbb{R}^4$ is the joint-angle vector and $\mathbf{r}_{\mathrm{a},k+1} \in \mathbb{R}^2$ is the actual end-effector position vector. In addition, the actual end-effector velocity vector $\dot{\mathbf{r}}_{\mathrm{a},k+1} \in \mathbb{R}^2$ and the joint velocity vector $\dot{\vartheta}_{k+1} \in \mathbb{R}^4$ have such a relation: $J(\vartheta_{k+1})\dot{\vartheta}_{k+1} = \dot{\mathbf{r}}_{\mathrm{a},k+1}$. We call the term $J(\vartheta_{k+1}) \in \mathbb{R}^{2\times 4}$ as the Jacobi matrix of the redundant manipulator [93, 297, 350]. In accordance with the above known conditions, a ZF is first structured as $\bar{\mathbf{z}}_{k+1} = \mathbf{r}_{\mathrm{a},k+1} - \mathbf{r}_{\mathrm{d},k+1}$, with $\mathbf{r}_{\mathrm{d},k+1} \in \mathbb{R}^2$ denoting the end-effector desired path. Then, adopting the ZNN design formula, we obtain $J(\vartheta_{k+1})\dot{\vartheta}_{k+1} = \dot{\mathbf{r}}_{\mathrm{d},k+1} - \eta(\mathbf{f}(\vartheta_{k+1}) - \mathbf{r}_{\mathrm{d},k+1})$ so that the end-effector can track the desired path. Note that, for the FDLES solving, the matrix M_{k+1} corresponds to $J(\vartheta_{k+1})$ and the vector $\mathbf{v}_{k+1}$ corresponds to $\dot{\mathbf{r}}_{\mathrm{d},k+1} - \eta(\mathbf{f}(\vartheta_{k+1}) - \mathbf{r}_{\mathrm{d},k+1})$ in this section. Besides, we might as well consider $\varphi(\vartheta_{k+1}, t_{k+1}) = \vartheta_{1,k+1} + \vartheta_{2,k+1} + \vartheta_{3,k+1} + \vartheta_{4,k+1} - \pi/3$. In order to solve this FDLES, the 7S-DTZNN algorithm (12.11) is firstly adopted. Thereinto, the task duration T is set as 50 s, the step length $\hbar$ is set as 0.1, and the sampling gap g is set as 0.001 s. The initial joint-angle vector ϑ_0 is set as $[\pi/5, -\pi/5, \pi/9, \pi/3]^{\mathrm{T}}$. The end-effector of redundant manipulator is expected to track a seven-petal flower path expressed as below:

$$\mathbf{r}_{\mathrm{d},k} = \begin{bmatrix} 9/5 + \cos(t_k)/2 + \cos(4t_k/3)/6 \\ 5/2 + \sin(t_k)/2 - \sin(4t_k/3)/6 \end{bmatrix}.$$

TABLE 12.4: MSSTEs synthesized by DTZNN algorithms when $\hbar = 0.1$ in Section 12.5.

DTZNN algorithm	$g = 0.1$ s	$g = 0.01$ s	$g = 0.001$ s
7S-DTZNN algorithm (12.11)	1.517×10^{-4} m	5.207×10^{-9} m	6.439×10^{-14} m
4S-DTZNN algorithm (12.14)	3.119×10^{-4} m	8.857×10^{-8} m	9.257×10^{-12} m
3S-DTZNN algorithm (12.15)	2.894×10^{-3} m	5.702×10^{-6} m	5.890×10^{-9} m

The corresponding numerical experimental results are shown in Figure 12.7(a)–(c). Thereinto, Figure 12.7(a) depicts the trajectories of the manipulator, which can complete the task of tracking a seven-petal flower path. Besides, Figure 12.7(b) depicts the end-effector actual trajectory, which can quickly converge to one location and then almost completely track the desired path (i.e., seven-petal flower). From Figure 12.7(c), we can see that the sum of joint angles $\sum_{i=1}^{4} \vartheta_{i,k+1}$ is identically equal to $\pi/3$ rad, which means that the angle between the fourth link and the X-axis is fixed at $\pi/3$ rad; i.e., the end-effector orientation control is achieved. We define the tracking error as $\tilde{e}_{k+1} = \|\mathbf{r}_{\mathrm{a},k+1} - \mathbf{r}_{\mathrm{d},k+1}\|_2$. To compare with the 4S-DTZNN algorithm (12.14) and the 3S-DTZNN algorithm (12.15) under the same initial conditions, the X-axis and Y-axis tracking errors (i.e., $\tilde{e}_{\mathrm{X},k+1}$ and $\tilde{e}_{\mathrm{Y},k+1}$) are shown in Figure 12.7(d)–(f). As seen from Figure 12.7(d), the X-axis and Y-axis tracking errors synthesized by (12.11) are both of orders 10^{-14} m. Comparatively, in Figure 12.7(e), the X-axis and Y-axis tracking errors synthesized by (12.14) are both of orders 10^{-12} m. Besides, in Figure 12.7(f), the X-axis and Y-axis tracking errors synthesized by (12.15) are both of orders 10^{-9} m. Evidently, in terms of the tracking performance, the 7S-DTZNN algorithm (12.11) is much superior to the two other DTZNN algorithms.

Besides, the maximal steady-state tracking errors (MSSTEs) $\lim_{k\to+\infty} \sup \tilde{e}_{k+1}$ synthesized by the three DTZNN algorithms with different values of g are presented in Table 12.4. As observed from the table, the MSSTEs synthesized by (12.11), (12.14), and (12.15) are of orders 10^{-4} m, 10^{-4} m, and 10^{-3} m, respectively, when $g = 0.1$ s. With g decreased by a factor of 10 to be 0.01 s, their MSSTEs reduced by factors of 10^5, 10^4, and 10^3, respectively. Likewise, with g decreased by a factor of 100 to be 0.001 s, the MSSTEs reduced by factors of 10^{10}, 10^8, and 10^6, respectively. That is, the computational precision of (12.11), (12.14), and (12.15), corresponding to $\mathcal{O}(g^5)$, $\mathcal{O}(g^4)$, and $\mathcal{O}(g^3)$, respectively, is further verified.

12.6 Chapter Summary

In this chapter, the FDLES has been investigated. On the basis of the ZNN method, the ZE theorem has been presented. Besides, the 7S-ZTD formula (12.10) has been presented for discretizing the CTZNN model (12.9), and then the corresponding 7S-DTZNN algorithm (12.11) has been developed for the FDLES solving. Likewise, the 4S-DTZNN algorithm (12.14) and the 3S-DTZNN algorithm (12.15) have also been obtained for the FDLES solving. The corresponding numerical experimental results have substantiated the validity and superiority of the developed 7S-DTZNN algorithm (12.11). Finally, the path-tracking control problem of the four-link redundant manipulator has been formulated as a specific FDLES problem, and the above three DTZNN algorithms have been adopted to solve it. The corresponding numerical experimental results have further substantiated the validity and superiority of the developed 7S-DTZNN algorithm (12.11).

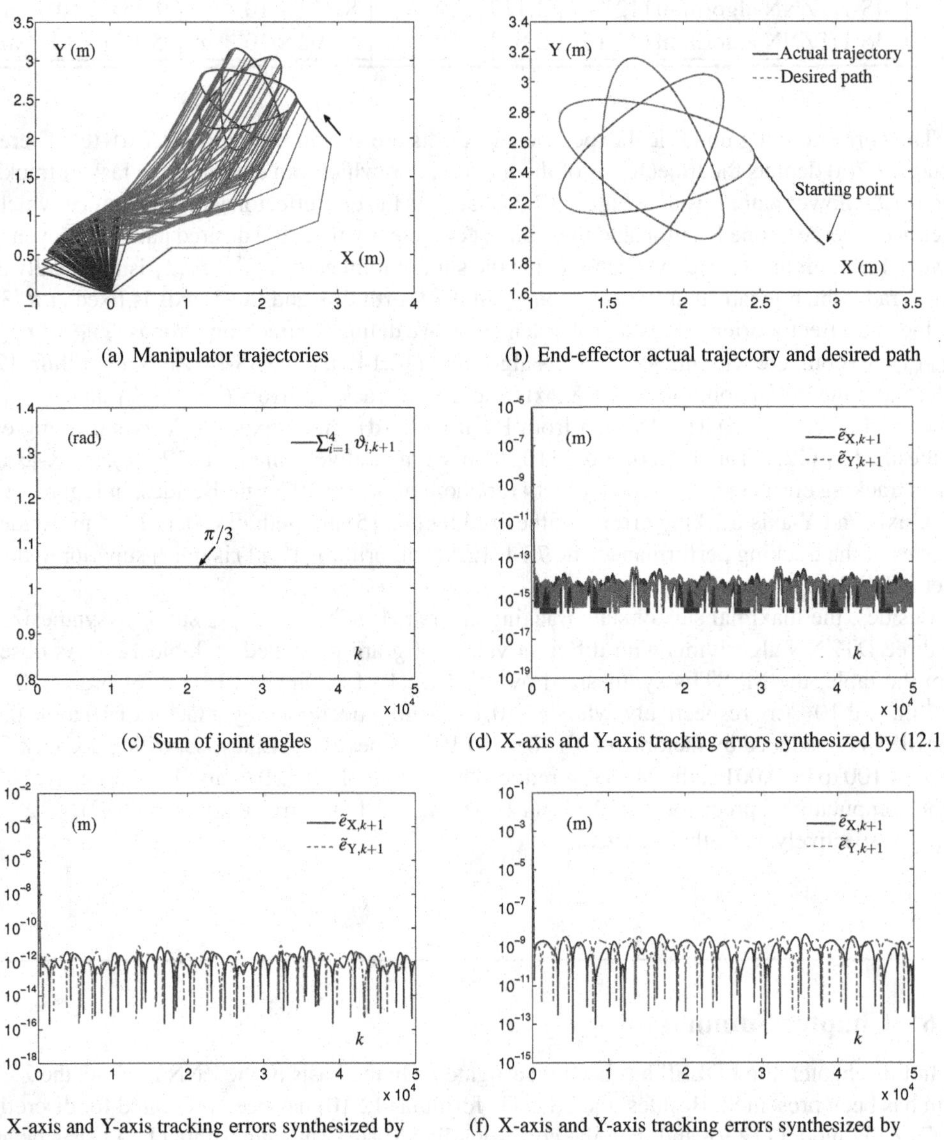

(a) Manipulator trajectories

(b) End-effector actual trajectory and desired path

(c) Sum of joint angles

(d) X-axis and Y-axis tracking errors synthesized by (12.11)

(e) X-axis and Y-axis tracking errors synthesized by algorithm (12.14)

(f) X-axis and Y-axis tracking errors synthesized by algorithm (12.15)

FIGURE 12.7: Trajectories of redundant manipulator, end-effector, and sum of joint angles $\sum_{i=1}^{4} \vartheta_{i,k+1}$ generated by 7S-DTZNN algorithm (12.11), as well as X-axis and Y-axis tracking errors synthesized by 7S-DTZNN algorithm (12.11), 4S-DTZNN algorithm (12.14), and 3S-DTZNN algorithm (12.15), respectively, with $\hbar = 0.1$ and $g = 0.001$ s.

Appendix N: Derivation Process of 7S-ZTD Formula (12.10)

According to Taylor expansion [161], one has

$$\zeta_{k+1} = \zeta_k + g\dot{\zeta}_k + \frac{g^2}{2}\ddot{\zeta}_k + \frac{g^3}{6}\dddot{\zeta}_k + \frac{g^4}{24}\zeta_k^{(4)} + \mathcal{O}(g^5), \tag{12.16}$$

$$\zeta_{k-1} = \zeta_k - g\dot{\zeta}_k + \frac{g^2}{2}\ddot{\zeta}_k - \frac{g^3}{6}\dddot{\zeta}_k + \frac{g^4}{24}\zeta_k^{(4)} + \mathcal{O}(g^5), \tag{12.17}$$

$$\zeta_{k-2} = \zeta_k - 2g\dot{\zeta}_k + 2g^2\ddot{\zeta}_k - \frac{4}{3}g^3\dddot{\zeta}_k + \frac{2}{3}g^4\zeta_k^{(4)} + \mathcal{O}(g^5), \tag{12.18}$$

$$\zeta_{k-3} = \zeta_k - 3g\dot{\zeta}_k + \frac{9}{2}g^2\ddot{\zeta}_k - \frac{9}{2}g^3\dddot{\zeta}_k + \frac{27}{8}g^4\zeta_k^{(4)} + \mathcal{O}(g^5), \tag{12.19}$$

$$\zeta_{k-4} = \zeta_k - 4g\dot{\zeta}_k + 8g^2\ddot{\zeta}_k - \frac{32}{3}g^3\dddot{\zeta}_k + \frac{32}{3}g^4\zeta_k^{(4)} + \mathcal{O}(g^5), \tag{12.20}$$

$$\zeta_{k-5} = \zeta_k - 5g\dot{\zeta}_k + \frac{25}{2}g^2\ddot{\zeta}_k - \frac{125}{6}g^3\dddot{\zeta}_k + \frac{625}{24}g^4\zeta_k^{(4)} + \mathcal{O}(g^5), \tag{12.21}$$

and

$$\zeta_{k-6} = \zeta_k - 6g\dot{\zeta}_k + 18g^2\ddot{\zeta}_k - 36g^3\dddot{\zeta}_k + 54g^4\zeta_k^{(4)} + \mathcal{O}(g^5), \tag{12.22}$$

in which $\ddot{\zeta}_k$, $\dddot{\zeta}_k$, and $\zeta_k^{(4)}$ represent the second-order, third-order, and fourth-order time derivatives of $\zeta(t)$ at time instant t_k, respectively. Let (12.16) multiply 1, let (12.17) multiply $-4/5$, let (12.18) multiply $-9/10$, let (12.19) multiply $1/5$, let (12.20) multiply $1/5$, let (12.21) multiply $-2/125$, and let (12.22) multiply $-1/30$. Adding them all together, we finally obtain

$$\begin{aligned}\dot{\zeta}_k = {} & \frac{25}{62g}\zeta_{k+1} + \frac{131}{930g}\zeta_k - \frac{10}{31g}\zeta_{k-1} - \frac{45}{124g}\zeta_{k-2} + \frac{5}{62g}\zeta_{k-3} \\ & + \frac{5}{62g}\zeta_{k-4} - \frac{1}{155g}\zeta_{k-5} - \frac{5}{372g}\zeta_{k-6} + \mathcal{O}(g^4),\end{aligned}$$

which is just the 7S-ZTD formula (12.10). The proof is therefore completed. □

Appendix O: Effective Interval Proof of Step Length $\hbar$ of 7S-DTZNN Algorithm (12.11)

By adopting the vector form of the 7S-ZTD formula (12.10) to discretize the ZNN design formula (12.7) directly, the following equation is obtained:

$$\begin{aligned}& \frac{25}{62}\mathbf{z}_{k+1} + \left(\hbar + \frac{131}{930}\right)\mathbf{z}_k - \frac{10}{31}\mathbf{z}_{k-1} - \frac{45}{124}\mathbf{z}_{k-2} + \frac{5}{62}\mathbf{z}_{k-3} \\ & + \frac{5}{62}\mathbf{z}_{k-4} - \frac{1}{155}\mathbf{z}_{k-5} - \frac{5}{372}\mathbf{z}_{k-6} + \mathbf{O}(g^5) = \mathbf{0},\end{aligned}$$

of which the characteristic equation is presented as

$$\frac{25}{62}\iota^7 + \left(\hbar + \frac{131}{930}\right)\iota^6 - \frac{10}{31}\iota^5 - \frac{45}{124}\iota^4 + \frac{5}{62}\iota^3 + \frac{5}{62}\iota^2 - \frac{1}{155}\iota - \frac{5}{372} = 0. \tag{12.23}$$

Provided that seven roots' moduli of (12.23) are all less than one, the 7S-DTZNN algorithm (12.11) is stable [351,352]. It may be hard to solve all seven roots directly inside the unit circle. Nevertheless, $|\iota| < 1$ can be transformed as $\mathrm{rea}(\omega) < 0$ by utilizing bilinear transformation (also termed as Tustin transformation [162,163]) $\iota = (\omega+1)/(\omega-1)$, where $\mathrm{rea}(\cdot)$ denotes the operation of taking the real part of the argument. Therefore, (12.23) is rewritten as below:

$$\hbar\omega^7 + (5\hbar+2)\omega^6 + (9\hbar+10)\omega^5 + \left(5\hbar+\frac{56}{3}\right)\omega^4 - \left(5\hbar-\frac{40}{3}\right)\omega^3$$
$$-\left(9\hbar-\frac{882}{155}\right)\omega^2 - \left(5\hbar-\frac{50}{31}\right)\omega - \hbar + \frac{48}{155} = 0.$$

According to the Routh stability criterion [164], the effective interval of the step length $\hbar$ of the 7S-DTZNN algorithm (12.11) is finally obtained as $(0, 48/155)$. The proof is therefore completed. □

Part VI

$\mathscr{O}(g^5)$ ZTD Formulas and Applications

Chapter 13

Future Matrix Equations Solving

Abstract

In this chapter, time-dependent matrix equation problems, including the Lyapunov equation, the matrix inversion, and the generalized matrix inversion, are investigated in a future (or say, discrete time-dependent) perspective. Then, in order to develop a unified solution algorithm for solving the above three future problems, a future matrix equation (FME) is investigated. A discrete-time unified solution algorithm, which is based on zeroing neural network (ZNN) method and an eight-step Zhang time discretization (8S-ZTD) formula, is thus developed and termed as eight-step discrete-time ZNN (8S-DTZNN) algorithm. Meanwhile, theoretical analyses on the stability and precision of the 8S-DTZNN algorithm are provided. In addition, other DTZNN algorithms obtained from a 6S-ZTD formula, Zhang–Taylor discretization formula, and Euler forward formula are also presented for comparison. Furthermore, numerical experiments, including manipulator motion generation, are conducted and analyzed to substantiate the efficacy and superiority of the 8S-DTZNN algorithm.

13.1 Introduction

Time-dependent matrix equation problems, including the Lyapunov equation, the matrix inversion, and the generalized matrix inversion, are popular subjects. As one of the most common matrix equations, the Lyapunov equation occurs in many fields of science and engineering, such as linear algebra [353], control theory [354], and optimization [355]. Specifically, the Lyapunov equation, especially the time-dependent one, is encountered in many branches of control theory, when Lyapunov's methods are applied to analyze the stability of nonlinear systems or designing an optimal controller [356]. Thus, different algorithms have been derived for solving the Lyapunov equation. For example, Sun *et al* presented an explicit iterative method by adding a parameter on the basis of fixed-point theory about dynamic equations in [357].

The problem of matrix inversion, as a traditional research hotspot, is an essential part in many science fields and engineering applications, such as manipulator kinematics [121], multiple-input multiple-output (MIMO) systems [358], and signal processing [359]. As a basic matrix operation, many various methods have been reported for the matrix inversion [181, 358–360]. In [358], Ma *et al* presented the QR decomposition algorithm for the matrix inversion on the basis of the modified squared Givens rotations, which can be applied to the MIMO systems. Leithead and Zhang proposed a method using the quasi-Newton BFGS $O(N^2)$-operation formula to approximate the inverse of a covariance matrix in Gaussian process regression [360].

Apart from the matrix inversion, finding the generalized inverse of a matrix is also a fundamental matrix operation. Performing quick and accurate generalized matrix inversion contributes significantly in many scientific and engineering aspects [248, 361, 362]. In consideration of its

DOI: 10.1201/9781003497783-13

important role, many efforts have been devoted to developing algorithms for the generalized matrix inversion [5,363,364]. The weighted Moore–Penrose generalized inverse of an arbitrary matrix was solved by Huang and Zhang through Newton iteration [5]. Besides, an algorithm based on the conjugate Gram–Schmidt process was presented for computing the pseudoinverse of a real matrix in [363].

As discussed above, the Lyapunov equation, the matrix inversion, and the generalized matrix inversion are meaningful research topics in engineering and science. In previous works [322,365–367], they were considered in static or continuous time-dependent perspectives and studied separately and individually. However, in consideration of easier hardware implementation and development of numerical methods, investigating time-dependent problems in discrete-time form is significant. Thus, the related three matrix equations are investigated in a discrete time-dependent perspective. That is, we focus on the solution $X_{k+1}=X(t_{k+1})$ at time instant t_{k+1}. Note that only current and previous information is available, and future information remains unknown. Solving these discrete time-dependent problems to obtain X_{k+1} means predicting the solution at the forthcoming future time instant t_{k+1} with the help of current and previous information. Moreover, the requirement of real-time computation is also needed to be satisfied, as X_{k+1} should be obtained before t_{k+1} arrives. In this case, such discrete time-dependent problems are termed as future problems in this chapter [368].

More importantly, considering the problem formulation of the future Lyapunov equation (FLE), future matrix inversion (FMI), and future generalized matrix inversion (FGMI), one observes that they all appear as matrix equations, but with different coefficient matrices. On the basis of this observation, they are able to be formulated into a unified problem, i.e., a future matrix equation (FME) problem. Focused on the FME problem, a unified solution algorithm is developed to solve the FLE problem, the FMI problem, and the FGMI problem together by setting corresponding coefficient matrices.

Neural networks and dynamics methods have been considered as powerful tools for real-time processing due to their nature of high-speed parallel distributed processing and feasible implementation on digital hardware [320,369,370]. Being a special class of recurrent neural networks (RNNs) [43], zeroing neural network (ZNN) is a systematic alternative for solving time-dependent problems. Since it was proposed by Zhang *et al* in 2002 [160], ZNN has been applied by researchers to solving time-dependent problems in different fields [321,323,346]. In [346], four complex ZNN models were developed to deal with the complex-variable time-dependent quadratic programming problem. A class of finite-time ZNN was established to solve linear and nonlinear equations by Xiao *et al* [223,371]. In [223], two robust nonlinear ZNN models were designed to solve the Lyapunov equation with various noises. In [371], two modified ZNN models with nonlinear activation functions were developed and exploited to time-dependent nonlinear equations and the motion tracking control of manipulator devices.

To deal with the FME problem, we develop a continuous-time unified solution model by adopting the ZNN method in this chapter [368]. However, to strictly satisfy the requirement of real-time computation and to take full advantage of ZNN's capability of predicting future solutions, a continuous-time ZNN (CTZNN) model is not yet enough, and a discrete-time ZNN (DTZNN) algorithm is desired. A DTZNN algorithm should be an effective discretization of a corresponding CTZNN model [22, 188, 192, 193]. Thus, effective discretization formulas become the keys to the discrete time-dependent (or say, future) problems.

An effective discretization formula for solving future problems should meet the following two requirements. On the one hand, it must be one-step-ahead (i.e., discretizing ζ_k with ζ_{k+1}, ζ_k, and ζ_{k-1}, $\cdots$). On the other hand, it must lead to a stable and convergent discrete-time algorithm. Zhang time discretization (ZTD) is a class of one-step-ahead numerical-differentiation formulas, which satisfies the above two conditions. Specifically, the Euler forward formula can be seen as the

TABLE 13.1: Comparison among different models and algorithms for solving matrix equations.

Model/Algorithm	Oriented problem	Solution form	Precision
In [223, 373]	Lyapunov equation	Continuous-time	– –
In [181, 322]	Matrix inversion	Continuous-time	– –
In [366, 367]	Generalized matrix inversion	Continuous-time	– –
In [22, 97]	Generalized matrix inversion	Discrete-time	$\mathscr{O}(g^3)$
In [193]	Matrix inversion	Discrete-time	$\mathscr{O}(g^3)$
In [188]	Matrix inversion	Discrete-time	$\mathscr{O}(g^4)$
In this chapter [368]	Unified matrix equation	Discrete-time	$\mathscr{O}(g^6)$

simplest ZTD formula. In recent years, some other ZTD formulas have been proposed and applied by Zhang *et al* [22, 97, 188, 193, 372]. In this chapter [368], an eight-step ZTD (8S-ZTD) formula with high precision is presented to obtain an eight-step DTZNN (8S-DTZNN) algorithm for solving the FME problem. A comparison of the 8S-DTZNN algorithm with existing models and algorithms is presented in Table 13.1, and the corresponding differences and specialties are illustrated. In summary, the 8S-DTZNN algorithm solves different kinds of matrix equations with high precision in a unified manner.

13.2 Problem Formulation of Future Matrix Equations

In real-time solving processing and hardware implementation, especially of engineering problems, time-dependent problems are usually formulated in discrete-time form. In this chapter [368], discrete time-dependent problems are named future problems, as their solutions at the future time instant t_{k+1} are desired, i.e., to obtain solution $X_{k+1} = X(t_{k+1})$ at each computational time interval $[t_k, t_{k+1}) = [kg, (k+1)g)$ with g denoting the sampling gap and $k = 0, 1, 2, \cdots$ denoting the updating index. Thus, in this section, we present the problem formulation of three common matrix equations in a future perspective.

13.2.1 Problem formulation of FLE

Given two time-dependent matrices $A_1(t)$ and $B_1(t)$, the FLE problem is formulated as follows with X_{k+1} to be generated at each computational time interval $[t_k, t_{k+1}) \subset [t_{\text{ini}}, t_{\text{fin}}] \subset [0, +\infty)$:

$$A_{1,k+1}X_{k+1} + X_{k+1}A_{1,k+1}^{\mathrm{T}} = B_{1,k+1}, \tag{13.1}$$

where t_{ini} and t_{fin} represent the initial and final time instants, respectively. Besides, $A_{1,k+1} = A_1(t_{k+1}) = A_1((k+1)g) \in \mathbb{R}^{n\times n}$ and $B_{1,k+1} = B_1(t_{k+1}) = B_1((k+1)g) \in \mathbb{R}^{n\times n}$ are time-dependent square matrices sampled at t_{k+1}; the superscript ^{T} stands for the transpose operator of a matrix; $X_{k+1} \in \mathbb{R}^{n\times n}$ is the solution matrix to be generated for the future equation. Note that it is necessary to deal with future problems because the requirement of real-time computation is desired in applications. However, before time instant t_{k+1} arrives, $A_{1,k+1}$ and $B_{1,k+1}$ remain unavailable. Thus, the challenge of satisfying the condition of real-time computation is to generate the future unknown solution on the basis of present and previous information.

13.2.2 Problem formulation of FMI

As known to us, matrix inversion is often encountered in different applications and problems in fields of engineering and science. The problem formulation of the FMI is presented as below with X_{k+1} to be generated at each computational time interval $[t_k, t_{k+1}) \subset [t_{\text{ini}}, t_{\text{fin}}] \subset [0, +\infty)$:

$$A_{2,k+1}X_{k+1} = I_{n\times n}, \tag{13.2}$$

where $A_{2,k+1} \in \mathbb{R}^{n\times n}$ is a time-dependent matrix sampled from $A_2(t) \in \mathbb{R}^{n\times n}$ at t_{k+1}; $I_{n\times n}$ denotes an $n \times n$ identity matrix; $X_{k+1} \in \mathbb{R}^{n\times n}$ is the unknown inverse of $A_{2,k+1}$. In this chapter [368], we suppose that $A_2(t)$ is nonsingular at any time instant $t \in [t_{\text{ini}}, t_{\text{fin}})$. The objective of the FMI is to generate X_{k+1} at each computational time interval $[t_k, t_{k+1})$, when $A_{2,k+1}$ is not available yet, such that (13.2) holds true and the requirement of real-time computation is satisfied.

13.2.3 Problem formulation of FGMI

To lay a solid foundation for the FGMI, the following lemma is presented.

Lemma 12 *For any time-dependent matrix $A(t) \in \mathbb{R}^{m\times n}$, $\forall t \in [0, +\infty)$, if $\operatorname{rank}(A(t)) = \min\{m,n\}$, then the unique time-dependent generalized inverse of $A(t)$ is given as*

$$A^{\dagger}(t) = \begin{cases} \left(A(t)^{\mathrm{T}}A(t)\right)^{-1}A(t)^{\mathrm{T}}, & \text{when } m > n, \\ A(t)^{\mathrm{T}}\left(A(t)A(t)^{\mathrm{T}}\right)^{-1}, & \text{when } m \le n. \end{cases}$$

Without loss of generality, by assuming $m \le n$ in this chapter [368], the FGMI problem is formulated as follows with X_{k+1} to be generated at each computational time interval $[t_k, t_{k+1}) \subset [t_{\text{ini}}, t_{\text{fin}}] \subset [0, +\infty)$:

$$X_{k+1}(A_{3,k+1}A_{3,k+1}^{\mathrm{T}}) = A_{3,k+1}^{\mathrm{T}}, \tag{13.3}$$

where $A_{3,k+1} \in \mathbb{R}^{m\times n}$ is measured from the smoothly time-dependent matrix $A_3(t)$ by sampling at time instant t_{k+1}; $X_{k+1} \in \mathbb{R}^{n\times m}$ is the unknown generalized inverse of $A_{3,k+1}$. Similarly, the computation of X_{k+1} needs to be completed during $[t_k, t_{k+1})$, with information at present and previous instants.

13.2.4 Unified formulation

Usually, the FLE problem (13.1), the FMI problem (13.2), and the FGMI problem (13.3) are investigated separately [279,364,373]. However, by taking the above three future problems together and comparing them, it is not difficult to see inner connections among them and notice that they can be regarded as specific situations of a unified future equation. Thus, in this chapter [368], different from other research articles that study matrix equations separately and individually, we tend to deal with the above three future problems uniformly. Furthermore, the unified formulation of the FLE problem (13.1), the FMI problem (13.2), and the FGMI problem (13.3) as an FME is presented as follows:

$$A_{k+1}X_{k+1}B_{k+1} + C_{k+1}X_{k+1}D_{k+1} = E_{k+1}, \tag{13.4}$$

where $A_{k+1} \in \mathbb{R}^{m\times n}$, $B_{k+1} \in \mathbb{R}^{m\times n}$, $C_{k+1} \in \mathbb{R}^{m\times n}$, and $D_{k+1} \in \mathbb{R}^{m\times n}$ as well as $E_{k+1} \in \mathbb{R}^{m\times n}$ are matrices sampled from corresponding time-dependent matrices at t_{k+1}; $X_{k+1} \in \mathbb{R}^{n\times m}$ is the solution to be computed at each computational time interval $[t_k, t_{k+1}) \subset [t_{\text{ini}}, t_{\text{fin}}]$.

Note that the FLE problem (13.1), the FMI problem (13.2), and the FGMI problem (13.3) are specific situations of the above FME problem (13.4). Thus, in the ensuing sections, focusing on the unified formulation, we develop a unified solution algorithm and consequently utilize it to solve (13.1), (13.2), and (13.3).

Remark 16 *The inner connections between the FLE problem (13.1), the FMI problem (13.2), the FGMI problem (13.3), and their unified formulation (13.4), are recapped here.*

- *Let A_{k+1} be set as $A_{1,k+1}$; let D_{k+1} be set as $A^{\mathrm{T}}_{1,k+1}$; let E_{k+1} be set as $B_{1,k+1}$; let $B_{k+1} = C_{k+1} = I_{n\times n}$. Then, the FME problem (13.4) degenerates into the FLE problem (13.1).*
- *Suppose that $O_{n\times n}$ denotes an $n\times n$ zero matrix. Let A_{k+1} be set as $A_{2,k+1}$; let $B_{k+1} = E_{k+1} = I_{n\times n}$; let $C_{k+1} = D_{k+1} = O_{n\times n}$. Then, the FME problem (13.4) degenerates into the FMI problem (13.2).*
- *Suppose that $O_{n\times m}$ and $O_{m\times m}$ denote $n\times m$ and $m\times m$ zero matrices, respectively, and $I_{m\times m}$ denotes an $m\times m$ identity matrix. Let A_{k+1} be set as $I_{m\times m}$; let $B_{k+1} = A_{3,k+1}A^{\mathrm{T}}_{3,k+1}$; let E_{k+1} be set as $A^{\mathrm{T}}_{3,k+1}$; let $C_{k+1} = O_{n\times m}$ and $D_{k+1} = O_{m\times m}$. Then, the FME problem (13.4) degenerates into the FGMI problem (13.3).*

Remark 17 *Unification and specialization are both important and interesting directions and contributions of scientific research. Through unification, we may be able to build a unified platform for solving many various problems effectively in a consistent manner and in batch mode. For example, in this chapter [368], we unify and then solve matrix equations, hoping to partially lay the engineering mathematical foundation for the development of future matrix processors or coprocessors, as well as matrix computers. On the other hand, through specialization, we can further improve solution technique and efficiency by considering the characteristics of a specific problem. Such particular and flexible advantages can be taken when using current computers, future matrix processors/coprocessors, and matrix computers for algorithmic development. The combination of the two directions, i.e., unification and also specialization, may be able to help us finally solve different and even all kinds of matrix problems more effectively and more efficiently in the future.*

13.3 Unified Solution Model and Algorithms

In this section, in order to obtain a unified solution algorithm for solving the aforementioned future problems, the unified formulation (13.4) is firstly converted to its continuous-time form. By employing the ZNN method, vectorization technique, and an 8S-ZTD formula with high precision, the 8S-DTZNN algorithm is finally developed.

13.3.1 CTZNN model

According to previous work, the ZNN method has shown its powerful ability to solve time-dependent problems. To employ the ZNN method, the continuous-time form of the unified formulation (13.4) is investigated first:

$$A(t)X(t)B(t)+C(t)X(t)D(t)=E(t),$$

with $X(t)$ denoting the time-dependent solution. Then, the following zeroing function (ZF) is defined:

$$Z(t)=A(t)X(t)B(t)+C(t)X(t)D(t)-E(t). \tag{13.5}$$

To zero out all the elements of $Z(t)$, the ZNN design formula is applied:

$$\dot{Z}(t)=-\eta Z(t), \tag{13.6}$$

with the ZNN design parameter $\eta > 0$. By substituting (13.5) into (13.6), the following equation is obtained:

$$A(t)\dot{X}(t)B(t)+C(t)\dot{X}(t)D(t)=\dot{E}(t)-\dot{A}(t)X(t)B(t)-A(t)X(t)\dot{B}(t)-\dot{C}(t)X(t)D(t) \\ -C(t)X(t)\dot{D}(t)-\eta Z(t). \tag{13.7}$$

For simplicity in representation, we define

$$P(t)=\dot{E}(t)-\dot{A}(t)X(t)B(t)-A(t)X(t)\dot{B}(t)-\dot{C}(t)X(t)D(t)-C(t)X(t)\dot{D}(t)-\eta Z(t),$$

and (13.7) is formulated as

$$A(t)\dot{X}(t)B(t)+C(t)\dot{X}(t)D(t)=P(t). \tag{13.8}$$

In order to solve (13.8) for the solution $X(t)$, we turn to the Kronecker product and the vectorization technique for more convenient matrix operations. Specifically, (13.8) is transformed into

$$\Big(\big(B^{\mathrm{T}}(t)\otimes A(t)\big)+\big(D^{\mathrm{T}}(t)\otimes C(t)\big)\Big)\dot{\mathbf{x}}(t)=\mathbf{p}(t), \tag{13.9}$$

where $\otimes$ denotes the Kronecker product, $\dot{\mathbf{x}}(t)=\mathrm{vec}\big(\dot{X}(t)\big)$, and $\mathbf{p}(t)=\mathrm{vec}\big(P(t)\big)$. Note that $\mathrm{vec}(\cdot)$ denotes the operator of vectorizing a matrix. For example, for a matrix $Q=[\mathbf{q}_1,\mathbf{q}_2,\cdots,\mathbf{q}_n]$, supposing that $\mathbf{q}_i$ (with $i=1,2,\cdots,n$) denotes the ith column of Q, we have

$$\mathrm{vec}(Q)=\mathbf{q}=\begin{bmatrix}\mathbf{q}_1\\ \mathbf{q}_2\\ \vdots\\ \mathbf{q}_n\end{bmatrix}.$$

Furthermore, by defining $L(t)$ as $\big(B^{\mathrm{T}}(t)\otimes A(t)\big)+\big(D^{\mathrm{T}}(t)\otimes C(t)\big)$, we obtain the following equation system:

$$L(t)\dot{\mathbf{x}}(t)=\mathbf{p}(t).$$

With the knowledge of solving linear equation systems, we have the following general solution for $\dot{\mathbf{x}}(t)$:

$$\dot{\mathbf{x}}(t)=L^{+}(t)\mathbf{p}(t)+\big(I_{mn\times mn}-L^{+}(t)L(t)\big)\,\mathbf{y},$$

where $L^{+}(t)$ denotes the conventional pseudoinverse of $L(t)$, $I_{mn\times mn}$ denotes an $mn\times mn$ identity matrix, and $\mathbf{y}\in\mathbb{R}^{mn}$ is any vector. Note that $L^{+}(t)$ is directly computed by MATLAB routine "pinv()" [20]. For convenience in further discussion, by setting $\mathbf{y}=\mathbf{0}$, a particular solution is obtained, and formulated as

$$\dot{\mathbf{x}}(t)=L^{+}(t)\mathbf{p}(t). \tag{13.10}$$

The model (13.10) is named as CTZNN model, and it is the unified solution model for solving the FME problem (13.4).

13.3.2 8S-ZTD formula and 8S-DTZNN algorithm

To solve the unified FME problem (13.4), i.e., to obtain the solution X_{k+1}, a discrete-time unified solution algorithm is desired. We first employ an 8S-ZTD formula to discretize the CTZNN model (13.10). The 8S-ZTD formula is presented by the following theorem.

Theorem 53 *With the sufficiently small sampling gap $g \in (0,1)$, let $\mathscr{O}(g^5)$ denote the error (especially, the truncation error) positively or negatively proportional to g^5, i.e., of the order of g^5. Suppose that $\zeta(t)$ is sufficiently smooth. With $\zeta_{k+1} = \zeta(t_{k+1}) = \zeta((k+1)g)$, the 8S-ZTD formula is formulated as follows:*

$$\begin{aligned}\dot{\zeta}_k = &\frac{140}{393g}\zeta_{k+1} + \frac{4923}{18340g}\zeta_k - \frac{140}{393g}\zeta_{k-1} - \frac{196}{393g}\zeta_{k-2} + \frac{35}{393g}\zeta_{k-3} + \frac{385}{1572g}\zeta_{k-4} \\ &- \frac{98}{1965g}\zeta_{k-5} - \frac{35}{393g}\zeta_{k-6} + \frac{97}{2751g}\zeta_{k-7} + \mathscr{O}(g^5).\end{aligned} \tag{13.11}$$

Proof. The proof is presented in Appendix P. □

By utilizing the 8S-ZTD formula (13.11), the 8S-DTZNN algorithm for solving the FME problem (13.4) is obtained as

$$\mathbf{x}_{k+1} \doteq \frac{393}{140}L_k^+\bar{\mathbf{p}}_k - \frac{14769}{19600}\mathbf{x}_k + \mathbf{x}_{k-1} + \frac{7}{5}\mathbf{x}_{k-2} - \frac{1}{4}\mathbf{x}_{k-3} - \frac{11}{16}\mathbf{x}_{k-4} + \frac{7}{50}\mathbf{x}_{k-5} + \frac{1}{4}\mathbf{x}_{k-6} - \frac{97}{980}\mathbf{x}_{k-7}, \tag{13.12}$$

where $\bar{\mathbf{p}}_k = g\mathbf{p}_k = g\text{vec}(R_k) = \text{vec}(g\dot{E}_k - g\dot{A}_kX_kB_k - gA_kX_k\dot{B}_k - g\dot{C}_kX_kD_k - gC_kX_k\dot{D}_k - \hbar Z_k)$, with $\hbar = g\eta$ denoting the step length, and $\doteq$ stands for the computational assignment operator.

Remark 18 *Normally, before t_{k+1} arrives, the values of the coefficient matrices at t_{k+1} are unavailable, and thus $\mathbf{x}_{k+1}$ cannot be obtained through $\mathbf{x}_{k+1} = (B_{k+1}^{\mathrm{T}} \otimes A_{k+1} + D_{k+1}^{\mathrm{T}} \otimes C_{k+1})^+\text{vec}(E_{k+1})$. With the 8S-DTZNN algorithm (13.12), $\mathbf{x}_{k+1}$ is generated on the basis of current and previous information. Consequently, X_{k+1} is obtained by reconstructing $\mathbf{x}_{k+1}$. It means that the requirement of future solving (computing X_{k+1} at each computational time interval $[t_k, t_{k+1})$) can be satisfied as long as the computing time for per updating is smaller than the sampling gap $g = t_{k+1} - t_k$.*

It is worth pointing out that, for time-independent generalized matrix inversion (i.e., not a future problem), the CTZNN model (13.10) may not be a good choice as the dimension of L is getting larger, which leads to extra amount of computation. However, when it comes to solving the FGMI problem (13.3), we accept the trade off that the 8S-DTZNN algorithm (13.12) needs to compute L_k^+, in light of its capability to predict $X_{k+1} = A_{3,k+1}^{\dagger}$ with current and previous information.

Next, the stability and convergence of the 8S-DTZNN algorithm (13.12) are presented and analyzed in the following theorems. The relevant analyses are based on Definitions 2–4 in Chapter 1.

Theorem 54 *With the sufficiently small sampling gap $g \in (0,1)$, let $\mathbf{O}(g^6)$ denote the error (especially, the truncation error) with each element being $\mathscr{O}(g^6)$. The 8S-DTZNN algorithm (13.12) is zero-stable, consistent, and convergent, which converges with the order of truncation error being $\mathbf{O}(g^6)$.*

Proof. The 8S-DTZNN algorithm (13.12) is considered an eight-step method. According to Definition 2 in Chapter 1, its characteristic polynomial $\Gamma_8(\iota)$ is

$$\Gamma_8(\iota) = \iota^8 + \frac{14769}{19600}\iota^7 - \iota^6 - \frac{7}{5}\iota^5 + \frac{1}{4}\iota^4 + \frac{11}{16}\iota^3 - \frac{7}{50}\iota^2 - \frac{1}{4}\iota + \frac{97}{980}.$$

The roots of $\Gamma_8(\iota)$ are 1, -0.6837 ± 0.6822i, -0.8415 ± 0.3066i, 0.4199 ± 0.3362i, and 0.4572, all of which satisfy $|\iota| \leq 1$ with $|\iota| = 1$ being simple. It is concluded from Definition 2 in Chapter 1 that the 8S-DTZNN algorithm (13.12) is zero-stable.

With (13.10) and (13.11), we have

$$\begin{aligned}\mathbf{x}_{k+1} = &\frac{393}{140}L_k^+\bar{\mathbf{p}}_k - \frac{14769}{19600}\mathbf{x}_k + \mathbf{x}_{k-1} + \frac{7}{5}\mathbf{x}_{k-2} - \frac{1}{4}\mathbf{x}_{k-3} - \frac{11}{16}\mathbf{x}_{k-4} + \frac{7}{50}\mathbf{x}_{k-5} + \frac{1}{4}\mathbf{x}_{k-6} \\ &- \frac{97}{980}\mathbf{x}_{k-7} + \mathbf{O}(g^6).\end{aligned}$$

Thus, the truncation error of the 8S-DTZNN algorithm (13.12) is $\mathbf{O}(g^6)$. On the basis of Definitions 3 and 4 in Chapter 1, the 8S-DTZNN algorithm (13.12) is consistent and converges with the order of truncation error being $\mathbf{O}(g^6)$. The proof is therefore completed. □

Note that the residual error is defined as $\hat{e}_{k+1} = \|A_{k+1}X_{k+1}B_{k+1} + C_{k+1}X_{k+1}D_{k+1} - E_{k+1}\|_{\text{F}}$ in this chapter [368], where $\|\cdot\|_{\text{F}}$ denotes the Frobenius norm of a matrix.

Theorem 55 *Suppose that A_k, B_k, C_k, and D_k are uniformly norm bounded. With the sufficiently small sampling gap $g \in (0,1)$, the maximal steady-state residual error (MSSRE) $\lim_{k\to\infty}\sup\hat{e}_{k+1}$ synthesized by the 8S-DTZNN algorithm (13.12) is $\mathscr{O}(g^6)$.*

Proof. Suppose that X^*_{k+1} is the theoretical solution of the FME problem (13.4) and X_{k+1} is reconstructed from $\mathbf{x}_{k+1}$ obtained by the 8S-DTZNN algorithm (13.12). From Theorem 54, we have $X_{k+1} = X^*_{k+1} + \mathbf{O}(g^6)$ and $A_{k+1}X^*_{k+1}B_{k+1} + C_{k+1}X^*_{k+1}D_{k+1} - E_{k+1} = O_{m\times n}$ with the sufficiently large k and $O_{m\times n}$ denoting an $m \times n$ zero matrix. Thus, it follows that

$$\begin{aligned}
&\lim_{k\to+\infty}\sup\left\|A_{k+1}X_{k+1}B_{k+1} + C_{k+1}X_{k+1}D_{k+1} - E_{k+1}\right\|_{\text{F}}\\
&= \lim_{k\to+\infty}\sup\left\|A_{k+1}X_{k+1}B_{k+1} + C_{k+1}X_{k+1}D_{k+1} - E_{k+1} - O_{m\times n}\right\|_{\text{F}}\\
&= \lim_{k\to+\infty}\sup\left\|A_{k+1}X_{k+1}B_{k+1} + C_{k+1}X_{k+1}D_{k+1} - E_{k+1} - A_{k+1}X^*_{k+1}B_{k+1} - C_{k+1}X^*_{k+1}D_{k+1} + E_{k+1}\right\|_{\text{F}}\\
&= \lim_{k\to+\infty}\sup\left\|A_{k+1}(X_{k+1} - X^*_{k+1})B_{k+1} + C_{k+1}(X_{k+1} - X^*_{k+1})D_{k+1}\right\|_{\text{F}}\\
&= \lim_{k\to+\infty}\sup\left\|A_{k+1}\mathbf{O}(g^6)B_{k+1} + C_{k+1}\mathbf{O}(g^6)D_{k+1}\right\|_{\text{F}} = \mathscr{O}(g^6),
\end{aligned}$$

with A_{k+1}, B_{k+1}, C_{k+1}, and D_{k+1} being uniformly norm bounded. The proof is therefore completed. □

As a conventional numerical method, the order-4 Runge–Kutta method, which is the fundamental of MATLAB routine "ode45()", is a typical tool to solve CTZNN models when dealing with continuous time-dependent problems. For a CTZNN model in the form of $\dot{x}(t) = \varphi(x(t),t)$, the iterative computation steps of the order-4 Runge–Kutta method are expressed as

$$\begin{cases}
\delta_1 = \varphi(x_k, t_k),\\
\delta_2 = \varphi\left(x_k + \frac{g}{2}\delta_1, t_k + \frac{g}{2}\right),\\
\delta_3 = \varphi\left(x_k + \frac{g}{2}\delta_2, t_k + \frac{g}{2}\right),\\
\delta_4 = \varphi(x_k + g\delta_3, t_k + g),\\
x_{k+1} = x_k + \frac{g}{6}(\delta_1 + 2\delta_2 + 2\delta_3 + \delta_4).
\end{cases}$$

It is observed that the above iteration is not suitable for solving the future problems in this chapter [368] as δ_4 is needed to compute x_{k+1}, while it is still unknown during the computational time interval $[t_k, t_{k+1})$.

13.3.3 Other DTZNN algorithms

For further comparison, other DTZNN algorithms obtained by a 6S-ZTD formula [372], Zhang–Taylor discretization formula [22], and Euler forward formula [161] are also presented. Specifically, a 6S-DTZNN algorithm is given as

$$\mathbf{x}_{k+1} \doteq \frac{48}{19}L_k^+\bar{\mathbf{p}}_k - \frac{39}{95}\mathbf{x}_k + \frac{16}{19}\mathbf{x}_{k-1} + \frac{18}{19}\mathbf{x}_{k-2} - \frac{3}{19}\mathbf{x}_{k-3} - \frac{7}{19}\mathbf{x}_{k-4} + \frac{14}{95}\mathbf{x}_{k-5}. \tag{13.13}$$

Besides, a Zhang–Taylor DTZNN (ZT-DTZNN) algorithm is given as

$$\mathbf{x}_{k+1} \doteq L_k^{+}\bar{\mathbf{p}}_k + \frac{3}{2}\mathbf{x}_k - \mathbf{x}_{k-1} + \frac{1}{2}\mathbf{x}_{k-2}. \tag{13.14}$$

What is more, an Euler-type DTZNN (ET-DTZNN) algorithm is expressed as

$$\mathbf{x}_{k+1} \doteq L_k^{+}\bar{\mathbf{p}}_k + \mathbf{x}_k. \tag{13.15}$$

Corollary 13 *With the sufficiently small sampling gap $g \in (0,1)$, let $\mathbf{O}(g^5)$, $\mathbf{O}(g^3)$, or $\mathbf{O}(g^2)$ denote the error (especially, the truncation error) with each element being $\mathscr{O}(g^5)$, $\mathscr{O}(g^3)$, or $\mathscr{O}(g^2)$, respectively. The 6S-DTZNN algorithm (13.13), the ZT-DTZNN algorithm (13.14), and the ET-DTZNN algorithm (13.15) are zero-stable, consistent, and convergent, which converge with the orders of truncation errors being $\mathbf{O}(g^5)$, $\mathbf{O}(g^3)$, and $\mathbf{O}(g^2)$, respectively.*

Corollary 14 *Suppose that A_k, B_k, C_k, and D_k are uniformly norm bounded. With the sufficiently small sampling gap $g \in (0,1)$, the MSSREs synthesized by the 6S-DTZNN algorithm (13.13), the ZT-DTZNN algorithm (13.14), and the ET-DTZNN algorithm (13.15) are $\mathscr{O}(g^5)$, $\mathscr{O}(g^3)$, and $\mathscr{O}(g^2)$, respectively.*

Remark 19 *Before discussing the computation complexity of the four DTZNN algorithms, we suppose that the dimensions of all coefficient matrices in the FME problem (13.4) are $n \times n$. Taking the 8S-DTZNN algorithm (13.12) as an example, we divide it into three parts when analyzing its complexity. The first part is L_k^{+}, which involves the pseudoinverse operation. According to the theoretical analyses in Section 13.3.1, the dimension of L is $n^2 \times n^2$. Therefore, the computational complexity for L_k^{+} is $\mathscr{O}\left((n^2)^3\right)$. The second part is $\bar{\mathbf{p}}_k$, which involves the multiplication of $n \times n$-dimensional matrices and the vectorization operation. Thus, the computational complexity of the second part is $\mathscr{O}(n^3)$. The third part relates to the addition and subtraction of n^2-dimensional vectors, and its computational complexity is $\mathscr{O}(n^2)$. To sum up, the computational complexity is $\mathscr{O}((n^2)^3)$. Note that as the structures of the four DTZNN algorithms are similar, they have similar computational complexity.*

For a more intuitive understanding of the main content of this chapter [368], Table 13.2 lists the problem, scheme, model, and algorithms.

TABLE 13.2: Problem, scheme, model, and algorithms in this chapter.

Problem	$A_{k+1}X_{k+1}B_{k+1} + C_{k+1}X_{k+1}D_{k+1} = E_{k+1}$.
Scheme	*Step 1*: Define ZF as $Z(t) = A(t)X(t)B(t) + C(t)X(t)D(t) - E(t)$. *Step 2*: Adopt ZNN design formula as $\dot{Z}(t) = -\eta Z(t)$. *Step 3*: Adopt discretization formulas to discretize CTZNN model (13.10).
Model	$\dot{\mathbf{x}}(t) = L^{+}(t)\mathbf{p}(t)$.
Algorithms	$\mathbf{x}_{k+1} \doteq \frac{393}{140}L_k^{+}\bar{\mathbf{p}}_k - \frac{14769}{19600}\mathbf{x}_k + \mathbf{x}_{k-1} + \frac{7}{5}\mathbf{x}_{k-2} - \frac{1}{4}\mathbf{x}_{k-3} - \frac{11}{16}\mathbf{x}_{k-4} +$ $\frac{7}{50}\mathbf{x}_{k-5} + \frac{1}{4}\mathbf{x}_{k-6} - \frac{97}{980}\mathbf{x}_{k-7}$, $\mathbf{x}_{k+1} \doteq \frac{48}{19}L_k^{+}\bar{\mathbf{p}}_k - \frac{39}{95}\mathbf{x}_k + \frac{16}{19}\mathbf{x}_{k-1} + \frac{18}{19}\mathbf{x}_{k-2} - \frac{3}{19}\mathbf{x}_{k-3} - \frac{7}{19}\mathbf{x}_{k-4} + \frac{14}{95}\mathbf{x}_{k-5}$, $\mathbf{x}_{k+1} \doteq L_k^{+}\bar{\mathbf{p}}_k + \frac{3}{2}\mathbf{x}_k - \mathbf{x}_{k-1} + \frac{1}{2}\mathbf{x}_{k-2}$, $\mathbf{x}_{k+1} \doteq L_k^{+}\bar{\mathbf{p}}_k + \mathbf{x}_k$.

13.4 Numerical Experiments

In this section, numerical experiments are conducted and corresponding numerical experimental results are shown to verify the theoretical results of the 8S-DTZNN algorithm (13.12) in the previous section. Comparatively, the numerical experimental results synthesized by the 6S-DTZNN algorithm (13.13), the ZT-DTZNN algorithm (13.14), and the ET-DTZNN algorithm (13.15) are also presented. The following experiments are run by MATLAB R2014a on 64-bit Windows 10 platform with Intel Core i7-7700 CPU and 8-GB RAM.

Example 13.1 For the FME problem (13.4), let $B_{k+1} = C_{k+1} = I_{2\times 2}$, and let

$$A_{k+1} = \begin{bmatrix} -\cos(t_{k+1}) - 3 & \sin(t_{k+1}) \\ \sin(t_{k+1}) & \cos(t_{k+1}) - 1.5 \end{bmatrix}$$

and

$$E_{k+1} = \begin{bmatrix} \sin(t_{k+1}) + 1 & \cos(t_{k+1}) \\ \cos(t_{k+1}) & \cos(t_{k+1}) + 0.5 \end{bmatrix}.$$

Then, the unified FME problem (13.4) degenerates into the FLE problem (13.1). The initial state of X_{k+1} is randomly generated as

$$X_0 = \begin{bmatrix} 0.5 & 0.3455 \\ 0.6925 & 0.2613 \end{bmatrix}.$$

By utilizing the vectorization technique, we obtain $\mathbf{x}_0 = [0.5, 0.6925, 0.3455, 0.2613]^{\mathrm{T}}$ to initialize the DTZNN algorithms. In this example, the task duration T is set as 20 s and the step length $\hbar$ is set as 0.05.

First, we present the element trajectories of X_{k+1} synthesized by the 8S-DTZNN algorithm (13.12) with the sampling gap $g = 0.01$ s in Figure 13.1, where the element trajectories of X_{k+1} are depicted in solid curves, and the ones of the theoretical solution X^*_{k+1} are depicted in dash curves. It is observed that the element trajectories of X_{k+1} and X^*_{k+1} coincide after 100 updates, which substantiates the efficacy of the 8S-DTZNN algorithm (13.12).

Furthermore, the residual errors synthesized by different DTZNN algorithms with different values of g are presented in Figure 13.2 to show the precision and superiority of the 8S-DTZNN algorithm (13.12). As observed in Figure 13.2, with g reduced by a factor of 10, the MSSRE synthesized by the 8S-DTZNN algorithm (13.12) increases by a factor of 10^6, which substantiates that the precision of the 8S-DTZNN algorithm (13.12) is $\mathscr{O}(g^6)$ and that it outperforms three other DTZNN algorithms. As provided in Table 13.3, the average computing time per updating (ACTPU) data of the four DTZNN algorithms are provided, and they are all smaller than the chosen values of g. It means that the requirement of real-time computation is satisfied, and the solution X_{k+1} of the FLE problem (13.1) is successfully generated at each computational time interval $[t_k, t_{k+1})$.

Remark 20 *Observed from Figure 13.2, with the sampling gap g reduced by a factor of* 10, *the 6S-DTZNN algorithm (13.13), the ZT-DTZNN algorithm (13.14), and the ET-DTZNN algorithm (13.15) increase their precision by* 10^5, 10^3, *and* 10^2 *times, respectively, which substantiates the superiority of the 8S-DTZNN algorithm (13.12) in terms of precision. Besides, as seen in Table 13.3, the ACTPU data of the four algorithms are similar with different values of g.*

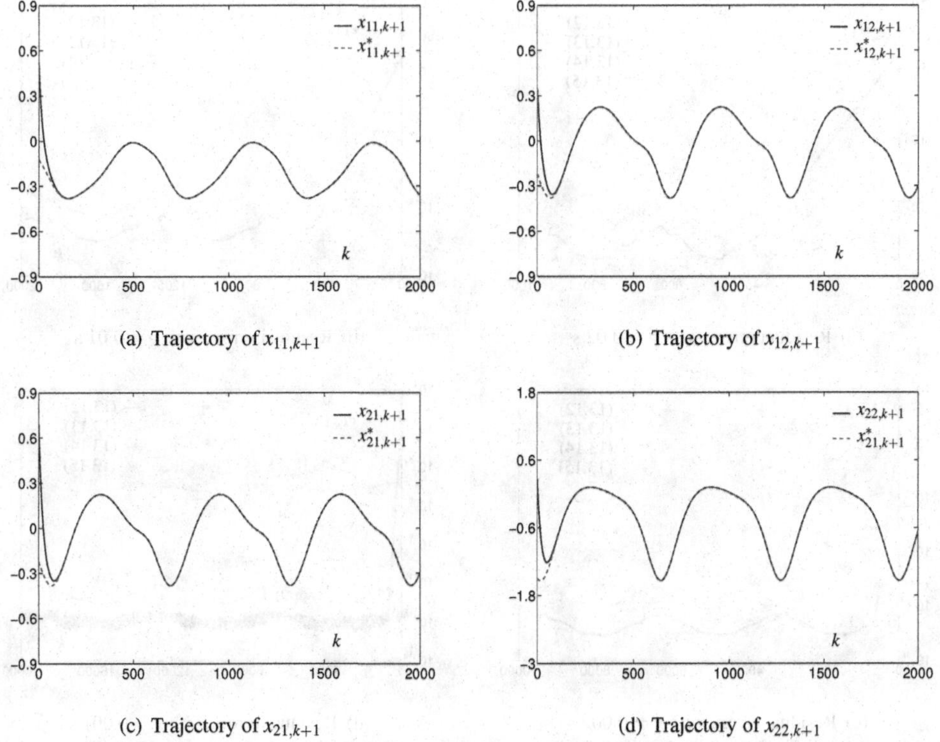

(a) Trajectory of $x_{11,k+1}$

(b) Trajectory of $x_{12,k+1}$

(c) Trajectory of $x_{21,k+1}$

(d) Trajectory of $x_{22,k+1}$

FIGURE 13.1: Element trajectories of X_{k+1} synthesized by 8S-DTZNN algorithm (13.12) with $g = 0.01$ s in Example 13.1.

Example 13.2 For the FME problem (13.4), let $B_{k+1} = E_{k+1} = I_{3\times 3}$ and $C_{k+1} = D_{k+1} = O_{3\times 3}$, and let $A_{k+1} = \bar{A}_{k+1} + S_{k+1}$ with

$$\bar{A}_{k+1} = \begin{bmatrix} \sin(2t_{k+1}) + 3 & \cos(2t_{k+1}) + 1.5 & \cos(2t_{k+1}) \\ 0.5\cos(2t_{k+1}) & \sin(2t_{k+1}) + 3 & 0.5\cos(2t_{k+1}) \\ \cos(2t_{k+1}) & 0.5\cos(2t_{k+1}) & \sin(2t_{k+1}) + 4 \end{bmatrix}$$

and

$$S_{k+1} = 0.01 \times \begin{bmatrix} \sin(4t_{k+1}) & 0 & 0 \\ 0 & \sin(4t_{k+1}) & 0 \\ 0 & 0 & \cos(4t_{k+1}) \end{bmatrix}.$$

Then, the FME problem (13.4) degenerates into the FMI problem (13.2). In this example, with the task duration $T = 20$ s, the step length $\hbar = 0.05$, and a random initial state

$$X_0 = \begin{bmatrix} 0.9649 & 0.9572 & 0.1419 \\ 0.1576 & 0.4854 & 0.4218 \\ 0.9706 & 0.8003 & 0.9157 \end{bmatrix},$$

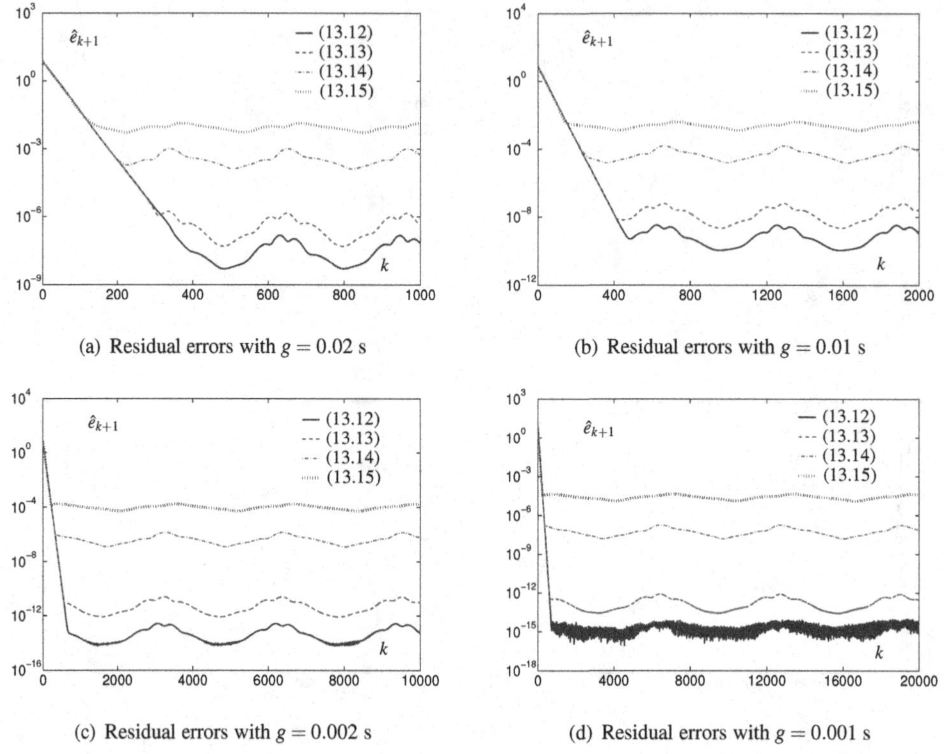

(a) Residual errors with $g = 0.02$ s

(b) Residual errors with $g = 0.01$ s

(c) Residual errors with $g = 0.002$ s

(d) Residual errors with $g = 0.001$ s

FIGURE 13.2: Trajectories of residual errors $\hat{e}_{k+1}$ synthesized by 8S-DTZNN algorithm (13.12), 6S-DTZNN algorithm (13.13), ZT-DTZNN algorithm (13.14), and ET-DTZNN algorithm (13.15) with different g values in Example 13.1.

the corresponding numerical experimental results are presented in Figure 13.3 and Table 13.4.

Specifically, the residual errors $\hat{e}_{k+1}$ synthesized by the 8S-DTZNN algorithm (13.12) as well as three other algorithms, i.e., (13.13), (13.14), and (13.15), are depicted in Figure 13.3 intuitively, and their MSSREs are listed in Table 13.4. It is concluded that the MSSRE synthesized by the 8S-DTZNN algorithm (13.12) is $\mathcal{O}(g^6)$. Furthermore, the ACTPU data of the four DTZNN algorithms are similar and around 0.3 ms. Thus, the requirement of real-time computation can be satisfied with an appropriate value of the sampling gap.

Example 13.3 Manipulator control is a popular subject in modern industrial applications [27, 46, 98, 130, 374]. In this example, the 8S-DTZNN algorithm (13.12) is applied to solve the FGMI problem in real-time motion generation process of a five-link redundant manipulator to examine its effectiveness and potential in practical problems.

Guided by [27], the kinematic equation of a five-link redundant manipulator is expressed as $\mathbf{f}(\vartheta(t)) = \mathbf{r}_\mathrm{a}(t)$, where $\mathbf{f}(\cdot) : \mathbb{R}^5 \to \mathbb{R}^2$ denotes a forward-kinematics mapping function with known structure and parameters; $\vartheta(t) \in \mathbb{R}^5$ denotes the joint-angle vector, and $\mathbf{r}_\mathrm{a}(t) \in \mathbb{R}^2$ denotes the actual position vector of the end-effector.

For real-time motion generation task of a manipulator, it can be regarded as a future problem since its objective is to predict or generate a joint-angle vector at the forthcoming instant $\vartheta(t_{k+1}) = \vartheta_{k+1}$ at the current computational time interval $[t_k, t_{k+1})$. As ϑ_{k+1} is obtained by real-time computation, pulses per second signal is generated in time to control the manipulator so that when the future time instant t_{k+1} arrives, the actual trajectory $\mathbf{r}_\mathrm{a}(t_{k+1}) = \mathbf{r}_{\mathrm{a},k+1}$ can coincide with a desired path $\mathbf{r}_\mathrm{d}(t_{k+1}) = \mathbf{r}_{\mathrm{d},k+1}$, i.e., $\mathbf{r}_{\mathrm{a},k+1} \to \mathbf{r}_{\mathrm{d},k+1}$.

On the basis of the results presented in [46, 98, 130], the kinematic equation of a serial manipulator at the joint-velocity layer with feedback control is expressed as $J(\vartheta_{k+1})\dot{\vartheta}_{k+1} = \dot{\mathbf{r}}_{\mathrm{d},k+1} +$

TABLE 13.3: MSSREs and ACTPU data synthesized by 8S-DTZNN algorithm (13.12), 6S-DTZNN algorithm (13.13), ZT-DTZNN algorithm (13.14), and ET-DTZNN algorithm (13.15) with different g values in Example 13.1.

g (ms)	DTZNN algorithm	MSSRE	ACTPU (ms)
20	8S-DTZNN algorithm (13.12)	1.5030×10^{-7}	0.3265
	6S-DTZNN algorithm (13.13)	1.4136×10^{-6}	0.3306
	ZT-DTZNN algorithm (13.14)	1.0141×10^{-3}	0.3293
	ET-DTZNN algorithm (13.15)	1.3658×10^{-2}	0.3192
10	8S-DTZNN algorithm (13.12)	3.2920×10^{-9}	0.2949
	6S-DTZNN algorithm (13.13)	6.2150×10^{-8}	0.2963
	ZT-DTZNN algorithm (13.14)	1.5680×10^{-4}	0.2980
	ET-DTZNN algorithm (13.15)	4.0272×10^{-3}	0.3013
2	8S-DTZNN algorithm (13.12)	2.6900×10^{-13}	0.3158
	6S-DTZNN algorithm (13.13)	2.4683×10^{-11}	0.3207
	ZT-DTZNN algorithm (13.14)	1.4131×10^{-6}	0.3298
	ET-DTZNN algorithm (13.15)	1.7359×10^{-4}	0.3336
1	8S-DTZNN algorithm (13.12)	9.9258×10^{-15}	0.3303
	6S-DTZNN algorithm (13.13)	7.8243×10^{-13}	0.3300
	ZT-DTZNN algorithm (13.14)	1.7749×10^{-7}	0.3321
	ET-DTZNN algorithm (13.15)	4.3502×10^{-5}	0.3344

$\Delta(\mathbf{r}_{\mathrm{d},k+1}-\mathbf{r}_{\mathrm{a},k+1})$, where Δ denotes a gain index and $J(\vartheta_{k+1})\in\mathbb{R}^{2\times5}$ denotes the Jacobi matrix. Note that $\mathbf{r}_{\mathrm{a},k+1}$ remains unknown in $[t_k,t_{k+1})$ and needs to be estimated by extrapolation formulas as $\hat{\mathbf{r}}_{\mathrm{a},k+1}$. During the motion generation, supposing that the Jacobi matrix $J(\vartheta_{k+1})$ is of full row rank, then $\dot{\vartheta}_{k+1}$ is predicted through $\dot{\vartheta}_{k+1}=J^{\dagger}(\vartheta_{k+1})(\dot{\mathbf{r}}_{\mathrm{d},k+1}+\Delta(\mathbf{r}_{\mathrm{d},k+1}-\hat{\mathbf{r}}_{\mathrm{a},k+1}))$. Furthermore, ϑ_{k+1} is generated in the following way.

$$\begin{cases}\hat{\mathbf{r}}_{\mathrm{a},k+1}\doteq 6\mathbf{r}_{\mathrm{a},k}-15\mathbf{r}_{\mathrm{a},k-1}+20\mathbf{r}_{\mathrm{a},k-2}-15\mathbf{r}_{\mathrm{a},k-3}+6\mathbf{r}_{\mathrm{a},k-4}-\mathbf{r}_{\mathrm{a},k-5},\\ \dot{\vartheta}_{k+1}\doteq J^{\dagger}(\vartheta_{k+1})(\dot{\mathbf{r}}_{\mathrm{d},k+1}+\Delta(\mathbf{r}_{\mathrm{d},k+1}-\hat{\mathbf{r}}_{\mathrm{a},k+1})),\\ \vartheta_{k+1}\doteq\dfrac{300}{137}\left(\dfrac{g}{5}\dot{\vartheta}_{k+1}+\vartheta_k-\vartheta_{k-1}+\dfrac{2}{3}\vartheta_{k-2}-\dfrac{1}{4}\vartheta_{k-3}+\dfrac{1}{25}\vartheta_{k-4}\right).\end{cases} \tag{13.16}$$

It is noticed that most computational operations in the algorithm (13.16) are vector addition and subtraction, which are not time-consuming. Consequently, obtaining $J^{\dagger}(\vartheta_{k+1})$, which is exactly the FGMI problem, becomes the key point of finishing the whole real-time task. Here, the 8S-DTZNN algorithm (13.12) is employed to obtain $J^{\dagger}(\vartheta_{k+1})$ during $[t_k,t_{k+1})$ and expedite the motion generation process.

Furthermore, two conventional pseudoinverse-based algorithms [22,97] are applied for comparison:

$$\vartheta_{k+1}\doteq\vartheta_k+gJ^{+}(\vartheta_k)\dot{\mathbf{r}}_{\mathrm{d},k} \tag{13.17}$$

and

$$\vartheta_{k+1}\doteq\vartheta_k+J^{+}(\vartheta_k)(g\dot{\mathbf{r}}_{\mathrm{d},k}+\hbar(\mathbf{r}_{\mathrm{d},k}-\mathbf{r}_{\mathrm{a},k})). \tag{13.18}$$

The step length $\hbar>0$ is usually set as an appropriate constant.

For simplicity, the five-link redundant manipulator with each link length being 1 m is considered to generate a Rhodonea curve, which is formulated as

$$\mathbf{r}_{\mathrm{d},k+1}=\begin{bmatrix}1+0.2\cos(\pi t_{k+1}/2)+0.5\cos(\pi t_{k+1}/3)\\ 1+0.2\sin(\pi t_{k+1}/2)-0.3\sin(\pi t_{k+1}/3)\end{bmatrix}.$$

TABLE 13.4: MSSREs and ACTPU data synthesized by 8S-DTZNN algorithm (13.12), 6S-DTZNN algorithm (13.13), ZT-DTZNN algorithm (13.14), and ET-DTZNN algorithm (13.15) with different g values in Example 13.2.

g (ms)	DTZNN algorithm	MSSRE	ACTPU (ms)
20	8S-DTZNN algorithm (13.12)	1.1212×10^{-6}	0.2239
	6S-DTZNN algorithm (13.13)	5.6634×10^{-6}	0.2341
	ZT-DTZNN algorithm (13.14)	1.2000×10^{-3}	0.2281
	ET-DTZNN algorithm (13.15)	1.1917×10^{-2}	0.2106
10	8S-DTZNN algorithm (13.12)	3.1659×10^{-8}	0.2270
	6S-DTZNN algorithm (13.13)	3.1312×10^{-7}	0.2257
	ZT-DTZNN algorithm (13.14)	2.1847×10^{-4}	0.2352
	ET-DTZNN algorithm (13.15)	4.0620×10^{-3}	0.2414
2	8S-DTZNN algorithm (13.12)	4.3808×10^{-12}	0.2637
	6S-DTZNN algorithm (13.13)	1.7498×10^{-10}	0.2507
	ZT-DTZNN algorithm (13.14)	2.3525×10^{-6}	0.2549
	ET-DTZNN algorithm (13.15)	2.0837×10^{-4}	0.2588
1	8S-DTZNN algorithm (13.12)	7.4433×10^{-14}	0.2868
	6S-DTZNN algorithm (13.13)	5.7063×10^{-12}	0.2903
	ZT-DTZNN algorithm (13.14)	2.9985×10^{-7}	0.2712
	ET-DTZNN algorithm (13.15)	5.2722×10^{-5}	0.2661

The task duration is set as $T = 20$ s, and the initial joint-angle vector is set as $\vartheta_0 = [3\pi/4, -\pi/2, -\pi/4, \pi/6, \pi/3]^{\mathrm{T}}$ rad. Besides, other parameters are set as $g = 0.01$ s and $\hbar = 0.05$. The corresponding numerical experimental results are depicted in Figure 13.4. The numerical experimental results of the motion generation, depicted in Figure 13.4(a) and (b), show that the actual trajectory generated by the algorithm (13.16) almost overlaps with the desired path after a short period of time. The trajectories of the joint-angle vector ϑ_{k+1} are presented in Figure 13.4(c). As seen from Figure 13.4(d), the algorithm (13.17) generates a Rhodonea curve, but with a deviation, while the algorithm (13.18) generates a desired Rhodonea curve, as shown in Figure 13.4(e). The tracking error of the end-effector between the actual trajectory $\mathbf{r}_{\mathrm{a},k+1}$ and the desired path $\mathbf{r}_{\mathrm{d},k+1}$ is defined as $\tilde{e}_{k+1} = \|\mathbf{r}_{\mathrm{a},k+1} - \mathbf{r}_{\mathrm{d},k+1}\|_2$. The tracking errors synthesized by the algorithms (13.16), (13.17), and (13.18) are displayed in Figure 13.4(f). Evidently, the tracking error synthesized by the algorithm (13.16) is the smallest among three algorithms, which illustrates the efficacy and superiority of the algorithm (13.16). In summary, the satisfying results synthesized by the 8S-DTZNN algorithm (13.12) further illustrate that the 8S-DTZNN algorithm (13.12) is effective for solving the FME problem (13.4) and that it may be efficacious in manipulator application.

13.5 Chapter Summary

In this chapter, the FLE problem (13.1), the FMI problem (13.2), and the FGMI problem (13.3) have been presented. In order to develop a unified solution for these problems, they have been seen as specific situations of the unified future matrix equation (13.4). Then, on the basis of the 8S-ZTD formula (13.11), a discrete-time unified solution algorithm termed as 8S-DTZNN algorithm has been developed. During the theoretical analyses on the 8S-DTZNN algorithm (13.12), it is found

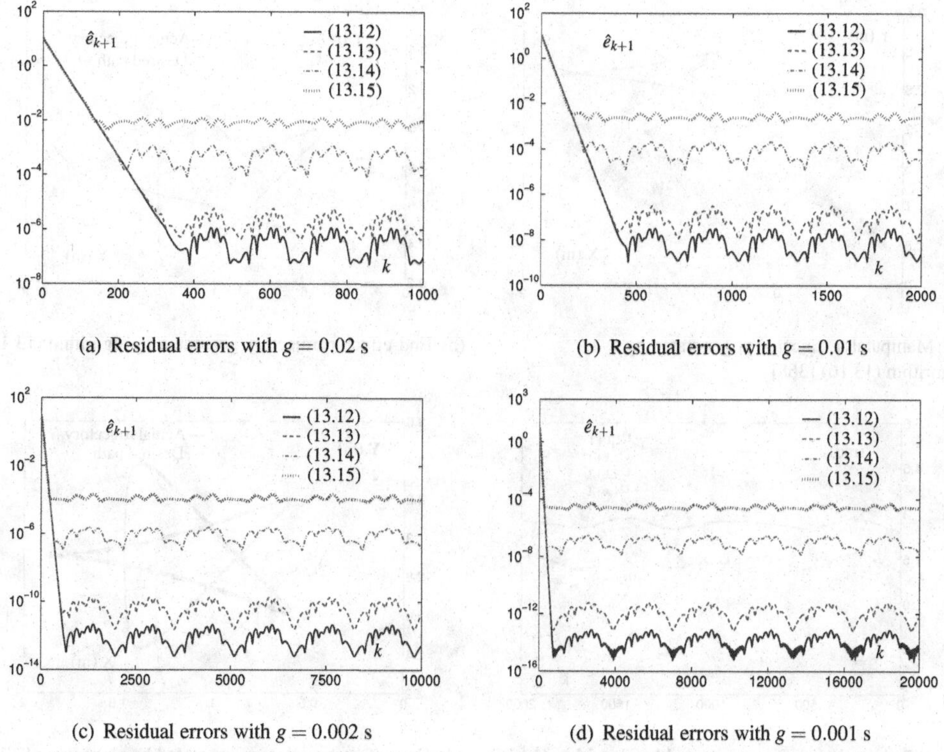

(a) Residual errors with $g = 0.02$ s

(b) Residual errors with $g = 0.01$ s

(c) Residual errors with $g = 0.002$ s

(d) Residual errors with $g = 0.001$ s

FIGURE 13.3: Trajectories of residual errors $\hat{e}_{k+1}$ synthesized by 8S-DTZNN algorithm (13.12), 6S-DTZNN algorithm (13.13), ZT-DTZNN algorithm (13.14), and ET-DTZNN algorithm (13.15) with different g values in Example 13.2.

that the MSSRE synthesized by the 8S-DTZNN algorithm (13.12) is $\mathscr{O}(g^6)$. For comparison, the 6S-DTZNN algorithm (13.13), the ZT-DTZNN algorithm (13.14), and the ET-DTZNN algorithm (13.15) have also been given. Finally, the numerical experimental results have substantiated not only the superiority of the 8S-DTZNN algorithm (13.12) (compared with three other DTZNN algorithms) but also its effectiveness in terms of real-time computation requirement and manipulator application.

Appendix P: Proof of Theorem 53

According to Taylor expansion [161], the following eight equations are obtained:

$$\zeta_{k+1} = \zeta_k + g\dot{\zeta}_k + \frac{g^2}{2}\ddot{\zeta}_k + \frac{g^3}{6}\dddot{\zeta}_k + \frac{g^4}{24}\zeta_k^{(4)} + \frac{g^5}{120}\zeta_k^{(5)} + \mathscr{O}(g^6), \tag{13.19}$$

$$\zeta_{k-1} = \zeta_k - g\dot{\zeta}_k + \frac{g^2}{2}\ddot{\zeta}_k - \frac{g^3}{6}\dddot{\zeta}_k + \frac{g^4}{24}\zeta_k^{(4)} - \frac{g^5}{120}\zeta_k^{(5)} + \mathscr{O}(g^6), \tag{13.20}$$

$$\zeta_{k-2} = \zeta_k - 2g\dot{\zeta}_k + 2g^2\ddot{\zeta}_k - \frac{4g^3}{3}\dddot{\zeta}_k + \frac{2g^4}{3}\zeta_k^{(4)} - \frac{4g^5}{15}\zeta_k^{(5)} + \mathscr{O}(g^6), \tag{13.21}$$

$$\zeta_{k-3} = \zeta_k - 3g\dot{\zeta}_k + \frac{9g^2}{2}\ddot{\zeta}_k - \frac{9g^3}{2}\dddot{\zeta}_k + \frac{27g^4}{8}\zeta_k^{(4)} - \frac{81g^5}{40}\zeta_k^{(5)} + \mathscr{O}(g^6), \tag{13.22}$$

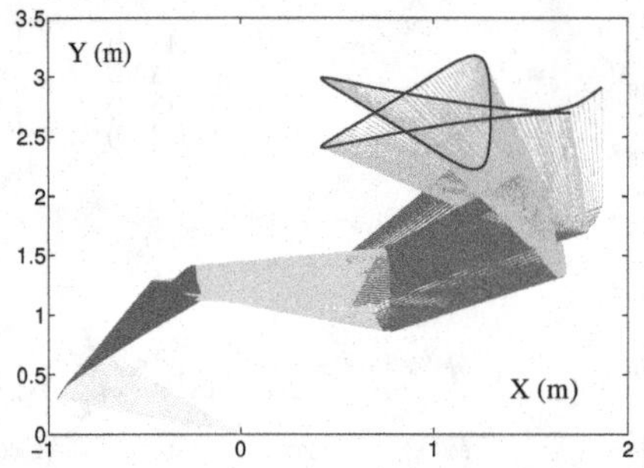

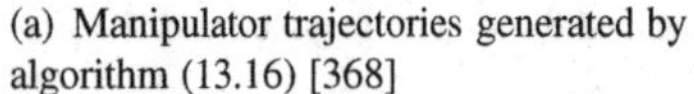
(a) Manipulator trajectories generated by algorithm (13.16) [368]

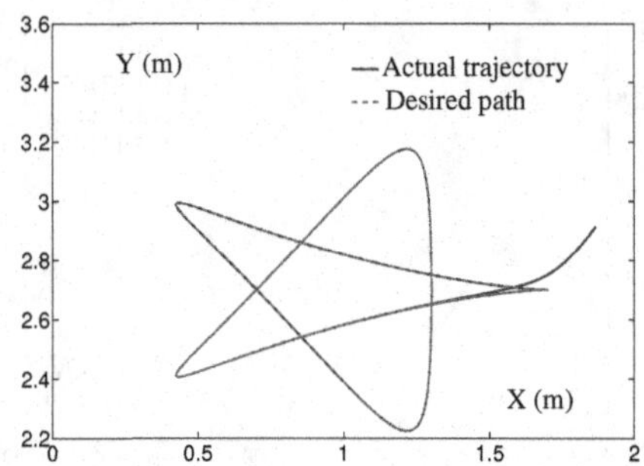

(b) End-effector trajectory generated by algorithm (13.16)

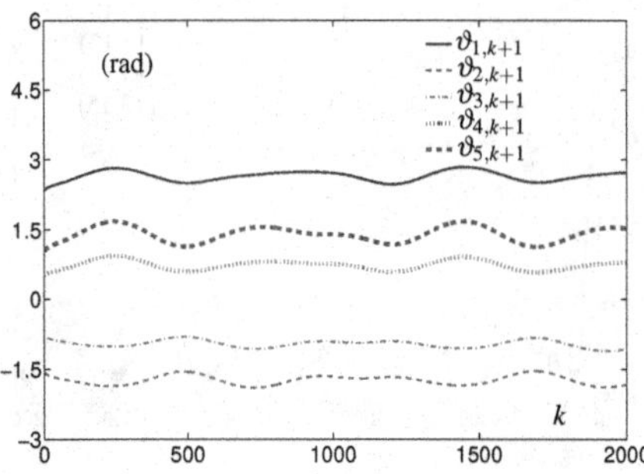

(c) Trajectories of ϑ_{k+1} generated by algorithm (13.16)

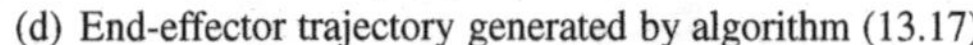
(d) End-effector trajectory generated by algorithm (13.17)

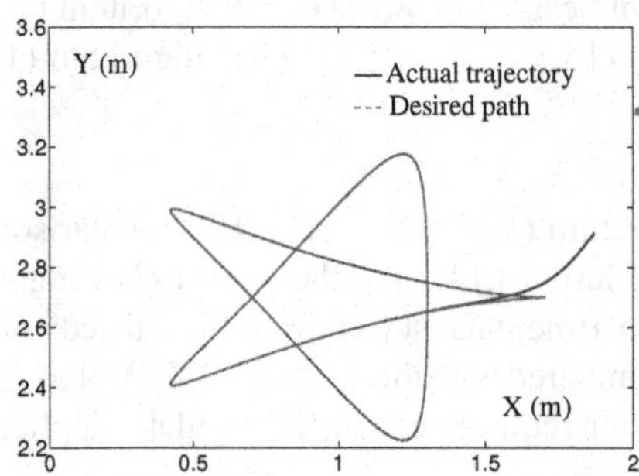

(e) End-effector trajectory generated by algorithm (13.18)

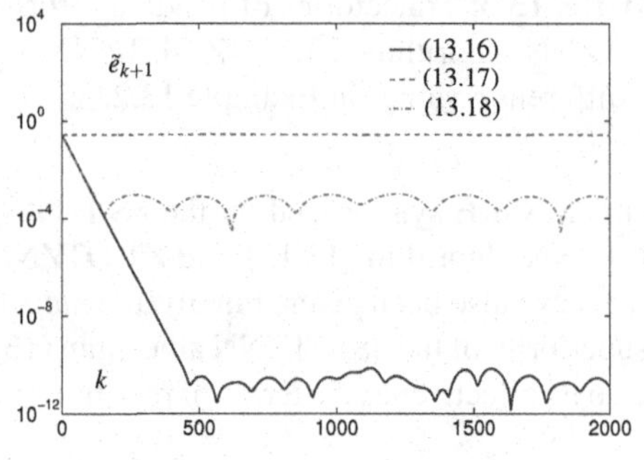

(f) Tracking errors synthesized by algorithms (13.16), (13.17), and (13.18)

FIGURE 13.4: Motion generation of five-link redundant manipulator synthesized by algorithms (13.16), (13.17), and (13.18) with $\hbar = 0.05$ and $g = 0.01$ s in Example 13.3.

$$\zeta_{k-4} = \zeta_k - 4g\dot{\zeta}_k + 8g^2\ddot{\zeta}_k - \frac{32g^3}{3}\dddot{\zeta}_k + \frac{32g^4}{3}\zeta_k^{(4)} - \frac{128g^5}{15}\zeta_k^{(5)} + \mathscr{O}(g^6), \tag{13.23}$$

$$\zeta_{k-5} = \zeta_k - 5g\dot{\zeta}_k + \frac{25g^2}{2}\ddot{\zeta}_k - \frac{125g^3}{6}\dddot{\zeta}_k + \frac{625g^4}{24}\zeta_k^{(4)} - \frac{625g^5}{24}\zeta_k^{(5)} + \mathscr{O}(g^6), \tag{13.24}$$

$$\zeta_{k-6} = \zeta_k - 6g\dot{\zeta}_k + 18g^2\ddot{\zeta}_k - 36g^3\dddot{\zeta}_k + 54g^4\zeta_k^{(4)} - \frac{324g^5}{5}\zeta_k^{(5)} + \mathscr{O}(g^6), \tag{13.25}$$

and

$$\zeta_{k-7} = \zeta_k - 7g\dot{\zeta}_k + \frac{49g^2}{2}\ddot{\zeta}_k - \frac{343g^3}{6}\dddot{\zeta}_k + \frac{2401g^4}{24}\zeta_k^{(4)} - \frac{16807g^5}{120}\zeta_k^{(5)} + \mathscr{O}(g^6), \tag{13.26}$$

where $\ddot{\zeta}_k$, $\dddot{\zeta}_k$, $\zeta_k^{(4)}$, and $\zeta_k^{(5)}$ represent the second-order through fifth-order time derivatives of $\zeta(t)$ at time instant t_k, respectively. Let (13.19) multiply 140, let (13.20) multiply -140, let (13.21) multiply -196, let (13.22) multiply 35, let (13.23) multiply $385/4$, let (13.24) multiply $-98/5$, let (13.25) multiply -35, and let (13.26) multiply $97/7$. Adding them together, we finally obtain

$$\begin{aligned}\dot{\zeta}_k = {} & \frac{140}{393g}\zeta_{k+1} + \frac{4923}{18340g}\zeta_k - \frac{140}{393g}\zeta_{k-1} - \frac{196}{393g}\zeta_{k-2} + \frac{35}{393g}\zeta_{k-3} + \frac{385}{1572g}\zeta_{k-4} \\ & - \frac{98}{1965g}\zeta_{k-5} - \frac{35}{393g}\zeta_{k-6} + \frac{97}{2751g}\zeta_{k-7} + \mathscr{O}(g^5),\end{aligned}$$

which is just the 8S-ZTD formula (13.11). The proof is therefore completed. □

Chapter 14

Minimum Joint Motion Control of Redundant Manipulators

Abstract

As a significant and basic sub topic of robotics, the problem of optimal motion planning and control of redundant manipulators is widely existing in many fields, such as industry and daily life. Following previous works, this chapter aims to solve the problem of velocity-layer minimum joint motion control (VLMJMC) of redundant manipulators in a discrete-time form. First, by applying the approach of Lagrange multipliers and zeroing neural network (ZNN) method, a continuous-time ZNN (CTZNN) model is presented. Additionally, a nine-step Zhang time discretization (9S-ZTD) formula is derived, constructed, and investigated. Second, by adopting the 9S-ZTD formula and other ZTD formulas with less steps, five discrete-time ZNN (DTZNN) algorithms are further acquired and presented, with corresponding theoretical analyses. Finally, numerical and physical experimental results both verify the feasibility, effectiveness, and correctness of the five DTZNN algorithms.

14.1 Introduction

In recent decades, with the development of information and computer technology, manipulator processing, manufacturing, and application have been unprecedentedly and rapidly developed. The problem of optimal motion planning and control of redundant manipulators, which is a significant and basic subtopic of robotics, exists diffusely in many industry, production, and medical fields, and the relevant theories and applications evolve at a faster pace than ever before [377–384]. Note that, in practical use, the minimum motion of redundant manipulators has some advantages [231,385–388], such as minimum energy consumption and collision avoidance. In [385], Zhang *et al* developed a feedback-aided minimum joint movement scheme for redundant manipulators. In [386], Ogbemhe *et al* presented an optimal trajectory scheme for robotic welding by using a genetic algorithm. An acceleration-layer minimum motion control scheme for redundant manipulators was developed and studied by Chen *et al* in [231]. Besides, an online time-optimal trajectory planning method for robotic manipulators was presented by Liu *et al* in [388].

As a promising and potential approach, the neural network has been paid more and more attention and research. Moreover, it has already been applied in nearly all fields of production, economy, and life [389–395]. Zeroing neural network (ZNN), which has the background of recurrent neural networks (RNNs), has been designed and proposed and then used to solve different kinds of time-dependent problems with good results [185, 223, 225, 227, 228, 396]. For instance, in [227], Jin *et al* successfully solved the pseudoinverse problem of time-dependent matrices by using this method. Xiao *et al* developed a neural network model for solving dynamic complex linear equations on the basis of the ZNN method in [396]. It is worth mentioning that when we employ the ZNN

DOI: 10.1201/9781003497783-14

method to solve time-dependent problems, a continuous-time ZNN (CTZNN) model is obtained first. However, it is not enough for practical use, since modern digital hardware is usually more suitable for discrete-time algorithms. Therefore, a kind of discretization formulas, which is termed as Zhang time discretization (ZTD) formulas, is proposed to acquire corresponding discrete-time ZNN (DTZNN) algorithms from the original CTZNN model [22, 188, 190, 193, 234]. According to the previous works, we have already known that the precision of a DTZNN algorithm is highly related to the accuracy of the corresponding ZTD formula. Hence, to obtain a DTZNN algorithm with higher precision, a nine-step ZTD (9S-ZTD) formula is constructed, studied, and used. The main work in this chapter [375, 376] is to solve the problem of velocity-layer minimum joint motion control (VLMJMC) of redundant manipulators by utilizing the ZNN method and the 9S-ZTD formula.

14.2 VLMJMC Problem and CTZNN Model

For further discussion, a CTZNN model for the VLMJMC of redundant manipulators is derived, discussed, and investigated at first. In the previous work [385], the VLMJMC problem is given as

$$\begin{aligned} &\min \ \frac{1}{2}\left(\dot{\vartheta}(t)+\mathbf{a}(t)\right)^{\mathrm{T}}\left(\dot{\vartheta}(t)+\mathbf{a}(t)\right), \\ &\text{s. t. } J(\vartheta(t))\,\dot{\vartheta}(t)=\dot{\mathbf{r}}_{\mathrm{d}}(t)+\eta_1\left(\mathbf{r}_{\mathrm{d}}(t)-\mathbf{f}(\vartheta(t))\right), \end{aligned} \tag{14.1}$$

where $\mathbf{a}(t)=\eta_2(\vartheta(t)-\vartheta(0))$; $\vartheta(t)\in\mathbb{R}^n$ and $\dot{\vartheta}(t)\in\mathbb{R}^n$ represent the joint-angle vector and joint-velocity vector, respectively; $\vartheta(0)$ is the initial value of $\vartheta(t)$; $\mathbf{r}_{\mathrm{d}}(t)\in\mathbb{R}^m$ represents a desired path for the end-effector and $\dot{\mathbf{r}}_{\mathrm{d}}(t)\in\mathbb{R}^m$ is the corresponding time derivative; $\eta_1,\eta_2\in\mathbb{R}^+$ are design parameters; $\mathbf{f}(\cdot)$ is a forward-kinematics mapping function with known structure and parameters; $J(\vartheta(t))=\partial\mathbf{f}(\vartheta(t))/\partial\vartheta(t)\in\mathbb{R}^{m\times n}$ is the Jacobian matrix; the superscript ^{T} is the transpose operator of a vector.

Besides, (14.1) is further represented as

$$\begin{aligned} &\min \ \frac{1}{2}\mathbf{x}^{\mathrm{T}}(t)\mathbf{x}(t)+\mathbf{a}^{\mathrm{T}}(t)\mathbf{x}(t), \\ &\text{s. t. } A(t)\mathbf{x}(t)=\mathbf{b}(t), \end{aligned}$$

where $\mathbf{x}(t)=\dot{\vartheta}(t)$, $A(t)=J(\vartheta(t))$, and $\mathbf{b}(t)=\dot{\mathbf{r}}_{\mathrm{d}}(t)+\eta_1(\mathbf{r}_{\mathrm{d}}(t)-\mathbf{f}(\vartheta(t))$; $\mathbf{a}(t)$ is defined as before. On the basis of the method of Lagrange multipliers [47, 48], the Lagrange function is defined as below:

$$L(\mathbf{x}(t),\mathbf{l}(t))=\frac{1}{2}\mathbf{x}^{\mathrm{T}}(t)\mathbf{x}(t)+\mathbf{a}^{\mathrm{T}}(t)\mathbf{x}(t)+\mathbf{l}^{\mathrm{T}}(t)\left(A(t)\mathbf{x}(t)-\mathbf{b}(t)\right),$$

with $\mathbf{l}(t)\in\mathbb{R}^m$ denoting a Lagrange-multiplier vector. Next, the following equations are obtained:

$$\begin{cases} \dfrac{\partial L(\mathbf{x}(t),\mathbf{l}(t))}{\partial\mathbf{x}(t)}=\mathbf{x}(t)+\mathbf{a}(t)+A^{\mathrm{T}}(t)\mathbf{l}(t)=\mathbf{0}, \\ \dfrac{\partial L(\mathbf{x}(t),\mathbf{l}(t))}{\partial\mathbf{l}(t)}=A(t)\mathbf{x}(t)-\mathbf{b}(t)=\mathbf{0}. \end{cases}$$

They are represented in the following compact form:

$$B(t)\mathbf{c}(t)+\mathbf{d}(t)=\mathbf{0}. \tag{14.2}$$

Thereinto, $B(t)=[I_{n\times n},\ A^{\mathrm{T}}(t);\ A(t),\ O_{m\times m}]\in\mathbb{R}^{(n+m)\times(n+m)}$ with $I_{n\times n}$ and $O_{m\times m}$ denoting an $n\times n$ identity matrix and an $m\times m$ zero matrix, respectively; $\mathbf{c}(t)=[\mathbf{x}(t);\ \mathbf{l}(t)]\in\mathbb{R}^{n+m}$ and $\mathbf{d}(t)=[\mathbf{a}(t);\ -\mathbf{b}(t)]\in\mathbb{R}^{n+m}$. Given that $A(t)$ is of full row rank, since $I_{n\times n}$ is positive definite, $B(t)$ is nonsingular at any time instant $t\in[0,+\infty)$. Therefore, the solution of (14.2) is unique.

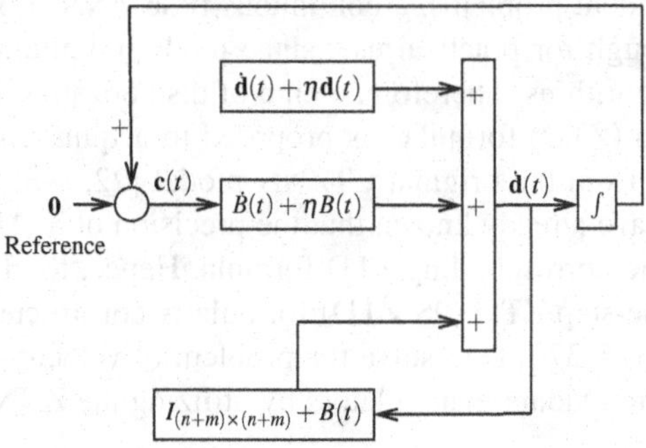

FIGURE 14.1: Block diagram of CTZNN model (14.3) for VLMJMC of redundant manipulators.

Moreover, by using the ZNN method, we define a zeroing function (ZF): $\mathbf{z}(t) = B(t)\mathbf{c}(t) + \mathbf{d}(t)$ firstly. Next, the ZNN design formula (i.e., $\dot{\mathbf{z}}(t) = -\eta\mathbf{z}(t)$) is adopted to make it converge to a zero vector. At last, the CTZNN model for the VLMJMC of redundant manipulators is acquired as

$$\dot{\mathbf{c}}(t) = -B^{-1}(t)\left(\left(\dot{B}(t) + \eta B(t)\right)\mathbf{c}(t) + \dot{\mathbf{d}}(t) + \eta\mathbf{d}(t)\right), \tag{14.3}$$

where $\dot{\mathbf{c}}(t)$, $\dot{\mathbf{d}}(t)$, and $\dot{B}(t)$ represent the time derivatives of $\mathbf{c}(t)$, $\mathbf{d}(t)$, and $B(t)$, respectively; $B^{-1}(t)$ is the inverse of $B(t)$; and $\eta \in \mathbb{R}^+$ denotes the ZNN design parameter. The CTZNN model (14.3) for the VLMJMC of redundant manipulators is shown as a control system in Figure 14.1.

14.3 DTZNN Algorithms

Due to the rapid development of digital hardware, we pay more attention to solve the VLMJMC problem of redundant manipulators in a discrete-time form. In other words, our object is to obtain $\mathbf{x}_{k+1}$ satisfying

$$\begin{aligned} \min\ & \frac{1}{2}\mathbf{x}_{k+1}^{\mathrm{T}}\mathbf{x}_{k+1} + \mathbf{a}_{k+1}^{\mathrm{T}}\mathbf{x}_{k+1}, \\ \text{s. t. } & A_{k+1}\mathbf{x}_{k+1} = \mathbf{b}_{k+1}, \end{aligned}$$

at each computational time interval $[t_k, t_{k+1}) = [kg, (k+1)g)$ with g denoting the sampling gap and $k = 0, 1, 2, \cdots$ denoting the updating index.

For the sake of solving the above discrete time-dependent problem, five DTZNN algorithms with different precision are developed and discussed. Moreover, to ensure the correctness of these algorithms, corresponding theoretical analyses are also provided in this section.

In order to obtain DTZNN algorithms, discretization formulas are needed to discretize the CTZNN model (14.3). First, the 9S-ZTD formula is presented by the following theorem.

Theorem 56 *With the sufficiently small sampling gap $g \in (0,1)$, let $\mathscr{O}(g^5)$ denote the error (especially, the truncation error) positively or negatively proportional to g^5, i.e., of the order of g^5. Suppose that $\zeta(t)$ is sufficiently smooth. With $\zeta_{k+1} = \zeta(t_{k+1}) = \zeta((k+1)g)$, the 9S-ZTD formula is formulated as follows:*

$$\begin{aligned} \dot{\zeta}_k = {} & \frac{350}{879g}\zeta_{k+1} + \frac{9683}{82040g}\zeta_k - \frac{70}{293g}\zeta_{k-1} - \frac{105}{293g}\zeta_{k-2} - \frac{70}{897g}\zeta_{k-3} + \frac{35}{293g}\zeta_{k-4} \\ & + \frac{182}{1465g}\zeta_{k-5} - \frac{35}{897g}\zeta_{k-6} - \frac{160}{2051g}\zeta_{k-7} + \frac{245}{7032g}\zeta_{k-8} + \mathscr{O}(g^5). \end{aligned} \tag{14.4}$$

Proof. The proof is presented in Appendix Q. □

By utilizing the 9S-ZTD formula (14.4) to discretize the CTZNN model (14.3), a 9S-DTZNN algorithm is developed as

$$\mathbf{c}_{k+1} \doteq \frac{879}{350}\tilde{\mathbf{c}}_k - \frac{29049}{98000}\mathbf{c}_k + \frac{3}{5}\mathbf{c}_{k-1} + \frac{9}{10}\mathbf{c}_{k-2} + \frac{1}{5}\mathbf{c}_{k-3} - \frac{3}{10}\mathbf{c}_{k-4} - \frac{39}{125}\mathbf{c}_{k-5} + \frac{1}{10}\mathbf{c}_{k-6} + \frac{48}{245}\mathbf{c}_{k-7} - \frac{7}{80}\mathbf{c}_{k-8}, \tag{14.5}$$

where $\tilde{\mathbf{c}}_k = -B_k^{-1}\left((g\dot{B}_k + \hbar B_k)\mathbf{c}_k + g\dot{\mathbf{d}}_k + \hbar\mathbf{d}_k\right)$ with the step length $\hbar = g\eta$, and $\doteq$ denotes the computational assignment operator.

Besides, a seven-step ZTD (7S-ZTD) formula, which is derived from [231] by setting values for parameters, is given as below:

$$\dot{\zeta}_k = \frac{200}{427g}\zeta_{k+1} - \frac{2861}{25620g}\zeta_k - \frac{200}{427g}\zeta_{k-2} + \frac{20}{427g}\zeta_{k-3} + \frac{15}{1708g}\zeta_{k-4} + \frac{228}{2135g}\zeta_{k-5} - \frac{65}{1281g}\zeta_{k-6} + \mathscr{O}(g^4),$$

and a corresponding 7S-DTZNN algorithm is presented as

$$\mathbf{c}_{k+1} \doteq \frac{427}{200}\tilde{\mathbf{c}}_k + \frac{2861}{12000}\mathbf{c}_k + \mathbf{c}_{k-2} - \frac{1}{10}\mathbf{c}_{k-3} - \frac{3}{160}\mathbf{c}_{k-4} - \frac{57}{250}\mathbf{c}_{k-5} + \frac{13}{120}\mathbf{c}_{k-6}. \tag{14.6}$$

For the comparisons purpose, three other ZTD formulas with different precision are employed and listed below. The first one is a five-step ZTD (5S-ZTD) formula [188]:

$$\dot{\zeta}_k = \frac{1}{2g}\zeta_{k+1} - \frac{5}{48g}\zeta_k - \frac{1}{4g}\zeta_{k-1} - \frac{1}{8g}\zeta_{k-2} - \frac{1}{12g}\zeta_{k-3} + \frac{1}{16g}\zeta_{k-4} + \mathscr{O}(g^3).$$

The second one is the Zhang–Taylor discretization formula [22]:

$$\dot{\zeta}_k = \frac{1}{g}\zeta_{k+1} - \frac{3}{2g}\zeta_k + \frac{1}{g}\zeta_{k-1} - \frac{1}{2g}\zeta_{k-2} + \mathscr{O}(g^2).$$

The third one is the Euler forward formula [251]:

$$\dot{\zeta}_k = \frac{1}{g}\zeta_{k+1} - \frac{1}{g}\zeta_k + \mathscr{O}(g).$$

Note that the Euler forward formula is regarded as the simplest one of ZTD formulas. Correspondingly, a 5S-DTZNN algorithm, a Zhang–Taylor DTZNN (ZT-DTZNN) algorithm, and an Euler-type DTZNN (ET-DTZNN) algorithm are developed as

$$\mathbf{c}_{k+1} \doteq 2\tilde{\mathbf{c}}_k + \frac{5}{24}\mathbf{c}_k + \frac{1}{2}\mathbf{c}_{k-1} + \frac{1}{4}\mathbf{c}_{k-2} + \frac{1}{6}\mathbf{c}_{k-3} - \frac{1}{8}\mathbf{c}_{k-4}, \tag{14.7}$$

$$\mathbf{c}_{k+1} \doteq \tilde{\mathbf{c}}_k + \frac{3}{2}\mathbf{c}_k - \mathbf{c}_{k-1} + \frac{1}{2}\mathbf{c}_{k-2}, \tag{14.8}$$

and

$$\mathbf{c}_{k+1} \doteq \tilde{\mathbf{c}}_k + \mathbf{c}_k. \tag{14.9}$$

Note that the residual error is defined as $\hat{e}_{k+1} = \|B_{k+1}\mathbf{c}_{k+1} + \mathbf{d}_{k+1}\|_2$ for the VLMJMC of redundant manipulators in this chapter [375, 376], where $\|\cdot\|$ denotes the 2-norm of a vector. Then, we have the following theorem for these DTZNN algorithms.

TABLE 14.1: Problem, scheme, model, and algorithms in this chapter.

Problem	$\min\ \frac{1}{2}\mathbf{x}_{k+1}^{\mathrm{T}}\mathbf{x}_{k+1}+\mathbf{a}_{k+1}^{\mathrm{T}}\mathbf{x}_{k+1}$, s. t. $A_{k+1}\mathbf{x}_{k+1}=\mathbf{b}_{k+1}$.
Scheme	*Step 1*: Define Lagrange function as $L(\mathbf{x}(t),\mathbf{l}(t))=\frac{1}{2}\mathbf{x}^{\mathrm{T}}(t)\mathbf{x}(t)+\mathbf{a}^{\mathrm{T}}(t)\mathbf{x}(t)+\mathbf{l}^{\mathrm{T}}(t)(A(t)\mathbf{x}(t)-\mathbf{b}(t))$. *Step 2*: Define ZF as $\mathbf{z}(t)=B(t)\mathbf{c}(t)+\mathbf{d}(t)$. *Step 3*: Adopt ZNN design formula as $\dot{\mathbf{z}}(t)=-\eta\mathbf{z}(t)$. *Step 4*: Adopt discretization formulas to discretize CTZNN model (14.3).
Model	$\dot{\mathbf{c}}(t)=-B^{-1}(t)\left(\left(\dot{B}(t)+\eta B(t)\right)\mathbf{c}(t)+\dot{\mathbf{d}}(t)+\eta\mathbf{d}(t)\right)$.
Algorithms	$\mathbf{c}_{k+1}\doteq\frac{879}{350}\tilde{\mathbf{c}}_k-\frac{29049}{98000}\mathbf{c}_k+\frac{3}{5}\mathbf{c}_{k-1}+\frac{9}{10}\mathbf{c}_{k-2}+\frac{1}{5}\mathbf{c}_{k-3}-\frac{3}{10}\mathbf{c}_{k-4}-\frac{39}{125}\mathbf{c}_{k-5}+\frac{1}{10}\mathbf{c}_{k-6}+\frac{48}{245}\mathbf{c}_{k-7}-\frac{7}{80}\mathbf{c}_{k-8}$, $\mathbf{c}_{k+1}\doteq\frac{427}{200}\tilde{\mathbf{c}}_k+\frac{2861}{12000}\mathbf{c}_k+\mathbf{c}_{k-2}-\frac{1}{10}\mathbf{c}_{k-3}-\frac{3}{160}\mathbf{c}_{k-4}-\frac{57}{250}\mathbf{c}_{k-5}+\frac{13}{120}\mathbf{c}_{k-6}$, $\mathbf{c}_{k+1}\doteq 2\tilde{\mathbf{c}}_k+\frac{5}{24}\mathbf{c}_k+\frac{1}{2}\mathbf{c}_{k-1}+\frac{1}{4}\mathbf{c}_{k-2}+\frac{1}{6}\mathbf{c}_{k-3}-\frac{1}{8}\mathbf{c}_{k-4}$, $\mathbf{c}_{k+1}\doteq\tilde{\mathbf{c}}_k+\frac{3}{2}\mathbf{c}_k-\mathbf{c}_{k-1}+\frac{1}{2}\mathbf{c}_{k-2}$, $\mathbf{c}_{k+1}\doteq\tilde{\mathbf{c}}_k+\mathbf{c}_k$.

Theorem 57 *Suppose that A_k is of full row rank and B_k is uniformly norm bounded. With the sufficiently small sampling gap $g\in(0,1)$, let $\mathbf{O}(g^6)$ denote the error (especially, the truncation error) with each element being $\mathscr{O}(g^6)$. The 9S-DTZNN algorithm (14.5) is zero-stable, consistent, and convergent, which converges with the order of truncation error being $\mathbf{O}(g^6)$. Besides, the maximal steady-state residual error (MSSRE) $\lim_{k\to\infty}\sup\hat{e}_{k+1}$ synthesized by the 9S-DTZNN algorithm (14.5) is $\mathscr{O}(g^6)$.*

Proof. The proof is presented in Appendix R. □

Corollary 15 *Suppose that A_k is of full row rank and B_k is uniformly norm bounded. With the sufficiently small sampling gap $g\in(0,1)$, let $\mathbf{O}(g^5)$ denote the error (especially, the truncation error) with each element being $\mathscr{O}(g^5)$. The 7S-DTZNN algorithm (14.6) is zero-stable, consistent, and convergent, which converges with the order of truncation error being $\mathbf{O}(g^5)$. Besides, the MSSRE $\lim_{k\to\infty}\sup\hat{e}_{k+1}$ synthesized by the 7S-DTZNN algorithm (14.6) is $\mathscr{O}(g^5)$.*

Corollary 16 *Suppose that A_k is of full row rank and B_k is uniformly norm bounded. With the sufficiently small sampling gap $g\in(0,1)$, let $\mathbf{O}(g^4)$ denote the error (especially, the truncation error) with each element being $\mathscr{O}(g^4)$. The 5S-DTZNN algorithm (14.7) is zero-stable, consistent, and convergent, which converges with the order of truncation error being $\mathbf{O}(g^4)$. Besides, the MSSRE $\lim_{k\to\infty}\sup\hat{e}_{k+1}$ synthesized by the 5S-DTZNN algorithm (14.7) is $\mathscr{O}(g^4)$.*

Corollary 17 *Suppose that A_k is of full row rank and B_k is uniformly norm bounded. With the sufficiently small sampling gap $g\in(0,1)$, let $\mathbf{O}(g^3)$ denote the error (especially, the truncation error) with each element being $\mathscr{O}(g^3)$. The ZT-DTZNN algorithm (14.8) is zero-stable, consistent, and convergent, which converges with the order of truncation error being $\mathbf{O}(g^3)$. Besides, the MSSRE $\lim_{k\to\infty}\sup\hat{e}_{k+1}$ synthesized by the ZT-DTZNN algorithm (14.8) is $\mathscr{O}(g^3)$.*

Corollary 18 *Suppose that A_k is of full row rank and B_k is uniformly norm bounded. With the sufficiently small sampling gap $g\in(0,1)$, let $\mathbf{O}(g^2)$ denote the error (especially, the truncation error) with each element being $\mathscr{O}(g^2)$. The ET-DTZNN algorithm (14.9) is zero-stable, consistent, and convergent, which converges with the order of truncation error being $\mathbf{O}(g^2)$. Besides, the MSSRE $\lim_{k\to\infty}\sup\hat{e}_{k+1}$ synthesized by the ET-DTZNN algorithm (14.9) is $\mathscr{O}(g^2)$.*

For a more intuitive understanding of the main content of this chapter [375,376], Table 14.1 lists the problem, scheme, model, and algorithms.

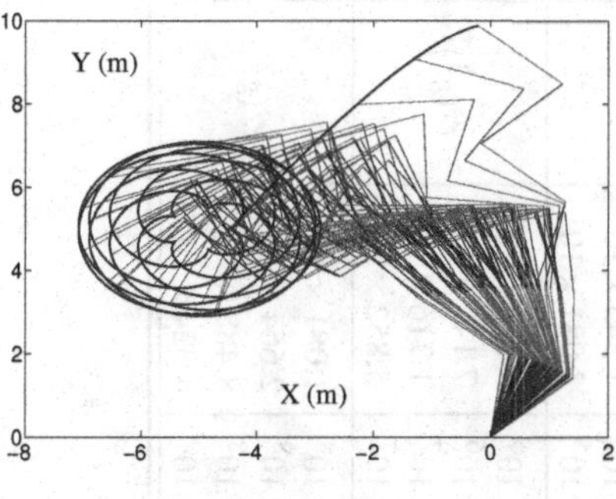

(a) Manipulator trajectories [375]

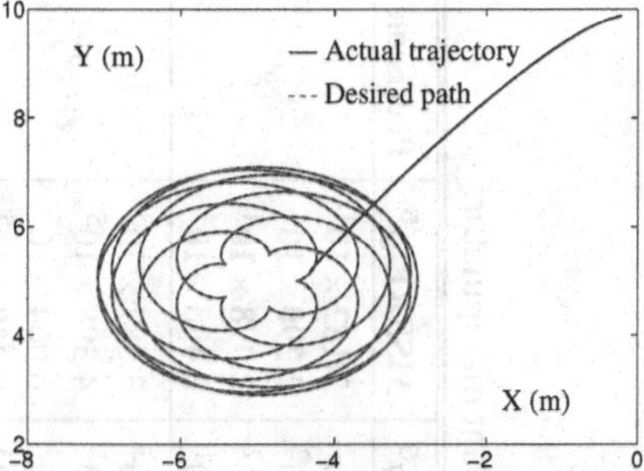

(b) End-effector actual trajectory and desired path

FIGURE 14.2: Motion generation of six-link redundant manipulator synthesized by 9S-DTZNN algorithm (14.5) with its end-effector tracking epicycloid path.

14.4 Numerical and Physical Experiments

To substantiate the performance and effectiveness of different DTZNN algorithms for solving the VLMJMC problem of redundant manipulator, the numerical and physical experiments are conducted in this section. Note that, except for the special description, the parameters are set as $\eta_1 = \eta_2 = 10$, $g = 0.01$ s, and $\hbar = 0.1$ uniformly. Additionally, the tracking error of the end-effector between the actual trajectory $\mathbf{r}_{\text{a},k+1} = \mathbf{f}(\vartheta_{k+1})$ and a desired path $\mathbf{r}_{\text{d},k+1}$ is defined as $\tilde{e}_{k+1} = \|\mathbf{r}_{\text{a},k+1} - \mathbf{r}_{\text{d},k+1}\|_2$. We use the residual error $\hat{e}_{k+1}$ and the tracking error $\tilde{e}_{k+1}$ to determine the accuracy of a DTZNN algorithm.

14.4.1 Six-link redundant manipulator

By using the five DTZNN algorithms, the real-time VLMJMC of a six-link redundant manipulator for tracking an epicycloid path is performed. The task duration and the initial joint-angle vector of the six-link redundant manipulator are set as $T = 60$ s and $\vartheta_0 = [\pi/3, \pi/5, -\pi/9, \pi/3, -\pi/2, \pi/2]^{\text{T}}$ rad, respectively. The corresponding numerical experimental results are shown in Figures 14.2 and 14.3. Note that, because of similarity, we only present the motion generation of the six-link redundant manipulator synthesized by the 9S-DTZNN algorithm (14.5), i.e., Figure 14.2. It is observed from Figure 14.2 that the six-link redundant manipulator tracks the desired path successfully. Besides, as spotted from Figure 14.3, the residual errors as well as the tracking errors synthesized by different DTZNN algorithms change regularly, and they are in accordance with Theorem 57 and Corollaries 15–18. Therefore, the effectiveness of the DTZNN algorithms is verified.

In order to validate the precision of different DTZNN algorithms, we run the numerical experiments with different g values, and the corresponding numerical experimental results are shown in Table 14.2. Evidently, it is observed from Table 14.2, the MSSREs synthesized by the 9S-DTZNN algorithm (14.5), the 7S-DTZNN algorithm (14.6), the 5S-DTZNN algorithm (14.7), the ZT-DTZNN algorithm (14.8), and the ET-DTZNN algorithm (14.9) are nearly proportional to $\mathcal{O}(g^6)$, $\mathcal{O}(g^5)$, $\mathcal{O}(g^4)$, $\mathcal{O}(g^3)$, and $\mathcal{O}(g^2)$, respectively. Therefore, the correctness of Theorem 57 and Corollaries 15–18 is verified.

TABLE 14.2: MSSREs synthesized by DTZNN algorithms with different values of g for VLMJMC of six-link redundant manipulator.

DTZNN algorithm	g (s)	MSSRE	MSSRE/g	MSSRE/g^2	MSSRE/g^3	MSSRE/g^4	MSSRE/g^5	MSSRE/g^6	Precision
9S-DTZNN algorithm (14.5)	0.01	2.182×10^{-8}	2.182×10^{-6}	2.182×10^{-4}	2.182×10^{-2}	2.182×10^{0}	2.182×10^{2}	$\mathbf{2.182\times10^{4}}$	$\mathcal{O}(g^6)$
	0.008	6.002×10^{-9}	7.503×10^{-7}	9.378×10^{-5}	1.172×10^{-2}	1.465×10^{0}	1.832×10^{2}	$\mathbf{2.290\times10^{4}}$	
	0.006	1.119×10^{-9}	1.865×10^{-7}	3.108×10^{-5}	5.181×10^{-3}	8.634×10^{-1}	1.439×10^{2}	$\mathbf{2.398\times10^{4}}$	
	0.004	1.023×10^{-10}	2.558×10^{-8}	6.394×10^{-6}	1.598×10^{-3}	3.996×10^{-1}	9.990×10^{1}	$\mathbf{2.498\times10^{4}}$	
7S-DTZNN algorithm (14.6)	0.01	3.387×10^{-7}	3.387×10^{-5}	3.387×10^{-3}	3.387×10^{-1}	3.387×10^{1}	$\mathbf{3.387\times10^{3}}$	3.387×10^{5}	$\mathcal{O}(g^5)$
	0.008	1.153×10^{-7}	1.441×10^{-5}	1.802×10^{-3}	2.252×10^{-1}	2.815×10^{1}	$\mathbf{3.519\times10^{3}}$	4.398×10^{5}	
	0.006	2.829×10^{-8}	4.715×10^{-6}	7.858×10^{-4}	1.310×10^{-1}	2.183×10^{1}	$\mathbf{3.638\times10^{3}}$	6.064×10^{5}	
	0.004	3.825×10^{-9}	9.563×10^{-7}	2.391×10^{-4}	5.977×10^{-2}	1.494×10^{1}	$\mathbf{3.735\times10^{3}}$	9.338×10^{5}	
5S-DTZNN algorithm (14.7)	0.01	4.627×10^{-6}	4.627×10^{-4}	4.627×10^{-2}	4.627×10^{0}	$\mathbf{4.627\times10^{2}}$	4.627×10^{4}	4.627×10^{6}	$\mathcal{O}(g^4)$
	0.008	1.942×10^{-6}	2.428×10^{-4}	3.034×10^{-2}	3.793×10^{0}	$\mathbf{4.741\times10^{2}}$	5.927×10^{4}	7.408×10^{6}	
	0.006	6.277×10^{-7}	1.046×10^{-4}	1.744×10^{-2}	2.906×10^{0}	$\mathbf{4.843\times10^{2}}$	8.072×10^{4}	1.345×10^{7}	
	0.004	1.262×10^{-7}	3.155×10^{-5}	7.888×10^{-3}	1.972×10^{0}	$\mathbf{4.930\times10^{2}}$	1.232×10^{5}	3.081×10^{7}	
ZT-DTZNN algorithm (14.8)	0.01	3.595×10^{-4}	3.595×10^{-2}	3.595×10^{0}	$\mathbf{3.595\times10^{2}}$	3.595×10^{4}	3.595×10^{6}	3.595×10^{8}	$\mathcal{O}(g^3)$
	0.008	1.872×10^{-4}	2.340×10^{-2}	2.925×10^{0}	$\mathbf{3.656\times10^{2}}$	4.570×10^{4}	5.713×10^{6}	7.141×10^{8}	
	0.006	8.005×10^{-5}	1.334×10^{-2}	2.224×10^{0}	$\mathbf{3.706\times10^{2}}$	6.177×10^{4}	1.029×10^{7}	1.716×10^{9}	
	0.004	2.397×10^{-5}	5.993×10^{-3}	1.498×10^{0}	$\mathbf{3.745\times10^{2}}$	9.363×10^{4}	2.341×10^{7}	5.852×10^{9}	
ET-DTZNN algorithm (14.9)	0.01	1.081×10^{-2}	1.081×10^{0}	$\mathbf{1.081\times10^{2}}$	1.081×10^{4}	1.081×10^{6}	1.081×10^{8}	1.081×10^{10}	$\mathcal{O}(g^2)$
	0.008	6.983×10^{-3}	8.729×10^{-1}	$\mathbf{1.091\times10^{2}}$	1.364×10^{4}	1.705×10^{6}	2.131×10^{8}	2.664×10^{10}	
	0.006	3.960×10^{-3}	6.600×10^{-1}	$\mathbf{1.100\times10^{2}}$	1.833×10^{4}	3.056×10^{6}	5.093×10^{8}	8.488×10^{10}	
	0.004	1.771×10^{-3}	4.428×10^{-1}	$\mathbf{1.107\times10^{2}}$	2.767×10^{4}	6.918×10^{6}	1.729×10^{9}	4.324×10^{11}	

14.4.2 PUMA560 manipulator

In this subsection, the DTZNN algorithms are applied to the real-time VLMJMC of a PUMA560 manipulator [27] for tracking a disc-spring path. Besides, the initial joint-angle vector of the PUMA560 manipulator is set as $\vartheta_0 = [0, -\pi/5, 0, -\pi/3, 0, \pi]^{\mathrm{T}}$ rad, and the task duration is set as $T = 15$ s.

The motion generation of the PUMA560 manipulator and the end-effector actual trajectory synthesized by the 9S-DTZNN algorithm (14.5) are shown in Figure 14.4, and those synthesized by other DTZNN algorithms are omitted because of similarity. It is seen from Figure 14.4 that the actual trajectory is in line with the desired path, which validates the correctness and feasibility of the DTZNN algorithms. Moreover, as seen in Figures 14.5 and 14.6, the residual errors and tracking errors synthesized by different DTZNN algorithms change regularly, and they are also in line with Theorem 57 and Corollaries 15–18.

14.4.3 Kinova Jaco^2 manipulator

Similar numerical experiments are performed on a Kinova Jaco^2 manipulator [374], but with a different desired path, i.e., a little-bee path. The initial joint-angle vector of the Kinova Jaco^2 manipulator is set as $\vartheta_0 = [1.675, 2.843, -3.216, 4.187, -1.71, -2.65]^{\mathrm{T}}$ rad, and the task duration is set as $T = 8$ s.

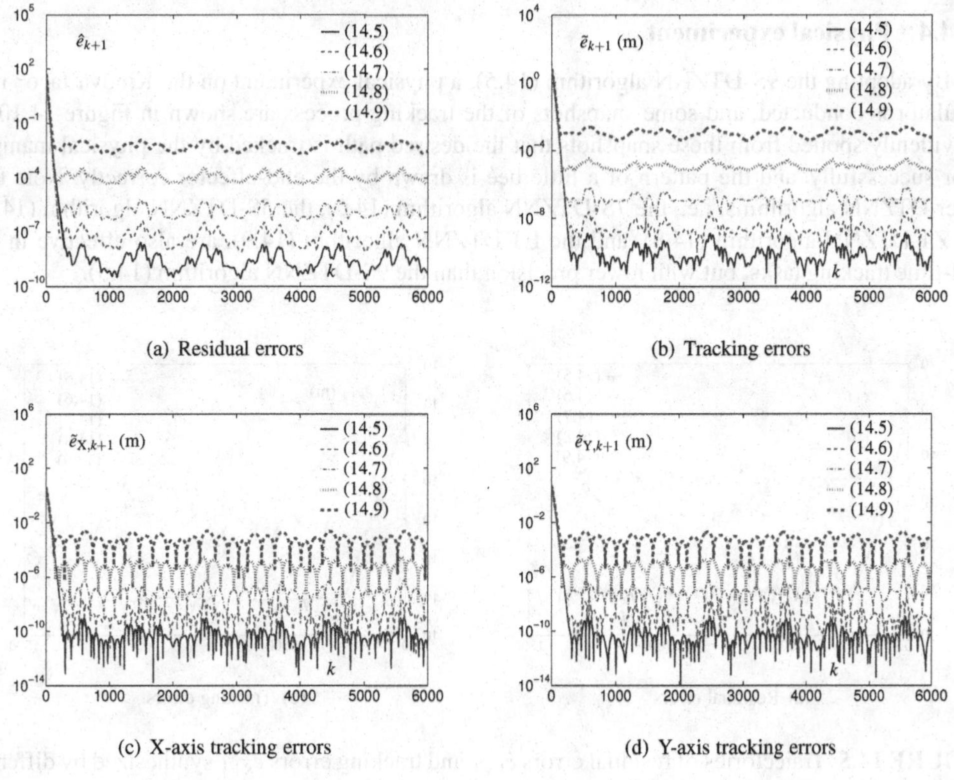

FIGURE 14.3: Trajectories of residual errors $\hat{e}_{k+1}$ and tracking errors $\tilde{e}_{k+1}$ synthesized by different DTZNN algorithms when six-link redundant manipulator tracking epicycloid path.

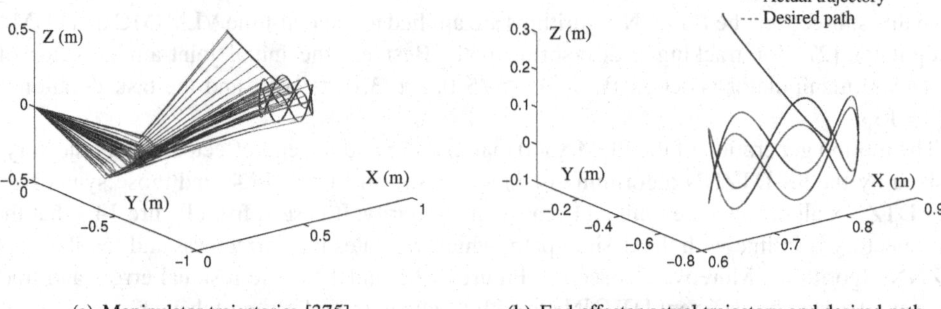

(a) Manipulator trajectories [375]

(b) End-effector actual trajectory and desired path

FIGURE 14.4: Motion generation of PUMA560 manipulator synthesized by 9S-DTZNN algorithm (14.5) with its end-effector tracking disc-spring path.

In the same way, only the motion generation of the Kinova Jaco^2 manipulator synthesized by the 9S-DTZNN algorithm (14.5) is given. As seen in Figure 14.7, the manipulator tracks the desired path successfully. In addition, the residual errors and tracking errors in Figures 14.8 and 14.9, confirm the correctness of Theorem 57 and Corollaries 15–18 again.

14.4.4 Physical experiment

By adopting the 9S-DTZNN algorithm (14.5), a physical experiment on the Kinova Jaco^2 manipulator is conducted, and some snapshots of the tracking process are shown in Figure 14.10. It is evidently spotted from these snapshots that the desired path is tracked by the physical manipulator successfully, and the pattern of a little bee is drawn by the end-effector correctly. Note that other DTZNN algorithms, i.e., the 7S-DTZNN algorithm (14.6), the 5S-DTZNN algorithm (14.7), the ZT-DTZNN algorithm (14.8), and the ET-DTZNN algorithm (14.9), are also effective in the real-time tracking tasks, but with lower precision than the 9S-DTZNN algorithm (14.5).

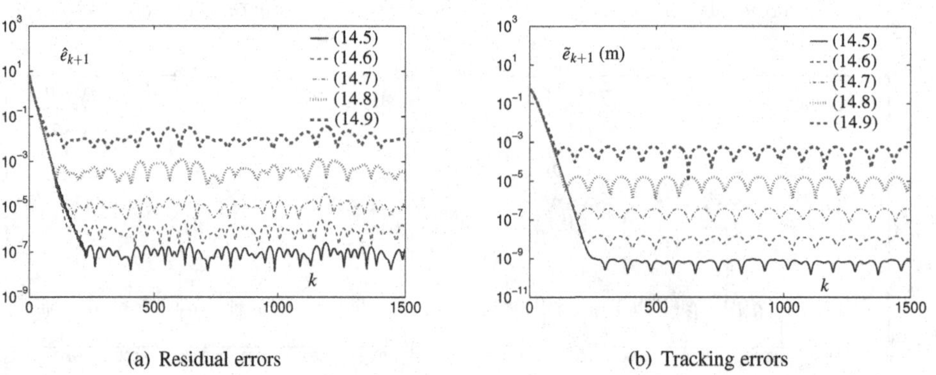

(a) Residual errors

(b) Tracking errors

FIGURE 14.5: Trajectories of residual errors $\hat{e}_{k+1}$ and tracking errors $\tilde{e}_{k+1}$ synthesized by different DTZNN algorithms when PUMA560 manipulator tracking disc-spring path.

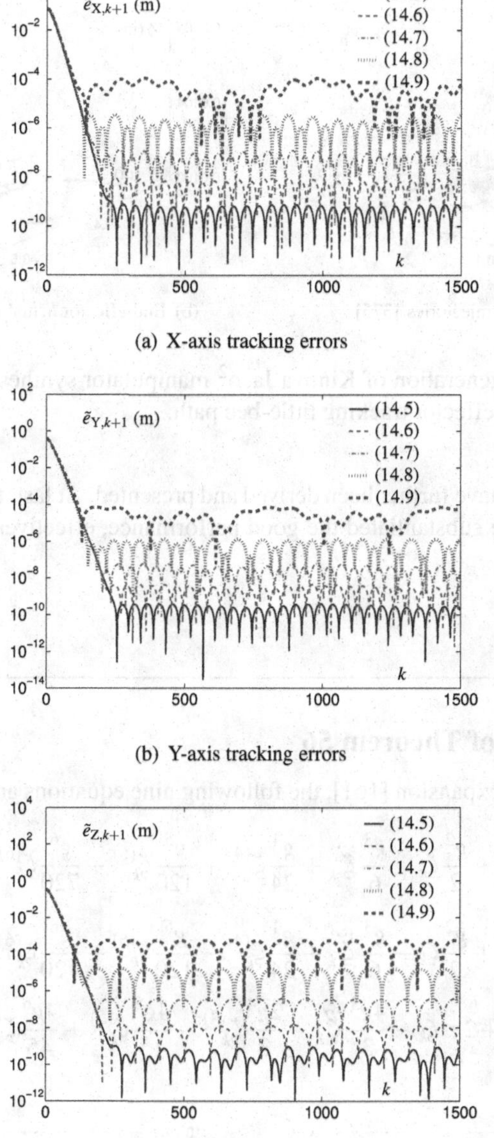

(a) X-axis tracking errors

(b) Y-axis tracking errors

(c) Z-axis tracking errors

FIGURE 14.6: Trajectories of X-axis, Y-axis, and Z-axis tracking errors synthesized by different DTZNN algorithms when PUMA560 manipulator tracking disc-spring path.

14.5 Chapter Summary

In this chapter, the VLMJMC problem of redundant manipulators has been investigated and solved in a discrete-time form. Specifically, the CTZNN model (14.3) for the VLMJMC of redundant manipulators has been presented by using the ZNN method and the approach of Lagrange multipliers. Besides, the 9S-ZTD formula (14.4) has been constructed and investigated. Then, the

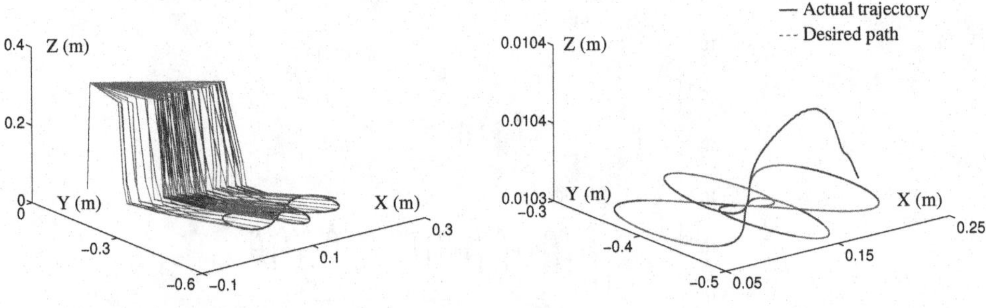

(a) Manipulator trajectories [375]

(b) End-effector actual trajectory and desired path

FIGURE 14.7: Motion generation of Kinova Jaco^2 manipulator synthesized by 9S-DTZNN algorithm (14.5) with its end-effector tracking little-bee path.

five DTZNN algorithms have further been derived and presented. At last, the numerical and physical experimental results have substantiated the good performance, effectiveness, and feasibility of the DTZNN algorithms.

Appendix Q: Proof of Theorem 56

According to Taylor expansion [161], the following nine equations are obtained:

$$\zeta_{k+1}=\zeta_k+g\dot{\zeta}_k+\frac{g^2}{2}\ddot{\zeta}_k+\frac{g^3}{6}\dddot{\zeta}_k+\frac{g^4}{24}\zeta_k^{(4)}+\frac{g^5}{120}\zeta_k^{(5)}+\frac{g^6}{720}\zeta_k^{(6)}+\mathcal{O}(g^7), \tag{14.10}$$

$$\zeta_{k-1}=\zeta_k-g\dot{\zeta}_k+\frac{g^2}{2}\ddot{\zeta}_k-\frac{g^3}{6}\dddot{\zeta}_k+\frac{g^4}{24}\zeta_k^{(4)}-\frac{g^5}{120}\zeta_k^{(5)}+\frac{g^6}{720}\zeta_k^{(6)}+\mathcal{O}(g^7), \tag{14.11}$$

$$\zeta_{k-2}=\zeta_k-2g\dot{\zeta}_k+2g^2\ddot{\zeta}_k-\frac{4g^3}{3}\dddot{\zeta}_k+\frac{2g^4}{3}\zeta_k^{(4)}-\frac{4g^5}{15}\zeta_k^{(5)}+\frac{4g^6}{45}\zeta_k^{(6)}+\mathcal{O}(g^7), \tag{14.12}$$

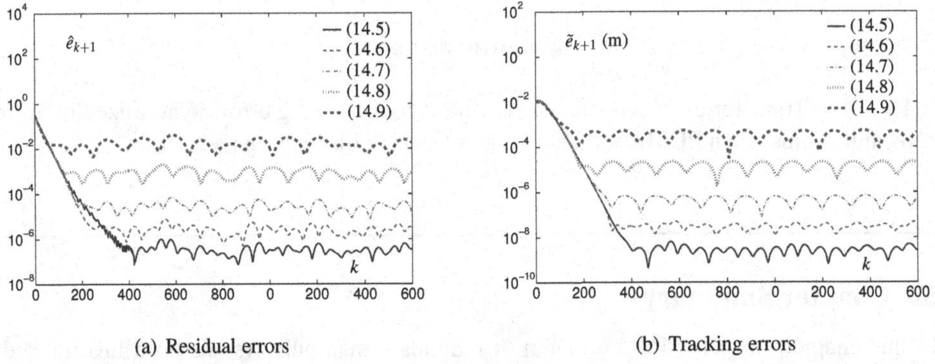

(a) Residual errors

(b) Tracking errors

FIGURE 14.8: Trajectories of residual errors $\hat{e}_{k+1}$ and tracking errors $\tilde{e}_{k+1}$ synthesized by different DTZNN algorithms when Kinova Jaco^2 manipulator tracking little-bee path.

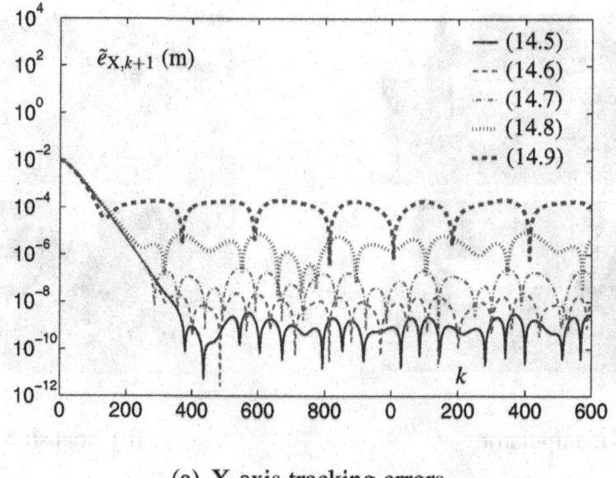

(a) X-axis tracking errors

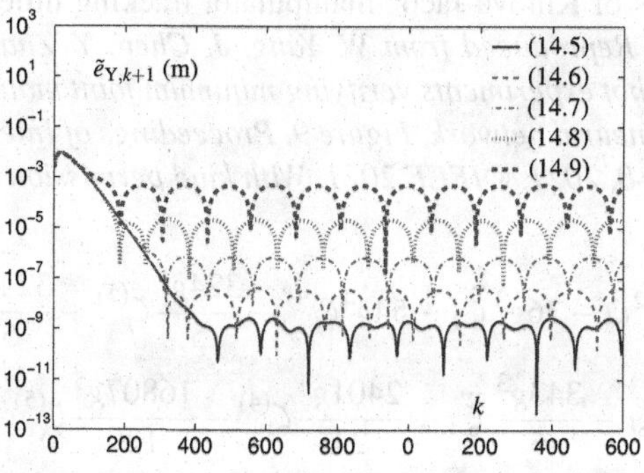

(b) Y-axis tracking errors

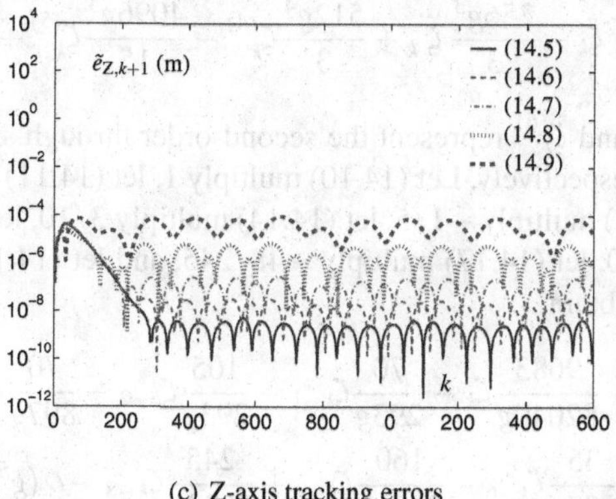

(c) Z-axis tracking errors

FIGURE 14.9: Trajectories of X-axis, Y-axis, and Z-axis tracking errors synthesized by different DTZNN algorithms when Kinova Jaco^2 manipulator tracking little-bee path.

$$\zeta_{k-3} = \zeta_k - 3g\dot{\zeta}_k + \frac{9g^2}{2}\ddot{\zeta}_k - \frac{9g^3}{2}\dddot{\zeta}_k + \frac{27g^4}{8}\zeta_k^{(4)} - \frac{81g^5}{40}\zeta_k^{(5)} + \frac{81g^6}{80}\zeta_k^{(6)} + \mathcal{O}(g^7), \quad (14.13)$$

$$\zeta_{k-4} = \zeta_k - 4g\dot{\zeta}_k + 8g^2\ddot{\zeta}_k - \frac{32g^3}{3}\dddot{\zeta}_k + \frac{32g^4}{3}\zeta_k^{(4)} - \frac{128g^5}{15}\zeta_k^{(5)} + \frac{256g^6}{45}\zeta_k^{(6)} + \mathcal{O}(g^7), \quad (14.14)$$

$$\zeta_{k-5} = \zeta_k - 5g\dot{\zeta}_k + \frac{25g^2}{2}\ddot{\zeta}_k - \frac{125g^3}{6}\dddot{\zeta}_k + \frac{625g^4}{24}\zeta_k^{(4)} - \frac{625g^5}{24}\zeta_k^{(5)} + \frac{3125g^6}{144}\zeta_k^{(6)} + \mathcal{O}(g^7), \quad (14.15)$$

(a) Snapshots of manipulator (b) Snapshots of end-effector

FIGURE 14.10: Snapshots of Kinova Jaco^2 manipulator tracking little-bee path by adopting 9S-DTZNN algorithm (14.5). *Reproduced from W. Yang, J. Chen, Y. Zhang, J. Sun, and Z. Zhang, Abundant computer and robot experiments verifying minimum joint motion planning and control of redundant arms via Zhang neural network, Figure 9, Proceedings of International Joint Conference on Neural Networks, pp. 1–8, 2021. ©IEEE 2021. With kind permission of IEEE.*

$$\zeta_{k-6} = \zeta_k - 6g\dot{\zeta}_k + 18g^2\ddot{\zeta}_k - 36g^3\dddot{\zeta}_k + 54g^4\zeta_k^{(4)} - \frac{324g^5}{5}\zeta_k^{(5)} + \frac{324g^6}{5}\zeta_k^{(6)} + \mathcal{O}(g^7), \quad (14.16)$$

$$\zeta_{k-7} = \zeta_k - 7g\dot{\zeta}_k + \frac{49g^2}{2}\ddot{\zeta}_k - \frac{343g^3}{6}\dddot{\zeta}_k + \frac{2401g^4}{24}\zeta_k^{(4)} - \frac{16807g^5}{120}\zeta_k^{(5)} + \frac{117649g^6}{720}\zeta_k^{(6)} + \mathcal{O}(g^7), \quad (14.17)$$

and

$$\zeta_{k-8} = \zeta_k - 8g\dot{\zeta}_k + 32g^2\ddot{\zeta}_k - \frac{256g^3}{3}\dddot{\zeta}_k + \frac{512g^4}{3}\zeta_k^{(4)} - \frac{4096g^5}{15}\zeta_k^{(5)} + \frac{16384g^6}{45}\zeta_k^{(6)} + \mathcal{O}(g^7), \quad (14.18)$$

where $\ddot{\zeta}_k$, $\dddot{\zeta}_k$, $\zeta_k^{(4)}$, $\zeta_k^{(5)}$, and $\zeta_k^{(6)}$ represent the second-order through sixth-order time derivatives of $\zeta(t)$ at time instant t_k, respectively. Let (14.10) multiply 1, let (14.11) multiply $-3/5$, let (14.12) multiply $-9/10$, let (14.13) multiply $-1/5$, let (14.14) multiply $3/10$, let (14.15) multiply $39/125$, let (14.16) multiply $-1/10$, let (14.17) multiply $-48/245$, and let (14.18) multiply $7/80$. Adding them together, we finally obtain

$$\dot{\zeta}_k = \frac{350}{879g}\zeta_{k+1} + \frac{9683}{82040g}\zeta_k - \frac{70}{293g}\zeta_{k-1} - \frac{105}{293g}\zeta_{k-2} - \frac{70}{897g}\zeta_{k-3} + \frac{35}{293g}\zeta_{k-4} + \frac{182}{1465g}\zeta_{k-5} - \frac{35}{897g}\zeta_{k-6} - \frac{160}{2051g}\zeta_{k-7} + \frac{245}{7032g}\zeta_{k-8} + \mathcal{O}(g^5),$$

which is just the 9S-ZTD formula (14.4). The proof is therefore completed. □

Appendix R: Proof of Theorem 57

According to Definition 2 in Chapter 1, the characteristic polynomial of the 9S-DTZNN algorithm (14.5) is expressed as

$$\Gamma_9(\iota) = \iota^9 + \frac{29049}{98000}\iota^8 - \frac{3}{5}\iota^7 - \frac{9}{10}\iota^6 - \frac{1}{5}\iota^5 + \frac{3}{10}\iota^4 + \frac{39}{125}\iota^3 - \frac{1}{10}\iota^2 - \frac{48}{245}\iota + \frac{7}{80}.$$

The roots of $\Gamma_9(\iota)$ are 1, 0.5026, −0.8111, −0.7205 ± 0.5496i, −0.2535 ± 0.8489i, and 0.4801 ± 0.3202i, where i is the imaginary unit. There is one simple root on the unit circle, and another eight roots lie inside the unit circle. Thus, the 9S-DTZNN algorithm (14.5) is zero-stable.

On the basis of (14.3) and (14.4), we have

$$\mathbf{c}_{k+1} = \frac{879}{350}\tilde{\mathbf{c}}_k - \frac{29049}{98000}\mathbf{c}_k + \frac{3}{5}\mathbf{c}_{k-1} + \frac{9}{10}\mathbf{c}_{k-2} + \frac{1}{5}\mathbf{c}_{k-3} - \frac{3}{10}\mathbf{c}_{k-4} - \frac{39}{125}\mathbf{c}_{k-5} + \frac{1}{10}\mathbf{c}_{k-6} + \frac{48}{245}\mathbf{c}_{k-7} - \frac{7}{80}\mathbf{c}_{k-8} + \mathbf{O}(g^6).$$

Thus, the truncation error of the 9S-DTZNN algorithm (14.5) is $\mathbf{O}(g^6)$. According to Definitions 3 and 4 in Chapter 1, the 9S-DTZNN algorithm (14.5) is consistent and converges with the order of truncation error being $\mathbf{O}(g^6)$.

Suppose that $\mathbf{c}^*_{k+1}$ is the theoretical solution of $B_{k+1}\mathbf{c}_{k+1} + \mathbf{d}_{k+1} = \mathbf{0}$. Besides, on the basis of the above proof, we have $\mathbf{c}_{k+1} = \mathbf{c}^*_{k+1} + \mathbf{O}(g^6)$ with the sufficiently large k. Thus, it follows that

$$\begin{aligned}
&\lim_{k\to+\infty} \sup \|B_{k+1}\mathbf{c}_{k+1} + \mathbf{d}_{k+1}\|_2 \\
&= \lim_{k\to+\infty} \sup \|B_{k+1}(\mathbf{c}^*_{k+1} + \mathbf{O}(g^6)) + \mathbf{d}_{k+1}\|_2 \\
&= \lim_{k\to+\infty} \sup \|B_{k+1}\mathbf{c}^*_{k+1} + \mathbf{d}_{k+1} + B_{k+1}\mathbf{O}(g^6)\|_2 \\
&= \lim_{k\to+\infty} \sup \|B_{k+1}\mathbf{O}(g^6)\|_2 = \mathcal{O}(g^6),
\end{aligned}$$

with B_{k+1} being uniformly norm bounded. The proof is therefore completed. □

Part VII

Miscellaneous

Chapter 15

Euler-Precision General Formula of ZTD

Abstract

In this chapter, we present and focus on a general two-step Zhang time discretization (2S-ZTD) formula with truncation error proportional to the sampling gap. To begin with, the stability and accuracy of the general 2S-ZTD formula are ensured by strict proof. Then, the general 2S-ZTD formula is used for the first-order derivative approximation, and numerical experimental results verify its stability and accuracy. Besides, the general 2S-ZTD formula is applied to discretizing continuous-time zeroing neural network (CTZNN) model, and thus the general two-step discrete-time zeroing neural network (2S-DTZNN) algorithm with square precision is developed for solving future minimization problem. Numerical experimental results verify the stability and accuracy of the general 2S-DTZNN algorithm again.

15.1 Introduction

The Euler forward formula, Euler-precision numerical-differentiation formula, Taylor numerical-differentiation, and Lagrange numerical-differentiation formulas are widely applied in different fields. In numerical analysis, they are often used to represent the numerical differential values of some specific functions and also to solve ordinary differential equations (ODEs), including initial value problems and boundary value problems [25,161,397]. In engineering applications, they can be regarded as powerful and essential tools when we need to build numerical models [77,398], since, in realistic cases, it might be challenging to implement continuous-time models in digital computers. Those numerical-differentiation formulas perform pretty well on numerical problems solving. Nevertheless, unfortunately, most of those formulas fail to solve discrete time-dependent problems. Note that numerical solution is generally off-line solution, while discrete-time solution is on-line solution. Therefore, stable and effective Euler-precision discretization formulas aiming at solving discrete time-dependent (also termed as future) problems are required to be presented.

In this chapter [399], we mainly present a general two-step Zhang time discretization (2S-ZTD) formula (i.e., Euler-precision general formula of ZTD) to solve a future minimization problem (i.e., future unconstrained nonlinear optimization problem in Chapter 6).

DOI: 10.1201/9781003497783-15

15.2 General 2S-ZTD Formula Derivation

In this section, we derive a general 2S-ZTD formula and analyze its stability and truncation error by strict theoretical proof.

Theorem 58 *With the sufficiently small sampling gap $g \in (0,1)$, let $\mathscr{O}(g)$ denote the error (especially, the truncation error) positively or negatively proportional to g, i.e., of the order of g. Suppose that $\zeta(t)$ is sufficiently smooth. With $\zeta_{k+1} = \zeta(t_{k+1}) = \zeta((k+1)g)$, the general 2S-ZTD formula is presented as*

$$\dot{\zeta}_k = \frac{(a_1+1)\zeta_{k+1} - (2a_1+1)\zeta_k + a_1\zeta_{k-1}}{g} + \mathscr{O}(g), \tag{15.1}$$

where $a_1 > -1/2$ and $a_1 \neq 0$.

Proof. The outline of the proof is to generate the linear combination of ζ_{k+1} and ζ_{k-1} in their Taylor expansions first [161, 397] and then to determine the proper relations of the coefficients via specific constraints.

Generally, the pth-order Taylor expansion of ζ_{k+1} is represented as $\zeta_{k+1} = \zeta_k + g\dot{\zeta}_k + g^2\ddot{\zeta}_k/2 + \cdots + g^p\zeta_k^{(p)}/p! + \mathscr{O}(g^{p+1})$. To get a general 2S-ZTD formula, we show the second-order Taylor expansions of ζ_{k+1} and ζ_{k-1} as

$$\zeta_{k+1} = \zeta_k + g\dot{\zeta}_k + \frac{g^2}{2}\ddot{\zeta}_k + \mathscr{O}(g^3) \tag{15.2}$$

and

$$\zeta_{k-1} = \zeta_k - g\dot{\zeta}_k + \frac{g^2}{2}\ddot{\zeta}_k + \mathscr{O}(g^3). \tag{15.3}$$

By assuming

$$a_1\zeta_{k-1} + a_2\zeta_k + a_3\zeta_{k+1} \doteq g\dot{\zeta}_k, \tag{15.4}$$

with $\doteq$ denoting the computational assignment operator, and substituting (15.2) and (15.3) into (15.4), it can be written as $b_0\zeta_k + b_1 g\dot{\zeta}_k + b_2 g^2\ddot{\zeta}_k + \mathscr{O}(g^3) = 0$, where $b_0 = a_1 + a_2 + a_3$, $b_1 = -a_1 + a_3 - 1$, and $b_2 = a_1/2 + a_3/2$. Noticing the error term of the left-hand-side of (15.4) being $\mathscr{O}(g^3)$, we could rewrite (15.4) as $\dot{\zeta}_k = (a_1\zeta_{k-1} + a_2\zeta_k + a_3\zeta_{k+1})/g + \mathscr{O}(g^2)$.

To guarantee the truncation error reaching $\mathscr{O}(g^2)$, b_0, b_1, and b_2 should be equal to zero, i.e.,

$$\begin{cases} b_0 = a_1 + a_2 + a_3 = 0, \\ b_1 = -a_1 + a_3 - 1 = 0, \\ b_2 = a_1/2 + a_3/2 = 0. \end{cases}$$

By solving the above linear system, we have

$$\begin{cases} a_1 = -1/2, \\ a_2 = 0, \\ a_3 = 1/2. \end{cases}$$

Therefore, the characteristic polynomial of (15.4) is $\Gamma_2(\iota) = \iota^2 - 1$. Because the formula, which is actually the simplest central numerical-differentiation formula [161] given as $\dot{\zeta}_k \doteq (\zeta_{k+1} - \zeta_{k-1})/(2g)$, does not satisfy the (strong) zero-stability condition by the definitions in [25], the formula should not be considered an acceptable 2S-ZTD formula. Therefore, this result should be discarded.

Again, to guarantee that the truncation error could reach $\mathscr{O}(g)$, b_0 and b_1 should be equal to zero. To be specific, we have

$$\begin{cases} b_0 = a_1 + a_2 + a_3 = 0, \\ b_1 = -a_1 + a_3 - 1 = 0. \end{cases}$$

The solution could be represented as

$$\begin{cases} a_2 = -2a_1 - 1, \\ a_3 = a_1 + 1. \end{cases} \tag{15.5}$$

Hence, we could use a_1 to present b_2 as $b_2 = a_1 + 1/2$. Moreover, we should constrain the range of the coefficient a_1 to guarantee the zero-stability condition. The characteristic polynomial of (15.4) becomes

$$\Gamma_2(\iota) = a_3\iota^2 + a_2\iota + a_1.$$

To analyze the property of its roots, we apply linear fractional transformation [400], or say, bilinear transformation (also termed as Tustin transformation [162, 163]):

$$\iota = \frac{\omega + 1}{\omega - 1},$$

which maps the area $\mathrm{Re}(\omega) \leq 0$ in the complex plane onto the area $|\iota| \leq 1$ (i.e., transforming the area $|\iota| \leq 1$ onto the area $\mathrm{Re}(\omega) \leq 0$ in the complex plane). Then, we have

$$c_2\omega^2 + c_1\omega + c_0 = 0,$$

where

$$\begin{cases} c_2 = a_1 + a_2 + a_3, \\ c_1 = -2a_1 + 2a_3, \\ c_0 = a_1 - a_2 + a_3. \end{cases}$$

Paying attention to the constraint (15.5), we obtain

$$2\omega + (4a_1 + 2) = 0.$$

From the Routh stability criterion [25, 401, 402], the zero-stable condition is

$$a_1 > -1/2.$$

Moreover, for the sake of not being degenerated, a_1, a_2, and a_3 should not be equal to zero, that is to say,

$$\begin{cases} a_1 \neq 0, \\ a_2 = -2a_1 - 1 \neq 0, \\ a_3 = a_1 + 1 \neq 0, \end{cases}$$

and thus the constraint $a_1 \neq 0$ is compulsory.

Finally, the general 2S-ZTD formula could be represented as

$$\dot{\zeta}_k = \frac{(a_1+1)\zeta_{k+1} - (2a_1+1)\zeta_k + a_1\zeta_{k-1}}{g} + (a_1 + 1/2)g\ddot{\zeta}(c).$$

where $a_1 > -1/2$, $a_1 \neq 0$, and $c \in (t_{k-1}, t_{k+1})$. The term of the truncation error is

$$(a_1 + 1/2)g\ddot{\zeta}(c) = \mathscr{O}(g),$$

and the value converges toward zero when a_1 approaches toward $-1/2$. The proof is therefore completed. □

Corollary 19 *With the sufficiently small sampling gap $g \in (0,1)$, let $\mathscr{O}(g)$ denote the error (especially, the truncation error) positively or negatively proportional to g, i.e., of the order of g. Suppose that $\zeta(t)$ is sufficiently smooth. With $\zeta_{k+1} = \zeta(t_{k+1}) = \zeta((k+1)g)$ and letting $a_1 = -1/3$, we have*

$$\dot{\zeta}_k = \frac{2\zeta_{k+1} - \zeta_k - \zeta_{k-1}}{3g} + \mathscr{O}(g). \tag{15.6}$$

This formula is also known as the Euler-precision ZFD formula 3NgPFD_G [403].

Corollary 20 *With the sufficiently small sampling gap $g \in (0,1)$, let $\mathscr{O}(g)$ denote the error (especially, the truncation error) positively or negatively proportional to g, i.e., of the order of g. Suppose that $\zeta(t)$ is sufficiently smooth. With $\zeta_{k+1} = \zeta(t_{k+1}) = \zeta((k+1)g)$ and letting $a_1 = 1/2$, we have*

$$\dot{\zeta}_k = \frac{3\zeta_{k+1} - 4\zeta_k + \zeta_{k-1}}{2g} + \mathscr{O}(g). \tag{15.7}$$

However, in practical applications, the performance of this formula may be poor, since the value of a_1 is too far from the critical value $-1/2$, giving a relatively large error term.

Corollary 21 *With the sufficiently small sampling gap $g \in (0,1)$, let $\mathscr{O}(g)$ denote the error (especially, the truncation error) positively or negatively proportional to g, i.e., of the order of g. Suppose that $\zeta(t)$ is sufficiently smooth. We could expand $-1/2$ to power series with the common ratio $q = 1/2$, that is,*

$$-\frac{1}{2} = -\frac{1}{4} - \frac{1}{8} - \frac{1}{16} - \frac{1}{32} - \cdots.$$

We take the sum of the first three terms as a_1. Numerically, $a_1 = -7/16$. Then, we have

$$\dot{\zeta}_k = \frac{9\zeta_{k+1} - 2\zeta_k - 7\zeta_{k-1}}{16g} + \mathscr{O}(g), \tag{15.8}$$

of which the coefficient of error term is relatively small.

15.3 Numerical Experiments for Derivative Approximations

In this section, we use the general 2S-ZTD formula (15.1) with different a_1 to approximate the first-order derivatives of target functions. The stability and accuracy can be verified by these numerical experiments.

Example 15.1 We consider the target function:

$$f_k = \ln(\arctan(1 + t_k^2)), \text{with } t_k \in [0,1] \text{ s},$$

whose first-order time derivative is

$$\dot{f}_k^* = \frac{2t_k}{(t_k^4 + 2t_k^2 + 2)\arctan(1 + t_k^2)},$$

where $\dot{f}_k^*$ denotes the theoretical value.

The corresponding numerical experimental results are displayed in Figures 15.1 and 15.2. The trajectories of the approximation values $\dot{f}_k$ are displayed in Figure 15.1. Besides, the trajectories of the approximation errors $\check{e}_k = |\dot{f}_k - \dot{f}_k^*|$ are displayed in Figure 15.2. The numerical experimental results verify that the approximation error term of the general 2S-ZTD formula (15.1) is $\mathscr{O}(g)$, with

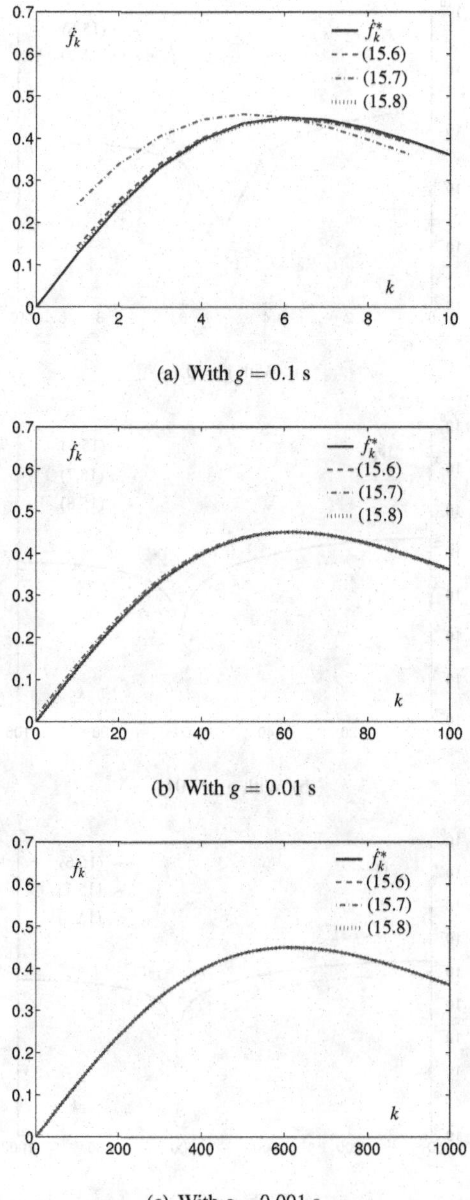

(a) With $g = 0.1$ s

(b) With $g = 0.01$ s

(c) With $g = 0.001$ s

FIGURE 15.1: Trajectories of approximation values $\dot{f}_k$ using 2S-ZTD formulas (15.6), (15.7), and (15.8) in Example 15.1.

the sampling gap g changing from 0.1 s to 0.01 s and then to 0.001 s. The leftmost and rightmost values should not be computed by the general 2S-ZTD formula (15.1), because, e.g., the leftmost value is $\dot{f}_0 = \dot{f}(0)$ and we have to use the value $f_{-1} = f(-g)$ to compute the derivative $\dot{f}_0$ while $-g$ is not in the domain.

Besides, from Figure 15.2, we see that the trajectory of the approximation error synthesized by the 2S-ZTD formula (15.7) with $g = 0.1$ s performs badly, and when $g = 0.01$ and 0.001 s, the

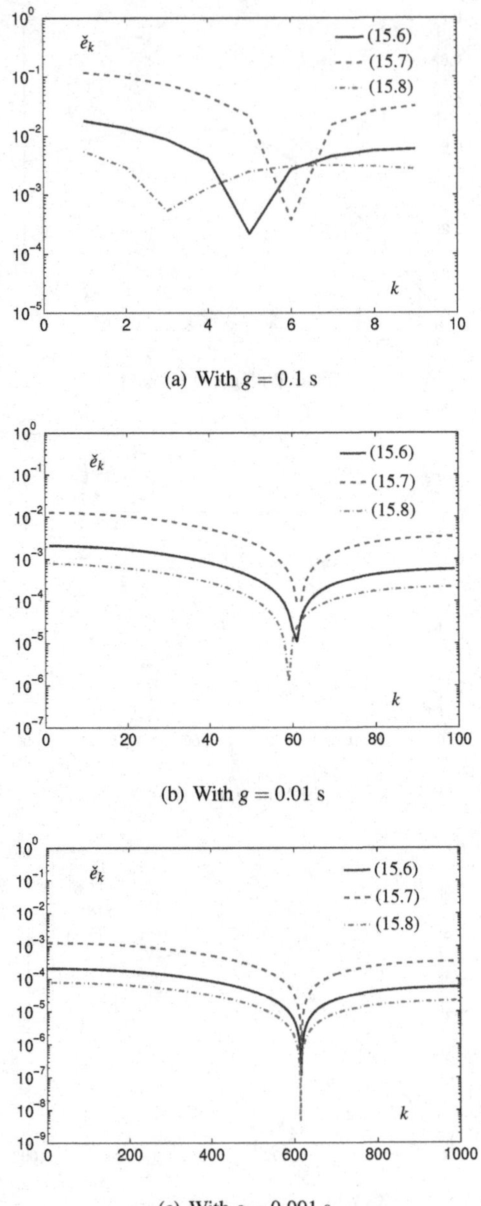

(a) With $g = 0.1$ s

(b) With $g = 0.01$ s

(c) With $g = 0.001$ s

FIGURE 15.2: Trajectories of approximation errors $\check{e}_k$ synthesized by 2S-ZTD formulas (15.6), (15.7), and (15.8) in Example 15.1.

results are acceptable. The 2S-ZTD formulas (15.6) and (15.8) perform well in all cases, with the approximation errors being acceptably small in all sample points.

Example 15.2 We consider another target function:

$$f_k = \frac{1}{5\exp(\sin(3t_k)) + 4}, \text{ with } t_k \in [0,2] \text{ s},$$

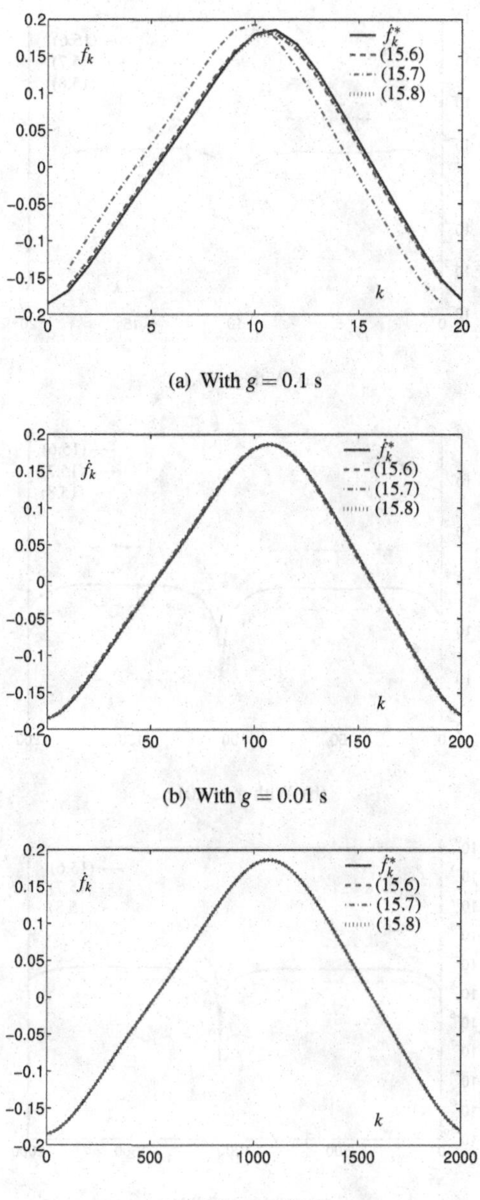

(a) With $g = 0.1$ s

(b) With $g = 0.01$ s

(c) With $g = 0.001$ s

FIGURE 15.3: Trajectories of approximation values $\dot{f}_k$ using 2S-ZTD formulas (15.6), (15.7), and (15.8) in Example 15.2.

whose first-order time derivative is

$$\dot{f}_k^* = -\frac{15\cos(3t_k)\exp(\sin(3t_k))}{(5\exp(\sin(3t_k))+4)^2}.$$

The corresponding numerical experimental results are displayed in Figures 15.3 and 15.4. The trajectories of the approximation values $\dot{f}_k$ are displayed in Figure 15.3. Besides, the trajectories of the approximation errors $\breve{e}_k$ are displayed in Figure 15.4. Again, the numerical experimental results

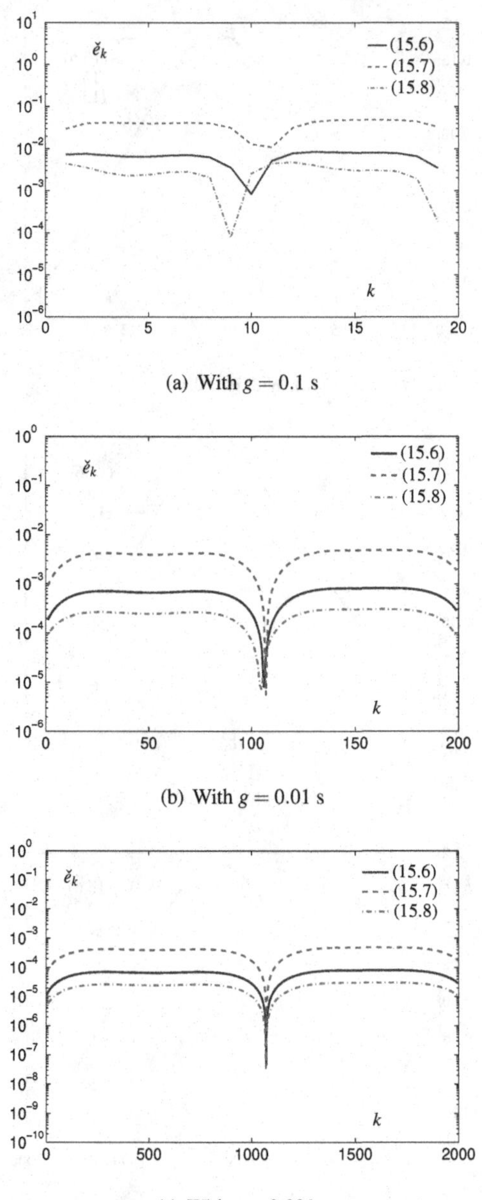

(a) With $g = 0.1$ s

(b) With $g = 0.01$ s

(c) With $g = 0.001$ s

FIGURE 15.4: Trajectories of approximation errors $\check{e}_k$ synthesized by 2S-ZTD formulas (15.6), (15.7), and (15.8) in Example 15.2.

verify that the approximation error term of the general 2S-ZTD formula (15.1) is $\mathscr{O}(g)$. Evidently, we see that, as predicted in Corollaries 19–21, the third 2S-ZTD formula performs best, the first 2S-ZTD formula follows, then the second 2S-ZTD formula. Their performances are satisfying.

In summary, the results substantiate that the 2S-ZTD formulas are zero-stable and accurate.

15.4 Discretization Theory and Numerical Experiments

In this section, we investigate and solve the future minimization problem.

Example 15.3 We consider the following future minimization problem [111], with $\mathbf{x}_{k+1}$ to be computed at each computational time interval $[t_k, t_{k+1}) \subset [0, 10]$ s:

$$\min_{\mathbf{x}_{k+1} \in \mathbb{R}^4} \varphi(\mathbf{x}_{k+1}, t_{k+1}) \in \mathbb{R}, \tag{15.9}$$

where $\mathbf{x}_k = [x_{1,k}, x_{2,k}, x_{3,k}, x_{4,k}]^{\mathrm{T}}$, $t_k = kg$, and

$$\begin{aligned}\varphi(\mathbf{x}_k, t_k) &= \cosh(t_k)x_{1,k}^2 + 4x_{2,k}^2 + \cosh(t_k)x_{3,k}^2 + 7x_{4,k}^2 \\ &+ \sin(2t_k)x_{1,k} - x_{2,k} - 2\sinh(t_k)x_{1,k}x_{3,k} - \cos(t_k)x_{4,k}.\end{aligned} \tag{15.10}$$

To begin with, we define the gradient of $\varphi(\mathbf{x}(t), t)$ (corresponding to continuous form of (15.9)) as $\mathbf{z}(t) = \partial\varphi(\mathbf{x}(t), t)/\partial\mathbf{x}(t) = \Psi(\mathbf{x}(t), t) \in \mathbb{R}^n$, i.e., zeroing function (ZF). The goal is to make the residual error $\hat{e}(t)=\|\Psi(\mathbf{x}(t), t)\|_2$ approach toward zero, where $\|\cdot\|_2$ denotes the 2-norm of a vector. Applying the ZNN design formula [45, 404, 405], we have $\dot{\mathbf{z}}(t) = \mathrm{d}\mathbf{z}(t)/\mathrm{d}t = -\eta\mathbf{z}(t)$, where η is a positive real number representing the convergent rate of the continuous-time ZNN (CTZNN) model. Then, we obtain the following CTZNN model by expanding the left-hand side of the above equation as

$$H(\mathbf{x}(t), t)\dot{\mathbf{x}}(t) + \Psi_t'(\mathbf{x}(t), t) = -\eta\Psi(\mathbf{x}(t), t), \tag{15.11}$$

where $H(\mathbf{x}(t), t) = \partial\Psi(\mathbf{x}(t), t)/\partial\mathbf{x}^{\mathrm{T}}(t) = \partial^2\varphi(\mathbf{x}(t), t)/\ (\partial\mathbf{x}(t)\partial\mathbf{x}^{\mathrm{T}}(t)) \in \mathbb{R}^{n\times n}$ (known as the Hessian matrix of the target function $\varphi(\mathbf{x}(t), t)$ [191, 406]), and $\Psi_t'(\mathbf{x}(t), t) = \partial\Psi(\mathbf{x}(t), t)/\partial t = \partial^2\varphi(\mathbf{x}(t), t)/(\partial\mathbf{x}(t)\partial t) \in \mathbb{R}^n$. Substituting the general 2S-ZTD formula (15.1) into the CTZNN model (15.11), we get

$$H(\mathbf{x}_k, t_k)\frac{(a_1+1)\mathbf{x}_{k+1} - (2a_1+1)\mathbf{x}_k + a_1\mathbf{x}_{k-1}}{g} + \Psi_t'(\mathbf{x}_k, t_k) \doteq -\eta\Psi(\mathbf{x}_k, t_k). \tag{15.12}$$

Suppose that $H(\mathbf{x}_k, t_k)$ is always nonsingular in this chapter [399], the general two-step discrete-time zeroing neural network (2S-DTZNN) algorithm is further obtained as

$$\mathbf{x}_{k+1} \doteq -\frac{1}{a_1+1}H^{-1}(\mathbf{x}_k, t_k)(\hbar\Psi(\mathbf{x}_k, t_k) + g\Psi_t'(\mathbf{x}_k, t_k)) + \frac{2a_1+1}{a_1+1}\mathbf{x}_k - \frac{a_1}{a_1+1}\mathbf{x}_{k-1}, \tag{15.13}$$

with $\hbar = g\eta$ representing the step length. The truncation error of the general 2S-ZTD formula (15.1) is $\mathscr{O}(g)$. Therefore, the truncation error of (15.12) is $\mathbf{O}(g)$, in which the truncation error $\mathbf{O}(g)$ represents a vector with each element being $\mathscr{O}(g)$. Because we derive (15.13) from (15.12) by multiplying g simultaneously to both sides of (15.12), the truncation error of (15.13) is $\mathbf{O}(g^2)$.

Note that the residual error is defined as $\hat{e}_{k+1} = \|\partial\varphi(\mathbf{x}_{k+1}, t_{k+1})/\partial\mathbf{x}_{k+1}\|_2 = \|\Psi(\mathbf{x}_{k+1}, t_{k+1})\|_2$ for the future minimization (15.9) in this chapter [399].

Theorem 59 *Consider the future minimization (15.9) with $\varphi(\cdot,\cdot)$ being second-order differentiable and bounded. Suppose that $H(\mathbf{x}_k, t_k)$ is always nonsingular and uniformly norm bounded. With the coefficient $a_1 > -1/2$ and $a_1 \neq 0$ as well as with the sufficiently small sampling gap $g \in (0, 1)$, the maximal steady-state residual error (MSSRE) $\lim_{k\to+\infty}\sup\hat{e}_{k+1}$ synthesized by the general 2S-DTZNN algorithm (15.13) is $\mathscr{O}(g^2)$.*

Proof. Notice that the continuous time t and the discrete-time instant t_k are actually always in the same physical system of time and that they are different but (closely) related descriptions of such same physical system of time. To prove that the MSSRE synthesized by the general 2S-DTZNN algorithm (15.13), i.e., $\lim_{k\to+\infty}\sup\hat{e}_{k+1}$, is $\mathscr{O}(g^2)$, we know that (15.12) can actually be written as

$$H(\mathbf{x}_k,t_k)(\dot{\mathbf{x}}_k+\mathbf{O}(g))+\dot{\Psi}(\mathbf{x}_k,t_k)=-\eta\Psi(\mathbf{x}_k,t_k). \tag{15.14}$$

Because the truncation error of the general 2S-ZTD formula (15.1) is $\mathscr{O}(g)$. By expanding the left-hand side of (15.14), we have

$$H(\mathbf{x}_k,t_k)\dot{\mathbf{x}}_k+\dot{\Psi}(\mathbf{x}_k,t_k)+H(\mathbf{x}_k,t_k)\mathbf{O}(g)=-\eta\Psi(\mathbf{x}_k,t_k). \tag{15.15}$$

Note that $H(\mathbf{x}_k,t_k)$ can be absorbed in the error term $\mathbf{O}(g)$ and that $H(\mathbf{x}_k,t_k)\dot{\mathbf{x}}_k+\Psi'_t(\mathbf{x}_k,t_k)=\dot{\Psi}(\mathbf{x}_k,t_k)$. Then, (15.15) is written as

$$\dot{\Psi}(\mathbf{x}_k,t_k)+\mathbf{O}(g)=-\eta\Psi(\mathbf{x}_k,t_k). \tag{15.16}$$

The analytic solution of (15.16) is represented as

$$\Psi(\mathbf{x}_k,t_k)=\mathbf{O}(g)/\eta+(\Psi(\mathbf{x}_0,t_0)-\mathbf{O}(g)/\eta)\exp(-\eta t_k). \tag{15.17}$$

By noticing $\hbar=g\eta$, i.e., $\eta=\hbar/g$, (15.17) becomes

$$\begin{aligned}\Psi(\mathbf{x}_k,t_k)=&\mathbf{O}(g^2)/\hbar+(\Psi(\mathbf{x}_0,t_0)-\mathbf{O}(g^2)/\hbar)\exp(-\eta t_k)\\=&\mathbf{O}(g^2)+(\Psi(\mathbf{x}_0,t_0)-\mathbf{O}(g^2))\exp(-\eta t_k).\end{aligned} \tag{15.18}$$

From (15.18), we have

$$\begin{aligned}\lim_{k\to+\infty}\sup\Psi(\mathbf{x}_{k+1},t_{k+1})=&\mathbf{O}(g^2)+\lim_{k\to+\infty}\sup(\Psi(\mathbf{x}_0,t_0)-\mathbf{O}(g^2))\exp(-\eta t_{k+1})\\=&\mathbf{O}(g^2)+\lim_{k\to+\infty}\sup(\Psi(\mathbf{x}_0,t_0)-\mathbf{O}(g^2))\exp(-\eta(k+1)g)\\=&\mathbf{O}(g^2)+\mathbf{0}=\mathbf{O}(g^2).\end{aligned}$$

Therefore, the MSSRE $\lim_{k\to+\infty}\sup\hat{e}_{k+1}$ synthesized by the general 2S-DTZNN algorithm (15.13) is $\mathscr{O}(g^2)$. The proof is therefore completed. □

To solve the future minimization (15.9), we choose $g=0.1$, 0.01, and 0.001 s but keep $\hbar=0.3$ unchanged. The numerical experimental results are shown in Figure 15.5. Specifically, Figure 15.5(a), (c), and (e) shows that the residual errors $\hat{e}_{k+1}$ converge at a high rate. Besides, Figure 15.5(b), (d), and (f) displays the trajectories of the function $\varphi(\mathbf{x}_{k+1},t_{k+1})$ generated by the general 2S-DTZNN algorithm (15.13) with different a_1.

In summary, the above numerical experimental results verify that the general 2S-DTZNN algorithm (15.13) can solve the future minimization problem not only correctly but also efficiently.

For a more intuitive understanding of the main content of this chapter [399], Table 15.1 lists the problem, scheme, model, and algorithm.

15.5 Chapter Summary

In this chapter, the general 2S-ZTD formula (15.1) has been presented to approximate the first-order derivative, and the numerical experimental results have verified its stability and accuracy. Moreover, we have constructively used the general 2S-ZTD formula (15.1) to discretize the CTZNN model (15.11) and obtain the general 2S-DTZNN algorithm (15.13) for solving the future minimization (15.9). Meanwhile, the stability and efficacy of the general 2S-DTZNN algorithm (15.13) have been substantiated via the numerical experimental results.

TABLE 15.1: Problem, scheme, model, and algorithm in this chapter.

Problem	$\min_{\mathbf{x}_{k+1}\in\mathbb{R}^4} \varphi(\mathbf{x}_{k+1}, t_{k+1}) \in \mathbb{R}.$
Scheme	*Step 1*: Define ZF as $\mathbf{z}(t) = \boldsymbol{\Psi}(\mathbf{x}(t), t)$. *Step 2*: Adopt ZNN design formula as $\dot{\mathbf{z}}(t) = -\eta \mathbf{z}(t)$. *Step 3*: Adopt general 2S-ZTD formula (15.1) to discretize CTZNN model (15.11).
Model	$H(\mathbf{x}(t), t)\dot{\mathbf{x}}(t) + \boldsymbol{\Psi}'_t(\mathbf{x}(t), t) = -\eta \boldsymbol{\Psi}(\mathbf{x}(t), t).$
Algorithm	$\mathbf{x}_{k+1} \doteq -\frac{1}{a_1+1} H^{-1}(\mathbf{x}_k, t_k)(\hbar \boldsymbol{\Psi}(\mathbf{x}_k, t_k) + g \boldsymbol{\Psi}'_t(\mathbf{x}_k, t_k)) + \frac{2a_1+1}{a_1+1}\mathbf{x}_k - \frac{a_1}{a_1+1}\mathbf{x}_{k-1}.$

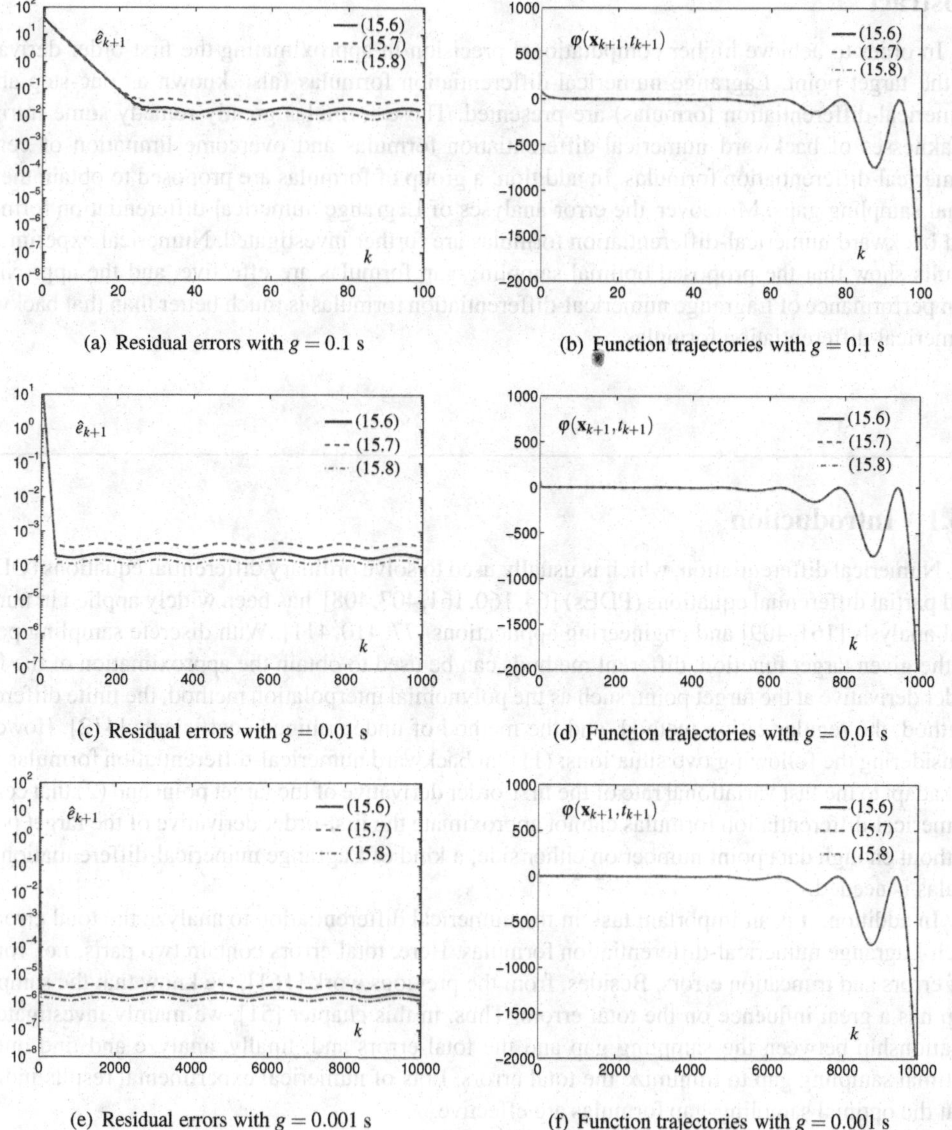

(a) Residual errors with $g = 0.1$ s

(b) Function trajectories with $g = 0.1$ s

(c) Residual errors with $g = 0.01$ s

(d) Function trajectories with $g = 0.01$ s

(e) Residual errors with $g = 0.001$ s

(f) Function trajectories with $g = 0.001$ s

FIGURE 15.5: Trajectories of residual errors $\hat{e}_{k+1}$ and function $\varphi(\mathbf{x}_{k+1}, t_{k+1})$ generated by general 2S-DTZNN algorithm (15.13) with $\hbar = 0.3$ in Example 15.3.

Chapter 16

Lagrange Numerical-Differentiation Formulas

Abstract

In order to achieve higher computational precision in approximating the first-order derivative of the target point, Lagrange numerical-differentiation formulas (also known as one-step-ahead numerical-differentiation formulas) are presented. These formulas greatly remedy some intrinsic weaknesses of backward numerical-differentiation formulas and overcome limitation of central numerical-differentiation formulas. In addition, a group of formulas are proposed to obtain the optimal sampling gaps. Moreover, the error analyses of Lagrange numerical-differentiation formulas and backward numerical-differentiation formulas are further investigated. Numerical experimental results show that the proposed optimal sampling-gap formulas are effective, and the approximation performance of Lagrange numerical-differentiation formulas is much better than that backward numerical-differentiation formulas.

16.1 Introduction

Numerical differentiation, which is usually used to solve ordinary differential equations (ODEs) and partial differential equations (PDEs) [64, 160, 161, 407, 408], has been widely applied in numerical analysis [161, 409] and engineering applications [77, 410, 411]. With discrete sampling points of the given target function, different methods can be used to obtain the approximation of the first-order derivative at the target point, such as the polynomial interpolation method, the finite difference method, the regularization method, and the method of undetermined coefficients [412]. However, considering the following two situations: (1) that backward numerical-differentiation formulas may not adapt to the fast variational rate of the first-order derivative of the target point and (2) that central numerical-differentiation formulas cannot approximate the first-order derivative of the target points without enough data point number on either side, a kind of Lagrange numerical-differentiation formulas is needed.

In addition, it is an important task in the numerical differentiation to analyze the total errors of such Lagrange numerical-differentiation formulas. Here, total errors contain two parts, i.e., round-off errors and truncation errors. Besides, from the previous work [161], we know that the sampling gap has a great influence on the total errors. Thus, in this chapter [51], we mainly investigate the relationship between the sampling gap and the total errors and, finally, analyze and find out the optimal sampling gap to minimize the total errors. Lots of numerical experimental results indicate that the optimal sampling-gap formulas are effective.

DOI: 10.1201/9781003497783-16

16.2 Formula Derivation with Alternative Proof

Based on the polynomial interpolation theory, an interpolation polynomial $\phi(x)$ is constructed to approximate the unknown target function $f(x)$, that is, $f(x) \approx \phi(x)$. Therefore, we can obtain the first-order derivative of the unknown target function $f(x)$ by computing the first-order derivative of $\phi(x)$, that is, $f'(x) \approx \phi'(x)$ [161]. Besides, in practical applications, sampling data points are collected with equal space in the digital discrete system, i.e., $x_{i+1} - x_i = g$ $(i = 0, 1, 2, \cdots, n)$, where $g > 0$ is the sampling gap. Hence, we present and investigate Lagrange numerical-differentiation formulas in the following. First, the following definition and lemma [51] are presented for further discussion.

Definition 5 *Assuming that the value of the unknown target function $f(x)$ at the discrete-sampling data point x_i is $f(x_i)$ $(i = 0, 1, 2, \cdots, n)$ and the n-degree polynomial $\phi_n(x_i) = \alpha_0 + \alpha_1 x + \cdots + \alpha_n x^n$ satisfies $\phi_n(x_i) = f(x_i)$, then we name $\phi_n(x)$ as the n-degree interpolation polynomial of the unknown target function $f(x)$.*

Lemma 13 *Assuming that $x_0, x_1, x_2, \cdots, x_n$ are $(n+1)$ mutually different data points in the sampling interval $[a, b]$, and the $(n+1)$th-order derivative of the unknown target function $f(x)$ is continuous (marked as $f \in C^{(n+1)}[a, b]$), then for any $x \in [a, b]$, there exists a number $c \in (a, b)$ that satisfies*

$$f(x) = \phi_n(x) + \sigma_{n+1}(x),$$

where $\phi_n(x)$ is the interpolation polynomial of the unknown target function $f(x)$, and the remainder term $\sigma_{n+1}(x)$ can be expressed as

$$\sigma_{n+1}(x) = \frac{f^{n+1}(c) \prod_{i=0}^{n} (x - x_i)}{(n+1)!}.$$

According to Definition 5 and Lemma 13 [51], we construct an n-order interpolation polynomial $\phi_n(x)$ to approximate the unknown target function $f(x)$. Therefore, we have the following theorem.

Theorem 60 *Assuming that the unknown target function $f(x)$ is smooth and differentiable, then the approximation of the first-order derivative of $f(x)$ is determined by calculating that of the interpolation polynomial $\phi_n(x)$, that is,*

$$f'(x) = \phi_n'(x) + \sigma_{n+1}'(x),$$

where $\sigma_{n+1}'(x)$ is the first-order derivative of the remainder term $\sigma_{n+1}(x)$. Considering that the data points are sampled with equal space g, the first-order derivative of $f(x)$ can be formulated as

$$f'(x_i) = \frac{1}{g} \sum_{j=0,\, j \neq i}^{n} \frac{(-1)^{i-j} C_n^j / C_n^i f(x_j) + f(x_i)}{i - j} + \frac{(-1)^{n-i} g^n f^{n+1}(c)}{(n+1) C_n^i}, \tag{16.1}$$

where $C_n^i = n!/((n-i)!i!)$, $C_n^j = n!/((n-j)!j!)$, and $c \in [a, b]$.

Proof. The proof is presented in Appendix S. □

It is worth pointing out that, by letting $i = n - 1$ and ignoring the first-order derivative of the remainder item in the numerical-differentiation formula (16.1), we can approximate the first-order derivative of the unknown target function $f(x)$ as follows:

$$f'(x_{n-1}) \approx \frac{1}{g} \sum_{j=0,\, j \neq n-1}^{n} \frac{(-1)^{n-j-1} C_n^j f(x_j)/n + f(x_{n-1})}{n - j - 1}. \tag{16.2}$$

TABLE 16.1: Lagrange numerical-differentiation formulas using two through seven data points.

Data point number	Lagrange numerical-differentiation formula	Truncation error
Two	$f'(x_0) \approx (f(x_1) - f(x_0))/g$	$\mathcal{O}(g)$
Three	$f'(x_1) \approx (f(x_2) - f(x_0))/(2g)$	$\mathcal{O}(g^2)$
Four	$f'(x_2) \approx (2f(x_3) + 3f(x_2) - 6f(x_1) + f(x_0))/(6g)$	$\mathcal{O}(g^3)$
Five	$f'(x_3) \approx (3f(x_4) + 10f(x_3) - 18f(x_2)$ $+6f(x_1) - f(x_0))/(12g)$	$\mathcal{O}(g^4)$
Six	$f'(x_4) \approx (12f(x_5) + 65f(x_4) - 120f(x_3)$ $+60f(x_2) - 20f(x_1) + 3f(x_0))/(60g)$	$\mathcal{O}(g^5)$
Seven	$f'(x_5) \approx (10f(x_6) + 77f(x_5) - 150f(x_4)$ $+100f(x_3) - 50f(x_2) + 15f(x_1) - 2f(x_0))/(60g)$	$\mathcal{O}(g^6)$

For formula (16.2), let $n = 1, 2, \cdots, 15$, and then we can derive the equally spaced Lagrange numerical-differentiation formulas using two through sixteen data points, respectively. The equally spaced Lagrange numerical-differentiation formulas using two through seven data points are shown in Table 16.1, while those using eight through sixteen data points are shown in Appendix T.

As we can see from Table 16.1, the Lagrange numerical-differentiation formula using two data points is in the same form as the forward numerical-differentiation formula using two data points. Moreover, the one using three data points is the same with the central numerical-differentiation formula using two data points. Hence, we mainly discuss the Lagrange numerical-differentiation formulas using four through seven data points.

16.3 Total Error Analyses and Numerical Experiments

In this section, a special kind of formula is proposed to determine the optimal sampling gap of Lagrange numerical-differentiation formulas, and then related numerical experiments are executed to substantiate the correctness of these optimal sampling-gap formulas.

16.3.1 Optimal sampling-gap formulas

As we mentioned above, the sampling gap has a great influence on the total errors. Thus, in practical engineering applications, the optimal sampling gap is generally expected for obtaining a relatively higher accuracy. In this subsection, we propose a special kind of formula to determine the optimal sampling gaps of Lagrange numerical-differentiation formulas.

For better understanding, we first give the derivation of the optimal sampling-gap formulas for the Lagrange numerical-differentiation formulas using four and five data points in detail. The following derivation is about the optimal sampling-gap formula of the Lagrange numerical-differentiation formula using four data points.

In digital computers, there always exist round-off errors in the numerical computations [161], which can be simplified as the following equations:

$$f(x_3) = y_3 + \varepsilon_3,$$

$$f(x_2) = y_2 + \varepsilon_2,$$

$$f(x_1) = y_1 + \varepsilon_1,$$

$$f(x_0) = y_0 + \varepsilon_0,$$

where $f(x_3), f(x_2), f(x_1)$, and $f(x_0)$ are approximated by numerical values y_3, y_2, y_1, and y_0, respectively, while ε_3, ε_2, ε_1, and ε_0 are the corresponding round-off errors.

According to the Lagrange numerical-differentiation formula using four data points, we can obtain

$$f'(x_2) \approx \frac{2y_3 + 3y_2 - 6y_1 + y_0}{6g}.$$

Then, the error analysis can be explained by the following equation:

$$f'(x_2) = \frac{2y_3 + 3y_2 - 6y_1 + y_0}{6g} + E(f,g),$$

in which

$$E(f,g) = \frac{2\varepsilon_3 + 3\varepsilon_2 - 6\varepsilon_1 + \varepsilon_0}{6g} - \frac{g^3 f^{(4)}(c)}{12},$$

where the total error term $E(f,g)$ contains two parts, i.e., a part due to the round-off error, and a part due to the truncation error.

Assuming that $|\varepsilon_i| \leq \rho$ ($i = 0, 1, 2, 3$, and ρ denotes a positive constant), which is accumulative, and that $|f^{(4)}(c)| \leq c_4$ with $f \in C^{(n+1)}[a,b]$ and c_4 denoting a positive constant, then

$$|E(f,g)| \leq \frac{2\rho}{g} + \frac{c_4 g^3}{12}. \quad (16.3)$$

Thus, the value of g that minimizes the right-hand side of the formula (16.3) is

$$g = \left(\frac{8\rho}{c_4}\right)^{1/4}.$$

In addition, the following derivation is given for the optimal sampling-gap formula of the Lagrange numerical-differentiation formula using five data points.

Similarly, $f(x_4), f(x_3), f(x_2), f(x_1)$, and $f(x_0)$ are respectively approximated by numerical values y_4, y_3, y_2, y_1, and y_0 with the corresponding round-off errors $\varepsilon_4, \varepsilon_3, \varepsilon_2, \varepsilon_1$, and ε_0. That is,

$$f(x_4) = y_4 + \varepsilon_4,$$

$$f(x_3) = y_3 + \varepsilon_3,$$

$$f(x_2) = y_2 + \varepsilon_2,$$

$$f(x_1) = y_1 + \varepsilon_1,$$

$$f(x_0) = y_0 + \varepsilon_0.$$

Based on the Lagrange numerical-differentiation formula using five data points, we obtain

$$f'(x_3) \approx \frac{3y_4 + 10y_3 - 18y_2 + 6y_1 - y_0}{12g}.$$

Then, the error analysis is explained by the following equation:

$$f'(x_3) = \frac{3y_4 + 10y_3 - 18y_2 + 6y_1 - y_0}{12g} + E(f,g),$$

of which

$$E(f,g) = \frac{3\varepsilon_4 + 10\varepsilon_3 - 18\varepsilon_2 + 6\varepsilon_1 - \varepsilon_0}{12g} - \frac{g^4 f^{(5)}(c)}{20}.$$

TABLE 16.2: Optimal sampling-gap formulas of four through seven data points about Lagrange numerical-differentiation formulas.

Data point number	Optimal sampling-gap formula
Four	$(8\rho/c_4)^{1/4}$
Five	$(95\rho/6c_5)^{1/5}$
Six	$(28\rho/c_6)^{1/6}$
Seven	$(707\rho/15c_7)^{1/7}$

Assuming that $|\varepsilon_i| \leq \rho$ $(i = 0,1,2,3,4)$, which is accumulative, and $|f^{(5)}(c)| \leq c_5$ with $f \in C^{(n+1)}[a,b]$ and c_5 denoting a positive constant, then

$$|E(f,g)| \leq \frac{38\rho}{12g} + \frac{c_5 g^4}{20}, \tag{16.4}$$

and the value of g that minimizes the right-hand side of the formula (16.4) is

$$g = \left(\frac{95\rho}{6c_5}\right)^{1/5}.$$

Following the above two derivations, we similarly obtain the optimal sampling-gap formulas of other data points about Lagrange numerical-differentiation formulas. Specifically, the optimal sampling-gap formulas of four through seven data points about Lagrange numerical-differentiation formulas are shown in Table 16.2.

16.3.2 Numerical experiments

As we mentioned above, different from the backward numerical-differentiation formula, the Lagrange numerical-differentiation formula can adapt to the fast variational rate of the first-order derivative of the target point for the reason that the latter one takes the data points on both sides into consideration. It is worth noting that we carry 16 decimal places in all the computations, and thus ρ is set as 0.5×10^{-16}. To analyze the total errors of Lagrange numerical-differentiation formulas, we use the following function as the target function in this subsection:

$$f(x) = \cos(x).$$

Since the first-order derivative of the target function $f'(x) = -\sin(x)$ has the fastest changes at $x = \pm k\pi$ $(k = 0,1,2,3,\cdots)$, we use $x = 0$ (i.e., $k = 0$) as the target point in the following numerical experiments. Additionally, 18 different sampling gaps g are investigated to verify the efficacy of Lagrange numerical-differentiation formulas. Besides, the errors between the first-order derivative of target function values $f'(x)$ and the first-order derivative of interpolation polynomial values $\phi'(x)$ at the target point are presented in Table 16.3 (note that we only show ten decimal places of errors due to space limitation).

In addition, for the target function $f(x) = \cos(x)$, $|f^{(4)}(x)| = |\cos(x)| \leq 1 = c_4$. From Table 16.2, we can get the optimal sampling gap $g = 1.4142 \times 10^{-4}$ for the Lagrange numerical-differentiation formula using four data points. To be more intuitive, we can present the relationship between the errors and the sampling gap g (varying from 10^{-6} through 0.5) in Figure 16.1 for the Lagrange numerical-differentiation formula using four data points.

From Figure 16.1, we see the minimal error occurs approximately at about the sampling gap $g = 10^{-4}$, which substantiates that the above optimal sampling-gap formulas for the Lagrange numerical-differentiation formula using four data points are effective and accurate.

TABLE 16.3: Errors in approximation to $f'(x) = -\sin(x)$ using Lagrange numerical-differentiation formulas with different sampling gaps g.

g	Error using four data points	Error using five data points	Error using six data points	Error using seven data points
0.5	$9.9906861022 \times 10^{-3}$	$1.2230341975 \times 10^{-3}$	$7.9876250224 \times 10^{-4}$	$2.7011594455 \times 10^{-4}$
0.2	$6.6223553159 \times 10^{-4}$	$1.3200620420 \times 10^{-5}$	$1.0244736087 \times 10^{-5}$	$5.1787483101 \times 10^{-7}$
0.1	$8.3194548564 \times 10^{-5}$	$4.1562621196 \times 10^{-7}$	$3.3000929278 \times 10^{-7}$	$4.1361971625 \times 10^{-9}$
0.05	$1.0412327201 \times 10^{-5}$	$1.3012699066 \times 10^{-5}$	$1.0390640644 \times 10^{-8}$	$3.2486013878 \times 10^{-11}$
0.02	$6.6662223148 \times 10^{-7}$	$1.3333038377 \times 10^{-10}$	$1.0662877987 \times 10^{-10}$	$4.7369515717 \times 10^{-14}$
0.01	$8.3331930245 \times 10^{-8}$	$4.1892415462 \times 10^{-12}$	$3.2921813423 \times 10^{-12}$	$3.2566542055 \times 10^{-14}$
0.005	$1.0416652725 \times 10^{-8}$	$1.5543122344 \times 10^{-13}$	$1.1842378929 \times 10^{-13}$	$3.1086244689 \times 10^{-14}$
0.002	$6.6671668186 \times 10^{-10}$	$1.3877787807 \times 10^{-14}$	$5.1810407815 \times 10^{-14}$	$2.5905203907 \times 10^{-14}$
0.001	$8.3488771451 \times 10^{-11}$	$1.5728159515 \times 10^{-13}$	$7.4014868308 \times 10^{-15}$	$1.9984014443 \times 10^{-14}$
5×10^{-4}	$1.0214051826 \times 10^{-11}$	$1.8503717077 \times 10^{-13}$	$2.8125649957 \times 10^{-13}$	$1.9984014443 \times 10^{-13}$
2×10^{-4}	$4.6259292692 \times 10^{-13}$	$3.2381504884 \times 10^{-13}$	$2.2204460492 \times 10^{-13}$	$2.2204460492 \times 10^{-13}$
1×10^{-4}	$0.0000000000 \times 10^{-0}$	$1.0177044392 \times 10^{-12}$	$1.4802973661 \times 10^{-12}$	$4.8109664400 \times 10^{-13}$
5×10^{-5}	$1.4802973661 \times 10^{-12}$	$1.2952601953 \times 10^{-12}$	$2.9605947323 \times 10^{-12}$	$4.0708177569 \times 10^{-12}$
2×10^{-5}	$9.2518585385 \times 10^{-13}$	$3.2381504884 \times 10^{-12}$	$3.7007434154 \times 10^{-12}$	$3.7007434154 \times 10^{-12}$
1×10^{-5}	$0.0000000000 \times 10^{-0}$	$2.2204460492 \times 10^{-11}$	$5.1810407815 \times 10^{-12}$	$2.3314683517 \times 10^{-11}$
5×10^{-6}	$2.9605947323 \times 10^{-11}$	$2.5905203907 \times 10^{-11}$	$2.3684757858 \times 10^{-11}$	$1.0362081563 \times 10^{-11}$
2×10^{-6}	$9.2518585385 \times 10^{-11}$	$6.4763009769 \times 10^{-11}$	$7.4014868308 \times 10^{-11}$	$1.4802973661 \times 10^{-11}$
1×10^{-6}	$3.7007434154 \times 10^{-11}$	$3.3306690738 \times 10^{-10}$	$2.9605947323 \times 10^{-11}$	$2.2944609175 \times 10^{-10}$

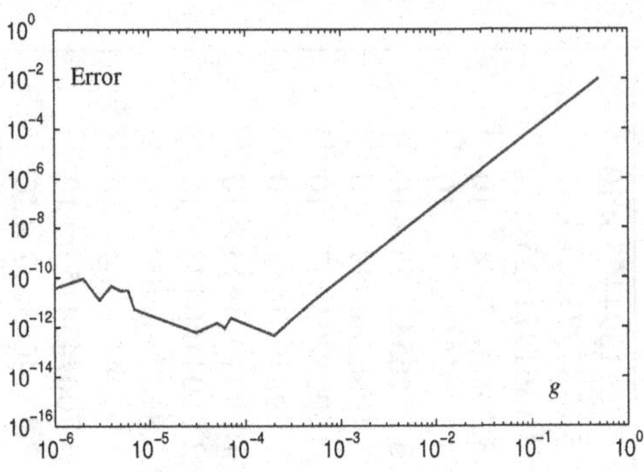

FIGURE 16.1: Errors with sampling gap g changing from 10^{-6} through 0.5 using four data points.

In order to further verify Lagrange numerical-differentiation formulas, we present another target function $f(x) = \arctan(x)$ with the target point being $x = 1/\sqrt{3}$. With the sampling gap g changing from 10^{-6} through 0.5, Table 16.4 presents the errors between the first-order derivative of target function values $f'(x)$ and the first-order derivative of interpolation polynomial values $\phi'(x)$ at the target point.

16.4 Comparisons with Backward Numerical-Differentiation Formulas

Backward numerical-differentiation formulas can be used to approximate the first-order derivative of the target function. In order to illustrate the superiority of Lagrange numerical-differentiation formulas, we present the backward numerical-differentiation formulas using four through seven data points in Table 16.5. With the sampling gap g changing from 10^{-6} through 0.5, the approximation errors of backward numerical-differentiation formulas using four through seven data points are shown in Tables 16.6 and 16.7 for the target functions $f(x) = \cos(x)$ and $f(x) = \arctan(x)$, respectively.

By comparing Tables 16.3 and 16.4 with Tables 16.6 and 16.7 at the same sampling gap, the approximation errors of the first-order derivative of the target function using the Lagrange numerical-differentiation formulas are much smaller than those using the backward numerical-differentiation formulas. This can be explained as that Lagrange numerical-differentiation formulas make use of a future data point in approximating the first-order derivative of the target function, and these formulas can thus adapt to accelerating changes when the target point is close to the boundary.

In summary, from the above verifications and comparisons about Lagrange numerical-differentiation formulas and backward numerical-differentiation formulas, we conclude that Lagrange numerical-differentiation formulas are not only effective in computing the first-order derivative of the target function but also superior to the backward numerical-differentiation formulas in numerical computations and applications.

16.5 Chapter Summary

In this chapter, we have presented a special kind of numerical-differentiation formulas called Lagrange numerical-differentiation formulas to approximate the first-order derivative of the target function. Specifically, different from the traditional forward/backward numerical-differentiation

TABLE 16.4: Errors in approximation to $f'(x) = \arctan'(x)$ using Lagrange numerical-differentiation formulas by different sampling gaps g.

g	Error using four data points	Error using five data points	Error using six data points	Error using seven data points
0.5	$3.4322597261 \times 10^{-2}$	$2.6735325849 \times 10^{-2}$	$5.9998178013 \times 10^{-3}$	$1.5076288427 \times 10^{-2}$
0.2	$2.4164707297 \times 10^{-3}$	$3.3921025627 \times 10^{-4}$	$7.5974285402 \times 10^{-4}$	$9.6439958186 \times 10^{-5}$
0.1	$2.7655834630 \times 10^{-4}$	$4.3829933915 \times 10^{-5}$	$1.3503825063 \times 10^{-5}$	$8.0717829157 \times 10^{-6}$
0.05	$3.2576901872 \times 10^{-5}$	$3.0670502828 \times 10^{-6}$	$1.8806123514 \times 10^{-7}$	$1.2431557017 \times 10^{-7}$
0.02	$2.0048580308 \times 10^{-6}$	$8.0622992282 \times 10^{-8}$	$6.9323313756 \times 10^{-10}$	$4.2022285651 \times 10^{-10}$
0.01	$2.4723914515 \times 10^{-7}$	$5.0565872600 \times 10^{-9}$	$1.0508149905 \times 10^{-11}$	$6.0000893142 \times 10^{-12}$
0.005	$3.0694074393 \times 10^{-8}$	$3.1631985919 \times 10^{-10}$	$1.8152146452 \times 10^{-13}$	$1.0269562977 \times 10^{-13}$
0.002	$1.9563585196 \times 10^{-8}$	$8.0330186946 \times 10^{-12}$	$7.8936857050 \times 10^{-14}$	$7.8936857050 \times 10^{-14}$
0.001	$2.4413560062 \times 10^{-10}$	$7.7959860789 \times 10^{-13}$	$2.7633451082 \times 10^{-13}$	$5.1314508198 \times 10^{-14}$
5×10^{-4}	$3.0750735291 \times 10^{-11}$	$3.9412917374 \times 10^{-14}$	$4.3420822493 \times 10^{-13}$	$4.3420822493 \times 10^{-13}$
2×10^{-4}	$1.6628920462 \times 10^{-12}$	$9.2770235937 \times 10^{-13}$	$3.9523939676 \times 10^{-14}$	$1.2236878177 \times 10^{-12}$
1×10^{-4}	$9.2770235937 \times 10^{-13}$	$5.5266902165 \times 10^{-13}$	$3.9523939676 \times 10^{-14}$	$2.3289148387 \times 10^{-12}$
5×10^{-5}	$5.5266902165 \times 10^{-13}$	$5.5266902165 \times 10^{-13}$	$3.9523939676 \times 10^{-14}$	$3.9523939676 \times 10^{-14}$
2×10^{-5}	$1.2927436898 \times 10^{-12}$	$2.4079627181 \times 10^{-12}$	$2.4079627181 \times 10^{-12}$	$2.4079627181 \times 10^{-11}$
1×10^{-5}	$2.4079627181 \times 10^{-12}$	$2.4079627181 \times 10^{-12}$	$3.3119174069 \times 10^{-11}$	$9.4344532186 \times 10^{-12}$
5×10^{-6}	$1.7211010394 \times 10^{-11}$	$3.2013947048 \times 10^{-11}$	$3.7935099506 \times 10^{-11}$	$3.7935099506 \times 10^{-11}$
2×10^{-6}	$1.2927436898 \times 10^{-12}$	$7.1606942597 \times 10^{-11}$	$5.6804005943 \times 10^{-11}$	$2.9365154752 \times 10^{-10}$
1×10^{-6}	$2.4079627181 \times 10^{-12}$	$1.5043766232 \times 10^{-10}$	$5.6804005943 \times 10^{-11}$	$2.9365154752 \times 10^{-10}$

TABLE 16.5: Backward numerical-differentiation formulas using four through seven data points.

Data point number	Backward numerical-differentiation formula	Truncation error
Four	$f'(x_3) \approx (11f(x_3) - 18f(x_2) + 9f(x_1) - 2f(x_0))/6g$	$\mathcal{O}(g^3)$
Five	$f'(x_4) \approx (25f(x_4) - 48f(x_3) + 36f(x_2)$ $-16f(x_1) + 3f(x_0))/12g$	$\mathcal{O}(g^4)$
Six	$f'(x_5) \approx (137f(x_5) - 300f(x_4) + 300f(x_3)$ $-200f(x_2) + 75f(x_1) - 12f(x_0))/60g$	$\mathcal{O}(g^5)$
Seven	$f'(x_6) \approx (147f(x_6) - 360f(x_5) + 450f(x_4)$ $-400f(x_3) + 225f(x_2) - 72f(x_1) + 10f(x_0))/60g$	$\mathcal{O}(g^6)$

formulas, Lagrange numerical-differentiation formulas make use of a future data point in the approximation of the first-order derivative at the target point. In addition, we have presented the derivation for a group of formulas that can obtain the optimal sampling gaps for Lagrange numerical-differentiation formulas. Finally, we have verified the efficiency and efficacy of the optimal sampling-gap formulas by computing the first-order derivative at the target point with different sampling gaps. Moreover, the comparisons between the approximation errors of Lagrange numerical-differentiation formulas and backward numerical-differentiation formulas have further substantiated the superiority of Lagrange numerical-differentiation formulas.

Appendix S: Proof of Formula (16.1)

Proof. According to [161], the Lagrange interpolation polynomial $\phi_n(x)$ of the degree n is formulated as follows:

$$\phi_n(x) = \sum_{i=0}^{n} f(x_i)\mathcal{L}_i(x), \tag{16.5}$$

where $\mathcal{L}_i(x)$ is the Lagrange basis polynomial using given data points:

$$\mathcal{L}_i(x) = \prod_{j=0,\ j\neq i}^{n} \frac{x - x_j}{x_i - x_j}.$$

Then, let

$$\omega(x) = (x - x_0)(x - x_1)\cdots(x - x_n) = \prod_{i=0}^{n}(x - x_i).$$

The first-order derivative of $\omega(x)$ is thus obtained as

$$\omega'(x) = \sum_{i=0}^{n}((x - x_0)(x - x_1)\cdots(x - x_{i-1})(x - x_{i+1})\cdots(x - x_n)).$$

Hence,

$$\mathcal{L}_i(x) = \prod_{j=0,\ j\neq i}^{n} \frac{x - x_j}{x_i - x_j} = \frac{\omega(x)}{(x - x_i)\omega'(x_i)}.$$

The formula (16.5) is rewritten as

$$\phi_n(x) = \sum_{i=0}^{n} f(x_i)\mathcal{L}_i(x) = \sum_{i=0}^{n} f(x_i)\frac{\omega(x)}{(x - x_i)\omega'(x_i)}.$$

With $i \neq j$, let

$$\omega_i(x) = \frac{\omega(x)}{(x - x_i)} \text{ and } \omega_{i,j}(x) = \frac{\omega(x)}{(x - x_i)(x - x_j)}.$$

TABLE 16.6: Errors in approximation to $f'(x) = -\sin(x)$ using backward numerical-differentiation formulas by different sampling gaps g.

g	**Error using four data points**	**Error using five data points**	**Error using six data points**	**Error using seven data points**
0.5	$2.5079921516 \times 10^{-2}$	$8.8859493015 \times 10^{-3}$	$2.3731168439 \times 10^{-3}$	$2.0270607771 \times 10^{-3}$
0.2	$1.9339041131 \times 10^{-3}$	$1.0402616212 \times 10^{-4}$	$4.8116431434 \times 10^{-5}$	$4.5366627337 \times 10^{-6}$
0.1	$2.4792114083 \times 10^{-4}$	$3.3125513110 \times 10^{-6}$	$1.6252292311 \times 10^{-6}$	$3.6977686098 \times 10^{-8}$
0.05	$3.1184930826 \times 10^{-5}$	$1.0400401132 \times 10^{-7}$	$5.1758282400 \times 10^{-8}$	$2.9194779926 \times 10^{-10}$
0.02	$1.9993333710 \times 10^{-6}$	$1.0663710655 \times 10^{-9}$	$5.3281231278 \times 10^{-10}$	$4.8405723873 \times 10^{-13}$
0.01	$2.4997920030 \times 10^{-7}$	$3.3388107093 \times 10^{-11}$	$1.6620778827 \times 10^{-11}$	$7.9936057773 \times 10^{-14}$
0.005	$3.1249284641 \times 10^{-8}$	$9.4739031434 \times 10^{-13}$	$6.2764608325 \times 10^{-13}$	$1.7763568394 \times 10^{-13}$
0.002	$1.9999372528 \times 10^{-9}$	$1.8503717077 \times 10^{-13}$	$2.3684757858 \times 10^{-13}$	$3.7007434154 \times 10^{-13}$
0.001	$2.5020726231 \times 10^{-10}$	$1.1102230246 \times 10^{-13}$	$1.1842378929 \times 10^{-13}$	$9.1778436702 \times 10^{-13}$
5×10^{-4}	$3.1530333899 \times 10^{-11}$	$2.2204460492 \times 10^{-13}$	$1.1842378929 \times 10^{-13}$	$4.7369515717 \times 10^{-13}$
2×10^{-4}	$2.7755575615 \times 10^{-12}$	$1.1102230246 \times 10^{-12}$	$2.5165055224 \times 10^{-12}$	$2.9605947323 \times 10^{-13}$
1×10^{-4}	$1.1102230246 \times 10^{-12}$	$0.0000000000 \times 10^{-0}$	$4.7369515717 \times 10^{-12}$	$5.3290705182 \times 10^{-12}$
5×10^{-5}	$7.4014868308 \times 10^{-13}$	$5.9211894646 \times 10^{-12}$	$4.1448326252 \times 10^{-12}$	$2.0724163126 \times 10^{-11}$
2×10^{-5}	$1.2952601953 \times 10^{-11}$	$2.5905203907 \times 10^{-11}$	$1.9243865760 \times 10^{-11}$	$2.8125649957 \times 10^{-11}$
1×10^{-5}	$2.9605947323 \times 10^{-11}$	$3.7007434154 \times 10^{-12}$	$7.4014868308 \times 10^{-11}$	$8.8817841970 \times 10^{-12}$
5×10^{-6}	$1.4802973661 \times 10^{-11}$	$1.1842378929 \times 10^{-10}$	$1.1842378929 \times 10^{-11}$	$1.7763568394 \times 10^{-11}$
2×10^{-6}	$1.1102230246 \times 10^{-10}$	$3.7007434154 \times 10^{-10}$	$2.9605947323 \times 10^{-11}$	$5.9211894646 \times 10^{-11}$
1×10^{-6}	$4.4408920985 \times 10^{-10}$	$1.4802973661 \times 10^{-10}$	$5.3290705182 \times 10^{-10}$	$3.8487731520 \times 10^{-10}$

TABLE 16.7: Errors in approximation to $f'(x) = \arctan'(x)$ using backward numerical-differentiation formulas by different sampling gaps g.

g	**Error using four data points**	**Error using five data points**	**Error using six data points**	**Error using seven data points**
0.5	$3.9735116141 \times 10^{-3}$	$7.6942214392 \times 10^{-2}$	$1.2045681957 \times 10^{-1}$	$1.3317102817 \times 10^{-1}$
0.2	$8.6062532141 \times 10^{-3}$	$2.4418732451 \times 10^{-3}$	$3.2200745211 \times 10^{-3}$	$3.7563832623 \times 10^{-3}$
0.1	$1.0049947745 \times 10^{-3}$	$1.0780061034 \times 10^{-4}$	$1.1594982281 \times 10^{-4}$	$3.1613369791 \times 10^{-5}$
0.05	$1.0999890675 \times 10^{-4}$	$1.1327894944 \times 10^{-5}$	$1.6861995943 \times 10^{-6}$	$8.1402131191 \times 10^{-7}$
0.02	$6.3370660817 \times 10^{-6}$	$3.1902580333 \times 10^{-7}$	$5.9874910585 \times 10^{-9}$	$2.7270551372 \times 10^{-9}$
0.01	$7.6194379206 \times 10^{-7}$	$2.0173808290 \times 10^{-8}$	$8.8731022529 \times 10^{-11}$	$3.7650882411 \times 10^{-11}$
0.005	$9.3347413798 \times 10^{-8}$	$1.2644897351 \times 10^{-9}$	$1.4763745781 \times 10^{-12}$	$4.1844305798 \times 10^{-13}$
0.002	$5.9010968334 \times 10^{-9}$	$3.2527092130 \times 10^{-11}$	$5.1314508198 \times 10^{-13}$	$3.9412917374 \times 10^{-14}$
0.001	$7.3485906249 \times 10^{-10}$	$1.1447509606 \times 10^{-12}$	$9.8676622428 \times 10^{-13}$	$1.9343415758 \times 10^{-14}$
5×10^{-4}	$9.0633611726 \times 10^{-11}$	$1.1447509606 \times 10^{-12}$	$1.8552936964 \times 10^{-12}$	$1.8552936964 \times 10^{-12}$
2×10^{-4}	$6.8488548166 \times 10^{-12}$	$2.4079627181 \times 10^{-12}$	$3.9523939676 \times 10^{-14}$	$4.7765125188 \times 10^{-12}$
1×10^{-4}	$2.4079627181 \times 10^{-12}$	$2.4079627181 \times 10^{-12}$	$3.9523939676 \times 10^{-14}$	$9.5133900757 \times 10^{-15}$
5×10^{-5}	$3.5131897391 \times 10^{-12}$	$2.4079627181 \times 10^{-12}$	$9.4344532186 \times 10^{-12}$	$2.8382185490 \times 10^{-11}$
2×10^{-5}	$2.4079627181 \times 10^{-12}$	$2.7197910590 \times 10^{-11}$	$9.4344532186 \times 10^{-12}$	$3.7935099506 \times 10^{-11}$
1×10^{-5}	$2.4079627181 \times 10^{-12}$	$2.4079627181 \times 10^{-12}$	$1.0417344764 \times 10^{-10}$	$9.4344532186 \times 10^{-12}$
5×10^{-6}	$6.1619931379 \times 10^{-11}$	$6.1619931379 \times 10^{-11}$	$9.4344532186 \times 10^{-12}$	$1.8004364665 \times 10^{-10}$
2×10^{-6}	$1.4562184791 \times 10^{-10}$	$2.9365154752 \times 10^{-10}$	$2.9365154752 \times 10^{-10}$	$7.6734674170 \times 10^{-10}$
1×10^{-6}	$2.4079627181 \times 10^{-12}$	$2.9846736193 \times 10^{-10}$	$7.6734674170 \times 10^{-10}$	$1.1274339239 \times 10^{-9}$

Then,

$$\frac{\omega_{i,j}(x)}{\omega_i(x)} = \frac{1}{(x-x_j)}.$$

Thus, we get

$$\omega_i(x_i) = \omega'(x_i).$$

In order to get the first-order derivative of $\phi_n(x)$, we rewrite $\phi_n(x)$ as

$$\phi_n(x) = \sum_{j=0,\ j\neq i}^{n} f(x_j)\frac{\omega(x)}{(x-x_j)\omega'(x_j)} + f(x_i)\frac{\omega_i(x)}{\omega'(x_i)}.$$

Thus,

$$\phi_n'(x) = \sum_{j=0,\ j\neq i}^{n} f(x_j)\frac{\omega'(x)(x-x_j)-\omega(x)}{(x-x_j)^2\omega'(x_j)} + f(x_i)\frac{\omega_i'(x)}{\omega'(x_i)}.$$

It follows that

$$\phi_n'(x) = \sum_{j=0,\ j\neq i}^{n} f(x_j)\left(\frac{\omega'(x)}{(x-x_j)\omega'(x_j)} - \frac{\omega(x)}{(x-x_j)^2\omega'(x_j)}\right) + f(x_i)\frac{\omega_i'(x)}{\omega'(x_i)}.$$

Noting that, for $i = 0,1,2,\cdots,n$, $\omega(x_i) = 0$ and $\omega_i'(x) = \sum_{j=0,\ j\neq i}^{n}\omega_{i,j}(x)$, we get $\phi_n'(x_i)$ as

$$\phi_n'(x_i) = \sum_{j=0,\ j\neq i}^{n} f(x_j)\frac{\omega'(x_i)}{(x_i-x_j)\omega'(x_j)} + f(x_i)\frac{\sum_{j=0,\ j\neq i}^{n}\omega_{i,j}(x_i)}{\omega'(x_i)},$$

i.e.,

$$\phi_n'(x_i) = \sum_{j=0,\ j\neq i}^{n} f(x_j)\frac{\omega'(x_i)}{(x_i-x_j)\omega'(x_j)} + f(x_i)\sum_{j=0,\ j\neq i}^{n}\frac{1}{x_i-x_j}.$$

When x_i $(i = 0,1,2,3,\cdots,n)$ is equally spaced, i.e., $x_{i+1}-x_i = g$, we can obtain the equally spaced differentiation formula as follows:

$$\phi_n'(x_i) = \frac{1}{g}\sum_{j=0,\ j\neq i}^{n}\frac{(-1)^{i-j}C_n^j/C_n^i f(x_j) + f(x_i)}{i-j}.$$

According to Lemma 1 [51], the first-order derivative of the remainder term of the unknown target function $f(x)$ is written as

$$\sigma_{n+1}'(x_i) = \frac{(-1)^{n-i}g^n f^{n+1}(c)}{(n+1)C_n^i}.$$

Therefore,

$$f'(x) = \phi_n'(x) + \sigma_{n+1}'(x).$$

The proof is therefore completed. □

Appendix T: Equally Spaced Lagrange Numerical-Differentiation Formulas Using Eight Through Sixteen Data Points

The equally spaced Lagrange numerical-differentiation formulas using eight through sixteen data points are shown in Table 16.8.

TABLE 16.8: Lagrange numerical-differentiation formulas using eight through sixteen data points.

Data point number	Lagrange numerical-differentiation formula	Truncation error
Eight	$f'(x_6) \approx (60f(x_7)+609f(x_6)-1260f(x_5)+1050f(x_4)$ $-700f(x_3)+315f(x_2)-84f(x_1)+10f(x_0))/420g$	$\mathcal{O}(g^7)$
Nine	$f'(x_7) \approx (105f(x_8)+1338f(x_7)-2940f(x_6)+2940f(x_5)$ $-2450f(x_4)+1470f(x_3)-588f(x_2)+140f(x_1)$ $-15f(x_0))/(840g)$	$\mathcal{O}(g^8)$
Ten	$f'(x_8) \approx (280f(x_9)+4329f(x_8)-10080f(x_7)$ $+11760f(x_6)-11760f(x_5)+8820f(x_4)-4704f(x_3)$ $+1680f(x_2)-360f(x_1)+35f(x_0))/(2520g)$	$\mathcal{O}(g^9)$
Eleven	$f'(x_9) \approx ((252f(x_{10})+4609f(x_9)-11340f(x_8)$ $+15120f(x_7)-17640f(x_6)+15876f(x_5)-10584f(x_4)$ $+5040f(x_3)-1620f(x_2)+315f(x_1)-28f(x_0))/(2520g)$	$\mathcal{O}(g^{10})$
Twelve	$f'(x_{10}) \approx ((2520f(x_{11})+53471f(x_{10})-138600f(x_9)$ $+207900f(x_8)-277200f(x_7)+291060f(x_6)$ $-232848f(x_5)+138600f(x_4)-59400f(x_3)$ $+17325f(x_2)-3080f(x_1)+252f(x_0))/(27720g)$	$\mathcal{O}(g^{11})$
Thirteen	$f'(x_{11}) \approx (2310f(x_{12})+55991f(x_{11})-152460f(x_{10})$ $+254100f(x_9)-381150f(x_8)+457380f(x_7)$ $-426888f(x_6)+304920f(x_5)-163350f(x_4)$ $+63525f(x_3)-16940f(x_2)+2772f(x_1)$ $-210f(x_0))/(27720g)$	$\mathcal{O}(g^{12})$
Fourteen	$f'(x_{12}) \approx (27720f(x_{13})+757913f(x_{12})-2162160f(x_{11})$ $+3963960f(x_{10})-6606600f(x_9)+8918910f(x_8)$ $-9513504f(x_7)+7927920f(x_6)-5096520f(x_5)$ $+2477475f(x_4)-880880f(x_3)+216216f(x_2)$ $-32760f(x_1)+2310f(x_0))/(360360g)$	$\mathcal{O}(g^{13})$
Fifteen	$f'(x_{13}) \approx (25740f(x_{14})+785633f(x_{13})-2342340f(x_{12})$ $+4684680f(x_{11})-8588580f(x_{10})+12882870f(x_9)$ $-15459444f(x_8)+14723280f(x_7)-11042460f(x_6)$ $+6441435f(x_5)-2862860f(x_4)+936936f(x_3)$ $-212940f(x_2)+30030f(x_1)-1980f(x_0))/(360360g)$	$\mathcal{O}(g^{14})$
Sixteen	$f'(x_{14}) \approx (24024f(x_{15})+811373f(x_{14})-2522520f(x_{13})$ $+5465460f(x_{12})-10930920f(x_{11})+18036018f(x_{10})$ $-24048024f(x_9)+25765740f(x_8)-22084920f(x_7)$ $+15030015f(x_6)-8016008f(x_5)+3279276f(x_4)$ $-993720f(x_3)+210210f(x_2)-27720f(x_1)$ $+1716f(x_0))/(360360g)$	$\mathcal{O}(g^{15})$

Bibliography

[1] B. Nemec and L. Zlajpah. Null space velocity control with dynamically consistent pseudo-inverse. *Robotica*, 18:513–518(5), 2000.

[2] S. Raudys and R.P.W. Duin. Expected classification error of the Fisher linear classifier with pseudo-inverse covariance matrix. *Pattern Recognition Letters*, 19:385–392, 1998.

[3] B.L. Zhang, H. Zhang, and S.S. Ge. Face recognition by applying wavelet subband representation and kernel associative memory. *IEEE Transactions on Neural Networks*, 15:166–177(1), 2004.

[4] H.H. Bauschke and J.M. Borwein. Fitzpatrick functions and continuous linear monotone operators. *SIAM Journal on Optimization*, 18:789–809(3), 2007.

[5] F. Huang and X. Zhang. An improved Newton iteration for the weighted Moore–Penrose inverse. *Applied Mathematics and Computation*, 174:1460–1486(2), 2006.

[6] Y. Wei, J. Cai, and M.K. Ng. Computing Moore–Penrose inverses of Toeplitz matrices by Newton's iteration. *Mathematical and Computer Modelling*, 40:181–191, 2004.

[7] P. Courrieu. Fast computation of Moore–Penrose inverse matrices. *Neural Information Processing-Letters and Reviews*, 8:25–29(2), 2005.

[8] M.D. Petkovi and P.S. Stanimirovi. Symbolic computation of the Moore–Penrose inverse using partitioning method. *International Journal of Computer Mathematics*, 82:355–367(3), 2005.

[9] J. Lin, C.C. Lin, and H.-S. Lo. Pseudo-inverse Jacobian control with grey relation alanalysis for robot manipulators mounted on oscillatory bases. *Journal of Sound and Vibration*, 326:421–437, 2009.

[10] O. Ludwig, U. Nunes, and R. Araujo. Eigenvalue decay: A new method for neural network regularization. *Neurocomputing*, 124:33–42, 2014.

[11] Y. Bai and J. Chen. New stability criteria for recurrent neural networks with interval time-varying delay. *Neurocomputing*, 121:179–184, 2013.

[12] X. Wang, L. Ma, B. Wang, and T. Wang. A hybrid optimization-based recurrent neural network for real-time data prediction. *Neurocomputing*, 120:547–559, 2013.

[13] A. Hosseinia, J. Wang, and S.M. Hosseinia. A recurrent neural network for solving a class of generalized convex optimization problems. *Neural Networks*, 44:78–86, 2013.

[14] S. Qin, W. Bian, and W. Xue. A new one-layer recurrent neural network for nonsmooth pseudoconvex optimization. *Neurocomputing*, 120:655–662, 2013.

[15] J. Wang. Recurrent neural networks for computing pseudoinverses of rank-deficient matrices. *SIAM Journal on Scientific Computing*, 19:1479–1493(5), 1997.

[16] D. Guo and Y. Zhang. Zhang neural network, Getz–Marsden dynamic system, and discrete-time algorithms for time-varying matrix inversion with application to robots' kinematic control. *Neurocomputing*, 97:22–32, 2012.

[17] Y. Zhang, Y. Yang, and N. Tan, Zhang neural network solving for time-varying full-rank matrix Moore-Penrose inverse. *Computing*, 92:97–121(2), 2011.

[18] Y. Zhang, Y. Xie, and H. Tan. Time-varying Moore–Penrose inverse solving shows different Zhang functions leading to different ZNN models. In *Proceedings of International Symposium on Neural Networks*, pages 98–105, 2012.

[19] B. Liao and Y. Zhang. From different ZFs to different ZNN models accelerated via Li activation functions to finite-time convergence for time-varying matrix pseudoinversion. *Neurocomputing*, 133:512–522, 2014.

[20] J.H. Mathews and K.D. Fink. *Numerical Methods Using MATLAB*. Prentice-Hall, New Jersey, USA, 2004.

[21] A. Ben-Israel and T.N.E. Greville. *Generalized Inverse: Theory and Applications, Second Edition*. Springer-Verlag, New York, USA, 2003.

[22] L. Jin and Y. Zhang. Discrete-time Zhang neural network of $O(\tau^3)$ pattern for time-varying matrix pseudoinversion with application to manipulator. *Neurocomputing*, 142:165–173, 2014.

[23] Y. Zhang, G. Shi, J. Li, G. Wu, and Z. Qi. Zhang matrix found as an exception with its time-dependent pseudoinverse unsolvable by Getz–Masden dynamic system. In *Proceedings of International Conference on Systems and Informatics*, pages 757–762, 2018.

[24] Y. Zhang, Z. Li, Y. Ling, M. Yang, and B. Qiu. Time-varying complex Zhang matrix (ZM) with its pseudoinverse not solvable directly by Getz–Masden (GM) dynamic system. In *Proceedings of IEEE Symposium Series on Computational Intelligence*, pages 518–525, 2019.

[25] D.F. Griffiths and D.J. Higham. *Numerical Methods for Ordinary Differential Equations: Initial Value Problems*. Springer Press, London, UK, 2010.

[26] O. Kanoun, F. Lamiraux, and P.B. Wieber. Kinematic control of redundant manipulators: Generalizing the task-priority framework to inequality task. *IEEE Transactions on Robotics*, 27:785–792(4), 2011.

[27] Y. Zhang and Z. Zhang. *Repetitive Motion Planning and Control of Redundant Robot Manipulators*. Springer Verlag, New York, USA, 2013.

[28] Y. Wang and S. Boyd. Fast model predictive control using online optimization. *IEEE Transactions on Control Systems Technology*, 18:267–278(2), 2010.

[29] J. Mattingley and S. Boyd. Real-time convex optimization in signal processing. *IEEE Signal Processing Magazine*, 27:50–61(3), 2010.

[30] Q. Liu, J. Cao, and G. Chen. A novel recurrent neural network with finite-time convergence for linear programming. *Neural Computation*, 22:2962–2978(11), 2010.

[31] Q. Liu and J. Cao. A recurrent neural network based on projection operator for extended general variational inequalities. *IEEE Transactions on Systems, Man, and Cybernetics*, 40:928–938(3), 2010.

[32] J.J. Hopfield and D.W. Tank. Neural computation of decisions in optimization problems. *Biological Cybernetics*, 52:141–152(3), 1985.

[33] Y. Xia and J. Wang. A recurrent neural network for solving nonlinear convex programs subject to linear constraints. *IEEE Transactions on Neural Networks*, 16:379–386(2), 2005.

[34] S. Liu and J. Wang. A simplified dual neural network for quadratic programming with its KWTA application. *IEEE Transactions on Neural Networks*, 17:1500–1510(6), 2006.

[35] M.P. Barbarosou and N.G. Maratos. A nonfeasible gradient projection recurrent neural network for equality-constrained optimization problems. *IEEE Transactions on Neural Networks*, 19:1665–1677(10), 2008.

[36] M.J. Perez-Ilzarbe. Convergence analysis of a discrete-time recurrent neural network to perform quadratic real optimization with bound constraints. *IEEE Transactions on Neural Networks*, 9:1344–1351(6), 1998.

[37] H. Tang, H. Li, and Z. Yi. A discrete-time neural network for optimization problems with hybrid constraints. *IEEE Transactions on Neural Networks*, 21:1184–1189(7), 2010.

[38] Q. Liu and J. Cao. Global exponential stability of discrete-time recurrent neural network for solving quadratic programming problems subject to linear constraints. *Neurocomputing*, 74:3494–3501(17), 2011.

[39] M.J. Perez-Ilzarbe. New discrete-time recurrent neural network proposal for quadratic optimization with general linear constraints. *IEEE Transactions on Neural Networks and Learning Systems*, 24:322–328(2), 2013.

[40] H.C. Lee and J.W. Choi. Linear time-varying eigenstructure assignment with flight control application. *IEEE Transactions on Aerospace and Electronic Systems*, 40:145–157(1), 2004.

[41] Y. Zhang and Z. Li. Zhang neural network for online solution of time-varying convex quadratic program subject to time-varying linear-equality constraints. *Physics Letters A*, 373:1639–1643(18–19), 2009.

[42] Y. Zhang, B. Mu, and H. Zheng. Link between and comparison and combination of Zhang neural network and quasi-Newton BFGS method for time-varying quadratic minimization. *IEEE Transactions on Cybernetics*, 43:490–503(2), 2013.

[43] Y. Zhang and C. Yi. *Zhang Neural Networks and Neural-Dynamic Method*. Nova, New York, USA, 2011.

[44] D. Guo and Y. Zhang. Zhang neural network for online solution of time-varying linear matrix inequality aided with an equality conversion. *IEEE Transactions on Neural Networks and Learning Systems*, 25:370–382(2), 2014.

[45] Y. Zhang, W. Ma, and B. Cai. From Zhang neural network to Newton iteration for matrix inversion. *IEEE Transactions on Circuits and Systems I*, 56:1405–1415(7), 2009.

[46] B. Liao, Y. Zhang, and L. Jin. Taylor $O(h^3)$ discretization of ZNN models for dynamic equality-constrained quadratic programming with application to manipulators. *IEEE Transactions on Neural Networks and Learning Systems*, 27:225–237(2), 2016.

[47] S. Boyd and L. Vandenberghe. *Convex Optimization*. Cambridge University Press, Cambridge, UK, 2004.

[48] J. Nocedal and S.J. Wright. *Numerical Optimization*. Springer Verlag, New York, USA, 1999.

[49] J. Piepmeier, G. McMurray, and H. Lipkin. A dynamic quasi-Newton method for uncalibrated visual servoing. In *Proceedings of International Conference on Robotics and Automation*, pages 1595–1600, 1999.

[50] R. Setiono and L.C.K. Hui. Use of a quasi-Newton method in a feedforward neural network construction algorithm. *IEEE Transactions on Neural Networks*, 6:273–277(1), 1995.

[51] Y. Zhang, Y. Chou, J. Chen, Z. Zhang, and L. Xiao. Presentation, error analysis and numerical experiments on a group of 1-step-ahead numerical differentiation formulas. *Journal of Computational and Applied Mathematics*, 239:406–414, 2013.

[52] S. Gigola, L. Lebtahi, and N. Thomec. The inverse eigenvalue problem for a Hermitian reflexive matrix and the optimization problem. *Journal of Computational and Applied Mathematics*, 291:449–457, 2016.

[53] J. Chen, D. Han, H. Nie, and M. Cheng. Dual quaternion-based inverse kinematics of dexterous finger. *Journal of Vibroengineering*, 16:2813–2820, 2014.

[54] Y. Fan and J.G. Nagy. An efficient computational approach for multiframe blind deconvolution. *Journal of Computational and Applied Mathematics*, 236:2112–2125(8), 2012.

[55] L. Lu. Gram matrix of Bernstein basis: Properties and applications. *Journal of Computational and Applied Mathematics*, 280:37–41(1), 2015.

[56] X. Ma. Two matrix inversions associated with the Hagen–Rothe formula, their q-analogues and applications. *Journal of Combinatorial Theory, Series A*, 118:1475–1493, 2011.

[57] G. Sharma, A. Agarwala, and B. Bhattacharya. A fast parallel Gauss Jordan algorithm for matrix inversion using CUDA. *Computers and Structures*, 128:31–37, 2013.

[58] V. Strassen. The asymptotic spectrum of tensors. *Journal fur die reine und angewandte Mathematic*, 384:102–152, 1988.

[59] D. Coppersmith and S. Winograd. Matrix multiplication via arithmetic progressions. *Journal of Symbolic Computation*, 9:251–280, 1990.

[60] B.F. Vajargah. A way to obtain Monte Carlo matrix inversion with minimal error. *Applied Mathematics and Computation*, 191:225–233(1), 2007.

[61] A.H. Bajodah. Inertia-independent generalized dynamic inversion feedback control of spacecraft attitude maneuvers. *Acta Astronautica*, 68:1742–1751(11), 2011.

[62] I. Haneduddin and A.H. Bajodah. Nonlinear generalised dynamic inversion for aircraft manoeuvring control. *International Journal of Control Automation and Systems*, 85:437–450(4), 2012.

[63] Y. Zhang, Z. Li, and K. Li. Complex-valued Zhang neural network for online complex-valued time-varying matrix inversion. *Applied Mathematics and Computation*, 217:10066–10073(24), 2011.

[64] Y. Zhang and S. S. Ge. Design and analysis of a general recurrent neural network model for time-varying matrix inversion. *IEEE Transactions on Neural Networks*, 16:1477–1490(6), 2005.

[65] Y. Zhang, K. Chen, and H. Tan. Performance analysis of gradient neural network exploited for online time-varying matrix inversion. *IEEE Transations on Automatic Control*, 54:1940–1945(8), 2009.

[66] S. Wen, Z. Zeng, and T. Huang. Exponential stability analysis of memristor-based recurrent neural networks with time-varying delays. *Neurocomputing*, 97:233–240, 2012.

[67] L. Li and J. Jian. Exponential convergence and Lagrange stability for impulsive Cohen–Grossberg neural networks with time-varying delays. *Journal of Computational and Applied Mathematics*, 277:23–35, 2015.

[68] S. Li, B. Liu, and Y. Li. Selective positive-negative feedback produces the winner-take-all competition in recurrent neural networks. *IEEE Transactions on Neural Networks and Learning Systems*, 24:301–309(2), 2013.

[69] L. Jin, Y. Zhang, and S. Li. Integration-enhanced Zhang neural network for real-time-varying matrix inversion in the presence of various kinds of noises. *IEEE Transactions on Neural Networks and Learning Systems*, 27:2615-2627(12), 2016.

[70] Y. Zhang, L. Jin, D. Guo, Y. Yin, and Y. Chou. Taylor-type 1-step-ahead numerical differentiation rule for first-order derivative approximation and ZNN discretization. *Journal of Computational and Applied Mathematics*, 273:29–40, 2015.

[71] Y. Zhang, J. Li, Y. Shi, M. Mao, and H. Tan. New formula of 4-instant g-square finite difference (4IgSFD) applied to time-variant matrix inversion. In *Proceedings of Chinese Control and Decision Conference*, 1714–1719, 2015.

[72] M. Mao, J. Li, L. Jin, S. Li, and Y. Zhang. Enhanced discrete-time Zhang neural network for time-variant matrix inversion in the presence of bias noises. *Neurocomputing*, 207:220–230, 2016.

[73] N.H. Getz and J.E. Marsden. Dynamical methods for polar decomposition and inversion of matrices. *Linear Algebra and Its Applications*, 258:311–343(1–3), 1997.

[74] N.H. Getz and J.E. Marsden. Joint-space tracking of workspace trajectories in continuous time. In *Proceedings of Conference on Decision and Control*, 1001–1006, 1995.

[75] P. Miao, Y. Shen, Y. Huang, and Y.-W. Wang. Solving time-varying quadratic programs based on finite-time Zhang neural networks and their application to robot tracking. *Neural Computing and Applications*, 26:693–703(3), 2015.

[76] Z. Zhang and Y. Zhang. Design and experimentation of acceleration level drift-free scheme aided by two recurrent neural networks. *IET Control Theory and Applications*, 7:25–42, 2013.

[77] S.C. Chapra and R.P. Canale. *Numerical Methods for Engineers.* McGraw-Hill, New York, USA, 2014.

[78] M. Combrinck. Analysis of numerical differentiation methods applied to time domain electromagnetic (TDEM) geophysical data in the S-layer differential transform. *Computers and Geosciences*, 35:1563–1573(8), 2009.

[79] I. Salgado, O. Camacho, C. Yanez, and I. Chairez. Proportional derivative fuzzy control supplied with second order sliding mode differentiation. *Engineering Applications of Artificial Intelligence*, 35:84–94, 2014.

[80] P.E. Hadjidoukas, P. Angelikopoulos, C. Voglis, D.G. Papageorgiou, and I.E. Lagaris. NDL-v2.0: A new version of the numerical differentiation library for parallel architectures. *Computer Physics Communications*, 185:2217–2219(7), 2014.

[81] J.S.C. Prentice. Truncation and roundoff errors in three-point approximations of first and second derivatives. *Applied Mathematics and Computation*, 217:4576–4581(9), 2011.

[82] I.R. Khan and R. Ohba. Closed-form expressions for the finite difference approximations of first and higher derivatives based on Taylor series. *Journal of Computational and Applied Mathematics*, 107:179–193(2), 1999.

[83] Y. Liu, S.M. Lee, O.M. Kwon, and J.H. Park. A study on H_∞ state estimation of static neural networks with time-varying delays. *Applied Mathematics and Computation*, 226:589–597(1), 2014.

[84] M. Qasim and V. Khadkikar. Application of artificial neural networks for shunt active power filter control. *IEEE Transactions on Industrial Informatics*, 10:1765–1774(3), 2014.

[85] Y. Yang, J. Cao, X. Xu, M. Hu, and Y. Gao. A new neural network for solving quadratic programming problems with equality and inequality constraints. *Mathematics and Computers in Simulation*, 101:103–112, 2014.

[86] F. Ortega-Zamorano, J.M. Jerez, and L. Franco. FPGA implementation of the c-mantec neural network constructive algorithm. *IEEE Transactions on Industrial Informatics*, 10:1154–1161(2), 2014.

[87] G. Acciani, G. Brunetti, and G. Fornarelli. Application of neural networks in optical inspection and classification of solder joints in surface mount technology. *IEEE Transactions on Industrial Informatics*, 2:200–209(3), 2006.

[88] S. Maiti, V. Verma, C. Chakraborty, and Y. Hori. An adaptive speed sensorless induction motor drive with artificial neural network for stability enhancement. *IEEE Transactions on Industrial Informatics*, 8:757–766(4), 2012.

[89] R. Rakkiyappan, K. Sivaranjani, and G. Velmurugan. Passivity and passification of memristor-based complex-valued recurrent neural networks with interval time-varying delays. *Neurocomputing*, 144:391–407(20), 2014.

[90] S. Li and F. Qin. A dynamic neural network approach for solving nonlinear inequalities defined on a graph and its application to distributed, routing-free, range-free localization of WSNs. *Neurocomputing*, 117:72–80(6), 2013.

[91] S. Li, S. Chen, B. Liu, Y. Li, and Y. Liang. Decentralized kinematic control of a class of collaborative redundant manipulators via recurrent neural networks. *Neurocomputing*, 91:1–10, 2012.

[92] D. Guo and Y. Zhang. Novel recurrent neural network for time-varying problems solving. *IEEE Computational Intelligence Magazine*, 7:61–65(4): 2012.

[93] Y. Shi, B. Qiu, D. Chen, J. Li, and Y. Zhang. Proposing and validation of a new four-point finite-difference formula with manipulator application. *IEEE Transactions on Industrial Informatics*, 14:1323–1333(4), 2018.

[94] N.H. Getz. *Dynamic Inversion of Nonlinear Maps with Applications to Nonlinear Control and Robotics*. Ph.D. Dissertation, University of California Berkeley, USA, 1995.

[95] B. Liao and Y. Zhang. Different complex ZFs leading to different complex ZNN models for time-varying complex generalized inverse matrices. *IEEE Transactions on Neural Networks and Learning Systems*, 25:1621–1631(9), 2014.

[96] J. Li, M. Mao, F. Uhlig, and Y. Zhang. A 5-instant finite difference formula to find discrete time-varying generalized matrix inverses, matrix inverses, and scalar reciprocals. *Numerical Algorithms*, 81:609–629, 2019.

[97] Y. Zhang, Y. Ling, M. Yang, S. Yang, and Z. Zhang. Inverse-free discrete ZNN models solving for future matrix pseudoinverse via combination of extrapolation and ZeaD formulas. *IEEE Transactions on Neural Networks and Learning Systems*, 32:2663–2675(6), 2021.

[98] L. Jin and S. Li. Distributed task allocation of multiple robots: A control perspective. *IEEE Transactions on Systems, Man, and Cybernetics: Systems*, 48:693–701(5), 2018.

[99] T. Yoshikawa. Manipulability of robotic mechanisms. *International Journal of Robotics Research*, 4:3–9(2), 1985.

[100] Y. Zhang, J. Li, and Z. Zhang. A time-varying coefficient-based manipulability-maximizing scheme for motion control of redundant robots subject to varying joint-velocity limits. *Optimal Control Applications and Methods*, 34:202–215(2), 2013.

[101] M.S. Bazaraa, H.D. Sherali, and C.M Shetty. *Nonlinear Programming: Theory and Algorithms*. Wiley, New York, USA, 2006.

[102] R. Rakkiyappan, S. Dharani, and J. Cao. Synchronization of neural networks with control packet loss and time-varying delay via stochastic sampled-data controller. *IEEE Transactions on Neural Networks and Learning Systems*, 26:3215–3226(12), 2015.

[103] R. Rakkiyappan, J. Cao, and G. Velmurugan. Existence and uniform stability analysis of fractional-order complex-valued neural networks with time delays. *IEEE Transactions on Neural Networks and Learning Systems*, 26:84–97(1), 2015.

[104] W. Xiong, X. Yu, Y. Chen, and J. Gao. Quantized iterative learning consensus tracking of digital networks with limited information communication. *IEEE Transactions on Neural Networks and Learning Systems*, 28:1473–1480(6), 2017.

[105] W. Xiong, R. Patel, J. Cao, and W. Zheng. Synchronization of hierarchical time-varying neural networks based on asynchronous and intermittent sampled-data control. *IEEE Transactions on Neural Networks and Learning Systems*, 28:2837–2843(11), 2017.

[106] J. Li, M. Mao, F. Uhlig, and Y. Zhang. Z-type neural-dynamics for time-varying nonlinear optimization under a linear equality constraint with robot application. *Journal of Computational and Applied Mathematics*, 327:155–166, 2018.

[107] Y. Zhang, M. Yang, J. Li, L. He, and S. Wu. ZFD formula 4IgSFD_Y applied to future minimization. *Physics Letters A*, 381:1677–1681(19), 2017.

[108] J.R. Johnson, A.J. Fenn, H.M. Aumann, and F.G. Willwerth. An experimental adaptive nulling receiver utilizing the sample matrix inversion algorithm with channel equalization. *IEEE Transactions on Microwave Theory and Techniques*, 39:798–808(5), 1991.

[109] C. Liu and C. Lu. A view of Gaussian elimination applied to early-stopped Berlekam–Massey algorithm. *IEEE Transactions on Communications*, 55:1131–1143(6), 2007.

[110] W.F. Tinney. Compensation methods for network solutions by optimally ordered triangular factorization. *IEEE Transactions on Power Systems*, 91:123–127(1), 1972.

[111] L. Jin and Y. Zhang. Continuous and discrete Zhang dynamics for real-time varying nonlinear optimization. *Numerical Algorithms*, 73:115–140(1), 2016.

[112] A. Simonetto and E. Dall'Anese. Prediction-correction algorithms for time-varying constrained optimization. *IEEE Transactions on Signal Processing*, 65:5481–5494(20), 2017.

[113] A. Simonetto, A. Koppel, A. Mokhtari, G. Leusx, and A. Ribeiro. Decentralized prediction-correction methods for networked time-varying convex optimization. *IEEE Transactions on Automatic Control*, 62:5724–5738(11), 2017.

[114] B. Zhou and T. Zhao. On asymptotic stability of discrete-time linear time-varying systems. *IEEE Transactions on Automatic Control*, 62:4274–4281(8), 2017.

[115] J. Wang, X. Zhang, and Q. Han. Event-triggered generalized dissipativity filtering for neural networks with time-varying delays. *IEEE Transactions on Neural Networks and Learning Systems*, 27:77–88(1), 2016.

[116] P.S. Stanimirovi, I.S. Ivkovi, and Y. Wei. Recurrent neural network for computing the Drazin inverse. *IEEE Transactions on Neural Networks and Learning Systems*, 26:2830–2843(11), 2015.

[117] H. Wang, X. Liu, and K. Liu. Robust adaptive neural tracking control for a class of stochastic nonlinear interconnected systems. *IEEE Transactions on Neural Networks and Learning Systems*, 27:510–523(3), 2016.

[118] H. Wang, B. Chen, X. Liu, K. Liu, and C. Lin. Robust adaptive fuzzy tracking control for pure-feedback stochastic nonlinear systems with input constraints. *IEEE Transactions on Cybernetics*, 43:2093–2104(6), 2013.

[119] A. Arbi, J. Cao, and A. Alsaedif. Improved synchronization analysis of competitive neural networks with time-varying delays. *Nonlinear Analysis: Modelling and Control*, 23:82–102(1), 2018.

[120] A. Arbi, C. Aouiti, F. Cherif, A. Touati, and A.M. Alimi. Stability analysis for delayed high-order type of Hopfield neural networks with impulses. *Neurocomputing*, 165:312–329, 2015.

[121] L. Jin, S. Li, L. Xiao, R. Lu, and B. Liao. Cooperative motion generation in a distributed network of redundant robot manipulators with noises. *IEEE Transactions on Systems, Man, and Cybernetics: Systems*, 48:1715–1724(10), 2018.

[122] Z. Zhang, A. Beck, and N. Magnenat-Thalmann. Human-like behavior generation based on head-arms model for robot tracking external targets and body parts. *IEEE Transactions on Cybernetics*, 45:1390–1400(8), 2015.

[123] B. Cai and Y. Zhang. Different-level redundancy-resolution and its equivalent relationship analysis for robot manipulators using gradient-descent and Zhang et al's neural-dynamic methods. *IEEE Transactions on Industrial Electronics*, 59:3146–3155(8), 2012.

[124] Y. Zhang, B. Qiu, B. Liao, and Z. Yang. Control of pendulum tracking (including swinging up) of IPC system using zeroing-gradient method. *Nonlinear Dynamics*, 89:1–25(1), 2017.

[125] J. Li, M. Mao, Y. Zhang, D. Chen, and Y. Yin. ZD, ZG and IOL controllers and comparisons for nonlinear system output tracking with DBZ problem conquered in different relative-degree cases. *Asian Journal of Control*, 19:1–14(4), 2017.

[126] K. Atkinson. *An Introduction to Numerical Analysis*. John Wiley & Sons, Inc., New York, USA, 1989.

[127] Y. Zhang, C. Li, P. He, M. Yang, and X. Yang. New ZFD (Zhang finite difference) formula 4IgSFD_L for time-varying reciprocal and inverse computation. In *Proceedings of Chinese Control and Decision Conference*, pages 2894–2899, 2017.

[128] J. Li, Y. Zhang, and M. Mao. General square-pattern discretization formulas via second-order derivative elimination for zeroing neural network illustrated by future optimization. *IEEE Transactions on Neural Networks and Learning Systems*, 30:891–901(3), 2019.

[129] L. Jin, Y. Zhang, S. Li, and Y. Zhang. Modified ZNN for time-varying quadratic programming with inherent tolerance to noises and its application to kinematic redundancy resolution of robot manipulators. *IEEE Transactions on Industrial Electronics*, 63:6978–6988(11), 2016.

[130] J. Li, Y. Zhang, S. Li, and M. Mao. New discretization-formula-based zeroing dynamics for real-time tracking control of serial and parallel manipulators. *IEEE Transactions on Industrial Informatics*, 14:3416–3425(8), 2018.

[131] B. Cai and Y. Zhang. Bi-criteria optimal control of redundant robot manipulators using LVI-based primal-dual neural network. *Optimal Control Applications and Methods*, 31:213–229, 2010.

[132] Y.-J. Liu, S. Li, S. Tong, and C.L.P. Chen. Neural approximation-based adaptive control for a class of nonlinear nonstrict feedback discrete-time systems. *IEEE Transactions on Neural Networks and Learning Systems*, 28:1531–1541(7), 2017.

[133] J. Lee and S. Leyffer. *Mixed Integer Nonlinear Programming*. Springer, New York, USA, 2012.

[134] D. Guo and Y. Zhang. Neural dynamics and Newton–Raphson iteration for nonlinear optimization. *Journal of Computational and Nonlinear Dynamics*, 9:1016–1026(2), 2014.

[135] Y. Zhang, S.S. Ge, and T.H. Lee. A unified quadratic-programming-based dynamical system approach to joint torque optimization of physically constrained redundant manipulators. *IEEE Transactions on Systems, Man, and Cybernetics, Part B: Cybernetics*, 34:2126–2132(5), 2004.

[136] Y. Zhao and S. Liu. Global optimization algorithm for mixed integer quadratically constrained quadratic program. *Journal of Computational and Applied Mathematics*, 319:159–169, 2017.

[137] Y. Zhang, W. Li, B. Qiu, Y. Ding, and D. Zhang. Three-state space reformulation and control of MD-included one-link robot system using direct-derivative and Zhang-dynamics methods. In *Proceedings of Chinese Control and Decision Conference*, pages 3785–3790, 2017.

[138] Y. Zhao and C. Feng. Time-dependent optimization for information processing and its applications. *Journal of Southeast Univresity*, 29:1038–1041(4), 1999.

[139] Y. Zhao and M.N.S. Swamy. A novel technique for tracking time-varying minimum and its applications. In *Proceedings of Canadian Electrical and Computer Engineering Conference*, pages 910–913, 1998.

[140] M.B. Arouxet, N.E. Echebest, and E.A. Pilotta. Inexact restoration method for nonlinear optimization without derivatives. *Journal of Computational and Applied Mathematics*, 290:26–43, 2015.

[141] J.-H. Hours and C.N. Jones. Parametric non-convex decomposition algorithm for real-time and distributed NMPC. *IEEE Transactions on Automatic Control*, 61:287–302(2), 2016.

[142] S. Rahili and W. Ren. Distributed convex optimization for continuous-time dynamics with time-varying cost functions. *IEEE Transactions on Automatic Control*, 62:1590–1605(4), 2017.

[143] M. Fazlyab, C. Nowzari, G.J. Pappas, A. Ribeiro, and V.M. Preciado. Self-triggered time-varying convex optimization. In *Proceedings of Conference on Decision and Control*, pages 3090–3097, 2016.

[144] F.Y. Jakubiec and A. Ribeiro. D-MAP: Distributed maximum a posteriori probability estimation of dynamic systems. *IEEE Transactions on Signal Processing*, 61:450–466(2), 2013.

[145] Q. Ling and A. Ribeiro. Decentralized dynamic optimization through the alternating direction method of multipliers. *IEEE Transactions on Signal Processing*, 62:1185–1197(5), 2014.

[146] A. Simonetto, A. Mokhtari, A. Koppel, G. Leus, and A. Ribeiro. A class of prediction-correction methods for time-varying convex optimization. *IEEE Transactions on Signal Processing*, 64:4576–4591(17), 2016.

[147] M. Fatemi. A new efficient conjugate gradient method for unconstrained optimization. *Journal of Computational and Applied Mathematics*, 300:207–216, 2016.

[148] J. Cu, L. Zhang, and X. Xiao. Log-sigmoid nonlinear Lagrange method for nonlinear optimization problems over second-order cones. *Journal of Computational and Applied Mathematics*, 229:129–144, 2009.

[149] E.G. Birgin and J.M. Martinez. A spectral conjugate gradient method for unconstrained optimization. *Applied Mathematics and Optimization*, 43:117–128(2), 2001.

[150] Y. Dai and L. Liao. New conjugacy conditions and related nonlinear conjugate gradient methods. *Applied Mathematics and Optimization*, 43:87–101(1), 2001.

[151] Y. Narushima and H. Yabe. Conjugate gradient methods based on secant conditions that generate descent search directions for unconstrained optimization. *Journal of Computational and Applied Mathematics*, 236:4303–4317(17), 2012.

[152] A.L. Dontchev, M.I. Krastanov, R.T. Rockafellar, and V.M. Veliov. An Euler–Newton continuation method for tracking solution trajectories of parametric variational inequalities. *SIAM Journal on Control and Optimization*, 51:1823–1840(51), 2013.

[153] V.M. Zavala and M. Anitescu. Real-time nonlinear optimization as a generalized equation. *SIAM Journal on Control and Optimization*, 48:5444–5467(8), 2010.

[154] A. Nagurney and J. Pan. Evolution variational inequalities and projected dynamical systems with application to human migration. *Mathematical and Computer Modelling*, 43:646–657(5-6), 2006.

[155] W. Su. *Traffic Engineering and Time-Varying Convex Optimization*. Ph.D. Dissertation, Pennsylvania State University, USA, 2009.

[156] E. Dall'Anese and A. Simonetto. Optimal power flow pursuit. *IEEE Transactions on Smart Grid*, 9:942–952(2), 2016.

[157] Y. Zhang, L. He, C. Hu, J. Guo, J. Li, and Y. Shi. General four-step discrete-time zeroing and derivative dynamics applied to time-varying nonlinear optimization. *Journal of Computational and Applied Mathematics*, 347:314–329, 2019.

[158] S. Li, Y. Li, and Z. Wang. A class of finite-time dual neural networks for solving quadratic programming problems and its k-winners-take-all application. *Neural Networks*, 39:27–39, 2013.

[159] P. Miao, Y. Shen, Y. Li, and L. Bao. Finite-time recurrent neural networks for solving nonlinear optimization problems and their application. *Neurocomputing*, 177:120–129, 2016.

[160] Y. Zhang, D. Jiang, and J. Wang. A recurrent neural network for solving Sylvester equation with time-varying coefficients. *IEEE Transactions on Neural Networks and Learning Systems*, 13:1053–1063(5), 2002.

[161] J.H. Mathews and K.D. Fink. *Numerical Methods Using MATLAB*. Prentice-Hall, Englewood Cliffs, USA, 2005.

[162] Y. Jiang, X. Hu, and S. Wu. Transformation matrix for time discretization based on Tustin's method. *Mathematical Problems in Engineering*, 2014:1–9, 2014.

[163] C. Zhu and Y. Zou. Improved recursive algorithm for fractional-order system solution based on PSE and Tustin transform. *Systems Engineering and Electronics*, 31:2736–2741(11), 2009.

[164] K. Ogata. *Modern Control Engineering*. Prentice-Hall, Englewood Cliffs, USA, 2001.

[165] A. Klapper. Improved multicovering bounds from linear inequalities and supercodes. *IEEE Transactions on Information Theory*, 50:532–536(3), 2004.

[166] L. Xiao and Y. Zhang. Solving time-varying nonlinear inequalities using continuous and discrete-time Zhang dynamics. *International Journal of Computer Mathematics*, 90:1114–1127(5), 2013.

[167] S.P. Shary. New characterizations for the solution set to interval linear systems of equations. *Applied Mathematics and Computation*, 265:570–573, 2015.

[168] M.T. Darvishi and R. Khosro-Aghdam. Symmetric successive overrelaxation methods for rank deficient linear systems. *Applied Mathematics and Computation*, 173:404–420(1), 2006.

[169] H. Tian. Accelerate overrelaxation methods for rank deficient linear systems. *Applied Mathematics and Computation*, 140:485–499(2), 2003.

[170] W.S. Cheung. Some new nonlinear inequalities and applications to boundary value problems. *Nonlinear Analysis-Theory Methods & Applications*, 64:2112–2128(9), 2006.

[171] N.S. Hoang and A.G. Ramm. A nonlinear inequality and applications. *Nonlinear Analysis-Theory Methods & Applications*, 71:2744–2752(7), 2009.

[172] D.Q. Mayne, E. Polak, and A.J. Heunis. Solving nonlinear inequalities in a finite number of iterations. *Journal of Optimization Theory and Applications*, 33:207–221(2), 1981.

[173] D. Guo, L. Yan, and Z. Nie. Design, analysis, and representation of novel five-step DTZD algorithm for time-varying nonlinear optimization. *IEEE Transactions on Neural Networks and Learning Systems*, 29:4248–4260(9), 2018.

[174] L. Jin, S. Li, B. Hu, M. Liu, and J. Yu. A noise-suppressing neural algorithm for solving time-varying system of linear equations: A control-based approach. *IEEE Transactions on Industrial Informatics*, 15:236–246(1), 2019.

[175] L. Xiao and Y. Zhang. Two new types of Zhang neural networks solving systems of time-varying nonlinear inequalities. *IEEE Transactions on Circuits and Systems I-Regular Papers*, 59:2363–2373(10), 2012.

[176] L. Xiao, B. Liao, S. Li, and K. Chen. Nonlinear recurrent neural networks for finite-time solution of general time-varying linear matrix equations. *Neural Networks*, 98:102–113, 2018.

[177] L. Xiao, S. Li, J. Yang, and Z. Zhang. A new recurrent neural network with noise-tolerance and finite-time convergence for dynamic quadratic minimization. *Neurocomputing*, 285:125–132, 2018.

[178] L. Xiao. A finite-time recurrent neural network for solving online time-varying Sylvester matrix equation based on a new evolution formula. *Nonlinear Dynamics*, 90:1581–1591(3), 2017.

[179] S. Li, J. He, Y. Li, and M.U. Rafique. Distributed recurrent neural networks for cooperative control of manipulators: A game-theoretic perspective. *IEEE Transactions on Neural Networks and Learning Systems*, 28:415–426(2), 2017.

[180] J.J. Hopfield. Neural networks and physical systems with emergent collective computational abilities. *The Proceedings of the National Academy of Sciences*, 79:2554–2558(8), 1982.

[181] L. Jin, S. Li, and B. Hu. RNN models for dynamic matrix inversion: A control-theoretical perspective. *IEEE Transactions on Industrial Informatics*, 14:189–199(1), 2018.

[182] L. Jin, S. Li, X. Luo, Y. Li, and B. Qin. Neural dynamics for cooperative control of redundant robot manipulators. *IEEE Transactions on Industrial Informatics*, 14:3812–3821(9), 2018.

[183] F. Xu, Z. Li, Z. Nie, H. Shao, and D. Guo. Zeroing neural network for solving time-varying linear equation and inequality systems. *IEEE Transactions on Neural Networks and Learning Systems*, 30:2346–2357(8), 2019.

[184] Y. Zhang, H. Gong, M. Yang, J. Li, and X. Yang. Stepsize range and optimal value for Taylor–Zhang discretization formula applied to zeroing neurodynamics illustrated via future equality-constrained quadratic programming. *IEEE Transactions on Neural Networks and Learning Systems*, 30:959–966(3), 2019.

[185] L. Xiao, K. Li, and M. Duan. Computing time-varying quadratic optimization with finite-time convergence and noise tolerance: A unified framework for zeroing neural network. *IEEE Transactions on Neural Networks and Learning Systems*, 30:3360–3369(11), 2019.

[186] Z. Zhang, L. Kong, and L. Zheng. Power-type varying-parameter RNN for solving TVQP problems: Design, analysis, and applications. *IEEE Transactions on Neural Networks and Learning Systems*, 30:2419–2433(8), 2019.

[187] B. Qiu, Y. Zhang, and Z. Yang. New discrete-time ZNN models for least-squares solution of dynamic linear equation system with time-varying rank-deficient coefficient. *IEEE Transactions on Neural Networks and Learning Systems*, 29:5767–5776(11), 2018.

[188] D. Guo, Z. Nie, and L. Yan. Novel discrete-time Zhang neural network for time-varying matrix inversion. *IEEE Transactions on Systems, Man, and Cybernetics: Systems*, 47:2301–2310(8), 2017.

[189] D. Guo, Z. Nie, and L. Yan. Theoretical analysis, numerical verification and geometrical representation of new three-step DTZD algorithm for time-varying nonlinear equations solving. *Neurocomputing*, 214:516–526, 2016.

[190] M. Yang, Y. Zhang, H. Hu, and B. Qiu. General 7-instant DCZNN model solving future different-level system of nonlinear inequality and linear equation. *IEEE Transactions on Neural Networks and Learning Systems*, 31:3204–3214(9), 2020.

[191] L. Jin and Y. Zhang. Discrete-time Zhang neural network for online time-varying nonlinear optimization with application to manipulator motion generation. *IEEE Transactions on Neural Networks and Learning Systems*, 26:1525–1531(7), 2015.

[192] D. Guo, F. Xu, Z. Li, Z. Nie, and H. Shao. Design, verification, and application of new discrete-time recurrent neural network for dynamic nonlinear equations solving. *IEEE Transactions on Industrial Informatics*, 14:3936–3945(9), 2018.

[193] C. Hu, X. Kang, and Y. Zhang. Three-step general discrete-time Zhang neural network design and application to time-variant matrix inversion. *Neurocomputing*, 306:108–118, 2018.

[194] C.K. Alexander and M.N.O. Sadiku. *Fundamentals of Electric Circuits*. McGraw-Hill, New York, USA, 2000.

[195] A.V. Oppenheim and R.W. Schafer. *Discrete-Time Signal Processing, Third Edition*. Prentice-Hall, New Jersey, USA, 2009.

[196] L. Xiao, B. Liao, S. Li, Z. Zhang, L. Ding, and L. Jin. Design and analysis of FTZNN applied to real-time solution of nonstationary Lyapunov equation and tracking control of wheeled mobile manipulator. *IEEE Transactions on Industrial Informatics*, 14:98–105(1), 2018.

[197] Z. Zhang, Z. Li, Y. Zhang, Y. Luo, and Y. Li. Neural-dynamic-method-based dual-arm CMG scheme with time-varying constraints applied to humanoid robots. *IEEE Transactions on Neural Networks and Learning Systems*, 26:3251–3262(12), 2015.

[198] L. Xiao and Y. Zhang. Solving time-varying inverse kinematics problem of wheeled mobile manipulators using Zhang neural network with exponential convergence. *Nonlinear Dynamics*, 76:1543–1559(2), 2014.

[199] Z. Zhang, L. Zheng, J. Yu, Y. Li, and Z. Yu. Three recurrent neural networks and three numerical methods for solving a repetitive motion planning scheme of redundant robot manipulators. *IEEE/ASME Transactions on Mechatronics*, 22:1423–1434(3), 2017.

[200] L. Jin, S. Li, H.M. La, and X. Luo. Manipulability optimization of redundant manipulators using dynamic neural networks. *IEEE Transactions on Industrial Electronics*, 64:4710–4720(6), 2017.

[201] S. Arslan and F. Koken. The Pell and Pell–Lucas numbers via square roots of matrices. *Journal of Informatics and Mathematical Sciences*, 8:159–166(3), 2016.

[202] L. Wei. An adaptive expectation genetic algorithm based on ANFIS and multinational stock market volatility causality for TAIEX forecastion. *Cybernetics and Systems*, 43:410–425(4), 2012.

[203] L.-H. Ma, Z.-B. Feng, B.-H. Ying, and Z.-Y. Wang. Application of fixed matrix square root UKF in the ultra-tightly coupled integrated GPS/SINS navigation system. *ICIC Express Letters, Part B: Applications*, 6:175–180(1), 2015.

[204] G.Y. Kulikov and M.V. Kulikova. NIRK-based Cholesky-factorized square-root accurate continuous-discrete unscented Kalman filters for state estimation in nonlinear continuous-time stochastic models with discrete measurements. *Applied Numerical Mathematics*, 147:196–221, 2020.

[205] H. Nguyen, X.N. Bui, Q.H. Tran, and N.L. Mai. A new soft computing model for estimating and controlling blast-produced ground vibration based on Hierarchical K-means clustering and Cubist algorithms. *Applied Soft Computing*, 77:376–386, 2019.

[206] A. Haridas, R. Marimuthu, and B. Chakraborty. A novel approach to improve the speech intelligibility using fractional delta-amplitude modulation spectrogram. *Cybernetics and systems*, 49:421–451(7–8), 2018.

[207] H. Waadeland. Computation of continued fractions by square-root modification: Reflections and examples. *Applied Numerical Mathematics*, 4:361–375(2–4), 1988.

[208] J. Brankart, E. Cosme, C. Testut, P. Brasseur, and J. Verron. Efficient adaptive error parameterizations for square root or ensemble Kalman filters: Application to the control of ocean mesoscale signals. *Monthly Weather Review*, 138:932–950(3), 2010.

[209] J.R. Cardoso, C.S. Kenney, and F.S. Leite. Computing the square root and logarithm of a real P-orthogonal matrix. *Applied Numerical Mathematics*, 46:173–196(2), 2003.

[210] Z. Liu, Y. Zhang, J. Santos, and R. Ralha. On computing complex square roots of real matrices. *Applied Mathematics Letters*, 25:1565–1568(10), 2012.

[211] Y. Zhang, L. Jin, and Z. Ke. Superior performance of using hyperbolic sine activation functions in ZNN illustrated via time-varying matrix square roots finding. *Computer Science and Information Systems*, 9:1603–1625(4), 2012.

[212] E.S. Gawlik. Zolotarev iterations for the matrix square root. *SIAM Journal on Matrix Analysis and Applications*, 40:696–719(2), 2019.

[213] W. Li, B. Liao, L. Xiao, and R. Lu. A recurrent neural network with predefined-time convergence and improved noise tolerance for dynamic matrix square root finding. *Neurocomputing*, 337:262–273, 2019.

[214] S. Sra. On the matrix square root via geometric optimization. *The Electronic Journal of Linear Algebra*, 31:433–443, 2016.

[215] S. Qin and X. Xue. A two-layer recurrent neural network for non-smooth convex optimization problems. *IEEE Transactions on Neural Networks and Learning Systems*, 26:1149–1160(6), 2015.

[216] S. Qin, X. Yang, X. Xue, and J. Song. A one-layer recurrent neural network for pseudoconvex optimization problems with equality and inequality constraints. *IEEE Transactions on Cybernetics*, 47:3063–3074(10), 2017.

[217] Z. Li and D. Huang. Robust control of two-link manipulator with disturbance torque and time-varying mass loads. *Transactions of the Institute of Measurement and Control*, 42:1667–1674(9), 2020.

[218] C.S. de Oliveira, C. Sanin, and E. Szczerbicki. Flexible knowledge-vision-integration platform for personal protective equipment detection and classification using hierarchical convolutional neural networks and active leaning. *Cybernetics and Systems*, 49:335–367(5–6), 2018.

[219] Z. Li, C. Li, S. Li, and X. Cao. A fault-tolerant method for motion planning of industrial redundant manipulator. *IEEE Transactions on Industrial Informatics*, 16:7469–7478(12), 2020.

[220] N. Liu and S. Qin. A novel neurodynamic approach to constrained complex-variable pseudoconvex optimization. *IEEE Transactions on Cybernetics*, 49:3946–3956(11), 2019.

[221] N. Liu and S. Qin. A neurodynamic approach to nonlinear optimization problems with affine equality and convex inequality constraints. *Neural Networks*, 109:147–158, 2019.

[222] L. Xiao. A nonlinearly-activated neurodynamic model and its finite-time solution to equality-constrained quadratic optimization with nonstationary coefficients. *Applied Soft Computing*, 40:252–259, 2016.

[223] L. Xiao, Y. Zhang, Z. Hu, and J. Dai. Performance benefits of robust nonlinear zeroing neural network for finding accurate solution of Lyapunov equation in presence of various noises. *IEEE Transactions on Industrial Informatics*, 15:5161–5171(9), 2019.

[224] D. Guo and Y. Zhang. Li-function activated ZNN with finite-time convergence applied to redundant-manipulator kinematic control via time-varying Jacobian matrix pseudoinversion. *Applied Soft Computing*, 24:158–168, 2014.

[225] L. Jin, S. Li, J. Yu, and J. He. Robot manipulator control using neural networks: A survey. *Neurocomputing*, 285:23–34, 2018.

[226] D. Guo, F. Xu, and L. Yan. New pseudoinverse-based path-planning scheme with PID characteristic for redundant robot manipulators in the presence of noise. *IEEE Transactions on Control Systems Technology*, 26:2008–2019(6), 2018.

[227] L. Jin, S. Li, H. Wang, and Z. Zhang. Nonconvex projection activated zeroing neurodynamic models for time-varying matrix pseudoinversion with accelerated finite-time convergence. *Applied Soft Computing*, 62:840–850, 2018.

[228] J. Chen and Y. Zhang. Continuous and discrete zeroing neural dynamics handling future unknown-transpose matrix inequality as well as scalar inequality of linear class. *Numerical Algorithms*, 83:529–547, 2020.

[229] X. Liu, C. Hu, X. Kang, M. Mao, Y. Zhang, and B. Qiu. New five-step discrete-time zeroing neural network for time-varying matrix square root finding. In *Proceedings of International Conference on Systems and Informatics*, pages 738–744, 2019.

[230] J. Guo, B. Qiu, J. Chen, and Y. Zhang. Solving future different-layer nonlinear and linear equation system using new eight-node DZNN model. *IEEE Transactions on Industrial Informatics*, 16:2280–2289(4), 2020.

[231] J. Chen and Y. Zhang. Discrete-time ZND models solving ALMMPC via eight-instant general and other formulas of ZeaD. *IEEE Access*, 7:125909–125918, 2019.

[232] W. Li, L. Xiao, and B. Liao. A finite-time convergent and noise rejection recurrent neural network and its discretization for dynamic nonlinear equations solving. *IEEE Transactions on Cybernetics*, 50:3195–3207(7), 2020.

[233] D. Guo, X. Lin, Z. Su, S. Sun, and Z. Huang. Design and analysis of two discrete-time ZD algorithms for time-varying nonlinear minimization. *Numerical Algorithms*, 77:23–36(1), 2018.

[234] M. Sun, M. Tian, and Y. Wang. Discrete-time Zhang neural networks for time-varying nonlinear optimization. *Discrete Dynamics in Nature and Society*, 2019:1–14, 2019.

[235] J. Chen, J. Guo, and Y. Zhang. General ten-instant DTDMSR model for dynamic matrix square root finding. *Cybernetics and Systems*, 52:127–143(1), 2020.

[236] Y.-J. Liu, S. Tong, and C.L.P. Chen. Adaptive fuzzy control via observer design for uncertain nonlinear systems with unmodeled dynamics. *IEEE Transactions on Fuzzy Systems*, 21:275–288(2), 2013.

[237] C.L.P. Chen, G. Wen, Y. Liu, and Z. Liu. Observer-based adaptive backstepping consensus tracking control for high-order nonlinear semi-strict-feedback multiagent systems. *IEEE Transactions on Cybernetics*, 46:1591–1601(7), 2016.

[238] Y.-J. Liu, C.L.P. Chen, G. Wen, and S. Tong. Adaptive neural output feedback tracking control for a class of uncertain discrete-time nonlinear systems. *IEEE Transactions on Neural Networks and Learning Systems*, 22:1162–1167(7), 2011.

[239] C. Yang, Y. Jiang, Z. Li, W. He, and C. Su. Neural control of bimanual robots with guaranteed global stability and motion precision. *IEEE Transactions on Industrial Informatics*, 13:1162–1171(3), 2017.

[240] J. Baek, M. Jin, and S. Han. A new adaptive sliding-mode control scheme for application to robot manipulators. *IEEE Transactions on Industrial Electronics*, 63:3628–3637(6), 2016.

[241] B. D'Andrea-Novel, G. Campion, and G. Bastin. Control of nonholonomic wheeled mobile robots by state feedback linearization. *International Journal of Robotics Research*, 14:543–559(6), 1995.

[242] D.H. Kim and J.H. Oh. Tracking control of a two-wheeled mobile robot using input–output linearization. *Control Engineering Practice*, 7:369–373(3), 1999.

[243] Q. Zhang, J. Shippen, and B. Jones. Robust backstepping and neural network control of a low-quality nonholonomic mobile robot. *International Journal of Machine Tools and Manufacture*, 39:1117–1134(7), 1999.

[244] M.L. Corradini, V. Fossi, A. Giantomassi, G. Ippoliti, S. Longhi, and G. Orlando. Minimal resource allocating networks for discrete time sliding mode control of robotic manipulators. *IEEE Transactions on Industrial Informatics*, 8:733–745(4), 2012.

[245] Q. Zhang, L. Lapierre, and X. Xiang. Distributed control of coordinated path tracking for networked nonholonomic mobile vehicles. *IEEE Transactions on Industrial Informatics*, 9:472–484(1), 2013.

[246] Y. Wang, L. Gu, Y. Xu, and X. Cao. Practical tracking control of robot manipulators with continuous fractional-order nonsingular terminal sliding mode. *IEEE Transactions on Industrial Electronics*, 63:6194–6204(10), 2016.

[247] J.H. Yang and S.H. Shen. Novel approach for adaptive tracking control of a 3-D overhead crane system. *Journal of Intelligent and Robotic Systems*, 62:59–80(1), 2011.

[248] B. Cai and X. Jiang. A novel artificial neural network method for biomedical prediction based on matrix pseudo-inversion. *Journal of Biomedical Informatics*, 48:114–121, 2014.

[249] K. Chen. Robustness analysis of Wang neural network for online linear equation solving. *Electronics Letters*, 48:1391–1392(22), 2012.

[250] X. Li and S. Song. Impulsive control for existence, uniqueness and global stability of periodic solutions of recurrent neural networks with discrete and continuously distributed delays. *IEEE Transactions on Neural Networks and Learning Systems*, 24:868–877(6), 2013.

[251] E. Suli and D.F. Mayers. *An Introduction to Numerical Analysis*. Cambridge University Press, Oxford, UK, 2003.

[252] R.J. LeVeque. *Finite Difference Methods for Ordinary and Partial Differential Equations: Steady-State and Time-Dependent Problems*. SIAM, Washington, USA, 2007.

[253] A.M. Mohammed and S. Li. Dynamic neural networks for kinematic redundancy resolution of parallel Stewart platforms. *IEEE Transactions on Cybernetics*, 46:1538–1550(7), 2016.

[254] X. Hu and J. Wang. Design of general projection neural networks for solving monotone linear variational inequalities and linear and quadratic optimization problems. *IEEE Transactions on Systems, Man, and Cybernetics, Part B: Cybernetics*, 37:1414–1421(5), 2007.

[255] W.-P. Zhu, M.O. Ahmad, and M.N.S. Swamy. Weighted least-square design of FIR filters using a fast iterative matrix inversion algorithm. *IEEE Transactions on Circuits and Systems I Fundamental Theory and Applications*, 49:1620–1628(11), 2002.

[256] S. Li, Z.-H. You, H. Guo, X. Luo, and Z.-Q. Zhao. Inverse-free extreme learning machine with optimal information updating. *IEEE Transactions on Cybernetics*, 46:1229–1241(5), 2016.

[257] J. Cao and X. Wang. New recursive algorithm for matrix inversion. *Journal of Systems Engineering and Electronics*, 19:381–384(2), 2008.

[258] B.F. Vajargah. Different stochastic algorithms to obtain matrix inversion. *Applied Mathematics and Computation*, 189:1841–1846(2), 2007.

[259] A. Storjohann and S. Yang. A relaxed algorithm for online matrix inversion. *ACM Communications in Computer Algebra*, 48:140–142(3), 2014.

[260] F.K. Haghani and F. Soleymani. An improved Schulz-type iterative method for matrix inversion with application. *Transactions of the Institute of Measurement and Control*, 36:983–991(8), 2014.

[261] D.W. Tank and J.J. Hopfield. Simple 'neural' optimization networks: An A/D converter, signal decision circuit, and a linear programming circuit. *IEEE Transactions on Circuits and Systems*, 33:533–541(5), 1986.

[262] J. Wang. A recurrent neural network for real-time matrix inversion. *Applied Mathematics and Computation*, 55:89–100(1), 1993.

[263] Y. Zhang and J. Wang. Global exponential stability of recurrent neural networks for synthesizing linear feedback control systems via pole assignment. *IEEE Transactions on Neural Networks*, 13:633–644(3), 2002.

[264] J. Cao and J. Wang. Global exponential stability and periodicity of recurrent neural networks with time delays. *IEEE Transactions on Circuits and Systems I: Regular Chapters*, 52:920–931(5), 2005.

[265] Y. Zhang, Y. Shi, K. Chen, and C. Wang. Global exponential convergence and stability of gradient-based neural network for online matrix inversion. *Applied Mathematics and Computation*, 215:1301–1306(3), 2009.

[266] C.L.P. Chen, Y.-J. Liu, and G.-X. Wen. Fuzzy neural network-based adaptive control for a class of uncertain nonlinear stochastic systems. *IEEE Transactions on Cybernetics*, 44:583–593(5), 2014.

[267] X. Le, S. Chen, Z. Yan, and J. Xi. A neurodynamic approach to distributed optimization with globally coupled constraints. *IEEE Transactions on Cybernetics*, 48:3149–3158(11), 2017.

[268] M. Eshaghnezhad, S. Effati, and A. Mansoori. A neurodynamic model to solve nonlinear pseudo-monotone projection equation and its applications. *IEEE Transactions on Cybernetics*, 47:3050–3062(10), 2017.

[269] S.S. Ge, C. Yang, and T.H. Lee. Adaptive predictive control using neural network for a class of pure-feedback systems in discrete time. *IEEE Transactions on Neural Networks*, 19:1599–1614(9), 2008.

[270] Y.-J. Liu and S. Tong. Adaptive NN tracking control of uncertain nonlinear discrete-time systems with nonaffine dead-zone input. *IEEE Transactions on Cybernetics*, 45:497–505(3), 2015.

[271] Y.-J. Liu and S. Tong. Optimal control-based adaptive NN design for a class of nonlinear discrete-time block-triangular systems. *IEEE Transactions on Cybernetics*, 46:2670–2680(11), 2016.

[272] C.-K. Zhang, Y. He, L. Jiang, Q.-G. Wang, and M. Wu. Stability analysis of discrete-time neural networks with time-varying delay via an extended reciprocally convex matrix inequality. *IEEE Transactions on Cybernetics*, 47:3040–3049(10), 2017.

[273] H. Wang, K. Liu, X. Liu, B. Chen, and C. Lin. Neural-based adaptive output-feedback control for a class of nonstrict-feedback stochastic nonlinear systems. *IEEE Transactions on Cybernetics*, 45:1977–1987(9), 2015.

[274] S. Yang, Q. Liu, and J. Wang. A collaborative neural network approach to multiple-objective distributed optimization. *IEEE Transactions on Neural Networks and Learning Systems*, 29:981–992(4), 2017.

[275] J. Fan and J. Wang. A collective neural network optimization approach to nonnegative matrix factorization. *IEEE Transactions on Neural Networks and Learning Systems*, 28:2344–2356(10), 2017.

[276] W. He, Y. Chen, and Z. Yin. Adaptive neural network control of an uncertain robot with full-state constraints. *IEEE Transactions on Cybernetics*, 46:620–629(3), 2016.

[277] W. He, Z. Yin, and C. Sun. Adaptive neural network control of a marine vessel with constraints using the asymmetric barrier Lyapunov function. *IEEE Transactions on Cybernetics*, 47:1641–1651(7), 2017.

[278] K. Chen. Recurrent implicit dynamics for online matrix inversion. *Applied Mathematics and Computation*, 219:10218–10224(20), 2013.

[279] K. Chen and C. Yi. Robustness analysis of a hybrid of recursive neural dynamics for online matrix inversion. *Applied Mathematics and Computation*, 273:969–975, 2016.

[280] S. Li and Y. Li. Nonlinearly activated neural network for solving time-varying complex Sylvester equation. *IEEE Transactions on Cybernetics*, 44:1397–1407(8), 2014.

[281] Y. Zhang, L. Xiao, Z. Xiao, and M. Mao. *Zeroing Dynamics, Gradient Dynamics, and Newton Iterations*. CRC Press, Boca Raton, USA, 2015.

[282] C. Yi, Y. Chen, and X. Lan. Comparison on neural solvers for the Lyapunov matrix equation with stationary & nonstationary coefficients. *Applied Mathematical Modelling*, 37:2495–2502(4), 2013.

[283] L. Xiao. A new design formula exploited for accelerating Zhang neural network and its application to time-varying matrix inversion. *Theoretical Computer Science*, 647:50–58, 2016.

[284] Q. Wei, D. Liu, Q. Lin, and R. Song. Discrete-time optimal control via local policy iteration adaptive dynamic programming. *IEEE Transactions on Cybernetics*, 47:3367–3379(10), 2017.

[285] D.-J. Li and D.-P. Li. Adaptive control via neural output feedback for a class of nonlinear discrete-time systems in a nested interconnected form. *IEEE Transactions on Cybernetics*, 48:2633–2642(9), 2017.

[286] Z.-H. Zhang and G.-H. Yang. Interval observer-based fault isolation for discrete-time fuzzy interconnected systems with unknown interconnections. *IEEE Transactions on Cybernetics*, 47:2413–2424(9), 2017.

[287] H. Zhang, H. Zhong, and C. Dang. Delay-dependent decentralized H_∞ filtering for discrete-time nonlinear interconnected systems with time-varying delay based on the T-S fuzzy model. *IEEE Transactions on Fuzzy Systems*, 20:431–443(3), 2012.

[288] R.D. Richtmyer and K.W. Morton. *Difference Methods for Initial-Value Problems, Second Edition*. Interscience Publishers, New York, USA, 1967.

[289] G.D. Smith. *Numerical Solution of Partial Differential Equations: Finite Difference Methods*. Oxford University Press, Oxford, UK, 1985.

[290] Y. Xia, J. Wang, and D.L. Hung. Recurrent neural networks for solving linear inequalities and equations. *IEEE Transactions on Circuits and Systems I Fundamental Theory and Applications*, 46:452–462(4), 1999.

[291] B. Qiu and Y. Zhang. Two new discrete-time neurodynamic algorithms applied to online future matrix inversion with nonsingular or sometimes-singular coefficient. *IEEE Transactions on Cybernetics*, 49:2032–2045(6), 2019.

[292] D.A. Bini, G. Codevico, and M. Van Barel. Solving Toeplitz least squares problems by means of Newton's iteration. *Numerical Algorithms*, 33:93–103(1–4), 2003.

[293] Z. Li, W. Ma, Z. Yin, and H. Guo. Tracking control of time-varying knee exoskeleton disturbed by interaction torque. *ISA Transactions*, 71:458–466, 2017.

[294] X.-B. Liang and S.K. Tso. An improved upper bound on step-size parameters of discrete-time recurrent neural networks for linear inequality and equation system. *IEEE Transactions on Circuits and Systems I Fundamental Theory and Applications*, 49:695–698(5), 2002.

[295] Y. Zhang, J. Wang, and Y. Xia. A dual neural network for redundancy resolution of kinematically redundant manipulators subject to joint limits and joint velocity limits. *IEEE Transactions on Neural Networks*, 14:658–667(3), 2003.

[296] B. Qiu, Y. Zhang, and Z. Yang. Revisit and compare Ma equivalence and Zhang equivalence of minimum velocity norm (MVN) type. *Advanced Robotics*, 30:416–430(6), 2016.

[297] Z. Zhang, Y. Lin, S. Li, Y. Li, Z. Yu, and Y. Luo. Tricriteria optimization-coordination motion of dual-redundant-robot manipulators for complex path planning. *IEEE Transactions on Control Systems Technology*, 26:1345–1357(4), 2018.

[298] B. Siciliano, L. Sciavicco, L. Villani, and G. Oriolo. *Robotics: Modelling, Planning and Control*. Springer-Verlag, London, UK, 2009.

[299] S. Wang, J. Na, and X. Ren. RISE-based asymptotic prescribed performance tracking control of nonlinear servo mechanisms. *IEEE Transactions on Systems, Man, and Cybernetics: Systems*, 48:2359–2370(12), 2018.

[300] C. Yang, J. Luo, Y. Pan, Z. Liu, and C. Su. Personalized variable gain control with tremor attenuation for robot teleoperation. *IEEE Transactions on Systems, Man, and Cybernetics: Systems*, 48:1759–1770(10), 2018.

[301] J. Na, Y. Huang, X. Wu, G. Gao, G. Herrmann, and J.Z. Jiang. Active adaptive estimation and control for vehicle suspensions with prescribed performance. *IEEE Transactions on Control Systems Technology*, 26:2063–2077(6), 2018.

[302] W. He and Y. Dong. Adaptive fuzzy neural network control for a constrained robot using impedance learning. *IEEE Transactions on Neural Networks and Learning Systems*, 29:1174–1186(4), 2018.

[303] C. Zhang, J. Na, J. Wu, Q. Chen, and Y. Huang. Proportional-integral approximation-free control of robotic systems with unknown dynamics. *IEEE/ASME Transactions on Mechatronics*, 26:2226–2236(4), 2021.

[304] J. Na, B. Jing, Y. Huang, G. Gao, and C. Zhang. Unknown system dynamics estimator for motion control of nonlinear robotic systems. *IEEE Transactions on Industrial Electronics*, 67:3850–3859(5), 2020.

[305] D. Guo, Z. Nie, and L. Yan. The application of noise-tolerant ZD design formula to robots' kinematic control via time-varying nonlinear equations solving. *IEEE Transactions on Systems, Man, and Cybernetics: Systems*, 48:2188–2197(12), 2018.

[306] Z. Li, F. Xu, Q. Feng, J. Cai, and D. Guo. The application of ZFD formula to kinematic control of redundant robot manipulators with guaranteed motion precision. *IEEE Access*, 6:64777–64783, 2018.

[307] Z. Li, B. Liao, F. Xu, and D. Guo. A new repetitive motion planning scheme with noise suppression capability for redundant robot manipulators. *IEEE Transactions on Systems, Man, and Cybernetics: Systems*, 50:5244–5254(12), 2020.

[308] W. Li. Predefined-time convergent neural solution to cyclical motion planning of redundant robots under physical constraints. *IEEE Transactions on Industrial Electronics*, 67:10732–10743(12), 2020.

[309] D. Guo, Z. Li, A.H. Khan, Q. Feng, and J. Cai. Repetitive motion planning of robotic manipulators with guaranteed precision. *IEEE Transactions on Industrial Informatics*, 17:356–366(1), 2021.

[310] Y. Zhang, D. Guo, B. Cai, and K. Chen. Remedy scheme and theoretical analysis of joint-angle drift phenomenon for redundant robot manipulators. *Robotics and Computer-Integrated Manufacturing*, 27:860–869(4), 2011.

[311] R.G. Roberts and A.A. Maciejewski. Repeatable generalized inverse control strategies for kinematically redundant manipulators. *IEEE Transactions on Automatic Control*, 38:689–699(5), 2002.

[312] K. Tchon and J. Jakubiak. A repeatable inverse kinematics algorithm with linear invariant subspaces for mobile manipulators. *IEEE Transactions on Systems, Man, and Cybernetics, Part B (Cybernetics)*, 35:1051–1057(5), 2005.

[313] D. Wang, D. Liu, Q. Zhang, and D. Zhao. Data-based adaptive critic designs for nonlinear robust optimal control with uncertain dynamics. *IEEE Transactions on Systems, Man, and Cybernetics: Systems*, 46:1544–1555(11), 2016.

[314] S. Li, Z. Shao, and Y. Guan. A dynamic neural network approach for efficient control of manipulators. *IEEE Transactions on Systems, Man, and Cybernetics: Systems*, 49:932–941(5), 2019.

[315] S. Li, M. Zhou, and X. Luo. Modified primal-dual neural networks for motion control of redundant manipulators with dynamic rejection of harmonic noises. *IEEE Transactions on Neural Networks and Learning Systems*, 29:4791–4801(10), 2018.

[316] C. Yang, X. Wang, Z. Li, Y. Li, and C. Su. Teleoperation control based on combination of wave variable and neural networks. *IEEE Transactions on Systems, Man, and Cybernetics: Systems*, 47:2125–2136(8), 2017.

[317] T. Li, S. Duan, J. Liu, L. Wang, and T. Huang. A spintronic memristor-based neural network with radial basis function for robotic manipulator control implementation. *IEEE Transactions on Systems, Man, and Cybernetics: Systems*, 46:582–588(4), 2016.

[318] Z. Yao, J. Yao, and W. Sun. Adaptive RISE control of hydraulic systems with multilayer neural-networks. *IEEE Transactions on Industrial Electronics*, 66:8638–8647(11), 2019.

[319] S. Li, H. Wang, and M.U. Rafique. A novel recurrent neural network for manipulator control with improved noise tolerance. *IEEE Transactions on Neural Networks and Learning Systems*, 29:1908–1918(5), 2017.

[320] L. Xiao, S. Li, K. Li, L. Jin, and B. Liao. Co-design of finite-time convergence and noise suppression: A unified neural model for time varying linear equations with robotic applications. *IEEE Transactions on Systems, Man, and Cybernetics: Systems*, 50:5233–5243(12), 2020.

[321] J. Li, Y. Zhang, and M. Mao. Continuous and discrete zeroing neural network for different-level dynamic linear system with robot manipulator control. *IEEE Transactions on Systems, Man, and Cybernetics: Systems*, 50:4633–4642(11), 2020.

[322] W. Li. Design and analysis of a novel finite-time convergent and noise tolerant recurrent neural network for time-variant matrix inversion. *IEEE Transactions on Systems, Man, and Cybernetics: Systems*, 50:4362–4376(11), 2020.

[323] Y. Shi and Y. Zhang. New discrete-time models of zeroing neural network solving systems of time-variant linear and nonlinear inequalities. *IEEE Transactions on Systems, Man, and Cybernetics: Systems*, 50:565–576(2), 2020.

[324] L. Xiao and Y. Zhang. A new performance index for the repetitive motion of mobile manipulators. *IEEE Transactions on Cybernetics*, 44:280–292(2), 2014.

[325] L. Jin, S. Li, B. Liao, and Z. Zhang. Zeroing neural networks: A survey. *Neurocomputing*, 267:597–604, 2017.

[326] D. Guo, F. Xu, Z. Li, Z. Nie, and H. Shao. Design, verification and application of new discrete-time recurrent neural network for dynamic nonlinear equations solving. *IEEE Transactions on Industrial Informatics*, 14:3936–3945(9), 2018.

[327] M. Yang, Y. Zhang, Z. Zhang, and H. Hu. 6-step discrete ZNN model for repetitive motion control of redundant manipulator. *IEEE Transactions on Systems, Man, and Cybernetics: Systems*, 52:4969–4980(8), 2022.

[328] L. Jin and S. Li. Nonconvex function activated zeroing neural network models for dynamic quadratic programming subject to equality and inequality constraints. *Neurocomputing*, 267:107–113, 2017.

[329] Q. Ma, S. Qin, and T. Jin. Complex Zhang neural networks for complex-variable dynamic quadratic programming. *Neurocomputing*, 330:56–69, 2019.

[330] Y. Zhang, D. Guo, S. Xu, and H. Li. Verification and practice on first-order numerical differentiation formulas for unknown target functions. *Journal of Gansu Sciences*, 21:13–18(1), 2009.

[331] Y. Zhu and W.X. Zheng. Multiple Lyapunov functions analysis approach for discrete-time switched piecewise-affine systems under dwell-time constraints. *IEEE Transactions on Automatic Control*, 65:2177–2184(5), 2020.

[332] Y. Zhu, W. X. Zheng, and D. Zhou. Quasi-synchronization of discrete-time Luré-type switched systems with parameter mismatches and relaxed PDT constraints. *IEEE Transactions on Cybernetics*, 50:2026–2037(5), 2020.

[333] Y. Zhang, S. Li, J. Zou, and A.H. Khan. A passivity-based approach for kinematic control of redundant manipulators with constraints. *IEEE Transactions on Industrial Informatics*, 16:3029–3038(5), 2020.

[334] L. Xiao, K. Li, Z. Tan, Z. Zhang, B. Liao, K. Chen, L. Jin, and S. Li. Nonlinear gradient neural network for solving system of linear equations. *Information Processing Letters*, 142:35–40, 2019.

[335] Z. Liao, W. Gong, X. Yan, L. Wang, and C. Hu. Solving nonlinear equations system with dynamic repulsion-based evolutionary algorithms. *IEEE Transactions on Systems, Man, and Cybernetics: Systems*, 50:1590–1601(4), 2020.

[336] A. Amiri, A. Cordero, M.T. Darvishi, and J.R. Torregrosa. A fast algorithm to solve systems of nonlinear equations. *Journal of Computational and Applied Mathematics*, 354:242–258, 2019.

[337] K. Goulianas, A. Margaris, I. Refanidis, and K. Diamantaras. An adaptive learning rate backpropagation-type neural network for solving $n \times n$ systems on nonlinear algebraic equations. *Mathematical Methods in the Applied Sciences*, 39:2602–2616(10), 2016.

[338] M. Sun and Y. Wang. General five-step discrete-time Zhang neural network for time-varying nonlinear optimization. *Bulletin of the Malaysian Mathematical Sciences Society*, 43:1741–1760, 2020.

[339] K. Chen and Z. Zhang. A primal neural network for online equality-constrained quadratic programming. *Cognitive Computation*, 10:381–388(2), 2018.

[340] W. Li. A recurrent neural network with explicitly definable convergence time for solving time-variant linear matrix equations. *IEEE Transactions on Industrial Informatics*, 14:5289–5298(12), 2018.

[341] Y.-J. Liu, S. Lu, and S. Tong. Neural network controller design for an uncertain robot with time-varying output constraint. *IEEE Transactions on Systems, Man, and Cybernetics: Systems*, 47:2060–2068(8), 2017.

[342] L. Xiao, Z. Zhang, and S. Li. Solving time-varying system of nonlinear equations by finite-time recurrent neural networks with application to motion tracking of robot manipulators. *IEEE Transactions on Systems, Man, and Cybernetics: Systems*, 49:2210–2220(11), 2019.

[343] M. Di Marco, M. Forti, P. Nistri, and L. Pancioni. Discontinuous neural networks for finite-time solution of time-dependent linear equations. *IEEE Transactions on Cybernetics*, 46:2509–2520(11), 2016.

[344] X. Liu, F. Zhao, S.S. Ge, Y. Wu, and X. Mei. End-effector force estimation for flexible-joint robots with global friction approximation using neural networks. *IEEE Transactions on Industrial Informatics*, 15:1730–1741(3), 2019.

[345] L. Jin and S. Li. Nonconvex function activated zeroing neural network models for dynamic quadratic programming subject to equality and inequality constraints. *Neurocomputing*, 267:107–113, 2017.

[346] Q. Ma, S. Qin, and T. Jin. Complex Zhang neural networks for complex-variable dynamic quadratic programming. *Neurocomputing*, 330:56–69, 2019.

[347] M.D. Petkovic, P.S. Stanimirovic, and V.N. Katsikis. Modified discrete iterations for computing the inverse and pseudoinverse of the time-varying matrix. *Neurocomputing*, 289:155–165, 2018.

[348] F. Uhlig. The construction of high order convergent look-ahead finite difference formulas for Zhang neural networks. *Journal of Difference Equations and Applications*, 25:930–941(7), 2019.

[349] J. Na, Q. Chen, X. Ren, and Y. Guo. Adaptive prescribed performance motion control of servo mechanisms with friction compensation. *IEEE Transactions on Industrial Electronics*, 61:486–494(1), 2014.

[350] Z. Zhang, Z. Yan, and T. Fu. Varying-parameter RNN activated by finite-time functions for solving joint-drift problems of redundant robot manipulators. *IEEE Transactions on Industrial Informatics*, 14:5359–5367(12), 2018.

[351] B.M. Chen. Simple algorithm for the stable/unstable decomposition of a linear discrete-time system. *International Journal of Control*, 61:255–260(1), 1995.

[352] Z. Guo, S. Yang, and J. Wang. Global synchronization of stochastically disturbed memristive neurodynamics via discontinuous control laws. *IEEE/CAA Journal of Automatica Sinica*, 3:121–131(2), 2016.

[353] Z. Luo, J. Tao, and N. Xiu. Lowest-rank solutions of continuous and discrete Lyapunov equations over symmetric cone. *Linear Algebra and Its Applications*, 452:68–88, 2014.

[354] B. Wang, J. Wang, B. Zhang, and X. Li. Global cooperative control framework for multiagent systems subject to actuator saturation with industrial applications. *IEEE Transactions on Systems, Man, and Cybernetics: Systems*, 47:1270–1283(7), 2017.

[355] L. Zou, Z. Wang, H. Gao, and X. Liu. Event-triggered state estimation for complex networks with mixed time delays via sampled data information: The continuous-time case. *IEEE Transactions on Cybernetics*, 45:2804–2815(10), 2015.

[356] M. Barreau, A. Seuret, F. Gouaisbaut, and L. Baudouin. Lyapunov stability analysis of a string equation coupled with an ordinary differential system. *IEEE Transactions on Automatic Control*, 63:3850–3857(11), 2018.

[357] H.-J. Sun, W. Liu, and Y. Teng. Explicit iterative algorithms for solving coupled discrete-time Lyapunov matrix equations. *IET Control Theory and Applications*, 10:2565–2573(18), 2016.

[358] L. Ma, K. Dickson, J. McAllister, and J. McCanny. QR decomposition-based matrix inversion for high performance embedded MIMO receivers. *IEEE Transactions on Signal Processing*, 59:1858–1867(4), 2011.

[359] A. Asif and J.M.F. Moura. Block matrices with L-block-banded inverse: Inversion algorithms. *IEEE Transactions on Signal Processing*, 52:630–642(2), 2005.

[360] W.E. Leithead and Y. Zhang. $O(N^2)$-operation approximation of covariance matrix inverse in Gaussian process regression based on quasi-Newton BFGS methods. *Communications in Statistics-Simulation and Computation*, 36:367–380(2), 2007.

[361] B. Jin, Z. Jing, and H. Zhao. Incremental and decremental extreme learning machine based on generalized inverse. *IEEE Access*, 7:20852–20865, 2017.

[362] H. Kim. Necessary and sufficient characterisation for output synchronisation of linear heterogeneous agents using reflexive generalised inverses. *IET Control Theory and Applications*, 12:2534–2540(18), 2018.

[363] F. Toutounian and A. Ataei. New method for computing Moore–Penrose inverse matrices. *Journal of Computational and Applied Mathematics*, 228:412–417(1), 2009.

[364] J. Uhlmann. A rank-preserving generalized matrix inverse for consistency with respect to similarity. *IEEE Control Systems Letters*, 3:91–95(1), 2019.

[365] L. Xiao, Y. Zhang, Q. Zuo, J. Dai, J. Li, and W. Tang. A noise-tolerant zeroing neural network for time-dependent complex matrix inversion under various kinds of noises. *IEEE Transactions on Industrial Informatics*, 16:3757–3766(6), 2020.

[366] Z. Tan, W. Li, L. Xiao, and Y. Hu. New varying-parameter ZNN models with finite-time convergence and noise suppression for time-varying matrix Moore–Penrose inversion. *IEEE Transactions on Neural Networks and Learning Systems*, 31:2980–2991(8), 2020.

[367] Z. Tan, L. Xiao, S. Chen, and X. Lv. Noise-tolerant and finite-time convergent ZNN models for dynamic matrix Moore–Penrose inversion. *IEEE Transactions on Industrial Informatics*, 16:1591–1601(3), 2020.

[368] Y. Zhang, M. Yang, H. Huang, J. Chen, and Z. Li. Unified solution of different-kind future matrix equations using new nine-instant discretization formula and zeroing neural dynamics. *IEEE Transactions on Systems, Man, and Cybernetics: Systems*, 52:4993–5003(8), 2022.

[369] Z. Zhang, L. Kong, L. Zheng, P. Zhang, X. Qu, B. Liao, and Z. Yu. Robustness analysis of a power-type varying-parameter recurrent neural network for solving time-varying QM and QP problems and applications. *IEEE Transactions on Systems, Man, and Cybernetics: Systems*, 50:5106–5118(12), 2020.

[370] Z. Zhang, S. Chen, J. Xie, and S. Yang. Two hybrid multiobjective motion planning schemes synthesized by recurrent neural networks for wheeled mobile robot manipulators. *IEEE Transactions on Systems, Man, and Cybernetics: Systems*, 51:3270–3281(5), 2021.

[371] L. Xiao, Z. Zhang, and S. Li. Solving time-varying system of nonlinear equations by finite-time recurrent neural networks with application to motion tracking of robot manipulators. *IEEE Transactions on Systems, Man, and Cybernetics: Systems*, 49:2210–2220(11), 2019.

[372] Y. Zhang, M. Yang, H. Huang, M. Xiao, and H. Hu. New discrete-solution model for solving future different-level linear inequality and equality with robot manipulator control. *IEEE Transactions on Industrial Informatics*, 15:975–1984(4), 2019.

[373] X. Lv, L. Xiao, Z. Tan, and Z. Yang. Wsbp function activated Zhang dynamic with finite-time convergence applied to Lyapunov equation. *Neurocomputing*, 314:310–315, 2018.

[374] Y. Zhang, S. Chen, S. Li, and Z. Zhang. Adaptive projection neural network for kinematic control of redundant manipulators with unknown physical parameters. *IEEE Transactions on Industrial Electronics*, 65:4909–4920(6), 2018.

[375] W. Yang, J. Chen, Y. Zhang, J. Sun, and Z. Zhang. Abundant computer and robot experiments verifying minimum joint motion planning and control of redundant arms via Zhang neural network. In *Proceedings of International Joint Conference on Neural Networks*, pages 1–8, 2021.

[376] Z. Tang, J. Guo, J. Chen, and Y. Zhang. Redundant-manipulator minimal motion via different-precision discrete-time Zhang neural dynamics algorithms especially ten-instant one. In *Proceedings of China Automation Congress*, pages 288–293, 2021.

[377] I. Ullah, P. Chikontwe, and P. SangHyun. Real-time tracking of guidewire robot tips using deep convolutional neural networks on successive localized frames. *IEEE Access*, 7:159743–159753, 2019.

[378] S. Bo, S. Xie, L. Tang, C. Deng, and Y. Zhang. An industrial robot-based rehabilitation system for bilateral exercises. *IEEE Access*, 7:151282–151294, 2019.

[379] B. Zhou and W. Gu. Numerical study of some intelligent robot systems governed by the fractional differential equations. *IEEE Access*, 7:138548–138555, 2019.

[380] D. Chen, S. Li, Q. Wu, and X. Luo. Super-twisting ZNN for coordinated motion control of multiple robot manipulators with external disturbances suppression. *Neurocomputing*, 371:78–90, 2020.

[381] S. Jia and J. Shan. Finite-time trajectory tracking control of space manipulator under actuator saturation. *IEEE Transactions on Industrial Electronics*, 67:2086–2096(3), 2020.

[382] J. Gao and G. Yan. Design and implementation of a clamper-based and motor-driven capsule robot powered by wireless power transmission. *IEEE Access*, 7:138151–138161, 2019.

[383] L. Zhang, Y. Wang, Y. Hou, and H. Li. Fixed-time sliding mode control for uncertain robot manipulators. *IEEE Access*, 7:149750–149763, 2019.

[384] Y. Ge, Y. Xiong, L. Tenorio, and P.J. From. Fruit localization and environment perception for strawberry harvesting robots. *IEEE Access*, 7:147642–147652, 2019.

[385] Y. Zhang and Z. Zhang. Feedback-aided minimum joint movement (FAMJM) scheme for redundant manipulators with simulations and experiments. In *Proceedings of Chinese Control Conference*, pages 5656–5661, 2013.

[386] J. Ogbemhe, K. Mpofu, and N. Tlale. Optimal trajectory scheme for robotic welding along complex joints using a hybrid multi-objective genetic algorithm. *IEEE Access*, 7:158753–158769, 2019.

[387] Y. Huang, H. Ding, Y. Zhang, H. Wang, D. Cao, N. Xu, and C. Hu. A motion planning and tracking framework for autonomous vehicles based on artificial potential field elaborated resistance network approach. *IEEE Transactions on Industrial Electronics*, 67:1376–1386(2), 2020.

[388] Y. Liu, C. Guo, and Y. Weng. Online time-optimal trajectory planning for robotic manipulators using adaptive elite genetic algorithm with singularity avoidance. *IEEE Access*, 7:146301–146308, 2019.

[389] D. Ding, Z. Wang, Q. Han, and G. Wei. Neural-network-based output-feedback control under round-robin scheduling protocols. *IEEE Transactions on Cybernetics*, 49:2372–2384(6), 2019.

[390] M. Sheikholeslami, M.B. Gerdroodbary, R. Moradi, A. Shafee, and Z. Li. Application of neural network for estimation of heat transfer treatment of Al_2O_3-H_2O nanofluid through a channel. *Computer Methods in Applied Mechanics and Engineering*, 344:1–12, 2019.

[391] W. Wang, J. Shen, and H. Ling. A deep network solution for attention and aesthetics aware photo cropping. *IEEE Transactions on Pattern Analysis and Machine Intelligence*, 41:1531–1544(7), 2019.

[392] H. Nguyen and X. Bui. Predicting blast-induced air overpressure: A robust artificial intelligence system based on artificial neural networks and random forest. *Natural Resources Research*, 28:893–907(3), 2019.

[393] J.J.A. Armenteros, K.D. Tsirigos, C.K. Sonderby, T.N. Petersen, O. Winther, S. Brunak, G. Heijne, and H. Nielsen. Signal P 5.0 improves signal peptide predictions using deep neural networks. *Nature Biotechnology*, 37:420–430(4), 2019.

[394] K. Muhammad, J. Ahmad, I. Mehmood, S. Rho, and S.W. Baik. Convolutional neural networks based fire detection in surveillance videos. *IEEE Access*, 6:18174–18183, 2018.

[395] D. Wang, D.R. Liu, C.X. Mu, and Y. Zhang. Neural network learning and robust stabilization of nonlinear systems with dynamic uncertainties. *IEEE Transactions on Neural Networks and Learning Systems*, 29:1342–1351(4), 2018.

[396] L. Xiao, Q. Yi, J. Dai, K. Li, and Z. Hu. Design and analysis of new complex zeroing neural network for a set of dynamic complex linear equations. *Neurocomputing*, 363:171–181, 2019.

[397] R.W. Hamming. *Introduction to Applied Numerical Analysys*. Dover Publications, New York, USA, 2012.

[398] S. Anita, V. Arnautu, and V. Capasso. *An Introduction to Optimal Control Problems in Life Sciences and Economics*. Springer, New York, USA, 2011.

[399] Y. Zhang, M. Zhu, C. Hu, J. Li, and M. Yang. Euler-precision general-form of Zhang et al discretization (ZeaD) formulas, derivation, and numerical experiments. In *Proceedings of Chinese Control and Decision Conference*, pages 6273–6278, 2018.

[400] J.W. Brown and R.V. Churchill. *Complex Variables and Applications, Eighth Edition*. McGraw-Hill Higher Education, New York, USA, 2009.

[401] R.C. Dorf and R.H. Bishop. *Modern Control Systems, Twelfth Edition*. Prentice Hall, Englewood, USA, 2001.

[402] Q.I. Rahman and G. Schmeisser. *Analytic Theory of Polynomials*. Oxford University Press, Oxford, UK, 2002.

[403] Y. Zhang, H. Gong, J. Li, H. Huang, and M. Yang. Euler-precision ZFD formula 3NgPFD_G extended to future minimization with theoretical guarantees and numerical experiments. In *Proceedings of Advanced Information Technology, Electronic and Automation Control Conference*, pages 171–176, 2017.

[404] Y. Zhang, Y. Fang, B. Liao, T. Qiao, and H. Tan. New DTZNN model for future minimization with cube steady-state error pattern using Taylor finite-difference formula. In *Proceedings of International Conference on Intelligent Control and Information Processing*, pages 128–133, 2015.

[405] Y. Zhang, Z. Ke, Z. Li, and D. Guo. Comparison on continuous-time Zhang dynamics and Newton-Raphson iteration for online solution of nonlinear equations. In *Proceedings of International Symposium on Neural Networks*, pages 393–402, 2011.

[406] J.J. Callahan. *Advanced Calculus: A Geometric View*. Springer, New York, USA, 2010.

[407] Y. Zhang and K. Chen. Comparison on Zhang neural network and gradient neural network for time-varying linear matrix equation AXB=C solving. In *Proceedings of International Conference on Industrial Technology*, pages 1–6, 2008.

[408] W. Ma, Y. Zhang, and J. Wang. MATLAB simulink modeling and simulation of Zhang neural networks for online time-varying Sylvester equation solving. In *Proceedings of International Joint Conference on Neural Networks*, pages 286–290, 2008.

[409] R.L. Burden and J.D. Faires. *Numerical Analysis*. Brooks/Cole, Pacific Grove, USA, 2001.

[410] D. Baleanu, O. Defterli, and O.P. Agrawl. A central difference numerical scheme for fractional optimal control problems. *Journal of Vibration and Control*, 15:583–597(4), 2009.

[411] T.N. Krishnamurti and L. Bounoua. *An Introduction to Numerical Weather Prediction Technique Techniques*. CRC Press, Boca Raton, USA, 1995.

[412] J.P. Li. General explicit difference formulas for numerical differentiation. *Journal of Computational and Applied Mathematics*, 183:29–52, 2005.

Glossary

ACTPU: Average computing time per updating

CTCZNN: Continuous-time conventional zeroing neural network

CTDD: Continuous-time derivative dynamics

CTDDLES: Continuous time-dependent different-layer equation system

CTDDLIES: Continuous time-dependent different-layer inequation-equation system

CTDMI: Continuous time-dependent matrix inversion

CTDMP: Continuous time-dependent matrix pseudoinversion

CTDMSRF: Continuous time-dependent matrix square root finding

CTDUNO: Continuous time-dependent unconstrained nonlinear optimization

CTEZNN: Continuous-time enhanced zeroing neural network

CTGNN: Continuous-time gradient neural network

CTZNN: Continuous-time zeroing neural network

DTCZNN: Discrete-time conventional zeroing neural network

DTDD: Discrete-time derivative dynamics

DTEZNN: Discrete-time enhanced zeroing neural network

DTGNN: Discrete-time gradient neural network

DTZNN: Discrete-time zeroing neural network

8S-DTZNN: Eight-step discrete-time zeroing neural network

8S-ZTD: Eight-step Zhang time discretization

ET-DTPB: Euler-type discrete-time pseudoinverse-based

ET-DTGNN: Euler-type discrete-time gradient neural network

ET-DTZNN: Euler-type discrete-time zeroing neural network

ET-DTZNN-K: Euler-type discrete-time zeroing neural network with $\dot{A}_k$ known

ET-DTZNN-KPM: Euler-type discrete-time zeroing neural network with $\dot{\mathbf{r}}_{\mathrm{d},k}$ known for parallel manipulator

ET-DTZNN-KSM: Euler-type discrete-time zeroing neural network with $\dot{\mathbf{r}}_{\mathrm{d},k}$ known for serial manipulator

ET-DTZNN-U: Euler-type discrete-time zeroing neural network with $\dot{A}_k$ unknown

ET-DTZNN-UPM: Euler-type discrete-time zeroing neural network with $\dot{\mathbf{r}}_{\mathrm{d},k}$ unknown for parallel manipulator

ET-DTZNN-USM: Euler-type discrete-time zeroing neural network with $\dot{\mathbf{r}}_{\mathrm{d},k}$ unknown for serial manipulator

FDLES: Future different-layer equation system

FDLIES: Future different-layer inequation-equation system

FGMI: Future generalized matrix inversion

FLE: Future Lyapunov equation

FME: Future matrix equation

FMI: Future matrix inversion

FMLP: Future matrix left pseudoinversion

FMP: Future matrix pseudoinversion

FMRP: Future matrix right pseudoinversion

FMSRF: Future matrix square root finding

FNES: Future nonlinear equation system

5S-DTGNN: Five-step discrete-time gradient neural network

5S-DTZNN: Five-step discrete-time zeroing neural network

4S-DTZNN: Four-step discrete-time zeroing neural network

4S-DTZNN-KPM: Four-step discrete-time zeroing neural network with $\dot{\mathbf{r}}_{\mathrm{d},k}$ known for parallel manipulator

4S-DTZNN-KSM: Four-step discrete-time zeroing neural network with $\dot{\mathbf{r}}_{\mathrm{d},k}$ known for serial manipulator

4S-DTZNN-UPM: Four-step discrete-time zeroing neural network with $\dot{\mathbf{r}}_{\mathrm{d},k}$ unknown for parallel manipulator

4S-DTZNN-USM: Four-step discrete-time zeroing neural network with $\dot{\mathbf{r}}_{\mathrm{d},k}$ unknown for serial manipulator

5S-ZTD: Five-step Zhang time discretization

4S-ZTD: Four-step Zhang time discretization

FUNO: Future unconstrained nonlinear optimization

GNN: Gradient neural network

MIMO: Multiple-input multiple-output

MSSRE: Maximal steady-state residual error

MSSSE: Maximal steady-state solution error

MSSTE: Maximal steady-state tracking error

NI: Newton iteration

9S-DTZNN: Nine-step discrete-time zeroing neural network

***N*S-ZTD:** N-step Zhang time discretization

9S-ZTD: Nine-step Zhang time discretization

ODE: Ordinary differential equation

1S-DTZNN: One-step discrete-time neural network

1S-ZTD: One-step Zhang time discretization

PDE: Partial differential equation

PPS: Pulses per second

QP: Quadratic programing

RNN: Recurrent neural networks

SODE: Second-order derivative elimination

7S-DTZNN: Seven-step discrete-time zeroing neural network

7S-ZTD: Seven-step Zhang time discretization

6S-DTZNN: Six-step discrete-time zeroing neural network

6S-ZTD: Six-step Zhang time discretization

3S-DTZNN: Three-step discrete-time zeroing neural network

2S-DTZNN: Two-step discrete-time zeroing neural network

3S-ZTD: Three-step Zhang time discretization

2S-ZTD: Two-step Zhang time discretization

UNO: Unconstrained nonlinear optimization

VLMJMC: Velocity-layer minimum joint motion control

VLSI: Very large scale integration

ZE: Zeroing equivalency

ZF: Zeroing function

ZNN: Zeroing neural network

ZTD: Zhang time discretization

ZT-DTZNN: Zhang–Taylor discrete-time zeroing neural network

ZT-DTZNN-K: Zhang–Taylor discrete-time zeroing neural network with $\dot{A}_k$ known

ZT-DTZNN-U: Zhang–Taylor discrete-time zeroing neural network with $\dot{A}_k$ unknown

Index

Printed in the United States
by Baker & Taylor Publisher Services